Edwards, Jonathan

An Account of the Life of the Late Reverend Mr. David Brainerd

ISBN: 978-0-9998644-7-0

This classic reprint was produced from digital files in the Google Books digital collection, which may be found at http://www.books.google.com. The artwork used on the cover is from Wikimedia Commons and remains in the public domain. Omissions and/or errors in this book are due to either the physical condition of the original book or due to the scanning process by Google or its agents.

This edition of Jonathan Edwards's **An Account of the Life of the Late Revered Mr. David Brainerd** was originally published in 1765 (Edinburgh). Pages 428 and 429 of this book were missing in the Google document, and were subsequently reconstructed from the 1824 edition of Edwards's book by the same title.

Townsends
PO Box 415, Pierceton, IN 46562
www.Townsends.us

AN
ACCOUNT of the LIFE

Of the late REVEREND

Mr *David Brainerd*,

Minister of the Gospel,

Missionary to the Indians, from the Honourable Society in Scotland, for the Propagation of Christian Knowledge, and Pastor of a Church of *Christian Indians* in New-Jersey.

Who died at Northampton in New-England, October 9. 1747, in the 30th Year of his Age.

Chiefly taken from his own *Diary*, and other private Writings, written for his own Use; and now published,

By JONATHAN EDWARDS, A. M.
Then Minister of the Gospel at Northampton, afterwards President of the College of New-Jersey.

To which is annexed,

I. Mr Brainerd's JOURNAL while among the Indians.

II. Mr Pemberton's Sermon at his ORDINATION. With an APPENDIX relative to the Indian Affairs.

EDINBURGH:
Printed by JOHN GRAY and GAVIN ALSTON,
For WILLIAM GRAY in the Front of the Exchange.
MDCCLXV.

THE

PREFACE.

THERE are two ways of reprefenting and recommending true religion and virtue to the world, which God hath made ufe of; the one is by doctrine and precept, the other is by inftance and example; both are abundantly ufed in the *holy fcriptures.* Not only are the grounds, nature, defign, and importance of religion clearly exhibited in the doctrines of fcripture, and its exercife and practice plainly delineated, and abundantly enjoined and enforced, in its commands and counfels; but there we have many excellent examples of religion, in its power and practice, fet before us, in the hiftories both of the Old Teftament and New. ——JESUS CHRIST, the great Prophet of God, when he came into the world to be "the light of the world," to teach and enforce true religion, in a greater degree than ever had been before, he made ufe of both thefe methods. In his doctrine he declared the mind and will of God, and the nature and properties of that virtue which becomes creatures of our make and in our circumftances, more clearly and fully than ever it had been before, and more powerfully inforced it by what he declared of the obligations and inducements to holinefs; and he alfo in his own practice gave a moft perfect example of the virtue he taught. He exhibited to the world fuch an illuftrious pattern of humility, divine love, difcreet zeal, felf-denial, obedience, patience, refignation, fortitude, meeknefs, forgivenefs, compaffion, benevolence, and univerfal holinefs, as neither men nor angels ever faw before. God alfo in his providence has been wont to make ufe of both thefe methods to hold forth light to mankind, and inducement to their duty, in all ages: he has from time to time raifed up eminent teachers, to exhibit and bear teftimony to the truth in their *doctrine,* and oppofe the errors, darknefs, and wickednefs of the world; and alfo has, from age to age, raifed up fome eminent perfons that have fet bright *examples* of that religion that is taught and prefcribed in the word of God; whofe examples have in divine providence been fet forth to public view. Thefe have a great tendency to engage the attention of men to the doctrines and rules that are taught, and greatly to confirm and enforce them; and efpecially when thefe bright examples have been exhibited in the fame perfons that have been eminent *teachers,* fo that the world has

had

had opportunity to ſee ſuch a confirmation of the truth, efficacy, and amiableneſs of the religion taught, in the practice of the ſame perſons that have moſt clearly and forceably taught it; and above all, when theſe bright examples have been ſet by eminent teachers in a variety of unuſual circumſtances of remarkable *trial;* and God has withal remarkably diſtinguiſhed them with wonderful *ſucceſs* of their inſtructions and labours, conſiſting in glorious events that have been in many reſpects new and ſtrange.

Such an inſtance we have in the *excellent perſon,* whoſe *life* is publiſhed in the following pages. His example is attended with a great variety of circumſtances, tending to engage the attention of religious people, eſpecially in theſe parts of the world: he was one of diſtinguiſhed natural abilities; as all are ſenſible, that had acquaintance with him: he was a miniſter of the goſpel, and one who was called to unuſual ſervices in that work, whoſe miniſtry was attended with very remarkable and unuſual events, an account of which has already been given to the public; one whoſe courſe of religion began before the late times of extraordinary religious commotion, but yet one that lived in thoſe times, and went through them, and was very much in the way of the various extraordinary effects and unuſual appearances of that day, and was not an idle ſpectator, but had a near concern in many things that paſſed at that time; one that had a very extenſive acquaintance with thoſe that have been the ſubjects of the late religious operations, in many of theſe Britiſh colonies, in places far diſtant one from another, in people of many different nations, of different educations, manners, and cuſtoms; one who had peculiar opportunity of acquaintance with the falſe appearances and counterfeits of religion: one who himſelf was the inſtrument of a moſt remarkable awakening, and an exceeding wonderful and abiding alteration and moral transformation of ſuch ſubjects as do peculiarly render the change rare and aſtoniſhing.

In the following account, the reader will have opportunity to ſee, not only what were the external circumſtances and remarkable incidents of the life of this perſon, and how he ſpent his time from day to day, as to his external behaviour; but alſo what paſſed in his own heart, the wonderful change that he experienced in his mind and diſpoſition, the manner in which that change was brought to paſs, how it continued, what were its conſequences in his inward frames, thoughts, affections, and ſecret exerciſes, through many viciſſitudes and trials, from thenceforth for more than eight years, till his death;

death; and also to see how all ended at last, in his sentiments, frame, and behaviour, during a long season of the gradual and sensible approach of death, under a lingering illness, and what were the effects of his religion in dying circumstances, or in the last stages of his dying illness. The account being written, the reader may have opportunity at his leisure to compare the various parts of the story, and deliberately to view and weigh the whole, and consider how far what is related is agreeable to the dictates of right reason and the holy word of God.

I am far from supposing, that Mr Brainerd's inward exercises and experiences, or his external conduct, were free from all imperfection: the example of *Jesus Christ* is the only example that ever was set in the human nature, that was altogether perfect; which therefore is a rule, to try all other examples by; and the dispositions, frames, and practices of others must be commended and followed no further, than they were *followers of Christ*.

There is one thing in Mr Brainerd, easily discernible by the following account of his life, that may be called an imperfection in him, which though not properly an imperfection of a moral nature, yet may possibly be made an objection against the extraordinary appearances of religion and devotion in him, by such as seek for objections against every thing that can be produced in favour of true vital religion; and that is, that he was one who by his constitution and natural temper was so prone to *melancholy* and dejection of spirit. There are some who think that all serious strict religion is a melancholy thing, and that what is called Christian experience, is little else besides melancholy vapours disturbing the brain, and exciting enthusiastical imaginations. But that Mr Brainerd's temper or constitution inclined him to despondency, is no just ground to suspect his extraordinary devotion, as being only the fruit of a warm imagination. I doubt not but that all who have well observed mankind, will readily grant this, that it is not all those who by their natural constitution or temper are most disposed to *dejection*, that are the persons who are the most susceptive of lively and strong impressions on their imagination, or the most subject to those vehement impetuous affections, which are the fruits of such impressions; but that many who are of a very *gay* and *sanguine* natural temper are vastly more so, and if their affections are turned into a religious channel, are much more exposed to *enthusiasm*, than many of the former. And as to Mr Brainerd in particular, notwithstanding his inclination to despondency, he was evidently one of that sort of persons who usually are the

the furtheſt from a teeming imagination; being one of a penetrating genius, of clear thought, of cloſe reaſoning, and a very exact judgment; as all know, that knew him. As he had a great inſight into human nature, and was very *diſcerning* and *judicious* in things in general, ſo he excelled in his judgment and knowledge of things in divinity, but eſpecially in things appertaining to inward experimental religion; moſt accurately diſtinguiſhing between real ſolid piety and enthuſiaſm, between thoſe affections that are rational and ſcriptural, having their foundation in light and judgment, and thoſe that are founded in whimſical conceits, ſtrong impreſſions on the imagination, and thoſe vehement emotions of the animal ſpirits that ariſe from them. He was exceeding ſenſible of mens expoſedneſs to theſe things, how much they had prevailed, and what multitudes had been deceived by them, of the pernicious conſequences of them, and the fearful miſchief they had done in the Chriſtian world. He greatly abhorred ſuch a ſort of religion, and was abundant in bearing teſtimony againſt it, living and dying; and was quick to diſcern when any thing of that nature aroſe, though in its firſt buddings, and appearing under the moſt fair and plauſible diſguiſes; and had that talent at deſcribing the various workings of this *imaginary enthuſiaſtical* religion, evincing the falſeneſs and vanity of it, and demonſtrating the great difference between this and true *ſpiritual* devotion, which I ſcarcely ever knew equalled in any other perſon.———And his judicioufneſs did not only appear in diſtinguiſhing among the experiences of *others*, but alſo among the various exerciſes of *his own mind;* and particularly in diſcerning what within himſelf was to be laid to the ſcore of *melancholy;* in which he exceeded all melancholy perſons that ever I was acquainted with, (though I have been in the way of acquaintance with very many); which was doubtleſs owing to a peculiar ſtrength in his *judgment:* it is a rare thing indeed, that melancholy people are well ſenſible of their own diſeaſe, and fully convinced that ſuch and ſuch things are to be aſcribed to it, as are indeed its genuine operations and fruits.———Mr Brainerd did not obtain that degree of ſkill, which he had in this matter, at once, but gained it gradually; as the reader may diſcern by the following account of his life. In the former part of his religious courſe, he imputed much of that kind of gloomineſs of mind and thoſe dark thoughts, to ſpiritual *deſertion*, which in the latter part of his life, he was abundantly ſenſible, were owing to the diſeaſe of *melancholy;* accordingly he often expreſsly ſpeaks of them in his diary as ariſing from this cauſe;

and

and he was often in conversation speaking of the difference between melancholy and godly sorrow, true humiliation, and spiritual desertion, and the great danger of mistaking the one for the other, and the very hurtful nature of melancholy, discoursing with great judgment upon it, and doubtless much more judiciously for what he knew by his own experience.

But besides what may be argued from Mr Brainerd's strength of judgment, it is apparent in *fact*, that he was not a person of a warm imagination. His inward experiences, either in his convictions or his conversion, and his religious views and impressions through the course of his life to his death, (of which he has left a very particular account), none of them consisted in, or were excited by, strong and lively images formed in his imagination; there is nothing at all appears of it in his *diary*, from beginning to end: yea, he told me on his death-bed, that, although once when he was very young in years and in experience, he was deceived into a high opinion of such things, looking on them as superior attainments in religion, beyond what he had ever arrived to, and was ambitious of them and earnestly sought them, yet he never could obtain them; and that he never in his life had a strong impression on his imagination, of any visage, outward form, external glory, or any other thing of that nature; which kind of impressions abound among the wild enthusiastic people of the late and present day.

As Mr Brainerd's religious impressions, views, and affections in their nature were vastly different from enthusiasm, so were their *effects* in him as contrary as possible to the ordinary effects of that. Nothing so puffs men up, as *enthusiasm*, with a high conceit of their own wisdom, holiness, eminency, and sufficiency, and makes them so bold, forward, assuming, and arrogant: but the reader will see, that Mr Brainerd's religion constantly disposed him to a most mean thought of himself, an abasing sense of his own exceeding sinfulness, deficiency, unprofitableness, and ignorance; looking on himself as worse than others; disposing him to universal benevolence, meekness, and in honour to prefer others, and to treat all with kindness and respect. And when *melancholy* prevailed, though the effects of it were very prejudicial to him, yet it had not those effects of *enthusiasm*; but operated by dark and discouraging thoughts of himself, as ignorant, wicked, and wholly unfit for the work of the ministry, or even to be seen among mankind, *&c.*——Indeed, at the time forementioned, when he had not learned well to distinguish between enthusiasm and solid religion, he joining and keeping company with some that

that were tinged with no ſmall degree of the former, for a ſeaſon partook with them in a degree of their diſpoſitions and behaviours; though, as was obſerved before, he could not obtain thoſe things wherein their *enthuſiaſm* itſelf conſiſted, and ſo could not become like them in that reſpect, however he erroneouſly deſired and ſought it. But certainly it is not at all to be wondered at, that a youth and a young convert, one that had his heart ſo ſwallowed up in religion, and ſo earneſtly deſired the flouriſhing of it, but had had ſo little opportunity for reading, obſervation, and experience, ſhould for a while be dazzled and deceived with the glaring appearances of that miſtaken devotion and zeal; eſpecially conſidering what the extraordinary circumſtances of that day were. He told me on his death-bed, that while he was in theſe circumſtances he was out of his element, and did violence to himſelf, while complying, in his conduct, with perſons of a fierce and imprudent zeal, from his great veneration of ſome that he looked upon much better than himſelf. So that it would be very unreaſonable, that his error at that time ſhould nevertheleſs be eſteemed a juſt ground of prejudice againſt the whole of his religion, and his character in general; eſpecially conſidering, how greatly his mind was ſoon changed, and how exceedingly he afterwards lamented his error, and abhorred himſelf for his imprudent zeal and miſconduct at that time, even to the breaking of his heart, and almoſt to the overbearing and breaking the ſtrength of his nature; and how much of a Chriſtian ſpirit he ſhewed, in his condemning himſelf for that miſconduct, as the reader will ſee.

What has been now mentioned of Mr Brainerd, is ſo far from being juſt ground of prejudice againſt what is related in the following account of his life, that, if duly conſidered, it will render the hiſtory the more ſerviceable. For by his thus joining for a ſeaſon with *enthuſiaſts*, he had a more full and intimate acquaintance with what belonged to that ſort of religion, and ſo was under better advantages to judge of the difference between that and the other, which he finally approved and ſtrove to his utmoſt to promote, in oppoſition to it: and hereby the reader has the more to demonſtrate to him, that Mr Brainerd, in his teſtimony againſt it, and the ſpirit and behaviour of thoſe that are influenced by it, ſpeaks from impartial conviction, and not from prejudice; becauſe therein he openly condemns his own former opinion and conduct, on account of which he had greatly ſuffered from his oppoſers, and for which ſome continued to reproach him as long as he lived.

Another

Another imperfection in Mr Brainerd, which may be observed in the following account of his life, was his being *excessive in his labours;* not taking due care to proportion his fatigues to his strength. Indeed the case was very often so, and such the seeming calls of Providence, that it was extremely difficult for him to avoid doing more than his strength would well admit of; yea, his circumstances, and the business of his mission among the Indians, were such, that great fatigues and hardships were altogether inevitable. However, he was finally convinced, that he had erred in this matter, and that he ought to have taken more thorough care, and been more resolute to withstand temptations to such degrees of labour as injured his health; and accordingly warned his brother, who succeeds him in his mission, to be careful to avoid this error.

Besides the imperfections already mentioned, it is readily allowed, that there were some imperfections that ran through his whole life, and were mixed with all his religious affections and exercises, some mixture of what was natural with that which was spiritual; as it evermore is in the best saints in this world. Doubtless there was some influence that natural temper had in the religious exercises and experiences of Mr Brainerd, as there most apparently was in the exercises of devout David, and the apostles Peter, John, and Paul: there was undoubtedly very often some influence of his natural disposition to dejection in his religious mourning, some mixture of melancholy with truly godly sorrow and real Christian humility, and some mixture of the natural fire of youth with his holy zeal for God, and some influence of natural principles mixed with grace in various other respects, as it ever was and ever will be with the saints while on this side heaven. Perhaps none were more sensible of Mr Brainerd's imperfections than he himself; or could distinguish more accurately, than he, between what was natural and what was spiritual. It is easy for the judicious reader to observe, that his graces ripened, and the religious exercises of his heart became more and more pure, and he more and more distinguishing in his judgment the longer he lived; he had much to teach and purify him, and he failed not to make his advantage thereby.

But notwithstanding all these imperfections, I am persuaded, every pious and judicious reader will acknowledge, that what is here set before him is indeed a remarkable instance of true and eminent Christian piety in heart and practice, tending greatly to confirm the reality of vital religion, and the power of of godliness, most worthy of imitation, and many ways tending to the spiritual benefit of the careful observer.

It is fit the reader should be aware, that what Mr Brainerd wrote in his *diary*, out of which the following account of his life is chiefly taken, was written only for his own private use, and not to get honour and applause in the world, nor with any design that the world should ever see it, either while he lived or after his death, excepting some few things that he wrote in a dying state, after he had been persuaded, with difficulty, not entirely to suppress all his private writings. He shewed himself almost invincibly averse to the publishing of any part of his *diary* after his death; and when he was thought to be dying at Boston, gave the most strict peremptory orders to the contrary: but being by some of his friends there prevailed upon to withdraw so strict and absolute a prohibition, he was pleased finally to yield so far as that "his papers "should be left in my hands, that I might dispose of them as "I thought would be most for God's glory and the interest of "religion."——But a few days before his death, he ordered some part of his *diary* to be destroyed, (as will afterwards be observed), which renders the account of his life the less complete. And there are some parts of his *diary* here left out for brevity's sake, that would (I am sensible) have been a great advantage to the history, if they had been inserted; particularly the account of his wonderful successes among the Indians; which for substance is the same in his private *diary* with that which has already been made public, in the *Journal* he kept by order of the Society in Scotland, for their information. That account, I am of opinion, would be more entertaining and more profitable, if it were published as it is written in his *diary*, in connection with his secret religion and the inward exercises of his mind, and also with the preceding and following parts of the story of his life. But because that account has been published already, and because the adding it here would make the book much more bulky and more costly, which might tend to discourage the purchase and perusal of it, and so render it less extensively useful, I have therefore omitted that part. However, this defect may in a great measure be made up to the reader, by his purchasing his public *Journal*, and reading it in its place, with this history of his life; which undoubtedly would be well worth the while for every reader, and would richly recompense the additional cost of the purchase. I hope therefore, that those of my readers who are not furnished with *that book*, will, for their own profit and entertainment, and that they may have the story of

this

this excellent person more complete, procure one of those books; without which he must have a very imperfect view of the most important part of his life, and (on some accounts) of the most remarkable and wonderful things in it *.——I should also observe, that besides that book, and antecedent to it, there is a *narrative* relating to the Indian affairs, annexed to Mr Pemberton's sermon at Mr Brainerd's ordination †; which likewise may the more profitably be read in conjunction with his *diary* previous to November 5. 1744.

But it is time to end this preface, that the reader may be no longer detained from the history itself.

N. B. Those parts of the following history that are included between *brackets* thus [ ], are the words of the *publisher*, for the most part, summarily representing (for brevity's sake) the substance or chief things contained in Mr Brainerd's diary, for such a certain space of time as is there specified: the rest is the account that he gives of himself in his private writings, in his own words.

I presume, scarce any reader needs to be told, that [*A. Æt.*] on the top of the page, signifies, *the year of his age*, and [*A. D.*] *the year of our Lord*.

* To supply the defect here mentioned, the publisher of this edition of Mr Brainerd's life procured a copy of the Journal referred to, which the reader will find subjoined at the end of the life.

† In order that Mr Brainerd's life might be complete, the reader will also have the pleasure of perusing, at the end of the Journal, Mr Pemberton's sermon, together with the narrative relating to the Indian affairs, here referred to.

EDINBURGH, March 18. 1765.

PROPOSALS

For printing, by SUBSCRIPTION,

A TREATISE concerning RELIGIOUS AFFECTIONS.

In three parts.

PART 1. Concerning the nature of the affections, and their importance in religion.

PART 2. Shewing what are no certain signs that religious affections are gracious, or that they are not.

PART 3. Shewing what are distinguishing signs of truly gracious and holy affections.

By JONATHAN EDWARDS, A.M.

President of the College of New-Jersey.

CONDITIONS.

I. The book will be printed on a coarse and fine paper; and on the same type with the Life and Journal of Mr David Brainerd.

II. It will consist of about 400 pages large 8vo, and will be delivered to subscribers the fine paper neatly bound in calf at 5 s. and the coarse paper neatly bound in sheep at 4 s.

III. The book will be put to the press as soon as 200 copies are subscribed for.

A formal recommendation of this treatise is unnecessary. The subject treated of is of the utmost importance, even the nature of true religion, and the distinguishing marks of genuine holiness and virtue. The eminent piety of the author, his penetrating philosophical genius, his freedom from the least tincture of Enthusiasm, and the uncommon religious appearances in New-England, of which he had been long an attentive and critical observer, afforded him peculiar advantages, for conducting so difficult an inquiry with judgment and precision. Accordingly the book was so well received, that an impression of near 1300 copies was soon sold off. An excellent abridgment of it has been published by the Reverend Mr Gordon at London. It is hoped, that through the blessing of God, the republishing the complete treatise may prove a seasonable preservative against the increasing evils of formality on the one hand, and Enthusiasm on the other; while some imagine that vigorous lively affections in religion are unnecessary, nay, are to be guarded against as of pernicious tendency; and while others, without inquiring into the nature, source, and effects of religious affections, rashly conclude, that every one is truly gracious, who appears to be much moved by divine things, and expresses himself about them with warmth and earnestness.

It is intreated, that all who are for encouraging these proposals, will send in their names, designations, and places of abode immediately, to WILLIAM GRAY the Publisher, front of the Exchange, Edinburgh, that the book may be put to the press without loss of time.

An ACCOUNT
Of the LIFE of
The late Reverend
Mr *David Brainerd.*

PART I.

From his *birth*, to the time when he began to devote himſelf to the *ſtudy of divinity*, in order to his being fitted for the work of the miniſtry.

MR David Brainerd was born April 20. 1718, at Haddam, a town belonging to the county of Hartford, in the colony of Connecticut, New-England. His father, who died when this his ſon was about nine years of age, was the Worſhipful Hezekiah Brainerd Eſq; an aſſiſtant, or one of his Majeſty's council for that colony, and the ſon of Daniel Brainerd Eſq; a juſtice of the peace, and a deacon of the church of Chriſt in Haddam. His mother was Mrs Dorothy Hobart, daughter to the Reverend Mr Jeremiah Hobart, who preached a while at Topsfield, and then removed to Hempſtead on Long-Iſland, and afterwards removed from Hempſtead, (by reaſon of numbers turning Quakers, and many others being ſo irreligious, that they would do nothing towards the ſupport of the miniſtry), and came and ſettled in the work of the miniſtry at Haddam; where he died in the 85th year of his age: of whom it is remarkable, that he went to the public worſhip in the forenoon, and died in his chair between meetings. And this reverend gentleman was ſon of the Reverend Mr Peter Hobart, who was, firſt, miniſter of the goſpel at Hingham, in the county of Norfolk in England;

land; and, by reaſon of the perſecution of the Puritans, removed with his family to New-England, and was ſettled in the miniſtry at Hingham, in the Maſſachuſetts. He had five ſons, *viz.* Joſhua, Jeremiah, Gerſhom, Japheth, and Nehemiah. His ſon Joſhua was miniſter at Southold on Long-Iſland; Jeremiah was Mr David Brainerd's grandfather, miniſter at Haddam, *&c.* as was before obſerved; Gerſhom was miniſter of Groton in Connecticut; Japheth was a phyſician, and went in the quality of a doctor of a ſhip to England, (before the time for the taking his ſecond degree at college), and deſigned to go from thence to the Eaſt-Indies, and never was heard of more; Nehemiah was ſometime fellow of Harvard college, and afterwards miniſter at Newton in the Maſſachuſetts. The mother of Mrs Dorothy Hobart (who was afterwards Brainerd) was daughter to the Reverend Mr Samuel Whiting, miniſter of the goſpel, firſt at Boſton in Lincolnſhire, and afterwards at Lynn in the Maſſachuſetts, New-England: he had three ſons that were miniſters of the goſpel.

Mr David Brainerd was the third ſon of his parents. They had five ſons, and four daughters. Their eldeſt ſon is Hezekiah Brainerd, Eſq; a juſtice of the peace, and for ſeveral years paſt a repreſentative of the town of Haddam, in the general aſſembly of Connecticut colony; the ſecond was the Reverend Mr Nehemiah Brainerd, a worthy miniſter at Eaſtbury in Connecticut, who died of a conſumption Nov. 10. 1742.; the fourth is Mr John Brainerd, who ſucceeds his brother David, as miſſionary to the Indians, and paſtor of the ſame church of Chriſtian Indians in New-Jerſey; and the fifth was Iſrael, lately ſtudent at Yale-college in New-Haven, and died ſince his brother David.—Mrs Dorothy Brainerd having lived ſeveral years a widow, died, when her ſon, whoſe life I am about to give an account of, was about fourteen years of age: ſo that in his youth he was left both fatherleſs and motherleſs. What account he has given of himſelf, and his own life, may be ſeen in what follows.]

I Was, I think, from my youth, ſomething ſober, and inclined rather to melancholy, than the contrary extreme; but do not remember any thing of conviction of ſin, worthy of remark, till I was, I believe, about ſeven or eight years of age; when I became ſomething concerned for my ſoul, and terrified at the thoughts of death, and was driven to the performance of duties: but it appeared a melancholy buſineſs, and deſtroyed my eagerneſs for play. And, alas! this religious concern was but ſhort-lived. However, I ſometimes attended

attended secret prayer; and thus lived at "ease in Zion, "without God in the world," and without much concern, as I remember, till I was above thirteen years of age. But sometime in the winter 1732, I was something roused out of carnal security, by I scarce know what means at first; but was much excited by the prevailing of a mortal sickness in Haddam. I was frequent, constant, and something fervent in duties, and took delight in reading, especially Mr Janeway's *Token for children;* I felt sometimes much melted in duties, and took great delight in the performance of them; and I sometimes hoped, that I was converted, or at least in a good and hopeful way for heaven and happiness, not knowing what conversion was. The Spirit of God at this time proceeded far with me; I was remarkably dead to the world, and my thoughts were almost wholly employed about my soul's concerns; and I may indeed say, "Almost I was persuaded to be "a Christian." I was also exceedingly distressed and melancholy at the death of my mother, in March 1732. But afterwards my religious concern began to decline, and I by degrees fell back into a considerable degree of security, though I still attended secret prayer frequently.

About the 15th of April 1733, I removed from my father's house to East-Haddam, where I spent four years, but still "without God in the world;" though, for the most part, I went a round of secret duty. I was not exceedingly addicted to young company, or frolicking (as it is called). But this I know, that when I did go into company, I never returned from a frolick in my life, with so good a conscience as I went with; it always added new guilt to me, and made me afraid to come to the throne of grace, and spoiled those good frames I was wont sometimes to please myself with. But, alas! all my good frames were but self-righteousness, not bottomed on a desire for the glory of God.

About the latter end of April 1737, being full nineteen years of age, I removed to Durham, and began to work on my farm, and so continued the year out, or near, till I was twenty years old; frequently longing, from a natural inclination, after a liberal education. When I was about twenty years of age, I applied myself to study; and sometime before, was more than ordinarily excited to and in duty: but now engaged more than ever in the duties of religion. I became very strict, and watchful over my thoughts, words, and actions; and thought I must be sober indeed, because I designed to devote myself to the ministry; and imagined I did dedicate myself to the Lord.

Some time in April 1738, I went to Mr Fiske's, and lived with him during his life *. And I remember, he advised me wholly to abandon young company, and associate myself with grave elderly people: which counsel I followed; and my manner of life was now exceeding regular, and full of religion, such as it was; for I read my Bible more than twice through in less than a year, I spent much time every day in secret prayer, and other secret duties; I gave great attention to the word preached, and endeavoured to my utmost to retain it. So much concerned was I about religion, that I agreed with some young persons to meet privately on Sabbath-evenings for religious exercises, and thought myself sincere in these duties; and after our meeting was ended, I used to repeat the discourses of the day to myself, and recollect what I could, though sometimes it was very late in the night. Again, on Monday-mornings I used sometimes to recollect the same sermons. And I had sometimes considerable movings of affections in duties, and much pleasure, and had many thoughts of joining to the church. In short, I had a very good outside, and rested entirely on my duties, though I was not sensible of it.

After Mr Fiske's death, I proceeded in my learning with my brother; and was still very constant in religious duties, and often wondered at the levity of professors; it was a trouble to me, that they were so careless in religious matters.—Thus I proceeded a considerable length on a *self-righteous* foundation; and should have been entirely lost and undone, had not the mere mercy of God prevented.

Some time in the beginning of winter, *anno* 1738, it pleased God, on one Sabbath-day morning, as I was walking out for some secret duties, (as I remember), to give me on a sudden such a sense of my danger, and the wrath of God, that I stood amazed, and my former good frames, that I had pleased myself with, all presently vanished; and from the view that I had of my sin and vileness, I was much distressed all that day, fearing the vengeance of God would soon overtake me; I was much dejected, and kept much alone, and sometimes begrutched the birds and beasts their happiness, because they were not exposed to eternal misery, as I evidently saw I was. And thus I lived from day to day, being frequently in great distress: sometimes there appeared mountains before me to obstruct my hopes of mercy; and the work of conversion appeared so great, I thought I should never be the subject of it:

* Mr Fiske was the pastor of the church in Haddam.

but

but used, however, to pray and cry to God, and perform other duties with great earnestness, and hoped by some means to make the case better. And though I hundreds of times renounced all pretences of any *worth* in my duties, (as I thought), even in the season of the performance of them, and often confessed to God that I deserved nothing for the very best of them, but eternal condemnation; yet still I had a secret latent hope of *recommending* myself to God by my religious duties; and when I prayed affectionately, and my heart seemed in some measure to melt, I hoped God would be thereby moved to pity me, my prayers then looked with some appearance of *goodness* in them, and I seemed to *mourn* for sin: and then I could in some measure venture on the mercy of God in Christ, (as I thought), though the preponderating thought and foundation of my hope was some imagination of *goodness* in my heart-meltings, and flowing of affections in duty, and (sometimes) extraordinary enlargements therein, *&c.* Though at some times the gate appeared so very strait, that it looked next to impossible to enter, yet at other times I flattered myself that it was not so very difficult, and hoped I should by diligence and watchfulness soon gain the point. Sometimes after enlargement in duty and considerable affection, I hoped I had made a *good step* towards heaven, and imagined that God was affected as I was, and that he would hear such *sincere cries*, (as I called them): and so sometimes when I withdrew for secret duties in great distress, I returned something comfortable; and thus healed myself with my duties.

Some time in February 1738-9, I set apart a day for secret fasting and prayer, and spent the day in almost incessant cries to God for mercy, that he would open my eyes to see the evil of sin, and the way of life by Jesus Christ. And God was pleased that day to make considerable discoveries of my heart to me. But still I *trusted* in all the duties I performed; though there was no manner of *goodness* in the duties I then performed, there being no manner of respect to the glory of God in them, nor any such principle in my heart; yet God was pleased to make my endeavours that day, a means to shew me my *helplessness* in some measure.

Sometimes I was greatly *encouraged*, and imagined that God loved me, and was pleased with me, and thought I should soon be fully reconciled to God; while the whole was founded on mere *presumption*, arising from enlargement in duty, or flowing of affections, or some good resolutions, and the like. And when, at times, great distress began to arise, on a sight of my vileness and nakedness, and inability to de-

liver

liver myſelf from a ſovereign God, I uſed to put off the diſcovery, as what I could not bear. Once, I remember, a terrible pang of diſtreſs ſeized me, and the thoughts of renouncing myſelf, and ſtanding naked before God, ſtripped of all goodneſs, were ſo dreadful to me, that I was ready to ſay to them as Felix to Paul, "Go thy way for this time." Thus, though I daily longed for greater conviction of ſin, ſuppoſing that I muſt ſee more of my dreadful ſtate in order to a remedy; yet when the diſcoveries of my vile helliſh heart were made to me, the ſight was ſo dreadful, and ſhewed me ſo plainly my expoſedneſs to damnation, that I could not endure it.——I conſtantly ſtrove after whatever *qualifications* I imagined others obtained before the reception of Chriſt, in order to *recommend* me to his favour. Sometimes I felt the power of an *hard heart*, and ſuppoſed it muſt be *ſoftened* before Chriſt would accept of me; and when I felt any meltings of heart, I hoped now the work was almoſt done: and hence, when my diſtreſs ſtill remained, I was wont to murmur at God's dealings with me; and thought, when others felt their hearts ſoftened, God ſhewed them mercy; but my diſtreſs remained ſtill.

Sometimes I grew *remiſs* and *ſluggiſh*, without any great convictions of ſin, for a conſiderable time together; but after ſuch a ſeaſon, convictions ſometimes ſeized me more violently. One night I remember in particular, when I was walking ſolitarily abroad, I had opened to me ſuch a view of my ſin, that I feared the ground would cleave aſunder under my feet, and become my grave, and ſend my ſoul quick into hell, before I could get home. And though I was forced to go to bed, leſt my diſtreſs ſhould be diſcovered by others, which I much feared; yet I ſcarce durſt ſleep at all, for I thought it would be a great wonder if I ſhould be out of hell in the morning. And though my diſtreſs was ſometimes thus great, yet I greatly dreaded the loſs of convictions, and returning back to a ſtate of carnal ſecurity, and to my former inſenſibility of impending wrath; which made me exceeding exact in my behaviour, leſt I ſhould ſtifle the motions of God's Spirit. When at any time I took a view of my convictions of my own ſinfulneſs, and thought the degree of them to be conſiderable, I was wont to truſt in my convictions: but this confidence, and the hopes that aroſe in me from it, of ſoon making ſome notable advances towards deliverance, would eaſe my mind, and I ſoon became more ſenſeleſs and remiſs: but then again, when I diſcerned my convictions to grow languid, and I thought them about to leave me, this immediately

immediately alarmed and distressed me. Sometimes I expected to take a large step, and get very far towards conversion, by some particular opportunity or means I had in view.

The many disappointments, and great distresses and perplexity I met with, put me into a most *horrible frame* of *contesting* with the Almighty; with an inward vehemence and virulence, finding fault with his ways of dealing with mankind. I found great fault with the imputation of Adam's sin to his posterity: and my wicked heart often wished for some other way of salvation, than by Jesus Christ. And being like the troubled sea, and my thoughts confused, I used to contrive to escape the wrath of God by some other means, and had strange projections, full of Atheism, contriving to disappoint God's designs and decrees concerning me, or to escape God's notice, and hide myself from him. But when, upon reflection, I saw these projections were vain, and would not serve me, and that I could contrive nothing for my own relief, this would throw my mind into the most horrid frame, to wish there was no God, or to wish there were some other God that could controul him, *&c.* These thoughts and desires were the secret inclinations of my heart, that were frequently acting before I was aware; but, alas! they were *mine*, although I was affrighted with them, when I came to reflect on them: when I considered of it, it distressed me, to think, that my heart was so full of enmity against God; and it made me tremble, lest God's vengeance should suddenly fall upon me. I used before, to imagine my heart was not so bad, as the scriptures and some other books represented. Sometimes I used to take much pains to work it up into a good frame, a humble submissive disposition; and hoped there was then some goodness in me: but it may be on a sudden, the thoughts of the strictness of the law, or the sovereignty of God, would so irritate the corruption of my heart, that I had so watched over, and hoped I had brought to a good frame, that it would break over all bounds, and burst forth on all sides, like floods of waters when they break down their damm. But being sensible of the necessity of a deep humiliation in order to a saving close with Christ, I used to set myself to work in my own heart those convictions that were requisite in such an humiliation; as, a conviction, that God would be just, if he cast me off for ever; and that if ever God should bestow mercy on me, it would be mere grace, though I should be in distress many years first, and be never so much engaged in duty; that God was not in the least obliged to

pity

pity me the more for all past duties, cries, and tears, &c. These things I strove to my utmost to bring myself to a firm belief of, and hearty assent to; and hoped that now I was brought off from myself, and truly humbled and bowed to the divine sovereignty; and was wont to tell God in my prayers, that now I had those very dispositions of soul that he required, and on which he shewed mercy to others, and thereupon to beg and plead for mercy to me. But when I found no relief, and was still oppressed with guilt, and fears of wrath, my soul was in a tumult, and my heart rose against God, as dealing hardly with me. Yet then my conscience flew in my face, putting me in mind of my late confession to God of his justice in my condemnation, &c. And this giving me a sight of the badness of my heart, threw me again into distress, and I wished I had watched my heart more narrowly, to keep it from breaking out against God's dealings with me, and I even wished I had not pleaded for mercy on account of my humiliation, because thereby I had lost all my seeming goodness.

Thus, scores of times, I vainly imagined myself humbled and prepared for saving mercy.

While I was in this distressed, bewildered, and tumultuous state of mind, the *corruption* of my heart was especially *irritated* with these things following.

1. The *strictness* of the divine *law*. For I found it was impossible for me (after my utmost pains) to answer the demands of it. I often made new resolutions, and as often broke them. I imputed the whole to carelessness, and the want of being more watchful, and used to call myself a fool for my negligence. But when, upon a stronger resolution, and greater endeavours, and close application of myself to fasting and prayer, I found all attempts fail, then I quarrelled with the law of God, as unreasonably rigid. I thought, if it extended only to my outward actions and behaviours, I could bear with it; but I found it condemned me for my evil thoughts, and sins of my heart, which I could not possibly prevent. I was extremely loth to give out, and own my utter helplessness in this matter: but after repeated disappointments, thought that, rather than perish, I could do a little more still, especially if such and such circumstances might but attend my endeavours and strivings; I hoped, that I should strive more earnestly than ever, if the matter came to extremity, (though I never could find the time to do my utmost, in the manner I intended): and this hope of future more favourable circumstances, and of doing something great

great hereafter, kept me from utter despair in myself, and from seeing myself fallen into the hands of a sovereign God, and dependent on nothing but free and boundless grace.

2. Another thing was, that *faith alone* was the *condition of salvation;* and that God would not come down to lower terms, that he would not promise life and salvation upon my sincere and hearty prayers and endeavours. That word, Mark xvi. 16. "He that believeth not, shall be damned," cut off all hope there: and I found, faith was the sovereign gift of God; that I could not get it as of myself, and could not oblige God to bestow it upon me, by any of my performances, (Eph. ii. 1. 8.) "This," I was ready to say, "is a hard saying, who can hear it?" I could not bear, that all I had done should stand for mere nothing, who had been very conscientious in duty, and had been exceeding religious a great while, and had (as I thought) done much more than many others that had obtained mercy. I confessed indeed the vileness of my duties; but then, what made them at that time seem vile, was my wandering thoughts in them; not because I was all over defiled like a devil, and the principle corrupt from whence they flowed, so that I could not possibly do any thing that was good. And therefore I called what I did, by the name of honest faithful endeavours; and could not bear it, that God had made no promises of salvation to them.

3. Another thing was, that I could not find out *what* faith was; or *what* it was to believe, and come to Christ. I read the calls of Christ, made to the *weary* and *heavy laden;* but could find no way that he directed them to come in. I thought, I would gladly come, if I knew *how*, though the path of duty directed to were never so difficult. I read Mr Stoddard's *Guide to Christ*, (which I trust was, in the hand of God, the happy means of my conversion), and my heart rose against the author; for though he told me my very heart all along under convictions, and seemed to be very beneficial to me in his directions; yet here he failed, he did not tell me any thing I could do, that would bring me to Christ, but left me as it were with a great gulph between me and Christ, without any direction to get through. For I was not yet effectually and experimentally taught, that there could be no way prescribed, whereby a natural man could, of his own strength, obtain that which is supernatural, and which the highest angel cannot give.

4. Another thing that I found a great inward opposition to, was the *sovereignty* of God. I could not bear, that it should be wholly at God's pleasure, to save or damn me,

just as he would. That passage, Rom. ix. 11.—23. was a constant vexation to me, especially vers. 21. The reading or meditating on this always destroyed my seeming good frames: when I thought I was almost humbled, and almost resigned to God's sovereignty, the reading or thinking on this passage would make my enmity against the sovereignty of God appear. And when I came to reflect on my inward enmity and blasphemy, that arose on this occasion, I was the more afraid of God, and driven further from any hopes of reconciliation with him; and it gave me such a dreadful view of myself, that I dreaded more than ever to see myself in God's hands, and at his sovereign disposal, and it made me more opposite than ever to submit to his sovereignty; for I thought God designed my damnation.——

All this time the Spirit of God was powerfully at work with me; and I was inwardly pressed to relinquish all *self-confidence*, all hopes of ever helping myself by any means whatsoever: and the conviction of my *lost* estate was sometimes so clear and manifest before my eyes, that it was as if it had been declared to me in so many words, "It is done, it is done, it "is for ever impossible to deliver yourself." For about three or four days, my soul was thus distressed, especially at some turns, when for a few moments I seemed to myself lost and undone; but then would shrink back immediately from the sight, because I dared not venture myself into the hands of God, as wholly helpless, and at the disposal of his sovereign pleasure. I dared not see that important truth concerning myself, that I was *dead in trespasses and sins*. But when I had as it were thrust away these views of myself at any time, I felt distressed to have the same discoveries of myself again; for I greatly feared being given over of God to final stupidity. When I thought of putting it off to a *more convenient season*, the conviction was so close and powerful with regard to the present time, that it was the best time, and probably the only time, that I dared not put it off. It was the sight of *truth*, concerning myself, *truth* respecting my state, as a creature fallen and alienated from God, and that consequently could make no demands on God for mercy, but must subscribe to the absolute sovereignty of the divine Being; the sight of the *truth*, I say, my soul shrank away from, and trembled to think of beholding. Thus, "He that doth evil," as all unregenerate men continually do, "hates the light of truth," neither cares to *come to it*, because it will *reprove his deeds*, and shew him his just deserts, John iii. 20. And though some time before, I had taken much pains (as I thought) to sub-

mit

mit to the ſovereignty of God, yet I miſtook the thing; and did not once imagine, that ſeeing and being made experimentally ſenſible of this truth, which my ſoul now ſo much dreaded and trembled at a ſenſe of, was the frame of ſoul that I had been ſo earneſt in purſuit of heretofore: for I had ever hoped, that when I had attained to that *humiliation*, which I ſuppoſed neceſſary to go before faith, then it would not be fair for God to *caſt me off;* but now I ſaw it was ſo far from any goodneſs in me, to own myſelf ſpiritually dead, and deſtitute of all goodneſs, that, on the contrary, *my mouth* would be for ever *ſtopped* by it; and it looked as dreadful to me, to ſee myſelf, and the relation I ſtood in to God, as a ſinner and I criminal, and he a great Judge and Sovereign, as it would be to a poor trembling creature, to venture off ſome high precipice. And hence I put it off for a minute or two, and tried for better circumſtances to do it in; either I muſt read a paſſage or two, or pray firſt, or ſomething of the like nature; or elſe put off my ſubmiſſion to God's ſovereignty, with an objection, that I did not know how to ſubmit. But the truth was, I could ſee no ſafety in owning myſelf in the hands of a ſovereign God, and that I could lay no claim to any thing better than damnation.

But after a conſiderable time ſpent in ſuch like exerciſes and diſtreſſes, one morning, while I was walking in a ſolitary place, as uſual, I at once ſaw that all my contrivances and projections to effect or procure deliverance and ſalvation for myſelf, were utterly *in vain;* I was brought quite to a ſtand as finding myſelf totally *loſt*. I had thought many times before, that the difficulties in my way were very great; but now I ſaw, in another and very different light, that it was for ever impoſſible for me to do any thing towards helping or delivering myſelf. I then thought of blaming myſelf, that I had not done more, and been more engaged, while I had opportunity; (for it ſeemed now as if the ſeaſon of doing was for ever over and gone): but I inſtantly ſaw, that let me have done what I would, it would no more have tended to my helping myſelf, than what I had done; that I had made all the pleas I ever could have made to all eternity; and that all my pleas were vain. The *tumult* that had been before in my mind, was now *quieted;* and I was ſomething eaſed of that diſtreſs, which I felt, while ſtruggling againſt a ſight of myſelf, and of the divine ſovereignty. I had the greateſt certainty, that my ſtate was for ever miſerable, for all that I could do; and wondered, and was almoſt aſtoniſhed, that I had never been ſenſible of it before.

In the time while I remained in this ſtate, my *notions* reſpecting my *duties*, were quite different from what I had ever entertained in times paſt. Before this, the more I did in duty, the more I thought God was obliged to me; or at leaſt the more hard I thought it would be for God to caſt me off; though at the ſame time I confeſſed, and thought I ſaw, that there was no goodneſs or merit in my duties: but now the more I did in prayer or any other duty, the more I ſaw I was indebted to God for allowing me to aſk for mercy; for I ſaw, it was ſelf-intereſt had led me to pray, and that I had never once prayed from any reſpect to the glory of God. Now I ſaw, there was no neceſſary connection between my prayers and the beſtowment of divine mercy; that they laid not the leaſt obligation upon God to beſtow his grace upon me; and that there was no more virtue or goodneſs in them, than there would be in my paddling with my hand in the water, (which was the compariſon I had then in my mind); and this becauſe they were not performed from any love or regard to God. I ſaw, that I had been heaping up my devotions before God, faſting, praying, &c. pretending, and indeed really thinking, at ſome times, that I was aiming at the glory of God; whereas I never once truly intended it, but only my own happineſs. I ſaw, that as I had never done any thing *for* God, I had no claim to lay to any thing *from* him, but perdition, on account of my hypocriſy and mockery. Oh how different did my duties now appear from what they uſed to do! I uſed to charge them with ſin and imperfection; but this was only on account of the wanderings and vain thoughts attending them, and not becauſe I had no regard to God in them; for this I thought I had: but when I ſaw evidently that I had regard to nothing but ſelf-intereſt, then they appeared vile mockery of God, ſelf-worſhip, and a continual courſe of lies; ſo that I ſaw now, there was ſomething worſe had attended my duties, than barely a few wanderings, &c.; for the whole was nothing but ſelf-worſhip, and an horrid abuſe of God.

I continued, as I remember, in this ſtate of mind, from Friday morning till the Sabbath-evening following, July 12. 1739. when I was walking again in the ſame ſolitary place, where I was brought to ſee myſelf loſt and helpleſs, (as was before mentioned): and here, in a mournful melancholy ſtate, was attempting to pray; but found no heart to engage in that or any other duty; my former concern and exerciſe, and religious affections were now gone. I thought, the Spirit of God had quite left me; but ſtill was not diſtreſſed: yet diſ-

conſolate,

consolate, as if there was nothing in heaven or earth could make me happy. And having been thus endeavouring to pray (though being, as I thought, very stupid and senseless) for near half an hour, (and by this time the sun was about half an hour high, as I remember), then, as I was walking in a dark thick grove, *unspeakable glory* seemed to open to the view and apprehension of my soul: I do not mean any external brightness, for I saw no such thing; nor do I intend any imagination of a body of light, some where away in the third heavens, or any thing of that nature; but it was a new inward apprehension or view that I had of God, such as I never had before, nor any thing which had the least resemblance of it. I stood still, and wondered and admired! I knew that I never had seen before any thing comparable to it for excellency and beauty; it was widely different from all the conceptions that ever I had had of God, or things divine. I had no particular apprehension of any one person in the Trinity, either the Father, the Son, or the Holy Ghost; but it appeared to be *divine glory*, that I then beheld: and my soul *rejoiced with joy unspeakable*, to see such a God, such a glorious divine Being; and I was inwardly pleased and satisfied, that he should be *God over all* for ever and ever. My soul was so captivated and delighted with the excellency, loveliness, greatness, and other perfections of God, that I was even swallowed up in him; at least to that degree, that I had no thought (as I remember) at *first*, about my own salvation, and scarce reflected there was such a creature as myself.

Thus God, I trust, brought me to a hearty disposition to *exalt him*, and set him on the throne, and principally and ultimately to aim at his honour and glory, as King of the universe.

I continued in this state of inward joy and peace, yet astonishment, till near dark, without any sensible abatement; and then began to think and examine what I had seen; and felt sweetly *composed* in my mind all the evening following. I felt myself in a new world, and every thing about me appeared with a different aspect from what it was wont to do.

At this time, the *way of salvation* opened to me with such infinite wisdom, suitableness, and excellency, that I wondered I should ever think of any other way of salvation; was amazed, that I had not dropped my own contrivances, and complied with this lovely, blessed, and excellent way before. If I could have been saved by my own duties, or any other way

way that I had formerly contrived, my whole ſoul would now have refuſed. I wondered, that all the world did not ſee and comply with this way of ſalvation, entirely by the *righteouſneſs of Chriſt*.

The ſweet reliſh of what I then felt, continued with me for ſeveral days, almoſt conſtantly, in a greater or leſs degree; I could not but ſweetly rejoice in God, lying down and riſing up. The next Lord's day I felt ſomething of the ſame kind, though not ſo powerful as before. But, not long after, was again involved in *thick darkneſs*, and under great diſtreſs; yet not of the ſame kind with my diſtreſs under convictions. I was guilty, afraid, and aſhamed to come before God; was exceedingly preſſed with a ſenſe of guilt: but it was not long before I felt (I truſt) true repentance and joy in God.

About the latter end of Auguſt, I again fell under great darkneſs; it ſeemed as if the preſence of God was *clean gone for ever;* though I was not ſo much diſtreſſed about my ſpiritual ſtate, as I was at my being ſhut out from God's preſence, as I then ſenſibly was. But it pleaſed the Lord to return graciouſly to me, not long after.

In the beginning of September I went to college *, and entered there; but with ſome degree of reluctancy, fearing leſt I ſhould not be able to lead a life of ſtrict religion, in the midſt of ſo many temptations.——After this, in the vacancy, before I went to tarry at college, it pleaſed God to viſit my ſoul with clearer manifeſtations of himſelf and his grace. I was ſpending ſome time in prayer, and ſelf-examination; and the Lord by his grace ſo ſhined into my heart, that I enjoyed full aſſurance of his favour, for that time; and my ſoul was unſpeakably refreſhed with divine and heavenly enjoyments. At this time eſpecially, as well as ſome others, ſundry paſſages of God's word opened to my ſoul with divine clearneſs, power, and ſweetneſs, ſo as to appear exceeding precious, and with clear and certain evidence of its being *the word of God*. I enjoyed conſiderable ſweetneſs in religion all the winter following.

In Jan. 1739—40, the meaſles ſpread much in college; and I having taken the diſtemper, went home to Haddam. But ſome days before I was taken ſick, I ſeemed to be greatly deſerted, and my ſoul mourned the abſence of the Comforter exceedingly: it ſeemed to me, all comfort was for ever gone; I prayed and cried to God for help, yet found no preſent comfort or relief. But through divine goodneſs, a night

* Yale-college in New-Haven.

on

or two before I was taken ill, while I was walking alone in a very retired place, and engaged in meditation and prayer, I enjoyed a ſweet refreſhing viſit, as I truſt, from above, ſo that my ſoul was raiſed far above the fears of death; indeed I rather longed for death, than feared it. O how much more refreſhing this one ſeaſon was, than all the pleaſures and delights that earth can afford! After a day or two I was taken with the meaſles, and was very ill indeed, ſo that I almoſt deſpaired of life; but had no diſtreſſing fears of death at all. However, through divine goodneſs I ſoon recovered: yet, by reaſon of hard and cloſe ſtudies, and being much expoſed on account of my freſhman-ſhip, I had but little time for ſpiritual duties; my ſoul often mourned for want of more time and opportunity to be alone with God. In the Spring and Summer following, I had better advantages for retirement, and enjoyed more comfort in religion: though indeed my ambition in my ſtudies greatly wronged the activity and vigour of my ſpiritual life: yet this was uſually the caſe with me, that "in the multitude of my thoughts "within me, God's comforts *principally* delighted my ſoul;" theſe were my greateſt conſolations day by day.

One day I remember in particular, (I think it was in June 1740), I walked to a conſiderable diſtance from the college, in the fields alone at noon, and in prayer found ſuch unſpeakable ſweetneſs and delight in God, that I thought, if I muſt continue ſtill in this evil world, I wanted always to be there, to behold God's glory: my ſoul dearly loved all mankind, and longed exceedingly that they ſhould enjoy what I enjoyed. ——It ſeemed to be a little reſemblance of heaven.

On Lord's day, July 6. being ſacrament-day, I found ſome divine life and ſpiritual refreſhment in that holy ordinance. When I came from the Lord's table, I wondered how my fellow-ſtudents could live as I was ſenſible moſt did.——Next Lord's day, July 13. I had ſome ſpecial ſweetneſs in religion. ——Again, Lord's day, July 20. my ſoul was in a ſweet and precious frame.

Some time in Auguſt following, I became ſo weakly and diſordered, by too cloſe application to my ſtudies, that I was adviſed by my tutor to go home, and diſengage my mind from ſtudy, as much as I could; for I was grown ſo weak, that I began to ſpit blood. I took his advice, and endeavoured to lay aſide my ſtudies. But being brought very low, I looked death in the face more ſtedfaſtly; and the Lord was pleaſed to give me renewedly a ſweet ſenſe and reliſh of divine things; and particularly in October 13. I found divine help

help and consolation in the precious duties of secret prayer and self-examination, and my soul took delight in the blessed God:—so likewise on the 17th of October.

Saturday, October 18. in my morning devotions, my soul was exceedingly melted for, and bitterly mourned over my exceeding *sinfulness* and *vileness*. I never before had felt so pungent and deep a sense of the odious nature of sin, as at this time. My soul was then unusually carried forth in love to God, and had a lively sense of God's love to me. And this love and hope, at that time, cast out fear. Both morning and evening I spent some time in self-examination, to find the truth of grace, as also my fitness to approach to God at his table the next day; and through infinite grace, found the holy Spirit influencing my soul with love to God, as a witness within myself.

Lord's day, October 19. in the morning I felt my soul *hungering and thirsting after righteousness*. In the forenoon, while I was looking on the sacramental elements, and thinking that Jesus Christ would soon be "set forth crucified before me," my soul was filled with light and love, so that I was almost in an ecstasy; my body was so weak, I could scarcely stand. I felt at the same time an exceeding tenderness and most fervent love towards all mankind; so that my soul and all the powers of it seemed, as it were, to melt into softness and sweetness. But in the season of the communion, there was some abatement of this sweet life and fervour. This love and joy cast out fear; and my soul longed for perfect grace and glory. This sweet frame continued till the evening, when my soul was sweetly spiritual in secret duties.

Monday, October 20. I again found the sweet assistance of the holy Spirit in secret duties, both morning and evening, and life and comfort in religion through the whole day.

Tuesday, October 21. I had likewise experience of the goodness of God in "shedding abroad his love in my heart," and giving me delight and consolation in religious duties; and all the remaining part of the week, my soul seemed to be taken up with divine things. I now so longed after God, and to be freed from sin, that when I felt myself recovering, and thought I must return to college again, which had proved so hurtful to my spiritual interest the year past, I could not but be grieved, and I thought I had much rather have died; for it distressed me, to think of getting away from God. But before I went, I enjoyed several other sweet and precious seasons of communion with God, (particularly October 30.

and Nov. 4.), wherein my ſoul enjoyed unſpeakable comfort.

I returned to college about November 6. and through the goodneſs of God, felt the power of religion almoſt daily, for the ſpace of ſix weeks.

November 28. In my evening-devotion, I enjoyed precious diſcoveries of God, and was unſpeakably refreſhed with that paſſage, Heb. xii. 22. 23. 24. that my ſoul longed to wing away for the paradiſe of God; I longed to be conformed to God in all things.——A day or two after, I enjoyed much of the light of God's countenance, moſt of the day; and my ſoul reſted in God.

Tueſday, December 9. I was in a comfortable frame of ſoul moſt of the day; but eſpecially in evening-devotions, when God was pleaſed wonderfully to aſſiſt and ſtrengthen me; ſo that I thought nothing ſhould ever move me from the love of God in Chriſt Jeſus my Lord.—O! *one hour with God* infinitely exceeds all the pleaſures and delights of this lower world.

Some time towards the latter end of January 1740,-41. I grew more *cold* and *dull* in matters of religion, by means of my old temptation, *viz.* ambition in my ſtudies.—But through divine goodneſs, a great and general *awakening* ſpread itſelf over the college, about the latter end of February, in which I was much quickened, and more abundantly engaged in religion.

[This awakening here ſpoken of, was at the beginning of that extraordinary religious commotion through the land, which is freſh in every one's memory. This awakening was for a time very great and general at New-Haven; and the college had no ſmall ſhare in it: that ſociety was greatly reformed, the ſtudents in general became ſerious, and many of them remarkably ſo, and much engaged in the concerns of their eternal ſalvation. And however undeſirable the iſſue of the awakenings of that day have appeared in many others, there have been manifeſtly happy and abiding effects of the impreſſions then made on the minds of many of the members of that college. And by all that I can learn concerning Mr Brainerd, there can be no reaſon to doubt but that he had much of God's gracious preſence, and of the lively actings of true grace, at that time: but yet he was afterwards abundantly ſenſible, that his religious experiences and affections at that time were not free from a corrupt mixture, nor his conduct to be acquitted from many things that were imprudent and blameable; which he greatly lamented himſelf, and was willing that others ſhould forget, that none might make an ill improvement of ſuch an example. And therefore although in the time of it, he kept a conſtant diary, containing a very particular account of what paſſed from day to day, for the next thirteen months, from the latter end of January 1740,—41: forementioned, in two ſmall books, which he called the two firſt volumes of his diary, next following the account before given of his convictions, converſion, and conſequent comforts; yet, when he lay on his death-bed, he gave order (unknown to me, till after his death) that theſe two volumes ſhould be deſtroyed, and in the beginning of the third book of his diary, he wrote thus, (by the hand of another, he not being able to write himſelf), "The two preceding volumes immediately following the account of the author's converſion, are loſt. If any are deſirous to know how the author lived, in general, during that ſpace of time, let them read the firſt thirty pages of this volume; where they will find ſomething of a ſpecimen of his ordinary manner of living, through that whole ſpace of time, which was about thirteen months; excepting that here he was more refined from ſome *imprudencies* and *indecent heats*, than there; but the ſpirit of devotion running through the whole, was the ſame."

It could not be otherwiſe than that one whoſe heart had been ſo prepared and drawn to God, as Mr Brainerd's had been, ſhould be mightily enlarged, animated, and engaged at the ſight of ſuch an alteration made in the college, the town, and land; and ſo great an appearance of mens reforming their lives, and turning from their profaneneſs and immorality, to ſeriouſneſs and concern for their ſalvation, and of religion's reviving and flouriſhing almoſt every where. But as an intemperate imprudent zeal, and a degree of enthuſiaſm ſoon crept in, and mingled itſelf with that revival of religion; and ſo great and general an awakening being quite a new thing in the land, at leaſt as to all the living inhabitants of it; neither people nor miniſters had learned thoroughly to diſtinguiſh between ſolid religion and its deluſive counterfeits; even many miniſters of the goſpel, of long ſtanding and the beſt reputation, were for a time overpowered with the glaring appearances of the latter: and therefore ſurely it was not to be wondered at, that young Brainerd, but a ſophimore at college, ſhould be ſo; who was not only young in years, but very young in religion and experience, and had had but little opportunity

opportunity for the study of divinity, and still less for observation of the circumstances and events of such an extraordinary state of things: a man must divest himself of all reason, to make strange of it. In these disadvantageous circumstances, Brainerd had the unhappiness to have a tincture of that intemperate indiscreet zeal, which was at that time too prevalent; and was led, from his high opinion of others that he looked upon better than himself, into such errors as were really contrary to the habitual temper of his mind. One instance of his misconduct at that time, gave great offence to the rulers of the college, even to that degree that they expelled him the society; which it is necessary should here be particularly related, with its circumstances.

In the time of the awakening at college, there were several religious students that associated themselves one with another for mutual conversation and assistance in spiritual things, who were wont freely to open themselves one to another, as special and intimate friends: Brainerd was one of this company. And it once happened, that he and two or three more of these his intimate friends were in the hall together, after Mr Whittelsey, one of the tutors, had been to prayer there with the scholars; no other person now remaining in the hall, but Brainerd and these his companions. Mr Whittelsey having been unusually pathetical in his prayer, one of Brainerd's friends on this occasion asked him what he thought of Mr Whittelsey; he made answer, "He has no more grace than "this chair." One of the freshmen happening at that time to be near the hall (though not in the room) over-heard those words of his; though he heard no name mentioned, and knew not who the person was, which was thus censured: he informed a certain woman that belonged to the town, withal telling her his own suspicion, *viz.* that he believed Brainerd said this of some one or other of the rulers of the college. Whereupon she went and informed the rector, who sent for this freshman and examined him; and he told the rector the words that he heard Brainerd utter, and informed him who were in the room with him at that time. Upon which the rector sent for them: they were very backward to inform against their friend, of that which they looked upon as private conversation, and especially as none but they had heard or knew of whom he had uttered those words; yet the rector compelled them to declare what he said, and of whom he said it.——Brainerd looked on himself greatly abused in the management of this affair; and thought, that what he said in private, was injuriously extorted from his friends, and that then it was injuriously required of him (as it was wont to be of such as had been guilty of some open notorious crime) to make a public confession, and to humble himself before the whole college in the hall, for what he had said only in private conversation.——He not complying with this demand, and having gone once to the separate meeting at New-Haven, when forbidden by the rector, and also having been accused by one person of saying concerning the rector, that he wondered he did not expect to drop down dead for fining the scholars who followed Mr Tennent to Milford, though there was no proof of it, (and Mr Brainerd ever professed that he did not remember his saying any thing to that purpose); for these things he was expelled the college.

Now, how far the circumstances and exigences of that day might justify such great severity in the governors of the college, I will not undertake to determine; it being my aim, not to bring reproach on the authority of the college, but only to do justice to the memory of a person, who I think to be eminently one of those whose *memory is blessed*.——The reader will see, in the sequel of the story of Mr Brainerd's life *, what his own thoughts afterwards were of his behaviour in these things, and in how Christian a manner he conducted himself, with respect to this affair: though he ever, as long as he lived, supposed himself much abused, in the management of it, and in what he suffered in it.

His expulsion was in the winter *anno* 1741–2. while he was in his third year in college.]

* Particularly under the date, Wednesday, Sept. 14. 1743.

PART

PART II.

From about the time that he first began to devote himself more especially to the *study of divinity*, till he was examined and licensed to *preach*, by the Association of ministers belonging to the Eastern district of the county of Fairfield in Connecticut.

[MR Brainerd, the Spring after his expulsion, went to live with the Reverend Mr Mills of Ripton, to follow his studies with him, in order to his being fitted for the work of the ministry; where he spent the greater part of the time till the Association licensed him to preach; but frequently rode to visit the neighbouring ministers, particularly Mr Cooke of Stratfield, Mr Graham of Southbury, and Mr Bellamy of Bethlehem.

Here (at Mr Mills's) he began the third book of his diary, in which the account he wrote of himself, is as follows.]

Thursday, April 1. 1742. I seem to be declining with respect to my life and warmth in divine things; had not so free access to God in prayer as usual of late. O that God would humble me deeply in the dust before him! I deserve hell every day, for not loving my Lord more, "who has (I trust) loved me, and given himself for me;" and every time I am enabled to exercise any grace renewedly, I am renewedly indebted to the God of all grace for special assistance. "Where then is boasting?" Surely "it is excluded," when we think how we are dependent on God for the being and every act of grace. Oh, if ever I get to heaven, it will be because God will, and nothing else; for I never did any thing of myself, but get away from God! My soul will be astonished at the unsearchable riches of divine grace, when I arrive at the mansions, which the blessed Saviour is gone before to prepare.

Friday, April 2. In the afternoon I felt something sweetly

ly in ſecret prayer, much reſigned, calm, and ſerene. What are all the ſtorms of this lower world, if *Jeſus* by his Spirit does but come *walking on the ſeas!*—Some time paſt, I had much pleaſure in the proſpect of the Heathen's being brought home to Chriſt, and deſired that the Lord would improve *me* in that work:—but now my ſoul more frequently deſires to die, *to be with Chriſt.* O that my ſoul were wrapt up in divine love, and my longing deſires after God increaſed!—In the evening, was refreſhed in prayer, with the hopes of the advancement of Chriſt's kingdom in the world.

Saturday, April 3. Was very much amiſs this morning, and had an ill night laſt night. I thought, if God would take me to himſelf now, my ſoul would exceedingly rejoice. O that I may be always humble and reſigned to God, and that God would cauſe my ſoul to be more fixed on himſelf, that I may be more fitted both for doing and ſuffering!

Lord's day, April 4. My heart was wandering and lifeleſs. ——In the evening God gave me faith in prayer, and made my ſoul melt in ſome meaſure, and gave me to taſte a divine ſweetneſs.—O my bleſſed God! Let me climb up near to him, and love, and long, and plead, and wreſtle, and reach, and ſtretch after him, and for deliverance from the body of ſin and death.—Alas! my ſoul mourned to think I ſhould ever loſe ſight of its beloved again. "O come, Lord Jeſus, "Amen."

[On the evening of the next day, he complains that he ſeemed to be void of all reliſh of divine things, felt much of the prevalence of corruption, and ſaw in himſelf a diſpoſition to all manner of ſin; which brought a very great gloom on his mind, and caſt him down into the depths of melancholy; ſo that he ſpeaks of himſelf as aſtoniſhed, amazed, having no comfort, being filled with horror, ſeeing no comfort in heaven or earth.]

Tueſday, April 6. I walked out this morning to the ſame place where I was laſt night, and felt ſomething as I did then; but was ſomething relieved by reading ſome paſſages in my diary, and ſeemed to feel as if I might pray to the great God again with freedom; but was ſuddenly ſtruck with a damp, from the ſenſe I had of my own vileneſs.——Then I cried to God to waſh my ſoul, and cleanſe me from my exceeding filthineſs, to give me repentance and pardon; and it began to be ſomething ſweet, to pray.——And I could think of undergoing the greateſt ſufferings in the cauſe of Chriſt, with pleaſure; and found myſelf willing (if God ſhould ſo order it) to

ſuffer

suffer banishment from my native land, among the Heathen, that I might do something for their souls salvation, in distresses and deaths of any kind.——Then God gave me to wrestle earnestly for others, for the kingdom of Christ in the world, and for dear Christian friends.——I felt weaned from the world, and from my own reputation amongst men, willing to be despised, and to be a gazing-stock for the world to behold.——It is impossible for me to express how I then felt: I had not much joy, but some sense of the majesty of God, which made me as it were tremble: I saw myself mean and vile, which made me more willing that God should do what he would with me; it was all infinitely reasonable.

Wednesday, April 7. I had not so much fervency, but felt something as I did yesterday-morning, in prayer.——At noon I spent some time in secret, with some fervency, but scarce any sweetness; and felt very dull in the evening.

Thursday, April 8. Had raised hopes to-day respecting the Heathen. O that God would bring in great numbers of them to Jesus Christ! I cannot but hope I shall see that glorious day.——Every thing in this world seems exceeding vile and little to me: I look so to myself.——I had some little dawn of comfort to-day in prayer: but especially to-night I think I had some faith and power of intercession with God, was enabled to plead with God for the growth of grace in myself: and many of the dear children of God then lay with weight upon my soul. Blessed be the Lord! It is good to wrestle for divine blessings.

Friday, April 9. Most of my time in morning-devotion was spent without sensible sweetness; yet I had one delightful prospect of arriving at the heavenly world. I am more amazed than ever at such thoughts; for I see myself infinitely vile and unworthy. I feel very heartless and dull; and though I long for the presence of God, and seem constantly to reach towards God in desires, yet I cannot feel that divine and heavenly sweetness that I used to enjoy.——No poor creature stands in need of divine grace more than I, and none abuse it more than I have done, and still do.

Saturday, April 10. Spent much time in secret prayer this morning, and not without some comfort in divine things, and I hope had some faith in exercise: but am so low, and feel so little of the sensible presence of God, that I hardly know what to call faith, and am made to "possess the sins of my "youth," and the dreadful sin of my nature, and am all sin; I cannot think, nor act, but every motion is sin.——I feel some faint hopes, that God will, of his infinite mercy, return

again

again with ſhowers of converting grace to poor goſpel-abuſing ſinners; and my hopes of being improved in the cauſe of God, which of late have been almoſt extinct, ſeem now a little revived. O that all my late diſtreſſes and awful apprehenſions might prove but Chriſt's ſchool, to make me fit for greater ſervice, by learning me the great leſſon of humility!

Lord's day, April 11. In the morning, felt but little life, excepting that my heart was ſomething drawn out in thankfulneſs to God for his amazing grace and condeſcenſion to me, in paſt influences and aſſiſtances of his Spirit.——Afterwards had ſome ſweetneſs in the thoughts of arriving at the heavenly world. O for the happy day!——After public worſhip God gave me ſpecial aſſiſtance in prayer; I wreſtled with my dear Lord, with much ſweetneſs; and interceſſion was made a ſweet and delightful employment to me.——In the evening, as I was viewing the light in the north, was delighted in contemplation on the glorious morning of the reſurrection.

Monday, April 12. This morning the Lord was pleaſed to lift up the light of his countenance upon me in ſecret prayer, and made the ſeaſon very precious to my ſoul. And though I have been ſo depreſſed of late, reſpecting my hopes of future ſerviceableneſs in the cauſe of God; yet now I had much encouragement reſpecting that matter. I was ſpecially aſſiſted to intercede and plead for poor ſouls, and for the enlargement of Chriſt's kingdom in the world, and for ſpecial grace for myſelf, to fit me for ſpecial ſervices. I felt exceeding calm, and quite reſigned to God, reſpecting my future improvement, *when* and *where* he pleaſed: my faith lifted me above the world, and removed all thoſe mountains, that I could not look over of late: I thought I wanted not the favour of man to lean upon; for I knew Chriſt's favour was infinitely better, and that it was no matter *when*, nor *where*, nor *how* Chriſt ſhould ſend me, nor what trials he ſhould ſtill exerciſe me with, if I might be prepared for his work and will. I now found ſweetly revived in my mind the wonderful diſcovery of infinite wiſdom in all the diſpenſations of God towards me, which I had a little before I met with my great trial at college; every thing appeared full of the wiſdom of God.

Tueſday, April 13. Saw myſelf to be very mean and vile; wondered at thoſe that ſhewed me reſpect. Afterwards was ſomething comforted in ſecret retirement, and was aſſiſted to wreſtle with God, with ſome power, ſpirituality, and ſweetneſs.

ness. Blessed be the Lord, he is never unmindful of me, but always sends me needed supplies; and from time to time, when I am like one dead, raises me to life. O that I may never distrust infinite goodness!

Wednesday, April 14. My soul longed for communion with Christ, and for the mortification of indwelling corruption, especially spiritual pride. O there is a sweet day coming, wherein "the weary will be at rest!" My soul has enjoyed much sweetness this day in the hopes of its speedy arrival.

Thursday, April 15. My desires apparently centered in God, and I found a sensible attraction of soul after him sundry times to-day: I know *I long for God*, and a conformity to his will, in inward purity and holiness, ten thousand times more than for any thing here below.

Friday and Saturday, April 16. 17. Seldom prayed without some sensible sweetness and joy in the Lord. Sometimes I longed much "to be dissolved, and to be with Christ." O that God would enable me to grow in grace every day! Alas! my barrenness is such, that God might well say, "Cut it down."——I am afraid of a dead heart on the Sabbath now begun: O that God would quicken me by his grace!

Lord's day, April 18. Retired early this morning into the woods for prayer; had the assistance of God's Spirit, and faith in exercise, and was enabled to plead with fervency for the advancement of Christ's kingdom in the world, and to intercede for dear absent friends.——At noon, God enabled me to wrestle with him, and to feel (as I trust) the power of divine love in prayer.——At night, saw myself infinitely indebted to God, and had a view of my shortcomings: it seemed to me, that I had done as it were nothing for God, and that I never had *lived to him* but a few hours of my life.

Monday, April 19. I set apart this day for fasting and prayer to God for his grace, especially to prepare me for the work of the ministry, to give me divine aid and direction in my preparations for that great work, and in his own time to "send me into his harvest." Accordingly, in the morning, endeavoured to plead for the divine presence for the day, and not without some life. In the forenoon, I felt a power of intercession for precious immortal souls, for the advancement of the kingdom of my dear Lord and Saviour in the world; and withal, a most sweet resignation, and even consolation and joy in the thoughts of suffering hardships, distresses, and even death itself, in the promotion of it; and had special enlargement in pleading for the enlightening and conversion of the poor Heathen. In the afternoon, "God was with me of a "truth." O it was blessed company indeed! God enabled me so to agonize in prayer, that I was quite wet with sweat, though in the shade, and the wind cool. My soul was drawn out very much for the world: I grasped for multitudes of souls. I think I had more enlargement for sinners, than for the children of God; though I felt as if I could spend my life in cries for both. I enjoyed great sweetness in communion with my dear Saviour. I think I never in my life felt such an entire weanedness from this world, and so much resigned to God in every thing.——O that I may always live *to* and *upon* my blessed God! Amen, Amen.

Tuesday, April 20. This day I am twenty-four years of age. O how much mercy have I received the year past! How often has God "caused his goodness to pass before me!" And how poorly have I answered the vows I made this time twelvemonth, to be wholly the Lord's, to be for ever devoted to his service! The Lord help me to live more to his glory for time to come.——This has been a sweet, a happy day to me: blessed be God. I think my soul was never so drawn out in intercession for *others*, as it has been this night. Had a most fervent wrestle with the Lord to-night for my *enemies;* and I hardly ever so longed to *live to God*, and to be altogether devoted to him; I wanted to wear out my life in his service, and for his glory.

Wednesday, April 21. Felt much calmness and resignation, and God again enabled me to wrestle for numbers of souls, and had much fervency in the sweet duty of intercession. I enjoy of late more sweetness in intercession for others, than in any other part of prayer. My blessed Lord really let me "come near to him, and plead with him."

[The frame of mind, and exercises of soul, that he expresses the three days next following, Thursday, Friday, and Saturday, are much of the same kind with those expressed the two days past.]

Lord's day, April 25. This morning spent about two hours in secret duties, and was enabled more than ordinarily to agonize for immortal souls; though it was early in the morning, and the sun scarcely shined at all, yet my body was quite wet with sweat. Felt much pressed now, as frequently of late, to plead for the meekness and calmness of the Lamb of God in my soul; through divine goodness felt much of it

this

this morning. O it is a ſweet diſpoſition, heartily to forgive all injuries done us; to wiſh our greateſt enemies as well as we do our own ſouls! Bleſſed Jeſus, may I daily be more and more conformed to thee. At night was exceedingly melted with divine love, and had ſome feeling ſenſe of the bleſſedneſs of the upper world. Thoſe words hung upon me, with much divine ſweetneſs, Pſal. lxxxiv. 7. "They go "from ſtrength to ſtrength, every one of them in Zion ap-"peareth before God." O the *near acceſs* that God ſometimes gives us in our addreſſes to him! This may well be termed *appearing before God:* it is ſo indeed, in the true ſpiritual ſenſe, and in the ſweeteſt ſenſe.——I think I have not had ſuch power of interceſſion theſe many months, both for God's children, and for dead ſinners, as I have had this evening. I wiſhed and longed for the coming of my dear Lord: I longed to join the angelic hoſts in praiſes, wholly free from imperfection. O the bleſſed moment haſtens! All I want is to be more holy, more like my dear Lord. O for ſanctification! My very ſoul pants for the complete reſtoration of the bleſſed image of my ſweet Saviour; that I may be fit for the bleſſed enjoyments and employments of the heavenly world.

Farewell, vain world; *my ſoul can bid Adieu:*
My SAVIOUR'*s taught me to abandon you.*
Your charms may gratify a ſenſual mind;
Not pleaſe a ſoul wholly for GOD *deſign'd.*
Forbear t'entice, ceaſe then my ſoul to call:
'Tis fix'd through grace; my GOD *ſhall be my* all.
While he thus lets me heavenly glories view,
Your beauties fade, my heart's no room for you.

The Lord refreſhed my ſoul with many ſweet paſſages of his word. O the new Jeruſalem! my ſoul longed for it. O the ſong of Moſes and the Lamb! And that bleſſed ſong, that no man can learn, but they that are "redeemed from "the earth!" and the glorious *white robes*, that were given to "the ſouls under the altar!"

Lord, I'm a ſtranger *here alone;*
Earth *no true comforts can afford:*
Yet, abſent from my deareſt one,
My ſoul delights to cry, My Lord!
JESUS, *my Lord, my only love,*
Poſſeſs my ſoul, nor thence depart:

Grant me kind visits, heavenly dove;
My God shall then have all my heart.

Monday, April 26. Continued in a sweet frame of mind; but in the afternoon felt something of spiritual pride stirring. God was pleased to make it a humbling season at first; though afterwards he gave me sweetness. O my soul exceedingly longs for that blessed state of perfection of deliverance from all sin!——At night, God enabled me to give my soul up to him, to cast myself upon him, to be ordered and disposed of according to his sovereign pleasure; and I enjoyed great peace and consolation in so doing. My soul took sweet delight in God to-night: my thoughts freely and sweetly centered in him. O that I could spend every moment of my life to his glory!

Tuesday, April 27. Retired pretty early for secret devotions; and in prayer God was pleased to pour such ineffable comforts into my soul, that I could do nothing for some time but say over and over, "O my sweet Saviour! O my sweet "Saviour! whom have I in heaven but thee? and there is "none upon earth, that I desire beside thee." If I had had a thousand lives, my soul would gladly have laid them all down at once to have been with CHRIST. My soul never enjoyed so much of heaven before; it was the most refined and most spiritual season of communion with God I ever yet felt: I never felt so great a degree of resignation in my life: I felt very sweetly all the forenoon.——In the afternoon I withdrew to meet with my God, but found myself much declined, and God made it a humbling season to my soul: I mourned over *the body of death* that is in me: it grieved me exceedingly, that I could not pray to and praise God with my heart full of divine heavenly *love*.—O that my soul might never offer any dead cold services to my God!——In the evening had not so much sweet divine *love*, as in the morning; but had a sweet season of fervent *intercession*.

Wednesday, April 28. Withdrew to my usual place of retirement in great peace and tranquillity, and spent about two hours in secret duties. I felt much as I did yesterday-morning, only weaker and more overcome. I seemed to hang and depend wholly on my dear Lord; wholly weaned from all other dependances. I knew not what to say to my God, but only *lean on his bosom*, as it were, and breathe out my desires after a perfect conformity to him in all things. Thirsting desires, and insatiable longings, possessed my soul after perfect holiness: God was so precious to my soul, that the

the world with all its enjoyments was infinitely vile: I had no more value for the favour of men, than for pebbles: The LORD was my ALL; and *he* over-ruled all; which greatly delighted me. I think, my faith and dependance on God scarce ever rose so high. I saw him such a fountain of goodness, that it seemed impossible I should distrust him again, or be any way anxious about any thing that should happen to me. I now enjoyed great sweetness in praying for absent friends, and for the enlargement of Christ's kingdom in the world.—Much of the power of these divine enjoyments remained with me through the day.——In the evening my heart seemed sweetly to melt, and, I trust, was really humbled for indwelling corruption, and I "mourned like a dove." I felt that all my unhappiness arose from my being a sinner; for with resignation I could bid welcome all other trials; but sin hung heavy upon me; for God discovered to me the corruption of my heart: so that I went to bed with a heavy heart, because I was a sinner; though I did not in the least doubt of God's love. O that God would "purge away my dross, and take away my tin," and make me seven times refined!

Thursday, April 29. Was kept off at a distance from God;—but had some enlargement in intercession for precious souls.

Friday, April 30. Was something dejected in spirit: nothing grieves me so much, as that I cannot live constantly to God's glory. I could bear any desertion or spiritual conflicts, if I could but have *my heart* all the while *burning within me* with love to God and desires of his glory: but this is impossible; for when I *feel* these, I cannot be dejected in my soul, but only *rejoice in my Saviour*, who has delivered me from the reigning power, and will shortly deliver me from the indwelling of sin.

Saturday, May 1. Was enabled to cry to God with fervency for ministerial qualifications, and that God would appear for the advancement of his own kingdom, and that he would bring in the Heathen world, *&c.* Had much assistance in my studies.——This has been a profitable week to me; I have enjoyed many communications of the blessed Spirit in my soul.

Lord's day, May 2. God was pleased this morning to give me such a sight of myself, as made me appear very vile in my own eyes: I felt corruption stirring in my heart, which I could by no means suppress: felt more and more deserted: was exceeding weak, and almost sick with my inward trials.

Monday,

Monday, May 3. Had a ſenſe of vile ingratitude. In the morning I withdrew to my uſual place of retirement, and mourned for my abuſe of my dear Lord: ſpent the day in faſting and prayer: God gave me much power of wreſtling for his cauſe and kingdom: and it was a happy day to my ſoul. God was with me all the day, and I was more above the world, than ever in my life.

[Through the remaining part of this week, he complains almoſt every day of deſertion, and inward trials and conflicts, attended with dejection of ſpirit; but yet ſpeaks of times of relief and ſweetneſs, and daily refreſhing viſits of the divine Spirit, affording ſpecial aſſiſtance and comfort, and enabling, at ſome times, to much fervency and enlargement in religious duties.]

Lord's day, May 9. I think I never felt ſo much of the curſed pride of my heart, as well as the ſtubbornneſs of my will before. Oh dreadful! what a vile wretch I am! I could not ſubmit to be nothing, and to lie down in the duſt. Oh that God would humble me in the duſt! I felt myſelf ſuch a ſinner, all day, that I had ſcarce any comfort. Oh when ſhall I be "delivered from the body of this death!" I greatly feared, leſt through ſtupidity and careleſſneſs I ſhould loſe the benefit of theſe trials. O that they might be ſanctified to my ſoul! Nothing ſeemed to touch me but only this, that I was a ſinner.——Had fervency and refreſhment in ſocial prayer in the evening.

Monday, May 10. Rode to New-Haven; ſaw ſome Chriſtian friends there; had comfort in joining in prayer with them, and hearing of the goodneſs of God to them ſince I laſt ſaw them.

Tueſday, May 11. Rode from New-Haven to Weatherſfield; was very dull moſt of the day; had little ſpirituality in this journey, though I often longed to be alone with God; was much perplexed with vile thoughts; was ſometimes afraid of every thing: but God was *my helper*.—Catched a little time for retirement in the evening, to my comfort and rejoicing. Alas! I cannot live in the midſt of a tumult. I long to enjoy God alone.

Wedneſday, May 12. Had a diſtreſſing view of the pride, and enmity, and vileneſs of my heart.--Afterwards had ſweet refreſhment in converſing, and worſhipping God, with Chriſtian friends.

Thurſday, May 13. Saw ſo much of the wickedneſs of my heart,

heart, that I longed to get away from myself. I never before thought there was so much spiritual pride in my soul: I felt almost pressed to death with my own vileness. Oh what *a body of death* is there in me! *Lord, deliver my soul.* I could not find any convenient place for retirement, and was greatly exercised.——Rode to Hartford in the afternoon: had some refreshment and comfort in religious exercises with Christian friends; but longed for more retirement. O the closest walk with God is the sweetest heaven that can be enjoyed on earth!

Friday, May 14. Waited on a council of ministers convened at Hartford, and spread before them the treatment I had met with from the rector and tutors of Yale College; who thought it adviseable to intercede for me with the rector and trustees, and to intreat them to restore me to my former privileges in college *.——After this, spent some time in religious exercises with Christian friends.

Saturday, May 15. Rode from Hartford to Hebron; was something dejected on the road; appeared exceeding vile in my own eyes, saw much pride and stubbornness in my heart. Indeed I never saw such a week before, as this; for I have been almost ready to die with the view of the wickedness of my heart. I could not have thought I had such *a body of death* in me. Oh that God would *deliver my soul!*

[The three next days (which he spent at Hebron, Lebanon, and Norwich) he complains still of dulness and desertion, and expresses a sense of his vileness, and longing to hide himself in some cave or den of the earth: but yet speaks of some intervals of comfort and soul-refreshment each day.]

Wednesday, May 19. [At Millington] I was so amazingly deserted this morning, that I seemed to feel a sort of horror in my soul. Alas! when God withdraws, what is there that can afford any comfort to the soul!

[Through the eight days next following, he expresses more calmness and comfort, and considerable life, fervency, and sweetness in religion.]

Friday, May 28. [At New-Haven] I think I scarce ever felt

* The application which was then made on his behalf, had not the desired success.

felt so calm in my life; I rejoiced in resignation, and giving myself up to God, to be wholly and entirely devoted to him for ever.

[On the three following days, there was, by the account he gives, a continuance of the same excellent frame of mind, last expressed: but it seems not to be altogether to so great a degree.]

Tuesday, June 1. Had much of the presence of God in family-prayer, and had some comfort in secret. I was greatly refreshed from the word of God this morning, which appeared exceeding sweet to me: some things that appeared mysterious were opened to me. O that the kingdom of the dear Saviour might come with power, and the healing waters of the sanctuary spread far and wide for the healing of the nations!——Came to Ripton; but was very weak. However, being visited by a number of young people in the evening, I prayed with them.

[The remaining part of this week, he speaks of being much diverted and hindered in the business of religion, by great weakness of body, and necessary affairs, that he had to attend, and complains of having but little power in religion; but signifies, that God hereby shewed him, he was like a helpless infant cast out in the open field.]

Lord's day, June 6. I feel much deserted: but all this teaches me my nothingness and vileness more than ever.

Monday, June 7. Felt still powerless in secret prayer. Afterwards I prayed and conversed with some little life. God feeds me with crumbs: blessed be his name for any thing. I felt a great desire, that all God's people might know how mean and little and vile I am; that they might see I am nothing, that so they may pray for me aright, and not have the least dependance upon me.

Tuesday, June 8. I enjoyed one sweet and precious season this day: I never felt it so sweet to be nothing, and less than nothing, and to be accounted nothing.

[The three next days he complains of desertion, and want of fervency in religion; but yet his diary shews that every day his heart was engaged in religion, as his great, and, as it were, only business.]

Saturday,

Saturday, June 12. Spent much time in prayer this morning, and enjoyed much ſweetneſs:——Felt inſatiable longings after God much of the day: I wondered how poor ſouls do to live, that have *no God*.——The world, with all its enjoyments, quite vaniſhed. I ſee myſelf very helpleſs: but I have a bleſſed God to go to. I longed exceedingly "to be "diſſolved, and to be with Chriſt, to behold his glory." Oh, my weak weary ſoul longs to arrive at *my Father's houſe!*

Lord's day, June 13. Felt ſomething calm and reſigned in the public worſhip: at the ſacrament ſaw myſelf very vile and worthleſs. O that I may always lie low in the duſt. My ſoul ſeemed ſteadily to go forth after God, in longing deſires to live upon him.

Monday, June 14. Felt ſomething of the ſweetneſs of communion with God, and the *conſtraining* force of *his love*: how admirably it captivates the ſoul, and makes all the deſires and affections to center in God!——I ſet apart this day for ſecret faſting and prayer, to intreat God to direct and bleſs me with regard to the great work I have in view, of *preaching the goſpel;* and that the Lord would return to me, and "ſhew me the light of his countenance." Had little life and power in the forenoon: near the middle of the afternoon, God enabled me to wreſtle ardently in interceſſion for abſent friends:—but juſt at night, the Lord viſited me marvellouſly in prayer; I think my ſoul never was in ſuch an agony before: I felt no reſtraint; for the treaſures of divine grace were opened to me: I wreſtled for abſent friends, for the ingathering of ſouls, for multitudes of poor ſouls, and for many that I thought were the children of God, perſonally, in many diſtant places. I was in ſuch an agony, from ſun half an hour high, till near dark, that I was all over wet with ſweat; but yet it ſeemed to me that I had waſted away the day, and had done nothing. Oh, my dear Jeſus did *ſweat blood* for poor ſouls! I longed for more compaſſion towards them.——Felt ſtill in a ſweet frame, under a ſenſe of divine love and grace; and went to bed in ſuch a frame, with my heart ſet on God.

Tueſday, June 15. Had the moſt ardent longings after God, that ever I felt in my life: at noon, in my ſecret retirement, I could do nothing but tell my dear Lord, in a ſweet calm, that he knew I longed for nothing but *himſelf*, nothing but *holineſs;* that *he* had given me theſe deſires, and he *only* could give me the thing deſired. I never ſeemed to be ſo unhinged from myſelf, and to be ſo wholly devoted to God. My heart was ſwallowed up in God moſt of the day.

In the evening I had ſuch a view of the ſoul's being as it were enlarged, to contain more holineſs, that my ſoul ſeemed ready to ſeparate from my body, and ſtretch to obtain it. I then wreſtled in an agony for divine bleſſings; had my heart drawn out in prayer for ſome Chriſtian friends, beyond what I ever had before.——I feel differently now from what ever I did under any ſweet enjoyments before, more engaged to *live to God* for ever, and leſs pleaſed with my own frames: I am not ſatisfied with my frames, nor feel at all more eaſy after ſuch ſweet ſtrugglings than before; for it ſeems far too little, if I could always be ſo. Oh how ſhort do I fall of my duty in my ſweeteſt moments!

[In his diary for the two next days, he expreſſes ſomething of the ſame frame, but in a far leſs degree *.]

Friday, June 18. Conſidering my great unfitneſs for the work of the *miniſtry*, my preſent deadneſs, and total inability to do any thing for the glory of God that way, feeling myſelf very helpleſs, and at a great loſs "what the Lord would "have me to do;" I ſet apart this day for prayer to God, and ſpent moſt of the day in that duty, but amazingly deſerted moſt of the day: yet I found God graciouſly near; once in particular, while I was pleading for more compaſſion for immortal ſouls, my *heart* ſeemed to be *opened* at once, and I was enabled to cry with great ardency, for a few minutes. Oh, I was diſtreſſed, to think, that I ſhould offer ſuch dead cold ſervices to the *living God!* My ſoul ſeemed to breathe after holineſs, a life of conſtant devotedneſs to God. But I am almoſt loſt ſometimes in the purſuit of this bleſſedneſs, and ready to ſink, becauſe I continually fall ſhort and miſs of my deſire. O that the Lord would help me to hold out, yet a little while, till the happy hour of deliverance comes!

Saturday, June 19. Felt much diſordered; my ſpirits were very low: but yet enjoyed ſome freedom and ſweetneſs in the duties of religion. Bleſſed be God.

Lord's day, June 20. Spent much time alone. My ſoul longed to be holy, and reached after God; but ſeemed not to obtain my deſire: I *hungered* and *thirſted;* but was not ſweet-

* Here end the 30 firſt pages of the third volume of his diary, which he ſpeaks of in the beginning of this volume, (as was obſerved before), as containing a ſpecimen of his ordinary manner of living, through the whole ſpace of time, from the beginning of thoſe two volumes that were deſtroyed.

ly refreſhed and ſatisfied. My ſoul hung on God, as my only portion. O that I could grow in grace more abundantly every day!

[The next day he ſpeaks of his having aſſiſtance in his ſtudies, and power, fervency, and comfort in prayer.]

Tueſday, June 22. In the morning, ſpent about two hours in prayer and meditation, with conſiderable delight. Towards night, felt my ſoul go out in longing deſires after God, in ſecret retirement. In the evening, was ſweetly compoſed and reſigned to God's will; was enabled to leave myſelf and all my concerns with him, and to have my whole dependance upon him: my ſecret retirement was very refreſhing to my ſoul; it appeared ſuch a happineſs to have God for my portion, that I had rather be any other creature in this lower creation, than not come to the enjoyment of God: I had rather be a beaſt, than a man, without God, if I were to live here to eternity. Lord, endear thyſelf more to me!

[In his diary for the next ſeven days, he expreſſes a variety of exerciſes of mind: he ſpeaks of great longings after God and holineſs, and earneſt deſires for the converſion of others, of fervency in prayer, and power to wreſtle with God, and of compoſure, comfort, and ſweetneſs, from time to time; but expreſſes a ſenſe of the vile abomination of his heart, and bitterly complains of his barrenneſs, and the preſſing body of death; and ſays, he "ſaw clearly, that whatever he enjoyed, better than hell, was free grace." Complains of his being exceeding low, much below the character of a child of God; and is ſometimes very diſconſolate and dejected.]

Wedneſday, June 30. Spent this day alone in the woods, in faſting and prayer; underwent the moſt dreadful conflicts in my ſoul, that ever I felt, in ſome reſpects: I ſaw myſelf ſo vile, that I was ready to ſay, "I ſhall now periſh by the hand of Saul." I thought, and almoſt concluded, I had no power to ſtand for the cauſe of God, but was almoſt "afraid of the ſhaking of a leaf." Spent almoſt the whole day in prayer, inceſſantly. I could not bear to think of Chriſtians ſhewing me any reſpect. I almoſt deſpaired of doing any ſervice in the world: I could not feel any hope or comfort reſpecting the Heathen, which uſed to afford me ſome refreſhment in the darkeſt hours of this nature. I ſpent away the day *in the bitterneſs of my ſoul*. Near night, I felt a little better; and afterwards enjoyed ſome ſweetneſs in ſecret prayer.

Thurſday, July 1. Had ſome ſweetneſs in prayer this morning.--Felt exceeding ſweetly in ſecret prayer to-night, and deſired nothing ſo ardently as that *God ſhould do with me juſt as he pleaſed.*

Friday, July 2. Felt compoſed in ſecret prayer in the morning.——My deſires ſweetly aſcended to God this day, as I was travelling: and was comfortable in the evening. Bleſſed be God for all my conſolations.

Saturday, July 3. My heart ſeemed again to ſink. The diſgrace I was laid under at college, ſeemed to damp me, as it opens the mouths of oppoſers. I had no refuge but in God only. Bleſſed be his name, that I may go to *him* at all times, and find him a *preſent help*.

Lord's day, July 4. Had conſiderable aſſiſtance. In the evening I withdrew, and enjoyed a happy ſeaſon in ſecret prayer: God was pleaſed to give me the exerciſe of faith, and thereby brought the inviſible and eternal world near to my ſoul; which appeared ſweetly to me. I hoped, that my weary *pilgrimage* in the world would be *ſhort*; and that it would not be long before I was brought to my heavenly home and Father's houſe: I was ſweetly reſigned to God's will, to tarry his time, to do his work, and ſuffer his pleaſure. I felt *thankfulneſs* to God for all my preſſing *deſertions* of late; for I am perſuaded they have been made a means of making me more humble, and much more reſigned. I felt pleaſed, to be *little*, to be *nothing*, and to *lie in the duſt*. I enjoyed life and ſweet conſolation in pleading for the dear children of God, and the kingdom of Chriſt in the world; and my ſoul earneſtly breathed after holineſs, and the enjoyment of God. "O come, Lord Jeſus! come quickly. Amen."

[By his diary for the remaining days of this week, it appears that he enjoyed conſiderable compoſure and tranquillity, and had ſweetneſs and fervency of ſpirit in prayer, from day to day.]

Lords day, July 11. Was deſerted and exceeding dejected in the morning. In the afternoon, had ſome life and aſſiſtance, and felt reſigned; I ſaw myſelf exceeding vile.

[On the two next days he expreſſes inward comfort, reſignation, and ſtrength in God.]

Wedneſday,

Wednesday, July 14. Felt a kind of humble resigned sweetness: spent a considerable time in secret, giving myself up wholly to the Lord.—Heard Mr Bellamy preach towards night: felt very sweetly part of the time: longed for nearer *access to God.*

[The four next days, he expresses considerable comfort and fervency of spirit in Christian conversation and religious exercises.]

Monday, July 19. My desires seem especially to be carried out after weanedness from the *world,* perfect deadness to it, and to be even *crucified* to all its allurements. My soul longs to feel itself more of a *pilgrim* and *stranger* here below; that nothing may divert me from pressing through the lonely desart, till I arrive at my Father's house.

Tuesday, July 20. It was sweet, to give away myself to God, to be disposed of at his pleasure; and had some feeling sense of the sweetness of being a *pilgrim on earth.*

[The next day, he expresses himself as determined to be wholly devoted to God; and it appears by his diary, that he spent the whole day in a most diligent exercise of religion, and exceeding comfortably.]

Thursday, July 22. Journeying from Southbury to Ripton, called at a house by the way, where being very kindly entertained and refreshed, I was filled with amazement and shame, that God should stir up the hearts of any to shew so much kindness to such a *dead dog* as I; was made sensible, in some measure, how exceeding vile it is, not to be wholly devoted to God. I wondered, that God would suffer any of his creatures to feed and sustain me from time to time.

[In his diary for the six next days, are expressed various exercises and experiences, such as, sweet composure and fervency of spirit in meditation and prayer, weanedness from the world, being sensibly a pilgrim and stranger on the earth, engagedness of mind to spend every inch of time for God, *&c.*]

Thursday, July 29. Was examined by the Association met at Danbury, as to my learning, and also my experiences in religion, and received a licence from them to preach the gospel of Christ. Afterwards felt much devoted to God; joined in prayer with one of the ministers, my peculiar friend, in a convenient place; went to bed resolving to live devoted to God all my days.

PART

PART III.

From the time of his being licensed to preach, by the *Association*, till he was examined in New-York, by the *Correspondents* or commissioners of the *Society* in Scotland for propagating Christian knowledge, and approved and appointed as their *Missionary* to the *Indians*.

FRiday, July 30. 1742. Rode from Danbury to Southbury; preached there from 1 Pet. iv. 8. Had much of the comfortable presence of God in the exercise: I seemed to have power with God in prayer, and power to get hold of the hearts of the people in preaching.

Saturday, July 31. Exceeding calm and composed, and was greatly refreshed and encouraged.

[It appears by his diary, that he continued in this sweetness and tranquillity, almost through the whole of the next week.]

Lord's day, August 8. In the morning felt comfortably in secret prayer; my soul was refreshed with the hopes of the Heathen's coming home to Christ; was much resigned to God, I thought it was no matter what became of *me*.——Preached both parts of the day at Bethlehem, from Job xiv. 14. It was sweet to me to meditate on *death*. In the evening, felt very comfortably, and cried to God fervently, in secret prayer.

[It appears by his diary, that he continued through the three next days, engaged with all his might in the business of religion, and in almost a constant enjoyment of the comforts of it.]

Thursday, August 12. This morning and last night was exercised with sore inward trials: I had no power to pray; but

but ſeemed ſhut out from God. I had in a great meaſure loſt my hopes of God's ſending me among the Heathen afar off; and of ſeeing them flock home to Chriſt. I ſaw ſo much of my helliſh vileneſs, that I appeared worſe to myſelf than any devil: I wondered that God would let me live, and wondered that people did not ſtone me, much more that they would ever hear me preach! It ſeemed as though I never could nor ſhould preach any more; yet about nine or ten o'clock, the people came over, and I was forced to preach. And bleſſed be God, he gave me his preſence and Spirit in prayer and preaching: ſo that I was much aſſiſted, and ſpake with power from Job xiv. 14. Some Indians cried out in great diſtreſs *, and all appeared greatly concerned. After we had prayed and exhorted them to ſeek the Lord with conſtancy, and hired an Engliſh woman to keep a kind of *ſchool* among them, we came away about one o'clock, and came to Judea, about fifteen or ſixteen miles. There God was pleaſed to viſit my ſoul with much comfort. Bleſſed be the Lord for all things I meet with.

[It appears, that the two next days he had much comfort, and had his heart much engaged in religion.]

Lord's day, Auguſt 13. Felt much comfort and devotedneſs to God this day. At night, it was refreſhing, to get alone with God, and *pour out my ſoul*. O who can conceive of the ſweetneſs of communion with the bleſſed God, but thoſe that have experience of it! Glory to God for ever, that I may taſte heaven below.

Monday, Auguſt 16. Had ſome comfort in ſecret prayer, in the morning.——Felt ſweetly ſundry times in prayer this day: but was much perplexed in the evening with vain converſation.

Tueſday, Auguſt 17. Exceedingly depreſſed in ſpirit, it cuts and wounds my heart, to think how much *ſelf-exaltation*, *ſpiritual pride*, and *warmth of temper*, I have *formerly* had intermingled with my endeavours to promote God's work: and ſometimes I long to lie down at the feet of oppoſers, and confeſs what a poor imperfect creature I have been, and ſtill am. Oh, the Lord forgive me, and make me for the future "wiſe as a ſerpent, and harmleſs as a dove!"—Afterwards enjoyed conſiderable comfort and delight of ſoul.

* It was in a place near Kent, in the weſtern borders of Connecticut, where there is a number of Indians.

Wedneſday,

Wednesday, August 18. Spent most of this day in prayer and reading.—I see so much of my own extreme vileness, that I feel ashamed and guilty before God and man; I look to myself like the vilest fellow in the land: I wonder that God stirs up his people to be so kind to me.

Thursday, August 19. This day, being about to go from Mr Bellamy's at Bethlehem, where I had resided some time, prayed with him, and two or three other Christian friends, and gave ourselves to God with all our hearts, to be his for ever: eternity looked very near to me, while I was praying. If I never should see these Christians again in this world, it seemed but a few moments before I should meet them in another world.—Parted with them sweetly.

Friday, August 20. I appeared so vile to myself, that I hardly dared to think of being seen, especially on account of spiritual pride. However, to-night I enjoyed a sweet hour alone with God, (at Ripton): I was lifted above the frowns and flatteries of this lower world, had a sweet relish of heavenly joys, and my soul did as it were get into the eternal world, and really taste of heaven. I had a sweet season of intercession for dear friends in Christ; and God helped me to cry fervently for Zion. Blessed be God for this season.

Saturday, August 21. Was much perplexed in the morning.———Towards noon enjoyed more of God in secret, was enabled to see that it was best to throw myself into the hands of God, to be disposed of according to his pleasure, and rejoiced in such thoughts. In the afternoon, rode to New-Haven; was much confused all the way.——Just at night, underwent such a dreadful conflict, as I have scarce ever felt. I saw myself exceeding vile and unworthy; so that I was guilty, and ashamed, that any body should bestow any favour on me, or shew me any respect.

Lord's day, August 22. In the morning, continued still in perplexity.—In the evening, enjoyed that comfort that seemed to me sufficient to overbalance all my late distresses. I saw that God is the only soul-satisfying portion, and I really found satisfaction in him: my soul was much enlarged in sweet intercession for my fellow-men every where, and for many Christian friends, in particular, in distant places.

Monday, August 23. Had a sweet season in secret prayer: the Lord drew near to my soul, and filled me with peace and divine consolation. O my soul tasted the sweetness of the upper world; and was sweetly drawn out in prayer for the world, that it might come home Christ! Had much comfort

fort in the thoughts and hopes of the ingathering of the Heathen; was greatly affifted in interceffion for Chriftian friends.

[He continued ftill in the fame frame of mind the next day, but in a leffer degree.]

Wednefday, Auguft 25. In family-prayer, God helped me to climb up near him, fo that I fcarce ever got nearer.

[The four next days, he appears to have been the fubject of defertion, and of comfort and fervency in religion, interchangeably, together with a fenfe of vilenefs and unprofitablenefs.]

Monday, Auguft 30. Felt fomething comfortably in the morning; converfed fweetly with fome friends; was in a ferious compofed frame; prayed at a certain houfe with fome degree of fweetnefs. Afterwards, at another houfe, prayed privately with a dear Chriftian friend or two; and, I think, I fcarce ever launched fo far into the eternal world, as then; I got fo far out on the broad ocean, that my foul with joy triumphed over all the evils on the fhores of mortality. I think, time, and all its gay amufements and cruel difappointments, never appeared fo inconfiderable to me before: I was in a fweet frame; I faw myfelf nothing, and my foul reached after God with intenfe defire. O! I faw what I owed to God, in fuch a manner, as I fcarce ever did: I knew, I had never lived a moment to him, as I fhould do; indeed it appeared to me, I had never done any thing in Chriftianity: my foul longed with a vehement defire to *live to God.*——In the evening, fung and prayed with a number of Chriftians: felt "the powers of the world to come" in my foul, in prayer. Afterwards prayed again privately, with a dear Chriftian or two, and found the prefence of God; was fomething humbled in my fecret retirement; felt my ingratitude, becaufe I was not wholly fwallowed up in God.

[He was in a fweet frame great part of the next day.]

Wednefday, September 1. Went to Judea, to the ordination of Mr Judd. Dear Mr Bellamy preached from Matth. xxiv. 46. "Bleffed is that fervant," &c. I felt very folemn, and very fweetly, moft of the time; had my thoughts much on that time when *our Lord will come*; that time refrefhed my foul much; only I was afraid, I fhould not be found *faithful*, because I have so vile a heart. My thoughts were much in eternity, where I love to dwell. Blessed be God for this solemn season.——Rode home to-night with Mr Bellamy, felt something sweetly on the road; conversed with some friends till it was very late, and then retired to rest in a comfortable frame.

Thursday, September 2. About two in the afternoon, I preached from John vi. 67. and God assisted me in some comfortable degree; but more especially in my first prayer; my soul seemed then to launch quite into the eternal world, and to be as it were separated from this lower world.——Afterwards preached again from Is. v. 4. God gave me some assistance; but I saw myself a poor worm.

[On Friday, September 3. He complains of having but little life in the things of God, the former part of the day, but afterwards speaks of sweetness and enlargement.]

Saturday, September 4. Much out of health, and exceedingly depressed in my soul, and was at an awful distance from God.——Towards night, spent some time in profitable thoughts on Rom. viii. 2.——Near night, had a very sweet season in prayer; God enabled me to wrestle ardently for the advancement of the Redeemer's kingdom; pleaded earnestly for my own dear brother John, that God would make him more of a pilgrim and stranger on the earth, and fit him for singular serviceableness in the world; and my heart sweetly exulted in the Lord, in the thoughts of any distresses that might alight on him or me, in the advancement of Christ's kingdom.——It was a sweet and comfortable hour unto my soul, while I was indulged freedom to plead, not only for myself, but for many other souls.

Lord's day, September 5. Preached all day: was something strengthened and assisted in the afternoon; more especially in the evening: had a sense of my unspeakable shortcomings in all my duties. I found, alas! that I had never lived to God in my life.

Monday, September 6. Was informed, that they only waited for an opportunity to apprehend me for preaching at New-Haven lately, that so they might imprison me. This made me more solemn and serious, and to quit all hopes of the world's friendship: it brought me to a further sense of my vileness, and just desert of this, and much more, from the hand of God, though not from the hand of man. Retired

red into a convenient place in the woods, and ſpread the matter before God.

Tueſday, September 7. Had ſome reliſh of divine things in the morning. Afterwards felt more barren and melancholy. Rode to New-Haven, to a friend's houſe at a diſtance from the town; that I remain undiſcovered, and yet have opportunity to do buſineſs privately with friends which come to Commencement.

Wedneſday, September 8. Felt very ſweetly, when I firſt roſe in the morning. In family-prayer, had ſome enlargement, but not much ſpirituality, till eternity came up before me, and looked near; I found ſome ſweetneſs in the thoughts of bidding a dying farewell to this tireſome world. Though ſome time ago I reckoned upon ſeeing my dear friends at Commencement; yet being now denied the opportunity, for fear of impriſonment, I felt totally reſigned, and as contented to ſpend this day alone in the woods, as I could have done, if I had been allowed to go to town. Felt exceedingly weaned from the world to-day.——In the afternoon diſcourſed ſomething on ſome divine things with a dear Chriſtian friend, whereby we were both refreſhed. Then I prayed, with a ſweet ſenſe of the bleſſedneſs of communion with God: I think I ſcarce ever enjoyed more of God in any one prayer. O it was a bleſſed ſeaſon indeed to my ſoul! I knew not that ever I ſaw ſo much of my own nothingneſs in my life; never wondered ſo, that God allowed me to preach his word; never was ſo aſtoniſhed as now.——This has been a ſweet and comfortable day to my ſoul. Bleſſed be God.——Prayed again with my dear friend, with ſomething of the divine preſence. ——I long to be wholly conformed to God, and transformed into his image.

Thurſday, September 9. Spent much of the day alone: enjoyed the preſence of God in ſome comfortable degree: was viſited by ſome dear friends, and prayed with them: wrote ſundry letters to friends; felt religion in my ſoul while writing: enjoyed ſome ſweet meditations on ſome ſcriptures. —In the evening, went very privately into town, from the place of my reſidence at the farms, and converſed with ſome dear friends; felt ſweetly in ſinging hymns with them: and made my eſcape to the farms again, without being diſcovered by any enemies, as I knew of. Thus the Lord preſerves me continually.

Friday, September 10. Longed with intenſe deſire after God; my whole ſoul ſeemed impatient to be conformed to him, and to become "holy, as he is holy."—In the afternoon, prayed with a dear friend privately, and had the preſence of

God with us; our souls united together to reach after a blessed immortality, to be unclothed of the body of sin and death, and to enter the blessed world, where no unclean thing enters. O, with what intense desire did our souls long for that blessed day, that we might be freed from sin, and for ever live *to* and *in* our God!--In the evening, took leave of that house; but first kneeled down and prayed; the Lord was of a truth in the midst of us; it was a sweet parting season; felt in myself much sweetness and affection in the things of God. Blessed be God for every such divine gale of his Spirit, to speed me on in my way to the new Jerusalem!——Felt some sweetness afterwards, and spent the evening in conversation with friends, and prayed with some life, and retired to rest very late.

[The five next days, he appears to have been in an exceeding comfortable, sweet frame of mind, for the most part, and to have been the subject of the like heavenly exercises as are often expressed in preceding passages of his diary; such as, having his heart much engaged for God, wrestling with God in prayer with power and ardency, enjoying at times sweet calmness and composure of mind, giving himself up to God to be his for ever, with great complacence of mind, being wholly resigned to the will of God, that God might do with him what he pleased, longing well to improve time, having the eternal world as it were brought nigh, longing after God and holiness, earnestly desiring a complete conformity to him, and wondering how poor souls do to exist without God.]

Thursday, September 16. At night, felt exceeding sweetly: enjoyed much of God in secret prayer: felt an uncommon resignation, to *be* and *do* what God pleased. Some days past, I felt *great perplexity* on account of my past conduct: *my bitterness*, and want of Christian kindness and love, has been *very distressing* to my soul: the Lord forgive me my *unchristian warmth*, and want of a spirit of meekness!

[The next day, he speaks of much resignation, calmness, and peace of mind, and near views of the eternal world.]

Saturday, September 18. Felt some compassion for souls, and mourned I had no more. I feel much more kindness, meekness, gentleness, and love towards all mankind, than ever. I long to be at the feet of my enemies and persecutors: enjoyed ed some sweetness, in feeling my soul conformed to Christ Jesus, and given away to him for ever, in prayer to-day.

[The next day, he speaks of much dejection and discouragement, from an apprehension of his own unfitness ever to do any good in preaching; but blesses God for all dispensations of providence and grace; finding that by all God weaned him more from the world, and made him more resigned.

The next ten days, he appears to have been for the most part under great degrees of melancholy, exceedingly dejected and discouraged: speaks of his being ready to give up all for gone respecting the cause of Christ, and exceedingly longing to die: yet had some sweet seasons and intervals of comfort, and special assistance and enlargement in the duties of religion, and in performing public services, and considerable success in them.]

Thursday, September 30. Still very low in spirits, and did not know how to engage in any work or business, especially to *correct some disorders among Christians*; felt as though I had no power to be faithful in that regard. However, towards noon, preached from Deut. viii. 2. and was enabled with freedom to reprove some things in Christians conduct, that I thought very unsuitable and irregular; insisted near two hours on this subject.

[Through this, and the two following weeks, he passed through a variety of exercises: he was frequently dejected, and felt inward distresses: and sometimes sunk into the depths of melancholy: at which turns, he was not exercised about the state of his soul, with regard to the favour of God, and his interest in Christ, but about his own sinful infirmities, and unfitness for God's service. His mind appears sometimes extremely depressed and sunk with a sense of inexpressible vileness. But in the mean time, he speaks of many seasons of comfort and spiritual refreshment, wherein his heart was encouraged and strengthened in God, and sweetly resigned to his will, and of some seasons of very high degrees of spiritual consolation, and of his great longings after holiness and conformity to God, of his great fear of offending God, of his heart's being sweetly melted in religious duties, of his longing for the advancement of Christ's kingdom, and of his having at some times much assistance in preaching, and of remarkable effects on the auditory.]

Lord's

Lord's day, October 17. Had a considerable sense of my helplessness and inability; saw that I must be dependent on God for all I want; and especially when I went to the place of public worship: I found I could not speak a word for God without his special help and assistance: I went into the assembly trembling, as I frequently do, under a sense of my insufficiency to do any thing in the cause of God, as I ought to do.——But it pleased God to afford me much assistance, and there seemed to be a considerable effect on the hearers.——In the evening, I felt a disposition to praise God for his goodness to me, in special, that he had enabled me in some measure to be faithful; and my soul rejoiced to think, that I had thus performed the work of one day more, and was one day nearer my eternal, and (I trust) my heavenly home. O that I might be "faithful to the death, fulfilling as an hireling my day," till the shades of the evening of life shall free my soul from the toils of the day! This evening, in secret prayer, I felt exceeding solemn, and such longing desires after deliverance from sin, and after conformity to God, as melted my heart. Oh, I longed to be "delivered from this body of death!" I felt inward pleasing pain, that I could not be conformed to God entirely, fully, and for ever.——I scarce ever preach without being first visited with inward conflicts and sore trials. Blessed be the Lord for these trials and distresses, as they are blessed for my humbling.

Monday, October 18. In the morning, felt some sweetness, but still pressed through some trials of soul. My life is a constant mixture of consolations and conflicts, and will be so till I arrive at the world of spirits.

Tuesday, October 19. This morning and last night, felt a sweet longing in my soul after holiness: my soul seemed so to reach and stretch towards the mark of perfect sanctity, that it was ready to break with longings.

Wednesday, October 20. Exceeding infirm in body, exercised with much pain, and very lifeless in divine things.——Felt a little sweetness in the evening.

Thursday, October 21. Had a very deep sense of the vanity of the world, most of the day; had little more regard to it, than if I had been to go into eternity the next hour. Through divine goodness, I felt very serious and solemn. O, I love to live on the brink of eternity, in my views and meditations! This gives me a sweet, awful, and reverential sense and apprehension of God and divine things, when I see myself as it were *standing before the judgment-seat of Christ*.

Friday, October 22. Uncommonly weaned from the world to-day;

to-day: my soul delighted to be a *stranger and pilgrim on the earth;* I felt a disposition in me never to have any thing to do with this world: the character given of some of the ancient people of God, in Heb. xi. 13. was very pleasing to me, "They confessed that they were pilgrims and strangers on the "earth," by their daily practice; and O that I could always do so!——Spent some considerable time, in a pleasant grove, in prayer and meditation. O it is sweet, to be thus weaned from friends, and from myself, and dead to the present world, that so I may live wholly *to* and *upon* the blessed God! Saw myself little, low, and vile in myself.——In the afternoon, preached at Bethlehem, from Deut. viii. 2. and felt sweetly both in prayer and preaching: God helped me to speak to the hearts of dear Christians. Blessed be the Lord for this season: I trust, they and I shall rejoice on this account to all eternity. ——Dear Mr Bellamy came in, while I was making the first prayer, (being returned home from a journey); and after meeting, we walked away together, and spent the evening in sweetly conversing on divine things, and praying together, with sweet and tender love to each other, and returned to rest with our hearts in a serious spiritual frame.

Saturday, October 23. Something perplexed and confused. Rode this day from Bethlehem to Simsbury.

Lord's day, October 24. Felt so vile and unworthy, that I scarce knew how to converse with human creatures.

Monday, October 25. [At Turky-Hills] In the evening enjoyed the divine presence in secret prayer: it was a sweet and comfortable season to me: my soul *longed for God, for the living God:* enjoyed a sweet solemnity of spirit, and longing desire after the recovery of the divine image in my soul: "Then shall I be satisfied, when I shall awake in God's like-"ness," and never before.

Tuesday, October 26. [At West-Suffield] Underwent the most dreadful distresses, under a sense of my own unworthiness: it seemed to me, I deserved rather to be driven out of the place, than to have any body treat me with any kindness, or come to hear me preach. And verily my spirits were so depressed at this time, as well as at many others, that it was impossible I should treat immortal souls with faithfulness: I could not deal closely and faithfully with them, I felt so infinitely vile in myself. Oh, what *dust and ashes* I am, to think of preaching the gospel to others! Indeed I never can be faithful for one moment, but shall certainly "daub with un-"tempered mortar," if God do not grant me special help.——In the evening, I went to the meeting-house, and it looked to me near as easy for one to rise out of the grave and preach, as for me. However, God afforded me some life and power, both in prayer and sermon: God was pleased to lift me up, and shew me that he could enable me to preach. O the wonderful goodness of God to so vile a sinner!——Returned to my quarters; and enjoyed some sweetness in prayer alone, and mourned that I could not live more to God.

Wednesday, October 27. Spent the forenoon in prayer and meditation: was not a little concerned about preaching in the afternoon: felt exceedingly *without strength*, and very helpless indeed: went into the meeting-house, ashamed to see any come to hear such an unspeakably worthless wretch. However, God enabled me to speak with clearness, power, and pungency. But there was some noise and tumult in the assembly, that I did not well like, and endeavoured to bear public testimony against, with moderation and mildness, through the current of my discourse.——In the evening, was enabled to be in some measure thankful and devoted to God.

[The frames and exercises of his mind, during the four next days, were mostly very similar to those of the two days past; excepting intervals of considerable degrees of divine peace and consolation.

The things expressed within the space of the three following days are such as these; some seasons of dejection, mourning for being so destitute of the exercises of grace, longing to be delivered from sin, pressing after more of God, seasons of sweet consolation, precious and intimate converse with God in secret prayer, sweetness of Christian conversation, &c.——Within this time he rode from Suffield to Eastbury, Hebron, and Lebanon.]

Thursday, November 4. [At Lebanon] Saw much of my nothingness most of this day: but felt concerned that I had no more sense of my insufficiency and unworthiness. O it is sweet *lying in the dust!* But it is distressing to feel in my soul that hell of corruption, which still remains in me.——In the afternoon, had a sense of the sweetness of a strict, close, and constant devotedness to God, and my soul was comforted with the consolations of God; my soul felt a pleasing, yet painful concern, lest I should spend some moments *without God*. O may I always *live to God!*——In the evening, was visited by some friends, and spent the time in prayer and such conversation as tended to our edification. It was a comfortable

able season to my soul: I felt an intense desire to spend every moment for God.——God is unspeakably gracious to me continually: in times past, he has given me inexpressible sweetness in the performance of duty: frequently my soul has enjoyed much of God; but has been ready to say, "Lord, "it is good to be here;" and so to indulge sloth, while I have lived on the sweetness of my feelings. But of late, God has been pleased to keep my soul *hungry*, almost continually; so that I have been filled with a kind of a pleasing pain. When I really enjoy God, I feel my desires of him the more insatiable, and my thirstings after holiness the more unquenchable; and the Lord will not allow me to feel as though I were fully supplied and satisfied, but keeps me still reaching forward; and I feel barren and empty, as though I could not live, without more of God in me; I feel ashamed and guilty *before God*. Oh! I see, "the law is spiritual, but I am carnal." I do not, I cannot live to God. Oh for holiness! Oh for more of God in my soul! Oh this pleasing pain! It makes my soul press after God; the language of it is, "Then "shall I be satisfied, when I awake in God's likeness," (Psal. xvii. *ult.*); but never, never before: and consequently I am engaged to "press towards the mark," day by day. O that I may feel this continual hunger, and not be retarded, but rather animated by every cluster from Canaan, to reach forward in the narrow way, for the full enjoyment and possession of the heavenly inheritance! O that I may never loiter in my heavenly journey!

[These insatiable desires after God and holiness continued the two next days, with a great sense of his own exceeding unworthiness, and the nothingness of the things of this world.]

Lord's day, November 7. [At Millington] It seemed as if such an unholy wretch as I never could arrive at that blessedness, to be "holy, as God is holy." At noon, I longed for sanctification, and conformity to God, Oh, that is THE ALL, THE ALL! The Lord help me to *press after God* for ever.

Monday, November 8. Towards night, enjoyed much sweetness in secret prayer, so that my soul longed for an arrival in the *heavenly country*, the blessed paradise of God. Through divine goodness, I have scarce seen the day, for two months, but *death* has looked so pleasant to me at one time or other of the day, that I could have rejoiced the *pre-*

sent should be my *last*, notwithstanding my pressing inward trials and conflicts: and I trust, the Lord will finally make me a *conqueror*, and *more than so*; that I shall be able to use that triumphant language, "O death, where is thy sting!" And, "O grave, where is thy victory!"

[Within the next ten days, the following things are expressed: longing and wrestling to be holy, and to live to God; a desire that every single thought might be for God; feeling guilty, that his thoughts were no more swallowed up in God; sweet solemnity and calmness of mind; submission and resignation to God; great weanedness from the world; abasement in the dust; grief at some vain conversation that was observed; sweetness from time to time in secret prayer, and in conversing and praying with Christian friends. And every day he appears to have been greatly engaged in the great business of religion and living to God, without interruption.]

Friday, November 19. [At New-Haven] Received a letter from the Reverend Mr Pemberton of New-York, desiring me speedily to go down thither, and consult about the Indian affairs in those parts, and to meet certain gentlemen there that were intrusted with those affairs. My mind was instantly seized with concern; so I retired with two or three Christian friends, and prayed; and indeed it was a sweet time with me; I was enabled to leave myself and all my concerns with God; and taking leave of friends, I rode to Ripton, and was comforted in an opportunity to see and converse with dear Mr Mills.

[In the four next following days, he was sometimes oppressed with the weight of that great affair, about which Mr Pemberton had written to him; but was enabled from time to time to "cast his burden on the Lord," and to commit himself and all his concerns to him: and he continued still in a sense of the excellency of holiness, and longings after it, and earnest desires of the advancement of Christ's kingdom in the world; and had from time to time sweet comfort in meditation and prayer.]

Wednesday, November 24. Came to New-York; felt still much concerned about the importance of my business; put up many earnest requests to God for his help and direction; was confused with the noise and tumult of the city; enjoyed but little time alone with God; but my soul longed after him.

Thursday,

Thursday, November 25. Spent much time in prayer and supplication: was examined by some gentlemen, of my Christian experiences, and my acquaintance with divinity, and some other studies, in order to my improvement in that important affair of gospellizing the Heathen *: was made sensible of my great ignorance and unfitness for public service: I had the most abasing thoughts of myself, I think, that ever I had; I thought myself the worst wretch that ever lived: it hurt me, and pained my very heart, that any body should shew me any respect. Alas! methought, how sadly they are deceived in me! how miserably would they be disappointed, if they knew my inside! Oh my heart!——And in this depressed condition, I was forced to go and preach to a considerable assembly, before some grave and learned ministers; but felt such a pressure from a sense of my vileness, ignorance, and unfitness to appear in public, that I was almost overcome with it; my soul was grieved for the congregation, that they should sit there to hear such a *dead dog* as I preach; I thought myself infinitely indebted to the people, and longed that God would reward them with the rewards of his grace.——I spent much of the evening alone.

* These gentlemen that examined Mr Brainerd, were the correspondents in New-York, New-Jersey, and Pensylvania, of the honourable society in Scotland for propagating Christian knowledge; to whom was committed the management of their affairs in those parts, and who were now met at New-York.

PART IV.

From the time of his examination by the *Correspondents* of the society for propagating Christian knowledge, and being appointed their *Missionary*, to his first entrance on the business of his mission among the Indians at Kaunaumeek.

FRiday, November 26. Had still a sense of my great vileness, and endeavoured as much as I could to keep alone. Oh, what a nothing, what dust and ashes am I!---Enjoyed some peace and comfort in spreading my complaints before the God of all grace.

Saturday, November 27. Committed my soul to God with some degree of comfort; left New-York about nine in the morning; came away with a distressing sense still of my unspeakable unworthiness. Surely I may well love all my brethren; for none of them all is so vile as I; whatever they do outwardly, yet it seems to me none is conscious of so much guilt before God. Oh my leanness, my barrenness, my carnality, and past bitterness, and want of a gospel-temper! These things oppress my soul.——Rode from New-York, thirty miles, to White Plains, and most of the way continued lifting up my heart to God for mercy and purifying grace; and spent the evening much dejected in spirit.

[The three next days, he continued in this frame, in a great sense of his own vileness, with an evident mixture of melancholy, in no small degree; but had some intervals of comfort, and God's sensible presence with him.]

Wednesday, December 1. My soul breathed after God, in sweet spiritual and longing desires of conformity to him; my soul was brought to rest itself and all on his rich grace, and felt strength and encouragement to do or suffer any thing that

that divine providence ſhould allot me.——Rode about twenty miles from Stratfield to Newton.

[Within the ſpace of the next nine days, he went a journey from Newton to Haddam, his native town; and after ſtaying there ſome days, returned again into the weſtern part of Connecticut, and came to Southbury. In his account of the frames and exerciſes of his mind, during this ſpace of time, are ſuch things as theſe; frequent turns of dejection, a ſenſe of his vileneſs, emptineſs, and an unfathomable abyſs of deſperate wickedneſs in his heart, attended with a conviction that he had never ſeen but little of it; bitterly mourning over his barrenneſs, being greatly grieved that he could not live to God, to whom he owed his all *ten thouſand times*, crying out, "My leanneſs, my leanneſs!" a ſenſe of the meetneſs and ſuitableneſs of his lying in the duſt beneath God's feet; fervency and ardour in prayer; longing to live to God; a being afflicted with ſome impertinent trifling converſation that he heard; but enjoying ſweetneſs in Chriſtian converſation.]

Saturday, December 11. Converſed with a dear friend, to whom I had thought of giving a liberal education, and being at the whole charge of it, that he might be fitted for the goſpel-miniſtry *. I acquainted him with my thoughts in that matter, and ſo left him to conſider of it, till I ſhould ſee him again. Then I rode to Bethlehem, and ſo came to Mr Bellamy's lodgings; ſpent the evening with him in ſweet converſation

* Mr Brainerd having now undertaken the buſineſs of a miſſionary to the Indians, and expecting in a little time to leave his native country, to go among the ſavages, into the wilderneſs, far diſtant, and ſpend the remainder of his life among them, and having ſome eſtate left him by his father, and thinking he ſhould have no occaſion for it among them, (though afterwards, as he told me, he found himſelf miſtaken), he ſet himſelf to think which way he might ſpend it moſt to the glory of God; and no way preſenting to his thoughts, wherein he could do more good with it, than by being at the charge of educating ſome young perſon for the miniſtry, that appeared to be of good abilities, and well diſpoſed, he pitched upon this perſon here ſpoken of, to this end: who accordingly was ſoon put to learning; and Mr Brainerd continued to be at the charge of his education from year to year, ſo long as he (Mr Brainerd) lived, which was till this young man was carried through his third year in college.

fation and prayer: we recommended the important concern before mentioned (of sending my friend to college) unto the God of all grace. Blessed be the Lord for this evening's opportunity together.

Lord's day, December 12. I felt, in the morning, as if I had little or no power either to pray or preach, and felt a distressing need of divine help; I went to meeting trembling: but it pleased God to assist me in prayer and sermon: I think, my soul scarce ever penetrated so far into the immaterial world, in any one prayer that ever I made, nor were my devotions ever so much refined, and free from gross conceptions and imaginations framed from beholding material objects. I preached with some sweetness, from Matth. vi. 33. "But "seek ye first the kingdom of God," *&c.*; and in the afternoon from Rom. xv. 30. "And now I beseech you, brethren," *&c.* There was much affection in the assembly. This has been a sweet Sabbath to me; and blessed be God, I have reason to think, that my religion is become more refined and spiritual, by means of my late inward conflicts. Amen. May I always be willing that God should use his own methods with me!

Monday, December 13. Joined in prayer with Mr Bellamy; and found sweetness and composure in parting with him, who went a journey. Enjoyed some sweetness through the day; and just at night rode down to Woodbury.

Tuesday, December 14. Some perplexity hung on my mind: was distressed last night and this morning, for the interest of Zion, especially on account of the *false appearances of religion*, that do but rather breed confusion, especially in some places. I cried to God for help, to enable me to bear testimony against those things, which instead of promoting, do but hinder the progress of vital piety. In the afternoon, rode down to Southbury, and conversed again with my friend about the important affair of his following the work of the ministry; and he appeared much inclined to devote himself to that work, if God should succeed his attempts to qualify himself for so great a work. In the evening I preached from 1 Thess. iv. 8.; and endeavoured, though with tenderness, to undermine false religion. The Lord gave me some assistance; but, however, I seemed so vile, I was ashamed to be seen when I came out of the meeting-house.

Wednesday, December 15. Enjoyed something of God today, both in secret and social prayer; but was sensible of much barrenness, and defect in duty, as well as my inability to help myself for the time to come, or to perform the work

and

and business I have to do. Afterwards, felt much of the sweetness of religion, and the tenderness of the gospel-temper: was far from bitterness, and found a dear love to all mankind, and was afraid of scarcely any thing so much as lest some motion of anger or resentment should, some time or other, creep into my heart. Had some comforting soul-refreshing discourse with some dear friends, just as we took our leave of each other, and supposed it might be likely we should not meet again till we came to the eternal world *. But I doubt not, through grace, but that some of us shall have a happy meeting there, and bless God for this season, as well as many others. Amen.

Thursday, December. 16. Rode down to Derby; had some sweet thoughts on the road: my thoughts were very clear, especially on the essence of our salvation by Christ, from those words, "Thou shalt call his name Jesus," &c.

Friday, December 17. Spent much time in sweet conversation on spiritual things with dear Mr Humphreys. Rode to Ripton; spent some time in prayer with dear Christian friends.

Saturday, December 18. Spent much time in prayer in the woods: seemed raised above the things of the world: my soul was strong in the Lord of hosts: but was sensible of great barrenness.

Lord's day, December 19. At the sacrament of the Lord's supper, seemed strong in the Lord; and the world, with all its frowns and flatteries, in a great measure disappeared, so that my soul had nothing to do with them: and I felt a disposition to be wholly and for ever the Lord's.—In the evening, enjoyed something of the divine presence; had a humbling sense of my vileness, barrenness, and sinfulness. Oh, it wounded me, to think of the misimprovement of time! "God be merciful to me a sinner."

Monday, December 20. Spent this day in prayer, reading, and writing; and enjoyed some assistance, especially in correcting some thoughts on a certain subject; but had a mournful sense of my barrenness.

* It had been determined by the commissioners, who employed Mr Brainerd as a missionary, that he should go as soon as might be conveniently to the Indians living near the Forks of Delaware river in Pensylvania, and the Indians on Susquehanneh river; which being far off, where he would be exposed to many hardships and dangers; this was the occasion of his taking leave of his friends in this manner.

Tuesday,

Tuesday, December 21. Had a ſenſe of my inſufficiency for any public work and buſineſs, as well as to live to God. I rode over to Derby, and preached there: it pleaſed God to give me very ſweet aſſiſtance and enlargement, and to enable me to ſpeak with a ſoft and tender power and energy.—— We had afterwards a comfortable evening in ſinging and prayer: God enabled me to pray with as much ſpirituality and ſweetneſs as I have done for ſome time: my mind ſeemed to be unclothed of ſenſe and imagination, and was in a meaſure let into the immaterial world of ſpirits. This day and evening was, I truſt, through infinite goodneſs, made very profitable to a number of us, to advance our ſouls in holineſs and conformity to God: the glory be to him for ever. Amen. How bleſſed it is to grow more and more like God!

Wedneſday, December 22. Enjoyed ſome aſſiſtance in preaching at Ripton; but my ſoul mourned within me for my barrenneſs.

Thurſday, December 23. Enjoyed, I truſt, ſomething of God this morning in ſecret. Oh how divinely ſweet is it to come into the ſecret of his preſence, and abide in his pavilion! ——Took an affectionate leave of friends, not expecting to ſee them again for a very conſiderable time, if ever in this world. Rode with Mr Humphreys to his houſe at Derby; ſpent the time in ſweet converſation; my ſoul was refreſhed and ſweetly melted with divine things. Oh that I was always conſecrated to God! Near night, I rode to New-Haven, and there enjoyed ſome ſweetneſs in prayer and converſation, with ſome dear Chriſtian friends: my mind was ſweetly ſerious and compoſed: but alas! I too much loſt the ſenſe of divine things.

[He continued much in the ſame frame of mind, and in like exerciſes, the two following days.]

Lord's day, December 26. Felt much ſweetneſs and tenderneſs in prayer, eſpecially my whole ſoul ſeemed to love my worſt enemies, and was enabled to pray for thoſe that are ſtrangers and enemies to God with a great degree of ſoftneſs and pathetic fervour. In the evening, rode from New-Haven to Branford, after I had kneeled down and prayed with a number of dear Chriſtian friends in a very retired place in the woods, and ſo parted.

Monday, December 27. Enjoyed a precious ſeaſon indeed; had a ſweet melting ſenſe of divine things, of the pure ſpirituality

rituality of the religion of Chriſt Jeſus. In the evening, I preached from Matth. vi. 33. with much freedom, and ſweet power and pungency: the preſence of God attended our meeting. O the ſweetneſs, the tenderneſs I felt in my ſoul! if ever I felt the temper of Chriſt, I had ſome ſenſe of it now. Bleſſed be my God, I have ſeldom enjoyed a more comfortable and profitable day than this. O that I could ſpend all my time for God!

Tueſday, December 28. Rode from Branford to Haddam. In the morning, my clearneſs and ſweetneſs in divine things continued; but afterwards my ſpiritual life ſenſibly declined.

[The next twelve days, he was for the moſt part extremely dejected, diſcouraged, and diſtreſſed, and was evidently very much under the power of melancholy; and there are from day to day moſt bitter complaints of exceeding vileneſs, ignorance, corruption, an amazing load of guilt, unworthineſs to creep on God's earth, everlaſting uſeleſſneſs, fitneſs for nothing, *&c.*; and ſometimes expreſſions even of horror at the thoughts of ever preaching again. But yet in this time of great dejection, he ſpeaks of ſeveral intervals of divine help and comfort.

The three next days, which were ſpent at Hebron and the Crank, (a pariſh in Lebanon), he had relief, and enjoyed conſiderable comfort.]

Friday, January 14. 1742-3. My ſpiritual conflicts to-day were unſpeakably dreadful, heavier than the mountains and overflowing floods: I ſeemed incloſed, as it were, in hell itſelf: I was deprived of all ſenſe of God, even of the being of a God; and that was my miſery. I had no awful apprehenſions of God as angry. This was diſtreſs, the neareſt a-kin to the damned's torments, that I ever endured: their torment, I am ſure, will conſiſt much in a privation of God, and conſequently of all good. This taught me the abſolute dependance of a creature upon God the Creator, for every crumb of happineſs it enjoys. Oh! I feel that if there is no God, though I might live for ever here, and enjoy not only this, but all other worlds, I ſhould be ten thouſand times more miſerable than a toad. My ſoul was in ſuch anguiſh I could not eat, but felt as I ſuppoſed a poor wretch would that is juſt going to the place of execution. I was almoſt ſwallowed up with anguiſh, when I ſaw people gathering together to hear me preach. However, I went in that diſtreſs to the house of God, and found not much relief in the first prayer: it seemed as if God would let loose the people upon me to destroy me; nor were the thoughts of death distressing to me, like my own vileness. But afterwards in my discourse from Deut. viii. 2. God was pleased to give me some freedom and enlargement, some power and spirituality; and I spent the evening something comfortably.

[The two next days, his comfort continues, and he seems to enjoy an almost continual sweetness of soul in the duties and exercises of religion and Christian conversation. On Monday was a return of the gloom he had been under the Friday before. He rode to Coventry this day, and the latter part of the day had more freedom. On Tuesday he rode to Canterbury, and continued more comfortable.]

Wednesday, January 19. [At Canterbury] In the afternoon preached the lecture at the meeting-house: felt some tenderness, and something of the gospel-temper: exhorted the people to love one another, and not to set up their own frames as a standard to try all their brethren by. But was much pressed, most of the day, with a sense of my own badness, inward impurity, and unspeakable corruption. Spent the evening in loving Christian conversation.

Thursday, January 20. Rode to my brother's house between Norwich and Lebanon; and preached in the evening to a number of people: enjoyed neither freedom nor spirituality, but saw myself exceeding unworthy.

Friday, January 21. Had great inward conflicts; enjoyed but little comfort. Went to see Mr Williams of Lebanon, and spent several hours with him; and was greatly delighted with his serious, deliberate, and impartial way of discourse about religion.

[The next day, he was much dejected.]

Lord's-day, January 23. Scarce ever felt myself so unfit to exist, as now: I saw I was not worthy of a place among the Indians, where I am going, if God permit: I thought I should be ashamed to look them in the face, and much more to have any respect shewn me there. Indeed I felt myself banished from the earth, as if all places were too good for such a wretch as I: I thought I should be ashamed to go among the very savages of Africa; I appeared to myself a creature

creature fit for nothing, neither heaven nor earth.——None knows, but thoſe that feel it, what the ſoul endures that is ſenſibly ſhut out from the preſence of God: alas! it is more bitter than death.

[On Monday, he rode to Stoningtown, Mr Fiſh's pariſh.——On Tueſday he expreſſes conſiderable degrees of ſpiritual comfort and refreſhment.]

Wedneſday, January 26. Preached to a pretty large aſſembly at Mr Fiſh's meeting-houſe: inſiſted on humility, and ſtedfaſtneſs in keeping God's commands; and that through humility we ſhould prefer one another in love, and not make our own frames the rule by which we judge others. I felt ſweetly calm, and full of brotherly love; and never more free from party-ſpirit. I hope, ſome good will follow, that Chriſtians will be freed from falſe joy, and party-zeal, and cenſuring one another.

[On Thurſday, after conſiderable time ſpent in prayer and Chriſtian converſation, he rode to New-London.]

Friday, January 28. Here I found ſome fallen into ſome extravagances, too much carried away with a falſe zeal and bitterneſs. Oh, the want of a goſpel-temper is greatly to be lamented. Spent the evening in converſing with ſome about ſome points of conduct in both miniſters and private Chriſtians; but did not agree with them; God had not *taught them with briars and thorns* to be of a kind diſpoſition toward mankind.

[On Saturday, he rode to Eaſt-Haddam, and ſpent the three following days there; and in that ſpace of time he ſpeaks of his feeling weanedneſs from the world, a ſenſe of the nearneſs of eternity, ſpecial aſſiſtance in praying for the enlargement of Chriſt's kingdom, times of ſpiritual comfort, &c.]

Wedneſday, February 2. Preached my farewell-ſermon, laſt night, at the houſe of an aged man, who had been unable to attend on the public worſhip for ſome time; and this morning ſpent the time in prayer, almoſt where-ever I went; and having taken leave of friends, I ſet out on my journey towards the Indians; though by the way I was to ſpend ſome time at Eaſt-Hampton on Long-Iſland, by the leave of the commiſſioners who employed me in the Indian affair *; and being accompanied by a meſſenger from Eaſt-Hampton, we travelled to Lyme. On the road I felt an uncommon preſſure of mind: I ſeemed to ſtruggle hard for ſome pleaſure in ſomething here below, and ſeemed loth to give up all for gone; but then ſaw myſelf evidently throwing myſelf into all hardſhips and diſtreſſes in my preſent undertaking: I thought it would be leſs difficult to lie down in the grave: but yet I choſe to go, rather than ſtay.——Came to Lyme that night.

[He waited the two next days for a paſſage over the Sound, and ſpent much of the time in inward conflicts and dejection, but had ſome comfort.

On Saturday he croſſed the Sound, landed at Oyſter-Ponds on Long-Iſland, and travelled from thence to Eaſt-Hampton. And the ſeven following days he ſpent there, for the moſt part, under extreme dejection and gloomineſs of mind, with great complaints of darkneſs, ignorance, *&c.* Yet his heart appears to have been conſtantly engaged in the great buſineſs of religion, much concerned for the intereſt of religion in Eaſt-Hampton, and praying and labouring much for it.]

Saturday, February 12. Enjoyed a little more comfort, was enabled to meditate with ſome compoſure of mind; and eſpecially in the evening, found my ſoul more refreſhed in prayer, than at any time of late; my ſoul ſeemed to "take hold of "God's ſtrength," and was comforted with his conſolations. O how ſweet are ſome glimpſes of divine glory! how ſtrengthening and quickening!

Lord's day, February 13. At noon, under a great degree of diſcouragement; knew not how it was poſſible for me to preach in the afternoon, was ready to give up all for gone; but God was pleaſed to aſſiſt me in ſome meaſure. In the evening, my heart was ſweetly drawn out after God, and devoted to him.

[The next day, he had comfort and dejection intermingled.]

* The reaſon why the commiſſioners or correſpondents did not order Mr Brainerd to go immediately to the Indians, and enter on his buſineſs as a miſſionary to them, was, that the *Winter* was not judged to be a convenient ſeaſon for him firſt to go out into the wilderneſs, and enter on the difficulties and hardſhips he muſt there be expoſed to.

Tuesday, February 15. Early in the day I felt some comfort; afterwards I walked into a neighbouring grove, and felt more as a stranger on earth, I think, than ever before; dead to any of the enjoyments of the world, as if I had been dead in a natural sense.——In the evening, had divine sweetness in secret duty: God was then my portion, and my soul rose above those *deep waters*, into which I have sunk so low of late.—My soul then cried for Zion, and had sweetness in so doing.

[This sweet frame continued the next morning; but afterwards his inward distress returned.]

Thursday, February 17. In the morning, found myself something comfortable, and rested on God in some measure.——Preached this day at a little village belonging to East-Hampton; and God was pleased to give me his gracious presence and assistance, so that I spake with freedom, boldness, and some power. In the evening, spent some time with a dear Christian friend; felt sweetly serious, as on the brink of eternity; my soul enjoyed sweetness in lively apprehensions of standing before the glorious God: prayed with my dear friend with sweetness, and discoursed with utmost solemnity. And truly it was a little emblem of heaven itself.——I find my soul is more refined and weaned from a dependance on my frames and spiritual feelings.

Friday, February 18. Felt something sweetly most of the day, and found access to the throne of grace. Blessed be the Lord for any intervals of heavenly delight and composure, while I am engaged in the field of battle. O that I might be serious, solemn, and always vigilant, while in an evil world! Had some opportunity alone to-day, and found some freedom in study. O, I long to *live to God!*

Saturday, February 19. Was exceeding infirm to-day, greatly troubled with pain in my head and dizziness, scarce able to sit up. However, enjoyed something of God in prayer, and performed some necessary studies. I exceedingly long to die; and yet, through divine goodness, have felt very willing to live, for two or three days past.

Lord's day, February 20. Was something perplexed on account of my carelessness; I thought I could not be suitably concerned about the important work of the day, and so was restless with my easiness.——Was exceeding infirm again today; but the Lord strengthened me, both in the outward and inward man, so that I preached with some life and spirituality, ty, eſpecially in the afternoon, wherein I was enabled to ſpeak cloſely againſt ſelfiſh religion, that loves Chriſt for his benefits, but not for himſelf.

[During the next fortnight, it appears that he, for the moſt part, enjoyed much ſpiritual peace and comfort. In his diary for this ſpace of time, are expreſſed ſuch things as theſe; mourning over indwelling ſin and unprofitableneſs; deadneſs to the world; longing after God, and to live to his glory; heart-melting deſires after his eternal home; fixed reliance on God for his help; experience of much divine aſſiſtance both in the private and public exerciſes of religion; inward ſtrength and courage in the ſervice of God; very frequent refreſhment, conſolation, and divine ſweetneſs in meditation, prayer, preaching, and Chriſtian converſation. And it appears by his account, that this ſpace of time was filled up with great diligence and earneſtneſs in ſerving God, in ſtudy, prayer, meditation, preaching, and private inſtructing and counſelling.]

Monday, March 7. This morning when I aroſe, I found my heart go forth after God in longing deſires of conformity to him, and in ſecret prayer found myſelf ſweetly quickened and drawn out in praiſes to God for all he had done to and for me, and for all my inward trials and diſtreſſes of late; my heart aſcribed glory, glory, glory to the bleſſed God! and bid welcome all inward diſtreſs again, if God ſaw meet to exerciſe me with it: time appeared but an inch long, and eternity at hand; and I thought I could with patience and chearfulneſs bear any thing for the cauſe of God; for I ſaw that a moment would bring me to a world of peace and bleſſedneſs; and my ſoul, by the ſtrength of the Lord, roſe far above this lower world, and all the vain amuſements and frightful diſappointments of it. Afterwards, was viſited by ſome friends, but loſt ſome ſweetneſs by the means. After that, had ſome ſweet meditation on Gen. v. 24. "And "Enoch walked with God," &c.——This was a comfortable day to my ſoul.

[The next day, he ſeems to have continued in a conſiderable degree of ſweetneſs and fervency in religion.]

Wedneſday, March 9. Endeavoured to commit myſelf and all my concerns to God. Rode ſixteen miles to Mantauk *, and had

* Mantauk is the eaſtern cape or end of Long-Iſland, inhabited chiefly by Indians.

had ſome inward ſweetneſs on the road; but ſomething of flatneſs and deadneſs after I came there and had ſeen the Indians: I withdrew, and endeavoured to pray, but found myſelf awfully deſerted and left, and had an afflicting ſenſe of my vileneſs and meanneſs. However, I went and preached from Iſ. liii. 10. Had ſome aſſiſtance; and, I truſt, ſomething of the divine preſence was among us. In the evening, again I prayed and exhorted among them, after having had a ſeaſon alone, wherein I was ſo preſſed with the blackneſs of my nature, that I thought it was not fit for me to ſpeak ſo much as to Indians.

[The next day, he returned to Eaſt-Hampton; was exceeding infirm in body through the remaining part of this week; but ſpeaks of aſſiſtance and enlargement in ſtudy and religious exerciſes, and of inward ſweetneſs and breathing after God.]

Lord's day, March 13. At noon, I thought it impoſſible for me to preach, by reaſon of bodily weakneſs and inward deadneſs; and in the firſt prayer, was ſo weak that I could hardly ſtand; but in ſermon, God ſtrengthened me, ſo that I ſpake near an hour and half with ſweet freedom, clearneſs, and ſome tender power, from Gen. v. 24. "And Enoch walked with God." I was ſweetly aſſiſted to inſiſt on a cloſe *walk with God*, and to leave this as my parting advice to God's people here, that *they ſhould walk with God*. May the God of all grace ſucceed my poor labours in this place!

Monday, March 14. In the morning, was very buſy in preparation for my journey, and was almoſt continually engaged in ejaculatory prayer. About ten, took leave of the dear people of Eaſt-Hampton; my heart grieved and mourned, and rejoiced at the ſame time; rode near fifty miles to a part of Brook-Haven, and lodged there, and had refreſhing converſation with a Chriſtian friend.

[In two days more he reached New-York; but complains of much deſertion and deadneſs on the road. He ſtayed one day in New-York, and on Friday went to Mr Dickinſon's at Eliſabeth-Town. His complaints are the ſame as on the two preceding days.]

Saturday, March 19. Was bitterly diſtreſſed under a ſenſe of my ignorance, darkneſs, and unworthineſs; got alone, and poured

poured out my complaint to God in the bitterneſs of my ſoul.——In the afternoon, rode to Newark, and had ſome ſweetneſs in converſation with Mr Burr, and in praying together. O bleſſed be God for ever and ever, for any enlivening and quickening.

Lord's day, March 20. Preached in the forenoon: God gave me ſome aſſiſtance and ſweetneſs, and enabled me to ſpeak with real tenderneſs, love, and impartiality. In the evening, preached again; and, of a truth, God was pleaſed to aſſiſt a poor worm. Bleſſed be God, I was enabled to ſpeak with life, power, and paſſionate deſire of the edification of God's people, and with ſome power to ſinners. In the evening, I felt ſomething ſpiritual and watchful, leſt my heart ſhould by any means be drawn away from God. Oh, when ſhall I come to that bleſſed world, where every power of my ſoul will be inceſſantly and eternally wound up, in heavenly employments and enjoyments, to the higheſt degree!

[On Monday he went to Woodbridge, where he ſpeaks of his being with a number of miniſters *; and the day following of his travelling part of the way towards New-York, and lodging at a tavern. On Wedneſday, he came to New-York. On Thurſday, he rode near fifty miles, from New-York to North-Caſtle. On Friday, went to Danbury. On Saturday to New-Milford. On the Sabbath, he rode five or ſix miles to a place near Kent in Connecticut, called Scaticoke, where dwell

* Theſe miniſters were the *Correſpondents*, who now met at Woodbridge, and gave Mr Brainerd new directions; and inſtead of ſending him to the Indians at the Forks of Delaware, as before intended, they ordered him to go to a number of Indians, at Kaunaumeek, a place in the province of New York, in the woods between Stockbridge and Albany. This alteration was occaſioned by two things, *viz.* 1. Information that the correſpondents had received of ſome contention now ſubſiſting between the white people and the Indians at Delaware, concerning their lands, which they ſuppoſed would be a hinderance at preſent to their entertainment of a miſſionary, and to his ſucceſs among them. And, 2. Some intimations they had received from Mr Sergeant, miſſionary to the Indians at Stockbridge, concerning the Indians at Kaunaumeek, and the hopeful proſpect of ſucceſs that a miſſionary might have among them.

dwell a number of Indians *, and preached to them. On Monday, being detained by the rain, he tarried at Kent. On Tuesday, he rode from Kent to Salsbury. Wednesday, he went to Sheffield. Thursday, March 31. he went to Mr Sergeant's at Stockbridge. He was dejected and very disconsolate, through the main of this journey from New-Jersey to Stockbridge; and especially on the last day his mind was overwhelmed with an exceeding gloominess and melancholy.]

* These were the same Indians that Mr Brainerd mentions in his diary, on August 12. the preceding year.

*****************)(*****************

PART V.

From his first beginning to instruct the Indians at Kaunaumeek, to his *Ordination*.

FRiday, April 1. 1743. I rode to Kaunaumeek, near twenty miles from Stockbridge, where the Indians live, with whom I am concerned, and there lodged on a little heap of straw: was greatly exercised with inward trials and distresses all day; and in the evening, my heart was sunk, and I seemed to have no God to go to. O that God would help me!

[The next five days, he was for the most part in a dejected depressed state of mind, and sometimes extremely so. He speaks of God's "waves and billows rolling over his soul;" and of his being ready sometimes to say, "Surely his mercy "is clean gone for ever, and he will be favourable no more;" and says, the anguish he endured, was nameless and inconceivable; but at the same time speaks thus concerning his distresses, "What God designs by all my distresses I know not; "but this I know, I deserve them all, and thousands more." ——He gives an account of the Indians kindly receiving him, and being seriously attentive to his instructions.]

Thursday, April 7. Appeared to myself exceeding ignorant, weak, helpless, and unworthy, and altogether unequal to my work. It seemed to me, I should never do any service, or have any success among the Indians. My soul was weary of my life: I longed for death, beyond measure. When I thought of any godly soul departed, my soul was ready to envy him his privilege, thinking, "Oh, when will my turn "come! must it be years first!"——But I know, those ardent desires, at this and other times, rose partly for want of resignation to God under all miseries; and so were but impatience. Towards night, I had (I think) the exercise of faith in prayer, and some assistance in writing. O that God would keep me near him!

Friday,

Friday, April 8. Was exceedingly pressed under a sense of my *pride*, *selfishness*, *bitterness*, and *party-spirit*, in times past, while I attempted to promote the cause of God: its vile nature and dreadful consequences appeared in such odious colours to me, that my very heart was pained: I saw how poor souls stumbled over it into everlasting destruction, that I was constrained to make that prayer in the bitterness of my soul, "O Lord, deliver me from blood-guiltiness." I saw my desert of hell on this account. My soul was full of inward anguish and shame before God, that I had spent so much time in conversation tending only to promote a *party-spirit*. Oh, I saw I had not suitably prized mortification, self-denial, resignation under all adversities, meekness, love, candour, and holiness of heart and life: and this day was almost wholly spent in such bitter and soul-afflicting reflections on my past frames and conduct.——Of late, I have thought much of having the kingdom of Christ advanced in the world; but now I saw I had enough to do within myself. The Lord be merciful to me a sinner, and wash my soul!

Saturday, April 9. Remained much in the same state as yesterday; excepting that the sense of my vileness was not so quick and acute.

Lord's day, April 10. Rose early in the morning, and walked out, and spent considerable time in the woods, in prayer and meditation. Preached to the Indians, both forenoon and afternoon. They behaved soberly in general: two or three in particular appeared under some religious concern; with whom I discoursed privately; and one told me, "her "heart had cried, ever since she heard me preach first."

[The next day, he complains of much desertion.]

Tuesday, April 12. Was greatly oppressed with grief and shame, reflecting on my past conduct, my *bitterness* and *party-zeal*. I was ashamed, to think that such a wretch as I had ever preached.—Longed to be excused from that work. And when my soul was not in anguish and keen distress, I felt senseless "as a beast before God," and felt a kind of guilty amusement with the least trifles; which still maintained a kind of stifled horror of conscience, so that I could not rest any more than a condemned malefactor.

Wednesday, April 13. My heart was overwhelmed within me: I verily thought I was the meanest, vilest, most helpless, guilty, ignorant, benighted creature living. And yet I knew what God had done for my soul, at the same time: though

 sometimes

ſometimes I was aſſaulted with damping doubts and fears, whether it was poſſible for ſuch a wretch as I to be in a ſtate of grace.

Thurſday, April 14. Remained much in the ſame ſtate as yeſterday.

Friday, April 15. In the forenoon, very diſconſolate. In the afternoon, preached to my people, and was a little encouraged in ſome hopes God might beſtow mercy on their ſouls. ——Felt ſomething reſigned to God under all diſpenſations of his providence.

Saturday, April 16. Still in the depths of diſtreſs.——In the afternoon, preached to my people; but was more diſcouraged with them than before; feared that nothing would ever be done for them to any happy effect. I retired and poured out my ſoul to God for mercy; but without any ſenſible relief. Soon after came an Iriſh-man and a Dutch-man, with a deſign, as they ſaid, to hear me preach the next day; but none can tell how I felt, to hear their profane talk. Oh, I longed that ſome dear Chriſtian knew my diſtreſs. I got into a kind of hovel, and there groned out my complaint to God; and withal felt more ſenſible gratitude and thankfulneſs to God, that he had made me to differ from theſe men, as I knew through grace he had.

Lord's day, April 17. In the morning was again diſtreſſed as ſoon as I waked, hearing much talk about the world and the things of it. Though I perceived the men were in ſome meaſure afraid of me; and I diſcourſed ſomething about ſanctifying the Sabbath, if poſſible, to ſolemnize their minds: but when they were at a little diſtance, they again talked freely about ſecular affairs. Oh, I thought what a *hell* it would be, to live with ſuch men to eternity! The Lord gave me ſome aſſiſtance in preaching, all day, and ſome reſignation, and a ſmall degree of comfort in prayer at night.

[He continued in this diſconſolate frame the next day.]

Tueſday, April 19. In the morning, enjoyed ſome ſweet repoſe and reſt in God; felt ſome ſtrength and confidence in God; and my ſoul was in ſome meaſure refreſhed and comforted. Spent moſt of the day in writing, and had ſome exerciſe of grace ſenſible and comfortable: my ſoul ſeemed lifted above the *deep waters*, wherein it has been ſo long almoſt drowned; felt ſome ſpiritual longings and breathings of ſoul after God; found myſelf engaged for the advancement of

Christ's kingdom in my own soul, more than in others, more than in the Heathen world.

Wednesday, April 20. Set apart this day for fasting and prayer, to bow my soul before God for the bestowment of divine grace; especially that all my spiritual afflictions and inward distresses might be sanctified to my soul. And endeavoured also to remember the goodness of God to me in the year past, this day being my birth-day. Having obtained help of God, I have hitherto lived, and am now arrived at the age of twenty-five years. My soul was pained, to think of my barrenness and deadness; that I have lived so little to the glory of the eternal God. I spent the day in the woods alone, and there poured out my complaint to God. O that God would enable me to live to his glory for the future!

Thursday, April 21. Spent the forenoon in reading and prayer, and found myself something engaged; but still much depressed in spirit under a sense of my vileness and unfitness for any public service. In the afternoon, I visited my people, and prayed and conversed with some about their souls concerns: and afterwards found some ardour of soul in secret prayer. O that I might grow up into the likeness of God!

Friday, April 22. Spent the day in study, reading, and prayer; and felt a little relieved of my burden, that has been so heavy of late. But still in some measure oppressed: had a sense of barrenness. Oh my leanness testifies against me! my very soul abhors itself for its unlikeness to God, its inactivity and sluggishness. When I have done all, alas, what an unprofitable servant am I! My soul grones, to see the hours of the day roll away, because I do not fill them, in spirituality and heavenly-mindedness. And yet I long they should speed their pace, to hasten me to my eternal home, where I may fill up all my moments, through eternity, for God and his glory.

[On Saturday and Lord's day, his melancholy again prevailed: he cried out of his ignorance, stupidity, and senselessness; while yet he seems to have spent the time with utmost diligence, in study, in prayer, and in instructing and counselling the Indians. On Monday, he sunk into the deepest melancholy; so that he supposed he never spent a day in such distress in his life; not in fears of hell, (which, he says, he had no pressing fear of), but a distressing sense of his own vileness, *&c.* On Tuesday, he expresses some relief. Wednesday he kept as a day of fasting and prayer, but in great distress.

ſtreſs. The three days next following, his melancholy continued, but in a leſſer degree, and with intervals of comfort *.]

Lord's day, May 1. Was at Stockbridge to-day. In the forenoon had ſome relief and aſſiſtance; though not ſo much as uſual. In the afternoon, felt poorly in body and ſoul; while I was preaching, ſeemed to be rehearſing idle tales, without the leaſt life, fervour, ſenſe, or comfort: and eſpecially afterwards, at the ſacrament, my ſoul was filled with confuſion, and the utmoſt anguſh that ever I endured, under the feeling of my inexpreſſible vileneſs and meanneſs. It was a moſt bitter and diſtreſſing ſeaſon to me, by reaſon of the view I had of my own heart, and the ſecret abominations that lurk there: I thought the eyes of all in the houſe were upon me, and I dared not look any one in the face; for it verily ſeemed as if they ſaw the vileneſs of my heart, and all the ſins I had ever been guilty of. And if I had been baniſhed from the preſence of all mankind, never to be ſeen any more, or ſo much as thought of, ſtill I ſhould have been diſtreſſed with ſhame; and I ſhould have been aſhamed to ſee the moſt barbarous people on earth, becauſe I was viler, and ſeemingly more brutiſhly ignorant than they.—" I am made to " poſſeſs the ſins of my youth."

[The remaining days of this week were ſpent, for the moſt part, in inward diſtreſs and gloomineſs. The next Sabbath, he had encouragement, aſſiſtance, and comfort; but on Monday ſunk again.]

Tueſday, May 10. Was in the ſame ſtate, as to my mind, that I have been in for ſome time, extremely preſſed with a ſenſe of guilt, pollution, blindneſs: "The iniquity of my " heels have compaſſed me about; the ſins of my youth have " been ſet in order before me; they have gone over my head, " as an heavy burden, too heavy for me to bear." Almoſt all the actions of my life paſt ſeem to be covered over with ſin and guilt; and thoſe of them that I performed in the moſt conſcientious manner, now fill me with ſhame and confuſion, that I cannot hold up my face. Oh! the *pride*, *ſelfiſhneſs*, *hypocriſy*, *ignorance*, *bitterneſs*, *party-zeal*, and *the want of love*, *candour*, *meekneſs*, and *gentleneſs*, that have attended my

* On the laſt of theſe days he wrote the *firſt letter* added at the end of this hiſtory.

attempts

attempts to promote religion and virtue; and this when I have reason to hope I had real assistance from above, and some sweet intercourse with Heaven! But, alas, what corrupt mixtures attended my best duties!

[The next seven days, his gloom and distress continued, for the most part: but he had some turns of relief and spiritual comfort. He gives an account of his spending part of this time in hard labour, to build himself a little *cottage* to live in amongst the Indians, in which he might be by himself; having (it seems) hitherto lived with a poor Scotch-man, as he observes in the letter just now refered to in the margin; and afterwards, before his own house was habitable, lived in a wigwam among the Indians.]

Wednesday, May 18. My circumstances are such that I have no comfort, of any kind, but what I have in God. I live in the most lonesome wilderness; have but one single person to converse with, that can speak English *. Most of the talk I hear, is either Highland-Scotch or Indian. I have no fellow-Christian to whom I might unbosom myself, and lay open my spiritual sorrows, and with whom I might take sweet counsel in conversation about heavenly things, and join in social prayer. I live poorly with regard to the comforts of life: most of my diet consists of boiled corn, hasty-pudding, &c. I lodge on a bundle of straw, and my labour is hard and extremely difficult; and I have little appearance of success, to comfort me. The Indians affairs are very difficult; having no land to live on, but what the Dutch people lay claim to, and threaten to drive them off from; they have no regard to the souls of the poor Indians; and, by what I can learn, they hate me, because I come to preach to them.——But that which makes all my difficulties grievous to be borne, is, that "God hides his face from me."

Thursday, May 19. Spent most of this day in close studies: but was sometimes so distressed that I could think of nothing but my spiritual blindness, ignorance, pride, and misery.

* This person was Mr Brainerd's interpreter; who was an ingenious young Indian belonging to Stockbridge, whose name was John Wauwaumpequunnaunt, who had been instructed in the Christian religion by Mr Sergeant; and had lived with the Reverend Mr Williams of Long-Meadow, and had been further instructed by him, at the charge of Mr Hollis of London; and understood both English and Indian very well, and wrote a good hand.

Oh,

Oh, I have reason to make that prayer, "Lord, forgive my "sins of youth, and former trespasses!"

Friday, May 20. Was much perplexed, some part of the day; but towards night, had some comfortable meditations on Is. xl. 1. and enjoyed some sweetness in prayer. Afterwards my soul rose so far above the *deep waters*, that I dared to *rejoice in God*: I saw, there was sufficient matter of consolation in the blessed God.

[The next nine days, his burdens were for the most part alleviated, but with variety; at some times having considerable consolation, and at other times more depressed. The next day, Monday, May 30. he set out on a journey to New-Jersey, to consult the commissioners that employed him about the affairs of his mission *: performed his journey thither in four days; and arrived at Mr Burr's in Newark on Thursday. In great part of his journey, he was in the depths of melancholy, under like distresses with those already mentioned. On Friday, he rode to Elisabeth-Town; and on Saturday to New-York; and from thence on his way homewards as far as White-Plains; where he spent the Sabbath, and had considerable degrees of divine consolation and assistance in public services. On Monday, he rode about sixty miles to New-Haven. There he attempted a reconciliation with the authority of the *college*; and spent this week in visiting his friends in those parts, and in his journey homewards, till Saturday, in a pretty comfortable frame of mind. On Saturday, in his way from Stockbridge to Kaunaumeek, he was lost in the woods, and lay all night in the open air; but happily found his way in the morning, and came to his Indians on Lord's day, June 12. and had greater assistance in preaching among them than ever before, since his first coming among them.]

[From this time forward he was the subject of various frames and exercises of mind: but it seems, in the general, to have been with him much after the same manner as it had been hitherto from his first coming to Kaunaumeek, till he got into his own house, (a little hut, that he made chiefly with his own hands, with long and hard labour), which was

* His business with the commissioners now was, to obtain orders from them to set up a school among the Indians at Kaunaumeek, and that his interpreter might be appointed the schoolmaster: which was accordingly done.

near

near seven weeks from this time. Great part of this space of time, he was dejected and depressed with melancholy, and sometimes very extremely, his melancholy operating in like manner as has been related of times past. How it was with him in those dark seasons, he himself further describes in his diary for July 2. in the following manner. "My "soul is, and has for a long time been in a piteous condition, "wading through a series of sorrows, of various kinds. I "have been so crushed down sometimes with a sense of my "meanness and infinite unworthiness, that I have been a-"shamed that any, even the meanest of my fellow-creatures, "should so much as spend a thought about me, and have "wished sometimes while I have travelled among the thick "brakes, as one of them, to drop into everlasting oblivion. "In this case, sometimes, I have almost resolved never again "to see any of my acquaintance; and really thought, I could "not do it and hold up my face; and have longed for the re-"motest region, for a retreat from all my friends, that I "might not be seen or heard of any more.——Sometimes "the consideration of my ignorance has been a means of my "great distress and anxiety. And especially my soul has "been in anguish with fear, shame, and guilt, that ever I had "preached, or had any thought that way.——Sometimes my "soul has been in distress on feeling some particular corrup-"tions rise and swell like a mighty torrent, with present vio-"lence; having, at the same time, ten thousand former sins "and follies presented to view, in all their blackness and ag-"gravations.——And these attended with such external cir-"cumstances as mine at present are; destitute of most of the "conveniencies of life, and I may say, of all the pleasures of "it; without a friend to communicate any of my sorrows to, "and sometimes without any place of retirement, where I "may unburden my soul before God, which has greatly con-"tributed to my distress.——Of late, more especially, my "great difficulty has been a sort of carelessness, a kind of "regardless temper of mind, whence I have been disposed to "indolence and trifling: and this temper of mind has con-"stantly been attended with guilt and shame; so that some-"times I have been in a kind of horror, to find myself so un-"like the blessed God; and have thought I grew worse under "all my trials; and nothing has cut and wounded my soul "more than this. Oh, if I am one of God's chosen, as I "trust through infinite grace I am, I find of a truth, that *the "righteous are scarcely saved.*"

It is apparent, that one main occasion of that distressing

gloominess of mind which he was so much exercised with at Kaunaumeek, was reflection on his past errors and misguided zeal at *college*, in the beginning of the late religious commotions in the land. And therefore he repeated his endeavours this year for reconciliation with the governors of the college, whom he had in that time offended. Although he had been at New-Haven, in June, this year, and had attempted a reconciliation, as has been mentioned already; yet, in the beginning of July, he made another journey thither, and renewed his attempt, but still in vain.

Although he was much dejected, great part of that space of time that I am now speaking of; yet there were many intermissions of his melancholy, and some seasons of comfort, sweet tranquillity and resignation of mind, and frequent special assistance in public services, that he speaks of in his diary. The manner of his relief from his sorrow, once in particular, is worthy to be mentioned in his own words, in his diary for July 25. which are as follows. "Had little or no resolution "for a life of holiness; was ready almost to renounce my "hopes of living to God. And Oh how dark it looked, to "think of being unholy for ever! This I could not endure. "The cry of my soul was that, Psal. lxv. 3. *Iniquities pre-"vail against me.* But was in some measure relieved by a "comfortable meditation on God's eternity, that he never "had a beginning, &c. Whence I was led to admire his "greatness and power, &c. in such a manner, that I stood "still, and praised the Lord for his own glories and perfec-"tions; though I was (and if I should for ever be) an unholy "creature, my soul was comforted to apprehend an eternal, "infinite, powerful, holy God."]

Saturday, July 30. Just at night, moved into *my own house*, and lodged there that night; found it much better spending the time alone in my own house, than in the *wigwam* where I was before.

Lord's day, July 31. Felt more comfortably than some days past.——Blessed be the Lord, that has now given me a place of retirement.——O that I might *find God* in it, and that he would dwell with me for ever!

Monday, August 1. Was still busy in further labours on my house.—Felt a little of the sweetness of religion, and thought it was worth the while to *follow after God* through a thousand snares, desarts, and death itself. O that I might always *follow after holiness*, that I may be fully conformed to God! Had some

ſome degree of ſweetneſs, in ſecret prayer, though I had much ſorrow.

Tueſday, Auguſt 2. Was ſtill labouring to make myſelf more comfortable with regard to my houſe and lodging. Laboured under ſpiritual anxiety; it ſeemed to me, I deſerved to be kicked out of the world; yet found ſome comfort in "committing my cauſe to God. It is good for me to be "afflicted," that I may die wholly to this world, and all that is in it.

Wedneſday, Auguſt 3. Spent moſt of the day in writing. Enjoyed ſome ſenſe of religion. Through divine goodneſs I am now uninterruptedly alone; and find my retirement comfortable. I have enjoyed more ſenſe of divine things within a few days laſt paſt, than for ſome time before. I longed after holineſs, humility, and meekneſs: O that God would enable me to "paſs the time of my ſojourning here in his fear," and always *live to him!*

Thurſday, Auguſt 4. Was enabled to pray much, through the whole day; and through divine goodneſs found ſome intenſeneſs of ſoul in the duty, as I uſed to do, and ſome ability to perſevere in my ſupplications: had ſome apprehenſions of divine things, that were engaging, and that gave me ſome courage and reſolution. It is good, I find, to *perſevere in attempts* to pray, if I cannot *pray with perſeverance*, i. e. continue long in my addreſſes to the divine Being. I have generally found, that the more I do in ſecret prayer, the more I have delighted to do, and have enjoyed more of a ſpirit of prayer: and frequently have found the contrary, when with journeying or otherwiſe, I have been much deprived of retirement. A ſeaſonable ſteady performance of ſecret duties in their proper hours, and a careful improvement of all time, filling up every hour with ſome profitable labour, either of heart, head, or hands, are excellent means of ſpiritual peace and boldneſs before God. "Chriſt" indeed "is our peace, and "by him we have boldneſs of acceſs to God;" but a *good conſcience, void of offence*, is an excellent preparation for an approach into the divine preſence. There is difference between *ſelf-confidence* and a *ſelf-righteous pleaſing ourſelves* (with our own duties, attainments, and ſpiritual enjoyments), which godly ſouls ſometimes are guilty of, and that *holy confidence* ariſing from the teſtimony of a good conſcience, which good Hezekiah had, when he ſays, "Remember, O Lord, I "beſeech thee, how I have walked before thee in truth, and "with a perfect heart." "Then," ſays the holy pſalmiſt, "ſhall I not be aſhamed, when I have reſpect to all thy com- "mandments."

"mandments." Filling up our time *with* and *for* God, is the way to rise up and lie down in peace.

[The next eight days, he continued for the most part in a very comfortable frame, having his mind fixed and sweetly engaged in religion; and more than once blesses God, that he had given him a little *cottage*, where he might live alone, and enjoy a happy retirement, free from noise and disturbance, and could at any hour of the day lay aside all studies, and spend time in lifting up his soul to God for spiritual blessings.]

Saturday, August 13. Was enabled in secret prayer to raise my soul to God, with desire and delight. It was indeed a blessed season to my soul: I found the comfort of being a Christian: "I counted the sufferings of the present life "not worthy to be compared with the glory" of divine enjoyments even in this world. All my past sorrows seemed kindly to disappear, and I "remembered no more the sorrow "for joy."——O, how kindly, and with what a filial tenderness, the soul hangs on, and confides in *the Rock of ages*, at such a season, that he will "never leave it, nor forsake it," that he will cause "all things to work together for its good!" *&c.* I longed, that others should know how good a God the Lord is. My soul was full of tenderness and love, even to the most inveterate of my enemies: I longed they should share in the same mercy. I loved and longed that God should do just as he pleased with me and every thing else. I felt exceeding serious, calm, and peaceful, and encouraged to press after holiness as long as I live, whatever difficulties and trials may be in my way. May the Lord always help me so to do! Amen, and Amen.

Lord's day, August 14. I had much more freedom in public, than in private. God enabled me to speak with some feeling sense of divine things; but perceived no considerable effect.

Monday, August 15. Spent most of the day in labour to procure something to keep my horse on in the winter.—Enjoyed not much sweetness in the morning: was very weak in body, through the day, and thought this frail body would soon drop into the dust: had some very realizing apprehensions of a speedy entrance into another world. And in this weak state of body, was not a little distressed for want of suitable food. Had no bread, nor could I get any. I am forced to go or send ten or fifteen miles for all the bread I eat; and sometimes it is mouldy and soure, before I eat it, if I get any

considerable

considerable quantity: and then again I have none for some days together, for want of an opportunity to send for it, and cannot find my horse in the woods to go myself; and this was my case now: but through divine goodness I had some Indian *meal*, of which I made little cakes, and fried them. Yet felt contented with my circumstances, and sweetly resigned to God. In prayer I enjoyed great freedom; and blessed God as much for my present circumstances, as if I had been a king; and thought, I found a disposition to be contented in any circumstances. Blessed be God!

[The rest of this week, he was exceeding weak in body, and much exercised with pain; and yet obliged from day to day to labour hard, to procure fodder for his horse; excepting some part of the time he was so very ill, that he was neither able to work nor study: but speaks of longings after holiness and perfect conformity to God; complains of enjoying but little of God: yet says, *that little* was better to him, than *all the world* besides. In his diary for Saturday, he says, he was something melancholy and sorrowful in mind; and adds, "I never feel comfortably, but when I find my soul going "forth after God: if I cannot be holy, I must necessarily be "miserable for ever."]

Lord's day, August 21. Was much straitened in the forenoon-exercise: my thoughts seemed to be all scattered to the ends of the earth. At noon, I fell down before the Lord, and groned under my vileness, barrenness, deadness, and felt as if I was guilty of soul-murder, in speaking to immortal souls in such a manner as I had then done.——In the afternoon, God was pleased to give me some assistance, and I was enabled to set before my hearers the nature and necessity of true repentance, &c. Afterwards had some small degree of thankfulness. Was very ill and full of pain in the evening; and my soul mourned that I had spent so much time to so little profit.

Monday, August 22. Spent most of the day in study; and found my bodily strength in a measure restored. Had some intense and passionate breathings of soul after holiness, and very clear manifestations of my utter inability to procure, or work it in myself; it is wholly owing to the power of God. O, with what tenderness the love and desire of holiness fills the soul! I wanted to wing out of myself to God, or rather to get a conformity to him: but, alas! I cannot add to my stature in grace one cubit. However, my soul can never leave

striving

ſtriving for it; or at leaſt groning, that it cannot ſtrive for it, and obtain more purity of heart.——At night, I ſpent ſome time in inſtructing my poor people: Oh that God would pity their ſouls!

Tueſday, Auguſt 23. Studied in the forenoon, and enjoyed ſome freedom. In the afternoon, laboured abroad: endeavoured to pray much; but found not much ſweetneſs or intenſeneſs of mind. Towards night, was very weary, and tired of this world of ſorrow: the thoughts of death and immortality appeared very deſirable, and even refreſhed my ſoul. Thoſe lines turned in my mind with pleaſure,

Come, death, ſhake hands; I'll kiſs thy bands:
'Tis happineſs for me to die.
What! doſt thou think, that I will ſhrink?
I'll go to immortality.

In evening-prayer, God was pleaſed to draw near my ſoul, though very ſinful and unworthy: was enabled to wreſtle with God, and to perſevere in my requeſts for grace: I poured out my ſoul for all the world, friends, and enemies. My ſoul was concerned, not ſo much for ſouls as ſuch, but rather for Chriſt's kingdom, that it might appear in the world, that God might be known to be God, in the whole earth. And Oh, my ſoul abhorred the very thought of a *party* in religion! Let the truth of God appear, where-ever it is; and God have the glory for ever. Amen. This was indeed a comfortable ſeaſon: I thought I had ſome ſmall taſte of, and real reliſh for the enjoyments and employments of the upper world. O that my ſoul was more attempered to it!

Wedneſday, Auguſt 24. Spent ſome time, in the morning, in ſtudy and prayer. Afterwards, was engaged in ſome neceſſary buſineſs abroad. Towards night, found a little time for ſome particular ſtudies. I thought, if God ſhould ſay, "Ceaſe making any proviſion for this life, for you ſhall in a "few days go out of time into eternity," my ſoul would leap for joy. O that I may both "deſire to be diſſolved, to "be with Chriſt," and likewiſe "wait patiently all the days "of my appointed time till my change come!"—But, alas! I am very unfit for the buſineſs and bleſſedneſs of heaven.— O for more holineſs!

Thurſday, Auguſt. 25. Part of the day, engaged in ſtudies; and part, in labour abroad. I find it is impoſſible to enjoy peace and tranquillity of mind without a careful improvement of time. This is really an imitation of God and Chriſt Jeſus: "My Father worketh hitherto, and I work," ſays

says our Lord. But still, if we would be like God, we must see that we fill up our time for him.——I daily long to dwell in perfect light and love. In the mean time, my soul mourns that I make so little progress in grace, and preparation for the world of blessedness: I see and know that I am a very barren tree in God's vineyard, and that he might justly say, "Cut it "down," &c. O that God would make me more lively and vigorous in grace, for his own glory! Amen.

[The two next days, he was much engaged in some necessary labours, in which he extremely spent himself. He seems, these days to have had a great sense of the vanity of the world; and continued longings after holiness, and more fervency of spirit in the service of God.]

Lord's day, August. 28. Was much perplexed with some irreligious Dutch-men. All their discourse turned upon the things of the world; which was no small exercise to my mind. Oh, what a *hell* it would be to spend an eternity with such men! Well might David say, "I beheld the transgressors, "and was grieved."—But adored be God, *heaven* is a place "into which no unclean thing enters." Oh, I long for the holiness of that world! Lord, prepare me therefor.

[The next day, he set out on a journey to New-York. Was something dejected, the two first days of his journey; but yet seems to have enjoyed some degrees of the sensible presence of God.]

Wednesday, August 31. Rode down to Bethlehem: was in a sweet, serious, and, I hope, Christian frame, when I came there; eternal things engrossed all my thoughts; and I longed to be in the world of spirits. O how happy is it, to have all our thoughts swallowed up in that world; to feel one's self a serious considerate stranger in this world, diligently seeking a road through it, the best, the sure road to the heavenly Jerusalem!

Thursday, September 1. Rode to Danbury. Was more dull and dejected in spirit, than yesterday. Indeed, I always feel comfortably, when God realizes death, and the things of another world, to my mind: whenever my mind is taken off from the things of this world, and set on God, my soul is then at *rest*.

[He went forward on his journey, and came to New-York on

on the next Monday. And after tarrying there two or three days, set out from the city towards New-Haven, intending to be there at the commencement; and on Friday came to Horse-Neck. In the mean time, he complains much of dulness, and want of fervour in religion: but yet from time to time, speaks of his enjoying spiritual warmth and sweetness in conversation with Christian friends, assistance in public services, *&c.*]

Saturday, September 10. Rode six miles to Stanwich, and preached to a considerable assembly of people. Had some assistance and freedom, especially towards the close. Endeavoured much afterwards, in private conversation, to establish holiness, humility, meekness, *&c.* as the essence of true religion; and to moderate some noisy sort of persons, that appeared to me to be acted by unseen spiritual pride. Alas, what extremes men incline to run into!—Returned to Horse-Neck, and felt some seriousness and sweet solemnity in the evening.

Lord's day, September 11. In the afternoon, preached from Tit. iii. 8. I think, God never helped me more in painting out true religion, and in detecting clearly, and tenderly discountenancing false appearances of religion, wild-fire party-zeal, spiritual pride, *&c.* as well as a confident dogmatical spirit, and its spring, *viz.* ignorance of the heart.——In the evening, took much pains in private conversation to suppress some confusions, that I perceived were amongst that people.

Monday, September 12. Rode to Mr Mills's at Ripton. Had some perplexing hours; but was some part of the day very comfortable. It is "through great trials," I see, "that "we must enter the gates of paradise." If my soul could but be holy, that God might not be dishonoured, methinks I could bear sorrows.

Tuesday, September 13. Rode to New-Haven. Was sometimes dejected; not in the sweetest frame. Lodged at ****. Had some profitable Christian conversation, *&c.*——I find, though my inward trials are great, and a life of solitude gives them greater advantage to settle, and penetrate to the very inmost recesses of the soul; yet it is better to be alone, than incumbered with noise and tumult. I find it very difficult maintaining any sense of divine things, while removing from place to place, diverted with new objects, and filled with care and business. A settled steady business is best adapted to a life of strict religion.

Wednesday,

Wednesday, September 14. This day I ought to have taken my *degree* *; but God sees fit to deny it me. And though I was greatly afraid of being overwhelmed with perplexity and confusion, when I should see my *class-mates* take theirs; yet, in the very season of it, God enabled me with calmness and resignation to say, "The will of the Lord be "done." Indeed, through divine goodness, I have scarcely felt my mind so calm, sedate, and comfortable for some time. I have long feared this season, and expected my humility, meekness, patience, and resignation would be much tried †: but found much more pleasure and divine comfort, than I expected.—Felt spiritually serious, tender and affectionate in private prayer with a dear Christian friend to-day.

Thursday, September 15. Had some satisfaction in hearing the ministers discourse, *&c.* It is always a comfort to me, to hear religious and spiritual discourse. O that ministers and people were more spiritual and devoted to God!—Towards night, with the advice of Christian friends, I offered the following reflections in writing, to the rector and trustees of the college, (which are for substance the same that I had freely offered to the rector before, and intreated him to accept); and this I did, that if possible I might cut off all occasion of stumbling and offence, from those that seek occasion. What I offered, is as follows.

"Whereas I have said before several persons, concerning "Mr Whittelsey, one of the tutors of Yale-college, that I "did not believe he had any more grace than the chair I "then leaned upon; I humbly confess, that herein I have "sinned against God, and acted contrary to the rules of his "word, and have injured Mr Whittelsey. I had no right to "make thus free with his character; and had no just reason "to say as I did concerning him. My fault herein was the "more aggravated, in that I said this concerning one that "was so much my superior, and one that I was obliged "to treat with special respect and honour, by reason "of the relation I stood in to him in the college. Such

* This being *commencement*-day.

† His trial was the greater, in that, had it not been for the displeasure of the governors of the college, he would not only on that day have shared with his class-mates in the public honours which they then received, but would on that occasion have appeared at the head of that class; which, if he had been with them, would have been the most numerous of any that ever had been graduated at that college.

"a manner of behaviour, I confess, did not become a "Christian; it was taking too much upon me, and did "not savour of that humble respect, that I ought to have ex-"pressed towards Mr Whittelsey. I have long since been "convinced of the falseness of those apprehensions, by which "I then justified such a conduct. I have often reflected on "this act with grief; I hope, on account of the sin of it: "and am willing to lie low, and be abased before God and "man for it. And humbly ask the forgiveness of the gover-"nors of the college, and of the whole society; but of Mr "Whittelsey in particular. And whereas I have been accused "by one person of saying concerning the reverend rector, "of Yale-college, that I wondered he did not expect to drop "down dead for fining the scholars that followed Mr Ten-"nent to Milford; I seriously profess, that I do not remem-"ber my saying any thing to this purpose. But if I did, "which I am not certain I did not, I utterly condemn it, and "detest all such kind of behaviour; and especially in an un-"dergraduate towards the rector. And I now appear, to "judge and condemn myself for going once to the separate "meeting in New-Haven, a little before I was expelled, "though the rector had refused to give me leave. For this "I humbly ask the rector's forgiveness. And whether the "governors of the college shall ever see cause to remove "the academical censure I lie under, or no, or to admit me "to the privileges I desire; yet I am willing to appear, if "they think fit, openly to own, and to humble myself for "those things I have herein confessed."

God has made me willing to do any thing, that I can do, consistent with truth, for the sake of peace, and that I might not be a stumbling-block and offence to others. For this reason I can cheerfully forego, and give up what I verily believe, after the most mature and impartial search, is my right, in some instances. God has given me that disposition, that if this were the case, that a man has done me an hundred injuries, and I (though ever so much provoked to it) have done him one, I feel disposed, and heartily willing humbly to confess my fault to him, and on my knees to ask forgiveness of him; though at the same time he should justify himself in all the injuries he has done me, and should only make use of my humble confession to blacken my character the more, and represent me as the only person guilty, *&c.*; yea, though he should as it were insult me, and say, "he knew all this be-"fore, and that I was making work for repentance," *&c.* Though what I said concerning Mr Whittelsey was only spoken

ſpoken in private, to a friend or two; and being partly overheard, was related to the rector, and by him extorted from my friends; yet, ſeeing it was divulged and made public, I was willing to confeſs my fault therein publickly.—But I truſt, God will plead my cauſe *.

[The next day he went to Derby; then to Southbury, where he ſpent the Sabbath: and ſpeaks of ſome ſpiritual comfort; but complains much of unfixedneſs, and wanderings of mind in religion.]

Monday, September 19. In the afternoon, rode to Bethlehem, and there preached. Had ſome meaſure of aſſiſtance, both in prayer and preaching. I felt ſerious, kind and tender towards all mankind, and longed that holineſs might flouriſh more on earth.

Tueſday, September 20. Had thoughts of going forward on my journey to my Indians; but towards night was taken with a hard pain in my teeth, and ſhivering cold, and could not poſſibly recover a comfortable degree of warmth the

* I was witneſs to the very Chriſtian ſpirit Mr Brainerd ſhewed at that time, being then at New-Haven, and being one that he ſaw fit to conſult on that occaſion. (This was the firſt time that ever I had opportunity of perſonal acquaintance with him.) There truly appeared in him a great degree of calmneſs and humility; without the leaſt appearance of riſing of ſpirit for any ill treatment he ſuppoſed he had ſuffered, or the leaſt backwardneſs to abaſe himſelf before them who he thought had wronged him. What he did was without any objection or appearance of reluctance, even in private to his friends, that he freely opened himſelf to. Earneſt application was made on his behalf to the authority of the college, that he might have his degree then given him; and particularly by the Reverend Mr Burr of Newark, one of the correſpondents of the honourable ſociety in Scotland; he being ſent from New-Jerſey to New-Haven, by the reſt of the commiſſioners, for that end; and many arguments were uſed, but without ſucceſs. Indeed the governors of the college were ſo far ſatisfied with the reflections Mr Brainerd had made on himſelf, that they appeared willing to admit him again into college; but not to give him his degree, till he ſhould have remained there, at leaſt a twelve-month, which being contrary to what the correſpondents, to whom he was now engaged, had declared to be their mind, he did not conſent to it. He deſired his degree, as he thought it would tend to his being more extenſively uſeful; but ſtill when he was denied it, he manifeſted no diſappointment or reſentment.

whole night following. I continued very full of pain all night; and in the morning had a very hard fever, and pains almost all over my whole body. I had a sense of the divine goodness in appointing this to be the place of my sickness, *viz.* among my friends that were very kind to me. I should probably have perished, if I had first got home to my own house in the wilderness, where I have none to converse with but the poor rude ignorant Indians. Here I saw was mercy in the midst of affliction. I continued thus, mostly confined to my bed, till Friday night; very full of pain most of the time; but through divine goodness not afraid of death. Then the extreme folly of those appeared to me, who put off their turning to God till a sick-bed. Surely this is not a time proper to prepare for eternity.——On Friday evening my pains went off something suddenly; and I was exceeding weak, and almost fainted; but was very comfortable the night following. These words Psal. cxviii. 17. I frequently revolved in my mind; and thought we were to prize the continuation of life only on this account, that we may "shew forth God's "goodness and works of grace."

[From this time, he gradually recovered; and on the next Tuesday was so well as to be able to go forward on his journey homewards; but was till the Tuesday following before he reached Kaunaumeek. And seems, great part of this time, to have had a very deep and lively sense of the vanity and emptiness of all things here below, and of the reality, nearness, and vast importance of eternal things.]

Tuesday, October 4. This day rode home to my own house and people. The poor Indians appeared very glad of my return. Found my house and all things in safety. I presently fell on my knees, and blessed God for my safe return, after a long and tedious journey, and a season of sickness in several places where I had been, and after I had been sick myself. God has renewed his kindness to me, in preserving me one journey more. I have taken many considerable journeys since this time last year, and yet God has never suffered one of my bones to be broken, or any distressing calamity to befal me, excepting the ill turn I had in my last journey; though I have been often exposed to cold and hunger in the wilderness, where the comforts of life were not to be had; have frequently been lost in the woods; and sometimes obliged to ride much of the night; and once lay out in the woods all night. Blessed be God that has preserved me!

[In his diary for the next eleven days, are great complaints of distance from God, spiritual pride, corruption, and exceeding vileness. He once says, his heart was so pressed with a sense of his pollution, that he could scarcely have the face and impudence (as it then appeared to him) to desire that God should not damn him for ever. And at another time, he says, he had so little sense of God, or apprehension and relish of his glory and excellency, that it made him more disposed to kindness and tenderness towards those who are blind and ignorant of God and things divine and heavenly.]

Lord's day, October 16. In the evening, God was pleased to give me a feeling sense of my own unworthiness; but through divine goodness such as tended to draw, rather than drive me from God: it filled me with solemnity. I retired alone, (having at this time a friend with me), and poured out my soul to God with much freedom; and yet in anguish, to find myself so unspeakably sinful and unworthy before a holy God. Was now much resigned under God's dispensations towards me, though my trials had been very great. But thought whether I could be resigned, if God should let the French Indians come upon me, and deprive me of my life, or carry me away captive, (though I knew of no special reason then to propose this trial to myself, more than any other); and my soul seemed so far to rest and acquiesce in God, that the sting and terror of these things seemed in a great measure gone. Presently after I came to the Indians, whom I was teaching to sing psalm-tunes that evening, I received the following letter from Stockbrigde, by a messenger sent on the Sabbath on purpose, which made it appear of greater importance.

"Sir, Just now we received advices from Col. Stoddard, "that there is the utmost danger of a rupture with France. "He has received the same from his excellency our gover-"nor, ordering him to give notice to all the exposed places, "that they may secure themselves the best they can against "any sudden invasion. We thought best to send directly to "Kaunaumeek, that you may take the prudentest measures "for your safety that dwell there. I am, Sir, &c."

I thought, upon reading the contents, it came in a good season; for my heart seemed something fixed on God, and therefore I was not much surprised: but this news only made me more serious, and taught me that I must not please myself with any of the comforts of life which I had been preparing for my support. Blessed be God, that gave me any intenseness and fervency this evening!

Monday,

Monday, October 17. Had some rising hopes sometimes, that "God would arise and have mercy on Zion speedily." My heart is indeed refreshed, when I have any prevailing hopes of Zion's prosperity. O that I may see the glorious day, when Zion shall become the joy of the whole earth! Truly there is nothing that I greatly value in this lower world.

[On Tuesday, he rode to Stockbridge; complains of being much diverted, and having but little life. On Wednesday, he expresses some solemn sense of divine things, and a longing to be always doing for God with a godly frame of spirit.]

Thursday, October 20. Had but little sense of divine things this day. Alas, that so much of my precious time is spent with so little of God! Those are tedious days, wherein I have no spirituality.

Friday, October 21. Returned home to Kaunaumeek: was glad to get alone in my little cottage, and to cry to that God who seeth in secret, and is present in a wilderness.

Saturday, October 22. Had but little sensible communion with God. This world is a dark cloudy mansion. Oh, when will the Sun of righteousness shine on my soul without cessation or intermission!

Lord's day, October 23. In the morning, had a little dawn of comfort arising from hopes of seeing glorious days in the church of God: was enabled to pray for such a glorious day with some courage and strength of hope. In the forenoon, treated on the glories of heaven, &c.——In the afternoon, on the miseries of hell, and the danger of going there. Had some freedom and warmth, both parts of the day. And my people were very attentive. In the evening, two or three came to me under concern for their souls; to whom I was enabled to discourse closely, and with some earnestness and desire. O that God would be merciful to their poor souls!

[He seems, through the whole of this week, to have been greatly engaged to fill up every inch of time in the service of God, and to have been most diligently employed in study, prayer, and instructing the Indians; and from time to time expresses longings of soul after God, and the advancement of his kingdom, and spiritual comfort and refreshment.]

Lord's day, October 30. In the morning, enjoyed some

fixedness

fixedness of soul in prayer, which was indeed sweet and desirable; was enabled to leave myself with God, and to acquiesce in him. At noon, my soul was refreshed with reading Rev. iii. more especially the 11th and 12th verses. O my soul longed for that blessed day, when I should "dwell in "the temple of God," and "go no more out" of his immediate presence!

Monday, October 31. Rode to Kinderhook, about fifteen miles from my place. While riding, I felt some divine sweetness in the thoughts of being "a pillar in the temple of God" in the upper world, and being no more deprived of his blessed presence, and the sense of *his favour*, which is "better than "life." My soul was so lifted up to God, that I could pour out my desires to him, for more grace and further degrees of sanctification, with abundant freedom. Oh, I longed to be more abundantly prepared for that blessedness, with which I was then in some measure refreshed!——Returned home in the evening; but took an extremely bad cold by riding in the night.

Tuesday, November 1. Was very much disordered in body, and sometimes full of pain in my face and teeth; was not able to study much, and had not much spiritual comfort. Alas! when God is withdrawn, all is gone.—Had some sweet thoughts, which I could not but write down, on the *design*, *nature*, and *end* of *Christianity*.

Wednesday, November 2. Was still more indisposed in body, and in much pain, most of the day: had not much comfort; was scarcely able to study at all; and still entirely alone in the wilderness. But, blessed be the Lord, I be not exposed in the open air, I have a house, and many of the comforts of life, to support me. I have learned, in a measure, that all good things, relating both to time and eternity, come from God.——In the evening, had some degree of quickening in prayer: I think, God gave me some sense of his presence.

Thursday, November 3. Spent this day in secret fasting and prayer, from morning till night. Early in the morning, had (I think) some small degree of assistance in prayer. Afterwards, read the story of Elijah the prophet, 1 Kings xvii. xviii. and xix chapters, and also 2 Kings ii. and iv chapters. My soul was much moved, observing the faith, zeal, and power of that holy man; how he wrestled with God in prayer, &c. My soul then cried with Elisha, "Where is the Lord God of "Elijah?" Oh, I longed for more faith! My soul breathed after God, and pleaded with him, that a "double portion of "that

"that spirit," which was given to Elijah, might "rest on me." And that which was divinely refreshing and strengthening to my soul, was, I saw that God is the *same* that he was in the days of Elijah.——Was enabled to wrestle with God by prayer, in a more affectionate, fervent, humble, intense, and importunate manner, than I have for many months past. Nothing seemed too hard for God to perform; nothing too great for me to hope for from him.——I had for many months entirely lost all hopes of being made instrumental of doing any special service for God in the world; it has appeared entirely impossible, that one so black and vile should be thus improved for God. But at this time God was pleased to revive this hope.——Afterwards read the iiid chapter of Exodus and on to the xxth, and saw more of the *glory* and *majesty* of *God* discovered in those chapters, than ever I had seen before; frequently in the mean time falling on my knees, and crying to God for the faith of Moses, and for a manifestation of the *divine glory*. Especially the iiid and ivth, and part of the xivth and xvth chapters, were unspeakably sweet to my soul: my soul blessed God, that he had shewn himself so *gracious* to his servants of old. The xvth chapter seemed to be the very language which my soul uttered to God in the season of my first spiritual comfort, when I had just got through the *Red sea*, by a *way* that I had no expectation of. O how my soul then *rejoiced in God!* And now those things came fresh and lively to my mind; now my soul blessed God afresh, that he had opened that unthought-of *way* to deliver me from the fear of the Egyptians, when I almost despaired of life.——Afterwards read the story of Abraham's pilgrimage in the land of Canaan: my soul was melted, in observing his *faith*, how he leaned on God; how he *communed* with God, and what a *stranger* he was here in the world. After that, read the story of Joseph's sufferings, and God's goodness to him: blessed God for these examples of faith and patience. My soul was ardent in prayer, was enabled to wrestle ardently for myself, for Christian friends, and for the church of God. And felt more desire to see the power of God in the conversion of souls, than I have done for a long season. Blessed be God for this season of fasting and prayer! May his goodness always abide with me, and draw my soul to him!

Thursday, November 4. Rode to Kinderhook; went quite to Hudson's River, about twenty miles from my house; performed some business; and returned home in the evening to my own house. I had rather ride hard, and fatigue myself, to get home, than to spend the evening and night amongst those that have no regard for God.

[The two next days, he was very ill, and full of pain, probably through his riding in the night, after a fatiguing day's journey on Thursday: but yet seems to have been diligent in business.]

Monday, November 7. This morning the Lord afforded me some special assistance in prayer; my mind was solemn, fixed, affectionate, and ardent in desires after holiness; and felt full of tenderness and love; and my affections seemed to be dissolved into kindness and softness.——In the evening, enjoyed the same comfortable assistance in prayer, as in the morning: my soul longed after God, and cried to him with a filial freedom, reverence, and boldness. O that I might be entirely consecrated and devoted to God!

[The two next days, he complains of bodily illness and pain; but much more of spiritual barrenness and unprofitableness.]

Thursday, November 10. Spent this day in fasting and prayer alone. In the morning, was very dull and lifeless; was something melancholy and discouraged. But after some time, reading 2 Kings xix chapter, my soul was moved and affected; especially reading vers. 14. and onward. I saw there was no other way for the afflicted children of God to take, but to go to God with all their sorrows. Hezekiah, in his great distress, went and spread his complaint before the Lord. I was then enabled to see the mighty power of God, and my extreme need of that power: was enabled to cry to God affectionately and ardently for his divine power and grace to be exercised towards me.——Afterwards, read the story of David's trials, and observed the course he took under them, how he strengthened his hands in God; whereby my soul was carried out after God, enabled to cry to him, and rely upon him, and felt *strong in the Lord.* Was afterwards refreshed, observing the blessed temper that was wrought in David by his trials: all bitterness, and desire of revenge, seemed wholly taken away; so that he mourned for the death of his enemies; 2 Sam. i. 17. and iv. 9. *ad fin.*——Was enabled to bless God, that he had given me something of this divine temper, that my soul freely *forgives*, and heartily *loves my enemies.*

[It appears by his diary for the remaining part of this week, and for the two following weeks, that great part of the time he was very ill, and full of pain; and yet obliged, through his circumstances, in this ill state of body, to be at great fatigues, in labour, and travelling day and night, and to expose himself in stormy and severe seasons. He from time to time, within this space, speaks of outgoings of soul after God; his heart strengthened in God; seasons of divine sweetness and comfort; his heart affected with gratitude for mercies, &c. And yet there are many complaints of lifelessness, weakness of grace, distance from God, and great unprofitableness. But still there appears a constant care, from day to day, not to lose time, but to improve it all for God.]

Lord's day, November 27. In the evening, was greatly affected in reading an account of the very joyful death of a pious gentleman; which seemed to invigorate my soul in God's ways: I felt courageously engaged to pursue a life of holiness and self-denial as long as I live; and poured out my soul to God for his help and assistance in order thereto. Eternity then seemed near, and my soul rejoiced, and longed to meet it. O, I trust, that will be a blessed day, that finishes my toil here!

Monday, November 28. In the evening, was obliged to spend time in company and conversation that was unprofitable.——Nothing lies heavier upon me, than the misimprovement of time.

Tuesday, November 29. Began to study the Indian tongue, with Mr Sergeant at Stockbridge *.——Was perplexed for want of more retirement.——I love to live alone in my own little *cottage*, where I can spend much time in prayer, &c.

Wednesday, November 30. Pursued my study of Indian: but was very weak and disordered in body, and was troubled in mind at the barrenness of the day, that I had done so little for God. I had some enlargement in prayer at night. Oh, a barn, or stable, hedge, or any other place, is truly desirable, if God is there! Sometimes, of late, my hopes of Zion's pro-

* The commissioners that employed him, had directed him to spend much time this winter with Mr Sergeant, to learn the language of the Indians; which necessitated him very often to ride, backwards and forwards, twenty miles through the uninhabited woods between Stockbridge and Kaunaumeek; which many times exposed him to extreme hardship in the severe seasons of the winter.

sperity

sperity are more-raised, than they were in the Summer past. My soul seems to confide, in God, that he will yet "shew "forth his salvation" to his people, and make Zion "the "joy of the whole earth. O how excellent is the loving-"kindness of the Lord!" My soul sometimes inwardly exults at the lively thoughts of what God has already done for his church, and what "mine eyes have seen of the salvation "of God." It is sweet, to hear nothing but spiritual discourse from God's children; and sinners "enquiring the way "to Zion," saying, "What shall we do?" &c. O that I may see more of this blessed work!

Thursday, December 1. Both morning and evening, I enjoyed some intenseness of soul in prayer, and longed for the enlargement of Christ's kingdom in the world. My soul seems, of late, to *wait on God* for his blessing on Zion. O that religion might powerfully revive!

Friday, December 2. Enjoyed not so much health of body, or fervour of mind, as yesterday. If the chariot-wheels move with ease and speed at any time, for a short space; yet by and by they drive heavily again. "O that I had the wings "of a dove, that I might fly away" from sin and corruption, and be *at rest in God!*

Saturday, December 3. Rode home to my house and people. Suffered much with the extreme cold.——I trust, I shall ere long arrive safe to my journey's end, where my toils shall cease.

Lord's day, December 4. Had but little sense of divine and heavenly things. My soul mourns over my barrenness. Oh how sad is spiritual deadness!

Monday, December 5. Rode to Stockbridge. Was almost outdone with the extreme cold. Had some refreshing meditations by the way; but was barren, wandering, and lifeless, much of the day. Thus my days roll away, with but little done for God; and this is my burden.

Tuesday, December 6. Was perplexed to see the vanity and levity of professed Christians. Spent the evening with a Christian friend, that was able in some measure to sympathize with me in my spiritual conflicts. Was a little refreshed to find one with whom I could converse of *inward trials*, &c.

Wednesday, December 7. Spent the evening in perplexity, with a kind of guilty indolence. When I have no heart or resolution for God, and the duties incumbent on me, I feel guilty of negligence and misimprovement of time. Certainly I ought to be engaged in my work and business, to the utmost extent of my strength and ability.

Thurfday, December 8. My mind was much diftracted with different affections. Seemed to be at an amazing diftance from God: and looking round in the world, to fee if there was not fome happinefs to be derived from it, God, and fome certain objects in the world, feemed each to invite my heart and affections; and my foul feemed to be diftracted between them. I have not been fo much befet with the world for a long time; and that with relation to fome particular objects which I thought myfelf moft dead to. But even while I was defiring to pleafe myfelf with any thing below, guilt, forrow, and perplexity, attended the firft motions of defire. Indeed I cannot fee the appearance of pleafure and happinefs in the world, as I ufed to do: and bleffed be God for any habitual deadnefs to the world.——I found no peace, or deliverance from this diftraction and perplexity of mind, till I found accefs to the throne of grace: and as foon as I had any fenfe of God, and things divine, the allurements of the world vanifhed, and my heart was determined for God. But my foul mourned over my folly, that I fhould defire any pleafure, but only in God. God forgive my fpiritual idolatry!

[The next thirteen days, he appears to have been continually in deep concern about the improvement of precious time; and there are many expreffions of grief, that he improved time no better; fuch as, "Oh, what mifery do I feel, when "my thoughts rove after vanity! I fhould be happy if always "engaged for God! O wretched man that I am!" &c. Speaks of his being pained with a fenfe of his barrennefs, perplexed with his wanderings, longing for deliverance from the being of fin, mourning that time paffed away, and fo little was done for God, &c.——On Tuefday, December 20. he fpeaks of his being vifited at Kaunaumeek by fome under fpiritual concern.]

Thurfday, December 22. Spent this day alone in fafting and prayer, and reading in God's word the exercifes and deliverances of God's children. Had, I truft, fome exercife of faith, and realizing apprehenfion of divine power, grace, and holinefs; and alfo of the unchangeablenefs of God, that he is the fame as he was when he delivered his faints of old out of great tribulation. My foul was fundry times in prayer enlarged for God's church and people. O that Zion might become the "joy of the whole earth!" It is better to wait upon God with patience, than to put confidence in any thing in this

this lower world. "My soul, wait thou on the Lord; for "from him comes thy salvation."

Friday, December 23. Felt a little more courage and resolution in religion, than at some other times.

Saturday, December 24. Had some assistance, and longing desires after sanctification, in prayer this day; especially in the evening: was sensible of my own weakness and spiritual impotency: saw plainly, I should fall into sin, if God of his abundant mercy did not "uphold my soul, and with-hold me "from evil." O that God would "uphold me by his free "Spirit, and save me from the hour of temptation!"

Lord's day, December 25. Prayed much, in the morning, with a feeling sense of my own spiritual weakness and insufficiency for any duty. God gave me some assistance in preaching to the Indians; and especially in the afternoon, when I was enabled to speak with uncommon plainness, freedom, and earnestness. Blessed be God for any assistance granted to one so unworthy. Afterwards felt some thankfulness; but still sensible of barrenness.——Spent some time in the evening, with one or two persons under spiritual concern, and exhorting others to their duty, &c.

Monday, December 26. Rode down to Stockbridge. Was very much fatigued with my journey, wherein I underwent great hardship: was much exposed and very wet by falling into a river. Spent the day and evening without much sense of divine and heavenly things; but felt guilty, grieved, and perplexed with wandering, careless thoughts.

Tuesday, December 27. Had a small degree of warmth in secret prayer, in the evening; but, alas! had but little spiritual life, and consequently but little comfort. Oh, the pressure of a *body of death* *!

Wednesday, December 28. Rode about six miles to the ordination of Mr Hopkins. In the season of the solemnity was somewhat affected with a sense of the greatness and importance of the work of a minister of Christ. Afterwards was grieved to see the vanity of the multitude. In the evening, spent a little time with some Christian friends, with some degree of satisfaction; but most of the time, had rather have been alone.

Thursday, December 29. Spent the day mainly in conversing with friends; yet enjoyed little satisfaction, because I could find but few disposed to converse of divine and heaven-

* This day he wrote the *second letter* added at the end of this history.

ly things. Alas, what are things of this world, to afford satisfaction to the soul!—Near night, returned to Stockbridge; in secret blessed God for retirement, and that I be not always exposed to the company and conversation of the world. O that I could live "in the secret of God's presence!"

Friday, December. 30. Was in a solemn devout frame in the evening. Wondered that earth, with all its charms, should ever allure me in the least degree. O that I could always realize the being and holiness of God!

Saturday, December 31. Rode from Stockbridge home to my house: the air was clear and calm, but as cold as ever I felt it in the world, or near. I was in great danger of perishing by the extremity of the season.——Was enabled to meditate much on the road.

Lord's day, January 1. 1743-4. In the morning, had some small degree of assistance in prayer. Saw myself so vile and unworthy, that I could not look my people in the face, when I came to preach. Oh, my meanness, folly, ignorance, and inward pollution!——In the evening, had a little assistance in prayer, so that the duty was delightsome, rather than burdensome. Reflected on the goodness of God to me in the past year, *&c.* Of a truth God has been kind and gracious to me, though he has caused me to pass through many sorrows; he has provided for me bountifully, so that I have been enabled, in about fifteen months past, to bestow to charitable uses about an *hundred pounds* New-England money, that I can now remember*. Blessed be the Lord, that has so far used me as *his steward*, to distribute a *portion of his goods*. May I always remember, that all I have comes from God. Blessed be the Lord, that has carried me through all the toils, fatigues, and hardships of the year past, as well as the spiritual sorrows and conflicts that have attended it. O that I could begin this year *with God*, and spend the whole of it to *his glory*, either in life or death!

Monday, January 2. Had some affecting sense of my own impotency and spiritual weakness.—It is nothing but the power of God that keeps me from all manner of wickedness. I see, *I am nothing*, and can do nothing without help from

* Which was, I suppose, to the value of about *one hundred and eighty-five pounds* in our bills of the old tenor, as they now pass.—By this, as well as many other things, it is manifest, that his frequent melancholy did not arise from the consideration of any disadvantage he was laid under to get a living in the world, by his expulsion from the college.

above.

above. Oh, for divine grace! In the evening, had some ardour of soul in prayer, and longing desires to have God for my guide and safeguard at all times *.

Tuesday, January 3. Was employed much of the day in writing; and spent some time in other necessary employment. But my time passes away so swiftly, that I am astonished when I reflect on it, and see how little I do in it. My state of solitude does not make the hours hang heavy upon my hands. O what reason of thankfulness have I on account of this retirement! I find, that I do not, and it seems I cannot, lead a *Christian* life, when I am abroad, and cannot spend time in devotion, Christian conversation, and serious meditation, as I should do. Those weeks that I am obliged now to be from home, in order to learn the Indian tongue, are mostly spent in perplexity and barrenness, without much sweet relish of divine things; and I feel myself a stranger at the throne of grace, for want of more frequent and continued retirement. When I return home, and give myself to meditation, prayer, and fasting, a new scene opens to my mind, and my soul longs for mortification, self-denial, humility, and divorcement from all the things of the world. This evening, my heart was somewhat warm and fervent in prayer and meditation, so that I was loth to indulge sleep. Continued in those duties till about midnight.

Wednesday, January 4. Was in a resigned and mortified temper of mind, much of the day. Time appeared a *moment*; life a *vapour*, and all its enjoyments as *empty bubbles*, and fleeting blasts of wind.

Thursday, January 5. Had a humbling and pressing sense of my unworthiness. My sense of the badness of my own heart filled my soul with bitterness and anguish; which was ready to sink, as under the weight of a heavy burden. And thus spent the evening, till late.—Was somewhat intense and ardent in prayer.

Friday, January 6. Feeling and considering my extreme weakness, and want of grace, the pollution of my soul, and danger of temptations on every side, I set apart this day for fasting and prayer, neither eating nor drinking from evening to evening, beseeching God to have mercy on me. And my soul intensely longed, that the dreadful spots and stains of sin might be washed away from it. Saw something of the power and allsufficiency of God. My soul seemed to rest on his

* This day he wrote the *third letter*, published at the end of this account of his life.

power

power and grace; longed for resignation to his will, and mortification to all things here below. My mind was greatly fixed on divine things: my resolutions for a life of mortification, continual watchfulness, self-denial, seriousness, and devotion to God, were strong and fixed; my desires ardent and intense; my conscience tender, and afraid of every appearance of evil. My soul grieved with the reflection on past levity, and want of resolution for God. I solemnly renewed my dedication of myself to God, and longed for grace to enable me always to keep covenant with him. Time appeared very short, eternity near; and a great name, either in or after life, together with all earthly pleasures and profits, but an empty bubble, a deluding dream.

Saturday, January 7. Spent this day in seriousness, with stedfast resolutions for God and a life of mortification. Studied closely, till I felt my bodily strength fail. Felt some degree of resignation to God, with an acquiescence in his dispensations. Was grieved, that I could do so little for God before my bodily strength failed.——In the evening, though tired, yet was enabled to continue instant in prayer for some time. Spent the time in reading, meditation, and prayer, till the evening was far spent: was grieved, to think that I could not *watch unto prayer* the whole night.—— But blessed be God, heaven is a place of continual and incessant devotion, though earth is dull.

[The six days following, he continued in the same happy frame of mind; enjoyed the same composure, calmness, resignation, ardent desire, and sweet fervency of spirit, in a high degree, every day, not one excepted. Thursday, this week, he kept as a day of secret fasting and prayer.]

Saturday, January 14. This morning, enjoyed a most solemn season in prayer: my soul seemed enlarged, and assisted to pour out itself to God for grace, and for every blessing I wanted, for myself, my dear Christian friends, and for the church of God; and was so enabled to *see him who is invisible*, that my soul *rested upon him* for the performance of every thing I asked agreeable to his will. It was then my happiness, to "continue instant in prayer," and was enabled to continue in it for near an hour. My soul was then "strong in "the Lord, and in the power of his might." Longed exceedingly for angelic holiness and purity, and to have all my thoughts, at all times, employed in divine and heavenly things. O how blessed is an heavenly temper! O how unspeakably

ſpeakably bleſſed it is, to feel a meaſure of that rectitude, in which we were at firſt created!—Felt the ſame divine aſſiſtance in prayer ſundry times in the day. My ſoul confided in God for myſelf, and for his Zion; truſted in divine power and grace, that he would do glorious things in his church on earth, for his own glory.

[The next day he ſpeaks of ſome glimpſes he had of the divine glories, and of his being enabled to maintain his reſolutions in ſome meaſure; but complains, that he could not draw near to God: ſeems to be filled with trembling fears leſt he ſhould return to a life of vanity, to pleaſe himſelf with ſome of the enjoyments of this lower world; and ſpeaks of his being much troubled, and feeling guilty, that he ſhould addreſs immortal ſouls with no more ardency and deſire of their ſalvation.—On Monday, he rode down to Stockbridge, was diſtreſſed with the extreme cold: but notwithſtanding, his mind was in a devout and ſolemn frame in his journey. The four next days, he was very ill, probably by his ſuffering from the cold in his journey; yet he ſays he ſpent the time in a more ſolemn manner than he feared. On Friday-evening, he rode down and viſited Mr Hopkins; and on Saturday, rode eighteen miles to Solſbury, where he kept Sabbath, and enjoyed conſiderable degrees of God's gracious preſence, aſſiſtance in duty, and divine comfort and refreſhment, longing to give himſelf wholly to God, to be his for ever.]

Monday, January 23. I think I never felt more reſigned to God, nor ſo much dead to the world, in every reſpect, as now; was dead to all deſire of reputation and greatneſs, either in life, or after death; all I longed for, was to be holy, humble, crucified to the world, *&c.*

Tueſday, January 24. Near noon, rode over to Canaan. In the evening, was unexpectedly viſited by a conſiderable number of people, with whom I was enabled to converſe profitably of divine things: took pains to deſcribe the difference between a regular and irregular *ſelf-love*; the one conſiſting with a ſupreme love to God, but the other not; the former uniting God's glory, and the ſoul's happineſs, that they become one common intereſt, but the latter disjoining and ſeparating God's glory and the man's happineſs, ſeeking the latter with a neglect of the former. Illuſtrated this by that genuine love that is found between the ſexes; which is diverſe from that which is wrought up towards a perſon only by rational arguments, or hope of ſelf-intereſt. Love is a pleaſing paſſion, it it affords pleaſure to the mind where it is; but yet true genuine love is not, nor can be placed upon any object with that deſign of pleaſing itſelf with the feeling of it in a man's own breaſt.

[On Wedneſday he rode to Sheffield; the next day, to Stockbridge; and on Saturday, home to Kaunaumeek, though the ſeaſon was cold and ſtormy: which journey was followed with illneſs and pain. It appears by his diary, that he ſpent the time, while riding, in profitable meditations, and in lifting up his heart to God; and he ſpeaks of aſſiſtance, comfort, and refreſhment; but ſtill complains of barrenneſs, *&c.* His diary for the five next days is full of the moſt heavy bitter complaints; and he expreſſes himſelf as full of ſhame and ſelf-loathing for his lifeleſs temper of mind and ſluggiſhneſs of ſpirit, and as being in perplexity and extremity, and appearing to himſelf unſpeakably vile and guilty before God, on account of ſome inward workings of corruption he found in his heart, *&c.*]

Thurſday, February 2. Spent this day in faſting and prayer, ſeeking the preſence and aſſiſtance of God, that he would enable me to overcome all my corruptions and ſpiritual enemies.

Friday, February 3. Enjoyed more freedom and comfort than of late; was intenſely engaged in meditation upon the different whiſpers of the various powers and affections of a pious mind, exerciſed with a great variety of diſpenſations: and could not but write, as well as meditate, on ſo entertaining a ſubject *. I hope, the Lord gave me ſome true ſenſe of divine things this day: but, alas, how great and preſſing are the remains of indwelling corruption! I am now more ſenſible than ever, that God alone is "the author and finiſher of our "faith," *i. e.* that the whole, and every part of ſanctification, and every good word, work, or thought, that is found in me, is the effect of his power and grace; that, "without "him I can do nothing," in the ſtricteſt ſenſe, and that, "he "works in us to will and to do of his own good pleaſure," and from no other motive. Oh, how amazing it is that people can talk ſo much about mens power and goodneſs; when, if God did not hold us back every moment, we ſhould be devils

* I find what he wrote on this head among his papers that were left in my hand, and it is here publiſhed at the end of this account of his life.

incarnate! This my bitter experience, for several days last past, has abundantly taught me concerning myself.

Saturday, February 4. Enjoyed some degree of freedom and spiritual refreshment; was enabled to pray with some fervency, and longing desires of Zion's prosperity, and my faith and hope seems to *take hold of God*, for the performance of what I was enabled to plead for. Sanctification in myself, and the ingathering of God's elect, was all my desire; and the hope of its accomplishment, all my joy.

Lord's day, February 5. Was enabled in some measure to rest and confide in God, and to prize his presence, and some glimpses of the light of his countenance, above my necessary food. Thought myself, after the season of weakness, temptation, and desertion I endured the last week, to be somewhat like Samson, when his locks began to grow again. Was enabled to preach to my people with more life and warmth, than I have for some weeks past.

Monday, February 6. This morning, my soul again was strengthened in God, and found some sweet repose in him in prayer; longing especially for the complete mortification of sensuality and pride, and for resignation to God's dispensations, at all times, as through grace I felt it at this time. I did not desire deliverance from any difficulty that attends my circumstances, unless God was willing. O how comfortable is this temper!—Spent most of the day in reading God's word, in writing, and prayer. Enjoyed repeated and frequent comfort and intenseness of soul in prayer through the day. In the evening, spent some hours in private conversation with my people; and afterwards, felt some warmth in secret prayer.

Tuesday, February 7. Was much engaged in some sweet meditations on the powers and affections of the godly soul in their pursuit of their beloved object: wrote something of the native language of spiritual sensation, in its soft and tender whispers; declaring, that it now "feels and tastes that the "Lord is gracious;" that he is the supreme good, the only soul-satisfying happiness; that he is a complete, sufficient, and almighty portion: saying,

"*Whom have I in heaven but thee? and there is none upon* "*earth that I desire besides* this blessed portion. O, I feel it "is heaven to please him, and to be just what he would have "me to be! O that my soul were *holy, as he is holy!* O that "it were *pure, even as Christ is pure;* and *perfect, as my Fa-* "*ther in heaven is perfect!* These, I feel, are the sweetest "commands in God's book, comprising all others. And shall

"I break them! must I break them! am I under a necessity "of it as long as I live in the world! O my soul, wo, wo "is me that I am a sinner, because I now necessarily grieve "and offend this blessed God, who is infinite in goodness and "grace! Oh, methinks, if he would punish me for my sins, "it would not wound my heart so deep to offend him: but "though I sin continually, yet he continually repeats his "kindness to me! Oh, methinks I could bear any suffering; "but how can I bear to grieve and dishonour this blessed "God! How shall I yield ten thousand times more honour "to him? What shall I do to glorify and worship this best "of beings? O that I could consecrate myself, soul and bo- "dy, to his service for ever! O that I could give up myself "to him, so as never more to attempt to be my own, or to "have any will or affections that are not perfectly conform- "ed to him! But, alas, alas! I find I cannot be thus entire- "ly devoted to God; I cannot live, and not sin. O ye an- "gels, do ye glorify him incessantly; and if possible, pro- "strate yourselves lower before the blessed King of Heaven? "I long to bear a part with you; and, if it were possible, to "help you. Oh, when we have done all that we can, to "all eternity, we shall not be able to offer the ten thou- "sandth part of the homage that the glorious God deserves!"

Felt something spiritual, devout, resigned, and mortified to the world, much of the day; and especially towards and in the evening. Blessed be God, that he enables me to love him for himself.

Wednesday, February 8. Was in a comfortable frame of soul, most of the day; though sensible of, and restless under spiritual barrenness. I find that both mind and body are quickly tired with intenseness and fervour in the things of God. O that I could be as incessant as *angels* in devotion and spiritual fervour!

Thursday, February 9. Observed this day as a day of fasting and prayer, intreating of God to bestow upon me his blessing and grace; especially to enable me to live a life of mortification to the world, as well as of resignation and patience. Enjoyed some realizing sense of divine power and goodness in prayer, several times; and was enabled to roll the burden of myself and friends, and of Zion, upon the goodness and grace of God: but, in the general, was more dry and barren than I have usually been of late upon such occasions.

Friday, February 10. Was exceedingly oppressed, most of the day, with shame, grief, and fear, under a sense of my past folly, as well as present barrenness and coldness. When

God sets before me my past misconduct, especially any instances of *misguided zeal*, it sinks my soul into shame and confusion, makes me afraid of a shaking leaf. My fear is such as the prophet Jeremy complains of, Jer. xx. 10.—— I have no confidence to hold up my face, even before my fellow-worms; but only when my soul confides in God, and I find the sweet temper of Christ, the spirit of humility, solemnity, and mortification, and resignation, alive in my soul. ——But, in the evening, was unexpectedly refreshed in *pouring out my complaint to God*; my shame and fear was turned into a sweet composure and acquiescence in God.

Saturday, February 11. Felt much as yesterday: enjoyed but little sensible communion with God.

Lord's day, February 12. My soul seemed to confide in God, and to repose itself on him; and had outgoings of soul after God in prayer. Enjoyed some divine assistance, in the forenoon, in preaching; but in the afternoon, was more perplexed with shame, &c. Afterwards, found some relief in prayer; loved, as a feeble, afflicted, despised creature, to cast myself on a God of infinite grace and goodness, hoping for no happiness but from him.

Monday, February 13. Was calm and sedate in morning-devotions; and my soul seemed to rely on God.——Rode to Stockbridge, and enjoyed some comfortable meditations by the way; had a more refreshing taste and relish of heavenly blessedness, than I have enjoyed for many months past. I have many times, of late, felt as ardent desires of holiness as ever; but not so much sense of the sweetness and unspeakable pleasure of the enjoyments and employments of heaven. My soul longed to leave earth, and bear a part with angels in their celestial employments. My soul said, "Lord, it is good to "be here;" and it appeared to me better to die, than to lose the relish of these heavenly delights.

[A sense of divine things seemed to continue with him, in a lesser degree, through the next day. On Wednesday he was, by some discourse that he heard, cast into a melancholy gloom, that operated much in the same manner as his melancholy had formerly done, when he came first to Kaunaumeek; the effects of which seemed to continue in some degree the six following days.]

Wednesday, February 22. In the morning, had as clear a sense of the exceeding pollution of my nature, as ever I remember to have had in my life. I then appeared to myself inexpressibly

inexpressibly lothsome and defiled; sins of childhood, of early youth, and such follies as I had not thought of for years together, (as I remember), came now fresh to my view, as if committed but yesterday, and appeared in the most odious colours; they appeared more in number than the hairs of my head; yea, they "went over my head as an heavy burden." ——In the evening, the hand of faith seemed to be strengthened in God; my soul seemed to rest and acquiesce in him; was supported under my burdens, reading the cxxvth psalm; found that it was sweet and comfortable to lean on God.

Thursday, February 23. Was frequent in prayer, and enjoyed some assistance.——"There is a God in heaven," that over-rules all things for the best; and this is the comfort of my soul: "I had fainted, unless I had believed to see the good-"ness of God in the land of the living," notwithstanding present sorrows.——In the evening, enjoyed some freedom in prayer, for myself, friends, and the church of God.

Friday, February 24. Was exceeding restless and perplexed under a sense of the misimprovement of time; mourned to see time pass away; felt in the greatest hurry; seemed to have every thing to do: yet could do nothing, but only grieve and grone under my ignorance, unprofitableness, meanness, the foolishness of my actions and thoughts, the pride and bitterness of my past frames, (at some times, at least), all which at this time appeared to me in lively colours, and filled me with shame. I could not compose my mind to any profitable studies, by reason of this pressure. And the reason, I judge, why I am not allowed to study a great part of my time, is, because I am endeavouring to lay in such a stock of knowlegde, as shall be a self-sufficiency.——I know it to be my indispensable duty to study, and qualify myself in the best manner I can for public service: but this is my misery, I naturally study and prepare, that I may "consume it upon my "lusts" of pride and self-confidence.

[He continued in much the same frame of uneasiness at the misimprovement of time, and pressure of spirit under a sense of vileness, unprofitableness, *&c.* for the six next following days; excepting some intervals of calmness and composure, in resignation to, and confidence in God.]

Friday, March 2. Was most of the day employed in writing on a divine subject. Was frequent in prayer, and enjoyed some small degree of assistance. But in the evening, God was pleased to grant me a divine sweetness in prayer; especially

cially in the duty of interceſſion. I think, I never felt ſo much kindneſs and love to thoſe who I have reaſon to think are my enemies, (though at that time I found ſuch a diſpoſition to think the beſt of all, that I ſcarce knew how to think that any ſuch thing as enmity and hatred lodged in any ſoul; it ſeemed as if all the world muſt needs be friends); and never prayed with more freedom and delight, for myſelf, or deareſt friend, than I did now for my enemies.

Saturday, March 3. In the morning, ſpent (I believe) an hour in prayer, with great intenſeneſs and freedom, and with the moſt ſoft and tender affection towards mankind. I longed that thoſe who I have reaſon to think owe me ill-will, might be eternally happy: it ſeemed refreſhing, to think of meeting them in heaven, how much ſoever they had injured me on earth: had no diſpoſition to inſiſt upon any confeſſion from them, in order to reconciliation, and the exerciſe of love and kindneſs to them. O it is an emblem of heaven itſelf, to love all the world with a love of kindneſs, forgiveneſs, and benevolence; to feel our ſouls ſedate, mild, and meek; to be void of all evil ſurmiſings and ſuſpicions, and ſcarce able to think evil of any man upon any occaſion; to find our hearts ſimple, open, and free, to thoſe that look upon us with a different eye!——Prayer was ſo ſweet an exerciſe to me, that I knew not how to ceaſe, leſt I ſhould loſe the ſpirit of prayer. Felt no diſpoſition to eat or drink, for the ſake of the pleaſure of it, but only to ſupport my nature, and fit me for divine ſervice. Could not be content without a very particular mention of a great number of dear friends at the throne of grace; as alſo the particular circumſtances of many, ſo far as they were known.

Lord's day, November 4. In the morning, enjoyed the ſame intenſeneſs in prayer as yeſterday morning, though not in ſo great a degree: felt the ſame ſpirit of love, univerſal benevolence, forgiveneſs, humility, reſignation, mortification to the world, and compoſure of mind, as then. "My ſoul "reſted in God;" and I found, I wanted no other refuge or friend. While my ſoul thus truſts in God, all things ſeem to be at peace with me, even the ſtones of the earth: but when I cannot apprehend and confide in God, all things appear with a different aſpect.

[Through the four next days, he complains of barrenneſs, want of holy confidence in God, ſtupidity, wanderings of mind, *&c.* and ſpeaks of oppreſſion of mind under a ſenſe of exceeding meanneſs, paſt follies, as well as preſent workings of corruption.——On Friday, he seems to have been restored to a considerable degree of the same excellent frame that he enjoyed the Saturday before.]

Saturday, March 10. In the morning, felt exceeding dead to the world, and all its enjoyments: I thought, I was ready and willing to give up life and all its comforts, as soon as called to it; and yet then had as much comfort of life as almost ever I had. Life itself now appeared but an empty bubble; the riches, honours, and common enjoyments of life appeared extremely tasteless. I longed to be perpetually and entirely *crucified* to all things here below, by the *cross of Christ*. My soul was sweetly resigned to God's disposal of me, in every regard; and I saw, there had nothing happened to me but what was best for me. I confided in God, that he would "never leave me,' though I should "walk through the "valley of the shadow of death." It was then "my meat "and drink to be holy, to live to the Lord, and die to "the Lord." And I thought, that I then enjoyed such a heaven, as far exceeded the most sublime conceptions of an unregenerate soul; and even unspeakably beyond what I myself could conceive of at another time. I did not wonder, that Peter said, "Lord, it is good to be here," when thus refreshed with divine glories. My soul was full of love and tenderness in the duty of intercession; especially felt a most sweet affection to some precious godly ministers, of my acquaintance. Prayed earnestly for dear Christians, and for those I have reason to fear are my enemies; and could not have spoken a word of bitterness, or entertained a bitter thought, against the vilest man living. Had a sense of my own great unworthiness. My soul seemed to breathe forth love and praise to God afresh, when I thought he would let his children love and receive me as one of their brethren and fellow-citizens: and when I thought of their treating me in that manner, I longed to lie at their feet; and could think of no way to express the sincerity and simplicity of my love and esteem of them, as being much better than myself.—Towards night, was very sorrowful; seemed to myself the worst creature living; and could not pray, nor meditate, nor think of holding up my face before the world.—Was a little relieved in prayer, in the evening; but longed to get on my knees, and ask forgiveness of every body that ever had seen any thing amiss in my past conduct, especially in my *religious zeal*.—Was afterwards much perplexed, so that I could not sleep quietly.

Lord's day, March 11. My soul was in some measure *strengthened in God,* in morning-devotion; so that I was released from trembling fear and distress.——Preached to my people from the parable of the *sower,* Matth. xiii. and enjoyed some assistance, both parts of the day: had some freedom, affection, and fervency in addressing my poor people; longed that God should take hold of their hearts, and make them spiritually alive. And indeed I had so much to say to them, that I knew not how to leave off speaking *.

Monday, March 12. In the morning, was in a devout, tender, and loving frame of mind; and was enabled to cry to God, I hope, with a child-like spirit, with importunity, and resignation, and composure of mind. My spirit was full of quietness, and love to mankind; and longed that peace should reign on the earth: was grieved at the very thoughts of a *fiery, angry,* and *intemperate* zeal in religion; mourned over past follies in that regard; and my soul confided in God for strength and grace sufficient for my future work and trials.—Spent the day mainly in hard labour, making preparation for my intended journey.

Tuesday, March 13. Felt my soul going forth after God sometimes; but not with such ardency as I longed for. In the evening, was enabled to continue *instant in prayer,* for some considerable time together; and especially had respect to the journey I designed to enter upon, with the leave of divine providence, on the morrow. Enjoyed some freedom and fervency, intreating that the divine presence might attend me in *every place* where my business might lead me; and had a particular reference to the trials and temptations that I apprehended I might be more eminently exposed to in particular places. Was strengthened and comforted; although I was before very weary. Truly the *joy of the Lord* is *strength* and *life.*

Wednesday, March 14. Enjoyed some intenseness of soul in prayer, repeating my petitions for God's presence in every place where I expected to be in my journey. Besought the Lord that I might not be too much pleased and amused with dear friends and acquaintance, in one place and another.——

* This was the last Sabbath that ever he performed public service at Kaunaumeek, and these the last sermons that ever he preached there. It appears by his diary, that while he continued with these Indians, he took great pains with them, and did it with much discretion; but the particular manner how, has been omitted for brevity's sake.

Near ten set out on my journey, and near night came to Stockbridge.

Thursday, March 15. Rode down to Sheffield. Here I met a messenger from East-Hampton on Long-Island; who by the unanimous vote of that large town, was sent to invite me thither, in order to settle with that people, where I had been before frequently invited. Seemed more at a loss what was my duty, than before; when I heard of the great difficulties of that place, I was much concerned and grieved, and felt some desires to comply with their request; but knew not what to do: endeavoured to commit the case to God.

[The two next days, he went no further than Salisbury, being much hindered by the rain. When he came there, he was much indisposed.—He speaks of comfortable and profitable conversation with Christian friends, on these days.]

Lord's day, March 18. [At Salisbury] was exceeding weak and faint, so that I could scarce walk: but God was pleased to afford me much freedom, clearness, and fervency in preaching: I have not had the like assistance in preaching to sinners for many months past.——Here another messenger met me, and informed me of the vote of another congregation, to give me an invitation to come among them upon probation for settlement*. Was something exercised in mind with a weight and burden of care. O that God would "send forth "faithful labourers into his harvest!"

[After this, he went forward on his journey towards New-York and New-Jersey: in which he proceeded slowly; performing his journey under great degrees of bodily indisposition. However, he preached several times by the way, being urged by friends; in which he had considerable assistance. He speaks of comfort in conversation with Christian friends, from time to time, and of various things in the exercises and frames of his heart, that shew much of a divine influence on his mind in this journey: but yet complains of *the thing that he feared, viz.* a decline of his spiritual life, or vivacity in religion, by means of his constant removal from place to place, and want of retirement; and complains bitterly of his unworthiness, deadness, *&c.*——He came to New-York on Wednesday, March 28. and to Elisabeth-Town on the

* This congregation was that at Millington, near Haddam, They were very earnestly desirous of his coming among them.

Saturday

Saturday following, where it seems he waited till the commissioners came together.]

Thursday, April 5. Was again much exercised with weakness, and with pain in my head. Attended on the commissioners in their meeting *. Resolved to go on still with the Indian affair, if divine providence permitted; although I had before felt some inclination to go to East-Hampton, where I was solicited to go †.

* The Indians at Kaunaumeek being but few in number, and Mr Brainerd having now been labouring among them about a year, and having prevailed upon them to be willing to leave Kaunaumeek, and remove to Stockbridge, to live constantly under Mr Sergeant's ministry; he thought he might now do more service for Christ among the Indians elsewhere: and therefore went this journey to New-Jersey to lay the matter before the commissioners; who met at Elisabeth-Town, on this occasion, and determined that he should forthwith leave Kaunaumeek, and go to the Delaware Indians.

† By the invitations Mr Brainerd had lately received, it appears, that it was not from necessity, or for want of opportunities to settle in the ministry amongst the English, notwithstanding the disgrace he had been laid under at college, that he was determined to forsake all the outward comforts to be enjoyed in the English settlements, to go and spend his life among the brutish *savages*, and endure the difficulties and self-denials of an Indian *mission*. He had, just as he was leaving Kaunaumeek, had an earnest invitation to a settlement at East-Hampton on Long Island, the fairest, pleasantest town on the whole island, and one of its largest and most wealthy parishes. The people there were unanimous in their desires to have him for their pastor, and for a long time continued in an earnest pursuit of what they desired, and were hardly brought to relinquish their endeavours and give up their hopes of obtaining him. Besides the invitation he had to Millington; which was near his native town, and in the midst of his friends. Nor did Mr Brainerd chuse the business of a missionary to the Indians, rather than accept of those invitations, because he was unacquainted with the difficulties and sufferings which attended such a service: for he had had experience of these difficulties in summer and winter; having spent about a twelvemonth in a lonely desert among these savages, where he had gone through extreme hardships, and been the subject of a train of outward and inward sorrows, which were now fresh in his mind. Notwithstanding all these things, he chose still to go on with this business; and that although the place he was now going to, was at a still much greater distance from most of his friends, acquaintance, and native land.

 [After

[After this, he continued two or three days in the Jerseys, very ill; and then returned to New-York; and from thence into New-England; and went to his native town of Haddam; where he arrived on Saturday, April 14.——And he continues still his bitter complaints of want of retirement. While he was in New-York, he says thus, "Oh, it is not the "pleasures of the *world* can comfort me! If *God* deny his "presence, what are the pleasures of the *city* to me? One "hour of sweet retirement where *God is*, is better than the "whole world." And he continues to cry out of his ignorance, meanness, and unworthiness. However, he speaks of some seasons of special assistance, and divine sweetness.——He spent some days among his friends at East-Hampton and Millington.]

Tuesday, April 17. Rode to Millington again; and felt perplexed when I set out; was feeble in body, and weak in faith. I was going to preach a lecture; and feared I should never have assistance enough to get through. But contriving to ride alone, at a distance from the company that was going, I spent the time in lifting up my heart to God: had not gone far before my soul was abundantly strengthened with those words, "If God be for us, who can be against us?" I went on, confiding in God; and fearing nothing so much as self-confidence. In this frame I went to the house of God, and enjoyed some assistance. Afterwards felt the spirit of love and meekness in conversation with some friends. Then rode home to my brother's: and in the evening, singing hymns with friends, my soul seemed to melt: and in prayer afterwards, enjoyed the exercise of *faith*, and was enabled to be *fervent in spirit*: found more of God's presence, than I have done any time in my late wearisome journey. Eternity appeared very near; my nature was very weak, and seemed ready to be dissolved; the sun declining, and the shadows of the evening drawing on apace. O I longed to fill up the remaining moments all for God! Though my body was so feeble, and wearied with preaching, and much private conversation, yet I wanted to sit up all night to do something for God. To God, the giver of these refreshments, be glory for ever and ever. Amen.

Wednesday, April 18. Was very weak, and enjoyed but little spiritual comfort. Was exercised with one cavilling against *original sin*. May the Lord open his eyes to see the fountain of sin in *himself!*

[After this, he visited several ministers in Connecticut; and then

then travelled towards Kaunaumeek, and came to Mr Sergeant's at Stockbridge, Thursday, April 26. He performed this journey in a very weak state of body. The things he speaks of in the mean time, appertaining to the frames and exercises of his mind, are at some times deadness and a being void of spiritual comfort, at other times resting in God, spiritual sweetness in conversation, engagedness in meditation on the road, assistance in preaching, rejoicing to think that so much more of his work was done, and he so much nearer to the eternal world. And he once and again speaks of a sense of great ignorance, spiritual pollution, *&c.*]

Friday and Saturday, April 27. and 28. Spent some time in visiting friends, and discoursing with my people, (who were now moved down from their own place to Mr Sergeant's), and found them very glad to see me returned. Was exercised in my mind with a sense of my own unworthiness.

Lord's day, April 29. Preached for Mr Sergeant, both parts of the day, from Rev. xiv. 4. Enjoyed some freedom in preaching, though not much spirituality. In the evening, my heart was in some measure lifted up in thankfulness to God for any assistance.

Monday, April 30. Rode to Kaunaumeek, but was extremely ill; did not enjoy the comfort I hoped for in my own house.

Tuesday, May 1. Having received new orders to go to a number of Indians on Delaware river in Pensylvania, and my people here being mostly removed to Mr Sergeant's, I this day took all my clothes, books, *&c.* and disposed of them, and set out for Delaware river: but made it my way to return to Mr Sergeant's; which I did this day, just at night. Rode several hours in the rain through the howling wilderness, although I was so disordered in body, that little or nothing but blood came from me.

[He continued at Stockbridge the next day; and on Thursday rode a little way, to Sheffield, under a great degree of illness; but with encouragement and chearfulness of mind under his fatigues. On Friday, he rode to Salisbury, and continued there till after the Sabbath. He speaks of his soul's being, some part of this time, refreshed in conversation with some Christian friends, about their heavenly home and their journey thither. At other times, he speaks of himself as exceedingly perplexed with barrenness and deadness, and has this exclamation, "Oh, that time should pass with so little

" done

"done for God!"——On Monday he rode to Sharon; and speaks of himself as distressed at the consideration of the misimprovement of time.]

Tuesday, May 8. Set out from Sharon in Connecticut, and travelled about forty-five miles to a place called the *Fish-kit* *, and lodged there. Spent much of my time, while riding, in prayer, that God would go with me to Delaware. My heart sometimes was ready to sink with the thoughts of my work, and going alone in the wilderness, I knew not where: but still it was comfortable, to think, that others of God's children had "wandered about in caves and dens of the earth;" and Abraham, when he was called to go forth, "went out, "not knowing whither he went." O that I might follow after God!

[The next day, he went forward on his journey; crossed Hudson's river, and went to Goshen in the Highlands; and so travelled across the woods, from Hudson's river to Delaware, about an hundred miles, through a desolate and hideous country, above New-Jersey; where were very few settlements: in which journey he suffered much fatigue and hardship. He visited some Indians in the way †, and discoursed with them concerning Christianity. Was considerably melancholy and disconsolate, being alone in a strange wilderness. On Saturday, he came to a settlement of Irish and Dutch people, about twelve miles above the Forks of Delaware.]

Lord's day, May 13. Rose early; felt very poorly after my long journey, and after being wet and fatigued. Was very melancholy; have scarce ever seen such a gloomy morning in my life; there appeared to be no *Sabbath*; the children were all at play; I a stranger in the wilderness, and knew not where to go; and all circumstances seemed to conspire to render my affairs dark and discouraging. Was disappointed respecting an *interpreter*, and heard that the Indians were much scattered, *&c.* Oh, I mourned after the presence of God, and seemed like a creature banished from his sight! yet he was pleased to support my sinking soul, amidst all my sorrows; so that I never entertained any thought of quitting my business among

* A place so called in New-York government, near Hudson's river, on the west side of the river.

† See Mr Brainerd's *Narrative*, in a letter to Mr Pemberton, at the end of his ordination-sermon,---page 32, 33.

the poor Indians; but was comforted, to think, that death would ere long set me free from these distresses.——Rode about three or four miles to the Irish people, where I found some that appeared sober and concerned about religion. My heart then began to be a little encouraged: went and preached, first to the Irish, and then to the Indians: and in the evening, was a little comforted; my soul seemed to rest on God, and take courage. O that the Lord would be my support and comforter in an evil world!

Monday, May 14. Was very busy in some necessary studies. Felt myself very loose from all the world; all appeared "vanity and vexation of spirit." Seemed something lonesome and disconsolate, as if I was banished from all mankind, and bereaved of all that is called pleasurable in the world; but appeared to myself so vile and unworthy, it seemed fitter for me to be here than any where.

Tuesday, May 15. Still much engaged in my studies; and enjoyed more health, than I have for some time past: but was something dejected in spirit with a sense of my meanness; seemed as if I could never do any thing at all to any good purpose by reason of ignorance and folly. O that a sense of these things might work more habitual humility in my soul!

[He continued much in the same frame the next day.]

Thursday, May 17. Was this day greatly distressed with a sense of my vileness; appeared to myself too bad to walk on God's earth, or to be treated with kindness by any of his creatures. God was pleased to let me see my inward pollution and corruption, to such a degree, that I almost despaired of being made holy: "Oh! wretched man that I am! who "shall deliver me from the body of this death?" In the afternoon, met with the Indians, according to appointment, and preached to them. And while riding to them, my soul seemed to confide in God; and afterwards had some relief and enlargement of soul in prayer, and some assistance in the duty of intercession: vital piety and holiness appeared sweet to me, and I longed for the perfection of it.

Friday, May 18. Felt again something of the sweet spirit of religion; and my soul seemed to confide in God, that he would never leave me.—But oftentimes saw myself so mean a creature, that I knew not how to think of preaching. O that I could always live *to*, and *upon* God!

Saturday, May 19. Was, some part of the time, greatly oppressed with the weight and burden of my work; it seemed

impossible

impossible for me ever to go through with the business I had undertaken.——Towards night, was very calm and comfortable; and I think, my soul trusted in God for help.

Lord's day, May 20. Preached twice to the poor Indians, and enjoyed some freedom in speaking, while I attempted to remove their prejudices against Christianity. My soul longed for assistance from above, all the while; for I saw I had no strength sufficient for that work. Afterwards, preached to the Irish people; was much assisted in the first prayer, and something in sermon. Several persons seemed much concerned for their souls, with whom I discoursed afterwards with much freedom and some power. Blessed be God for any assistance afforded to an unworthy worm. O that I could live to him!

[Through the rest of this week, he was sometimes ready to sink with a sense of his unworthiness and unfitness for the work of the ministry; and sometimes encouraged and lifted above his fears and sorrows, and was enabled confidently to rely on God; and especially on Saturday, towards night, he enjoyed calmness and composure, and assistance in prayer to God. He rejoiced, (as he says), "That God remains "unchangeably powerful and faithful, a sure and sufficient "portion, and the dwelling-place of his children in all generations."]

Lord's day, May 27. Visited my Indians, in the morning, and attended upon a *funeral* among them; was affected to see their *Heathenish practices*. O that they might be "turned "from darkness to light!" Afterwards, got a considerable number of them together, and preached to them; and observed them very attentive. After this, preached to the white people from Heb. ii. 3. Was enabled to speak with some freedom and power: several people seemed much concerned for their souls; especially one who had been educated a Roman catholic. Blessed be the Lord for any help.

Monday, May 28. Set out from the Indians above the Forks of Delaware, on a journey towards Newark in New-Jersey, according to my orders. Rode through the wilderness; was much fatigued with the heat; lodged at a place called Black-River; was exceedingly tired and worn out.

[On Tuesday, he came to Newark. The next day, went to Elisabeth-Town; on Thursday, he went to New-York; and on Friday returned to Elisabeth-Town. These days were

were ſpent in ſome perplexity of mind. He continued at Eliſabeth-Town till Friday in the week following. Was enlivened, refreſhed, and ſtrengthened on the Sabbath at the Lord's table. The enſuing days of the week were ſpent chiefly in ſtudies preparatory to his *ordination*; and on ſome of them he ſeemed to have much of God's gracious preſence, and of the ſweet influences of his Spirit; but was in a very weak ſtate of body. On Saturday, he rode to Newark.]

Lord's day, June 10. [At Newark] in the morning, was much concerned how I ſhould perform the work of the day; and trembled at the thoughts of being left to myſelf.—Enjoyed very conſiderable aſſiſtance in all parts of the public ſervice. Had an opportunity again to attend on the ordinance of the Lord's ſupper, and through divine goodneſs was refreſhed in it: my ſoul was full of love and tenderneſs towards the children of God, and towards all men; felt a certain ſweetneſs of diſpoſition towards every creature. At night, I enjoyed more ſpirituality, and ſweet deſire of holineſs, than I have felt for ſome time: was afraid of every thought and every motion, leſt thereby my heart ſhould be drawn away from God. O that I might never leave the bleſſed God! "Lord, "in thy preſence is fulneſs of joy." O the bleſſedneſs of living to God!

Monday, June 11. This day the *preſbytery* met together at Newark, in order to my *ordination*. Was very weak and diſordered in body; yet endeavoured to repoſe my confidence in God. Spent moſt of the day alone; eſpecially the forenoon. At three in the afternoon preached my probation-ſermon, from Acts xxvi. 17. 18. being a text given me for that end. Felt not well, either in body or mind; however, God carried me through comfortably. Afterwards, paſſed an examination before the *preſbytery*. Was much tired, and my mind burdened with the greatneſs of that charge I was in the moſt ſolemn manner about to take upon me: my mind was ſo preſſed with the weight of the work incumbent upon me, that I could not ſleep this night, though very weary and in great need of reſt.

Tueſday, June 12. Was this morning further examined, reſpecting my experimental acquaintance with Chriſtianity *. At

* Mr Pemberton, in a letter to the Honourable ſociety in Scotland that employed Mr Brainerd, which he wrote concerning him, (publiſhed

At ten o'clock my *ordination* was attended; the sermon preached by the Reverend Mr Pemberton. At this time I was affected with a sense of the important trust committed to me; yet was composed, and solemn, without distraction: and I hope, I then (as many times before) gave myself up to God, to be for him, and not for another. O that I might always be engaged in the service of God, and duly remember the solemn charge I have received, in the presence of God, angels, and men. Amen. May I be assisted of God for this purpose.— Towards night, rode to Elisabeth-Town.

(published in Scotland, in *the Christian monthly history*), writes thus, "We can with pleasure say, that Mr Brainerd passed through "his ordination-trials, to the universal approbation of the *presbytery*, and appeared uncommonly qualified for the work of the "ministry. He seems to be armed with a great deal of self-denial, "and animated with a noble zeal to propagate the gospel among "those barbarous nations, who have long dwelt in the darkness of "Heathenism."

PART

******************)(******************

PART VI.

From his Ordination, till he first began to preach to the Indians at Crosweeksung, among whom he had his most remarkable Success.

WEdnesday, June 13. Spent some considerable time in writing an account of the Indian affairs to go to Scotland; spent some time in conversation with friends; but enjoyed not much sweetness and satisfaction.

Thursday, June 14. Received some particular kindness from friends; and wondered, that God should open the hearts of any to treat me with kindness: saw myself to be unworthy of any favour, from God, or any of my fellow-men. Was much exercised with pain in my head; however determined to set out on my journey towards Delaware in the afternoon: but in the afternoon my pain increased exceedingly; so that I was obliged to betake myself to the bed; and the night following, was greatly distressed with pain and sickness; was sometimes almost bereaved of the exercise of reason by the extremity of pain. Continued much distressed till Saturday, when I was something relieved by an emetic: but was unable to walk abroad till the Monday following, in the afternoon; and still remained very feeble. I often admired the goodness of God, that he did not suffer me to proceed on my journey from this place where I was so tenderly used, and to be sick by the way among strangers.—God is very gracious to me, both in health and sickness, and intermingles much mercy with all my afflictions and toils. Enjoyed some sweetness in things divine, in the midst of my pain and weakness. Oh that I could praise the Lord!

[On Tuesday, June 19. He set out on his journey home, and in three days reached his place, near the Forks of Dela-

ware.

ware. Performed the journey under much weakness of body; but had comfort in his soul, from day to day: and both his weakness of body, and consolation of mind, continued through the week.]

Lord's day, June 24. Extremely feeble; scarce able to walk: however, visited my Indians, and took much pains to instruct them; laboured with some that were much disaffected to Christianity. My mind was much burdened with the weight and difficulty of my work. My whole dependence and hope of success seemed to be on God; who alone I saw could make them willing to receive instruction. My heart was much engaged in prayer, sending up silent requests to God, even while I was speaking to them. O that I could always go in the strength of the Lord!

Monday, June 25. Was something better in health than of late; was able to spend a considerable part of the day in prayer and close studies. Had more freedom and fervency in prayer than usual of late; especially longed for the presence of God in my work, and that the poor Heathen might be converted. And in evening-prayer my faith and hope in God were much raised. To an eye of reason every thing that respects the conversion of the Heathen is as dark as midnight; and yet I cannot but hope in God for the accomplishment of something glorious among them. My soul longed much for the advancement of the Redeemer's kingdom on earth. Was very fearful lest I should admit some vain thought, and so lose the sense I then had of divine things. O for an abiding heavenly temper!

Tuesday, June 26. In the morning, my desires seemed to rise, and ascend up freely to God. Was busy most of the day in translating prayers into the language of the Delaware Indians; met with great difficulty, by reason that my interpreter was altogether unacquainted with the business. But though I was much discouraged with the extreme difficulty of that work, yet God supported me; and especially in the evening, gave me sweet refreshment: in prayer my soul was enlarged, and my faith drawn into sensible exercise; was enabled to cry to God for my poor Indians; and though the work of their conversion appeared "impossible with man, yet with God" I saw "all things were possible." My faith was much strengthened, by observing the wonderful assistance God afforded his servants Nehemiah and Ezra, in reforming his people, and re-establishing his ancient church. I was much assisted in prayer for dear Christian friends, and for others that I apprehended

prehended to be Christless; but was more especially concerned for the poor Heathen, and those of my own charge: was enabled to be instant in prayer for them; and hoped that God would bow the heavens and come down for their salvation. It seemed to me, there could be no impediment sufficient to obstruct that glorious work, seeing the living God, as I strongly hoped, was engaged for it. I continued in a solemn frame, lifting up my heart to God for assistance and grace, that I might be more mortified to this present world, that my whole soul might be taken up continually in concern for the advancement of Christ's kingdom: longed that God would purge me more, that I might be as a chosen vessel to bear his name among the Heathens. Continued in this frame till I dropped asleep.

Wednesday, June 27. Felt something of the same solemn concern, and spirit of prayer, that I enjoyed last night, soon after I rose in the morning.—In the afternoon, rode several miles to see if I could procure any lands for the poor Indians, that they might live together, and be under better advantages for instruction. While I was riding, had a deep sense of the greatness and difficulty of my work; and my soul seemed to rely wholly upon God for success, in the diligent and faithful use of means. Saw, with greatest certainty, that *the arm of the Lord* must be *revealed*, for the help of these poor Heathen, if ever they were delivered from the bondage of the powers of darkness. Spent most of the time, while riding, in lifting up my heart for grace and assistance.

Thursday, June 28. Spent the morning, in reading several parts of the holy scripture, and in fervent prayer for my Indians, that God would set up his kingdom among them, and bring them into his church.—About nine, I withdrew to my usual place of retirement in the woods; and there again enjoyed some assistance in prayer. My great concern was for the conversion of the Heathen to God; and the Lord helped me to plead with him for it. Towards noon, rode up to the Indians, in order to preach to them; and while going, my heart went up to God in prayer for them; could freely tell God, he knew that the cause was not mine, which I was engaged in; but it was his own cause, and it would be for his own glory to convert the poor Indians: and blessed be God, I felt no desire of their conversion, that I might receive honour from the world, as being the instrument of it. Had some freedom in speaking to the Indians.

[The next day, he speaks of some serious concern for the kingdom

kingdom of the blessed Redeemer; but complains much of barrenness, wanderings, inactivity, &c.]

Saturday, June 30. My soul was much solemnized in reading God's word; especially the ninth chapter of Daniel. I saw how God had called out his servants to prayer, and made them wrestle with him, when he designed to bestow any great mercy on his church. And, alas! I was ashamed of myself, to think of my dulness and inactivity, when there seemed to be so much to do for the upbuilding of Zion. Oh, how does Zion lie waste! I longed, that the church of God might be enlarged: was enabled to pray, I think, in faith; my soul seemed sensibly to confide in God, and was enabled to wrestle with him. Afterwards, walked abroad to a place of sweet retirement, and enjoyed some assistance in prayer again: had a sense of my great need of divine help, and felt my soul sensibly depend on God. Blessed be God, this has been a comfortable week to me.

Lord's day, July 1. In the morning, was perplexed with wandering vain thoughts; was much grieved, judged and condemned myself before God. And Oh, how miserable did I feel, because I could not live to God! At ten, rode away with a heavy heart, to preach to my Indians. Upon the road I attempted to lift up my heart to God; but was infested with an unsettled wandering frame of mind; and was exceeding restless and perplexed, and filled with shame and confusion before God. I seemed to myself to be "more brutish than "any man;" and thought, none deserved to be "cast out of "God's presence" so much as I. If I attempted to lift up my heart to God, as I frequently did by the way, on a sudden, before I was aware, my thoughts were wandering "to "the ends of the earth:" and my soul was filled with surprise and anxiety, to find it thus. Thus also after I came to the Indians, my mind was confused; and I felt nothing sensibly of that sweet reliance on God, that my soul has been comforted with in days past. Spent the forenoon in this posture of mind, and preached to the Indians without any heart. In the afternoon, I felt still barren, when I began to preach; and after about half an hour, I seemed to myself to know nothing, and to have nothing to say to the Indians; but soon after, I found in myself a spirit of love, and warmth, and power, to address the poor Indians; and God helped me to plead with them, to "turn from all the vanities of the Heathen, to the "living God:" and I am persuaded, the Lord touched their consciences; for I never saw such attention raised in them before.

fore. And when I came away from them, I spent the whole time while I was riding to my lodgings, three miles distant, in prayer and praise to God. And after I had rode more than two miles, it came into my mind to dedicate myself to God again; which I did with great solemnity, and unspeakable satisfaction; especially gave up myself to him renewedly in the work of the ministry. And this I did by divine grace, I hope, without any exception or reserve; not in the least shrinking back from any difficulties, that might attend this great and blessed work. I seemed to be most free, chearful, and full in this dedication of myself. My whole soul cried, "Lord, to thee I dedicate myself: O accept of me, and let "me be thine for ever. Lord, I desire nothing else; I desire nothing more. O come, come, Lord, accept a poor "worm. *Whom have I in heaven but thee? and there is none "upon earth, that I desire besides thee.*" After this, was enabled to praise God with my whole soul, that he had enabled me to devote and consecrate all my powers to him in this solemn manner. My heart rejoiced in my particular work as a *missionary;* rejoiced in my necessity of self-denial in many respects; and still continued to give up myself to God, and implore mercy of him; praying incessantly, every moment, with sweet fervency. My nature being very weak of late, and much spent, was now considerably overcome: my fingers grew very feeble, and somewhat numb, so that I could scarcely stretch them out straight; and when I lighted from my horse, could hardly walk, my joints seemed all to be loosed. But I felt abundant *strength in the inner man.* Preached to the white people: God helped me much, especially in prayer. Sundry of my poor Indians were so moved as to come to meeting also; and one appeared much concerned.

Monday, July 2. Had some relish of the divine comforts of yesterday; but could not get that warmth and exercise of faith, that I desired. Had sometimes a distressing sense of my past follies, and present ignorance and barrenness: and especially in the afternoon, was sunk down under a load of sin and guilt, in that I had lived so little to God, after his abundant goodness to me yesterday. In the evening, though very weak, was enabled to pray with fervency, and to continue instant in prayer, near an hour. My soul mourned over the power of its corruption, and longed exceedingly to be *washed and purged as with hyssop.* Was enabled to pray for my dear absent friends, Christ's ministers, and his church; and enjoyed much freedom and fervency, but not so much comfort, by reason

reaſon of guilt and ſhame before God.—Judged and condemned myſelf for the follies of the day.

Tueſday, July 3. Was ſtill very weak. This morning, was enabled to pray under a feeling ſenſe of my need of help from God, and, I truſt, had ſome faith in exerciſe; and, bleſſed be God, was enabled to plead with God a conſiderable time. Truly God is good to me. But my ſoul mourned, and was grieved at my ſinfulneſs and barrenneſs, and longed to be more engaged for God. Near nine, withdrew again for prayer; and through divine goodneſs, had the bleſſed Spirit of prayer; my ſoul loved the duty, and longed for God in it. O it is ſweet to be *the Lord's*, to be ſenſibly devoted to him! What a bleſſed portion is God! How glorious, how lovely in himſelf! O my ſoul longed to improve time wholly for God!——Spent moſt of the day in tranſlating prayers into Indian.——In the evening, was enabled again to wreſtle with God in prayer with fervency. Was enabled to maintain a ſelf-diffident and watchful frame of ſpirit, in the evening, and was jealous and afraid leſt I ſhould admit careleſſneſs and ſelf-confidence.

[The next day, he ſeems to have had ſpecial aſſiſtance and fervency moſt of the day, but in a leſs degree than the preceding day. Thurſday was ſpent in great bodily weakneſs; yet ſeems to have been ſpent in continual and exceeding painfulneſs in religion; but in great bitterneſs of ſpirit by reaſon of his vileneſs and corruption; he ſays thus, "I thought "there was not one creature living ſo vile as I. Oh, my in"ward pollution! Oh, my guilt and ſhame before God! "——I know not what to do. Oh, I longed ardently to be "cleanſed and waſhed from the ſtains of inward pollution! "Oh, to be made like God, or rather to be made fit for God "to own!"]

Friday, July 6. Awoke this morning in the fear of God: ſoon called to mind my ſadneſs in the evening paſt; and ſpent my firſt waking minutes in prayer for ſanctification, that my ſoul might be waſhed from its exceeding pollution and defilement. After I aroſe, I ſpent ſome time in reading God's word and prayer: I cried to God under a ſenſe of my great indigency.——I am, of late, moſt of all concerned for miniſterial qualifications, and the converſion of the Heathen: laſt year, I longed to be prepared for a world of glory, and ſpeedily to depart out of this world; but of late all my concern almoſt is for the converſion of the Heathen; and for that end,

end, I long to live. But blessed be God, I have less desire to live for any of the pleasures of the world, than ever I had: I long and love to be a pilgrim; and want grace to imitate the life, labours, and sufferings of St Paul among the Heathen. And when I long for holiness now, it is not so much for myself as formerly; but rather that thereby I may become an "able minister of the New-Testament," especially to the Heathen. Spent about two hours this morning in reading and prayer by turns; and was in a watchful tender frame, afraid of every thing that might cool my affections, and draw away my heart from God. Was something strengthened in my studies; but near night was very weak and weary.

Saturday, July 7. Was very much disordered this morning, and my vigour all spent and exhausted: but was affected and refreshed in reading the sweet story of Elijah's translation, and enjoyed some affection and fervency in prayer: longed much for ministerial gifts and graces, that I might do something in the cause of God. Afterwards was refreshed and invigorated, while reading Mr Joseph Alleine's first case of conscience, *&c.* and enabled then to pray with some ardour of soul, and was afraid of carelessness and self-confidence, and longed for holiness.

Lord's day, July 8. Was ill last night, not able to rest quietly. Had some small degree of assistance in preaching to the Indians; and afterwards was enabled to preach to the white people with some power, especially in the close of my discourse, from Jer. iii. 23. The Lord also assisted me in some measure in the first prayer: blessed be his name. Near night, though very weary, was enabled to read God's word with some sweet relish of it, and to pray with affection, fervency, and (I trust) faith: my soul was more sensibly dependent on God than usual. Was watchful, tender, and jealous of my own heart, lest I should admit carelessness and vain thoughts, and grieve the blessed Spirit, so that he should withdraw his sweet, kind, and tender influences. Longed to "depart, and "be with Christ," more than at any time of late. My soul was exceedingly united to the saints of ancient times, as well as those now living; especially my soul melted for the society of Elijah and Elisha. Was enabled to cry to God with a child-like spirit, and to continue instant in prayer for some time. Was much enlarged in the sweet duty of intercession: was enabled to remember great numbers of dear friends, and precious souls, as well as Christ's ministers. Continued in this frame, afraid of every idle thought, till I dropped asleep.

Monday,

Monday, July 9. Was under much illness of body most of the day, and not able to sit up the whole day. Towards night, felt a little better. Then spent some time in reading God's word and prayer; enjoyed some degree of fervency and affection; was enabled to plead with God for his cause and kingdom: and, through divine goodness, it was apparent to me, that it was his cause I pleaded for, and not my own; and was enabled to make this an argument with God to answer my requests.

Tuesday, July 10. Was very ill, and full of pain, and very dull and spiritless.——In the evening, had an affecting sense of my ignorance, *&c.* and of my need of God at all times, to do every thing for me; and my soul was humbled before God.

Wednesday, July 11. Was still exercised with illness and pain. Had some degree of affection and warmth in prayer and reading God's word: longed for Abraham's faith and fellowship with God; and felt some resolution to spend all my time for God, and to exert myself with more fervency in his service; but found my body weak and feeble. In the afternoon, though very ill, was enabled to spend some considerable time in prayer; spent indeed most of the day in that exercise; and my soul was diffident, watchful, and tender, lest I should offend my blessed Friend, in thought or behaviour. I am persuaded my soul confided in, and leaned upon the blessed God. Oh, what need did I see myself to stand in of God at all times, to assist me and lead me!——Found a great want of strength and vigour, both in the outward and inner man.

[The exercises and experiences, that he speaks of in the next nine days, are very similar to those of the preceding days of this and the foregoing week; a sense of his own weakness, ignorance, unprofitableness, and vileness; lothing and abhorring himself; self-diffidence; sense of the greatness of his work, and his great need of divine help, and the extreme danger of self-confidence; longing for holiness and humility, and to be fitted for his work, and to live to God; and longing for the conversion of the Indians; and these things to a very great degree.]

Saturday, July 21. This morning, was greatly oppressed with guilt and shame, from a sense of inward vileness and pollution. About nine, withdrew to the woods for prayer; but had not much comfort; I appeared to myself the vilest, meanest

meanest creature upon earth, and could scarcely live with myself; so mean and vile I appeared, that I thought I should never be able to hold up my face in heaven, if God of his infinite grace should bring me thither. Towards night my burden respecting my work among the Indians began to increase much; and was aggravated by hearing sundry things that looked very discouraging, in particular that they intended to meet together the next day for an idolatrous feast and dance. Then I began to be in anguish: I thought I must in conscience go and endeavour to break them up; and knew not how to attempt such a thing. However, I withdrew for prayer, hoping for strength from above. And in prayer I was exceedingly enlarged, and my soul was as much drawn out as ever I remember it to have been in my life, or near. I was in such anguish, and pleaded with so much earnestness and importunity, that when I rose from my knees I felt extremely weak and overcome, I could scarcely walk straight, my joints were loosed, the sweat ran down my face and body, and nature seemed as if it would dissolve. So far as I could judge, I was wholly free from selfish ends in my fervent supplications for the poor Indians. I knew, they were met together to worship devils, and not God; and this made me cry earnestly, that God would now appear, and help me in my attempts to break up this idolatrous meeting. My soul pleaded long; and I thought, God would hear, and would go with me to vindicate his own cause: I seemed to confide in God for his presence and assistance. And thus I spent the evening, praying incessantly for divine assistance, and that I might not be self-dependent, but still have my whole dependence upon God. What I passed through was remarkable, and indeed inexpressible. All things here below vanished; and there appeared to be nothing of any considerable importance to me, but holiness of heart and life, and the conversion of the Heathen to God. All my cares, fears, and desires, which might be said to be of a worldly nature, disappeared; and were, in my esteem, of little more importance than a puff of wind. I exceedingly longed, that God would get to himself a name among the Heathen; and I appealed to him with the greatest freedom, that he knew I "preferred him above my chief joy." Indeed, I had no notion of joy from this world; I cared not where or how I lived, or what hardships I went through, so that I could but gain souls to Christ. I continued in this frame all the evening and night. While I was asleep, I dreamed of these things; and when I waked, (as I frequently did). the first thing I thought of was this great work of pleading for God against Satan.

Lord's day, July 22. When I waked, my soul was burdened with what seemed to be before me: I cried to God, before I could get out of my bed: and as soon as I was dressed, I withdrew into the woods, to pour out my burdened soul to God, especially for assistance in my great work; for I could scarcely think of any thing else: and enjoyed the same freedom and fervency as the last evening; and did with unspeakable freedom give up myself afresh to God, for life or death, for all hardships he should call me to among the Heathen; and felt as if nothing could discourage me from this blessed work. I had a strong hope, that God would "bow the heavens and "come down," and do some marvellous work among the Heathen. And when I was riding to the Indians, three miles, my heart was continually going up to God for his presence and assistance; and hoping, and almost expecting, that God would make this the day of his power and grace amongst the poor Indians. When I came to them, I found them engaged in their frolic; but through divine goodness I got them to break up and attend to my preaching: yet still there appeared nothing of the special power of God among them. Preached again to them in the afternoon; and observed the Indians were more sober than before: but still saw nothing special among them; from whence Satan took occasion to tempt and buffet me with these cursed suggestions, There is no God, or if there be, he is not able to convert the Indians, before they have more knowledge, &c. I was very weak and weary, and my soul borne down with perplexity; but was mortified to all the world, and was determined still to wait upon God for the conversion of the Heathen, though the devil tempted me to the contrary.

Monday, July 23. Retained still a deep and pressing sense of what lay with so much weight upon me yesterday: but was more calm and quiet; enjoyed freedom and composure, after the temptations of the last evening: had sweet resignation to the divine will; and desired nothing so much as the conversion of the Heathen to God, and that his kingdom might come in my own heart, and the hearts of others. Rode to a settlement of Irish people, about fifteen miles south-westward; spent my time in prayer and meditation by the way. Near night, preached from Matth. v. 3.——God was pleased to afford me some degree of freedom and fervency. Blessed be God for any measure of assistance.

Tuesday, July 24. Rode about seventeen miles westward, over

a

a hideous mountain, to a number of Indians. Got together near thirty of them: preached to them in the evening, and lodged among them *.—Was weak, and felt something disconsolate: yet could have no freedom in the thought of any other circumstances or business in life: all my desire was the conversion of the Heathen, and all my hope was in God: God does not suffer me to please or comfort myself with hopes of seeing friends, returning to my dear acquaintance, and enjoying worldly comforts.

[The next day, he preached to these Indians again; and then returned to the Irish settlement, and there preached to a numerous congregation: there was a considerable appearance of awakening in the congregation. Thursday, he returned home, exceedingly fatigued and spent; still in the same frame of mortification to the world, and solicitous for the advancement of Christ's kingdom: and on this day he says thus: "I have felt, this week, more of the spirit of a *pilgrim* " *on earth*, than perhaps ever before; and yet so desirous " to see Zion's prosperity, that I was not so willing to leave " this scene of sorrow as I used to be."—The two remaining days of the week, he was very ill, and cries out of wanderings, dulness, and want of spiritual fervency and sweetness. On the Sabbath, he was confined by illness, not able to go out to preach. After this, his illness increased upon him, and he continued very ill all the week †; and says, that "he " thought he never before endured such a season of distressing " weakness; and that his nature was so spent, that he could " neither stand, sit, nor lie with any quiet; and that he was " exercised with extreme faintness and sickness at his sto- " mach; and that his mind was as much disordered as his " body, seeming to be stupid, and without all kind of affec- " tions towards all objects; and yet perplexed, to think, " that he lived for nothing, that precious time rolled away, " and he could do nothing but trifle: and speaks of it as a " season wherein *Satan* buffeted him with some peculiar temp- " tations."—Concerning the next five days he writes thus, " On Lord's day, August 5. was still very poor. But " though very weak, I visited and preached to the poor " Indians twice, and was strengthened vastly beyond my ex-

* See Mr Brainerd's narrative at the end of his *ordination-sermon*, p. 34.

† This week, on Tuesday, he wrote the *fourth letter* added at the end of this account.

" pectations.

"pectations. And indeed, the Lord gave me some freedom and "fervency in addressing them; though I had not strength e-"nough to stand, but was obliged to sit down the whole time. "Towards night, was extremely weak, faint, sick, and full "of pain. And thus I have continued much in the same "state that I was in last week, through the most of this, (it "being now Friday), unable to engage in any business; fre-"quently unable to pray in the family. I am obliged to let "all my thoughts and concerns run at random; for I have "neither strength to read, meditate, or pray: and this natu-"rally perplexes my mind. I seem to myself like a man "that has all his estate embarked in one small boat, unhap-"pily going adrift, down a swift torrent. The poor owner "stands on the shore, and looks, and laments his loss.—— "But, alas! though my all seems to be adrift, and I stand "and see it, I dare not lament; for this sinks my spirits "more, and aggravates my bodily disorders! I am forced "therefore to divert myself with trifles; although at the "same time I am afraid, and often feel as if I was guilty of "the misimprovement of time. And oftentimes my con-"science is so exercised, with this miserable way of spending "time, that I have no peace; though I have no strength of "mind or body to improve it to better purpose. O that God "would pity my distressed state!"

The next three weeks after this, his illness was not so extreme; he was in some degree capable of business, both public and private; (although he had some turns wherein his indisposition prevailed to a great degree): he also in this space had, for the most part, much more inward assistance, and strength of mind: he often expresses great longings for the enlargement of Christ's kingdom; especially by the conversion of the Heathen to God: he speaks of his hope of this as all his delight and joy. He continues still to express his usual longings after holiness, and living to God, and his sense of his own unworthiness: he several times speaks of his appearing to himself the vilest creature on earth; and once says, that he verily thought there were none of God's children who fell so far short of that holiness, and perfection in their obedience, which God requires, as he. He speaks of his feeling more dead than ever to the enjoyments of the world. He sometimes mentions special assistance that he had in this space of time, in preaching to the Indians, and of appearances of religious concern among them. He speaks also of assistance in prayer for absent friends, and especially ministers and candidates for the ministry; and of much comfort he enjoyed

joyed in the company of ſome miniſters that came to viſit him.]

Saturday, September 1. Was ſo far ſtrengthened, after a ſeaſon of great weakneſs, that I was able to ſpend two or three hours in writing on a divine ſubject. Enjoyed ſome comfort and ſweetneſs in things divine and ſacred: and as my bodily ſtrength was in ſome meaſure reſtored, ſo my ſoul ſeemed to be ſomewhat vigorous, and engaged in the things of God.

Lord's day, September 2. Was enabled to ſpeak to my poor Indians with much concern and fervency; and I am perſuaded, God enabled me to exerciſe faith in him, while I was ſpeaking to them. I perceived, that ſome of them were afraid to hearken to, and embrace *Chriſtianity*, leſt they ſhould be inchanted and poiſoned by ſome of the *powows*: but I was enabled to plead with them not to fear theſe; and confiding in God for ſafety and deliverance, I bid a challenge to all theſe *powers of darkneſs*, to do their worſt upon *me* firſt: I told my people, I was a *Chriſtian*, and aſked them why the *powows* did not bewitch and poiſon me. I ſcarcely ever felt more ſenſible of my own unworthineſs, than in this action: I ſaw, that the honour of God was concerned in the affair; and I deſired to be preſerved, not from ſelfiſh views, but for a teſtimony of the divine power and goodneſs, and of the truth of Chriſtianity, and that God might be glorified. Afterwards, I found my ſoul rejoice in God for his aſſiſting grace.

[After this, he went a journey into New-England, and was abſent from the place of his abode, at the Forks of Delaware, about three weeks. He was in a feeble ſtate the greater part of the time. But in the latter part of the journey, he found he gained much in health and ſtrength. And as to the ſtate of his mind, and his religious and ſpiritual exerciſes, it was much with him as had been before uſual in journeys; excepting that the frame of his mind ſeemed more generally to be comfortable. But yet there are complaints of ſome uncomfortable ſeaſons, want of fervency, and want of retirements, and time alone with God. In this journey, he did not forget the Indians; but once and again ſpeaks of his longing for their converſion.]

Wedneſday, September 26. Rode home to the Forks of Delaware. What reaſon have I to bleſs God, who has preſerved

ſerved me in riding more than four hundred and twenty miles, and has "kept all my bones, that not one of them has been "broken!" My health likewiſe is greatly recovered. O that I could dedicate my all to God! This is all the return I can make to him.

Thurſday, September 27. Was ſomething melancholy; had not much freedom and comfort in prayer: my ſoul is diſconſolate, when God is withdrawn.

Friday, September 28. Spent the day in prayer, reading, and writing. Felt ſome ſmall degree of warmth in prayer, and ſome deſires of the enlargement of Chriſt's kingdom by the converſion of the Heathen, and that God would make me a "choſen veſſel, to bear his name before them:" longed for grace to enable me to be faithful.

[The next day, he ſpeaks of the ſame longings for the advancement of Chriſt's kingdom, and the converſion of the Indians; but complains greatly of the ill effects of the diverſions of his late journey, as unfixing his mind from that degree of engagedneſs, fervency, watchfulneſs, &c. which he enjoyed before. And the like complaints are continued the next day.]

Monday, October 1. Was engaged this day in making preparation for my intended journey to Suſquahannah: withdrew ſeveral times to the woods for ſecret duties, and endeavoured to plead for the divine preſence to go with me to the poor Pagans, to whom I was going to preach the goſpel. Towards night rode about four miles, and met brother Byram*; who was come, at my deſire, to be my companion in travel to the Indians. I rejoiced to ſee him; and, I truſt, God made his converſation profitable to me: I ſaw him, as I thought, more dead to the world, its anxious cares, and alluring objects, than I was: and this made me look within myſelf, and gave me a greater ſenſe of my guilt, ingratitude, and miſery.

Tueſday, October 2. Set out on my journey, in company with dear brother Byram, and my interpreter, and two chief Indians from the Forks of Delaware. Travelled about twenty-five miles, and lodged in one of the laſt houſes on our road; after which there was nothing but a hideous and howling *wilderneſs*.

* Miniſter at a place called *Rockciticus*, about forty miles from Mr Brainerd's lodgings.

Wedneſday,

Wednesday, October 3. We went on our way into the wilderness, and found the most difficult and dangerous travelling, by far, that ever any of us had seen; we had scarce any thing else but lofty mountains, deep valleys, and hideous rocks, to make our way through. However, I felt some sweetness in divine things, part of the day, and had my mind intensely engaged in meditation on a divine subject. Near night, my beast that I rode upon, hung one of her legs in the rocks, and fell down under me; but through divine goodness, I was not hurt. However, she broke her leg; and being in such a hideous place, and near thirty miles from any house, I saw nothing that could be done to preserve her life, and so was obliged to kill her, and to prosecute my journey on foot. This accident made me admire the divine goodness to me, that my bones were not broken, and the multitude of them filled with strong pain. Just at dark, we kindled a fire, cut up a few bushes, and made a shelter over our heads, to save us from the frost, which was very hard that night; and committing ourselves to God by prayer, we lay down on the ground, and slept quietly.

[The next day, they went forward on their journey, and at night took up their lodging in the woods in like manner.]

Friday, October 5. We arrived at Susquahannah river, at a place called *Opeholhaupung* *: found there twelve Indian houses: after I had saluted the king in a friendly manner, I told him my business, and that my desire was to teach them *Christianity*. After some consultation, the Indians gathered, and I preached to them. And when I had done, I asked, if they would hear me again. They replied, that they would consider of it; and soon after sent me word, that they would immediately attend, if I would preach: which I did, with freedom, both times. When I asked them again, whether they would hear me further, they replied, they would the next day. I was exceeding sensible of the impossibility of doing any thing for the poor Heathen without special assistance from above: and my soul seemed to rest on God, and leave it to him to do as he pleased in that which I saw was his own cause: and indeed, through divine goodness, I had felt some-

* See his narrative at the end of his ordination sermon, pag. 35. 36.

thing of this frame most of the time while I was travelling thither; and in some measure before I set out.

Saturday, October 6. Rose early, and besought the Lord for help in my great work. Near noon, preached again to the Indians: and in the afternoon, visited them from house to house, and invited them to come and hear me again the next day, and put off their hunting design, which they were just entering upon, till Monday. "This night," I trust, "the "Lord stood by me," to encourage and strengthen my soul: I spent more than an hour in secret retirement; was enabled to "pour out my heart before God," for the increase of grace in my soul, for ministerial endowments, for success among the poor Indians, for God's ministers and people, and for dear friends vastly distant, *&c.* Blessed be God!

[The next day, he complains of great want of fixedness and intenseness in religion, so that he could not keep any spiritual thought one minute without distraction; which occasioned anguish of spirit. He felt (he says) *amazingly guilty*, and *extremely miserable;* and cries out, "Oh my soul, what death "it is, to have the affections unable to centre in God, by reason of darkness, and consequently roving after that satisfaction elsewhere, that is only to be found here!" However, he preached twice to the Indians with some freedom and power; but was afterwards damped by the *objections* they made against *Christianity.* In the evening, in a sense of his great defects in preaching, he "intreated God not to impute "to him blood-guiltiness;" but yet was at the same time enabled to *rejoice in God.*]

Monday, October 8. Visited the Indians with a design to take my leave of them, supposing they would this morning go out to hunting early; but beyond my expectation and hope, they desired to hear me preach again. I gladly complied with their request, and afterwards endeavoured to answer their *objections* against Christianity. Then they went away; and we spent the rest of the afternoon in reading and prayer, intending to go home-ward very early the next day. My soul was in some measure refreshed in secret prayer and meditation. Blessed be the Lord for all his goodness.

Tuesday, October 9. We rose about four in the morning, and commending ourselves to God by prayer, and asking his special protection, we set out on our journey homewards about five, and travelled with great steadiness till past six at night. And then made us a fire, and a shelter of barks, and

so

so rested. I had some clear and comfortable thoughts on a divine subject, by the way, towards night.——In the night, the wolves howled around us; but God preserved us.

[The next day, they rose early, and set forward, and travelled that day, till they came to an Irish settlement, where Mr Brainerd was acquainted, and lodged there. He speaks of some sweetness in divine things, and thankfulness to God for his goodness to him in this journey, that he felt in his heart in the evening, though attended with shame for his barrenness. On Thursday, he continued in the same place; and he and Mr Byram preached there to the people.]

Friday, October 12. Rode home to my lodging; where I poured out my soul to God in secret prayer, and endeavoured to bless him for his abundant goodness to me in my late journey. I scarce ever enjoyed more health, at least, of later years; and God marvellously, and almost miraculously, supported me under the fatigues of the way, and travelling on foot. Blessed be the Lord, that continually preserves me in all my ways.

[On Saturday, he went again to the Irish settlement, to spend the Sabbath there, his Indians being gone.]

Lord's day, October 14. Was much confused and perplexed in my thoughts; could not pray; and was almost discouraged, thinking I should never be able to preach any more. But afterwards, God was pleased to give me some relief from these confusions: but still I was afraid, and even trembled before God. I went to the place of public worship, lifting up my heart to God for assistance and grace, in my great work: and God was gracious to me, and helped me to plead with him for holiness, and to use the strongest arguments with him, drawn from the incarnation and sufferings of Christ for this very end, that men might be made holy. Afterwards, I was much assisted in preaching. I know not that ever God helped me to preach in a more close and distinguishing manner for the trial of mens state. Through the infinite goodness of God, I felt what I spake; and God enabled me to treat on divine truth with uncommon clearness: and yet I was so sensible of my defects in preaching, that I could not be proud of my performance, as at some times; and blessed be the Lord for this mercy. In the evening, I longed to be entirely alone, to bless God for help in a time of extremity; and longed for great degrees of holiness, that I might shew my gratitude to God.

[The next morning, he spent some time before sun-rise in prayer, in the same sweet and grateful frame of mind, that he had been in the evening before: and afterwards went to his Indians, and spent some time in teaching and exhorting them.]

Tuesday, October 16. Felt a spirit of solemnity and watchfulness; was afraid I should not live *to* and *upon* God: longed for more intenseness and spirituality. Spent the day in writing; frequently lifting up my heart to God for more heavenly-mindedness. In the evening, enjoyed sweet assistance in prayer, and thirsted and pleaded to be as holy as the blessed *angels*: longed for ministerial gifts and graces, and success in my work: was sweetly assisted in the duty of intercession, and enabled to remember and plead for numbers of dear friends, and Christ's ministers.

[He seemed to have much of the same frame of mind, the two next days.]

Friday, October 19. Felt an abasing sense of my own impurity and unholiness; and felt my soul melt and mourn, that I had abused and grieved a very gracious God, who was still kind to me, notwithstanding all my unworthiness. My soul enjoyed a sweet season of bitter repentance and sorrow, that I had wronged that blessed God, who (I was persuaded) was reconciled to me in his dear Son. My soul was now tender, devout, and solemn. And I was afraid of nothing, but sin; and afraid of that in every action and thought.

[The four next days, were manifestly spent in a most constant tenderness, watchfulness, diligence, and self-diffidence. But he complains of wanderings of mind, languor of affections, *&c.*]

Wednesday, October 24. Near noon, rode to my people; spent some time, and prayed with them: felt the frame of a *pilgrim* on earth; longed much to leave this gloomy mansion; but yet found the exercise of patience and resignation. And as I returned home from the Indians, spent the whole time in lifting up my heart to God. In the evening, enjoyed a blessed season alone in prayer; was enabled to cry to God with a child-like ſpirit, for the ſpace of near an hour: enjoyed a ſweet freedom in ſupplicating for myſelf, for dear friends, miniſters, and ſome who are preparing for that work, and for the church of God; and longed to be as lively myſelf in God's ſervice as the angels.

Thurſday, October 25. Was buſy in writing. Was very ſenſible of my abſolute dependence on God in all reſpects; ſaw that I could do nothing in thoſe affairs, that I have ſufficient natural faculties for, unleſs God ſhould ſmile upon my attempt. "Not that we are ſufficient of ourſelves, to "think any thing, as of ourſelves," was a ſacred text that I ſaw the truth of.

Friday, October 26. In the morning, my ſoul was melted with a ſenſe of divine goodneſs and mercy to ſuch a vile unworthy worm as I: delighted to lean upon God, and place my whole truſt in him: my ſoul was exceedingly grieved for ſin, and prized and longed after holineſs; it wounded my heart deeply, yet ſweetly, to think how I had abuſed a kind God. I longed to be perfectly holy, that I might not grieve a gracious God; who will continue to love, notwithſtanding his love is abuſed! I longed for holineſs more for this end, than I did for my own happineſs ſake: and yet this was my greateſt happineſs, never more to diſhonour, but always to glorify the bleſſed God. Afterwards, rode up to the Indians, in the afternoon, &c.

[The four next days, he was exerciſed with much diſorder and pain of body, with a degree of melancholy and gloomineſs of mind, bitterly complaining of deadneſs and unprofitableneſs, yet mourning and longing after God.]

Wedneſday, October 31. Was ſenſible of my barrenneſs, and decays in the things of God: my ſoul failed when I remembered the fervency I had enjoyed at the throne of grace. Oh (I thought) if I could but be ſpiritual, warm, heavenly-minded, and affectionately breathing after God, this would be better than life to me! My ſoul longed exceedingly for death, to be looſed from this dulneſs and barrenneſs, and made for ever active in the ſervice of God. I ſeemed to live for nothing, and to do no good: and Oh, the burden of ſuch a life! Oh, death, death, my kind friend, haſten and deliver me from dull mortality, and make me ſpiritual and vigorous to eternity!

Thurſday, November 1. Had but little ſweetneſs in divine things. But afterwards, in the evening, felt ſome life, and longings

longings after God; I longed to be always solemn, devout, and heavenly-minded; and was afraid to leave off praying, lest I should again lose a sense of the sweet things of God.

Friday, November 2. Was filled with sorrow and confusion, in the morning, and could enjoy no sweet sense of divine things, nor get any relief in prayer. Saw I deserved, that every one of God's creatures should be let loose upon me to be the executioners of his wrath against me: and yet therein I saw I deserved what I did not fear as my portion. About noon, rode up to the Indians; and while going, could feel no desires for them, and even dreaded to say any thing to them; but God was pleased to give me some freedom and enlargement, and made the season comfortable to me. In the evening, had enlargement in prayer. But, alas! what comforts and enlargements I have felt for these many weeks past, have been only transient and short; and the greater part of my time has been filled up with deadness, or struggles with deadness, and bitter conflicts with corruption. I have found myself exercised sorely with some particular things that I thought myself most of all freed from. And thus I have ever found it, when I have thought the battle was over, and the conquest gained, and so let down my watch, the enemy has risen up and done me the greatest injury.

Saturday, November 3. I read the life and trials of a godly man, and was much warmed by it: I wondered at my past deadness; and was more convinced of it than ever. Was enabled to confess and bewail my sin before God, with self-abhorrence.

Lord's day, November 4. Had, I think, some exercise of faith in prayer, in the morning: longed to be spiritual. Had considerable help in preaching to my poor Indians: was encouraged with them, and hoped that God designed mercy for them.

[The next day *, he set out on a journey to New-York, to the meeting of the Presbytery there; and was gone from home more than a fortnight. He seemed to enter on this journey with great reluctance; fearing, that the diversions of it would prove a means of cooling his religious affections, as he had found in other journeys. But yet, in this journey he had some special seasons wherein he enjoyed extraordinary evidences and fruits of God's gracious presence. He was

* On this day he concluded his Narrative, that is at the end of his ordination-sermon.

greatly

greatly fatigued and exposed in this journey by cold and storms: and when he returned from New-York to New-Jersey, on Friday, was taken very ill, and was detained by his illness some time.]

Wednesday, November 21. Rode from Newark to Rockcitius in the cold, and was almost overcome with it. Enjoyed some sweetness in conversation with dear Mr Jones, while I dined with him: my soul loves the people of God, and especially the ministers of Jesus Christ, who feel the same trials that I do.

Thursday, November 22. Came on my way from Rockcitius to Delaware river. Was very much disordered with a cold and pain in my head. About six at night, I lost my way in the wilderness, and wandered over rocks and mountains, down hideous steeps, through swamps, and most dreadful and dangerous places; and the night being dark, so that few stars could be seen, I was greatly exposed: was much pinched with cold, and distressed with an extreme pain in my head, attended with sickness at my stomach; so that every step I took was distressing to me. I had little hope for several hours together, but that I must lie out in the woods all night, in this distressed case. But about nine o'clock, I found a house, through the abundant goodness of God, and was kindly entertained. Thus I have frequently been exposed, and sometimes lain out the whole night: but God has hitherto preserved me; and blessed be his name. Such fatigues and hardships as these serve to wean me more from the earth; and, I trust, will make heaven the sweeter. Formerly, when I was thus exposed to cold, rain, &c. I was ready to please myself with the thoughts of enjoying a comfortable house, a warm fire, and other outward comforts; but now these have less place in my heart, (through the grace of God), and my eye is more to God for comfort. In this world I expect tribulation; and it does not now, as formerly, appear strange to me; I do not in such seasons of difficulty flatter myself that it will be better hereafter; but rather think, how much worse it might be; how much greater trials others of God's children have endured; and how much greater are yet perhaps reserved for me. Blessed be God, that he makes the thoughts of my journey's end and of my dissolution a great comfort to me, under my sharpest trials; and scarce ever lets these thoughts be attended with terror or melancholy; but they are attended frequently with great joy.

Friday, November 23. Visited a sick man; discoursed and prayed

prayed with him. Then visited another house, where was one dead and laid out; looked on the corpse, and longed that my time might come to *depart*, that I might be *with Christ*. Then went home to my lodgings, about one o'clock. Felt poorly; but was able to read, most of the afternoon.

[Within the space of the next twelve days, he passed under many changes in the frames and exercises of his mind. He had many seasons of the special influences of God's Spirit, animating, invigorating, and comforting him in the ways of God and duties of religion: but had some turns of great dejection and melancholy. He spent much time, within this space, in hard labour, with others, to make for himself a little cottage or hut, to live in by himself through the winter. Yet he frequently preached to the Indians, and speaks of special assistance he had from time to time, in addressing himself to them; and of his sometimes having considerable encouragement, from the attention they gave. But on Tuesday, December 4. he was sunk into great discouragement, to see them (most of them) going in company to an idolatrous *feast* and *dance*, after he had taken abundant pains with them to dissuade them from these things.]

Thursday, December 6. Having now a happy opportunity of being retired in a house of my own, which I have lately procured and moved into, and considering that it is now a long time since I have been able, either on account of bodily weakness, or for want of retirement, or some other difficulty to spend any time in secret fasting and prayer; considering also the greatness of my work, and the extreme difficulties that attend it; and that my poor Indians are now *worshipping devils*, notwithstanding all the pains I have taken with them, which almost overwhelms my spirit; moreover, considering my extreme barrenness, spiritual deadness and dejection, of late; as also the power of some particular corruptions; I set apart this day for secret prayer and fasting, to implore the blessing of God on myself, on my poor people, on my friends, and on the church of God. At first, I felt a great backwardness to the duties of the day, on account of the seeming impossibility of performing them; but the Lord helped me to break through this difficulty. God was pleased, by the use of means, to give me some clear conviction of my sinfulness, and a discovery of *the plague of my own heart*, more affecting than what I have of late had. And especially I saw my sinfulness in this, that when God had *withdrawn* himself,

then,

then, instead of living and dying in *pursuit* of him, I have been disposed to one of these two things, either (*first*) to yield an unbecoming respect to some *earthly* objects, as if happiness were to be derived from them; or (*secondly*) to be secretly *froward* and impatient, and unsuitably desirous of *death*, so that I have sometimes thought I could not bear to think my life must be lengthened out. And that which often drove me to this impatient desire of death, was a despair of doing any good in life; and I chose death, rather than a life spent for nothing. But now God made me sensible of my sin in these things, and enabled me to cry to him for *forgiveness*. Yet this was not all I wanted; for my soul appeared exceedingly polluted, my heart seemed like a nest of vipers, or a cage of unclean and hateful birds: and therefore I wanted to be purified "by the blood of sprinkling, that cleanseth from all "sin." And this, I hope, I was enabled to pray for in faith. I enjoyed much more intenseness, fervency, and spirituality, than I expected; God was better to me than my fears. And towards night, I felt my soul rejoice, that God is unchangeably happy and glorious; that he will be glorified, whatever becomes of his creatures. I was enabled to persevere in prayer till sometime in the evening: at which time I saw so much need of divine help, in every respect, that I knew not how to leave off, and had forgot that I needed food. This evening, I was much assisted in meditating on Is. lii. 3. Blessed be the Lord for any help in the past day.

Friday, December 7. Spent some time in prayer, in the morning; enjoyed some freedom and affection in the duty, and had longing desires of being made "faithful to the death." Spent a little time in writing on a divine subject: then visited the Indians, and preached to them. But under inexpressible dejection: I had no heart to speak to them, and could not do it, but as I forced myself: I knew, they must hate to hear me, as having but just got home from their idolatrous feast and devil-worship.—In the evening, had some freedom in prayer and meditation.

Saturday, December 8. Have been uncommonly free this day from dejection, and from that distressing apprehension, that I could do nothing: was enabled to pray and study with some comfort; and especially was assisted in writing on a divine subject. In the evening, my soul rejoiced in God; and I blessed his name for shining on my soul. O the sweet and blessed change I then felt, when God "brought me out of "darkness into his marvellous light!"

Lord's day, December 9. Preached, both parts of the day,

 at

at a place called *Greenwich*, in New-Jersey, about ten miles from my own house. In the first discourse I had scarce any warmth or affectionate longing for souls. In the intermission-season I got alone among the bushes, and cried to God for pardon of my deadness; and was in anguish and bitterness, that I could not address souls with more compassion and tender affection: judged and condemned myself for want of this divine temper; though I saw I could not get it as of myself, any more than I could make a world. In the latter exercise, blessed be the Lord, I had some fervency, both in prayer and preaching; and especially in the application of my discourse was enabled to address precious souls with affection, concern, tenderness, and importunity. The Spirit of God, I think, was there; as the effects were apparent, tears running down many cheeks.

Monday, December 10. Near noon, I preached again: God gave me some assistance, and enabled me to be in some degree faithful; so that I had peace in my own soul, and a very comfortable composure, "although Israel should not be gathered." Came away from Greenwich, and rode home; arrived just in the evening. By the way, my soul blessed God for his goodness; and I rejoiced, that so much of my work was done, and I so much nearer my blessed reward. Blessed be God for grace to be faithful.

Tuesday, December 11. Felt very poorly in body, being much tired and worn out the last night. Was assisted in some measure in writing on a divine subject: but was so feeble and sore in my breast, that I had not much resolution in my work. Oh, how I long for that world "where the weary "are at rest!" and yet through the goodness of God I do not now feel impatient.

Wednesday, December 12. Was again very weak; but somewhat assisted in secret prayer, and enabled with pleasure and sweetness to cry, "Come, Lord Jesus! come, Lord Jesus! "come quickly." My soul "longed for God, for the living "God." O how delightful it is, to pray under such sweet influences! Oh how much better is this, than one's *necessary food!* I had at this time no disposition to eat, (though late in the morning); for earthly food appeared wholly tasteless. O how much "better is thy love than wine," than the sweetest wine!—I visited and preached to the Indians, in the afternoon; but under much dejection. Found my *interpreter* under some concern for his soul; which was some comfort to me; and yet filled me with new care. I longed greatly for his conversion; lifted up my heart to God for it, while I was talking

talking to him: came home, and poured out my ſoul to God for him: enjoyed ſome freedom in prayer, and was enabled, I think, to leave all with God.

Thurſday, December 13. Endeavoured to ſpend the day in faſting and prayer, to implore the divine bleſſing, more eſpecially on my poor people; and in particular, I ſought for converting grace for my *interpreter*, and three or four more under ſome concern for their ſouls. I was much diſordered in the morning when I aroſe; but having determined to ſpend the day in this manner, I attempted it. Some freedom I had in pleading for theſe poor concerned ſouls, ſeveral times; and when interceding for them, I enjoyed greater freedom from wandering and diſtracting thoughts, than in any part of my ſupplications: but, in the general, was greatly exerciſed with wanderings; ſo that in the evening it ſeemed as if I had need to pray for nothing ſo much as for the pardon of ſins committed in the day paſt, and the vileneſs I then found in myſelf. The ſins I had moſt ſenſe of, were pride, and wandering thoughts, whereby I mocked God. The former of theſe curſed iniquities excited me to think of writing, or preaching, or converting Heathen, or performing ſome other great work, that my name might live when I ſhould be dead. My ſoul was in anguiſh, and ready to drop into deſpair, to find ſo much of that curſed temper. With this, and the other evil I laboured under, *viz.* wandering thoughts, I was almoſt overwhelmed, and even ready to give over ſtriving after a ſpirit of devotion; and oftentimes ſunk into a conſiderable degree of deſpondency, and thought I was "more brutiſh than "any man." Yet after all my ſorrows, I truſt, through grace, this day and the exerciſes of it have been for my good, and taught me more of my corruption, and weakneſs without Chriſt, than I knew before.

Friday, December 14. Near noon, went to the Indians; but knew not what to ſay to them, and was aſhamed to look them in the face: I felt I had no power to addreſs their conſciences, and therefore had no boldneſs to ſay any thing. Was, much of the day, in a great degree of deſpair about ever "doing or ſeeing any good in the land of the living."

[He continued under the ſame dejection the next day.]

Lord's day, December 16. Was ſo overwhelmed with dejection, that I knew not how to live: I longed for death exceedingly: my ſoul was *ſunk into deep waters*, and *the floods* were ready to *drown me*: I was ſo much oppreſſed, that my

 ſoul

ſoul was in a kind of horror: I could not keep my thoughts fixed in prayer, for the ſpace of one minute, without fluttering and diſtraction: I was exceedingly aſhamed, that I did not live to God: I had no diſtreſſing doubt about my own ſtate; but would have cheerfully ventured (as far as I could poſſibly know) into eternity. While I was going to preach to the Indians, my ſoul was in anguiſh; I was ſo overborne with diſcouragement, that I deſpaired of doing any good, and was driven to my wits-end; I knew nothing what to ſay, nor what courſe to take. But at laſt I inſiſted on the evidence we have of the truth of Chriſtianity from the *miracles* of Chriſt; many of which I ſet before them: and God helped me to make a cloſe application to thoſe that refuſed to believe the truth of what I taught them: and indeed I was enabled to ſpeak to the conſciences of all, in ſome meaſure. I was ſomething encouraged, to find, that God enabled me to be faithful once more. Then came and preached to another company of them; but was very weary and faint. In the evening, I was ſomething refreſhed, and was enabled to pray and praiſe God with compoſure and affection: had ſome enlargement and courage with reſpect to my work: was willing to live, and longed to do more for God, than my weak ſtate of body would admit of. "I can do all things through "Chriſt that ſtrengthens me;" and by his grace, I am willing to *ſpend* and *be ſpent* in his ſervice, when I am not thus ſunk in dejection, and a kind of deſpair.

Monday, December 17. Was ſomething comfortable in mind, moſt of the day; and was enabled to pray with ſome freedom, cheerfulneſs, compoſure, and devotion; had alſo ſome aſſiſtance in writing on a divine ſubject.

Tueſday, December 18. Went to the Indians, and diſcourſed to them near an hour, without any power to come cloſe to their hearts. But at laſt I felt ſome fervency, and God helped me to ſpeak with warmth. My *interpreter* alſo was amazingly aſſiſted; and I doubt not but "the Spirit of "God was upon him," (though I had no reaſon to think he had any true and ſaving grace, but was only under conviction of his loſt ſtate); and preſently upon this moſt of the grown perſons were much affected, and the tears ran down their cheeks; and one *old man* (I ſuppoſe, an hundred years old) was ſo affected, that he wept, and ſeemed convinced of the importance of what I taught them. I ſtaid with them a conſiderable time, exhorting and directing them; and came away, lifting up my heart to God in prayer and praiſe, and encouraged and exhorted my *interpreter* to "ſtrive to enter

"in

"in at the ſtrait gate." Came home, and ſpent moſt of the evening in prayer and thankſgiving; and found myſelf much enlarged and quickened. Was greatly concerned, that the Lord's work which ſeemed to be begun, might be carried on with power, to the converſion of poor ſouls, and the glory of divine grace.

Wedneſday, December 19. Spent a great part of the day in prayer to God for the *outpouring of his Spirit* on my poor people; as alſo to bleſs his name for awakening my *intepreter* and ſome others, and giving us ſome tokens of his preſence yeſterday. And bleſſed be God, I had much freedom, five or ſix times in the day, in prayer and praiſe, and felt a weighty concern upon my ſpirit for the ſalvation of thoſe precious ſouls, and the enlargement of the Redeemer's kingdom among them. My ſoul hoped in God for ſome ſucceſs in my miniſtry; and bleſſed be his name for ſo much hope.

Thurſday, December 20. Was enabled to viſit the throne of grace frequently, this day; and through divine goodneſs enjoyed much freedom and fervency, ſundry times: was much aſſiſted in crying for mercy for my poor people, and felt cheerfulneſs and hope in my requeſts for them. I ſpent much of the day in writing; but was enabled to intermix prayer with my ſtudies.

Friday, December 21. Was enabled again to pray with freedom, chearfulneſs, and hope. God was pleaſed to make the duty comfortable and pleaſant to me; ſo that I delighted to perſevere, and repeatedly to engage in it. Towards noon viſited my people, and ſpent the whole time in the way to them in prayer, longing to "ſee the power of God" among them, as there appeared ſomething of it the laſt Tueſday; and I found it ſweet to reſt and hope in God. Preached to them twice, and at two diſtinct places: had conſiderable freedom each time, and ſo had my *interpreter*. Several of them followed me from one place to the other: and I thought, there was ſome divine influence diſcernible amongſt them. In the evening, was aſſiſted in prayer again. Bleſſed, bleſſed be the Lord!

[Very much the ſame things are expreſſed concerning his inward frame, exerciſes, and aſſiſtances on Saturday, as on the preceding days. He obſerves, that this was a comfortable week to him. But then concludes, "Oh that I had "no reaſon to complain of much barrenneſs! Oh that there "were no vain thoughts and evil affections lodging within me! "The Lord knows how I long for that world, where they "reſt

'rest not day nor night, saying, *Holy, holy, holy is the Lord* '*God Almighty*," &c. On the following Sabbath, he speaks of assistance and freedom in his public work, but as having less of the sensible presence of God, than frequently in the week past; but yet says, his soul was kept from sinking in discouragement. On Monday, again he seemed to enjoy very much the same liberty and fervency, through the day, that he enjoyed through the greater part of the preceding week *.]

Tuesday, December 25. Enjoyed very little quiet sleep last night, by reason of bodily weakness, and the closeness of my studies yesterday: yet my heart was somewhat lively in prayer and praise; I was delighted with the divine glory and happiness, and rejoiced that God was God, and that he was unchangeably possessed of glory and blessedness. Though God *held my eyes waking*, yet he helped me to improve my time profitably amidst my pains and weakness, in continued meditations on Luke xiii. 7. "Behold, these three years I come seek-" ing fruit," *&c.* My meditations were sweet; and I wanted to set before sinners their sin and danger.

[He continued in a very low state, as to his bodily health, for some days; which seems to have been a great hindrance to him in his religious exercises and pursuits. But yet he expresses some degree of divine assistance, from day to day, through the remaining part of this week. He preached several times this week to his Indians; and there appeared still some concern amongst them for their souls. On Saturday, he rode to the Irish settlement, about fifteen miles from his lodgings, in order to spend the Sabbath there.]

Lord's day, December 30. Discoursed, both parts of the day, from Mark viii. 34. "Whosoever will come after me," *&c.* God gave me very great freedom and clearness, and (in the afternoon especially) considerable warmth and fervency. In the evening also, had very great clearness while conversing with friends on divine things: I do not remember ever to have had more clear apprehensions of religion in my life: but found a struggle, in the evening, with spiritual pride.

[On Monday, he preached again in the same place with

* This day he wrote the *fifth letter* added at the end of this history.

freedom

freedom and fervency; and rode home to his lodging; and arrived in the evening, under a considerable degree of bodily illness, which continued the two next days. And he complains much of spiritual emptiness and barrenness on those days.]

Thursday, January 3. 1744-5. Being sensible of the great want of divine influences, and the outpouring of God's Spirit, I spent this day in fasting and prayer, to seek so great a mercy for myself, and my poor people in particular, and for the church of God in general. In the morning, was very lifeless in prayer, and could get scarce any sense of God. Near noon, enjoyed some sweet freedom to pray that the *will of God* might in every respect become *mine*; and I am persuaded, it was so at that time in some good degree. In the afternoon, I was exceeding weak, and could not enjoy much fervency in prayer; but felt a great degree of dejection; which, I believe, was very much owing to my bodily weakness and disorder.

Friday, January 4. Rode up to the Indians, near noon; spent some time there under great disorder: my soul was *sunk down into deep waters*, and I was almost overwhelmed with melancholy.

Saturday, January 5. Was able to do something at writing; but was much disordered with pain in my head. At night, was distressed with a sense of my spiritual pollution, and ten thousand youthful, yea, and childish follies, that no body but myself had any thought about; all which appeared to me now fresh, and in a lively view, as if committed yesterday, and made my soul ashamed before God, and caused me to hate myself.

Lord's day, January 6. Was still distressed with vapoury disorders. Preached to my poor Indians; but had little heart or life. Towards night, my soul was pressed under a sense of my unfaithfulness. O the joy and peace that arises from a sense of "having obtained mercy of God to be faithful!" And Oh the misery and anguish that spring from an apprehension of the contrary!

[His dejection continued the two next days; but not to so great a degree on Tuesday, when he enjoyed some freedom and fervency in preaching to the Indians.]

Wednesday, January 9. In the morning, God was pleased to remove that gloom which has of late oppressed my mind, and gave me freedom and sweetness in prayer. I was encouraged, and strengthened, and enabled to plead for grace for myself, and mercy for my poor Indians; and was sweetly assisted in my intercessions with God for others. Blessed be his holy name for ever and ever. Amen, and Amen. Those things that of late have appeared most difficult and almost impossible, now appeared not only possible, but easy. My soul so much delighted to continue instant in prayer, at this blessed season, that I had no desire for my *necessary food*: even dreaded leaving off praying at all, lest I should lose this spirituality, and this blessed thankfulness to God which I then felt. I felt now quite willing to live, and undergo all trials that might remain for me in a world of sorrow; but still longed for heaven, that I might glorify God in a perfect manner. O "come, Lord Jesus, come quickly." Spent the day in reading a little; and in some diversions, which I was necessitated to take by reason of much weakness and disorder. In the evening, enjoyed some freedom and intenseness in prayer.

[The three remaining days of the week, he was very low and feeble in body; but nevertheless continued constantly in the same comfortable sweet frame of mind, as is expressed on Wednesday. On the Sabbath, this sweetness in spiritual alacrity began to abate; but still he enjoyed some degree of comfort, and had assistance in preaching to the Indians.]

Monday, January 14. Spent this day under a great degree of bodily weakness and disorder; and had very little freedom, either in my studies or devotions: and in the evening, I was much dejected and melancholy. It pains and distresses me, that I live so much of my time for nothing. I long to do much in a little time, and if it might be the Lord's will, to *finish my work* speedily in this tiresome world. I am sure, I do not desire to live for any thing in this world; and through grace I am not afraid to look the *king of terrors* in the face: I know, I shall be afraid, if God leaves me; and therefore I think it always duty to lay in for that solemn hour. But for a very considerable time past, my soul has rejoiced to think of death in its nearest approaches; and even when I have been very weak, and seemed nearest eternity. "Not unto me, "not unto me, but to God be the glory." I feel that which convinces me, that if God do not enable me to maintain a holy dependence upon him, death will easily be a terror to me; but at present, I must say, "I long to depart, and to be "with

"with Christ," which is best of all. When I am in a sweet resigned frame of soul, I am willing to tarry a while in a world of sorrow, I am willing to be from home as long as God sees fit it should be so; but when I want the influence of this temper, I am then apt to be impatient to be gone.—Oh when will the day appear, that I shall be perfect in holiness, and in the enjoyment of God!

[The next day was spent under a great degree of dejection and melancholy; which (as he himself says, he was persuaded) was owing partly to bodily weakness, and vapoury disorders.]

Wednesday and Thursday, January 16. and 17. I spent most of the time in writing on a sweet divine subject, and enjoyed some freedom and assistance. Was likewise enabled to pray more frequently and fervently than usual: and my soul, I think, rejoiced in God; especially on the evening of the last of these days: *praise* then seemed *comely*, and I delighted to bless the Lord. O what reason have I to be thankful, that God ever helps me to labour and study for him! he does but *receive his own*, when I am enabled in any measure to praise him, labour for him, and live to him. Oh, how comfortable and sweet it is, to feel the assistance of divine grace in the performance of the duties God has enjoined us! "Bless the Lord, "O my soul."

[The same enlargement of heart, and joyful frame of soul, continued through the next day. But on the day following it began to decline; which decay seems to have continued the whole of the next week: yet he enjoyed some seasons of special and sweet assistance.]

Lord's day, January 27. Had the greatest degree of inward anguish, that almost ever I endured: I was perfectly overwhelmed, and so confused, that after I began to discourse to the Indians, before I could finish a sentence, sometimes I forgot entirely what I was aiming at; or if, with much difficulty, I had recollected what I had before designed, still it appeared strange, and like something I had long forgotten, and had now but an imperfect remembrance of. I know it was a degree of distraction, occasioned by vapoury disorders, melancholy, spiritual desertion, and some other things that particularly pressed upon me this morning, with an uncommon weight, the principal of which respected my Indians.

This distressing gloom never went off the whole day; but was so far removed, that I was enabled to speak with some freedom and concern to the Indians, at two of their settlements; and I think, there was some appearance of the presence of God with us, some seriousness, and seeming concern among the Indians, at least a few of them. In the evening, this gloom continued still, till family-prayer *, about nine o'clock, and almost through this, until I came near the close, when I was praying (as I usually do) for the illumination and conversion of my poor people; and then the cloud was scattered, so that I enjoyed sweetness and freedom, and conceived hopes, that God designed mercy for some of them. The same I enjoyed afterwards in secret prayer; in which precious duty I had for a considerable time sweetness and freedom, and (I hope) faith, in praying for myself, my poor Indians, and dear friends and acquaintance in New-England, and elsewhere, and for the dear interest of Zion in general. "Bless the Lord, "O my soul, and forget not all his benefits."

[He spent the rest of this week, or at least the most of it, under dejection and melancholy; which on Friday rose to an extreme height; he being then, as he himself observes, much exercised with vapoury disorders. This exceeding gloominess continued on Saturday, till the evening, when he was again relieved in family-prayer; and after it, was refreshed in secret, and felt willing to live, and endure hardships in the cause of God; and found his hopes of the advancement of Christ's kingdom, as also his hopes to *see the power of God* among the poor Indians, considerably raised.]

Lord's day, February 3. In the morning, I was somewhat relieved of that gloom and confusion, that my mind has of late been greatly exercised with: was enabled to pray with some composure and comfort. But, however, went to my Indians trembling; for my soul "remembered the wormwood "and the gall" (I might almost say the *hell*) of Friday last; and I was greatly afraid I should be obliged again to drink of that *cup of trembling*, which was inconceivably more bitter than death, and made me long for the grave more, unspeakably more, than for hid treasures, yea, inconceivably more

* Though Mr Brainerd now dwelt by himself in the forementioned little cottage, which he had built for his own use; yet that was near to a *family* of white people with whom he had lived before, and with whom he still attended family-prayer.

than

than the men of this world long for such treasures. But God was pleased to hear my cries, and to afford me great assistance; so that I felt peace in my own soul; and was satisfied, that if not one of the Indians should be profited by my preaching, but should all be damned, yet I should be accepted and rewarded as faithful; for I am persuaded, God enabled me to be so.——Had some good degree of help afterwards, at another place; and much longed for the conversion of the poor Indians. Was somewhat refreshed, and comfortable, towards night, and in the evening. O that my soul might praise the Lord for his goodness!——Enjoyed some freedom, in the evening, in meditation on Luke xiii. 24.

[In the three next days, he was the subject of much dejection: but the three remaining days of the week seem to have been spent with much composure and comfort. On the next Sabbath, he preached at Greenwich in New-Jersey. In the evening, he rode eight miles to visit a sick man at the point of death, and found him speechless and senseless.]

Monday, February 11. About break-of-day, the sick man died. I was affected at the sight: spent the morning with the mourners: and after prayer, and some discourse with them, I returned to Greenwich, and preached again from Psal. lxxxix. 15. and the Lord gave me assistance: I felt a sweet love to souls, and to the kingdom of Christ; and longed that poor sinners might *know the joyful sound*. Several persons were much affected. And after meeting, I was enabled to discourse, with freedom and concern, to some persons that applied to me under spiritual trouble. Left the place, sweetly composed, and rode home to my house about eight miles distant. Discoursed to friends, and inculcated divine truths upon some. In the evening, was in the most solemn frame that almost ever I remember to have experienced: I know not that ever death appeared more real to me, or that ever I saw myself in the condition of a dead corpse, laid out, and dressed for a lodging in the silent grave, so evidently as at this time. And yet I felt exceeding comfortably; my mind was composed and calm, and *death* appeared *without a sting*. I think, I never felt such an universal mortification to all created objects as now. Oh, how great and solemn a thing it appeared to die! Oh, how it lays the greatest honour in the dust! And oh, how vain and trifling did the riches, honours, and pleasures of the world appear! I could not, I dare not, so much as think of any of them; for *death, death*, solemn (though not frightful) *death* appeared at the door. Oh, I could see myself dead, and laid out, and inclosed in my coffin, and put down into the cold grave, with greatest solemnity, but without terror! I spent most of the evening in conversing with a dear Christian friend; and, blessed be God, it was a comfortable evening to us both.——What are friends? What are comforts? What are sorrows? What are distresses? —"The time is short: it remains, that they which weep, be "as though they wept not; and they which rejoice, as though "they rejoiced not: for the fashion of this world passeth "away. O come, Lord Jesus, come quickly. Amen."—— Blessed be God for the comforts of the past day.

Tuesday, February 12. Was exceeding weak; but in a sweet resigned, composed frame, most of the day: felt my heart freely go forth after God in prayer.

Wednesday, February 13. Was much exercised with vapoury disorders; but still enabled to maintain solemnity, and I think, spirituality.

Thursday, February 14. Spent the day in writing on a divine subject: enjoyed health, and freedom in my work: had a solemn sense of death; as I have indeed had every day this week, in some measure: what I felt on Monday last, has been abiding, in some considerable degree, ever since.

Friday, February 15. Was engaged in writing again almost the whole day. In the evening, was much assisted in meditating on that precious text, John vii. 37. "Jesus stood and "cried," &c. I had then a sweet sense of the free grace of the gospel: my soul was encouraged, warmed, and quickened, and my desires drawn out after God in prayer: my soul was watchful, and afraid of losing so sweet a guest as I then entertained. I continued long in prayer and meditation, intermixing one with the other; and was unwilling to be diverted by any thing at all from so sweet an exercise. I longed to proclaim the grace I then meditated upon, to the world of sinners.—O how *quick* and *powerful* is the *word* of the blessed God!

[The next day, he complains of great conflicts with corruption, and much discomposure of mind.]

Lord's day, February 17. Preached to the *white* people (my *interpreter* being absent) in the wilderness upon the sunny side of a hill: had a considerable assembly, consisting of people that lived (at least many of them) not less than thirty miles asunder;

asunder; some of them came near twenty miles. I discoursed to them, all day, from John vii. 37. "Jesus stood and cried, "saying, If any man thirst," &c. In the afternoon, it pleased God to grant me great freedom and fervency in my discourse; and I was enabled to imitate the example of Christ in the text, who *stood and cried.*—I think, I was scarce ever enabled to offer the free grace of God to perishing sinners with more freedom and plainness in my life. And afterwards, I was enabled earnestly to invite the children of God to come renewedly, and drink of this fountain of water of life, from whence they have heretofore derived unspeakable satisfaction. It was a very comfortable time to me: there were many tears in the assembly; and I doubt not but that the Spirit of God was there, convincing poor sinners of their need of Christ. In the evening, I felt composed, and comfortable, though much tired: I had some sweet sense of the excellency and glory of God; and my soul rejoiced, that he was "God over all, bless-"ed for ever;" but was too much crouded with company and conversation, and longed to be more alone with God. Oh that I could for ever bless God for the mercy of this day, who "answered me in the joy of my heart."

[The rest of this week seems to have been spent under a decay of this life and joy, and in distressing conflicts with corruption; but not without some seasons of refreshment and comfort.]

Lord's day, February 24. In the morning, was much perplexed: my *interpreter* being absent, I knew not how to perform my work among the Indians. However, I rode to the Indians, got a Dutchman to interpret for me, though he was but poorly qualified for the business. Afterwards, I came and preached to a few white people from John vi. 67. Here the Lord seemed to unburden me in some measure, especially towards the close of my discourse: I felt freedom to open the *love of Christ* to his own dear *disciples*: when the rest of the world *forsakes* him, and are *forsaken* by him, that he calls them no more, he then turns to his own, and says, "Will ye "also go away?" I had a sense of the free grace of Christ to his own people, in such seasons of general apostasy, and when they themselves in some measure backslide with the world. O the free grace of Christ, that he seasonably minds his people of their danger of *backsliding*, and invites them to persevere in their adherence to himself! I saw that *backsliding* souls, who seemed to be about to *go away* with the world, might

return,

return, and welcome, to him *immediately*; without any thing to recommend them; notwithstanding all their former backslidings. And thus my discourse was suited to my own soul's case: for, of late, I have found a great want of this sense and apprehension of divine grace; and have often been greatly distressed in my own soul, because I did not suitably apprehend this "fountain opened to purge away sin;" and so have been too much labouring for spiritual life, peace of conscience, and progressive holiness, in my own strength: but now God shewed me, in some measure, *the arm* of all strength, and *the fountain* of all grace.—In the evening, I felt solemn, devout, and sweet, resting on free grace for assistance, acceptance, and peace of conscience.

[Within the space of the next nine days, he had frequent refreshing, invigorating influences of God's Spirit; attended with complaint of dulness, and with longings after spiritual life and holy fervency.]

Wednesday, March 6. Spent most of the day in preparing for a journey to New-England. Spent some time in prayer, with a special reference to my intended journey. Was afraid I should forsake the *fountain of living waters*, and attempt to derive satisfaction from *broken cisterns*, my dear friends and acquaintance, with whom I might meet in my journey. I looked to God to keep me from this *vanity* in special, as well as others. Towards night, and in the evening, was visited by some friends, some of whom, I trust, were real Christians; who discovered an affectionate regard to me, and seemed grieved that I was about to leave them; especially seeing I did not expect to make any considerable stay among them, if I should live to return from New-England *. O how kind has God been to me! how has he raised up friends in every place, where his providence has called me! friends are a great comfort; and it is God that gives them; it is *he* makes them friendly to me. "Bless the Lord, O my soul, and forget not "all his benefits."

[The next day, he set out on his journey; and it was about five weeks before he returned.—The special design of this journey, he himself declares afterwards, in his diary for March 21. where, speaking of his conversing with a certain

* It seems, he had a design, by what afterwards appears, to remove and live among the Indians at Susquahannah river.

minister

minister in New-England, he says thus, "Contrived with him "how to raise some money among Christian friends, in order "to support a colleague with me in the wilderness, (I having "now spent two years in a very solitary manner), that we "might be together; as Christ sent out his disciples two and "two: and as this was the principal concern I had in view, "in taking this journey, so I took pains in it, and hope God "will succeed it, if for his glory." He first went into various parts of New-Jersey, and visited several ministers there; and then went to New-York; and from thence into New-England, going to various parts of Connecticut: and then returned into New-Jersey: he met a number of ministers at Woodbridge, "who," he says, "met there to consult about "the affairs of Christ's kingdom, in some important articles." He seems, for the most part, to have been free from melancholy in this journey; and many times to have had extraordinary assistance in public ministrations, and his preaching sometimes attended with very hopeful appearances of a good effect on the auditory. He also had many seasons of special comfort and spiritual refreshment, in conversation with ministers and other Christian friends, and also in meditation and prayer by himself alone.]

Saturday, April 13. Rode home to my own house at the Forks of Delaware: was enabled to remember the goodness of the Lord, who has now preserved me while riding full six hundred miles in this journey; has kept me that none of my bones have been broken. Blessed be the Lord, who has preserved me in this tedious journey, and returned me in safety to my own house. Verily it is God that has upheld me, and guarded my goings.

Lord's day, April 14. Was disordered in body with the fatigues of my late journey; but was enabled however to preach to a considerable assembly of white people, gathered from all parts round about, with some freedom, from Ezek. xxxiii. 11. "As I live, saith the Lord God," *&c.* Had much more assistance than I expected.

[This week, he went a journey to Philadelphia, in order to engage the *governor* there to use his interest with the chief man of the *Six Nations*, (with whom he maintained a strict friendship), that he would give him leave to live at Susquahannah, and instruct the Indians that are within their territories.

ries *. In his way to and from thence, he lodged with Mr Beaty, a young Presbyterian minister. He speaks of seasons of sweet spiritual refreshment that he enjoyed at his lodgings.]

Saturday, April 20. Rode with Mr Beaty to Abington, to attend Mr Treat's administration of the sacrament, according to the method of the church of Scotland. When we arrived, we found Mr Treat preaching: afterwards I preached a sermon from Matth. v. 3. "Blessed are the poor in spirit," *&c.* God was pleased to give me great freedom and tenderness, both in prayer and sermon: the assembly was sweetly melted, and scores were all in tears. It was, as I then hoped, and was afterwards abundantly satisfied by conversing with them, a "word spoken in season to many weary souls." I was extremely tired, and my spirits much exhausted, so that I could scarcely speak loud; yet I could not help rejoicing in God.

Lord's day, April 21. In the morning, was calm and composed, and had some outgoings of soul after God in secret duties, and longing desires of his presence in the *sanctuary* and at his *table;* that his presence might be in the assembly; and that his children might be entertained with a *feast of fat things.*—In the forenoon, Mr Treat preached. I felt some affection and tenderness in the season of the administration of the ordinance. Mr Beaty preached to the multitude abroad, who could not half have crouded into the meeting-house. In the season of the communion, I had comfortable and sweet apprehensions of the blissful communion of God's people, when they shall meet at their Father's table in his kingdom, in a state of perfection.—In the afternoon, I preached abroad to the whole assembly, from Rev. xiv. 4. "These are they that "follow the Lamb," *&c.* God was pleased again to give me very great freedom and clearness, but not so much warmth as before. However, there was a most amazing attention in the whole assembly; and, as I was informed afterwards, this was a sweet season to many.

Monday, April 22. I enjoyed some sweetness in retirement, in the morning. At eleven o'clock, Mr Beaty preach-

* The Indians at Susquahannah are a mixed company of many nations, speaking various languages, and few of them properly of the Six Nations. But yet the country having formerly been conquered by the Six Nations, they claim the land; and the Susquahannah-Indians are a kind of vassals to them.

ed, with freedom and life. Then I preached from Job vii. 37. and concluded the solemnity Had some freedom: but not equal to what I had enjoyed before: yet in the prayer, the Lord enabled me to cry (I hope) with a child-like temper, with tenderness and brokenness of heart.—Came home with Mr Beaty to his lodgings; and spent the time, while riding, and afterwards, very agreeably on divine things.

Tuesday, April 23. Left Mr Beaty's, and returned home to the Forks of Delaware: enjoyed some sweet meditations on the road, and was enabled to lift up my heart to God in prayer and praise.

[The two next days, he speaks of much bodily disorder, but of some degrees of spiritual assistance and freedom.]

Friday, April 26. Conversed with a Christian friend with some warmth; and felt a spirit of mortification to the world, in a very great degree. Afterwards, was enabled to pray fervently, and to rely on God sweetly, for "all things pertaining to life and godliness." Just in the evening, was visited by a dear Christian friend, with whom I spent an hour or two in conversation, on the very soul of religion. There are many with whom I can talk *about religion;* but, alas! I find few with whom I can talk *religion itself:* but, blessed be the Lord, there are some that love to feed on the kernel, rather than the shell.

[The next day, he went to the Irish settlement, often before mentioned, about fifteen miles distant; where he spent the Sabbath, and preached with some considerable assistance. On Monday, he returned, in a very weak state, to his own lodgings.]

Tuesday, April 30. Was scarce able to walk about, and was obliged to betake myself to the bed, much of the day; and spent away the time in a very solitary manner; being neither able to read, meditate, nor pray, and had none to converse with in that wilderness. Oh, how heavily does time pass away, when I can do nothing to any good purpose; but seem obliged to trifle away precious time! But of late, I have seen it my duty to *divert* myself by all lawful means, that I may be fit, at least some small part of my time, to labour for God. And here is the difference between my present diversions, and those I once pursued, when in a natural state. Then I made a god of diversions, delighted in them with a neglect of

God, and drew my highest satisfaction from them: now I use them as *means* to help me in *living to God;* fixedly delighting in *him*, and not in them, drawing my highest satisfaction from *him*. Then they were my *all;* now they are only means leading to my *all*. And those things that are the greatest diversion, when pursued with this view, do not tend to hinder, but promote my spirituality; and I see now, more than ever, that they are absolutely necessary.

Wednesday, May 1. Was not able to sit up more than half the day; and yet had such recruits of strength sometimes, that I was able to write a little on a divine subject. Was grieved that I could no more live to God. In the evening, had some sweetness and intenseness in secret prayer.

Thursday, May 2. In the evening, being a little better in health, I walked into the woods, and enjoyed a sweet season of meditation and prayer. My thoughts run upon Psal. xvii. 15. "I shall be satisfied, when I awake with thy likeness." And it was indeed a precious text to me. I longed to preach to the whole world; and it seemed to me, they must needs all be melted in hearing such precious divine truths, as I had then a view and relish of. My thoughts were exceeding clear, and my soul was refreshed.——Blessed be the Lord, that in my late and present weakness, now for many days together, my mind is not gloomy, as at some other times.

Friday, May 3. Felt a little vigour of body and mind, in the morning; had some freedom, strength, and sweetness in prayer. Rode to, and spent some time with my Indians. In the evening, again retiring into the woods, I enjoyed some sweet meditations on Isaiah liii. 1. "Yet it pleased the Lord "to bruise him," &c.

[The three next days were spent in much weakness of body: but yet he enjoyed some assistance in public and private duties; and seems to have remained free from melancholy.]

Tuesday, May 7. Spent the day mainly in making preparation for a journey into the wilderness. Was still weak, and concerned how I should perform so difficult a journey. Spent some time in prayer for the divine blessing, direction, and protection in my intended journey; but wanted bodily strength to spend the day in fasting and prayer.

[The next day, he set out on his journey to Susquahannah, with his interpreter. He endured great hardships and fatigues

in

in his way thither through a hideous wilderneſs; where, after having lodged one night in the open woods, he was overtaken with a north-earſterly ſtorm, in which he was almoſt ready to periſh. Having no manner of ſhelter, and not being able to make a fire in ſo great a rain, he could have no comfort if he ſtopt; therefore determined to go forward in hopes of meeting with ſome ſhelter, without which he thought it impoſſible he ſhould live the night through: but their horſes happening to have eat poiſon (for want of other food) at a place where they lodged the night before, were ſo ſick that they could neither ride nor lead them, but were obliged to drive them before them, and travel on foot; until through the mercy of God (juſt at duſk) they came to a bark-hut, where they lodged that night. After he came to Suſquahannah, he travelled about the length of an hundred miles on the river, and viſited many towns and ſettlements of the Indians; ſaw ſome of ſeven or eight diſtinct tribes; and preached to different nations, by different interpreters. He was ſometimes much diſcouraged, and ſunk in his ſpirits, through the oppoſition that appeared in the Indians to Chriſtianity. At other times, he was encouraged by the diſpoſition that ſome of theſe people manifeſted to hear, and willingneſs to be inſtructed. He here met with ſome that had formerly been his hearers at Kaunaumeek, and had removed hither; who ſaw and heard him again with great joy. He ſpent a fortnight among the Indians on this river; and paſſed through conſiderable labours and hardſhips, frequently lodging on the ground, and ſometimes in the open air; and at length he fell extremely ill, as he was riding in the wilderneſs, being ſeized with an ague, followed with a burning fever, and extreme pains in his head and bowels, attended with a great evacuation of blood; ſo that he thought he muſt have periſhed in the wilderneſs. But at laſt coming to an Indian trader's hut, he got leave to ſtay there; and though without phyſic or food proper for him, it pleaſed God, after about a week's diſtreſs, to relieve him ſo far that he was able to ride. He returned homewards from Juncauta, an iſland far down the river; where was a conſiderable number of Indians, who appeared more free from prejudices againſt Chriſtianity, than moſt of the other Indians. He arrived at the Forks of Delaware on Thurſday, May 30. after having rode in this journey about three hundred and forty miles *. He came home in a

* This is the journey which he occaſionally mentions in his printed Journal.

very weak state, and under dejection of mind; which was a great hindrance to him in religious exercises. However, on the Sabbath, after having preached to the Indians, he preached to the *white* people, with some success, from Is. liii. 10. "Yet it pleased the Lord to bruise him," &c. some being awakened by his preaching. The next day, he was much exercised for want of spiritual life and fervency.]

Tuesday, June 4. Towards evening, was in distress for God's presence, and a sense of divine things: withdrew myself to the woods, and spent near an hour in prayer and meditation; and I think, the Lord had compassion on me, and gave me some sense of divine things; which was indeed refreshing and quickening to me: my soul enjoyed intenseness and freedom in prayer, so that it grieved me to leave the place.

Wednesday, June 5. Felt thirsting desires after God, in the morning. In the evening, enjoyed a precious season of retirement: was favoured with some clear and sweet meditations upon a sacred text; divine things opened with clearness and certainty, and had a divine stamp upon them: my soul was also enlarged and refreshed in prayer; and I delighted to continue in the duty; and was sweetly assisted in praying for fellow-Christians, and my dear brethren in the ministry. Blessed be the dear Lord for such enjoyments. O how sweet and precious it is, to have a clear apprehension and tender sense of the *mystery of godliness*, of true holiness, and likeness to the best of beings! O what a blessedness it is, to be as much like God, as it is possible for a creature to be like his great Creator! Lord, give me more of *thy likeness*; "I "shall be satisfied, when I awake with it."

Thursday, June 6. Was engaged, a considerable part of the day, in meditation and study on divine subjects. Enjoyed some special freedom, clearness, and sweetness in meditation. O how refreshing it is, to be enabled to improve time well!

[The next day, he went a journey of near fifty miles to Neshaminy, to assist at a sacramental occasion, to be attended at Mr Beaty's meeting-house; being invited thither by him and his people.]

Saturday, June 8. Was exceeding weak and fatigued with riding in the heat yesterday: but being desired, I preached in the afternoon, to a crouded audience, from Is. xl. 1. "Com-

"fort

"fort ye, comfort ye my people, saith your God." God was pleased to give me great freedom, in opening the sorrows of God's people, and in setting before them comforting considerations. And, blessed be the Lord, it was a sweet melting season in the assembly.

Lord's day, June 9. Felt some longing desires of the presence of God to be with his people on the solemn occasion of the day. In the forenoon, Mr Beaty preached; and there appeared some warmth in the assembly. Afterwards, I assisted in the administration of the Lord's supper: and towards the close of it, I discoursed to the multitude *extempore*, with some reference to that sacred passage, Is. liii. 10. "Yet it "pleased the Lord to bruise him." Here God gave me great assistance in addressing sinners: and the word was attended with amazing power; many scores, if not hundreds, in that great assembly, consisting of three or four thousand, were much affected; so that there was a "very great mourning, "like the mourning of Hadadrimmon."——In the evening, I could hardly look any body in the face, because of the imperfections I saw in my performances in the day past.

Monday, June 10. Preached with a good degree of clearness and some sweet warmth, from Psal. xvii. 15. "I shall be satisfied, when I awake with thy likeness." And blessed be God, there was a great solemnity, and attention in the assembly, and sweet refreshment among God's people; as was evident then, and afterwards.

Tuesday, June 11. Spent the day mainly in conversation with dear Christian friends; and enjoyed some sweet sense of divine things. O how desirable it is, to keep company with God's dear children! These are the "excellent ones of the "earth, in whom," I can truly say, "is all my delight." O what delight will it afford, to meet them all in a state of perfection! Lord, prepare me for that state.

[The next day, he left Mr Beaty's, and went to Maidenhead in New-Jersey; and spent the next seven days in a comfortable state of mind, visiting several ministers in those parts.]

Tuesday, June 18. Set out from New-Brunswick with a design to visit some Indians at a place called *Crosweeksung* in New-Jersey, towards the sea*. In the afternoon, came to a place

* Mr Brainerd having, when at Boston, wrote and left with a friend

place called *Cranberry*, and meeting with a serious minister, Mr Macknight, I lodged there with him. Had some enlargement and freedom in prayer with a number of people.

friend a brief *relation* of facts touching his labours with the Indians, and reception among them, during the space of time between November 5. 1744. and June 19. 1745. (with a view to connect his *Narrative*, at the end of Mr Pemberton's ordination-sermon, and his *Journal*, in case they should ever be reprinted), concludes the same with this passage: "As my body was very feeble, so my mind "was scarce ever so much damped and discouraged about the conversion of the Indians, as at this time. And in this state of body "and mind I made my first visit to the Indians in New-Jersey, "where God was pleased to display his power and grace in the remarkable manner that I have represented in my printed Journal."

PART

PART VII.

From his first beginning to preach to the Indians at Crosweeksung, till he returned from his last journey to Susquahannah ill with the consumption, whereof he died.

[WE are now come to that part of Mr Brainerd's life, wherein he had his greatest *success*, in his labours for the good of souls, and in his particular business as a missionary to the *Indians*. An account of which, if here published, would doubtless be very entertaining to the reader, after he has seen by the preceding parts of this account of his life, how great and long-continued his desires for the spiritual good of this sort of people were; how he prayed, laboured, and wrestled, and how much he denied himself, and suffered, to this end. After all Mr Brainerd's agonizing in prayer, and travelling in birth, for the conversion of Indians, and all the interchanges of his raised hopes and expectations, and then disappointments and discouragements; and after waiting in a way of persevering prayer, labour, and suffering, as it were through a long *night*; at length the *day* dawns: "Weeping "continues for a night, but joy comes in the morning. He "went forth weeping, bearing precious seed, and now he "comes with rejoicing, bringing his sheaves with him." The desired event is brought to pass at last; but at a time, in a place, and upon subjects, that scarce ever entered into his heart. An account of this would undoubtedly now much gratify the Christian reader: and it should have been here inserted, as it stands in his diary, had it not been, that a particular account of this glorious and wonderful success was drawn up by Mr Brainerd himself, pursuant to the order of the honourable society in Scotland, and published by him in his lifetime; which account many have in their hands; and the inserting it here would too much swell this book, as was said

said before in the preface. However, I look upon the want of this account here, as a real defect in this history of Mr Brainerd's life; which, I would hope, those of my readers, who are not already possessed of his public *Journal*, will supply, by procuring one of those books, that they may not be without that which in some respects is the most remarkable, and to a Christian mind would be the most pleasant part of the whole story. That the reader who is furnished with one of those books, may know the *place* where the defects of this history are to be supplied from thence, I shall either expresly observe it as I go along, or else make a dash or stroke thus——; which when the reader finds in this 7th part of this history, he is to understand by it, that in that place something in Mr Brainerd's *diary*, worth observing, is *left out*, because the same for substance was published before in his printed *Journal* *.]

Wednesday, June 19. 1745. Rode to the Indians at Crossweeksung: found few at home; discoursed to them however, and observed them very serious and attentive. At night I was extremely worn out, and scarce able to walk or sit up. Oh, how tiresome is earth! how dull the body!

Thursday, June 20. Towards night, preached to the Indians again; and had more hearers than before. In the evening, enjoyed some peace and serenity of mind, some composure and comfort in prayer alone; and was enabled to lift up my head with some degree of joy, under an apprehension that my redemption draws nigh. Oh, blessed be God, that there remains a rest to his poor weary people!

Friday, June 21. Rode to Freehold, to see Mr William Tennent; and spent the day comfortably with him. My sinking spirits were a little raised and encouraged; and I felt my soul breathing after God, in the midst of Christian conversation. And in the evening, was refreshed in secret prayer; saw myself a poor worthless creature, without wisdom to direct, or strength to help myself. Oh, blessed be God, that lays me under a happy, a blessed necessity of living upon himself!

Saturday, June 22. About noon, rode to the Indians again; and near night, preached to them. Found my body much strengthened, and was enabled to speak with abundant plainness and warmth. And the power of God evidently attended

* This defect in the former edition of Mr Brainerd's life, here mentioned by Mr Edwards, is supplied in this, by annexing to it, the *Journal* here referred to.

the word; so that sundry persons were brought under great concern for their souls, and made to shed many tears, and to wish for Christ to save them. My soul was much refreshed, and quickened in my work; and I could not but spend much time with them, in order to open both their misery and remedy. This was indeed a sweet afternoon to me. While riding, before I came to the Indians, my spirits were refreshed, and my soul enabled to cry to God almost incessantly, for many miles together. In the evening also I found the consolations of God were not small: I was then willing to live, and in some respects desirous of it, that I might do something for the dear kingdom of Christ; and yet death appeared pleasant: so that I was in some measure in a strait between two, having a desire to depart. I am often weary of this world, and want to leave it on that account; but it is desirable to be drawn, rather than driven out of it.

[In the four next days is nothing remarkable in his diary, but what is in his public Journal.]

Thursday, June 27.——My soul rejoiced to find, that God enabled me to be faithful, and that he was pleased to awaken these poor Indians by my means. O how heart-reviving, and soul-refreshing is it to me to see the fruit of my labours!

Friday, June 28.——In the evening, my soul was revived, and my heart lifted up to God in prayer, for my poor Indians, myself, and friends, and the dear church of God. And O how refreshing, how sweet was this! Bless the Lord, O my soul, and forget not his goodness and tender mercy.

Saturday, June 29. Preached twice to the Indians; and could not but wonder at their seriousness, and the strictness of their attention.—Blessed be God that has inclined their hearts to hear. And O how refreshing it is to me, to see them attend with such uncommon diligence and affection, with tears in their eyes, and concern in their hearts! In the evening, could not but lift up my heart to God in prayer, while riding to my lodgings; and blessed be his name, had assistance and freedom. O how much *better than life* is the presence of God!

[His diary gives an account of nothing remarkable on the two next days, besides what is in his public Journal; excepting his heart's being lifted up with thankfulness, rejoicing in God, *&c*.]

X Tuesday,

Tuesday, July 2. Rode from the Indians to Brunswick, near forty miles, and lodged there. Felt my heart drawn out after God in prayer, almost all the forenoon; especially while riding. And in the evening, could not help crying to God for those poor Indians; and after I went to bed, my heart continued to go out to God for them, till I dropped asleep. O blessed be God that I may pray!

[He was so beat out by constant preaching to these Indians, yielding to their earnest and importunate desires, that he found it necessary to give himself some relaxation. He spent therefore about a week in New-Jersey, after he left these Indians, visiting several ministers, and performing some necessary business, before he went to the Forks of Delaware. And though he was very weak in body, yet he seems to have been strong in spirit. On Friday, July 12. he arrived at his own house in the Forks of Delaware; continuing still free from melancholy; from day to day, enjoying freedom, assistance, and refreshment in the inner man. But on Wednesday, the next week, he seems to have had some melancholy thoughts about his doing so little for God, being so much hindered by weakness of body.]

Thursday, July 18. Longed to spend the little inch of time I have in the world more for God. Felt a spirit of seriousness, tenderness, sweetness, and devotion, and wished to spend the whole night in prayer and communion with God.

Friday, July 19. In the evening, walked abroad for prayer and meditation, and enjoyed composure and freedom in these sweet exercises; especially in meditation on Rev. iii. 12. "Him that "overcometh, will I make a pillar in the temple of my God," *&c.* This was then a delightful theme to me, and it refreshed my soul to dwell upon it. Oh, when shall I *go no more out* from the service and enjoyment of the dear Lord! Lord, hasten the blessed day.

[Within the space of the next six days, he speaks of much inward refreshment and enlargement, from time to time.]

Friday, July 26. In the evening, God was pleased to help me in prayer, beyond what I have experienced for some time; especially my soul was drawn out for the enlargement of Christ's kingdom, and for the conversion of my poor people: and my soul relied on God for the accomplishment of that great

great work. Oh, how ſweet were the thoughts of death to me at this time! Oh, how I longed to be with Chriſt, to be employed in the glorious work of angels, and with an angel's freedom, vigour, and delight! And yet how willing was I to ſtay a while on earth, that I might do ſomething, if the Lord pleaſed, for his intereſt in the world! My ſoul, my very ſoul, longed for the ingathering of the poor Heathen; and I cried to God for them moſt willingly and heartily; and yet becauſe I could not but cry. This was a ſweet ſeaſon; for I had ſome lively taſte of heaven, and a temper of mind ſuited in ſome meaſure to the employments and entertainments of it. My ſoul was grieved to leave the place; but my body was weak and worn out, and it was near nine o'clock. Oh, I longed that the remaining part of my life might be filled up with more fervency and activity in the things of God! Oh the inward peace, compoſure, and God-like ſerenity of ſuch a frame! heaven muſt needs differ from this only in degree, and not in kind. "Lord, ever give me this bread of life."

[Much of this frame ſeemed to continue the next day.]

Lord's day, July 28. In the evening, my ſoul was melted, and my heart broken, with a ſenſe of paſt barrenneſs and deadneſs: and Oh, how I then longed to live to God, and bring forth much fruit to his glory!

Monday, July 29. Was much exerciſed with a ſenſe of vileneſs, with guilt and ſhame before God.

[For other things remarkable, while he was this time at the Forks of Delaware, the reader muſt be refered to his public Journal. As particularly for his labours and ſucceſs there among the Indians.

On Wedneſday, July 31. He ſet out on his return to Croſweekſung, and arrived there the next day. In his way thither, he had longing deſires that he might come to the Indians there, in the "fulneſs of the bleſſing of the goſpel of "Chriſt;" attended with a ſenſe of his own great weakneſs, dependence, and worthleſſneſs.]

Friday, Auguſt 2. In the evening I retired, and my ſoul was drawn out in prayer to God; eſpecially for my poor people, to whom I had ſent word that they might gather together, that I might preach to them the next day. I was much enlarged in praying for their ſaving converſion; and ſcarce ever found my deſires of any thing of this nature ſo sensibly and clearly (to my own satisfaction) disinterested, and free from selfish views. It seemed to me, I had no care, or hardly any desire to be the instrument of so glorious a work, as I wished and prayed for among the Indians: if the blessed work might be accomplished to the honour of God, and the enlargement of the dear Redeemer's kingdom, this was all my desire and care; and for this mercy I hoped, but with trembling; for I felt what Job expresses, chap. ix. 16. My rising hopes, respecting the conversion of the Indians, have been so often dashed, that my spirit is as it were broken, and courage wasted, and I hardly dare hope.

[Concerning his labours and marvellous success amongst the Indians, for the following ten days, let the reader see his public Journal. The things worthy of note in his *diary*, not there published, are his earnest and importunate prayers for the Indians, and the *travail of his soul* for them from day to day; and his great refreshment and joy in beholding the wonderful mercy of God, and the glorious manifestations of his power and grace in his work among them; and his ardent thanksgivings to God; his heart's rejoicing in Christ, as King of his church, and King of his soul; in particular, at the sacrament of the Lord's supper at Mr Macknight's meeting-house; a sense of his own exceeding unworthiness, which sometimes was attended with dejection and melancholy.]

Monday, August 19.—— Near noon, I rode to Freehold, and preached to a considerable assembly, from Matth. v. 3. It pleased God to leave me to be very dry and barren; so that I do not remember to have been so straitened for a whole twelvemonth past. God is just, and he has made my soul acquiesce in his will in this regard. It is contrary to *flesh and blood*, to be cut off from all freedom, in a large auditory, where their expectations are much raised; but so it was with me; and God helped me to say *Amen* to it; "Good is the "will of the Lord." In the evening I felt quiet and composed, and had freedom and comfort in secret prayer.

Tuesday, August 20. Was composed and comfortable, still in a resigned frame. Travelled from Mr Tennent's in Freehold to Elisabeth-Town. Was refreshed to see friends, and relate to them what God had done, and was still doing among my poor people.

Wednesday, August 21. Spent the forenoon in conversation with Mr Dickinson, contriving something for the settlement of the Indians together in a body, that they might be under

better

better advantages for instruction. In the afternoon, spent time agreeably with other friends; wrote to my brother at college: but was grieved that time slid away, while I did so little for God.

Friday, August 23. In the morning, was very weak; but favoured with some freedom and sweetness in prayer: was composed and comfortable in mind. After noon, rode to Crosweeksung to my poor people.——

Saturday, August 24.——Had composure and peace, while riding from the Indians to my lodgings: was enabled to pour out my soul to God for dear friends in New-England. Felt a sweet tender frame of spirit: my soul was composed and refreshed in God. Had likewise freedom and earnestness in praying for my dear people: blessed be God. "O the peace "of God that passeth all understanding!" it is impossible to describe the sweet peace of conscience, and tenderness of soul, I then enjoyed. O the blessed foretastes of heaven!

Lord's day, August 25.——I rode to my lodgings in the evening, blessing the Lord for his gracious visitation of the Indians, and the soul-refreshing things I had seen the day past amongst them, and praying that God would still carry on his divine work among them.

Monday, August 26.——I went from the Indians to my lodgings, rejoicing for the goodness of God to my poor people; and enjoyed freedom of soul in prayer, and other duties, in the evening. Bless the Lord, O my soul.

[The next day, he set out on a journey towards the Forks of Delaware, designing to go from thence to Susquahannah, before he returned to Crosweeksung. It was five days from his departure from Crosweeksung, before he reached the Forks, going round by the way of Philadelphia, and waiting on the governor of Pensylvania, to get a recommendation from him to the chiefs of the Indians; which he obtained. He speaks of much comfort and spiritual refreshment in this journey; and also a sense of his exceeding unworthiness, thinking himself the meanest creature that ever lived.]

Lord's day, September 1. [At the Forks of Delaware]——God gave me the *Spirit of prayer*, and it was a blessed season in that respect. My soul cried to God for mercy, in an affectionate manner. In the evening also my soul rejoiced in God.

[His

[His private *diary* has nothing remarkable, for the two next days, but what is in his public Journal.]

Wednesday, September 4. Rode fifteen miles to an Irish settlement, and preached there from Luke xiv. 22. "And yet "there is room." God was pleased to afford me some tenderness and enlargement in the first prayer, and much freedom, as well as warmth, in sermon. There were many tears in the assembly: the people of God seemed to melt, and others to be in some measure awakened. Blessed be the Lord, that lets me see his work going on in one place and another.

[The account for Thursday is the same for substance as in his public Journal.]

Friday, September 6. Enjoyed some freedom and intenseness of mind in prayer alone; and longed to have my soul more warmed with divine and heavenly things. Was somewhat melancholy towards night, and longed to die and quit a scene of sin and darkness; but was a little supported in prayer.

[This melancholy continued the next day.]

Lord's day, September 8.——In the evening, God was pleased to enlarge me in prayer, and give me freedom at the throne of grace: I cried to God for the enlargement of his kingdom in the world, and in particular among my dear people; was also enabled to pray for many dear ministers of my acquaintance, both in these parts, and in New-England; and also for other dear friends in New-England. And my soul was so engaged and enlarged in that sweet exercise, that I spent near an hour in it, and knew not how to leave the mercy-seat. Oh, how I delighted to pray and cry to God! I saw, God was both able and willing to do all that I desired, for myself and friends, and his church in general. I was likewise much enlarged and assisted in family-prayer. And afterwards, when I was just going to bed, God helped me to renew my petitions with ardency and freedom. Oh, it was to me a blessed evening of prayer! Bless the Lord, O my soul.

[The next day, he set out from the Forks of Delaware to go to Susquahannah. And on the fifth day of his journey, he he arrived at Shaumoking, a large Indian town on Susquahannah river. He performed the journey under a considerable degree of melancholy, occasioned at first by his hearing that the Moravians were gone before him to the Susquahannah-Indians.]

Saturday, September 14. [At Shaumoking]——In the evening, my soul was enlarged and sweetly engaged in prayer; especially, that God would set up his kingdom in this place, where the *devil* now reigns in the most eminent manner. And I was enabled to ask this for God, for his glory, and because I longed for the enlargement of his kingdom, to the honour of his dear name. I could appeal to God with the greatest freedom, that he knew it was *his* dear cause, and not my own, that engaged my heart: and my soul cried, "Lord, "set up thy kingdom, for thine own glory. Glorify thyself; "and I shall rejoice. Get honour to thy blessed name; and "this is all I desire. Do with me just what thou wilt. Blessed "be thy name for ever, that thou art God, and that thou "wilt glorify thyself. O that the whole world might glorify "thee! O let these poor people be brought to know thee, "and love thee, for the glory of thy dear ever-blessed name!" I could not but hope, that God would bring in these miserable, wicked Indians; though there appeared little human probability of it; for they were then *dancing* and *revelling*, as if possessed by the *devil*. But yet I *hoped*, though *against hope*, that God would be glorified, that God's name would be glorified by these poor Indians. I continued long in prayer and praise to God; and had great freedom, enlargement, and sweetness, remembering dear friends in New-England, as well as the people of my charge. Was entirely free from that dejection of spirit with which I am frequently exercised. Blessed be God!

[His *diary* from this time to September 22. (the last day of his continuance among the Indians at Susquahannah) is not legible, by reason of the badness of the ink. It was probably written with the juice of some berries found in the woods, having no other ink in that wilderness. So that for this space of time the reader must be wholly referred to his public Journal.

On Monday, September 23. He left the Indians, in order to his return to the Forks of Delaware, in a very weak state of body, and under dejection of mind, which continued the two first days of his journey.]

Wednesday,

Wednesday, September 25. Rode still homeward. In the forenoon, enjoyed freedom and intenseness of mind in meditation on Job xlii. 5, 6. "I have heard of thee by the hearing of the ear; but now mine eye seeth thee: wherefore I abhor myself, and repent in dust and ashes." The Lord gave me clearness to penetrate into the sweet truths contained in that text. It was a comfortable and sweet season to me.

Thursday, September 26. Was still much disordered in body, and able to ride but slowly. Continued my journey however. Near night, arrived at the Irish settlement, about fifteen miles from mine own house. This day, while riding, I was much exercised with a sense of my barrenness; and verily thought, there was no creature that had any true grace, but what was more spiritual and fruitful than I; I could not think that any of God's children made so poor a hand of living to God as I.

Friday, September 27. Spent considerable time, in the morning, in prayer and praise to God. My mind was somewhat intense in the duty, and my heart in some degree warmed with a sense of divine things: my soul was melted, to think, that "God had accounted me faithful, putting me into the ministry," notwithstanding all my barrenness and deadness. My soul was also in some measure enlarged in prayer for the dear people of my charge, as well as for other dear friends. In the afternoon, visited some Christian friends, and spent the time, I think, profitably: my heart was warmed, and more engaged in the things of God. In the evening, I enjoyed enlargement, warmth, and comfort in prayer: my soul relied on God for assistance and grace to enable me to do something in his cause: my heart was drawn out in thankfulness to God for what he had done for his own glory among my poor people of late: and I felt encouraged to proceed in his work, being persuaded of his power, and hoping *his arm* might be further *revealed*, for the enlargement of his dear kingdom: and my soul "rejoiced in hope of the glory of God," in hope of the advancement of his declarative glory in the world, as well as of enjoying him in a world of glory. Oh, blessed be God, the living God, for ever!

[He continued in this comfortable, sweet frame of mind, the two next days. On the day following, he went to his own house, in the Forks of Delaware, and continued still in the same frame. The next day, which was Tuesday, he visited his Indians.——Wednesday he spent mostly in writing the

the meditations he had had in his late journey to Susquahannah. On Thursday, he left the Forks of Delaware, and travelled towards Crosweeksung, where he arrived on Saturday, (October 5.) and continued from day to day in a comfortable state of mind. There is nothing material in his *diary* for this day and the next, but what is in his printed Journal.]

Monday, October 7. Being called by the church and people of East-Hampton on Long-Island, as a member of a council, to assist and advise in affairs of difficulty in that church, I set out on my journey this morning, before it was well light, and travelled to Elisabeth-Town, and there lodged. Enjoyed some comfort on the road, in conversation with Mr William Tennent, who was sent for on the same business.

[He prosecuted his journey with the other ministers that were sent for; and did not return till October 24. While he was at East-Hampton, the importance of the business that the council were come upon, lay with such weight on his mind, and he was so concerned for the interest of religion in that place, that he slept but little for several nights successively. In his way to and from East-Hampton, he had several seasons of sweet refreshment, wherein his soul was enlarged and comforted with divine consolations, in secret retirement; and he had special assistance in public ministerial performances in the house of God; and yet, at the same time, a sense of extreme vileness and unprofitableness. He from time to time speaks of soul-refreshment and comfort in conversation with the ministers that travelled with him; and seems to have little or nothing of melancholy, till he came to the west-end of Long-Island, in his return. After that, he was oppressed with dejection and gloominess of mind, for several days together.——For an account of the four first days after his return from his journey, I refer the reader to his public Journal.]

Monday, October 28.——Had an evening of sweet refreshing; my thoughts were raised to a blessed eternity; my soul was melted with desires of perfect holiness, and perfectly glorifying God.

Tuesday, October 29. About noon, rode and viewed the Indian lands at Cranberry: was much dejected, and greatly perplexed in mind; knew not how to see any body again, my soul was so sunk within me. Oh that these trials might make me more humble and holy. Oh that God would keep me from giving way to sinful dejection, which may hinder my usefulness.

Wednesday, October 30. My soul was refreshed with a view of the continuance of God's blessed work among the Indians.

Thursday, October 31. Spent most of the day in writing: enjoyed not much spiritual comfort; but was not so much sunk with melancholy as at some other times.

[Friday, November 1. See the public Journal.]

Saturday, November 2. Spent the day with the Indians, and wrote some things of importance; and longed to do more for God, than I did, or could do in this present feeble and imperfect state.

[November 3 and 4. See the public Journal.

Tuesday, November 5. He left the Indians, and spent the remaining part of this week in travelling to various parts of New-Jersey, in order to get a *collection* for the use of the Indians, and to obtain a *schoolmaster* to instruct them. And in the mean time, he speaks of very sweet refreshment and entertainment with Christian friends, and of his being sweetly employed, while riding, in meditation on divine subjects; his heart's being enlarged, his mind clear, his spirit refreshed with divine truths, and his "heart's burning within him, "while he went by the way, and the Lord opened to him the "scriptures."]

Lord's day, November 10. [At Elisabeth-Town] Was comfortable in the morning, both in body and mind; preached in the forenoon from 2 Cor. v. 20. God was pleased to give me freedom and fervency in my discourse; and the presence of God seemed to be in the assembly; numbers were affected, and there were many tears among them. In the afternoon, preached from Luke xiv. 22. "And yet there is room." Was favoured with divine assistance in the first prayer, and poured out my soul to God with a filial temper of mind; the living God also assisted me in sermon.

[The next day, he went to New-Town on Long-Island, to a meeting of the *Presbytery*. He speaks of some sweet meditations he had while there, on "Christ's delivering up the "kingdom to the Father;" and of his soul's being much refreshed

refreshed and warmed with the consideration of that blissful day.]

Friday, November 15. Could not cross the ferry by reason of the violence of the wind; nor could I enjoy any place of retirement at the ferry-house; so that I was in perplexity. Yet God gave me some satisfaction and sweetness in meditation, and lifting up my heart to God in the midst of company. And although some were drinking and talking profanely; which was indeed a grief to me, yet my mind was calm and composed. And I could not but bless God, that I was not like to spend an eternity in such company. In the evening, I sat down and wrote with composure and freedom; and can say (through pure grace) it was a comfortable evening to my soul, an evening I was enabled to spend in the service of God.

Saturday, November 16. Crossed the ferry about ten o'clock; arrived at Elisabeth-Town near night. Was in a calm composed frame of mind, and felt an entire resignation with respect to a loss I had lately sustained, in having my horse stolen from me the last Wednesday night, at New-Town. Had some longings of soul for the dear people of Elisabeth-Town, that God would *pour out his Spirit* upon them, and *revive his work* amongst them.

[He spent the four next days at Elisabeth-Town, for the most part, in a free and comfortable state of mind, intensely engaged in the service of God, and enjoying, at some times, the special assistances of his Spirit. On Thursday, this week, he rode to Freehold, and spent the day under considerable dejection.]

Friday, November 22. Rode to Mr Tennent's, and from thence to Crosweeksung. Had little freedom in meditation, while riding; which was a grief and burden to my soul. Oh that I could fill up all my time, whether in the house or by the way, for God! I was enabled, I think, this day to give up my soul to God, and put over all my concerns into his hands; and found some real consolation in the thought of being entirely at the divine disposal, and having no will or interest of my own. I have received my *all* from God; Oh that I could return my *all* to God! Surely God is worthy of my highest affection, and most devout adoration; he is infinitely worthy, that I should make him my last end, and live for ever to him: Oh that I might never more, in any one instance, live to myself!

Saturday, November 23. Visited my people; spent the day with them: wrote some things of importance. But was pretty much dejected, most of the day.

[There is nothing very material in his *diary* for the four next days, but what is also in his public Journal.]

Thursday, November 28.——I enjoyed some divine comfort, and fervency in the public exercise, and afterwards. And while riding to my lodgings, was favoured with some sweet meditations on Luke ix. 31. "Who appeared in glory, "and spake of his decease, which he should accomplish at "Jerusalem." My thoughts ran with freedom, and I saw and felt what a glorious subject the *death* of CHRIST is for *glorified* souls to dwell upon in their conversation. Oh, the *death* of CHRIST! how infinitely *precious!*

[For the three next days, see the public Journal.]

Monday, December 2. Was much affected with grief, that I had not lived more to God; and felt strong resolutions to double my diligence in my Master's service.

[After this, he went to a meeting of the *Presbytery*, at a place in New-Jersey, called *Connecticut-Farms;* which occasioned his absence from his people the rest of this week. He speaks of some seasons of sweetness, solemnity, and spiritual affection in his absence.

Lord's day, December 8. See his public Journal.]

Monday, December 9. Spent most of the day in procuring provisions, in order to my setting up house-keeping among the Indians. Enjoyed little satisfaction through the day, being very much out of my element.

Tuesday, December 10. Was engaged in the same business as yesterday. Towards night, got into my own house *.

Wednesday, December 11. Spent the forenoon in necessary labour about my house. In the afternoon, rode out

* This is the *third* house that he built to dwell in by himself among the Indians: the first at Kaunaumeek in the county of Albany; the second at the Forks of Delaware in Pensylvania; and now this at Crosweeksung in New-Jersey.

upon

upon business, and spent the evening with some satisfaction among friends in conversation on a serious and profitable subject.

[Thursday, December 12. See his public Journal.]

Friday, December 13. Spent the day mainly in labour about my house. In the evening, spent some time in writing; but was very weary, and much outdone with the labour of the day.

Saturday, December 14. Rose early, and wrote by candlelight some considerable time; spent most of the day in writing: but was somewhat dejected. In the evening, was exercised with a pain in my head.

[For the two next days, see his public Journal. The remainder of this week he spent chiefly in writing: some part of the time under a degree of melancholy; but some part of it with a sweet ardency in religion.]

Saturday, December 21.——After my labours with the Indians, I spent some time in writing some things divine and solemn; and was much wearied with the labours of the day; found that my spirits were extremely spent, and that I could do no more. I am conscious to myself that my labours are as great and constant as my nature will bear, and that ordinarily I go to the extent of my strength; so that I do all I can: but the misery is, I do not labour with that *heavenly* temper, that single eye to the *glory* of God, that I long for.

[Lord's day, December 22. See the public Journal.]

Monday, and Tuesday, December 23. and 24. Spent these days in writing, with the utmost diligence. Felt in the main a sweet mortification to the world, and a desire to live and labour only for God; but wanted more warmth and spirituality, a more sensible and affectionate regard to the glory of God.

[Wednesday, December 25. See the public Journal.]

Thursday, and Friday, December 26. and 27. Laboured in my studies, to the utmost of my strength: and though I felt a steady disposition of mind to live to God, and that I had

had nothing in this world to live for; yet I did not find that sensible affection in the service of God, that I wanted to have; my heart seemed barren, though my head and hands were full of labour.

[For the four next days, see his public Journal *.]

Wednesday, January 1. 1745-6.——I am this day beginning a *New Year;* and God has carried me through numerous trials and labours in the past. He has amazingly supported my feeble frame; for "having obtained help of God, I continue to this day." O that I might live nearer to God, this year, than I did the last! The business I have been called to, and enabled to go through, I know, has been as great as nature could bear up under, and what would have sunk and overcome me quite, without special support. But alas, alas! though I have done the labours, and endured the trials, with what spirit have I done the one, and borne the other? how cold has been the frame of my heart oftentimes! and how little have I sensibly eyed the glory of God, in all my doings and sufferings! I have found, that I could have no peace without filling up all my time with labours; and thus "necessity has been laid upon me;" yea, in that respect, I have loved to labour: but the misery is, I could not sensibly labour *for God*, as I would have done. May I for the future be enabled more sensibly to make the glory of God my *all!*

[For the space from this time till the next Monday, see the public Journal.]

Monday, January 6. Being very weak in body, I rode for my health. While riding, my thoughts were sweetly engaged, for a time, upon "the stone cut out of the mountain "without hands, which brake in pieces" all before it, and "waxed great, and became a great mountain, and filled the "whole earth:" and I longed that Jesus should "take to "himself his great power, and reign to the ends of the earth." And Oh, how sweet were the moments, wherein I felt my soul warm with hopes of the enlargement of the Redeemer's kingdom! I wanted nothing else but that Christ should reign, to the glory of his blessed name.

* On the first of these days he wrote the *sixth letter* here published at the end.

[The

[The next day he complains of want of fervency.]

Wednesday, January 8. In the evening, my heart was drawn out after God in secret: my soul was refreshed and quickened; and I trust, faith was in exercise. I had great hopes of the ingathering of precious souls to Christ; not only among my own people, but others also. I was sweetly resigned and composed under my bodily weakness; and was willing to live or die, and desirous to labour for God to the utmost of my strength.

Thursday, January 9. Was still very weak, and much exercised with vapoury disorders. In the evening, enjoyed some enlargement and spirituality in prayer. Oh that I could always spend my time profitably, both in health and weakness!

Friday, January 10. My soul was in a sweet, calm, composed frame, and my heart filled with love to all the world; and Christian simplicity and tenderness seemed then to prevail and reign within me. Near night, visited a serious baptist minister, and had some agreeable conversation with him; and found that I could taste God in friends.

[For the four next days, see the public Journal.]

Wednesday, January 15. My spirits were very low and flat, and I could not but think I was a burden to God's earth; and could scarcely look any body in the face, through shame and sense of barrenness. God pity a poor unprofitable creature!

[The two next days, he had some comfort and refreshment. For the two following days, see the public Journal.

The next day, he set out on a journey to Elisabeth-Town, to confer with the *Correspondents*, at their meeting there; and enjoyed much spiritual refreshment from day to day, through this week. The things expressed in this space of time, are such as these; serenity, composure, sweetness, and tenderness of soul; thanksgiving to God for his success among the Indians; delight in prayer and praise; sweet and profitable meditations on various divine subjects; longing for more love, for more vigour to live to God, for a life more entirely devoted to God, that he might spend all his time profitably for God and in his cause; conversing on spiritual subjects with affection; and lamentation for unprofitableness.]

Lord's

Lord's day, January 26. [At Connecticut-Farms] Was calm and composed. Was made sensible of my utter inability to preach, without divine help; and was in some good measure willing to leave it with God, to give or with-hold assistance, as he saw would be most for his own glory. Was favoured with a considerable degree of assistance in my public work. After public worship, I was in a sweet and solemn frame of mind, thankful to God that he had made me in some measure faithful in addressing precious souls, but grieved that I had been no more fervent in my work; and was tenderly affected towards all the world, longing that every sinner might be saved; and could not have entertained any bitterness towards the worst enemy living. In the evening, rode to Elisabeth-Town: while riding, was almost constantly engaged in lifting up my heart to God, lest I should lose that sweet heavenly solemnity and composure of soul I then enjoyed. Afterwards, was pleased, to think, that God *reigneth*; and thought, I could never be uneasy with any of his dispensations; but must be entirely satisfied, whatever trials he should cause me or his church to encounter. Never felt more sedateness, divine serenity and composure of mind: could freely have left the dearest earthly friend, for the society of "angels, and spirits of just men made perfect:" my affections soared aloft to the blessed Author of every dear enjoyment: I viewed the emptiness and unsatisfactory nature of the most desirable earthly objects, any further than God is seen in them: and longed for a life of spirituality and inward purity; without which, I saw, there could be no true pleasure.

[He retained a great degree of this excellent frame of mind, the four next days. As to his public services for and among the Indians, and his success in this time, see the public Journal.]

Saturday, February 1. Towards night, enjoyed some of the clearest thoughts on a divine subject (*viz.* that treated of 1 Cor. xv. 13.—16.) that ever I remember to have had upon any subject whatsoever; and spent two or three hours in writing them. I was refreshed with this intenseness: my mind was so engaged in these meditations, I could scarcely turn it to any thing else; and indeed I could not be willing to part with so sweet an entertainment.——

Lord's day, February 2.——After public worship, my bodily strength being much spent, my spirits sunk amazingly; and especially on hearing that I was so generally taken to be a

Roman

Roman Catholic, sent by the Papists to draw the Indians into an insurrection against the English, that some were in fear of me, and others were for having me taken up by authority and punished. Alas, what will not the devil do to bring a slur and disgrace on the work of God! Oh, how holy and circumspect had I need to be! Through divine goodness, I have been enabled to "mind my own business," in these parts, as well as elsewhere; and to let all men, and all denominations of men alone, as to their *party-notions*; and only preached the plain and necessary truths of *Christianity*, neither inviting to, nor excluding from *my meeting* any, of any sort or persuasion whatsoever. Towards night, the Lord gave me freedom at the throne of grace, in my first prayer before my *catechetical* lecture and in opening the xlvith Psalm to my people, my soul confided in God, although the wicked world should slander and persecute me, or even condemn and execute me as a traitor to my king and country. Truly God is a "present help in time of trouble." In the evening, my soul was in some measure comforted, having some hope that one poor soul was brought home to God this day; though the case did by no means appear clear. Oh that I could fill up every moment of time, during my abode here below, in the service of my God and King.

Monday, February 3. My spirits were still much sunk with what I heard the day before, of my being suspected to be engaged in the *Pretender's* interest: it grieved me, that after there had been so much evidence of a glorious *work of grace* among these poor Indians, as that the most carnal men could not but take notice of the great *change* made among them, so many poor souls should still suspect the whole to be only a *Popish* plot, and so cast an awful reproach on this blessed work of the divine Spirit; and at the same time wholly exclude themselves from receiving any benefit by this divine influence. This put me upon searching whether I had ever dropped any thing inadvertently, that might give *occasion* to any to suspect that I was stirring up the Indians against the English: and could think of nothing, unless it was my attempting sometimes to vindicate the rights of the Indians, and complaining of the horrid practice of making the Indians drunk, and then cheating them out of their lands and other properties: and once, I remembered, I had done this with too much warmth of spirit. And this much distressed me; thinking that this might possibly prejudise them against this work of grace, to their everlasting destruction. God, I believe, did me good

 by

by this trial; which served to humble me, and shew me the necessity of watchfulness, and of being "wise as a serpent," as well as "harmless as a dove." This exercise led me often to the throne of grace; and there I found some support: though I could not get the burden wholly removed. Was assisted in prayer, especially in the evening.

[He remained still under a degree of exercise of mind about this affair; which continued to have the same effect upon him, to cause him to reflect upon, and humble himself, and frequent the throne of grace: but soon found himself much more relieved and supported. He was, this week, in an extremely weak state, and obliged (as he expresses it) "to consume considerable time in diversions for his health."

For Saturday, February 7. and the Sabbath following, see his public Journal.

The Monday after, he set out on a journey to the Forks of Delaware, to visit the Indians there. He performed the journey under great weakness, and sometimes was exercised with much pain; but says nothing of dejection and melancholy. He arrived at his own house at the Forks, on Friday. The things appertaining to his inward frames and exercises, expressed within this week, are, sweet composure of mind; thankfulness to God for his mercies to him and others; resignation to the divine will; comfort in prayer and religious conversation; his heart drawn out after God, and affected with a sense of his own barrenness, as well as the fulness and freeness of divine grace.]

Lord's day, February 16.——In the evening, was in a sweet composed frame of mind. It was exceeding refreshing and comfortable, to think, that God had been with me, affording me some good measure of assistance. I then found freedom and sweetness in prayer and thanksgiving to God; and found my soul sweetly engaged and enlarged in prayer for dear friends and acquaintance. Blessed be the name of the Lord, that ever I am enabled to do any thing for his dear interest and kingdom. Blessed be God who enables me to be faithful. Enjoyed more resolution and courage for God, and more refreshment of spirit, than I have been favoured with for many weeks past.

Monday, February 17.——I was refreshed and encouraged: found a spirit of prayer, in the evening, and earnest longings for the illumination and conversion of these poor Indians.

[Tuesday,

[Tuesday, February 18. See the public Journal.]

Wednesday, February 19.——My heart was comforted and refreshed, and my soul filled with longings for the conversion of the Indians here.

Thursday, February 20.—— God was pleased to support and refresh my spirits, by affording me assistance this day, and so hopeful a prospect of success; and I returned home rejoicing, and blessing the name of the Lord; and found freedom and sweetness afterwards in secret prayer, and had my soul drawn out for dear friends. Oh, how blessed a thing is it, to labour for God faithfully, and with encouragement of success! Blessed be the Lord for ever and ever, for the assistance and comfort granted this day.

Friday, February 21.——My soul was refreshed and comforted, and I could not but bless God, who had enabled me in some good measure to be faithful in the day past. Oh, how sweet it is to be spent and worn out for God!

Saturday, February 22.——My spirits were much supported, though my bodily strength was much wasted. Oh that God would be gracious to the souls of these poor Indians!

God has been very gracious to me this week: he has enabled me to preach every day; and has given me some assistance, and encouraging prospect of success in almost every sermon. Blessed be his name. Divers of the white people have been awakened this week, and sundry of the Indians much cured of their prejudices and jealousies they had conceived against Christianity, and some seem to be really awakened.

[Lord's day, February 23. See the public Journal.

The next day, he left the Forks of Delaware, to return to Crosweeksung; and spent the whole week till Saturday, before he arrived there; but preached by the way every day, excepting one; and was several times greatly assisted; and had much inward comfort, and earnest longings to fill up all his time with the service of God. He utters such expressions as these, after preaching: "Oh that I may be enabled to "plead the cause of God faithfully, to my dying moment! "Oh how sweet it would be to spend myself wholly for "God, and in his cause, and to be freed from selfish motives "in my labours!"

For Saturday and Lord's day, March 1. and 2. see the public Journal. The four next days were spent in great bodily weakness; but he speaks of some seasons of considerable inward comfort.]

Thursday, March 6. I walked alone in the evening, and enjoyed sweetness and comfort in prayer, beyond what I have o late enjoyed: my soul rejoiced in my *pilgrimage state*, and I was delighted with the thoughts of labouring and *enduring hardness* for God: felt some longing desires to preach the gospel to dear immortal souls; and confided in God, that *he* would be *with me* in my work, and that he "never would "leave nor forsake me," to the end of my race. Oh, may I "obtain mercy of God to be faithful," to my dying moment!

Friday, March 7. In the afternoon, went on in my work with freedom and cheerfulness, God assisting me; and enjoyed comfort in the evening.

[For the two next days, see the public Journal.]

Monday, March 10.——My soul was refreshed with freedom and enlargement, and (I hope) the lively exercise of faith, in secret prayer, this night: my will was sweetly resigned to the divine will, and my hopes respecting the enlargement of the dear kingdom of Christ somewhat raised, and could commit Zion's cause to God as his own.

[On Tuesday he speaks of some sweetness and spirituality in Christian conversation. On Wednesday, complains that he enjoyed not much comfort and satisfaction, through the day, because he did but little for God. On Thursday, spent considerable time in company, on a special occasion; but in perplexity, because without savoury religious conversation. For Friday, Saturday, and Lord's day, see the public Journal.

In the former part of the week following he was very ill; and also under great dejection; being, as he apprehended, rendered unserviceable by his illness, and fearing that he should never be serviceable any more; and therefore exceedingly longed for death. But afterwards was more encouraged, and life appeared more desirable; because (as he says) he "had a "little dawn of hope, that he might be useful in the world." In the latter part of the week, he was in some measure relieved of his illness, in the use of means prescribed by a physician.

For Saturday and Lord's day, March 22. and 23. see his public Journal.]

Monday, March 24.——After the Indians were gone to their

their work, to clear their lands, I got alone, and poured out my soul to God, that he would smile upon these feeble beginnings, and that he would settle an Indian town, that might be *a mountain of holiness*; and found my soul much refreshed in these petitions, and much enlarged for Zion's interest, and for numbers of dear friends in particular. My sinking spirits were revived and raised, and I felt animated in the service God has called me to. This was the dearest hour I have enjoyed for many days, if not weeks. I found an encouraging hope, that something would be done for God, and that God would use and help me in his work. And Oh, how sweet were the thoughts of labouring for God, when I felt any spirit and courage, and had any hope that ever I should be succeeded!

[The next day, his *schoolmaster* was taken sick with a pleurisy; and he spent great part of the remainder of this week in tending him; which in his weak state was almost an over-bearing burden to him; he being obliged constantly to wait upon him, all day, from day to day, and to lie on the floor at night. His spirits sunk in a considerable degree, with his bodily strength, under this burden.

For Saturday and Lord's day, March 29. and 30. see the public Journal.]

Monday, March 31. Towards night, enjoyed some sweet meditations on those words: "It is good for me to draw "near to God." My soul, I think, had some sweet sense of what is intended in those words.

[The next day, he was extremely busy in tending the schoolmaster, and in some other necessary affairs, that greatly diverted him from what he looked upon as his proper business: but yet speaks of comfort and refreshment, at some times of the day.]

Wednesday, April 2. Was somewhat exercised with a spiritless frame of mind. Was a little relieved and refreshed in the evening, with meditation alone in the woods. But, alas! my days pass away as the *chaff!* it is but little I do, or can do, that turns to any account; and it is my constant misery and burden, that I am so fruitless in the vineyard of the Lord. Oh that I were *spirit*, that I might be active for God. This (I think) more than any thing else, makes me long, that "this "corruptible might put on incorruption, and this mortal

"put

"put on immortality." God deliver me from clogs, fetters, and a *body of death*, that impede my service for him.

[The next day, he complains bitterly of some exercises by corruption he found in his own heart.]

Friday, April 4. Spent most of the day in writing on Rev. xxii. 17. "And whosoever will," &c. Enjoyed some freedom and encouragement in my work; and found some comfort and composure in prayer.

Saturday, April 5.——After public worship, a number of my dear Christian Indians came to my house; with whom I felt a sweet union of soul: my heart was knit to them; and I cannot say, I have felt such a sweet and fervent *love to the brethren*, for some time past: and I saw in them appearances of the same love. This gave me something of a view of the heavenly state; and particularly that part of the happiness of heaven, which consists in the *communion of saints*: and this was affecting to me.

[For the two next days, see the public Journal.

On Tuesday, he went to a meeting of the Presbytery appointed at Elisabeth-Town. In his way thither, he enjoyed some sweet meditations: but after he came there, he was (as he expresses it) very *vapoury and melancholy, and under an awful gloom*, that oppressed his mind. And this continued till Saturday-evening, when he began to have some relief and encouragement. He spent the Sabbath at Staten-Island; where he preached to an assembly of Dutch and English, and enjoyed considerable refreshment and comfort, both in public and private. In the evening he returned to Elisabeth-Town.]

Monday, April 14. My spirits this day were raised and refreshed, and my mind composed, so that I was in a comfortable frame of soul, most of the day. In the evening my head was clear, my mind serene; I enjoyed sweetness in secret prayer, and meditation on Psal. lxxiii. 28. Oh, how free, how comfortable, chearful, and yet solemn, do I feel when I am in a good measure freed from those damps and melancholy glooms, that I often labour under! And blessed be the Lord, I find myself relieved in this respect.

Tuesday, April 15. My soul longed for more spirituality; and it was my burden, that I could do no more for God. Oh, my barrenness is my daily affliction and heavy load! Oh, how precious is time: and how it pains me, to see it slide away,

way, while I do so very little to any good purpose! Oh that God would make me more fruitful and spiritual.

[The next day, he speaks of his being almost overwhelmed with vapoury disorders; but yet not so as wholly to destroy the composure of his mind.]

Thursday, April 17. Enjoyed some comfort in prayer, some freedom in meditation, and composure in my studies. Spent some time in writing, in the forenoon. In the afternoon, spent some time in conversation with several dear ministers. In the evening, preached from Psal. lxxiii. 28. "But it is good for me to draw near to God." God helped me to feel the truth of my text, both in the first prayer and in sermon. I was enabled to pour out my soul to God, with great freedom, fervency, and affection: and, blessed be the Lord, it was a comfortable season to me. I was enabled to speak with tenderness, and yet with faithfulness: and divine truths seemed to fall with weight and influence upon the hearers. My heart was melted for the dear assembly, and I loved every body in it; and scarce ever felt more love to immortal souls in my life; my soul cried, "Oh that the dear "creatures might be saved! O that God would have mercy "on them!"

[He seems to have been in a very comfortable frame of mind the two next days.]

Lord's day, April 20. * Enjoyed some freedom, and, I hope, exercise of faith in prayer, in the morning; especially when I came to pray for Zion. I was free from that gloomy discouragement, that so often oppresses my mind; and my soul rejoiced in the hopes of Zion's prosperity, and the enlargement of the dear kingdom of the great Redeemer. O that his kingdom might come.——

Monday, April 21. Was composed and comfortable in mind, most of the day; was mercifully freed from those gloomy damps that I am frequently exercised with: had freedom and comfort in prayer, several times; especially had some rising hopes of Zion's enlargement and prosperity. And Oh, how refreshing were these hopes to my soul! Oh that the kingdom of the dear Lord might come. Oh that the poor Indians might quickly be gathered in, in great numbers!

* This day he entered into the 29th year of his age.

Tuesday,

Tuesday, April 22. My mind was remarkably free, this day, from melancholy damps and glooms, and animated in my work. I found such fresh vigour and resolution in the service of God, that the *mountains* seemed to become a *plain* before me. Oh, blessed be God for an interval of refreshment, and fervent resolution in my Lord's work! In the evening, my soul was refreshed in secret prayer, and my heart drawn out for divine blessings; especially for the church of God, and his interest among my own people, and for dear friends in remote places. Oh that Zion might prosper, and precious souls be brought home to God!

[In this comfortable fervent frame of mind he remained the two next days.

For the four days next following, *viz.* Friday, Saturday, Lord's day, and Monday, see his public Journal.——On Tuesday he went to Elisabeth-Town, to attend the meeting of the Presbytery there: and seemed to spend the time, while absent from his people on this occasion, in a free and comfortable state of mind.]

Saturday, May 3. Rode from Elisabeth-Town home to my people, at or near Cranberry; whither they are now removed, and where, I hope, God will settle them as a Christian congregation. Was refreshed in lifting up my heart to God, while riding; and enjoyed a thankful frame of spirit, for divine favours received the week past. Was somewhat uneasy and dejected, in the evening; having no house of my own to go into in this place: but God was my support.

[For Lord's day and Monday, see the public Journal.]

Tuesday, May 6. Enjoyed some spirit and courage in my work; was in a good measure free from melancholy: blessed be God for freedom from this *death*.

Wednesday, May 7. Spent most of the day in writing, as usual. Enjoyed some freedom in my work. Was favoured with some comfortable meditations, this day. In the evening, was in a sweet composed frame of mind; was pleased and delighted to leave all with God, respecting myself, for time and eternity, and respecting the people of my charge, and dear friends: had no doubt but that God would take care of me, and of his own interest among my people; and was

enabled

enabled to use freedom in prayer, as a child with a tender father. Oh, how sweet is such a frame!

Thursday, May 8. In the evening, was somewhat refreshed with divine things, and enjoyed a tender melting frame in secret prayer, wherein my soul was drawn out for the interest of Zion, and comforted with the lively hope of the appearing of the kingdom of the great Redeemer. These were sweet moments: I felt almost loth to go to bed, and grieved that sleep was necessary. However, I lay down with a tender reverential fear of God, sensible that "his favour is "life," and his smiles better than all that earth can boast of, infinitely better than life itself.

[Friday May 9. See the public Journal.]

Saturday, May 10. Rode to Allen's-Town, to assist in the administration of the Lord's supper. In the afternoon, preached from Tit. ii. 14. "Who gave himself for us," &c. God was pleased to carry me through with some competency of freedom; and yet to deny me that enlargement and power I longed for. In the evening, my soul mourned, and could not but mourn, that I had treated so excellent a subject in so defective a manner, that I had borne so broken a testimony for so worthy and glorious a Redeemer. And if my discourse had met with the utmost applause from all the world, (as I accidentally heard it applauded by some persons of judgment), it would not have given me any satisfaction: Oh, it grieved me, to think, that I had had no more holy warmth and fervency, that I had been no more melted in discoursing of Christ's death, and the end and design of it! Afterwards, enjoyed some freedom and fervency in secret and family prayer, and longed much for the presence of God to attend his word and ordinances the next day.

Lord's day, May 11. Assisted in the administration of the Lord's supper; but enjoyed little enlargement: was grieved and sunk with some things I thought undesirable, &c. In the afternoon, went to the house of God weak and sick in soul, as well as feeble in body: and longed, that the people might be entertained and edified with divine truths, and that an honest fervent testimony might be borne for God; but knew not how it was possible for *me* to do any thing of that kind, to any good purpose. Yet God, who is rich in mercy, was pleased to give me assistance, both in prayer and preaching: God helped me to wrestle for his presence, in prayer, and to tell him, that he had promised, "Where two or three are met "together in his name, there he would be in the midst of "them;" and that we were, at least some of us, so met; and pleaded, that for his truth's sake he would be with us. And blessed be God, it was sweet to my soul, thus to plead, and rely on God's promises. Discoursed upon Luke ix. 30. 31. "And behold, there talked with him two men, which "were Moses and Elias; who appeared in glory, and spake "of his decease, which he should accomplish at Jerusalem." Enjoyed special freedom, from the beginning to the end of my discourse, without interruption. Things pertinent to the subject were abundantly presented to my view; and such a fulness of matter, that I scarce knew how to dismiss the various heads and particulars I had occasion to touch upon. And, blessed be the Lord, I was favoured with some fervency and power, as well as freedom; so that the word of God seemed to awaken the attention of a stupid audience, to a considerable degree. I was inwardly refreshed with the consolations of God; and could with my whole heart say, "Though there be no fruit in the vine, &c. yet will I re-"joice in the Lord." After public service, was refreshed with the sweet conversation of some Christian friends.

[The four next days seem to have been mostly spent with spiritual comfort and profit.]

Friday, May 16. Near night, enjoyed some agreeable and sweet conversation with a dear minister, which, I trust, was blessed to my soul: my heart was warmed, and my soul engaged to live to God; so that I longed to exert myself with more vigour, than ever I had done, in his cause: and those words were quickening to me, "Herein is my Father glori-"fied, that ye bring forth much fruit." Oh, my soul longed, and wished, and prayed, to be enabled to live to God with utmost constancy and ardour! In the evening, God was pleased to shine upon me in secret prayer, and draw out my soul after himself; and I had freedom in supplication for myself, but much more in intercession for others: so that I was sweetly constrained to say, "Lord, use me as thou wilt; "do as thou wilt with me: but Oh, promote thine own "cause! Zion is thine; Oh visit thine heritage! Oh let thy "kingdom come! Oh let thy blessed interest be advanced "in the world!" When I attempted to look to God, respecting my worldly circumstances, and his providential dealings with me, in regard of my settling down in my congregation, which seems to be necessary, and yet very difficult, and

and contrary to my fixed intention for years past, as well as my disposition, which has been, and still is, at times especially, to go forth, and spend my life in preaching the gospel from place to place, and gathering souls *afar off* to Jesus the great Redeemer; when I attempted to look to God with regard to these things, and his designs concerning me, I could only say, "The will of the Lord be done: it is no matter "for me." The same frame of mind I felt with respect to another important affair I have lately had some serious thoughts of: I could say, with utmost calmness and composure, "Lord, if it be most for thy glory, let me proceed "in it; but if thou seest that it will in any wise hinder my "usefulness in thy cause, Oh prevent my proceeding: for "all I want, respecting this world, is such circumstances as "may best capacitate me to do service for God in the world." But blessed be God, I enjoyed liberty in prayer for my dear flock, and was enabled to pour out my soul into the bosom of a tender Father: my heart within me was melted, when I came to plead for my dear people, and for the kingdom of Christ in general. Oh, how sweet was this evening to my soul! I knew not how to go to bed; and when got to bed, longed for some way to improve time for God, to some excellent purpose. "Bless the Lord, O my soul."

Saturday, May 17. Walked out in the morning, and felt much of the same frame I enjoyed the evening before: had my heart enlarged in praying for the advancement of the kingdom of Christ, and found utmost freedom in leaving all my concerns with God.

I find *discouragement* to be an exceeding *hindrance* to my spiritual fervency and affection: but when God enables me sensibly to find that I have done something *for him*, this refreshes and animates me, so that I could break through all hardships, undergo any labours, and nothing seems too much either to do or to suffer. But Oh, what a death it is, to strive, and strive; to be always in a *hurry*, and yet do *nothing*, or at least nothing *for* God! Alas, alas, that time flies away, and I do so little for God!

Lord's day, May 18. I felt my own utter insufficiency for my work: God made me to see, that I was a *child*; yea, that I was a *fool*. I discoursed, both parts of the day, from Rev. iii. 20. "Behold, I stand at the door, and knock." God gave me freedom and power in the latter part of my (forenoon's) discourse; although, in the former part of it, I felt peevish and provoked with the unmannerly behaviour of the *white* people, who crouded in between my people and me; which proved a great temptation to me. But blessed be God, I got these shackles off before the middle of my discourse, and was favoured with a sweet frame of spirit in the latter part of the exercise; was full of love, warmth, and tenderness, in addressing my dear people.——In the intermission-season, could not but discourse to my people on the kindness and patience of Christ in *standing* and *knocking at the door*, &c.——In the evening, I was grieved, that I had done so little for God. Oh that I could be *a flame of fire* in the service of my God!

[Monday, May 19. See the public Journal.

On Tuesday, he complains of want of freedom and comfort; but had some return of these on Wednesday.]

Thursday, May 22. In the evening, was in a frame somewhat remarkable: had apprehended for several days before, that it was the design of providence I should *settle* among my people here; and had in my own mind begun to make provision for it, and to contrive means to hasten it; and found my heart something engaged in it, hoping I might then enjoy more agreeable circumstances of life, in several respects: and yet was never fully determined, never quite pleased with the thoughts of being settled and confined to one place. Nevertheless I seemed to have some freedom in that respect, because the congregation I thought of settling with, was one that God had enabled me to gather from amongst Pagans. For I never since I began to preach, could feel any freedom to "enter in-"to other mens labours," and settle down in the ministry where the "gospel was preached before;" I never could make that appear to be my providence: when I felt any disposition to consult my ease and worldly comfort, God has never given me any liberty in that respect, either since, or for some years before I began to preach. But God having succeeded my labours, and made me instrumental of gathering a church for him among these Indians, I was ready to think, it might be his design to give me a quiet settlement and a stated home of my own. And this, considering the late frequent sinking and failure of my spirits, and the need I stood in of some agreeable society, and my great desire of enjoying conveniencies and opportunities for profitable studies, was not altogether disagreeable to me: although I still wanted to go about far and wide, in order to spread the blessed gospel among benighted souls, far remote; yet I never had been so willing to settle

in

in any one place, for more than five years past, as I was in the foregoing part of this week. But now these thoughts seemed to be wholly dashed to pieces; not by necessity, but of choice: for it appeared to me, that God's dealings towards me had fitted me for a life of solitariness and hardship; it appeared to me I had nothing to lose, nothing to do with earth, and consequently nothing to lose by a total renunciation of it: and it appeared just right, that I should be destitute of house and home, and many comforts of life, which I rejoiced to see others of God's people enjoy. And at the same time, I saw so much of the excellency of Christ's kingdom, and the infinite desirableness of its advancement in the world, that it swallowed up all my other thoughts; and made me willing, yea, even rejoice, to be made a pilgrim or hermit in the wilderness, to my dying moment, if I might thereby promote the blessed interest of the great Redeemer. And if ever my soul presented itself to God for his service, without any reserve of any kind, it did so now. The language of my thoughts and disposition (although I spake no words) now were, "*Here I am, Lord, send me;* send me to *the ends of* "*the earth;* send me to the rough, the savage Pagans of the "wilderness; send me from all that is called comfort in earth, "or earthly comfort; send me even to death itself, if it be "but in thy service, and to promote thy kingdom." And at the same time I had as quick and lively a sense of the value of worldly comforts, as ever I had; but only saw them infinitely overmatched by the worth of Christ's kingdom, and the propagation of his blessed gospel. The quiet settlement, the certain place of abode, the tender friendship, which I thought I might be likely to enjoy in consequence of such circumstances, appeared as valuable to me, considered absolutely and in themselves, as ever before; but considered comparatively, they appeared nothing; compared with the value and preciousness of an enlargement of Christ's kingdom, they vanished like the stars before the rising sun. And sure I am, that although the comfortable accommodations of life appeared valuable and dear to me, yet I did surrender and resign myself, soul and body, to the service of God, and promotion of Christ's kingdom; though it should be in the loss of them all. And I could not do any other, because I could not will or chuse any other. I was constrained, and yet chose, to say, "Farewell, friends and earthly comforts, the dearest of "them all, the very dearest, if the Lord calls for it; adieu, "adieu; I'll spend my life, to my latest moments, *in caves* "*and dens of the earth,* if the kingdom of Christ may thereby

"be

"be advanced." I found extraordinary freedom at this time in pouring out my soul to God, for his cause; and especially that his kingdom might be extended among the Indians, far remote; and I had a great and strong hope, that God would do it. I continued wrestling with God in prayer for my dear little flock here; and more especially for the Indians elsewhere; as well as for dear friends in one place and another; till it was bed-time, and I feared I should hinder the family, &c. But Oh, with what reluctancy did I find myself obliged to consume time in sleep! I longed to be as *a flame of fire*, continually glowing in the divine service, preaching and building up Christ's kingdom, to my latest, my dying moment.

Friday, May 23. In the morning, was in the same frame of mind, as in the evening before. The glory of Christ's kingdom so much outshone the pleasure of earthly accommodations and enjoyments, that they appeared comparatively nothing, though in themselves good and desirable. My soul was melted in secret meditation and prayer, and I found myself divorced from any part in this world; so that in those affairs that seemed of the greatest importance to me, in respect of the present life, and those wherein the tender powers of the mind are most sensibly touched, I could only say, "The will "of the Lord be done." But just the same things that I felt the evening before, I felt now; and found the same freedom in prayer for the people of my charge, for the propagation of the gospel among the Indians, and for the enlargement and spiritual welfare of Zion in general, and my dear friends in particular, now, as I did then; and longed to burn out in one continued flame for God. Retained much of the same frame through the day. In the evening, was visited by my brother John Brainerd: the first visit I have ever received from any near relative, since I have been a missionary. Felt the same frame of spirit in the evening, as in the morning; and found that "it was good for me to draw near to God," and leave all my concerns and burdens with him. Was enlarged and refreshed in pouring out my soul for the propagation of the gospel of the Redeemer among the distant tribes of Indians. Blessed be God. If ever I filled up a day with studies and devotion, I was enabled so to fill up this day.

Saturday, May 24.——Enjoyed this day something of the same frame of mind as I felt the day before.

[Lord's day, May 25. See the public Journal.

This week, at least the former part of it, he was in a very weak state: but yet seems to have been free from melancholy, which

which often had attended the failing of his bodily strength. He from time to time speaks of comfort and inward refreshment, this week.

Lord's day, June 1. See the public Journal.]

Monday, June 2. In the evening, enjoyed some freedom in secret prayer and meditation.

Tuesday, June 3. My soul rejoiced, early in the morning, to think, that all things were at God's dispofal. Oh, it pleased me to leave them there! Felt afterwards much as I did, on Thursday evening, May 22. last; and continued in this frame for several hours. Walked out into the wilderness, and enjoyed freedom, fervency, and comfort, in prayer: and again enjoyed the same in the evening.

Wednesday, June 4. Spent the day in writing, and enjoyed some comfort, satisfaction, and freedom in my work. In the evening, I was favoured with a sweet refreshing frame of soul in secret prayer and meditation. Prayer was now wholly turned into praise, and I could do little else but try to adore and bless the living God: the wonders of his grace displayed in gathering to himself a church among the poor Indians here, were the subject-matter of my meditation, and the occasion of exciting my soul to praise and bless his name. My soul was scarce ever more disposed to inquire, "What I should "render to God for all his benefits," than at this time. Oh, I was brought into a strait, a sweet and happy strait, to know what to do! I longed to make some returns to God; but found I had nothing to return: I could only rejoice, that God had done the work himself; and that none in heaven or earth might pretend to share the honour of it with him; I could only be glad, that God's declarative glory was advanced by the conversion of these souls, and that it was to the enlargement of his kingdom in the world: but saw I was so poor, that I had nothing to offer to him. My soul and body, through grace, I could cheerfully surrender to him: but it appeared to me, this was rather a cumber, than a gift; and nothing could I do to glorify his dear and blessed name. Yet I was glad at heart, that he was unchangeably possessed of glory and blessedness. Oh that he might be adored and praised by all his intelligent creatures, to the utmost of their power and capacities! My soul would have rejoiced to see others praise him, though I could do nothing towards it myself.

[The next day, he speaks of his being subject to some degree

gree of melancholy; but of being something relieved in the evening.

Friday, June 6. See the public Journal.]

Saturday, June 7.——Rode to Freehold to assist Mr Tennent in the administration of the Lord's supper. In the afternoon, preached from Psal. lxxiii. 28. God gave me some freedom and warmth in my discourse: and I trust, his presence was in the assembly. Was comfortably composed, and enjoyed a thankful frame of spirit; and my soul was grieved that I could not render something to God for his benefits bestowed. Oh that I could be swallowed up in his praise!

Lord's day, June 8. Spent much time, in the morning, in secret duties; but between hope and fear, respecting the enjoyment of God in the business of the day then before us. Was agreeably entertained, in the forenoon, by a discourse from Mr Tennent, and felt somewhat melted and refreshed. In the season of communion, enjoyed some comfort; and especially in serving one of the tables. Blessed be the Lord, it was a *time of refreshing* to me, and I trust to many others. A number of my dear people sat down by themselves at the last table; at which time God seemed to be in the midst of them.——And the thoughts of what God had done among them were refreshing and melting to me. In the afternoon, God enabled me to preach with uncommon freedom, from 2 Cor. v. 20. Through the great goodness of God, I was favoured with a constant flow of pertinent matter, and proper expressions, from the beginning to the end of my discourse. In the evening, I could not but rejoice in God, and bless him for the manifestations of grace in the day past. Oh, it was a sweet and solemn day and evening! a season of comfort to the godly, and of awakening to some souls. Oh that I could praise the Lord!

Monday, June 9. Enjoyed some sweetness in secret duties.—Preached the concluding sermon from Gen. v. 24. "And "Enoch walked with God," &c. God gave me enlargement and fervency in my discourse; so that I was enabled to speak with plainness and power; and God's presence seemed to be in the assembly. Praised be the Lord, it was a sweet meeting, a desirable assembly. I found my strength renewed, and lengthened out, even to a wonder; so that I felt much stronger at the conclusion, than in the beginning of this sacramental solemnity. I have great reason to bless God for this solemnity, wherein I have found assistance in addressing others, and sweetness in my own soul.

[On

[On Tuesday, he found himself spent, and his spirits exhausted by his late labours; and on Wednesday, complains of vapoury disorders, and dejection of spirit, and of enjoying but little comfort or spirituality.]

Thursday, June 12. In the evening, enjoyed freedom of mind, and some sweetness in secret prayer: it was a desirable season to me; my soul was enlarged in prayer for my own dear people, and for the enlargement of Christ's kingdom, and especially for the propagation of the gospel among the Indians, back in the wilderness. Was refreshed in prayer for dear friends in New-England, and elsewhere: I found it sweet to pray at this time; and could with all my heart say, "It is good for me to draw near to God."

Friday, June 13.——I came away from the meeting of the Indians, this day, rejoicing and blessing God for his grace manifested at this season.

Saturday, June 14. Rode to Kingston, to assist the Rev. Mr Wales in the administration of the Lord's supper. In the afternoon, preached; but almost fainted in the pulpit: yet God strengthened me when I was just gone, and enabled me to speak his word with freedom, fervency, and application to the conscience. And praised be the Lord; "out of weakness I was made strong." I enjoyed some sweetness, in and after public worship; but was extremely tired. Oh, how many are the mercies of the Lord! "To them that have no might, he increaseth strength."

Lord's day, June 15. Was in a dejected spiritless frame, that I could not hold up my head, nor look any body in the face. Administered the Lord's supper at Mr Wales's desire: and found myself in a good measure unburdened and relieved of my pressing load, when I came to ask a blessing on the elements; here God gave me enlargement, and a tender affectionate sense of spiritual things; so that it was a season of comfort, in some measure, to me, and I trust, more so to others. In the afternoon, preached to a vast multitude, from Rev. xxii. 17. "And whosoever will," &c. God helped me to offer a testimony for himself, and to leave sinners inexcuseable in neglecting his grace. I was enabled to speak with such freedom, fluency, and clearness, as commanded the attention of the great. Was extremely tired, in the evening, but enjoyed composure and sweetness.

Monday, June 16. Preached again; and God helped me amazingly, so that this was a sweet refreshing season to my soul and others. Oh, for ever blessed be God for help afford-

 ed

ed at this time, when my body was so weak, and while there was so large an assembly to hear. Spent the afternoon in a comfortable agreeable manner.

[The next day was spent comfortably.

On Wednesday, he went to a meeting of ministers at Hopewell.

Thursday, June 19. See his public Journal *.

On Friday and Saturday, he was very much amiss; but yet preached to his people on Saturday. His illness continued on the Sabbath; but he preached, notwithstanding, to his people, both parts of the day: and after the public worship was ended, he endeavoured to apply divine truths to the consciences of some, and addressed them personally for that end: several were in tears, and some appeared much affected. But he was extremely wearied with the services of the day, and was so ill at night, that he could have no bodily rest; but remarks, that "God was his support, and that he was not "left destitute of comfort in him." On Monday, he continued very ill; but speaks of his mind's being calm and composed, resigned to the divine dispensations, and content with his feeble state. And by the account he gives of himself, the remaining part of this week, he continued very feeble, and for the most part dejected in mind, and enjoyed no great freedom nor sweetness in spiritual things; excepting that for some very short spaces of time he had refreshment and encouragement, which engaged his heart on divine things; and sometimes his heart was melted with spiritual affection.]

Lord's day, June 29. Preached, both parts of the day, from John xiv. 19. "Yet a little while, and the world seeth "me no more," &c. God was pleased to assist me, to afford me both freedom and power, especially towards the close of my discourses, both forenoon and afternoon. God's power appeared in the assembly, in both exercises. Numbers of God's people were refreshed and melted with divine things; one or two comforted, who had been long under distress: convictions, in divers instances, powerfully revived; and one man in years much awakened, who had not long frequented our meeting, and appeared before as stupid as a stock. God amazingly renewed and lengthened out my strength. I was so spent at noon, that I could scarce walk, and all my joints trembled; so that

* The public Journal that has been so often referred to, concludes with the account of this day.

I could not ſit, nor ſo much as hold my hand ſtill: and yet God ſtrengthened me to preach with power in the afternoon; although I had given out word to my people, that I did not expect to be able to do it. Spent ſome time afterwards in converſing, particularly, with ſeveral perſons, about their ſpiritual ſtate; and had ſome ſatisfaction concerning one or two. Prayed afterwards with a ſick child, and gave a word of exhortation. Was aſſiſted in all my work. Bleſſed be God. Returned home with more health, than I went out with; although my linen was wringing wet upon me, from a little after ten in the morning, till paſt five in the afternoon. My ſpirits alſo were conſiderably refreſhed; and my ſoul rejoiced in hope, that I had through grace done ſomething for God. In the evening, walked out, and enjoyed a ſweet ſeaſon in ſecret prayer and praiſe. But Oh, I found the truth of the Pſalmiſt's words, "My goodneſs extendeth not to thee!" I could not make any returns to God; I longed to live only to him, and to be in tune for his praiſe and ſervice for ever. Oh, for ſpirituality and holy fervency, that I might *ſpend and be ſpent* for God to my lateſt moment!

Monday, June 30. Spent the day in writing; but under much weakneſs and diſorder. Felt the labours of the preceding day; although my ſpirits were ſo refreſhed the evening before, that I was not then ſenſible of my being ſpent.

Tueſday, July 1. In the afternoon, viſited, and preached to my people, from Heb. ix. 27. on occaſion of ſome perſons lying at the point of death, in my congregation. God gave me ſome aſſiſtance; and his word made ſome impreſſions on the audience, in general. This was an agreeable and comfortable evening to my ſoul: my ſpirits were ſomewhat refreſhed, with a ſmall degree of freedom and help enjoyed in my work.

[On Wedneſday, he went to Newark, to a meeting of the Preſbytery: complains of lowneſs of ſpirits; and greatly laments his ſpending his time ſo unfruitfully. The remaining part of the week he ſpent there, and at Eliſabeth-Town; and ſpeaks of comfort and divine aſſiſtance, from day to day: but yet greatly complains for want of more ſpirituality.]

Lord's day, July 6. [At Eliſabeth-Town] Enjoyed ſome compoſure and ſerenity of mind, in the morning: heard Mr Dickinſon preach, in the forenoon, and was refreſhed with his diſcourſe; was in a melting frame, ſome part of the time of sermon: partook of the Lord's supper, and enjoyed some sense of divine things in that ordinance. In the afternoon, I preached from Ezek. xxxiii. 11. "As I live, saith the Lord "God," &c. God favoured me with freedom and fervency; and helped me to plead his cause, beyond my own power.

Monday, July 7. My spirits were considerably refreshed and raised, in the morning. There is no comfort, I find, in any enjoyment, without enjoying God and being engaged in his service. In the evening, had the most agreeable conversation that ever I remember in all my life, upon God's being *all in all*, and all enjoyments being just *that* to us which God makes them, and no more. It is good to begin and end with God. Oh, how does a sweet solemnity lay a foundation for true pleasure and happiness!

Tuesday, July 8. Rode home, and enjoyed some agreeable meditations by the way.

Wednesday, July 9. Spent the day in writing, enjoyed some comfort and refreshment of spirit in my evening retirement.

Thursday, July 10. Spent most of the day in writing. Towards night, rode to Mr Tennent's; enjoyed some agreeable conversation: went home, in the evening, in a solemn sweet frame of mind; was refreshed in secret duties, longed to live wholly and only for God, and saw plainly, there was nothing in the world worthy of my affection; so that my heart was dead to all below; yet not through dejection, as at some times, but from views of a better inheritance.

Friday, July 11. Was in a calm composed frame, in the morning, especially in the season of my secret retirement: I think, I was well pleased with the will of God, whatever it was, or should be, in all respects I had then any thought of. Intending to administer the Lord's supper the next Lord's day, I looked to God for his presence and assistance upon that occasion; but felt a disposition to say, "The will "of the Lord be done," whether it be to give me assistance, or not. Spent some little time in writing: visited the Indians, and spent some time in serious conversation with them; thinking it not best to preach, by reason that many of them were absent.

Saturday, July 12. This day was spent in fasting and prayer by my congregation, as preparatory to the sacrament. I discoursed, both parts of the day, from Rom. iv. 25. "Who was delivered for our offences," &c. God gave me some assistance in my discourses, and something of divine

power

power attended the word; so that this was an agreeable season. Afterwards led them to a solemn renewal of their covenant, and fresh dedication of themselves to God. This was a season both of solemnity and sweetness, and GOD seemed to be "in the midst of us." Returned to my lodgings, in the evening, in a comfortable frame of mind.

Lord's day, July 13. In the forenoon, discoursed on the *bread of life*, from John vi. 35. God gave me some assistance, in part of my discourse especially; and there appeared some tender affection in the assembly under divine truths; my soul also was somewhat refreshed. Administered the sacrament of the Lord's supper to thirty-one persons of the Indians. God seemed to be present in this ordinance; the communicants were sweetly melted and refreshed, most of them. Oh, how they melted, even when the elements were first uncovered! There was scarcely a dry eye among them, when I took off the linen, and shewed them the symbols of *Christ's broken body*.——Having rested a little, after the administration of the sacrament, I visited the communicants, and found them generally in a sweet loving frame; not unlike what appeared among them on the former sacramental occasion, on April 27. In the afternoon, discoursed upon *coming to Christ*, and the *satisfaction* of those who do so, from the same verse I insisted on in the forenoon. This was likewise an agreeable season, a season of much tenderness, affection, and enlargement in divine service: and God, I am persuaded, crowned our assembly with his divine presence. I returned home much spent, yet rejoicing in the goodness of God.

Monday, July 14. Went to my people, and discoursed to them from Psal. cxix. 106. "I have sworn, and I will perform it," &c. Observed, 1. That all God's *judgments* or commandments are *righteous*. 2. That God's people have *sworn to keep* them; and this they do especially at the Lord's table. There appeared to be a powerful divine influence on the assembly, and considerable melting under the word. Afterwards, I led them to a renewal of their covenant before God, (that they would watch over themselves and one another, lest they should fall into sin and dishonour the name of Christ), just as I did on Monday, April 28. This transaction was attended with great solemnity: and God seemed to own it by exciting in them a fear and jealousy of themselves, lest they should sin against God; so that the presence of God seemed to be amongst us in this conclusion of the sacramental solemnity.

[The

[The next day, he set out on a journey towards Philadelphia; from whence he did not return till Saturday. He went this journey, and spent the week, under a great degree of illness of body, and dejection of mind.]

Lord's day, July 20. Preached twice to my people, from John xvii. 24. "Father, I will that they also whom thou "hast given me, be with me, where I am, that they may "behold my glory, which thou hast given me." Was helped to discourse with great clearness and plainness in the forenoon. In the afternoon, enjoyed some tenderness, and spake with some influence. Divers were in tears; and some, to appearance, in distress.

Monday, July 21. Preached to the Indians, chiefly for the sake of some *strangers*. Then proposed my design of taking a journey speedily to Susquahannah: exhorted my people to pray for me, that God would be with me in that journey, *&c.* Then chose divers persons of the congregation to travel with me. Afterwards, spent time in discoursing to the *strangers*, and was somewhat encouraged with them. Took care of my people's secular business, and was not a little exercised with it. Had some degree of composure and comfort in secret retirement.

Tuesday, July 22. Was in a dejected frame, most of the day: wanted to wear out life, and have it at an end; but had some desires of *living to God*, and wearing out life *for him.* Oh that I could indeed do so!

[The next day, he went to Elisabeth-Town, to a meeting of the Presbytery; and spent this, and Thursday, and the former part of Friday, under a very great degree of melancholy, and exceeding gloominess of mind; not through any fear of future punishment, but as being distressed with a senselessness of all good, so that the whole world appeared empty and gloomy to him. But in the latter part of Friday, he was greatly relieved and comforted.]

Saturday, July 26. Was comfortable in the morning; my countenance and heart were not sad, as in days past; enjoyed some sweetness in lifting up my heart to God. Rode home to my people, and was in a comfortable pleasant frame by the way; my spirits were much relieved of their burden, and I felt free to go through all difficulties and labours in my Master's service.

Lord's day, July 27. Discoursed to my people, in the forenoon,

noon, from Luke xii. 37. on the duty and benefit of *watching:* God helped me in the latter part of my discourse, and the power of God appeared in the assembly. In the afternoon, discoursed from Luke xiii. 25. Here also I enjoyed some assistance, and the Spirit of God seemed to attend what was spoken, so that there was a great solemnity, and some tears among Indians and others.

Monday, July 28. Was very weak, and scarce able to perform any business at all; but enjoyed sweetness and comfort in prayer, both morning and evening; and was composed and comfortable through the day: my mind was intense, and my heart fervent, at least in some degree, in secret duties; and I longed to *spend and be spent for God.*

Tuesday, July 29. My mind was cheerful, and free from those melancholy damps, that I am often exercised with: had freedom in looking up to God, at sundry times in the day. In the evening, I enjoyed a comfortable season in secret prayer; was helped to plead with God for my own dear people, that he would carry on his own blessed work among them; was assisted also in praying for the divine presence to attend me in my intended journey to Susquahannah; was also helped to remember dear brethren and friends in New-England: scarce knew how to leave the throne of grace, and it grieved me that I was obliged to go to bed; I longed to do something for God, but knew not how. Blessed be God for this freedom from dejection.

Wednesday, July 30. Was uncommonly comfortable, both in body and mind; in the forenoon especially: my mind was solemn, I was assisted in my work, and God seemed to be near to me; so that the day was as comfortable as most I have enjoyed for some time. In the evening, was favoured with assistance in secret prayer, and felt much as I did the evening before. Blessed be God for that freedom I then enjoyed at the throne of grace, for myself, my people, and my dear friends, "It is "good for me to draw near to God."

[He seems to have continued very much in the same free, comfortable state of mind the next day.]

Friday, August 1. In the evening, enjoyed a sweet season in secret prayer; clouds of darkness and perplexing care were sweetly scattered, and nothing anxious remained. Oh, how serene was my mind at this season! how free from that distracting concern I have often felt! "Thy will be done," was a petition sweet to my soul; and if God had bidden me chuse

for

for myself in any affair, I should have chosen rather to have referred the choice to him; for I saw he was infinitely wise, and could not do any thing amiss, as I was in danger of doing. Was assisted in prayer, for my dear flock, that God would promote his own work among them, and that God would go with me in my intended journey to Susquahannah; was helped to remember dear friends in New-England, and my dear brethren in the ministry. I found enough in the sweet duty of prayer to have engaged me to continue in it the whole night, would my bodily state have admitted of it. Oh, how sweet it is, to be enabled heartily to say, "Lord, not my "will, but thine be done!"

Saturday, August 2. Near night, preached from Matth. xi. 29. Was considerably helped; and the presence of God seemed to be somewhat remarkably in the assembly; divine truths made powerful impressions, both upon saints and sinners. Blessed be God for such a revival among us. In the evening, was very weary, but found my spirits supported and refreshed.

Lord's day, August 3. Discoursed to my people, in the forenoon, from Col. iii. 4. observed, that *Christ* is the believer's *life*. God helped me, and gave me his presence in this discourse; and it was a season of considerable power in the assembly. In the afternoon, preached from Luke xix. 41. 42. I enjoyed some assistance; though not so much as in the forenoon. In the evening, I enjoyed freedom and sweetness in secret prayer; God enlarged my heart, freed me from melancholy damps, and gave me satisfaction in drawing near to himself. Oh that my soul could magnify the Lord, for these seasons of composure and resignation to his will!

Monday, August 4. Spent the day in writing; enjoyed much freedom and assistance in my work: was in a composed and comfortable frame, most of the day; and in the evening enjoyed some sweetness in prayer. Blessed be God, my spirits were yet up, and I was free from sinking damps; as I have been in general ever since I came from Elisabeth-Town last. Oh what a mercy is this!

Friday, August 5. Towards night, preached at the funeral of one of my Christians, from If. lvii. 2. was oppressed with the nervous head-ach, and considerably dejected: however, had a little freedom, some part of the time I was discoursing. Was extremely weary in the evening; but notwithstanding enjoyed some liberty and cheerfulness of mind in prayer; and found the dejection that I feared, much removed, and my spirits considerably refreshed.

[He

[He continued in a very comfortable cheerful frame of mind the next day, with his heart enlarged in the service of God.]

Thursday, August 7. Rode to my house, where I spent the last winter, in order to bring some things I needed for my Susquahannah journey: was refreshed to see that place, which God so marvellously visited with the showers of his grace. Oh how amazingly did the *power of God* often appear there! "Bless the Lord, O my soul, and forget not all his benefits."

[The next day, he speaks of liberty, enlargement, and sweetness of mind, in prayer and religious conversation.]

Saturday, August 9. In the afternoon, visited my people; set their affairs in order, as much as possible, and contrived for them the management of their worldly business; discoursed to them in a solemn manner, and concluded with prayer. Was composed, and comfortable in the evening, and somewhat fervent in secret prayer: had some sense and view of the eternal world, and found a serenity of mind. Oh that I could magnify the Lord for any freedom he affords me in prayer!

Lord's day, August 10. Discoursed to my people, both parts of the day, from Acts iii. 19. In discoursing of *repentance*, in the forenoon, God helped me, so that my discourse was searching, some were in tears, both of the Indians and white people; and the word of God was attended with some power. In the intermission-season, I was engaged in discoursing to some in order to their baptism; as well as with one who had then lately met with some comfort, after spiritual trouble and distress. In the afternoon, was somewhat assisted again, though weak and weary. Afterwards *baptized* six persons; three adults, and three children. Was in a comfortable frame in the evening, and enjoyed some satisfaction in secret prayer. I scarce ever in my life felt myself so full of tenderness, as this day.

Monday, August 11. Being about to set out on a journey to Susquahannah the next day, with leave of Providence, I spent some time this day in prayer with my people. that God would bless and succeed my intended journey; that he would send forth his blessed Spirit with his word, and set up his kingdom among the poor Indians in the wilderness. While I was opening and applying part of the cxth and iid Psalms,

 the

the *power of God* seemed to descend on the assembly in some measure; and while I was making the first prayer, numbers were melted, and I found some affectionate enlargement of soul myself. Preached from Acts iv. 31. God helped me, and my interpreter also: there was a shaking and melting among us; and divers, I doubt not, were in some measure "filled with the Holy Ghost." Afterwards, Mr Macknight prayed: I then opened the two last stanza's of the lxxiid Psalm; at which time God was present with us; especially while I insisted upon the promise of *all nations blessing* the great *Redeemer*: my soul was refreshed, to think, that this day, this blessed glorious season should surely come; and I trust, numbers of my dear people were also refreshed. Afterwards prayed; had some freedom, but was almost spent: then walked out, and left my people to carry on religious exercises among themselves: they prayed repeatedly, and sung, while I rested and refreshed myself. Afterwards, went to the meeting; prayed with, and dismissed the assembly. Blessed be God, this has been a day of grace. There were many tears and affectionate sobs among us this day. In the evening, my soul was refreshed in prayer: enjoyed liberty at the throne of grace, in praying for my people and friends, and the church of God in general. "Bless the Lord, O my soul."

[The next day, he set out on his journey towards Susquahannah, and six of his Christian Indians with him, whom he had chosen out of his congregation, as those that he judged most fit to assist him in the business he was going upon. He took his way through Philadelphia; intending to go to Susquahannah-river, far down along, where it is settled by the white people, below the country inhabited by the Indians; and so to travel up the river to the Indian habitations: for although this was much farther about, yet hereby he avoided the huge mountains, and hideous wilderness, that must be crossed in the nearer way; which in time past he had found to be extremely difficult and fatiguing. He rode this week as far as Charlestown, a place of that name about thirty miles westward of Philadelphia; where he arrived on Friday: and in his way hither, was for the most part in a composed comfortable state of mind.]

Saturday, August 16. [At Charlestown.] It being a day kept by the people of the place where I now was, as preparatory to the celebration of the Lord's supper, I tarried; heard Mr Treat preach; and then preached myself. God gave me some

ſome good degree of freedom, and helped me to diſcourſe with warmth, and application, to the conſcience. Afterwards, I was refreſhed in ſpirit, though much tired; and ſpent the evening agreeably, having ſome freedom in prayer, as well as Chriſtian converſation.

Lord's day, Auguſt 17. Enjoyed liberty, compoſure, and ſatisfaction, in the ſecret duties of the morning: had my heart ſomewhat enlarged in prayer for dear friends, as well as for myſelf. In the forenoon, attended Mr Treat's preaching, partook of the Lord's ſupper, five of my people alſo communicating in this holy ordinance: I enjoyed ſome enlargement and outgoing of ſoul in this ſeaſon. In the afternoon, preached from Ezek. xxxiii. 11. Enjoyed not ſo much ſenſible aſſiſtance as the day before; however, was helped to ſome fervency in addreſſing immortal ſouls. Was ſomewhat confounded in the evening, becauſe I thought I had done little or nothing for God; yet enjoyed ſome refreſhment of ſpirit in Chriſtian converſation and prayer. Spent the evening, till near mid-night, in religious exerciſes; and found my bodily ſtrength, which was much ſpent when I came from the public worſhip, ſomething renewed before I went to bed.

Monday, Auguſt 18. Rode on my way towards Paxton, upon Suſquahannah-river. Felt my ſpirits ſink, towards night, ſo that I had little comfort.

Tueſday, Auguſt 19. Rode forward ſtill; and at night lodged by the ſide of Suſquahannah. Was weak and diſordered both this and the preceding day, and found my ſpirits conſiderably damped, meeting with none that I thought godly people.

Wedneſday, Auguſt 20. Having lain in a cold ſweat all night, I coughed much bloody matter this morning, and was under great diſorder of body, and not a little melancholy; but what gave me ſome encouragement, was, I had a ſecret hope that I might ſpeedily get a diſmiſſion from earth, and all its toils and ſorrows. Rode this day to one Chambers's, upon Suſquahannah, and there lodged. Was much afflicted, in the evening, with an ungodly crew, drinking, ſwearing, &c. Oh, what a *hell* would it be, to be numbered with the *ungodly!* Enjoyed ſome agreeable converſation with a traveller, who ſeemed to have ſome reliſh of true religion.

Thurſday, Auguſt 21. Rode up the river about fifteen miles, and there lodged, in a family that appeared quite deſtitute of God. Laboured to diſcourſe with the man about the life of religion, but found him very artful in evading ſuch converſation. Oh, what a death it is to ſome, to hear of *the things of God!* Was out of my element; but was not so dejected as at some times.

Friday, August 22. Continued my course up the river; my people now being with me, who before were parted from me: travelled above all the English settlements; at night, lodged in the open woods; and slept with more comfort, than while among an ungodly company of white people. Enjoyed some liberty in secret prayer, this evening; and was helped to remember dear friends, as well as my dear flock, and the church of God in general.

Saturday, August 23. Arrived at the Indian town, called *Shaumoking*, near night. Was not so dejected as formerly; but yet somewhat exercised. Felt somewhat composed in the evening; enjoyed some freedom in leaving my *all* with God: through the great goodness of God, I enjoyed some liberty of mind; was not distressed with a despondency, as frequently heretofore.

Lord's day, August 24. Towards noon, visited some of the Delawares, and discoursed with them about Christianity. In the afternoon, discoursed to the *King*, and others, upon divine things; who seemed disposed to hear. Spent most of the day in these exercises. In the evening, enjoyed some comfort and satisfaction; and especially had some sweetness in secret prayer: this duty was made so agreeable to me, that I loved to walk abroad and repeatedly engage in it. Oh, how comfortable is a little glimpse of God!

Monday, August 25. Spent most of the day in writing. Sent out my people that were with me, to talk with the Indians, and contract a friendship and familiarity with them, that I might have a better opportunity of treating with them about Christianity. Some good seemed to be done by their visits this day, divers appeared willing to hearken to Christianity. My spirits were a little refreshed, this evening; and I found some liberty and satisfaction in prayer.

Tuesday, August 26. About noon, discoursed to a considerable number of Indians: God helped me, I am persuaded; I was enabled to speak with much plainness, and some warmth and power. The discourse had impression upon some, and made them appear very serious. I thought, things now appeared as encouraging, as they did at Crosweeks. At the time of my first visit to those Indians, I was a little encouraged: I pressed things with all my might; and called out my people, who were then present, to give in *their testimony* for God; which they did. Towards night, was refreshed; felt a heart to pray for the setting up of God's kingdom here; as well

well as for my dear congregation below, and my dear friends elsewhere.

Wednesday, August 27. There having been a thick smoak in the house where I lodged all night before, whereby I was almost choked, I was this morning distressed with pains in my head and neck, and could have no rest. In the morning, the smoak was still the same; and a cold easterly storm gathering, I could neither live within doors nor without any long time together; I was pierced with the rawness of the air abroad, in the house distressed with the smoak. I was this day very vapoury, and lived in great distress, and had not health enough to do any thing to any purpose.

Thursday, August 28. In the forenoon was under great concern of mind about my work. Was visited by some who desired to hear me preach; discoursed to them, in the afternoon, with some fervency, and laboured to persuade them to *turn to God*. Was full of concern for the kingdom of Christ, and found some enlargement of soul in prayer, both in secret and in my family. Scarce ever saw more clearly, than this day, that it is God's *work* to convert souls, and especially poor *Heathens*: I knew, I could not touch them; I saw, I could only speak to *dry bones*, but could give them no sense of what I said. My eyes were up to God for help: I could say, the *work* was *his*; and if done, the *glory* would be *his*.

Friday, August 29. Felt the same concern of mind, as the day before. Enjoyed some freedom in prayer, and a satisfaction to leave all with God. Travelled to the Delawares, found few at home: felt poorly, but was able to spend some time alone in reading God's word and in prayer, and enjoyed some sweetness in these exercises. In the evening, was assisted repeatedly in prayer, and found some comfort in coming to the throne of grace.

Saturday, August 30. Spent the forenoon in visiting a *trader*, that came down the river *sick*; who appeared as ignorant as any Indian. In the afternoon, spent some time in writing, reading, and prayer.

Lord's day, August 31. Spent much time, in the morning, in secret duties: found a weight upon my spirits, and could not but cry to God with concern and engagement of soul. Spent some time also in reading and expounding God's word to my dear family, that was with me, as well as in singing and prayer with them. Afterwards, spake the word of God, to some few of the Susquahannah-Indians. In the afternoon, felt very weak and feeble. Near night, was something refreshed in mind, with some views of things relating to my

great

great work. Oh, how heavy is my work, when *faith* cannot take hold of an *almighty arm*, for the performance of it! many times have I been ready to sink in this case. Blessed be God, that I may repair to a full *fountain*.

Monday, September 1. Set out on a journey towards a place called *The great island*, about fifty miles distant from Shaumoking, in the north-western branch of Susquahannah. Travelled some part of the way, and at night lodged in the woods. Was exceeding feeble, this day, and sweat much the night following.

Tuesday, September 2. Rode forward; but no faster than my people went on foot. Was very weak, on this as well as the preceding days: was so feeble and faint, that I feared it would kill me to lie out in the open air; and some of our company being parted from us, so that we had now no axe with us, I had no way but to climb into a young pine-tree, and with my knife to lop the branches, and so made a shelter from the dew. But the evening being cloudy, and very likely for rain, I was still under fears of being extremely exposed: sweat much in the night, so that my linen was almost wringing wet all night. I scarce ever was more weak and weary, than this evening, when I was able to sit up at all. This was a melancholy situation I was in; but I endeavoured to quiet myself with considerations of the possibility of my being in much worse circumstances, amongst enemies, &c.

Wednesday, September 3. Rode to the Delaware-town; found divers drinking and drunken. Discoursed with some of the Indians about Christianity; observed my *interpreter* much engaged and assisted in his work; some few persons seemed to hear with great earnestness and engagement of soul. About noon, rode to a small town of Shauwaunoes, about eight miles distant; spent an hour or two there, and returned to the Delaware-town, and lodged there. Was scarce ever more confounded with a sense of my own unfruitfulness and unfitness for my work, than now. Oh, what a dead, heartless, barren, unprofitable wretch did I now see myself to be! My spirits were so low, and my bodily strength so wasted, that I could do nothing at all. At length, being much overdone, lay down on a *buffalo-skin*; but sweat much the whole night.

Thursday, September 4. Discoursed with the Indians, in the morning, about Christianity; my *interpreter*, afterwards, carrying on the discourse, to a considerable length: some few appeared well-disposed, and somewhat affected. Left this place, and returned towards Shaumoking; and at night lodged

ged in the place where I lodged the Monday-night before: was in very uncomfortable circumstances in the evening, my people being belated, and not coming to me till past ten at night; so that I had no fire to dress any victuals, or to keep me warm, or keep off wild beasts; and I was scarce ever more weak and worn out in all my life. However, I lay down and slept before my people came up, expecting nothing else but to spend the whole night alone, and without fire.

Friday, September 5. Was exceeding weak, so that I could scarcely ride; it seemed sometimes as if I must fall off from my horse, and lie in the open woods: however, got to Shaumoking, towards night: felt something of a spirit of thankfulness, that God had so far returned me: was refreshed, to see one of my Christians, whom I left here in my late excursion.

Saturday, September 6. Spent the day in a very weak state; coughing and spitting blood, and having little appetite to any food I had with me: was able to do very little, except discourse a while of divine things to my own people, and to some few I met with. Had, by this time, very little life or heart to speak for God, through feebleness of body, and flatness of spirits. Was scarcely ever more ashamed and confounded in myself, than now. I was sensible, that there were numbers of God's people, who knew I was then out upon a design (or at least the pretence) of doing something for God, and in his cause, among the poor Indians; and they were ready to suppose, that I was *fervent in spirit*: but Oh, the heartless frame of mind that I felt, filled me with confusion! Oh (methought) if God's people knew me, as God knows, they would not think so highly of my zeal and resolution for God, as perhaps now they do! I could not but desire they should see how heartless and irresolute I was, that they might be undeceived, and "not think of me above what "they ought to think." And yet I thought, if they saw the utmost of my flatness and unfaithfulness, the smallness of my courage and resolution for God, they would be ready to shut me out of their doors, as unworthy of the company or friendship of Christians.

Lord's day, September 7. Was much in the same weak state of body, and afflicted frame of mind, as in the preceding day: my soul was grieved, and mourned that I could do nothing for God. Read and expounded some part of God's word to my own dear family, and spent some time in prayer with them; discoursed also a little to the Pagans: but spent the Sabbath with a little comfort.

Monday,

Monday, September 8. Spent the forenoon among the Indians; in the afternoon, left Shaumoking, and returned down the river, a few miles. Had proposed to have tarried a considerable time longer among the Indians upon Susquahannah; but was hindered from pursuing my purpose by the sickness that prevailed there, the weakly circumstances of my own people that were with me, and especially my own extraordinary weakness, having been exercised with great nocturnal sweats, and a coughing up of blood, in almost the whole of the journey; and was a great part of the time so feeble and faint, that it seemed as though I never should be able to reach home; and at the same time very destitute of the comforts, and even necessaries of life; at least, what was necessary for one in so weak a state. In this journey I sometimes was enabled to speak the word of God with some power, and divine truths made some impressions on divers that heard me; so that several, both men and women, old and young, seemed to *cleave to us*, and be well disposed towards *Christianity*; but *others mocked* and shouted, which damped those who before seemed friendly, at least some of them: yet God, at times, was evidently present, assisting me, my interpreter, and other dear friends who were with me: God gave, sometimes, a good degree of freedom in prayer for the ingathering of souls there; and I could not but entertain a strong hope, that the journey should not be wholly fruitless. Whether the issue of it would be the setting up Christ's kingdom *there*, or only the drawing of some few persons down to my congregation in New-Jersey; or whether they were now only preparing for some further attempts, that might be made among them, I did not determine: but I was persuaded, the journey would not be lost. Blessed be God, that I had any encouragement and hope.

Tuesday, September 9. Rode down the river, near thirty miles. Was extreme weak, much fatigued, and wet with a thunder-storm. Discoursed with some warmth and closeness to some poor ignorant souls, on the *life* and *power* of *religion*; what were, and what were not the *evidences* of it. They seemed much astonished, when they saw my Indians ask a blessing, and give thanks, at dinner; concluding *that* a very high evidence of grace in them: but were astonished, when I insisted, that neither that, nor yet secret prayer, was any sure evidence of grace. Oh the ignorance of the world! How are some empty outward *forms*, that may all be entirely *selfish*, mistaken for true religion, infallible evidences of it! The Lord pity a deluded world!

Wednesday,

Wednesday, September 10. Rode near twenty miles homeward. Was much solicited to preach, but was utterly unable, through bodily weakness. Was extremely overdone with the heat and showers this day, and coughed up considerable blood.

Thursday, September 11. Rode homeward; but was very weak, and sometimes scarce able to ride. Had a very importunate invitation to preach at a meeting-house I came by, the people being then gathering; but could not, by reason of weakness. Was resigned and composed under my weakness; but was much exercised with concern for my companions in travel, whom I had left with much regret, some lame, and some sick.

Friday, September 12. Rode about fifty miles; and came just at night to a Christian friend's house, about twenty-five miles westward from Philadelphia. Was courteously received, and kindly entertained, and found myself much refreshed in the midst of my weakness and fatigues.

Saturday, September 13. Was still agreeably entertained with Christian friendship, and all things necessary for my weak circumstances. In the afternoon, heard Mr Treat preach; and was refreshed in conversation with him, in the evening.

Lord's day, September 14. At the desire of Mr Treat and the people, I preached both parts of the day (but short) from Luke xiv. 23. God gave me some freedom and warmth in my discourse; and I trust, helped me in some measure to labour *in singleness of heart*. Was much tired in the evening, but was comforted with the most tender treatment I ever met with in my life. My mind, through the whole of this day, was exceeding calm; and I could ask for nothing in prayer, with any encouragement of soul, but that "the will "of God might be done."

Monday, September 15. Spent the whole day, in concert with Mr Treat, in endeavours to compose a difference, subsisting between certain persons in the congregation where we now were: there seemed to be a blessing on our endeavours. In the evening, baptized a child: was in a calm composed frame, and enjoyed (I trust) a spiritual sense of divine things, while administering the ordinance. Afterwards, spent the time in religious conversation, till late in the night. This was indeed a pleasant agreeable evening.

Tuesday, September 16. Continued still at my friend's house, about twenty-five miles westward of Philadelphia. Was very weak, unable to perform any business, and scarcely able to sit up.

Wednesday, September 17. Rode in to Philadelphia. Still very weak, and my cough and spitting of blood continued. Enjoyed some agreeable conversation with friends, but wanted more spirituality.

Thursday, September 18. Went from Philadelphia to Mr Treat's: was agreeably entertained on the road; and was in a sweet composed frame, in the evening.

Friday, September 19. Rode from Mr Treat's to Mr Stockston's at Prince-Town: was extreme weak, but kindly received and entertained. Spent the evening with some degree of satisfaction.

Saturday, September 20. Arrived among my own people, just at night: found them praying together: went in, and gave them some account of God's dealings with me and my companions in the journey; which seemed affecting to them. I then prayed with them, and thought the divine presence was amongst us; divers were melted into tears, and seemed to have a sense of divine things. Being very weak, I was obliged soon to repair to my lodgings, and felt much worn out, in the evening. Thus God has carried me through the fatigues and perils of another journey to Susquahannah, and returned me again in safety, though under a great degree of bodily indisposition. Oh that my soul were truly thankful for renewed instances of mercy! Many hardships and distresses I endured in this journey: but the Lord supported me under them all.

PART

****

PART VIII.

After his return from his laſt journey to Suſquahannah, until his *death*.

[*N. B.* HItherto Mr Brainerd had kept a conſtant *diary*, giving an account of what paſſed from day to day, with very little interruption: but henceforward his diary is very much interrupted by his illneſs; under which he was often brought ſo low, as either not to be capable of writing, or not well able to bear the burden of a care ſo conſtant, as was requiſite, to recollect, every evening, what had paſſed in the day, and digeſt it, and ſet down an orderly account of it in writing. However, his *diary* was not wholly neglected; but he took care, from time to time, to take ſome notice in it of the moſt material things concerning himſelf and the ſtate of his mind, even till within a few days of his death; as the reader will ſee afterwards *.]

Lord's day, September 21. 1746. I was ſo weak I could not preach, nor pretend to ride over to my people in the forenoon. In the afternoon, rode out; ſat in my chair, and

* Mr Shepard, in his *Select caſes reſolved*, under the firſt *caſe* ſays as follows. "I have lately known one very able, wiſe, and "godly, put upon the rack, by him that, envying God's people's "peace, knows how to change himſelf into an *angel of light* for "it being his uſual courſe, in the time of his health, to make a "*diary* of his hourly life, and finding much benefit by it he was "in conſcience preſſed, by the power and deluſion of *Satan*, to "make and take the ſame daily ſurvey of his life in the time of his "*ſickneſs*; by means of which he ſpent his enfeebled ſpirits, caſt "on fuel to fire his ſickneſs. Had not a friend of his convinced "him of his erroneous conſcience miſleading him at that time, he "had murdered his body, out of conſcience to ſave his ſoul, and "to preſerve his grace. And do you think *theſe* were the motions "of God's Spirit, which like thoſe *locuſts*, Rev ix. 9. 10. had faces like *men*, but had tails like *ſcorpions*, and ſtings in their "tails?"

discoursed to my people from Rom. xiv. 7. 8. I was strengthened and helped in my discourse: and there appeared something agreeable in the assembly. I returned to my lodgings extremely tired; but thankful, that I had been enabled to speak a word to my poor people I had been so long absent from. Was able to sleep very little this night, through weariness and pain. Oh, how blessed should I be, if the little I do were all done with right views! Oh that, "whether I live, "I might live to the Lord," &c.

Saturday, September 27. Spent this day, as well as the whole week past, under a great degree of bodily weakness, exercised with a violent cough, and a considerable fever; had no appetite to any kind of food; and frequently brought up what I eat, as soon as it was down; and oftentimes had little rest in my bed, by reason of pains in my breast and back: was able, however, to ride over to my people, about two miles, every day, and take some care of those who were then at work upon a small house for me to reside in amongst the Indians *. I was sometimes scarce able to walk, and never able to sit up the whole day, through the week. Was calm and composed, and but little exercised with melancholy damps, as in former seasons of weakness. Whether I should ever recover or no, seemed very doubtful; but this was many times a comfort to me, that *life* and *death* did not depend upon *my* choice, I was pleased to think, that he who is infinitely wise, had the determination of this matter; and that I had no trouble, to consider and weigh things upon all sides, in order to make the choice, whether I would live or die. Thus my time was consumed; I had little strength to pray, none to write or read, and scarce any to meditate: but through divine goodness, I could with great composure look *death* in the face, and frequently with sensible joy. Oh, how blessed it is, to be *habitually prepared* for death! The Lord grant, that I may be *actually ready also!*

Lord's day, September 28. Rode to my people; and, though under much weakness, attempted to preach from 2 Cor. xiii. 5. Discoursed about half an hour; at which season divine power seemed to attend the word: but being extreme weak, I was obliged to desist; and after a turn of faintness, with much difficulty rode to my lodgings; where beta-

* This was the *fourth* house he built for his residence among the Indians. Besides that at Kaunaumeek, and that at the Forks of Delaware, and another at Crosweeksung, he built one now at Cranberry.

king

king myself to my bed, I lay in a burning fever, and almost delirious, for several hours; till towards morning, my fever went off with a violent sweat. I have often been feverish, and unable to rest quietly after preaching: but this was the most severe distressing turn, that ever preaching brought upon me. Yet I felt perfectly at rest in my own mind, because I had made my utmost attempts to speak for God, and knew I could do no more.

Tuesday, September 30. Yesterday, and to-day, was in the same weak state, or rather weaker than in days past; was scarce able to sit up half the day. Was in a composed frame of mind, remarkably free from dejection and melancholy damps; as God has been pleased, in great measure, to deliver me from these unhappy glooms, in the general course of my present weakness hitherto, and also from a peevish froward spirit: And Oh how great a mercy is this! Oh that I might always be perfectly quiet in seasons of greatest weakness, although nature should sink and fail! Oh that I may always be able with utmost sincerity to say, "Lord, not my "will, but thine be done!" This, through grace, I can say at present, with regard to life or death, "The Lord do with "me as seems good in his sight;" that whether I live or die, I may *glorify him*, who is "worthy to receive blessing, and "honour, and dominion for ever. Amen."

Saturday, October 4. Spent the former part of this week under a great degree of infirmity and disorder, as I had done several weeks before: was able, however, to ride a little every day, although unable to sit up half the day, till Thursday. Took some care daily of some persons at work upon my house. On Friday, after noon found myself wonderfully revived and strengthened; and having some time before given notice to my people, and those of them at the Forks of Delaware in particular, that I designed, with leave of Providence, to administer the sacrament of the Lord's supper upon the first Sabbath in October, the Sabbath now approaching, on Friday-afternoon I preached, preparatory to the sacrament, from 2 Cor. xiii. 5. finishing what I had proposed to offer upon the subject the Sabbath before. The sermon was blessed of God to the stirring up religious affection, and a spirit of devotion, in the people of God; and to the greatly affecting one who had *backslidden* from God, which caused him to judge and condemn himself. I was surprisingly strengthened in my work, while I was speaking: but was obliged immediately after to repair to bed, being now removed into my own house among the Indians; which gave me such

speedy

ſpeedy relief and refreſhment, as I could not well have lived without. Spent ſome time on Friday night in converſing with my people about divine things, as I lay upon my bed; and found my ſoul refreſhed, though my body was weak. This being Saturday, I diſcourſed particularly with divers of the communicants; and this afternoon preached from Zech. xii. 10. There ſeemed to be a tender melting, and hearty mourning for ſin, in numbers in the congregation. My ſoul was in a comfortable frame, and I enjoyed freedom and aſſiſtance in public ſervice; was myſelf, as well as moſt of the congregation, much affected with the humble confeſſion, and apparent broken-heartedneſs of the forementioned *backſlider;* and could not but rejoice, that God had given him ſuch a ſenſe of his ſin and unworthineſs. Was extremely tired in the evening; but lay on my bed, and diſcourſed to my people.

Lord's day, October 5. Was ſtill very weak; and in the morning, conſiderably afraid I ſhould not be able to go through the work of the day; having much to do, both in private and public. Diſcourſed before the adminiſtration of the ſacrament, from John i. 29. "Behold the Lamb of God, "that taketh away the ſin of the world." Where I conſidered, I. In what reſpects Chriſt is called the *Lamb of God;* and obſerved that he is ſo called, (1.) From the *purity* and *innocency* of his nature. (2.) From his *meekneſs* and *patience* under ſufferings. (3.) From his being that *atonement,* which was pointed out in the *ſacrifice* of lambs, and in particular by the *paſchal* lamb. II. Conſidered how and in what ſenſe he "takes away the ſin of the world?" and obſerved, that the means and manner, in and by which he takes away the ſins of men, was his "giving himſelf for them," doing and ſuffering in their room and ſtead, *&c.* And he is ſaid to take away the ſin of *the world,* not becauſe *all* the world ſhall *actually* be redeemed from ſin by him; but becauſe, (1.) He has done and ſuffered *ſufficient* to anſwer for the ſins of the world, and ſo to redeem all mankind. (2.) He *actually* does take away the ſins of the *elect* world. And, III. Conſidered how we are to *behold* him, in order to have our ſins taken away. (1.) Not with our *bodily* eyes. Nor, (2.) By *imagining* him on the croſs, *&c.* But by a *ſpiritual* view of his glory and goodneſs, engaging the ſoul to *rely* on him, *&c.*——The divine preſence attended this diſcourſe; and the aſſembly was conſiderably melted with divine truths. After ſermon baptized two perſons. Then adminiſtered the Lord's ſupper to near forty communicants, of the Indians, beſides divers dear

Chriſtians

Christians of the white people. It seemed to be a season of divine power and grace; and numbers seemed to rejoice in God. Oh, the sweet union and harmony then appearing among the religious people! My soul was refreshed, and my religious friends, of the white people, with me. After the sacrament, could scarcely get home, though it was not more than twenty roods; but was supported and led by my friends, and laid on my bed; where I lay in pain till some time in the evening; and then was able to sit up and discourse with friends. Oh, how was this day spent in prayers and praises among my dear people! One might hear them, all the morning, before public worship, and in the evening, till near midnight, praying and singing praises to God, in one or other of their houses. My soul was refreshed, though my body was weak.

[This week, he went (in a very low state) in two days, to Elisabeth-Town, to attend the meeting of the *Synod* there; but was disappointed by its removal to New-York. He continued in a very composed comfortable frame of mind.]

Saturday, October 11. Towards night was seized with an ague, which was followed with a hard fever, and considerable pain: was treated with great kindness, and was ashamed to see so much concern about so unworthy a creature, as I knew myself to be. Was in a comfortable frame of mind, wholly submissive, with regard to *life* or *death*. It was indeed a peculiar satisfaction to me, to think, that it was not *my* concern or business to determine whether I should live or die. I likewise felt peculiarly satisfied, while under this uncommon degree of disorder; being now fully convinced of my being really weak, and unable to perform my work; whereas at other times my mind was perplexed with fears, that I was a misimprover of time, by conceiting I was sick, when I was not in reality so. Oh, how precious is time! And how guilty it makes me feel, when I think I have trifled away and misimproved it, or neglected to fill up each part of it with duty, to the utmost of my ability and capacity!

Lord's day, October 12. Was scarce able to sit up, in the forenoon: in the afternoon, attended public worship, and was in a composed comfortable frame.

Lord's day, October 19. Was scarcely able to do any thing at all in the week past, except that on Thursday I rode out about four miles; at which time I took cold. As I was able

to

to do little or nothing, so I enjoyed not much spirituality, or lively religious affection; though at some times I longed much to be more fruitful and full of heavenly affection; and was grieved to see the hours slide away, while I could do nothing for God.—Was able this week to attend public worship. Was composed and comfortable, willing either to die or live; but found it hard to be reconciled to the thoughts of living *useless*. Oh that I might never live to be a burden to God's creation; but that I might be allowed to repair *home*, when my *sojourning* work is done!

[This week, he went back to his Indians at Cranberry, to take some care of their spiritual and temporal concerns: and was much spent with riding; though he rode but a little way in a day.]

Thursday, October 23. Went to my own house, and set things in order. Was very weak, and somewhat melancholy: laboured to do something, but had no strength; and was forced to lie down on my bed, very solitary.

Friday, October 24. Spent the day in overseeing and directing my people, about mending their fence, and securing their wheat. Found, that all their concerns of a secular nature depended upon me.——Was somewhat refreshed in the evening, having been able to do something valuable in the day-time. Oh, how it pains me, to see time pass away, when I can do nothing to any purpose!

Saturday, October 25. Visited some of my people; spent some time in writing, and felt much better in body, than usual: when it was near night, I felt so well, that I had thoughts of expounding: but in the evening was much disordered again, and spent the night in coughing, and spitting of blood.

Lord's day, October 26. In the morning, was exceeding weak: spent the day, till near night, in pain to see my poor people wandering *as sheep not having a shepherd*, waiting and hoping to see me able to preach to them before night: it could not but distress me, to see them in this case, and to find myself unable to attempt any thing for their spiritual benefit. But towards night, finding myself a little better, I called them together to my house, and sat down, and read and expounded Matth. v. 1.—16. This discourse, though delivered in much weakness, was attended with power to many of the hearers; especially what was spoken upon the last of these verses; where I insisted on the infinite wrong done to religion, by having

having our *light* become *darkness*, instead of *shining before men*. As many in the congregation were now deeply affected with a sense of their deficiency, in regard of a spiritual conversation, that might recommend religion to others, and a spirit of concern and watchfulness seemed to be excited in them; so there was one, in particular, that had fallen into the sin of drunkenness, some time before, who was now deeply convinced of his sin, and the great dishonour done to religion by his misconduct, and discovered a great degree of grief and concern on that account. My soul was refreshed, to see this. And though I had no strength to speak so much as I would have done, but was obliged to lie down on the bed; yet I rejoiced to see such an humble melting in the congregation; and that divine truths, though faintly delivered, were attended with so much efficacy upon the auditory.

Monday, October 27. Spent the day in overseeing and directing the Indians, about mending the fence round their wheat: was able to walk with them, and contrive their business, all the forenoon. In the afternoon, was visited by two dear friends, and spent some time in conversation with them. Towards night, was able to walk out, and take care of the Indians again. In the evening, enjoyed a very peaceful frame.

Tuesday, October 28. Rode to Prince-Town, in a very weak state: had such a violent fever, by the way, that I was forced to alight at a friend's house, and lie down for some time. Near night, was visited by Mr Treat, Mr Beaty, and his wife, and another friend: my spirits were refreshed to see them; but I was surprized, and even ashamed, that they had taken so much pains as to ride thirty or forty miles to see me. Was able to sit up most of the evening; and spent the time in a very comfortable manner with my friends.

Wednesday, October 29. Rode about ten miles with my friends that came yesterday to see me; and then parted with them all but one, who stayed on purpose to keep me company, and cheer my spirits. Was extreme weak, and very feverish, especially towards night; but enjoyed comfort and satisfaction.

Thursday, October 30. Rode three or four miles, to visit Mr Wales: spent some time, in an agreeable manner, in conversation; and though extreme weak, enjoyed a comfortable composed frame of mind.

Friday, October 31. Spent the day among friends, in a comfortable frame of mind, though exceeding weak, and under a considerable fever.

Saturday, November 1. Took leave of friends, after having spent the forenoon with them, and returned home to my own house. Was much disordered in the evening, and oppressed with my cough; which has now been constant for a long time, with a hard pain in my breast, and fever.

Lord's day, November 2. Was unable to preach, and scarcely able to sit up, the whole day. Was grieved, and almost sunk, to see my poor people destitute of the means of grace; especially considering they could not read, and so were under great disadvantages for spending the Sabbath comfortably. Oh, methought, I could be contented to be sick, if my poor flock had a faithful pastor to feed them with spiritual knowledge! A view of their want of this was more afflictive to me, than all my bodily illness.

Monday, November 3. Being now in so weak and low a state, that I was utterly uncapable of performing my work, and having little hope of recovery, unless by much riding, I thought it my duty to take a lengthy journey into New-England, and to divert myself among my friends, whom I had not now seen for a long time. And accordingly took leave of my congregation this day.——Before I left my people, I visited them all in their respective houses, and discoursed to each one, as I thought most proper and suitable for their circumstances, and found great freedom and assistance in so doing: I scarcely left one house but some were in tears; and many were not only affected with my being about to *leave* them, but with the solemn *addresses* I made them upon divine things; for I was helped to be *fervent in spirit*, while I discoursed to them. When I had thus gone through my congregation, (which took me most of the day), and had taken leave of them, and of the school, I left home, and rode about two miles, to the house where I lived in the summer past, and there lodged. Was refreshed, this evening, in that I had left my congregation so well disposed and affected, and that I had been so much assisted in making my farewell-addresses to them.

Tuesday, November 4. Rode to Woodbridge, and lodged with Mr Pierson; continuing still in a very weak state.

Wednesday, November 5. Rode to Elisabeth-Town; intending, as soon as possible, to prosecute my journey into New-England. But was, in an hour or two after my arrival, taken much worse.

After this, for near a week, was confined to my chamber, and most of the time to my bed: and then so far revived as to

be

be able to walk about the house; but was still confined within doors.

In the beginning of this extraordinary turn of disorder, after my coming to Elisabeth-Town, I was enabled through mercy to maintain a calm, composed, and patient spirit, as I had been before from the beginning of my weakness. After I had been in Elisabeth-Town about a fortnight, and had so far recovered that I was able to walk about house, upon a day of thanksgiving kept in this place, I was enabled to recall and recount over the mercies of God, in such a manner as greatly affected me, and filled me (I think) with thankfulness and praise to God: especially my soul praised him for his work of grace among the Indians, and the enlargement of his dear kingdom: my soul blessed God for what he is in himself, and adored him, that he ever would display himself to creatures: I rejoiced, that he was God, and longed that all should know it, and feel it, and rejoice in it. "Lord, glorify thyself," was the desire and cry of my soul. Oh that *all people* might love and praise the blessed God; that he might have all possible honour and glory from the intelligent world *!

After this comfortable thanksgiving-season, I frequently enjoyed freedom and enlargement and engagedness of soul in prayer, and was enabled to intercede with God for my dear congregation, very often for every family, and every person, in particular; and it was often a great comfort to me, that I could pray heartily to God for those, to whom I could not speak, and whom I was not allowed to see. But at other times, my spirits were so flat and low, and my bodily vigour so much wasted, that I had scarce any affections at all.

In December, I had revived so far as to be able to walk abroad, and visit friends, and seemed to be on the gaining hand with regard to my health, in the main, until Lord's day, December 21. At which time I went to the public worship; and it being sacrament day, I laboured much, at the Lord's table, to bring forth a certain corruption, and have it *slain*, as being an *enemy* to God and my own soul; and could not but hope, that I had gained some strength against this, as well as other corruptions; and felt some brokenness of heart for my sin.

After this, having perhaps taken some cold, I began to decline as to bodily health; and continued to do so, till the latter

* About this time he wrote the *seventh letter*, published at the end of this account of his life.

end of January 1746-7. And having a violent cough, a considerable fever, and asthmatic disorder, and no appetite for any manner of food, nor any power of digestion. I was reduced to so low a state, that my friends (I believe) generally despaired of my life; and some of them, for some time together, thought I could scarce live a day to an end. In this time, I could think of nothing with any application of mind, and seemed to be in a great measure void of all affection, and was exercised with great temptations; but yet was not, ordinarily, afraid of death.

On Lord's day, February 1. Though in a very weak and low state, I enjoyed a considerable deal of comfort and sweetness in divine things; and was enabled to plead and use arguments with God in prayer, I think, with a child-like spirit. That passage of scripture occurred to my mind, and gave me great assistance, "If ye, being evil, know how to give good "gifts to your children, how much more will your heavenly "Father give the holy Spirit to them that ask him?" This text I was helped to plead, and insist upon; and saw the divine faithfulness engaged for dealing with me better than any earthly paren can do with his child. This season so refreshed my soul, that my body seemed also to be a gainer by it. And from this time, I began gradually to amend. And as I recovered some strength, vigour, and spirit, I found at times some freedom and life in the exercises of devotion, and some longings after spirituality and a life of usefulness to the interests of the great Redeemer: although at other times, I was awfully barren and lifeless, and out of frame for the things of God; so that I was ready often to cry out, "Oh that it were "with me as in months past! Oh that God had taken me away in the midst of my usefulness, with a sudden stroke, that I might not have been under a necessity of trifling away time in diversions! Oh that I had never lived to spend so much precious time, in so poor a manner, and to so little purpose! Thus I often reflected, was grieved, ashamed, and even confounded, sunk and discouraged.

On Tuesday, February 24. I was able to ride as far as Newark, (having been confined within Elisabeth-Town almost four months), and the next day returned to Elisabeth-Town. My spirits were somewhat refreshed with the ride, though my body was weary.

On Saturday, February 28. Was visited by an Indian of my own congregation; who brought me letters, and good news of the sober and good behaviour of my people in general: this refreshed my soul; I could not but soon retire, and

bless

bless God for his goodness; and found, I trust, a truly thankful frame of spirit, that God seemed to be building up that congregation for himself.

On Wednesday, March 4. I met with reproof from a friend, which, although I thought I did not deserve it from him, yet was (I trust) blessed of God to make me more tenderly afraid of sin, more jealous over myself, and more concerned to keep both heart and life pure and unblameable: it likewise caused me to reflect on my past deadness, and want of spirituality, and to abhor myself, and look on myself most unworthy. This frame of mind continued the next day; and for several days after, I grieved, to think, that in my necessary diversions I had not maintained more seriousness, solemnity, heavenly affection and conversation. And thus my spirits were often depressed and sunk; and yet, I trust, that reproof was made to be beneficial to me.

Wednesday, March 11. being kept in Elisabeth-Town as a day of fasting and prayer, I was able to attend public worship; which was the first time I was able so to do after December 21. Oh, how much weakness and distress did God carry me through in this space of time! But *having obtained help from him*, I yet live: Oh that I could live more to his glory!

Lord's day, March 15. Was able again to attend the public worship, and felt some earnest desires of being restored to the ministerial work: felt, I think, some spirit and life, to speak for God.

Wednesday, March 18. Rode out with a design to visit my people; and the next day arrived among them: was under great dejection in my journey.

On Friday morning, I rose early, walked about among my people, and inquired into their state and concerns; and found an additional weight and burden on my spirits, upon hearing some things disagreeable. I endeavoured to go to God with my distresses, and made some kind of lamentable complaint; and in a broken manner spread my difficulties before God; but notwithstanding, my mind continued very gloomy. About ten o'clock, I called my people together, and after having explained and sung a psalm, I prayed with them. There was a considerable deal of affection among them; I doubt not, in some instances, that which was more than merely natural.

[This was the *last interview* that he ever had with his people. About eleven o'clock the same day, he left them; and

and the next day came to Elisabeth-Town; his melancholy remaining still: and he continued for a considerable time under a great degree of dejection through vapoury disorders.]

Saturday, March 28. Was taken this morning with violent griping pains. These pains were extreme, and constant, for several hours; so that it seemed impossible for me, without a miracle, to live twenty-four hours in such distress. I lay confined to my bed, the whole day, and in distressing pain, all the former part of it: but it pleased God to bless means for the abatement of my distress. Was exceedingly weakened by this pain, and continued so for several days following; being exercised with a fever, cough, and nocturnal sweats. In this distressed case, so long as my head was free of vapoury confusions, *death* appeared agreeable to me; I looked on it as the end of toils, and an entrance into a place "where the "weary are at rest;" and, I think, I had some relish of the entertainments of the heavenly state; so that by these I was allured and drawn, as well as driven by the fatigues of life. Oh, how happy it is, to be drawn by desires of a state of perfect holiness!

Saturday, April 4. Was sunk and dejected, very restless and uneasy, by reason of the misimprovement of time; and yet knew not what to do: I longed to spend time in fasting and prayer, that I might be delivered from indolence and coldness in the things of God; but, alas, I had not bodily strength for these exercises! Oh, how blessed a thing is it, to enjoy peace of conscience! but how dreadful is a want of inward peace and composure of soul! It is impossible, I find, to enjoy this happiness without *redeeming time*, and maintaining a spiritual frame of mind.

Lord's day, April 5. It grieved me, to find myself so inconceivably barren. My soul thirsted for grace: but, alas, how far was I from obtaining what I saw so exceeding excellent! I was ready to despair of ever being a holy creature; and yet my soul was desirous of *following hard after God;* but never did I see myself so far from *having apprehended, or being already perfect*, as at this time. The Lord's supper being this day administered, I attended the ordinance: and though I saw in myself a dreadful emptiness, and want of grace, and saw myself as it were at an infinite distance from that purity which is becoming the gospel; yet in the season of communion, especially in the time of the distribution of the bread, I enjoyed some warmth of affection, and felt a tender *love to the brethren;* and, I think, to the glorious Redeemer,

deemer, the *first-born* among them. I endeavoured then to *bring forth* mine and *his enemies*, and *slay them before him*; and found great freedom in begging deliverance from this spiritual death, as well as in asking divine favours for my friends, and congregation, and the church of Christ in general.

Tuesday, April 7. In the afternoon, rode to Newark, in order to marry the Reverend Mr Dickinson *; and in the evening, performed that work. Afterwards, rode home to Elisabeth-Town, in a pleasant frame, full of composure and sweetness.

Thursday, April 9. Attended the ordination of Mr Tucker †, and afterwards the examination of Mr Smith: was in a comfortable frame of mind this day, and felt my heart, I think, sometimes in a spiritual frame.

Friday, April 10. Spent the forenoon in Presbyterial business: in the afternoon, rode to Elisabeth-Town; found my brother John there ‡: spent some time in conversation with him; but was extreme weak and outdone, my spirits considerably sunk, and my mind dejected.

Monday, April 13. Assisted in examining my brother. In the evening, was in a solemn devout frame; but was much overdone and oppressed with a violent head-ach.

* The late learned and very excellent Mr Jonathan Dickinson, pastor of a church in Elisabeth-Town, president of the college of New-Jersey, and one of the correspondents of the honourable society in Scotland for propagating Christian knowledge: who had a great esteem for Mr Brainerd, and had kindly entertained him in his house during his sickness in the winter past; and who, after a short illness, died in the next ensuing October, two days before Mr Brainerd.

† A worthy pious young gentleman; who lived in the ministry but a very short time: he died at Stratfield in Connecticut, the December following his ordination, being a little while after Mr Brainerd's death at Northampton. He was taken ill on a journey, returning from a visit to his friends at Milton (in the Massachusetts), which, as I take it, was his native place, and Harvard-college the place of his education.

‡ This brother of his had been sent for by the *correspondents*, to take care of, and instruct Mr Brainerd's congregation of Indians; he being obliged by his illness to be absent from them. And he continued to take care of them till Mr Brainerd's death: and since his death, has been ordained his *successor* in his mission, and to the charge of his congregation; which continues much to flourish under his pastoral care.

Tuesday,

Tuesday, April 14. Was able to do little or nothing: spent some time with Mr Byram and other friends. This day my brother went to my people.

Wednesday, April 15. Found some freedom at the throne of grace, several times this day. In the afternoon, was very weak, and spent the time to very little purpose; and yet in the evening, had (I thought) some religious warmth and spiritual desires in prayer: my soul seemed to go forth after God, and take complacence in his divine perfections. But, alas! afterwards awfully let down my watch, and grew careless and secure.

Thursday, April 16. Was in bitter anguish of soul, in the morning, such as I have scarce ever felt, with a sense of sin and guilt. I continued in distress the whole day, attempting to pray where-ever I went; and indeed could not help so doing: but looked upon myself so vile, I dared not look any body in the face; and was even grieved, that any body should shew me any respect, or at least, that they should be so deceived as to think I deserved it.

Friday, April 17. In the evening, could not but think, that God helped me to "draw near to the throne of grace," though most unworthy, and gave me a sense of his favour; which gave me inexpressible support and encouragement; though I scarcely dared to hope the mercy was real, it appeared so great: yet could not but rejoice, that ever God should discover his reconciled face to such a vile sinner. Shame and confusion, at times, covered me; and then hope, and joy, and admiration of divine goodness gained the ascendant. Sometimes I could not but admire the divine goodness, that the Lord had not let me fall into all the grossest vilest acts of sins and open scandal, that could be thought of; and felt myself so necessitated to praise God, that this was ready for a little while to swallow up my shame and pressure of spirit on account of my sins.

[After this, his dejection and pressure of spirit returned; and he remained under it the two next days.]

Monday, April 20. Was in a very disordered state, and kept my bed most of the day. I enjoyed a little more comfort, than in several of the preceding days. This day I arrived at the age of twenty-nine years.

Tuesday, April 21. I set out on my journey for New-England, in order (if it might be the will of God) to recover my my health by riding: travelled to New-York, and there lodged.

[This proved his final departure from New-Jersey.——He travelled slowly, and arrived among his friends at East-Haddam, about the beginning of May. There is very little account in his *diary*, of the time that passed from his setting out on this journey to May 10. He speaks of his sometimes finding his heart rejoicing in the glorious perfections of God, and longing to live to him; but complains of the unfixedness of his thoughts, and their being easily diverted from divine subjects, and cries out of his leanness, as testifying against him, in the loudest manner. And concerning those *diversions* he was obliged to use for his health, he says, that he sometimes found he could use diversions with "singleness of heart," aiming at the glory of God; but that he also found there was a necessity of great care and watchfulness, lest he should lose that spiritual temper of mind in his diversions, and lest they should degenerate into what was merely selfish, without any supreme aim at the glory of God in them.]

Lord's day, May 10. (At Had-Lime) I could not but feel some measure of gratitude to God at this time, (wherein I was much exercised), that he had always disposed me, in my ministry, to insist on the great doctrines of *regeneration*, the *new creature, faith in Christ, progressive sanctification, supreme love to God, living entirely to the glory of God, being not our own*, and the like. God has helped me to see, in the surest manner, from time to time, that these, and the like doctrines, necessarily connected with them, are the *only foundation* of safety and salvation for perishing sinners; and that those divine dispositions, which are consonant hereto, are that *holiness*, "without which no man shall see the Lord:" the exercise of these God-like tempers, wherein the soul acts in a kind of concert with God, and would be and do every thing that is pleasing to God; this, I saw, would stand by the soul in a dying hour; for God must, I think, *deny himself*, if he cast away *his own image*, even the soul that is one in desires with himself.

Lord's day, May 17. (At Millington) Spent the forenoon at home, being unable to attend the public worship. At this time, God gave me some affecting sense of my own vileness, and the exceeding sinfulness of my heart; that there seemed to be nothing but sin and corruption within me. "Innumerable evils compassed me about;" my want of spirituality

rituality and holy living, my neglect of God, and living to myself.——All the abominations of my heart and life seemed to be open to my view; and I had nothing to say, but, "God "be merciful to me a sinner."——Towards noon, I saw, that the grace of God in Christ is infinitely free towards sinners, and such sinners as I was; I also saw, that God is the supreme good, that in his presence is life; and I began to long to die, that I might *be with him*, in a state of freedom from all sin. Oh, how a small glimpse of his excellency refreshed my soul! Oh, how worthy is the blessed God to be loved, adored, and delighted in, for himself, for his own divine excellencies!

Though I felt much dulness, and want of a spirit of prayer, this week; yet I had some glimpses of the excellency of divine things; and especially one morning, in secret meditation and prayer, the excellency and beauty of holiness, as a likeness to the glorious God, was so discovered to me, that I began to long earnestly to be in that world where holiness dwells in perfection: and I seemed to long for this perfect holiness, not so much for the sake of my own happiness, (although I saw clearly that this was the greatest, yea, the only happiness of the soul), as that I might please God, live entirely to him, and glorify him to the utmost stretch of my rational powers and capacities.

Lord's day, May 24. (At Long-Meadow in Springfield) Could not but think, as I have often remarked to others, that much more of *true religion* consists in *deep humility, brokenness of heart, and an abasing sense of barrenness and want of grace and holiness*, than most who are called *Christians*, imagine; especially those who have been esteemed the converts of the *late* day; many of whom seem to know of no other religion but elevated *joys* and *affections*, arising only from some flights of *imagination*, or some *suggestion* made to their mind, of *Christ's* being *their's*, God's *loving them*, and the like.

[On Thursday, May 28. He came from Long-Meadow to Northampton; appearing vastly better than, by his account, he had been in the winter; indeed so well, that he was able to ride twenty-five miles in a day, and to walk half a mile; and appeared cheerful, and free from melancholy: but yet undoubtedly, at that time, in a confirmed, incurable consumption.

I had had much opportunity, before this, of particular information concerning him, from many that were well acquainted

quainted with him; and had myself once an opportunity of considerable conversation and some acquaintance with him, at New-Haven, near four years before, in the time of the *commencement* when he offered that confession to the rector of the college, that has been already mentioned in this history; I being one he was pleased then several times to consult on that affair: but now I had opportunity for a more full acquaintance with him. I found him remarkably sociable, pleasant, and entertaining in his conversation; yet solid, savoury, spiritual, and very profitable; appearing meek, modest, and humble, far from any stiffness, moroseness, superstitious demureness, or affected singularity in speech or behaviour, and seeming to nauseate all such things. We enjoyed not only the benefit of his conversation, but had the comfort and advantage of hearing him pray in the family, from time to time. His manner of praying was very agreeable; most becoming a worm of the dust, and a disciple of Christ, addressing to an infinitely great and holy God, and Father of mercies; not with florid expressions, or a studied eloquence; not with any intemperate vehemence, or indecent boldness; at the greatest distance from any appearance of ostentation, and from every thing that might look as though he meant to recommend himself to those that were about him, or set himself off to their acceptance; free too from vain repetitions, without impertinent excursions, or needless multiplying of words. He expressed himself with the strictest propriety, with weight, and pungency; and yet what his lips uttered seemed to flow from the *fulness of his heart*, as deeply impressed with a great and solemn sense of our necessities, unworthiness, and dependance, and of God's infinite greatness, excellency, and sufficiency, rather than merely from a warm and fruitful brain, pouring out good expressions. And I know not, that ever I heard him so much as ask a blessing or return thanks at table, but there was something remarkable to be observed both in the matter and manner of the performance. In his prayers, he insisted much on the prosperity of Zion, the advancement of Christ's kingdom in the world, and the flourishing and propagation of religion among the Indians. And he generally made it one petition in his prayer, "that we might not out-" live our usefulness."]

Lord's day, May 31. [At Northampton,] I had little inward sweetness in religion, most of the week past; not realising and beholding spiritually the *glory of God, and the blessed Redeemer:* from whence always arise *my comforts and joys* in

 religion,

religion, if I have any at all: and if I cannot so behold the excellencies and perfections of God, as to cause me to rejoice in him for what he is *in himself*, I have no solid foundation for joy. To rejoice, only because I apprehend I have an *interest in Christ*, and shall be finally saved, is a poor mean business indeed.

[This week, he consulted Dr Mather, at my house, concerning his illness; who plainly told him, that there were great evidences of his being in a confirmed *consumption*, and that he could give him no encouragement, that he should ever recover. But it seemed not to occasion the least discomposure in him, nor to make any manner of alteration as to the cheerfulness and serenity of his mind, or the freedom or pleasantness of his conversation.]

Lord's day, June 7. My attention was greatly engaged, and my soul so drawn forth, this day, by what I heard of the "exceeding preciousness of the saving grace of God's Spirit," that it almost overcame my body, in my weak state: I saw, that true grace is exceeding precious indeed; that it is very rare; and that there is but a very small degree of it, even where the reality of it is to be found; at least, I saw this to be *my* case.

In the preceding week, I enjoyed some comfortable seasons of meditation. One morning, the cause of God appeared exceeding precious to me: the Redeemer's kingdom is all that is valuable in the earth, and I could not but long for the promotion of it in the world: I saw also, that this cause is God's, that he has an infinitely greater regard and concern for it, than I could possibly have; that if I have any true love to this blessed interest, it is only a drop derived from that ocean; hence, I was ready to "lift up my head with joy;" and conclude, "Well, if God's cause be so dear and precious "to him, he will promote it." And thus I did as it were rest on God, that surely he would promote that which was so agreeable to his own will; though the time when, must still be left to his sovereign pleasure.

[He was advised by physicians still to continue riding, as what would tend, above any other means, to prolong his life. He was at a loss, for some time, which way to bend his course next; but finally determined to ride from hence to Boston; we having concluded that one of this family should go with him, and be helpful to him in his weak and low state.]

Tuesday,

Tuesday, June 9. I set out on a journey from Northampton to Boston. Travelled slowly, and got some acquaintance with divers ministers on the road.

I having now continued to ride for some considerable time together, felt myself much better than I had formerly done; and I found, that in proportion to the prospect I had of being restored to a state of usefulness, so I desired the continuance of life: but *death* appeared, inconceivably more desirable to me, than a *useless life*; yet blessed be God, I found my heart, at times, fully resigned and reconciled to this greatest of afflictions, if God saw fit thus to deal with me.

Friday, July 12. I arrived in Boston this day, somewhat fatigued with my journey. Observed, that there is no *rest*, but in God: fatigues of body, and anxieties of mind, attend us, both in town and country; no place is exempted.

Lord's day, June 14. I enjoyed some enlargement and sweetness in family-prayer, as well as in secret exercises; God appeared excellent, his ways full of pleasure and peace, and all I wanted was a spirit of holy fervency, to live to him.

Wednesday, June 17. This, and the two preceding days, I spent mainly in visiting the ministers of the town, and was treated with great respect by them.

On Thursday, June 18. I was taken exceeding ill, and brought to the gates of death, by the breaking of small ulcers in my lungs, as my physician supposed. In this extreme weak state I continued for several weeks, and was frequently reduced so low, as to be utterly speechless, and not able so much as to whisper a word; and even after I had so far revived, as to walk about house, and to step out of doors, I was exercised every day with a faint turn, which continued usually four or five hours; at which times, though I was not utterly speechless, so but that I could say *Yes* or *No*, yet I could not converse at all, nor speak one sentence, without making stops for breath; and divers times in this season, my friends gathered round my bed, to see me breathe my last, which they looked for every moment, as I myself also did.

How I was, the first day or two of my illness, with regard to the exercise of reason, I scarcely know; but I believe I was something shattered with the violence of the fever, at times: but the third day of my illness, and constantly afterwards, for four or five weeks together, I enjoyed as much serenity of mind, and clearness of thought, as perhaps I ever did in my life; and I think, my mind never penetrated with so much ease and freedom into divine things, as at this time;

and

and I never felt so capable of demonstrating the truth of many important doctrines of the gospel as now. And as I saw clearly the *truth* of those great doctrines, which are justly stiled the *doctrines of grace*; so I saw with no less clearness, that the *essence* of *religion* consisted in the soul's *conformity to God*, and acting above all selfish views, for *his glory*, longing to be *for him*, to live *to him*, and please and honour *him* in all things: and this from a clear view of his infinite excellency and worthiness *in himself*, to be loved, adored, worshipped, and served by all intelligent creatures. Thus I saw, that when a soul *loves* God with a supreme love, he therein acts *like* the blessed God himself, who most justly loves himself in that manner: so when God's interest and his are become one, and he longs that God should be *glorified*, and rejoices to think that he is unchangeably possessed of the highest glory and blessedness, herein also he acts in *conformity* to God: in like manner, when the soul is fully *resigned to*, and rests satisfied and contented *with* the divine will, here it is also *conformed* to God.

I saw further, that as this divine temper, whereby the soul exalts God, and treads self in the dust, is wrought in the soul by God's discovering his own glorious perfections *in the face of Jesus Christ* to it, by the special influences of the holy Spirit, so he cannot but have *regard to it*, as his own work; and as it is his image in the soul, he cannot but take *delight* in it. Then I saw again, that if God should slight and reject his own *moral image*, he must needs *deny himself*; which he cannot do. And thus I saw the *stability* and *infallibility* of this religion; and that those who are truly possessed of it, have the most complete and satisfying *evidence* of their being interested in all the benefits of Christ's redemption, having their hearts *conformed to him*; and that these, and these only, are qualified for the employments and entertainments of God's kingdom of glory; as none but these have any relish for the business of heaven, which is to ascribe glory to God, and not to themselves; and that God (though I would speak it with great reverence of his name and perfections) cannot, without denying himself, finally cast such away.

The next thing I had then to do, was to inquire, whether *this* was *my* religion: and here God was pleased to help me to the most easy remembrance and critical review of what had passed in course, of a religious nature, through several of the latter years of my life: and although I could discover much corruption attending my best duties, many selfish views and carnal ends, much spiritual pride and self-exaltation, and innumerable

innumerable other evils which compassed me about; I say, although I now discerned the sins of my holy things, as well as other actions; yet God was pleased, as I was reviewing, quickly to put this question out of doubt, by shewing me, that I had, from time to time, acted above the utmost influence of mere self-love; that I had longed to please and glorify him, as my highest happiness, *&c.* And this review was through grace attended with a present feeling of the same divine temper of mind; I felt now pleased, to think of the glory of God, and longed for heaven, as a state wherein I might glorify God perfectly, rather than a place of happiness for myself: and this feeling of the love of God in my heart, which I trust the Spirit of God excited in me afresh, was sufficient to give me full satisfaction, and make me long, as I had many times before done, to be with Christ: I did not now want any of the *sudden suggestions,* which many are so pleased with, "That Christ and his benefits are mine; that God "loves me," *&c.* in order to give me satisfaction about my state: no, my soul now abhorred those delusions of *Satan,* which are thought to be the *immediate witness of the Spirit,* while there is nothing but an *empty suggestion* of a certain fact, without any gracious discovery of the *divine glory,* or of the *Spirit's work* in their own hearts: I saw the awful delusion of this kind of confidences, as well as of the whole of *that* religion, which they usually spring from, or at least are the attendants of: the *false* religion of the late day, (though a day of wondrous grace), the *imaginations,* and impressions made only on the *animal* affections, together with the *sudden* suggestions made to the mind by *Satan, transformed into an angel of light,* of certain facts not revealed in scripture; these, and many like things, I fear, have made up the greater part of the religious appearance in many places.

These things I saw with great clearness, when I was thought to be dying. And God gave me great concern for his church and interest in the world, at this time: not so much because the late remarkable influence upon the minds of people was abated, and almost wholly gone, as because that false religion, those heats of imagination, and wild and selfish commotions of the animal affections, which attended the work of grace, had prevailed so far. *This* was that which my mind dwelt upon, almost day and night: and *this,* to me, was the darkest appearance, respecting religion, in the land; for it was *this* chiefly, that had prejudised the world against inward religion. And I saw, the great misery of all was, that so few saw any manner of *difference* between those exercises

ciſes that were ſpiritual and holy, and thoſe which have *ſelf-love* only for their beginning, centre, and end.

As God was pleaſed to afford me clearneſs of thought, and compoſure of mind, almoſt continually, for ſeveral weeks together, under my great weakneſs; ſo he enabled me, in ſome meaſure, to improve my time (as I hope) to valuable purpoſes. I was enabled to write a number of important *letters*, to friends in remote places*: and ſometimes I wrote when I was ſpeechleſs, *i. e.* unable to maintain converſation with any body; though perhaps I was able to ſpeak a word or two ſo as to be heard.—At this ſeaſon alſo, while I was confined at Boſton, I read with care and attention ſome papers of old Mr Shepard's, lately come to light, and deſigned for the preſs: and as I was deſired, and greatly urged, made ſome corrections, where the ſenſe was left dark, for want of a word or two.—Beſides this, I had many *viſitants*; with whom, when I was able to ſpeak, I always converſed of the things of religion; and was peculiarly diſpoſed and aſſiſted in diſtinguiſhing between the *true* and *falſe* religion of the times: there was ſcarce any ſubject, that has been matter of debate in the late day, but what I was at one time or other brought to a ſort of neceſſity to diſcourſe upon, and ſhew my opinion in; and that frequently before numbers of people; and eſpecially, I diſcourſed repeatedly on the nature and neceſſity of that *humiliation*, *ſelf-emptineſs*, or full conviction of a perſon's being utterly undone in himſelf, which is neceſſary in order to a ſaving *faith*, and the extreme *difficulty* of being brought to this, and the great danger there is of perſons taking up with ſome *ſelf-righteous appearances* of it. The *danger* of this I eſpecially dwelt upon, being perſuaded that multitudes periſh in this hidden way; and becauſe ſo little is ſaid from moſt pulpits to diſcover any danger here: ſo that perſons being never effectually brought to die in themſelves, are never truly united to Chriſt, and ſo periſh. I alſo diſcourſed much on what I take to be the eſſence of true religion, endeavouring plainly to deſcribe that God-like temper and diſpoſition of ſoul, and that holy converſation and behaviour, that may juſtly claim the honour of having God for its original and patron. And I have reaſon to hope God bleſſed my way of diſcourſing and diſtinguiſhing, to ſome, both miniſters and people; ſo that my time was not wholly loſt.

* Among theſe are the eighth, ninth, and tenth letters, at the end of this hiſtory.

[He

[He was much visited, while in Boston, by many persons of considerable note and figure, and of the best character, and by some of the first rank; who shewed him uncommon respect, and appeared highly pleased and entertained with his conversation. And besides his being honoured with the company and respect of ministers of the town, he was visited by several ministers from various parts of the country. And as he took all opportunities to discourse of the peculiar nature, and distinguishing characters of true spiritual and vital religion, and to bear his testimony against the various false appearances of it, consisting in, or arising from impressions on the imagination, and sudden and supposed immediate suggestions of truths, not contained in the scripture, and that faith which consists primarily in a person's "believing that "Christ died for him in particular," &c.; so what he said was for the most part heard with uncommon attention and regard; and his discourses and reasonings appeared manifestly to have great weight and influence, with many that he conversed with, both ministers and others *.

Also the honourable Commissioners in Boston, of the incorporated society in London for propagating the gospel in New-England, and parts adjacent, having newly had committed to them a legacy of the late reverend and famous Dr Daniel Williams of London, for the support of *two missionaries* to the Heathen, were pleased, while he was in Boston, to consult him about a mission to those Indians called the *Six Nations*, particularly about the qualifications requisite in a missionary to those Indians; and were so satisfied with his sentiments on this head, and had that confidence in his faithfulness, and his judgment and discretion in things of this nature, that they desired him to undertake to find and recommend a couple of persons fit to be employed in this business; and very much left the matter with him.

Likewise certain pious and generously disposed gentlemen in Boston, being moved by the wonderful narrative of his labours and success among the Indians, in New-Jersey, and more especially by their conversation with him on the same subject, took opportunity to inquire more particularly into the state and necessities of his congregation, and the school

* I have had advantage for the more full information of his conduct and conversation, the entertainment he met with, and what passed relating to him while in Boston; as he was constantly attended, during his continuance there, by one of my children, in order to his assistance in his illness.

among the Indians, with a charitable intention of contributing something of their substance to promote the excellent design of the advancement of the interests of Christianity among the Indians; and understanding that there was a want of Bibles for the school, three dozen of Bibles were immediately procured, and 14 *l.* in bills (of the old tenor) given over and above, besides more large benefactions made afterwards, which I shall have occasion to mention in their proper place.

Mr Brainerd's restoration from his extremely low state in Boston, so as to go abroad again and to travel, was very unexpected to him and his friends. My daughter who was with him, writes thus concerning him, in a letter dated June 23. "——On Thursday, he was very ill with a violent fever, "and extreme pain in his head and breast, and, at turns, de-"lirious. So he remained till Saturday evening, when he "seemed to be in the agonies of death: the family was up with "him till one or two o'clock, expecting every hour would be his "last. On Sabbath-day he was a little revived, his head was "better, but very full of pain, and exceeding sore at his "breast, much put to it for breath, *&c.* Yesterday he was "better upon all accounts. Last night he slept but little. "This morning he is much worse.——Dr Pynchon says, he "has no hopes of his life; nor does he think it likely he will "ever come out of the chamber; though he says, he may "be able to come to Northampton.——"

In another letter dated June 29. she says as follows. "Mr "Brainerd has not so much pain nor fever, since I last "wrote, as before: yet he is extremely weak and low, and "very faint, expecting every day will be his last. He says, "It is impossible for him to live, for want of life. He "has hardly vigour enough to draw his breath. I went this "morning into town, and when I came home, Mr Brom-"field said, he never expected I should see him alive; for he "lay two hours, as they thought, dying; one could scarcely "tell, whether he was alive, or not; he was not able to "speak, for some time: but now is much as he was before. The "*doctor* thinks, he will drop away in such a turn. Mr "Brainerd says, he never felt any thing so much like *dissolu-"tion*, as what he felt to-day; and says, he never had any "conception of its being possible for any creature to be alive, "and yet so weak as he is from day to day.——Dr Pynchon "says, he should not be surprised, if he should so recover "as to live half a year; nor would it surprise him, if he "should die in half a day. Since I began to write, he is "not so well, having had a faint turn again: yet patient

"and

"and resigned, having no distressing fears, but the con-
"trary."

His physician, the honourable Joseph Pynchon, Esq; when he visited him in his extreme illness in Boston, attributed his sinking so suddenly into a state so extremely low, and nigh unto death, to the breaking of ulcers, that had been long gathering in his lungs, (as Mr Brainerd himself intimates in a forementioned passage in his diary), and there discharging and diffusing their purulent matter; which, while nature was labouring and struggling to throw off, (that could be done no otherwise, than by a gradual straining of it through the small vessels of those vital parts), this occasioned an high fever, and violent coughing, and threw the whole frame of nature into the utmost disorder, and brought it near to a dissolution. But supposed, if the strength of nature held till the lungs had this way gradually cleared themselves of this putrid matter, he might revive, and continue better, till new ulcers gathered and broke; but then would surely sink again; and that there was no hope of his recovery; but (as he expressed himself to one of my neighbours, who at that time saw him in Boston) he was as certainly a dead man, as if he was shot through the heart.

But so it was ordered in divine providence, that the strength of nature held out through this great conflict, so as just to escape the grave at that turn; and then he revived, to the astonishment of all that knew his case.

After he began to revive, he was visited by his youngest brother, Mr Israel Brainerd, a student at Yale-college; who having heard of his extreme illness, went from thence to Boston, in order to see him, if he might find him alive, which he but little expected.

This visit was attended with a mixture of joy and sorrow to Mr Brainerd. He greatly rejoiced to see his brother, especially because he had desired an opportunity of some religious conversation with him before he died. But this meeting was attended with sorrow, as his brother brought to him the sorrowful tidings of his sister Spencer's death at Haddam; a sister, between whom and him had long subsisted a peculiarly dear affection, and much intimacy in spiritual matters, and whose house he used to make his home, when he went to Haddam, his native place. He had heard nothing of her sickness till this report of her death. But he had these comforts, together with the tidings, *viz.* a confidence of her being gone to heaven, and an expectation of his soon meeting her there.—His brother continued with him till he left the town, and came with him from thence to Northampton.

Concerning the last Sabbath Mr Brainerd spent in Boston, he writes in his *diary* as follows.]

Lord's day, July 19. I was just able to attend public worship, being carried to the house of God in a chaise. Heard Dr Sewall preach, in the forenoon: partook of the Lord's supper at this time. In this sacrament, I saw astonishing divine *wisdom* displayed; such wisdom as I saw required the tongues of angels and glorified saints to celebrate: it seemed to me, I never should do any thing at adoring the infinite *wisdom* of God discovered in the contrivance of man's redemption, until I arrived at a world of perfection; yet I could not help striving to "call upon my soul, and all within me, to bless "the name of God."——In the afternoon, heard Mr Prince preach.—I saw more of God in the *wisdom* discovered in the plan of man's redemption, than I saw of any other of his perfections, through the whole day.

[He left Boston the next day. But before he came away, he had occasion to bear a very full, plain, and open *testimony* against that opinion, that the *essence* of saving *faith* lies in *believing that Christ died for me in particular;* and that this is the *first* act of faith in a true believer's closing with Christ. He did it in a long conference he had with a gentleman, that has very publickly and strenuously appeared to defend that tenet. He had this discourse with him in the presence of a number of considerable persons, who came to visit Mr Brainerd before he left the town, and to take their leave of him. In which debate, he made this plain declaration, (at the same time confirming what he said by many arguments), That the *essence* of saving *faith* was wholly left out of that *definition* of saving faith which that gentleman has published; and that the faith which he had *defined,* had nothing of God in it, nothing above nature, nor indeed above the power of the devils; and that all such as had *this* faith, and had *no better,* though they might have this to never so high a degree, would surely perish. And he declared also, that he never had greater *assurance* of the *falseness* of the principles of those that maintained *such* a faith, and of their dangerous and destructive tendency, or a more affecting sense of the great delusion and misery of those that depended on getting to heaven by *such* a faith, (while they had *no better*), than he lately had when he was supposed to be at the point to *die,* and expected every minute

minute to paſs into *eternity*.—Mr Brainerd's diſcourſe at this time, and the forceable reaſonings, by which he confirmed what he aſſerted, appeared to be greatly to the ſatisfaction of thoſe preſent; as ſeveral of them took occaſion expreſsly to manifeſt to him, before they took leave of him.

When this converſation was ended, having bid an affectionate farewell to his friends, he ſet out in the cool of the afternoon, on his journey to Northampton, attended by his brother, and my daughter that went with him to Boſton; and would have been accompanied out of the town by a number of gentlemen, beſides that honourable perſon who gave him his company for ſome miles on that occaſion, as a teſtimony of their eſteem and reſpect, had not his averſion to any thing of pomp and ſhew prevented it.]

Saturday, July 25. I arrived here at Northampton; having ſet out from Boſton on Monday, about four o'clock P. M In this journey, I rode about ſixteen miles a day, one day with another. Was ſometimes extremely tired and faint on the road, ſo that it ſeemed impoſſible for me to proceed any further: at other times I was conſiderably better, and felt ſome freedom both of body and mind.

Lord's day, July 26. This day, I ſaw clearly, that I ſhould never be *happy*; yea, that God himſelf could not make me happy unleſs I could be in a capacity to "pleaſe and glorify "him for ever:" take away *this*, and admit me into all the fine *heavens* that can be conceived of by men or angels, and I ſhould ſtill be *miſerable* for ever.

[Though he had ſo far revived, as to be able to travel thus far, yet he manifeſted no expectation of recovery: he ſuppoſed, as his phyſician did, that his being brought ſo near to death at Boſton, was owing to the breaking of ulcers in his lungs: he told me that he had had ſeveral ſuch ill turns before, only not to ſo high a degree, but as he ſuppoſed, owing to the ſame cauſe, *viz.* the breaking of ulcers; and that he was brought lower and lower every time; and it appeared to him, that in his laſt ſickneſs (in Boſton) he was brought as low as it was poſſible, and yet live; and that he had not the leaſt expectation of ſurviving the next return of this breaking of ulcers: but ſtill appeared perfectly calm in the proſpect of death.

On Wedneſday morning, the week after he came to Northampton, he took leave of his brother Iſrael, and never expecting

ing to see him again in this world; he now setting out from hence on his journey to New-Haven.

When Mr Brainerd came hither, he had so much strength as to be able, from day to day, to ride out two or three miles, and to return; and sometimes to pray in the family; but from this time he gradually, but sensibly, decayed, and became weaker and weaker.

While he was here, his conversation from first to last was much on the same subjects as it had been when in Boston: he was much in speaking of the nature of *true religion* of heart and practice, as distinguished from its various *counterfeits;* expressing his great concern, that the latter did so much prevail in many places. He often manifested his great abhorrence of all such *doctrines* and *principles* in religion, as in any wise savoured of, and had any (though but a remote) tendency to Antinomianism; of all such notions, as seemed to diminish the necessity of holiness of life, or to abate mens regard to the commands of God, and a strict, diligent, and universal practice of virtue and piety, under a pretence of depreciating our works, and magnifying God's free grace. He spake often, with much detestation, of such *experiences* and pretended *discoveries* and *joys*, as have nothing of the nature of *sanctification* in them, and do not tend to strictness, tenderness, and diligence in religion, and meekness and benevolence towards mankind, and an humble behaviour: and he also declared, that he looked on such pretended *humility* as worthy of no regard, that was not manifested by *modesty* of *conduct* and *conversation*. He spake often, with abhorrence, of the spirit and practice that appears among the greater part of *separatists* at this day in the land, particularly, those in the Eastern parts of Connecticut; in their condemning and separating from the *standing* ministry and churches, their crying down *learning* and a *learned* ministry, their notion of an *immediate call* to the work of the ministry, and the forwardness of *laymen* to set up themselves as public teachers. He had been much conversant in the Eastern part of Connecticut, (his native place being near to it), when the same principles, notion, and spirit began to operate, which have since prevailed to a greater height; and had acquaintance with some of those persons who are become heads and leaders of the *separatists;* he had also been conversant with persons of the same way elsewhere: and I heard him say, once and again, he knew by his acquaintance with this sort of people, that what was chiefly and most generally in repute among *them* as the *power of godliness*, was an entirely *different* thing from that

true

true vital piety recommended in the *scriptures*, and had *nothing in it* of that nature. He manifested a great dislike of a disposition in persons to much *noise* and *show* in religion, and affecting to be abundant in proclaiming and publishing their own *experiences*: though at the same time he did not condemn, but approved of Christians speaking of their own experiences on some occasions, and to some persons, with due modesty and discretion. He *himself* sometimes, while at my house, spake of his own experiences: but it was always with apparent *reserve*, and in the exercise of care and judgment with respect to occasions, persons, and circumstances. He mentioned some remarkable things of his own religious experience to two young gentlemen, candidates for the ministry, who watched with him (each at a different time) when he was very low, and not far from his end; but he desired both of them not to speak of what he had told them till *after his death*.

The things which were the subject of that debate I mentioned before, that he had with a certain gentleman, the day he left Boston, seemed to lie with much weight on his mind after he came hither; and he began to write a *letter* to that gentleman, expressing his sentiments concerning the dangerous tendency of some of the tenets he had expressed in conversation, and in the writings he had published; with the considerations by which the exceeding hurtful nature of those notions is evident; but he had not strength to finish his letter.

After he came hither, as long as he lived, he was much in speaking of that future prosperity of Zion that is so often foretold and promised in the scripture: it was a theme he delighted to dwell upon; and his mind seemed to be carried forth with earnest concern about it, and intense desires, that religion might speedily and abundantly revive and flourish; though he had not the least expectation of recovery; yea, the nearer death advanced, and the more the symptoms of its approach increased, still the more did his mind seem to be taken up with this subject. He told me, when near his end, that "he never in all his life had his mind so led forth in desires "and earnest prayers for the flourishing of *Christ's kingdom* "on earth, as since he was brought so exceeding low at Boston." He seemed much to wonder, that there appeared no more of a disposition in ministers and people to pray for the flourishing of religion through the world; that so little a part of their *prayers* was generally taken up about it, in their families, and elsewhere; and particularly, he several times expressed his wonder, that there appeared no more forward-

ness

neſs to comply with the *propoſal* lately made, in a memorial from a number of miniſters in Scotland, and ſent over into America, for *united extraordinary prayer*, among Chriſt's miniſters and people, for the *coming of Chriſt's kingdom*: and he ſent it as his dying advice to *his own congregation*, that they ſhould practiſe agreeably to that propoſal *.

Though he was conſtantly exceeding weak, yet there appeared in him a continual care well to improve *time*, and fill it up with ſomething that might be profitable, and in ſome reſpect for the glory of God or the good of men; either profitable converſation, or writing letters to abſent friends, or noting ſomething in his diary, or looking over his former writings, correcting them, and preparing them to be left in the hands of others at his death, or giving ſome directions concerning a future conducting and management of his people, or employment in ſecret devotions. He ſeemed never to be eaſy, however ill, if he was not doing ſomething for God, or in his ſervice.

After he came hither, he wrote a *preface* to a *diary* of the famous Mr Shepard's, (in thoſe papers before mentioned, lately found), having been much urged to it by thoſe gentlemen in Boſton who had the care of the publication: which diary, with his *preface*, has ſince been publiſhed †.

In his diary for Lord's day, Auguſt 9. he ſpeaks of longing deſires after *death*, through a ſenſe of the excellency of a ſtate of *perfection*.

In his diary for Lord's day, Auguſt 16. he ſpeaks of his having ſo much refreſhment of *ſoul* in the houſe of God, that it ſeemed alſo to refreſh his *body*. And this is not only noted in his diary, but was very obſervable to others; it was very apparent, not only, that his *mind* was exhilarated with inward conſolation, but alſo that his *animal* ſpirits and *bodily* ſtrength ſeemed to be remarkably reſtored, as though he had forgot his illneſs.——But this was the laſt time that ever he attended public worſhip on the Sabbath.

* His congregation, ſince this, have with great cheerfulneſs and unanimity fallen in with this advice, and have practiſed agreeably to the propoſal from Scotland; and have at times appeared with uncommon engagedneſs and fervency of ſpirit in their meetings and united devotions, purſuant to that propoſal. Alſo the preſbyteries of New-York, and New Brunſwick, ſince this, have with one conſent, fallen in with the propoſal, as likewiſe ſome others of God's people in thoſe parts.

† A part of this *preface* is inſerted in the *appendix* to this hiſtory.

On

On Tuesday morning that week (I being absent on a journey) he prayed with my family; but not without much difficulty, for want of bodily strength; and this was the last family-prayer that ever he made.

He had been wont, till now, frequently to ride out, two or three miles: but this week, on Thursday, was the last time he ever did so.]

Lord's day, August 23. This morning, I was considerably refreshed with the thought, yea, the hope and expectation of the *enlargement* of *Christ's kingdom;* and I could not but hope, the time was at hand, when Babylon the great would *fall*, and *rise no more*: this led me to some spiritual meditations, that were very refreshing to me. I was unable to attend public worship, either part of the day; but God was pleased to afford me fixedness and satisfaction in divine thoughts. Nothing so refreshes my soul, as when I can *go to God*, yea, *to God my exceeding joy*. When he is so, sensibly, to my soul, Oh how unspeakably delightful is this!

In the week past, I had divers turns of inward refreshing; though my body was inexpressibly weak, followed continually with agues and fevers. Sometimes my soul centred in God, as my only *portion;* and I felt that I should be for ever unhappy, if *he* did not *reign*: I saw the sweetness and happiness of being *his* subject, at *his* disposal. This made all my difficulties quickly vanish.

From this Lord's day, *viz.* August 23. I was troubled very much with vapoury disorders, and could neither write nor read, and could scarcely live; although through mercy, was not so much oppressed with heavy melancholy and gloominess, as at many other times.

[Till this week he had been wont to lodge in a room above stairs; but he now grew so weak, that he was no longer able to go up stairs and down. Friday, August 28. was the last time he ever went above stairs, henceforward he betook himself to a lower room.

On Wednesday, September 2. being the day of our public lecture, he seemed to be refreshed with seeing the neighbouring ministers that came hither to the lecture, and expressed a great desire once more to go to the house of God on that day: and accordingly rode to the meeting, and attended divine service, while the Reverend Mr Woodbridge of Hatfield preached. He signified that he supposed it to be the last time that ever he should attend the public worship; as it proved. And indeed it was the last time that ever he went out at our gate alive.

On the Saturday-evening next following, he was unexpectedly visited by his brother Mr John Brainerd, who came to see him from New-Jersey. He was much refreshed by this unexpected visit, this brother being peculiarly dear to him; and he seemed to rejoice in a devout and solemn manner, to see him, and to hear the comfortable tidings he brought concerning the state of his dear congregation of Christian Indians: and a circumstance of this visit, that he was exceeding glad of, was, that his brother brought him some of his private writings from New-Jersey, and particularly his diary that he had kept for many years past.]

Lord's day, September 6. I began to read some of my private writings, which my brother brought me; and was considerably refreshed with what I met with in them.

Monday, September 7. I proceeded further in reading my old private writings, and found they had the same effect upon me as before: I could not but rejoice and bless God for what passed long ago, which without writing had been entirely lost.

This evening, when I was in great distress of body, my soul longed that God should be glorified: I saw there was no heaven but this. I could not but speak to the bystanders then of the only *happiness*, viz. *pleasing* God. Oh that I could for ever live to God! The day, I trust, is at hand, the perfect day: Oh, the day of deliverance from all sin!

Lord's day, September 13. I was much refreshed and engaged in meditation and writing, and found a heart to act for God. My spirits were refreshed, and my soul delighted to do something for God.

[On the evening following that Lord's day, his feet began to appear sensibly swelled; which thenceforward swelled more and more. A symptom of his dissolution coming on.

The next day, his brother John left him, being obliged to return to New-Jersey on some business of great importance and necessity; intending to return again with all possible speed, hoping to see his brother yet once more in the land of the living.

Mr Brainerd having now with much deliberation considered of the important affair forementioned, left with him by the honourable commissioners in Boston, of the corporation in London for the propagation of the gospel in New-England and parts adjacent, *viz.* the fixing upon and recommending

two

two persons proper to be employed as missionaries to the Six Nations, he about this time wrote a letter, recommending two young gentlemen of his acquaintance to those commissioners, *viz.* Mr Elihu Spencer of East-Haddam, and Mr Job Strong of Northampton. The commissioners on the receipt of this letter, cheerfully and unanimously agreed to accept of and employ the persons he had recommended: who accordingly have since waited on the commissioners to receive their instructions; and pursuant to their instructions, have applied themselves to a preparation for the business of their mission, in the manner to which they directed them; and one of them, *viz.* Mr Spencer, has been solemnly ordained to that work, by several of the ministers of Boston, in the presence of an ecclesiastical council convened for that purpose; and is now gone forth to the nation of the Oneidaes, about one hundred and seventy miles beyond Albany.

He also this week, *viz.* on Wednesday, September 16. wrote a letter to a particular gentleman in Boston (one of those charitable persons forementioned, who appeared so forward to contribute of their substance for the promoting Christianity among the Indians) relating to the growth of the Indian school, and the need of another schoolmaster, or some person to assist the schoolmaster in instructing the Indian children. These gentlemen, on the receipt of this letter, had a meeting, and agreed with great cheerfulness to give *L.* 200 (in bills of the old tenor) for the support of another schoolmaster; and desired the reverend Mr Pemberton of New-York, (who was then at Boston, and was also, at their desire, present at their meeting), as soon as possible to procure a suitable person for that service; and also agreed to allow *L.* 75 to defray some special charges that were requisite to encourage the mission to the Six Nations, (besides the salary allowed by the commissioners), which was also done on some intimations given by Mr Brainerd.

Mr Brainerd spent himself much in writing those letters, being exceeding weak: but it seemed to be much to his satisfaction, that he had been enabled to do it; hoping that it was something done for God, and which might be for the advancement of Christ's kingdom and glory. In writing the last of these letters, he was obliged to use the hand of another, not being able to write himself.

On the Thursday of this week (September 17.) was the last time that ever he went out of his lodging-room. That day, he was again visited by his brother Israel, who continued with him thenceforward till his death. On that evening, he was taken with something of a *diarrhea;* which he looked upon as another sign of his approaching *death:* whereupon he expressed himself thus; "Oh, the glorious time is now "coming! I have longed to serve God perfectly: now God "will gratify those desires!" And from time to time, at the several steps and new symptoms of the sensible approach of his dissolution, he was so far from being sunk or damped, that he seemed to be animated, and made more cheerful; as being glad at the appearances of *death's* approach. He often used the epithet, *glorious,* when speaking of the day of his *death,* calling it *that glorious day.* And as he saw his dissolution gradually approaching, he was much in talking about it, with perfect calmness speaking of a future state; and also settling all his affairs, very particularly and minutely giving directions concerning what he would have done in one respect and another after he was dead. And the nearer death approached, the more desirous he seemed to be of it. He several times spake of the different kinds of *willingness to die;* and spoke of it as an ignoble mean kind of willingness to die, to be willing to leave the body, only to get rid of pain; or to go to heaven, only to get honour and advancement there.]

Saturday, September 19. Near night, while I attempted to walk a little, my thoughts turned thus; "How infinitely "sweet it is, to love God, and be all for him!" Upon which it was suggested to me, "You are not an angel, not lively "and active." To which my whole soul immediately replied, "I as sincerely desire to love and glorify God, as any "angel in heaven." Upon which it was suggested again, "But you are filthy, not fit for heaven." Hereupon instantly appeared the blessed robes of Christ's *righteousness,* which I could not but exult and triumph in; and I viewed the infinite excellency of God, and my soul even broke with longings, that God should be *glorified.* I thought of dignity in heaven; but instantly the thought returned, "I do not go "to heaven to get honour, but to give all possible glory and "praise." Oh, how I longed that God should be glorified on *earth* also! Oh, I was made, for eternity, if God might be glorified! *Bodily pains* I cared not for; though I was then in extremity, I never felt easier; I felt willing to *glorify God* in that state of bodily distress, as long as he pleased I should continue in it. The *grave* appeared really sweet, and I longed to lodge my weary bones in it: but Oh, that God might be *glorified!* this was the burden of all my cry. Oh, I knew, I should be *active* as an angel, in heaven; and that I should be stripped of

my

my *filthy garments*; so that there was no objection.——But Oh, to *love* and *praise* God more, to *please* him for ever! this my soul panted after, and even now pants for while I write. Oh that *God* might be *glorified* in the whole earth! "Lord, "let thy kingdom come." I longed for a spirit of *preaching* to descend and rest on *ministers*, that they might address the consciences of men with closeness and power. I saw, God "had the residue of the Spirit;" and my soul longed it should be "poured from on high." I could not but plead with God for my dear *congregation*, that he would preserve it, and not suffer *his great name* to lose its glory in that work; my soul still longing, that God might be *glorified*.

[The extraordinary frame, that he was in, that evening, could not be hid; "his mouth spake out of the abundance of "his heart," expressing in a very affecting manner much the same things as are written in his *diary*: and among very many other extraordinary expressions, which he then uttered, were such as these; "*My heaven* is to *please* God, and *glorify* "him, and to give all to him, and to be wholly devoted to "his glory; that is the heaven I long for; that is my *re*-"*ligion*, and that is my *happiness*, and always was ever since "I suppose I had any true religion; and all those that are "of *that* religion shall meet *me* in heaven.—— I do not go "to heaven to be advanced, but to give honour to God. "It is no matter where I shall be stationed in heaven, whe-"ther I have a high or low seat there; but to love, and "please, and glorify God is all: had I a *thousand souls*, if "they were worth any thing, I would give them all to God; "but I have nothing to give, when all is done.——It is im-"possible for any rational creature to be *happy* without act-"ing all *for God*: God himself could not make him happy "any other way.——I long to be in heaven, *praising* and "*glorifying God* with the holy angels: all my desire is to "*glorify* God.——My heart goes out to the *burying-place*; it "seems to me a *desirable* place: but Oh to *glorify* God! that "is it; that is above all.——It is a great comfort to me, to "think, that I have done a little *for* God in the world: Oh! "it is but a *very small* matter; yet I *have* done a *little*; and "I lament it, that I have not done *more* for him.——There "is nothing in the world worth living for, but *doing good*, "and *finishing God's work*, doing the work that Christ did. "I see nothing else in the world, that can yield any satisfac-"tion, besides *living to God*, *pleasing him*, and *doing his* "*whole will*.——My greatest joy and comfort *has been*, to

"do

"do ſomething for promoting the intereſt of religion, and "the ſouls of particular perſons: and *now*, in my illneſs, "while I am full of pain and diſtreſs, from day to day, all "the comfort I have, is in being able to do ſome little *char* "(or ſmall piece of work) *for God;* either by ſomething that "I ſay, or by writing, or ſome other way."

He intermingled with theſe and other like expreſſions, many pathetical *counſels* to thoſe that were about him; particularly to my children and ſervants. He applied himſelf to ſome of my younger children at this time; calling them to him, and ſpeaking to them one by one; ſetting before them, in a very plain manner, the nature and eſſence of true piety, and its great importance and neceſſity; earneſtly warning them not to reſt in any thing ſhort of that true and thorough change of heart, and a life dovoted to God; counſelling them not to be ſlack in the great buſineſs of religion, nor in the leaſt to delay it; enforcing his counſels with this, that his words were the words of a *dying man:* ſaid he, "I ſhall die "here, and here I ſhall be buried, and here you will ſee my "grave, and do you remember what I have ſaid to you. I "am going into eternity: and it is ſweet to me to think of "eternity; the endleſſneſs of it makes it ſweet: but Oh, "what ſhall I ſay to the eternity of the *wicked!* I cannot "mention it, nor think of it; the thought is too dreadful. "When you ſee my grave, then remember what I ſaid to you "while I was alive; then think with yourſelf, how that man "that lies in that grave, counſelled and warned me to pre"pare for death."

His *body* ſeemed to be marvellouſly ſtrengthened, through the inward vigour and refreſhment of his *mind;* ſo that, although before he was ſo weak that he could hardly utter a ſentence, yet now he continued his moſt affecting and profitable diſcourſe to us for more than an hour, with ſcarce any intermiſſion; and ſaid of it, when he had done, "it was the "laſt ſermon that ever he ſhould preach."

This extraordinary frame of mind continued the next day; of which he ſays in his *diary* as follows.]

Lord's day, September 20. Was ſtill in a ſweet and comfortable frame: and was again melted with deſires that God might be *glorified,* and with longings to love and live to him. Longed for the influences of the divine Spirit to deſcend on *miniſters,* in a ſpecial manner. And Oh, I longed to be *with* God, to *behold his glory,* and to bow in his preſence!

[It

[It appears by what is noted in his *diary*, both of this day, and the evening preceding, that his mind at this time was much impressed with a sense of the importance of the work of the *ministry*, and the need of the grace of God, and his special spiritual assistance in this work: and it also appeared in what he expressed in conversation; particularly in his discourse to his brother Israel, who was then a member of Yale college at New-Haven, and had been prosecuting his studies, and academical exercises there, to that end, that he might be fitted for the work of the ministry, and was now with him *. He now, and from time to time, in this his dying state, recommended to his brother, a life of self-deniel, of weanedness from the world, and devotedness to God, and an earnest endeavour to obtain much of the grace of God's Spirit, and God's gracious influences on his heart; representing the great need which ministers stand in of them, and the unspeakable benefit of them from his own experience. Among many other expressions, he said thus; "When ministers feel these "special gracious influences on their hearts, it wonderfully "assists them to come at the consciences of men, and as it "were to handle them with hands; whereas, without them, "whatever reason and oratory we make use of, we do but "make use of stumps, instead of hands."

Monday, September 21. I began to correct a little volume of my private writings: God, I believe, remarkably helped me in it; my strength was surprisingly lengthened out, and my thoughts quick and lively, and my soul refreshed, hoping it might be a work for God. Oh, how good, how sweet it is, to labour for God!

Tuesday, September 22. Was again employed in reading and correcting, and had the same success, as the day before. I was exceeding weak; but it seemed to refresh my soul, thus to spend time.

Wednesday, September 23. I finished my corrections of the little piece forementioned, and felt uncommonly peaceful: it seemed as if I had now done all my work in this world, and stood ready for my call to a better. As long as I see any

* This young gentleman was an ingenious, serious, studious, and hopefully truly pious person: there appeared in him many qualities giving hope of his being a great blessing in his day. But it has pleased God, since the death of his brother, to take him away also. He died that winter, at New-Haven, on January 6. 1747-8. of a nervous fever, after about a fortnight's illness.

thing

thing to be done for God, life is worth having: but Oh, how vain and unworthy it is, to live for any lower end!——This day, I indited a letter, I think, of great importance, to the Reverend Mr Byram in New-Jersey: Oh that God would bless and succeed that letter, which was written for the benefit of his church *! Oh that God would *purify the sons of Levi*, that his glory may be advanced!——This night, I endured a dreadful turn, wherein my life was expected scarce an hour or minute together. But blessed be God, I have enjoyed considerable sweetness in divine things, this week, both by night and day.

Thursday, September 24. My strength began to fail exceedingly; which looked further as if I had done all my work: however, I had strength to fold and superscribe my letter. About two I went to bed, being weak and much disordered, and lay in a burning fever till night, without any proper rest. In the evening, I got up, having lain down in some of my cloaths; but was in the greatest distress, that ever I endured, having an uncommon kind of hiccough; which either strangled me, or threw me into a straining to vomit; and at the same time was distressed with griping pains. Oh, the distress of this evening! I had little expectation of my living the night through, nor indeed had any about me: and I longed for the *finishing* moment!——I was obliged to repair to bed by six o'clock; and through mercy enjoyed some rest; but was grievously distressed at turns with the hiccough.——My soul breathed after God, while the watcher was with me: ——"When shall I come to God, even to God, my exceeding joy? Oh for his blessed likeness!"

Friday, September 25. This day, I was unspeakably weak, and little better than speechless all the day: however, I was able to write a little, and felt comfortably in some part of the day. Oh, it refreshed my soul, to think of former things, of desires to glorify God, of the pleasures of living to him! "Oh my dear God, I am speedily coming to thee, I hope! hasten the day, O Lord, if it be thy blessed will: Oh come, Lord Jesus, come quickly. Amen †."

* It was concerning the qualifications of *ministers*, and the examination and licensing of *candidates* for the work of the ministry.

† This was the last that ever he wrote in his *diary* with his own hand: though it is continued a little farther, in a broken manner; written by his brother Israel, but indited by his mouth in this his weak and dying state.

Saturday,

Saturday, September 26. I felt the sweetness of divine things, this forenoon; and had the consolation of a consciousness that I was doing something for God.

Lord's day, September 27. This was a very comfortable day to my soul; I think, *I awoke with God.* I was enabled to *lift up my soul to God,* early this morning; and while I had little bodily strength, I found freedom to lift up my heart to God for myself and others. Afterwards, was pleased with the thoughts of speedily entering into the unseen world.

[Early this morning, as one of the family came into the room, he expressed himself thus: "I have had more *pleasure* "this morning, than all the *drunkards* in the world enjoy, "if it were all extracted!"——So much did he esteem the *joy of faith* above the *pleasures of sin.*

He felt, that morning, an unusual appetite to food; with which his mind seemed to be *exhilarated,* as looking on it a sign of the very near approach of *death;* and said upon it, "I was born on a *Sabbath-day;* and I have reason to think I "was new-born on a *Sabbath-day;* and I hope I shall die on "this *Sabbath-day:* I shall look upon it as a favour, if it "may be the will of God that it should be so: I long for the "time. Oh, *why is his chariot so long in coming? why* "*tarry the wheels of his chariots?* I am very willing to "part with all: I am willing to part with my dear brother "John, and never to see him again, to go to be for ever with "the Lord *. Oh, when I go there, how will God's dear "church on earth be upon my mind!"

Afterwards, the same morning, being asked, how he did? he answered, "I am almost in eternity: I long to be there. "My work is done: I have done with all my friends: all "the world is nothing to me. I long to be in heaven, *prai-* "*sing and glorifying God* with the holy *angels:* all my desire "is to glorify God."

During the whole of these last two weeks of his life, he seemed to continue in this frame of heart, loose from all the world, as having done his work, and done with all things here below, having nothing to do but to die, and abiding in an

* He had, before this, expressed a desire, if it might be the will of God, to live till his brother returned from New-Jersey: who, when he went away, intended, if possible, to perform his journey, and return in a fortnight; hoping once more to meet his brother in the land of the living. The fortnight was now near expired, it ended the next day.

 earnest

earnest desire and expectation of the happy moment, when his soul should take its flight, and go to a state of perfection of holiness and perfect glorifying and enjoying God, manifested in a variety of expressions. He said, "That the consideration of the day of death, and the day of judgment, had a long time been peculiarly sweet to him." He from time to time spake of his being willing to leave the body and the world *immediately*, that day, that night, and that moment, if it was the will of God. He also was much in expressing his longings that the church of Christ on *earth* might flourish, and Christ's kingdom here might be advanced, notwithstanding he was about to leave the *earth*, and should not with his eyes behold the desirable event, nor be instrumental in promoting it. He said to me, one morning, as I came into the room, "My thoughts have been employed on the old dear theme, *the prosperity* of God's church on *earth*. As I waked out of sleep, I was led to cry for the pouring out of God's Spirit, and the advancement of Christ's kingdom, which the dear Redeemer did and suffered so much for. It is that especially makes me long for it."——He expressed much hope that a glorious advancement of Christ's kingdom was *near* at hand.

He once told me, that "he had formerly longed for the outpouring of the Spirit of God, and the glorious times of the church, and hoped they were coming; and should have been willing to have lived to promote religion at that time, if that had been the will of God; but (says he) I am willing it should be as it is; I would not have the choice to make for myself, for ten thousand worlds." He expressed on his deathbed a full persuasion that he should in *heaven* see the prosperity of the church on *earth*, and should rejoice with Christ therein; and the consideration of it seemed to be highly pleasing and satisfying to his mind.

He also still dwelt much on the great importance of the work of *ministers* of the gospel; and expressed his longings, that they might be *filled with the Spirit of God;* and manifested much desire to see some of the neighbouring ministers, whom he had some acquaintance with, and whose sincere friendship he was confident of, that he might converse freely with them on that subject, before he died. And it so happened, that he had opportunity with some of them, according to his desire.

Another thing that lay much on his heart, and that he spake of, from time to time, in these near approaches of death, was the spiritual prosperity of his own congregation of of Christian Indians in New-Jersey: and when he spake of them, it was with peculiar tenderness; so that his speech would be presently interrupted and drowned with tears.

He also expressed much satisfaction in the disposals of Providence, with regard to the circumstances of his *death*; particularly that God had before his death given him the opportunity he had had in Boston, with so many considerable persons, ministers and others, to give in *his testimony* for God, and against false religion, and many mistakes that lead to it, and promote it; and there to lay before pious and charitable gentlemen, the state of the Indians, and their necessities, to so good effect; and that God had since given him opportunity to write to them further concerning these affairs; and to write other letters of importance, that he hoped might be of good influence with regard to the state of religion among the Indians, and elsewhere, after his death. He expressed great thankfulness to God for his mercy in these things. He also mentioned it as what he accounted a merciful circumstance of his death, that he should die *here* *. And speaking of these things, he said, "God had granted him all his desire;" and signified, that now he could with the greater alacrity leave the world.]

Monday, September 28. I was able to read, and make some few corrections in my private writings; but found I could not write, as I had done; I found myself sensibly declined in all respects. It has been only from a little while before noon, till about one or two o'clock, that I have been able to do any thing for some time past: yet this refreshed my heart, that I could do any thing, either public or private, that I hoped was for God.

[This evening, he was supposed to be dying: he thought so himself, and was thought so by those who were about him.

* The editor takes leave to make the remark, that when Mr Brainerd was at Boston, sick nigh unto death, it was with reluctance he thought of dying in a place where *funerals* are often attended with a *pomp* and *show*, which (especially on occasion of his own) he was very averse to any appearance of: and though it was with some difficulty he got his mind reconciled to the prospect then before him, yet at last he was brought to acquiesce in the divine will, with respect to this circumstance of his departure. However, it pleased God to order the event so as to gratify his *desire*, which he had expressed, of getting back to Northampton, with a view particularly to a more silent and private *burial*.

He seemed glad at the appearance of the near approach of death. He was almost speechless, but his lips appeared to move: and one that sat very near him, heard him utter such expressions as these, "Come, Lord Jesus, come quickly.—"Oh, why is his chariot so long in coming!"—After he revived, he blamed himself for having been too eager to be gone. And in expressing what he found in the frame of his mind at that time, he said, he then found an inexpressibly sweet love to those that he looked upon as *belonging to Christ*, beyond almost all that ever he felt before; so that it "seemed (to use his own words) like a little piece of *heaven* to have one of them near him." And being asked, whether he heard the prayer that was (at his desire) made with him; he said, "Yes, he heard every word, and had an uncommon sense of "the things that were uttered in that prayer, and that every "word reached his heart."

On the evening of the next, *viz.* Tuesday, September 29. as he lay in his bed, he seemed to be in an extraordinary frame; his mind greatly engaged in sweet meditations concerning the prosperity of Zion: there being present here at that time two young gentlemen of his acquaintance, that were *candidates* for the *ministry*, he desired us all to unite in singing a Psalm on that subject, even Zion's prosperity. And on his desire we sung a part of the ciid Psalm. This seemed much to refresh and revive him, and gave him new strength; so that, though before he could scarcely speak at all, now he proceeded, with some freedom of speech, to give his dying counsels to those two young gentlemen forementioned, relating to their preparation for, and prosecution of that great work of the ministry they were designed for; and in particular, earnestly recommended to them frequent secret *fasting* and *prayer*: and enforced his counsel with regard to this, from his own *experience* of the great comfort and benefit of it; which (said he) I should not mention, were it not that I am a *dying* person. And after he had finished his counsel, he made a prayer, in the audience of us all; wherein, besides praying for this family, for his brethren, and those candidates for the ministry, and for his own congregation, he earnestly prayed for the reviving and flourishing of religion in the world.

Till now, he had every day sat up part of the day; but after this he never rose from his bed.]

Wednesday, September 30. I was obliged to keep my bed the whole day, through weakness. However, redeemed a little time, and with the help of my brother, read and corrected about a dozen pages in my M. S. giving an account of my conversion.

Thursday, October 1. I endeavoured again to do something by way of writing, but soon found my powers of body and mind utterly fail. Felt not so sweetly, as when I was able to do something that I hoped would do some good. In the evening, was discomposed and wholly delirious; but it was not long before God was pleased to give me some sleep, and fully composed my mind*. Oh, blessed be God for his great goodness to me, since I was so low at Mr Bromfield's, on Thursday June 18. last past. He has, except those few minutes, given me the clear exercise of my reason, and enabled me to labour much for him, in things both of a public and private nature; and perhaps to do more good, than I should have done if I had been well; besides the comfortable influences of his blessed Spirit, with which he has been pleased to refresh my soul. May his name have all the glory for ever and ever. Amen.

Friday, October 2. My soul was this day, at turns, sweetly set on God: I longed to be *with him*, that I might *behold his glory*: I felt sweetly disposed to commit all to him, even my dearest friends, my dearest flock, and my absent brother, and all my concerns for time and eternity. Oh that *his kingdom* might come in the world; that they might all love and glorify him, for what he is in himself; and that the blessed Redeemer might "see of the travail of his soul, and be satisfied! Oh, come, Lord Jesus, come quickly! Amen †."

[The next evening, we very much expected his brother John from New-Jersey; it being about a week after the time that he proposed for his return, when he went away. And though our expectations were still disappointed; yet Mr Brainerd seemed to continue unmoved, in the same calm and peaceful frame, that he had before manifested; as having resigned all to God, and having done with his friends, and with all things here below.

On the morning of the next day, being Lord's day, October 4. as my daughter Jerusha (who chiefly tended him) came into the room, he looked on her very pleasantly, and said,

* From this time forward, he had the free use of his reason till the day before his death; excepting that at some times he appeared a little lost for a moment, at first waking out of sleep.

† Here ends his *diary*: these are the *last words*, that are written in it, either by his own hand, or by any other from his mouth.

said, "Dear Jerusha, are you willing to part with me?—I am "quite willing to part with you: I am willing to part with "all my friends: I am willing to part with my dear brother "John, although I love him the best of any creature living: "I have committed him and all my friends to God, and can "leave them with God. Though, if I thought I should not "see you, and be happy with you in another world I could "not bear to part with you. But we shall spend an happy "eternity together *!" In the evening, as one came into the room with a Bible in her hand, he expressed himself thus; "Oh, that dear book! that lovely book! I shall soon see it "opened! the mysteries that are in it, and the mysteries of "God's providence, will be all unfolded!"

His distemper now very apparently preyed on his vitals in an extraordinary manner: not by a sudden breaking of *ulcers* in his lungs, as at Boston, but by a constant discharge of purulent matter, in great quantities: so that what he brought up by expectoration, seemed to be as it were mouthfuls of almost clear *pus*; which was attended with very great inward pain and distress.

On Thursday, October 6. he lay, for a considerable time, as if he were dying. At which time, he was heard to utter,

* Since this, it has pleased a holy and sovereign God to take away this my dear child by death, on the 14th of February, next following; after a short illness of five days; in the eighteenth year of her age. She was a person of much the same spirit with Mr Brainerd. She had constantly taken care of, and attended him in his sickness, for nineteen weeks before his death; devoting herself to it with great delight, because she looked on him as an eminent servant of Jesus Christ. In this time, he had much conversation with her on things of religion; and in his dying state, often expressed to us, her parents, his great satisfaction concerning her true piety, and his confidence that he should meet her in heaven; and his high opinion of her, not only as a true Christian, but a very eminent saint; one whose soul was uncommonly fed and entertained with things that appertain to the most spiritual, experimental, and distinguishing parts of religion; and one who, by the temper of her mind, was fitted to deny herself for God, and to do good, beyond any young women whatsoever that he knew of. She had manifested a heart uncommonly devoted to God, in the course of her life, many years before her death; and said on her deathbed, that "she had not seen one minute for several years, wherein she "desired to live one minute longer, for the sake of any other good "in life, but doing good, living to God, and doing what might be "for his glory."

in broken whiſpers, ſuch expreſſions as theſe; "He will "come, he will not tarry.—I ſhall ſoon be in glory.—I ſhall "ſoon glorify God with the angels."——But after ſome time he revived.

The next day, *viz.* Wedneſday, October 7. his brother John arrived, being returned from New-Jerſey; where he had been detained much longer than he intended, by a mortal ſickneſs prevailing among the Chriſtian Indians, and by ſome other things in their circumſtances that made his ſtay with them neceſſary. Mr Brainerd was affected and refreſhed with ſeeing him, and appeared fully ſatisfied with the reaſons of his delay; ſeeing the intereſt of religion and of the ſouls of his people required it.

The next day, Thurſday, October 8. he was in great diſtreſs and agonies of body; and for the bigger part of the day, was much diſordered as to the exerciſe of his reaſon. In the evening, he was more compoſed, and had the uſe of his reaſon well; but the pain of his body continued and increaſed. He told me, it was impoſſible for any to conceive of the diſtreſs he felt in his breaſt. He manifeſted much concern leſt he ſhould diſhonour God by impatience, under his extreme agony; which was ſuch, that he ſaid, the thought of enduring it one minute longer was almoſt inſupportable. He deſired, that others would be much in lifting up their hearts continually to God for him, that God would ſupport him, and give him patience. He ſignified, that he expected to die that night; but ſeemed to fear a longer delay: and the diſpoſition of his mind with regard to death appeared ſtill the ſame that it had been all along. And notwithſtanding his bodily agonies, yet the intereſt of Zion lay ſtill with great weight on his mind; as appeared by ſome conſiderable diſcourſe he had that evening with the Reverend Mr Billing, one of the neighbouring miniſters, (who was then preſent), concerning the great importance of the work of the miniſtry, *&c.* And afterwards, when it was very late in the night, he had much very proper and profitable diſcourſe with his brother John, concerning his congregation in New-Jerſey, and the intereſt of religion among the Indians. In the latter part of the night, his bodily diſtreſs ſeemed to riſe to a greater height than ever; and he ſaid to thoſe then about him, that "it was another thing "to die, than people imagined;" explaining himſelf to mean that they were not aware what *bodily* pain and anguiſh is undergone before death. Towards day, his eyes fixed; and he continued lying immoveable, till about ſix o'clock in the morning, and then expired, on Friday, October 9. 1747. when

when his soul, as we may well conclude, was received by his dear Lord and Master, as an eminently faithful servant, into that state of perfection of holiness, and fruition of God, which he had so often and so ardently longed for; and was welcomed by the glorious assembly in the upper world, as one peculiarly fitted to join them in their blessed employments and enjoyments.

Much respect was shewn to his memory at his *funeral;* which was on the Monday following, after a sermon preached the same day, on that solemn occasion. His funeral was attended by eight of the neighbouring ministers, and seventeen other gentlemen of liberal education, and a great concourse of people.]

Some

****

Some further REMAINS of the Reverend Mr David Brainerd.

I. A Scheme of a *dialogue* between the various *powers* and *affections* of the mind, as they are found alternately whispering in the *godly soul*. (Mentioned in his diary, February 3. 1744.)

1. THE *understanding* introduced, (1.) As discovering its own excellency, and capacity of enjoying the most sublime pleasure and happiness. (2.) As observing its desire equal to its capacity, and incapable of being satisfied with any thing that will not fill it in the utmost extent of its exercise. (3.) As finding itself a dependent thing, not self-sufficient; and consequently unable to spin happiness (as the spider spins its web) out of its own bowels. This self-sufficiency observed to be the property and prerogative of God alone, and not belonging to any created being. (4.) As in vain seeking sublime pleasure, satisfaction, and happiness adequate to its nature, amongst created beings. The search and knowledge of the truth in the natural world allowed indeed to be refreshing to the mind; but still failing to afford complete happiness. (5.) As discovering the excellency and glory of God, that he is the fountain of goodness, and well-spring of happiness, and every way fit to answer the enlarged desires and cravings of our immortal souls.

2. The *will* introduced, as necessarily, yet freely chusing this God for its supreme happiness and only portion, fully complying with the understanding's dictates, acquiescing in God as the best good, his will as the best rule for intelligent creatures, and rejoicing that God is in every respect just what he is; and withal chusing and delighting to be a dependent creature, always subject to this God, not aspiring after self sufficiency and supremacy, but acquiescing in the contrary.

3. Ardent *love* or *desire* introduced, as passionately longing to please and glorify the divine Being, to be in every respect conformed to him, and in that way to enjoy him. This love or desire represented as most genuine; not induced by mean and mercenary views; not primarily springing from selfish hopes of salvation, whereby the divine glories would be sacrificed to the idol self: not arising from a slavish fear of divine anger in case of neglect, nor yet from hopes of feeling the sweetness of that tender and pleasant passion of love in one's own breast; but from a just esteem of the beauteous object beloved. This *love* further represented, as attended with vehement longings after the enjoyment of its object, but unable to find by what means.

4. The *understanding* again introduced, as informing, (1.) How God might have been enjoyed, yea, how he must necessarily have been enjoyed, had not man sinned against him; that as there was *knowledge*, *likeness*, and *love*, so there must needs be enjoyment, while there was no impediment. (2.) How he may be enjoyed in some measure now, *viz.* by the same *knowledge*, begetting *likeness* and *love*, which will be answered with returns of *love*, and the smiles of God's countenance, which are better than life. (3.) How God may be perfectly enjoyed, *viz.* by the soul's perfect freedom from sin. This perfect freedom never obtained till death; and then not by any unaccountable means, or in any unheard-of manner; but the same by which it has obtained some likeness to and fruition of God in this world, *viz.* a clear manifestation of him.

5. *Holy desire* appears, and inquires why the soul may not be perfectly holy; and so perfect in the enjoyment of God here; and expresses most insatiable thirstings after such a temper, and such fruition, and most consummate blessedness.

6. *Understanding* again appears, and informs, that God designs that those whom he sanctifies in part here, and intends for immortal glory, shall tarry a while in this present evil world, that their own experience of temptations, *&c.* may teach them how great the deliverance is, which God has wrought for them, that they may be swallowed up in thankfulness and admiration to eternity; as also that they may be instrumental of doing good to their fellow-men. Now if they were perfectly holy, *&c.* a world of sin would not be a fit habitation for them; and further, such manifestations of God as are necessary completely to sanctify the soul, would be insupportable to the body, so that we cannot *see God, and live.*

7. *Holy*

7. *Holy impatience* is next introduced, complaining of the ſins and ſorrows of life, and almoſt repining at the diſtance of a ſtate of perfection, uneaſy to ſee and feel the hours hang ſo dull and heavy, and almoſt concluding that the temptations, hardſhips, diſappointments, imperfections, and tedious employments of life will never come to a happy period.

8. *Tender conſcience* comes in, and meekly reproves the complaints of *impatience*; urging how careful and watchful we ought to be, leſt we ſhould offend the divine Being with complaints; alledging alſo the fitneſs of our waiting patiently upon God for all we want, and that in a way of doing and ſuffering; and at the ſame time mentioning the barrenneſs of the ſoul, how much precious time is miſimproved, and how little it has enjoyed of God, compared with what it might have done; as alſo ſuggeſting how frequently impatient complaints ſpring from nothing better than ſelf-love, want of reſignation, and a greater reverence of the divine Being.

9. *Judgment* or *ſound mind* next appears, and duly weighs the complaints of *impatience*, and the gentle admonitions of *tender conſcience*, and impartially determines between them. On the one hand, it concludes, that we may always be impatient with ſin; and ſuppoſes, that we may alſo with ſuch ſorrow, pain, and diſcouragement, as hinder our purſuit of holineſs, though they ariſe from the weakneſs of nature. It allows us to be impatient of the diſtance at which we ſtand from a ſtate of perfection and bleſſedneſs. It further indulges impatience at the delay of time, when we deſire the period of it for no other end than that we may with angels be employed in the moſt lively ſpiritual acts of devotion, and in giving all poſſible glory to him that lives for ever. Temptations and ſinful imperfections, it thinks we may juſtly be uneaſy with; and diſappointments, at leaſt thoſe that relate to our hopes of communion with God, and growing conformity to him. And as to the tedious employments and hardſhips of life, it ſuppoſes ſome longing for the end of them not inconſiſtent with a ſpirit of faithfulneſs, and a cheerful diſpoſition to perform the one and endure the other: it ſuppoſes, that a faithful ſervant, who fully deſigns to do all he poſſibly can, may ſtill juſtly long for the evening; and that no rational man would blame his kind and tender ſpouſe, if he perceived her longing to be with him, while yet faithfulneſs and duty to him might ſtill induce her to yield, for the preſent, to remain at a painful diſtance from him.—On the other hand, it approves of the caution, care, and watchfulneſs of *tender conſcience*, leſt the divine Being ſhould be offended with impatient complaints: it

 acknowledges

acknowledges the fitneſs of our *waiting upon God*, in a way of patient doing and ſuffering; but ſuppoſes this very conſiſtent with ardent deſires to *depart, and to be with Chriſt*. It owns it fit that we ſhould always remember our own barrenneſs, and thinks alſo that we ſhould be impatient of it, and conſequently long for a ſtate of freedom from it; and this, not ſo much that we may feel the happineſs of it, but that God may have the glory. It grants, that impatient complaints often ſpring from ſelf-love, and want of reſignation and humility. Such as theſe it diſapproves; and determines, we ſhould be impatient only of abſence from God, and diſtance from that ſtate and temper wherein we may moſt glorify him.

10. *Godly ſorrow* introduced, as making her ſad moan, not ſo much that ſhe is kept from the free poſſeſſion and full enjoyment of happineſs, but that God muſt be diſhonoured; the ſoul being ſtill in a world of ſin, and itſelf imperfect. She here, with grief, counts over paſt faults, preſent temptations, and fears for the future.

11. *Hope* or *holy confidence* appears, and ſeems perſuaded that "nothing ſhall ever ſeparate the ſoul from the love of "God in Chriſt Jeſus." It expects divine aſſiſtance and grace ſufficient for all the doing and ſuffering work of time, and that death will ere long put a happy period to all ſin and ſorrow; and ſo takes occaſion to rejoice.

12. *Godly fear*, or *holy jealouſy* here ſteps in, and ſuggeſts ſome timorous apprehenſions of the danger of deception; mentions the deceitfulneſs of the heart, the great influence of irregular ſelf-love in a fallen creature; inquires whether itſelf is not likely to have fallen in with deluſion, ſince the mind is ſo dark, and ſo little of God appears to the ſoul; and queries whether all its hopes of perſevering grace may not be preſumption, and whether its confident expectations of meeting death as a friend, may not iſſue in diſappointment.

13. Hereupon *reflection* appears, and minds the perſon of his paſt experiences; as to the preparatory work of conviction and humiliation; the view he then had of the impoſſibility of ſalvation, from himſelf, or any created arm: the manifeſtation he has likewiſe had of the glory of God in Jeſus Chriſt: how he then admired that glory, and choſe that God for his only portion, becauſe of the excellency and amiableneſs he diſcovered in him; not from ſlaviſh fear of being damned, if he did not, nor from baſe and mercenary hopes of ſaving himſelf; but from a juſt eſteem of that beauteous and

glorious

glorious object: as also how he had from time to time rejoiced and acquiesced in God, for what he is in himself; being delighted, that he is infinite in holiness, justice, power, sovereignty, as well as in mercy, goodness, and love: how he has likewise, scores of times, felt his soul mourn for sin, for this very reason, because it is contrary and grievous to God; yea, how he has mourned over one vain and impertinent thought, when he has been so far from fear of the divine vindictive wrath for it, that on the contrary he has enjoyed the highest assurance of the divine everlasting love: how he has from time to time, delighted in the commands of God, for their own purity and perfection, and longed exceedingly to be conformed to them, and even to be "holy, as God is holy;" and counted it present heaven, to be of a heavenly temper: how he has frequently rejoiced, to think of being for ever subject to, and dependent on God; accounting it infinitely greater happiness to glorify God in a state of subjection to, and dependence on him, than to be a *god* himself: and how heaven itself would be no heaven to him, if he could not there be every thing that God would have him be.

14. Upon this, *spiritual sensation* being awaked, comes in, and declares that she now feels and "tastes that the Lord is "gracious;" that he is the only supreme good, the only soul-satisfying happiness; that he is a complete, self-sufficient, and almighty portion. She whispers, "Whom have I in "heaven," but this God, this dear and blessed portion? "and "there is none upon earth I desire besides him." Oh, it is heaven, to please him, and to be just what he would have me be! O that my soul were "holy, as God is holy!" O that it was "pure, as Christ is pure;" and "perfect, as my Father "in heaven is perfect!" These are the sweetest commands in God's book, comprising all others; and shall I break them? must I break them? am I under a fatal necessity of it, as long as I live in this world? Oh my soul! wo, wo is me, that I am a sinner! because I now necessarily grieve and offend this blessed God, who is infinite in goodness and grace. Oh, methinks, should he punish me for my sins, it would not wound my heart so deep to offend him; but, though I sin continually, he continually repeats his kindness towards me! Oh, methinks I could bear any suffering; but how can I bear to grieve and dishonour this blessed God! How shall I give ten thousand times more honour to him? What shall I do, to glorify and worship this best of beings? O that I could consecrate myself, soul and body, to his service for ever!

O that I could give up myself to him, so as never more to attempt to be my own, or to have any will or affections that are not perfectly conformed to his! But Oh, alas, alas! I cannot, I feel I cannot, be thus entirely devoted to God: I cannot live and sin not. O ye *angels*, do ye glorify him incessantly: if possible, exert yourselves still more, in more lively and ardent devotion: if possible, prostrate yourselves still lower before the throne of the blessed King of heaven: I long to bear a part with you, and if it were possible, to help you. Yet when we have done, we shall not be able to offer the ten thousandth part of the homage he is worthy of. While *spiritual sensation* whispered these things, *fear* and *jealousy* were greatly overcome; and the soul replied, "Now "I know, and am assured," *&c.* and again it welcomed death as a friend, saying, "O death, where is thy sting!" *&c.*

15. Finally, *holy resolution* concludes the discourse, fixedly determining to *follow hard after God*, and continually to pursue a life of conformity to him. And the better to pursue this, enjoining it on the soul always to remember, that God is the only source of happiness, that his will is the only rule of rectitude to an intelligent creature, that earth has nothing in it desirable for itself, or any further than God is seen in it; and that the knowledge of God in Christ, begetting and maintaining love, and mortifying sensual and fleshly appetites, is the way to be holy on earth, and so to be attempered to the complete holiness of the heavenly world.

II. Some *gloomy* and *desponding* thoughts of a soul under *convictions of sin*, and concern for its eternal salvation.

1. I Believe, my case is *singular*, that none ever had so many strange and different thoughts and feelings as I.

2. I have been concerned much *longer* than many *others*, that I have known or read of, who have been savingly *converted*, and yet I am left.

3. I have *withstood* the power of *convictions* a long time; and therefore I fear, I shall be finally left of God.

4. I never shall be converted, without *stronger convictions*, and *greater terrors* of conscience.

5. I do not aim at the *glory* of God in any thing I do, and therefore I cannot hope for mercy.

6. I

6. I do not see the evil nature of *sin*, nor the sin of my *nature*; and therefore I am discouraged.

7. The more I *strive*, the more *blind* and *hard* my heart is, and the worse I grow continually.

8. I fear God never shewed *mercy* to one so *vile* as I.

9. I fear I am not *elected*, and therefore must perish.

10. I fear the *day* of grace is *past* with me.

11. I fear, I have committed the *unpardonable* sin.

12. I am an *old* sinner; and if God had designed mercy for me, he would have called me home to himself before now.

III. Some *signs* of *godliness*.

The distinguishing marks of a *true Christian*, taken from one of my old manuscripts; where I wrote as *I felt* and *experienced*, and not from any considerable degree of doctrinal knowledge, or acquaintance with the sentiments of others in this point.

1. HE has a true *knowledge* of the glory and excellency of God, that he is most worthy to be loved and praised for his own divine perfections. Psal. cxlv. 3.

2. God is his *portion*, Psal. lxxiii. 25. And God's *glory*, his great concern, Matth. vi. 22.

3. *Holiness* is his *delight*; nothing he so much longs for, as to be holy, as God is holy. Phil. iii. 9.——12.

4. *Sin* is his greatest *enemy*. This he hates, for its own nature, for what it is in itself, being contrary to a holy God, Jer. ii. 1. And consequently he hates all sin, Rom. vii. 24. 1 John iii. 9.

5. The *laws* of God also are his delight, Psal. cxix. 97. Rom. vii. 22. These he observes, not out of constraint, from a servile fear of hell; but they are his choice, Psal. cxix. 30. The strict observance of them is not his bondage, but his greatest liberty, vers. 45.

IV. LETTERS,

IV. LETTERS, written by Mr Brainerd to his friends.

ADVERTISEMENT.

MR Brainerd had a large acquaintance and correspondence, especially in the latter part of his life, and he did much at writing *letters* to his absent friends; but the most of his acquaintance living at a great distance from me, I have not been able to obtain copies of many that he wrote: however, the greater part of those which I have seen, are such as appear to me of profitable tendency, and worthy of the public view: I have therefore here added a few of his *letters*.

N. B. Several of these which follow, are not published at large, because some parts of them were concerning particular affairs of a private nature.

N° 1. To his brother John, then a student at Yale-college in New-Haven.

Dear Brother, *Kaunaumeek, April* 30. 1743.

I Should tell you, "I long to see you," but that my own experience has taught me, there is no happiness, and plenary satisfaction to be enjoyed, in *earthly friends*, though ever so near and dear, or in any other enjoyment, that is not God himself. Therefore, if the *God of all grace* would be pleased graciously to afford us each *his presence* and *grace*, that we may perform the work, and endure the trials he calls us to, in a most distressing tiresome wilderness, till we arrive at our journey's end; the local distance, at which we are held from each other at the present, is a matter of no great moment or importance to either of us. But, alas! the presence of God is what I want.——I live in the most lonely melancholy *desert*, about eighteen miles from Albany; (for it was not thought best that I should go to Delaware-river, as I believe I hinted to you in a letter from New-York). I board with a poor Scotchman: his wife can talk scarce any English. My *diet* consists mostly of hasty-pudding, boiled corn, and bread baked in the ashes, and sometimes a little meat and butter. My *lodging* is a little heap of straw, laid upon some boards, a little way from the ground; for it is a log-room, without any floor,

floor, that I lodge in. My *work* is exceeding hard and difficult: I travel on foot a mile and half, the worst of way, almost daily, and back again; for I live so far from my Indians.——I have not seen an English person this month.—These and many other circumstances, as uncomfortable, attend me; and yet my *spiritual conflicts* and *distresses* so far *exceed* all these, that I scarce think of them, or hardly mind but that I am entertained in the most sumptuous manner. The Lord grant that I may learn to "endure hardness, as a good "soldier of Jesus Christ!" As to my *success* here, I cannot say much as yet: the Indians seem generally kind, and well disposed towards me, and are mostly very attentive to my instructions, and seem willing to be taught further: two or three, I hope, are under some *convictions;* but there seems to be little of the special workings of the divine Spirit among them yet; which gives me many a heart-sinking hour. Sometimes I hope, God has abundant blessings in store for them and me; but at other times I am so overwhelmed with distress, that I cannot see how his dealings with me are consistent with covenant love and faithfulness, and I say, "Surely his tender mercies are clean gone for ever."——But however, I see, I *needed* all this *chastisement* already: "It is "good for me," that I have endured these trials, and have hitherto little or no apparent success. Do not be discouraged by my distresses: I was under great distress, at Mr Pomroy's, when I saw you last; but "God has been with me of a "truth," since that: he helped me sometimes, sweetly at Long-Island, and elsewhere. But let us always remember, that we must *through much tribulation* enter into God's eternal kingdom of rest and peace. The righteous are *scarcely* saved: it is an infinite wonder, that we have well-grounded hopes of being saved at all. For my part, I feel the most vile of any creature living; and I am sure sometimes, there is not such another existing on this side *hell.*——Now all you can do for me, is, to pray incessantly, that God would make me humble, holy, resigned, and heavenly-minded, by all my trials.———"Be strong in the Lord, and in the power of "his might." Let us *run, wrestle,* and *fight,* that we may win the *prize,* and obtain that complete happiness, to be "holy, as God is holy." So, wishing and praying that you may advance in learning and grace, and be fit for special service for God, I remain

Your affectionate brother,

DAVID BRAINERD.

N° 2.

N° 2. To his brother John, at Yale-college in New-Haven.

Dear brother, *Kaunaumeek, Dec.* 27. 1743.

I Long to see you, and know how you fare in your journey through a world of inexpressible sorrow, where we are compassed about with "vanity, confusion, and vexation of "spirit." I am more weary of life, I think, than ever I was. The whole *world* appears to me like a huge *vacuum*, a vast empty space, whence nothing desirable, or at least satisfactory, can possibly be derived; and I long, *daily* to *die* more and more to it; even though I obtain not that comfort from spiritual things, which I earnestly desire. *Worldly* pleasures, such as flow from greatness, riches, honours, and sensual gratifications, are infinitely *worse* than none. May the Lord deliver us more and more from these *vanities!* I have spent most of the fall and winter hitherto in a very weak state of body; and sometimes under pressing inward trials and spiritual conflicts: but "having obtained help from God, I continue to "this day;" and am now something better in health, than I was sometime ago. I find nothing more conducive to a life of *Christianity*, than a diligent, industrious, and faithful improvement of precious *time*. Let us then faithfully perform that business, which is allotted to us by divine providence, to the utmost of our bodily strength, and mental vigour. Why should we sink, and grow discouraged, with any particular trials, and perplexities, we are called to encounter in the world? *death* and *eternity* are just before us; a few tossing billows more will waft us into the world of spirits, and we hope (through infinite grace) into endless pleasures, and uninterrupted rest and peace. Let us then "run with patience the "race set before us," Heb. xii. 1. 2. And Oh that we could depend more upon the *living God*, and less upon our own wisdom and strength!——Dear brother, may the *God of all grace* comfort your heart, and succeed your studies, and make you an instrument of good to his people in your day. This is the constant prayer of

Your affectionate brother,

DAVID BRAINERD.

N° 3.

No 3. To his brother Israel, at Haddam.

My dear brother, *Kaunaumeek, January* 21. 1743-4.

—THere is but *one* thing, that deserves our highest care and most ardent desires; and that is, that we may answer the great *end,* for which we were made, *viz.* to *glorify* that God, who has given us our beings and all our comforts, and do all the *good,* we possibly can, to our *fellow-men,* while we live in the world: and verily life is not worth the having, if it be not improved for this noble end and purpose. Yet, alas, how little is this thought of among mankind! Most men seem to *live to themselves,* without much regard to the glory of God, or the good of their fellow-creatures: they earnestly desire, and eagerly pursue after the riches, the honours, and the pleasures of life, as if they really supposed, that wealth, or greatness, or mirriment, could make their immortal souls happy. But, alas, what false and delusive *dreams* are these! And how miserable will those 'ere long be, who are not *awaked* out of them, to see, that all their happiness consists in *living to God,* and becoming "holy, " as he is holy!" Oh, may you never fall into the tempers and vanities, the sensuality and folly of the present world! You are, by divine providence, left as it were *alone* in a wide world, to act for yourself: be sure then to remember, it is a world of *temptation.* You have no earthly parents to be the means of forming your youth to piety and virtue, by their pious examples, and seasonable counsels; let this then excite you with greater diligence and fervency to look up to the *Father of mercies* for grace and assistance against all the vanities of the world. And if you would glorify God, answer his just expectations from you, and make your own soul happy in this and the coming world, observe these few *directions;* though not from a father, yet from a brother who is touched with a tender concern for your present and future happiness. And,

First, Resolve upon, and daily endeavour to practise a life of *seriousness* and strict *sobriety.* The wise man will tell you the great advantage of such a life, Eccl. vii. 3. Think of the life of Christ; and when you can find that *he* was pleased with jesting and vain merriment, then you may indulge it in yourself.

Again, Be careful to make a good *improvement* of precious *time.* When you cease from labour, fill up your time in reading, meditation, and prayer: and while your hands are labouring, let your heart be employed, as much as possible, in divine thoughts.

Further, Take heed that you *faithfully* perform the *business* you have to do in the world, from a regard to the *commands* of God; and not from an ambitious desire of being esteemed better than others. We should always look upon ourselves as God's servants, placed in God's world, to do *his* work; and accordingly labour faithfully for *him*; not with a design to grow rich and great, but to glorify God, and do all the good we possibly can.

Again, Never expect any *satisfaction* or *happiness* from the *world*. If you hope for happiness *in* the world, hope for it from God, and not *from* the world. Do not think you shall be more *happy*, if you live to such or such a state of life, if you live to be for yourself, to be settled in the world, or if you should gain an estate in it: but look upon it that you shall then be *happy*, when you can be constantly employed for God, and not for yourself; and desire to live in this world, only to *do* and *suffer* what God allots to you. When you can be of the spirit and temper of angels, who are willing to come down into this lower world, to perform what God commands them, though their desires are *heavenly*, and not in the least set on *earthly* things, then you will be of that temper that you ought to have, Col. iii. 2.

Once more, Never think that you can live to God by *your own* power or strength; but always look to, and rely on *him* for assistance, yea, for all strength and grace. There is no greater *truth* than this, that "we can do nothing of our-"selves," John xv. 5. and 2 Cor. iii. 5.; yet nothing but our own *experience* can effectually teach it to us. Indeed we are a long time in learning, that *all* our strength and salvation is in God. This is a life, that I think no *unconverted* man can possibly live; and yet it is a life that every *godly* soul is pressing after, in some good measure. Let it then be your great concern, thus to devote yourself and your all to God.

I long to see you, that I may say much more to you than I now can, for your benefit and welfare; but I desire to commit you to, and leave you with the *Father of mercies*, and *God of all grace*; praying that you may be directed safely through an *evil world*, to God's *heavenly kingdom*.

I am your affectionate loving brother,

DAVID BRAINERD.

N° 4. To a special friend.

The Forks of Delaware, July 31. 1744.

CErtainly the greatest, the noblest pleasure of intelligent creatures must result from their acquaintance with the blessed God, and with their own rational and immortal souls. And Oh, how divinely sweet and entertaining is it, to look into our own souls, when we can find all our powers and passions united and engaged in pursuit after God, our whole souls longing and passionately breathing after a conformity to him, and the full enjoyment of him! Verily there are no hours pass away with so much divine pleasure, as those that are spent in communing with God and our own hearts. Oh, how sweet is a spirit of devotion, a spirit of seriousness and divine solemnity, a spirit of gospel simplicity, love, tenderness! Oh, how desirable, and how profitable to the Christian life, is a spirit of holy watchfulness, and godly jealousy over ourselves; when our souls are afraid of nothing so much as that we shall grieve and offend the blessed God, whom at such times we apprehend, or at least hope, to be a *father and friend;* whom we then love and long to *please*, rather than to be *happy* ourselves, or at least we delight to derive our happiness *from* pleasing and glorifying him! Surely this is a pious temper, worthy of the highest ambition and closest pursuit of intelligent creatures and holy Christians. Oh, how vastly superiour is the pleasure, peace, and satisfaction derived from these divine frames, to that which we (alas!) sometimes pursue in things impertinent and trifling! our own bitter experience teaches us, that "in the midst of such laughter the heart is sorrowful," and there is no true satisfaction but in God. But, alas! how shall we obtain and retain this sweet spirit of religion and devotion? Let us follow the apostle's direction, Phil. ii. 12. and labour upon the encouragement he there mentions, vers. 13. for it is God only can afford us this favour; and he will be *sought to*, and it is fit we should wait upon him for so rich a mercy. Oh, may the God of all grace afford us the grace and influences of his divine Spirit; and help us that we may from our hearts esteem it our greatest liberty and happiness, that "whether we live, we may live to "the Lord, or whether we die, we may die to the Lord;" that in *life* and *death*, we may be *his!*

I am in a very poor state of health; I think, scarce ever poorer:

poorer: but, through divine goodneſs, I am not diſcontented under my weakneſs, and confinement to this wilderneſs: I bleſs God for this retirement: I never was more thankful for any thing, than I have been of late for the neceſſity I am under of ſelf-denial in many reſpects: I love to be a *pilgrim* and *ſtranger* in this wilderneſs: it ſeems moſt fit for ſuch a poor ignorant, worthleſs, deſpiſed creature as I. I would not change my preſent *miſſion* for any other buſineſs in the whole world. I may tell you freely, without vanity and oſtentation, God has of late given me great freedom and fervency in prayer, when I have been ſo weak and feeble, my nature ſeemed as if it would ſpeedily diſſolve. I feel as if my *all* was loſt, and I was undone for this world, if the poor Heathen may not be converted. I feel, in general, different from what I did, when I ſaw you laſt; at leaſt more *crucified* to all the enjoyments of life. It would be very refreſhing to me, to ſee you here in this deſart; eſpecially in my weak diſconſolate hours: but, I think, I could be content never to ſee you, or any of my friends again in this world, if God would bleſs my labours here to the converſion of the poor Indians.

I have much that I could willingly communicate to you, which I muſt omit, till Providence gives us leave to ſee each other. In the mean time, I reſt

Your obliged friend and ſervant,

DAVID BRAINERD.

Nº 5. To a ſpecial friend, a miniſter of the goſpel in New-Jerſey.

The Forks of Delaware, Dec. 24. 1744.

Rev. and dear brother,

I Have little to ſay to you, about ſpiritual *joys*, and thoſe bleſſed *refreſhments*, and divine *conſolations*, with which I have been much favoured in times paſt: but this I can tell you, that if I gain experience in no other point, yet I am ſure I do in this, *viz.* that the *preſent world* has nothing in it to *ſatisfy* an immortal ſoul; and hence, that it is not to be *deſired for itſelf*, but only becauſe God may be *ſeen* and *ſerved* in it: and I wiſh I could be more patient and willing to live in it for *this end*, than I can uſually find myſelf to be. It is no virtue, I know, to deſire death, only to be freed from the

the miseries of life: but I want that divine hope, which you observed, when I saw you last, was the very sinews of vital religion. Earth can *do us no good*, and if there be no *hope* of our *doing good on earth*, how can we desire to live in it? And yet we ought to desire, or at least to be resigned, to tarry in it; because it is the will of our all-wise Sovereign. But perhaps these thoughts will appear melancholy and gloomy, and consequently will be very undesirable to you; and therefore I forbear to add. I wish you may not read them in the same circumstances in which I write them. I have a little more to *do* and *suffer* in a dark disconsolate world; and then I hope to be as happy as you are.——I should ask you to pray for me, were I worth your concern. May the Lord enable us both to "endure hardness as good soldiers of "Jesus Christ;" and may we "obtain mercy of God to be "faithful, to the death," in the discharge of our respective trusts!

I am your very unworthy brother,

and humble servant,

DAVID BRAINERD.

No 6. To his brother John, at college.

Crosweeksung, in New-Jersey, Dec. 28. 1745.

Very dear brother,

——I Am in one continued, perpetual, and uninterrupted hurry; and divine providence throws so much upon me, that I do not see it will ever be otherwise. May I "obtain mercy of God to be faithful to the death!" I cannot say, I am weary of my hurry; I only want strength and grace to do more for God, than I have ever yet done.

My dear brother; *The Lord of heaven*, that has carried me through many trials, *bless you;* bless you for time, and eternity; and fit you to do service for him in his church below, and to enjoy his blissful presence in his church triumphant. My brother; "the time is short:" Oh let us fill it up for God; let us "count the sufferings of this present time" as nothing, if we can but "run our race, and finish our "course with joy." Oh, let us strive to live to God. I bless the Lord, I have nothing to do with *earth*, but only to labour honestly in it for God, till I shall "accomplish as an "hireling my day." I think, I do not desire to live one minute

minute for any thing that *earth* can afford. Oh, that I could live for none but God, till my dying moment!

I am your affectionate brother,

DAVID BRAINERD.

N° 7. To his brother Israel, then a student at Yale-college in New-Haven.

Elisabeth-Town, New-Jersey, Nov. 24. 1746.

Dear brother,

I Had determined to make you and my other friends in New-England a visit, this fall; partly from an earnest desire I had to see you and them, and partly with a view to the recovery of my health; which has, for more than three months past, been much impaired. And in order to prosecute this design, I set out from my own people about three weeks ago, and came as far as to this place; where, my disorder greatly increasing, I have been obliged to keep house ever since, until the day before yesterday; at which time, I was able to ride about half a mile, but found myself much tired with the journey. I have now no hopes of prosecuting my journey into New-England this winter, supposing, my present state of health will by no means admit of it: although I am through divine goodness much better than I was some days ago, yet I have not strength now to ride more than ten miles a day, if the season were warm, and fit for me to travel in. My disorder has been attended with several symptoms of a *consumption;* and I have been at times apprehensive, that my great *change* was at hand: yet blessed be God, I have never been *affrighted;* but, on the contrary, at some times much *delighted* with a view of its approach. Oh, the blessedness of being delivered from the clogs of flesh and sense, from a *body of sin* and spiritual *death!* Oh, the unspeakable sweetness of being translated into a state of complete purity and perfection! believe me, my brother, a lively view and hope of these things, will make the king of terrors himself appear agreeable.——Dear brother, let me intreat you, to keep *eternity* in your view, and behave yourself as becomes one that must shortly "give an account of all things done in the body." That God may be *your* God, and prepare you for his service here, and his kingdom of glory hereafter, is the desire and daily prayer of

Your affectionate loving brother,

DAVID BRAINERD.

Nº 8. To his brother Israel, at college; written in the time of his extreme illness in Boston, a few months before his death.

My dear brother, *Boston, June* 30. 1747.

IT is from the sides of *eternity* I now address you. I am heartily sorry, that I have so little strength to write what I long so much to communicate to you. But let me tell you, my brother, *eternity* is another thing than we ordinarily take it to be in a healthful state. Oh, how vast and boundless! Oh, how fixed and unalterable! Oh, of what infinite importance is it, that we be prepared for *eternity!* I have been just a dying, now for more than a week; and all around me have thought me so: but in this time I have had clear views of *eternity;* have seen the blessedness of the *godly*, in some measure; and have longed to share their happy state; as well as been comfortably satisfied, that through grace, I shall do so: but Oh, what anguish is raised in my mind, to think of an *eternity* for those who are *Christless*, for those who are mistaken, and who bring their false hopes to the grave with them! The sight was so dreadful, I could by no means bear it: my thoughts recoiled, and I said, (but under a more affecting sense than ever before), "Who can dwell with everlasting "burnings!" Oh, methought, that I could now see my friends, that I might warn them, to see to it, they lay their foundation for *eternity* sure. And you, my dear brother, I have been particularly concerned for; and have wondered, I so much neglected conversing with you about your spiritual state at our last meeting. Oh, my brother, let me then beseech you now to examine, whether you are indeed a *new creature?* whether you have ever acted above *self?* whether the *glory* of God has ever been the sweetest highest concern with you? whether you have ever been reconciled to all the perfections of God? in a word, whether God has been your *portion*, and a holy *conformity* to him your chief delight? If you cannot answer positively, consider seriously the frequent breathings of your soul: but do not however put yourself off with a slight answer. If you have reason to think you are *graceless*, Oh give yourself and the throne of grace no rest, till God arise and save. But if the case should be otherwise, bless God for his grace, and press after holiness *.

* Mr Brainerd afterwards had greater satisfaction concerning the state of his brother's soul, by much opportunity of conversation with him before his death.

My soul longs, that you should be fitted for, and in due time go into the work of the *ministry*. I cannot bear to think of your going into any other business in life. Do not be discouraged, because you see your elder brothers in the ministry *die early*, one after another: I declare, now I am dying, I would not have spent my life *otherwise* for the whole world. But I must leave this with God.

If this line should come to your hands soon after the date, I should be almost desirous you should set out on a journey to me: it may be, you may see me alive; which I should much rejoice in. But if you cannot come, I must commit you to the grace of God, where you are. May he be your guide and counsellor, your sanctifier and eternal portion!

Oh, my dear brother, flee fleshly *lusts*, and the inchanting *amusements*, as well as corrupt *doctrines* of the present day; and strive to *live to God*. Take this as the *last* line from

Your affectionate dying brother,

DAVID BRAINERD.

N° 9. To a young gentleman, a *candidate* for the work of the *ministry*, for whom he had a special friendship; also written at the same time of his great illness and nearness to death in Boston.

Very dear Sir,

HOW amazing it is, that the *living* who *know they must die*, should notwithstanding "put far away the evil "day," in a season of health and prosperity; and live at such an awful distance from a familiarity with the grave, and the great concerns beyond it! and especially it may justly fill us with surprise, that any whose minds have been divinely *enlightened*, to behold the important things of *eternity* as they are, I say, that such should live in this manner. And yet, Sir, how frequently is this the case? how rare are the instances of those who live and act, from day to day, as on the verge of *eternity;* striving to fill up all their remaining moments, in the service, and to the honour of their great *Master?* We insensibly trifle away *time*, while we seem to have enough of it; and are so strangely amused, as in a great measure to lose a sense of the *holiness* and blessed qualifications necessary to prepare us to be inhabitants of the heavenly *paradise*. But Oh, dear Sir, a *dying bed*, if we enjoy our reason clearly, will

will give another view of things. I have now, for more than three weeks, lain under the greatest degree of weakness; the greater part of the time, expecting daily and hourly to enter into the eternal world: sometimes have been so far gone, as to be wholly speechless, for some hours together. And Oh, of what vast *importance* has a holy spiritual *life* appeared to me to be in this season! I have longed to call upon all my friends, to make it their business to *live to God;* and especially all that are designed for, or engaged in the service of the *sanctuary*. O dear Sir, do not think it enough, to live at the rate of *common Christians*. Alas, to how little purpose do they often converse, when they meet together! The *visits*, even of those who are called Christians indeed, are frequently extreme barren; and conscience cannot but condemn us for the misimprovement of time, while we have been conversant with them. But the way to enjoy the divine presence, and be fitted for distinguishing service for God, is to live a life of *great devotion* and *constant self-dedication* to him; observing the motions and dispositions of our own hearts, whence we may learn the corruptions that lodge there, and our constant need of help from God for the performance of the least duty. And Oh, dear Sir, let me beseech you frequently to attend the great and precious duties of *secret fasting* and *prayer*.

I have a secret thought, from some things I have observed, that God may perhaps design you for some singular service in the world. Oh then labour to be prepared and qualified to do much for God. Read Mr Edwards's piece on the *affections*, again and again; and labour to *distinguish* clearly upon experiences and affections in religion, that you may make a difference between the *gold* and the shining *dross;* I say, labour here, as ever you would be an *useful minister* of Christ: for nothing has put such a stop to the work of God in the late day as the false religion, the wild affections that attend it. Suffer me therefore, finally, to intreat you earnestly to "give "yourself to prayer, to reading and meditation" on divine truths: strive to penetrate to the bottom of them, and never be content with a superficial knowledge. By this means, your thoughts will gradually grow weighty and judicious; and you hereby will be possessed of a valuable *treasure*, out of which you may produce "things new and old," to the glory of God.

And now, "I commend you to the grace of God;" earnestly desiring, that a plentiful portion of the divine *Spirit* may rest upon you; that you may *live to God* in *every* capacity

capacity of life, and do abundant service for him in a *public*, if it be his will; and that you may be richly qualified for the "inheritance of the saints in light."

I scarce expect to see your face any more in the body; and therefore intreat you to accept this as the last token of love, from

Your sincerely affectionate dying friend,

DAVID BRAINERD.

P. S. I am now, at the dating of this letter, considerably recovered from what I was when I wrote it; it having lain by me some time, for want of an opportunity of conveyance; it was written in Boston.——I am now able to ride a little, and so am removed into the country: but I have no more expectation of recovering, than when I wrote, though I am a little better for the present; and therefore I still subscribe myself,

Your dying friend, &c.

D. B.

N° 10. To his brother John, at Bethel, the town of Christian Indians in New Jersey; written likewise at Boston, when he was there on the brink of the grave, in the summer before his death.

Dear brother,

I Am now just on the verge of *eternity*, expecting very speedily to appear in the unseen world. I feel myself no more an inhabitant of *earth*, and sometimes earnestly long to "depart and be with Christ." I bless God, he has for some *years* given me an abiding conviction, that it is impossible for any rational creature to enjoy true *happiness* without being entirely "devoted to him." Under the influence of this conviction I have in some measure acted: Oh that I had done more so! I saw both the excellency and necessity of *holiness* in life; but never in such a manner as now, when I am just brought to the sides of the grave. Oh, my brother, pursue after *holiness*; press towards this blessed mark; and let your thirsty soul continually say, "I shall never be satisfied till "I awake in thy likeness." Although there has been a great deal of *selfishness* in my views; of which I am ashamed, and for which my soul is humbled at every view: yet blessed be God, I find I have really had, for the most part, such a con-

cern

cern for *his glory*, and the advancement of *his kingdom* in the world, that it is a satisfaction to me to reflect upon *these years*.

And now, my dear brother, as I must press you to pursue after *personal* holiness, to be as much in *fasting* and *prayer* as your health will allow, and to live above the rate of *common Christians*; so I must intreat you solemnly to attend to your *public* work: labour to distinguish between *true* and *false* religion: and to that end, watch the motions of God's *Spirit* upon your own heart; look to *him* for help; and impartially compare your experiences with his *word*. Read Mr Edwards on the *affections*, where the essence and soul of religion is clearly distinguished from false affections *. Value religious *joys* according to the *subject-matter* of them: there are many that rejoice in their supposed *justification*; but what do these joys argue, but only that they *love themselves*? Whereas, in *true* spiritual joys, the soul rejoices in God for what he is *in himself*; blesses God for his holiness, sovereignty, power, faithfulness, and all his perfections; adores God, that he is what he is, that he is unchangeably possessed of infinite glory

* I had at first fully intended, in publishing this and the foregoing letters, to have suppressed these passages wherein *my name* is mentioned, and my *discourse on religious affections* recommended: and am sensible, that by my doing otherwise, I shall bring upon me the reproach of some. But how much soever I may be pleased with the commendation of any performance of mine, (and I confess, I esteem the judgment and approbation of such a person as Mr Brainerd, worthy to be valued, and look on myself as highly honoured by it), yet I can truly say, the things that governed me in altering my forementioned determination, with respect to these passages, were these two. (1.) What Mr Brainerd here says of that discourse, shews very fully and particularly what *his notions* were of experimental religion, and the nature of true piety, and how far *he* was from placing it in impressions on the imagination, or any enthusiastical impulses, and how essential in religion he esteemed holy practice, *&c. &c.* For all that have read that discourse, know what sentiments are there expressed concerning these things. (2.) I judged, that the *approbation* of so apparent and eminent a friend and example of inward vital religion, and evangelical piety in the height of it, would probably tend to make that *book* more serviceable; especially among some kinds of zealous persons, whose benefit was especially aimed at in the book; some of which are prejudiced against it, as written in too legal a strain, and opposing some things wherein the height of Christian experience consists, and tending to build men up on their own works.

and happiness. Now, when men thus rejoice in the "perfections of God," and in the "infinite excellency of the way of salvation by Christ," and in the holy *commands* of God, which are a transcript of his holy nature, *these* joys are divine and spiritual. Our joys will stand by us at the hour of *death*, if we can be then satisfied, that we have thus acted above *self*, and in a disinterested manner (if I may so express it) rejoiced in the *glory* of the blessed God.——I fear, you are not sufficiently aware how much *false* religion there is in the world: many serious Christians and valuable ministers are too easily imposed upon by this false *blaze*. I likewise fear, you are not sensible of the "dreadful effects and consequences" of this false religion. Let me tell you, it is the "devil transformed into an angel of light;" it is a brat of hell, that always springs up with every revival of religion, and stabs and murders the cause of God, while it passes current with multitudes of well-meaning people for the height of religion. Set yourselves, my brother, to crush all appearances of this nature, among the Indians, and never encourage any degrees of heat without light. Charge my people in the name of their *dying minister*, yea, in the name of *him who was dead and is alive*, to live and walk as becomes the gospel. Tell them, how great the expectations of God and his people are from them, and how awfully they will wound God's cause, if they fall into vice; as well as fatally prejudice other poor Indians. Always insist, that their experiences are *rotten*, that their joys are *delusive*, although they may have been rapt up into the *third heavens* in their own conceit by them, unless the main tenour of their *lives* be spiritual, watchful, and holy. In pressing these things, "thou shalt both save thyself, and those that hear thee."——

God knows, I was heartily willing to have served him *longer* in the work of the ministry, although it had still been attended with all the *labours* and *hardships* of past years, if he had seen fit that it should be so: but as his will now appears otherwise, I am fully content, and can with utmost freedom say, "The will of the Lord be done." It affects me, to think of leaving you in a world of sin: my heart pities you, that those storms and tempests are yet before you, which I trust, through grace I am almost delivered from. But "God lives, and blessed be my Rock:" he is the same almighty Friend; and will, I trust, be your Guide and Helper, as he has been mine.

And

And now, my dear brother, "I commend you to God and "to the word of his grace, which is able to build you up, and "give you inheritance among all them that are sanctified." May you enjoy the divine presence, both in private and public; and may "the arms of your hands be made strong, by the "right hand of the mighty God of Jacob!" Which are the passionate desires and prayers of

Your affectionate dying brother,

DAVID BRAINERD.

AN

AN APPENDIX.

Containing some Reflections and Observations on the preceding Memoirs of Mr Brainerd.

I. WE have here opportunity, as I apprehended, in a very lively *instance*, to see the *nature* of *true religion*; and the *manner* of its *operation* when exemplified in a *high degree* and *powerful exercise*. Particularly it may be worthy to be observed,

1. How greatly Mr Brainerd's religion *differed* from that of some pretenders to the experience of a *clear work* of saving *conversion* wrought on their hearts; who depending and living on that, settle in a *cold*, *careless*, and *carnal* frame of mind, and in a neglect of thorough, earnest religion, in the stated practice of it. Although his convictions and conversion were in all respects exceeding clear, and very remarkable; yet how far was he from acting as though he thought he had *got through his work*, when once he had obtained comfort, and satisfaction of his interest in Christ, and title to heaven? On the contrary, that work on his heart, by which he was brought to this, was with him evidently but the *beginning of his work*, his first entering on the great business of religion and the service of God, his first setting out in his race. His obtaining rest of soul in Christ, after earnest striving to enter in at the strait gate, and being violent to take the kingdom of heaven, he did not look upon as putting an end to any further occasion for striving and violence in religion; but these were continued still, and maintained constantly, through all changes, to the very end of life. His work was not finished, nor his race ended, till life was ended; agreeable to frequent *scripture-representations* of the Christian life. He continued pressing forward in a constant manner, forgetting the things that were behind, and reaching forth towards the things that

were

were before. His pains and earnestness in the business of religion were rather increased, than diminished, after he had received comfort and satisfaction concerning the safety of his state. Those divine principles, which after this he was actuated by, of love to God, and longings and thirstings after holiness, seem to be more effectual to engage him to pains and activity in religion, than fear of hell had been before.

And as his conversion was not the end of *his work*, or of the course of his diligence and strivings in religion; so neither was it the end of the *work of the Spirit* of God on his heart: but on the contrary, the beginning of that work; the beginning of his spiritual discoveries, and holy views; the first dawning of the light, which thenceforward increased more and more; the beginning of his holy affections, his sorrow for sin, his love to God, his rejoicing in Christ Jesus, his longings after holiness. And the powerful operations of the Spirit of God in these things, were carried on, from the day of his conversion, in a continued course, to his dying day. His religious experiences, his admiration, his joy, and praise, and flowing affections, did not only hold up to a considerable height for a few days, weeks, or months, at first, while hope and comfort were new things with him; and then gradually dwindle and die away, till they came to almost nothing, and so leave him without any sensible or remarkable experience of spiritual discoveries, or holy and divine affections, for months together; as it is with many, who after the newness of things is over, soon come to that pass, that it is again with them very much as it is used to be before their supposed conversion, with respect to any present views of God's glory, of Christ's excellency, or of the beauty of divine things; and with respect to any present thirstings for God, or ardent outgoings of their souls after divine objects: but only now and then they have a comfortable reflection on things they have met with in times past, and are something affected with them; and so rest easy, thinking all things are well; they have had a good *clear work*, and their state is safe, and they doubt not but they shall go to heaven when they die. How far otherwise was it with Mr Brainerd, than it is with such persons! His experiences, instead of dying away, were evidently of an increasing nature. His first love, and other holy affections, even at the beginning were very great; but after months and years, became much greater, and more remarkable; and the spiritual exercises of his mind continued exceeding great, (though not equally so at all times, yet usually so), without indulged remissness, and without habitual dwindling and dying

 away,

away, even till his decease. They began in a time of general deadness all over the land, and were greatly increased in a time of general riviving of religion. And when religion decayed again, and a general deadness returned, his experiences were still kept up in their height, and his holy exercises maintained in their life and vigour; and so continued to be, in a general course, where-ever he was, and whatever his circumstances were, among English and Indians, in company and alone, in towns and cities, and in the howling wilderness, in sickness and in health, living and dying. This is agreeable to scripture-descriptions of true and right religion, and of the Christian life. The change, that was wrought in him at his conversion, was agreeable to scripture-representations of that change which is wrought in true conversion; a great change, and an abiding change, rendering him a new man, a new creature: not only a change as to hope and comfort, and an apprehension of his own good estate; and a transient change, consisting in high flights of passing affections; but a change of *nature*, a change of the abiding habit and temper of the mind. Nor a partial change, merely in point of opinion, or outward reformation; much less a change from one error to another, or from one sin to another: but an universal change, both internal and external; as from corrupt and dangerous principles in religion, unto the belief of the truth, so from both the habits and ways of sin, unto universal holiness of heart and practice; from the power and service of Satan unto God.

2. His religion did apparently and greatly *differ* from that of many high pretenders to religion, who are frequently actuated by *vehement emotions* of mind, and are carried on in a course of *sudden* and *strong impressions*, and supposed *high illuminations* and *immediate discoveries*, and at the same time are persons of a virulent "zeal, not according to knowledge."

His convictions, preceding his conversion, did not arise from any frightful *impressions on his imagination*, or any external images and ideas of fire and brimstone, a sword of vengeance drawn, a dark pit open, devils in terrible shapes, *&c.* strongly fixed in his mind. His sight of his own sinfulness did not consist in any imagination of a heap of lothsome material filthiness within him; nor did his sense of the hardness of his heart consist in any bodily feeling in his breast something hard and heavy like a stone, nor in any imaginations whatever of such a nature.

His first discovery of God or Christ, at his conversion, was not

not any strong idea of any external glory or brightness, or majesty and beauty of countenance, or pleasant voice; nor was it any supposed immediate manifestation of God's love to *him* in particular; nor any imagination of Christ's smiling face, arms open, or words immediately spoken to him, as by name, revealing Christ's love to *him*; either words of scripture, or any other: but a manifestation of God's glory, and the beauty of his nature, as supremely excellent in itself; powerfully drawing, and sweetly captivating his heart; bringing him to a hearty desire to exalt God, set him on the throne, and give him supreme honour and glory, as the King and Sovereign of the universe; and also a new sense of the infinite wisdom, suitableness, and excellency of the way of salvation by Christ; powerfully engaging his whole soul to embrace this way of salvation, and to delight in it. His first faith did not consist in believing that Christ loved him, and died for him, in particular. His first comfort was not from any secret suggestion of God's eternal love to him, or that God was reconciled to him, or intended great mercy for him; by any such texts as these, "Son, be of good cheer, thy sins "are forgiven thee. Fear not, I am thy God," *&c.* or in any such way. On the contrary, when God's glory was first discovered to him, it was without any thought of salvation as his own. His first experience of the sanctifying and comforting power of God's Spirit did not begin in some bodily sensation, any pleasant warm feeling in his breast, that he (as some others) called the feeling the love of Christ in him, and being full of the Spirit. How exceeding far were his experiences at his first conversion from things of such a nature!

And if we look through the whole series of his experiences, from his conversion to his death, we shall find none of this kind. I have had occasion to read his *diary* over and over, and very particularly and critically to review every passage in it; and I find no one instance of a strong impression on his imagination, through his whole life: no instance of a strongly impressed idea of any external glory and brightness, of any bodily form or shape, any beautiful majestic countenance: no imaginary sight of Christ hanging on the cross, with his blood streaming from his wounds; or seated in heaven on a bright throne, with angels and saints bowing before him; or with a countenance smiling on him; or arms open to embrace him: no sight of heaven, in his imagination, with gates of pearl, and golden streets, and vast multitudes of glorious inhabitants, with shining garments: no sight of the book of life opened,

 with

with his name written in it: no hearing of the sweet music made by the songs of heavenly hosts; no hearing God or Christ immediately speaking to him; nor any sudden suggestions of words or sentences, either words of scripture, or any other, as then immediately spoken or sent to him: no new objective revelations, no sudden strong suggestions of secret facts. Nor do I find any one instance in all the records he has left of his own life, from beginning to end, of joy excited from a supposed *immediate* witness of the Spirit; or inward immediate suggestion, that his state was surely good, that God loved him with an everlasting love, that Christ died for him in particular, and that heaven was his; either with or without a text of scripture: no instance of comfort by a sudden bearing in upon his mind, as though at that very time directed by God to him in particular, any such kind of texts as these; "Fear not, I am with thee.—It is your Father's "good pleasure to give you the kingdom.—You have not "chosen me, but I have chosen you.—I have called thee by "thy name, thou art mine.—Before thou wast formed in the "belly, I knew thee," *&c.* No supposed communion and conversation with God carried on in this way; no such supposed tasting of the love of Christ. But the way he was satisfied of his own good estate, even to the entire abolishing of fear, was by feeling within himself the lively actings of a holy temper and heavenly disposition, the vigorous exercises of that divine love, which cast out fear. This was the way he had full satisfaction soon after his conversion, (see his diary on October 18. and 19. 1740). And we find no other way of satisfaction through his whole life afterwards: and this he abundantly declared to be the way, the only way, that he had complete satisfaction, when he looked death in the face, in its near approaches.

Some of the pretenders to an *immediate* witness by suggestion, and defenders of it, with an assuming confidence, would bear us in hand, that there is no full assurance without it; and that the way of being satisfied by signs, and arguing an interest in Christ from sanctification, if it will keep men quiet in life and health, yet will never do when they come to *die*: then (they say) men must have *immediate* witness, or else be in a dreadful uncertainty. But Mr Brainerd's experience is a confutation of this; for in him we have an instance of one that possessed as constant an unshaken an assurance, through the course of his life, after conversion, as perhaps can be produced in this age; which yet he obtained and enjoyed without any such sort of *testimony*, and without all

all manner of appearance of it, or pretence to it; yea, while utterly disclaiming any such thing, and declaring against it: and one whose assurance, we need not scruple to affirm, has as fair a claim, and as just a pretension to truth and genuineness, as any that the pretenders to *immediate witness* can produce: and not only an instance of one that had such assurance in life, but had it in a constant manner in his last illness; and particularly in the latter stages of it, through those last months of his life, wherein *death* was more sensibly approaching, without the least hope of life: and had it too in its *fulness*, and in the height of its exercise, under those repeated trials, that he had in this space of time; when brought from time to time to the very brink of the grave, expecting in a few minutes to be in eternity. He had "the full assurance of hope, unto the end." When on the verge of eternity, he then declares his assurance to be such as perfectly secluded all fear: and not only so, but it manifestly filled his soul with exceeding joy: he declaring at the same time, that this his consolation and good hope through grace arose wholly from the *evidence* he had of his good estate, by what he found of his sanctification, or the exercise of a holy heavenly temper of mind, supreme love to God, *&c.* and not in the least from any *immediate* witness by suggestion: yea, he declares that at these very times he saw the awful *delusion* of that confidence which is built on such a foundation, as well as of the whole of that religion which it usually springs from, or at least is the attendant of; and that his soul abhorred those delusions: and he continued in this mind, often expressing it with much solemnity, even till death.

Mr Brainerd's religion was not *selfish* and *mercenary:* his love to God was primarily and principally for the supreme excellency of his *own nature*, and not built on a preconceived notion that God loved *him*, had received *him* into favour, and had done great things *for him*, or promised great things *to him:* so his joy was joy in God, and not in himself. We see by his *diary* how, from time to time, through the course of his life, his soul was filled with ineffable sweetness and comfort. But what was the spring of this strong and abiding consolation? Not so much the consideration of the sure grounds he had to think that his state was good, that God had delivered him from hell, and that heaven was *his;* or any thoughts concerning his own distinguished happy and exalted circumstances, as a high favourite of Heaven: but the sweet meditations and entertaining views he had of divine things *without himself;* the affecting considerations and lively ideas

ideas of God's infinite glory, his unchangeable blessedness; his sovereignty and universal dominion; together with the sweet exercises of love to God, giving himself up to him, abasing himself before him, denying himself for him, depending upon him, acting for his glory, diligently serving him; and the pleasing prospects or hopes he had of a future advancement of the kingdom of Christ, &c.

It appears plainly and abundantly all along, from his conversion to his death, that that beauty, that sort of good, which was the great object of the new sense of his mind, the new relish and appetite given him in conversion, and thenceforward maintained and increased in his heart, was HOLINESS, conformity to God, living to God, and glorifying him. This was what drew his heart; this was the centre of his soul; this was the ocean to which all the streams of his religious affections tended: this was the object that engaged his eager thirsting desires and earnest pursuits: he knew no true excellency or happiness, but this: this was what he longed for most vehemently and constantly on *earth;* and this was with him the beauty and blessedness of *heaven;* which made him so much and so often to long for that world of glory: it was to be perfectly holy, and perfectly exercised in the holy employments of heaven; thus to glorify God, and enjoy him for ever.

His religious illuminations, affections, and comfort, seemed, to a great degree, to be attended with *evangelical humiliation;* consisting in a sense of his own utter insufficiency, despicableness, and odiousness; with an answerable disposition and frame of heart. How deeply affected was he almost continually with his great defects in religion; with his vast distance from that spirituality and holy frame of mind that became him; with his ignorance, pride, deadness, unsteadiness, barrenness? He was not only affected with the remembrance of his former sinfulness, before his conversion, but with the sense of his present vileness and pollution. He was not only disposed to think meanly of himself as *before God*, and in comparison of him; but *amongst men*, and as compared with them. He was apt to think other saints better than he; yea, to look on himself as the meanest and least of saints; yea, very often, as the vilest and worst of mankind. And notwithstanding his great attainments in *spiritual knowledge,* yet we find there is scarce any thing that he is more frequently affected and abased with a sense of, than his *ignorance*.

How eminently did he appear to be of a *meek* and *quiet* spirit, resembling the lamb-like, dove-like Spirit of Jesus Christ! how

how full of love, meeknefs, quietnefs, forgivenefs, and mercy! His love was not merely a fondnefs and zeal for a party, but an univerfal benevolence; very often exercifed in the moft fenfible and ardent love to his greateft oppofers and enemies. His love and meeknefs were not a mere pretence, and outward profeffion and fhew; but they were effectual things, manifefted in expenfive and painful deeds of love and kindnefs; and in a meek behaviour; readily confeffing faults under the greateft trials, and humbling himfelf even at the feet of thofe from whom he fuppofed he had fuffered moft; and from time to time very frequently praying for his enemies, abhorring the thoughts of bitternefs or refentment towards them. I fcarcely know where to look for any parallel inftance of felf-denial, in thefe refpects, in the prefent age. He was a perfon of great zeal; but how did he abhor a bitter zeal, and lament it where he faw it! and though he was once drawn into fome degrees of it, by the force of prevailing example, as it were in his childhood; yet how did he go about with a heart bruifed and broken in pieces for it all his life after!

Of how *foft* and *tender* a fpirit was he! How far were his experiences, hopes, and joys, from a tendency finally to ftupify and harden him, to leffen convictions and tendernefs of confcience, to caufe him to be lefs affected with prefent and paft fins, and lefs confcientious with refpect to future fins, more eafy in the neglect of duties that are troublefome and inconvenient, more flow and partial in complying with difficult commands, lefs apt to be alarmed at the appearance of his own defects and tranfgreffions, more eafily induced to a compliance with carnal appetites! On the contrary, how tender was his confcience! how apt was his heart to fmite him! how eafily and greatly was he alarmed at the appearance of moral evil! how great and conftant was his jealoufy over his own heart! how ftrict his care and watchfulnefs againft fin! how deep and fenfible were the wounds that fin made in his confcience! thofe evils that are generally accounted fmall, were almoft an infupportable burden to him; fuch as his inward deficiencies, his having no more love to God, finding within himfelf any flacknefs or dulnefs in religion, any unfteadinefs, or wandering frame of mind, *&c.* how did the confideration of fuch things as thefe opprefs and abafe him, and fill him with inward fhame and confufion! His love and hope, though they were fuch as caft out a fervile fear of hell, yet they were fuch as were attended with, and abundantly cherifhed and promoted a reverential filial fear of God, a dread of fin and of God's holy difpleafure. His joy feemed truly to to be a rejoicing with trembling. His assurance and comfort differed greatly from a false enthusiastic confidence and joy, in that it promoted and maintained mourning for sin: holy mourning, with him, was not only the work of an hour or a day, at his first conversion; but sorrow for sin was like a wound constantly running; he was a mourner for sin all his days. He did not, after he received comfort and full satisfaction of the forgiveness of all his sins, and the safety of his state, forget his past sins, the sins of his youth, that were committed before his conversion; but the remembrance of them, from time to time, revived in his heart, with renewed grief. That in Ezek. xvi. 63. was evidently fulfilled in him, "That "thou mayst remember, and be confounded, and never open "thy mouth any more, because of thy shame; when I am "pacified toward thee for all that thou hast done." And how lastingly did the sins that he committed after his conversion, affect and break his heart! if he did any thing whereby he thought he had in any respect dishonoured God, and wounded the interest of religion, he had never done with calling it to mind with sorrow and bitterness; though he was assured that God had forgiven it, yet he never forgave himself: his past sorrows and fears made no satisfaction, with him; but still the wound renews and bleeds afresh, again and again. And his present sins, that he daily found in himself, were an occasion of daily sensible and deep sorrow of heart.

His religion did not consist in unaccountable *flights* and vehement *pangs;* suddenly rising, and suddenly falling; at some turns exalted almost to the third heavens, and then at other turns negligent, vain, carnal, and swallowed up with the world, for days and weeks, if not months together. His religion was not like a blazing meteor, or like a flaming comet, (or a wandering star, as the apostle Jude calls it, verse 13.) flying through the firmament with a bright train, and then quickly going out in perfect darkness; but more like the steady lights of heaven, that are constant principles of light, though sometimes hid with clouds. Nor like a land-flood, which flows far and wide, with a rapid stream, bearing down all afore it, and then dried up; but more like a stream fed by living springs; which though sometimes increased by showers, and at other times diminished by drought, yet is a *constant stream.*

His religious affections and joys were not like those of some, who have rapture and mighty emotions from time to time in *company;* but have very little affection in *retirement* and secret places. Though he was of a very sociable temper, and

and loved the company of saints, and delighted very much in religious conversation, and in social worship; yet his warmest affections, and their greatest effects on animal nature, and his sweetest joys, were in his closet devotions, and solitary transactions between God and his own soul; as is very observable through his whole course, from his conversion to his death. He delighted greatly in sacred retirements; and loved to get quite away from all the world, to converse with God alone, in secret duties.

Mr Brainerd's experiences and comforts were very far from being like those of some persons, which are attended with a spiritual *satiety*, and put an end to their religious desires and longings, at least to the edge and ardency of them; resting satisfied in their own attainments and comforts, as having obtained their chief end, which is to extinguish their fears of hell, and give them confidence of the favour of God. How far were his religious affections, refreshments, and satisfactions, from such an operation and influence as this! On the contrary, how were they always attended with longings and thirstings after greater degrees of *conformity* to God! And the greater and sweeter his comforts were, the more vehement were his desires after *holiness*. For it is to be observed, that his longings were not so much after joyful discoveries of God's love, and clear views of his title to future advancement and eternal honours in heaven; as after more of present holiness, greater spirituality, an heart more engaged for God, to love, and exalt, and depend on him; an ability better to serve him, to do more for his glory, and to do all that he did with more of a regard to Christ as his righteousness and strength; and after the enlargement and advancement of Christ's kingdom in the earth. And his desires were not idle wishings and wouldings, but such as were powerful and effectual, to animate him to the earnest, eager pursuit of these things, with utmost diligence and unfainting labour and self-denial. His comforts never put an end to his seeking after God, and striving to obtain his grace; but, on the contrary, greatly engaged and enlarged him therein.

His religion did not consist only in *experience*, without *practice*. All his inward illuminations, affections, and comforts, seemed to have a direct tendency to practice, and to issue in it: and this, not merely a practice *negatively* good, free from gross acts of irreligion and immorality; but a practice *positively* holy and Christian, in a serious, devout, humble, meek, merciful, charitable, and beneficent conversation; making the service of God, and our Lord Jesus

Christ, the great business of life, which he was devoted to, and pursued with the greatest earnestness and diligence to the end of his days, through all trials. In him was to be seen the right way of being *lively in religion*: his *liveliness* in religion did not consist merely or mainly in his being lively with the *tongue*, but in *deed*; not in being forward in profession and outward shew, and abundant in declaring his own experiences; but chiefly in being active and abundant in the labours and duties of religion; "not slothful in business, but "fervent in spirit, serving the Lord, and serving his generation, according to the will of God."

By these things, many high pretenders to religion, and professors of extraordinary spiritual experience, may be sensible, that Mr Brainerd did greatly condemn *their* kind of religion; and that not only in word, but by example, both living and dying; as the whole series of his Christian experience and practice, from his conversion to his death, appears a constant condemnation of it.

It cannot be objected, that the reason why he so much disliked the religion of these pretenders, and why his own so much differed from it, was, that his *experiences* were not *clear*. There is no room to say, they were otherwise, in any respect, in which clearness of experience has been wont to be insisted on; whether it be the clearness of their *nature* or of their *order*, and the method his soul was at first brought to rest and comfort in his conversion. I am far from thinking (and so was he) that clearness of the *order* of experiences is, in any measure, of equal importance with the clearness of their *nature*: I have sufficiently declared in my discourse on *religious affections*, (which he expresly approved of and recommended), that I do not suppose, a sensible distinctness of the *steps* of the Spirit's operation and method of successive convictions and illuminations, is a necessary requisite to persons being received in full charity, as true saints; provided the *nature* of the things they profess be right, and their practice agreeable. Nevertheless, it is observable, (which cuts off all objection from such as would be most unreasonably disposed to object and cavil in the present case), so it was, that Mr Brainerd's experiences were not only clear in the latter respect, but remarkably so in the former: so that there is not perhaps one instance in five hundred true converts, that on this account can be parallelled with him.

It cannot be pretended, that the reason why he so much abhorred and condemned the notions and experiences of those whose

whose *first faith* consists in believing that Christ *is theirs*, and that Christ *died for them*; without any previous experience of union of heart to him, for his excellency, as he is in himself, and not for his supposed love to them; and who judge of their interest in Christ, their justification, and God's love to them, not by their sanctification, and the exercises and fruits of grace, but by a supposed *immediate* witness of the Spirit, by inward suggestion; I say, it cannot be pretended, that the reason why he so much detested and condemned such opinions and experiences, was, that he was of a too *legal* spirit; either that he never was dead to the law, never experienced a thorough work of conviction, was never fully brought off from his own righteousness, and weaned from the *old covenant*, by a thorough *legal* humiliation; or that afterwards, he had no great degree of *evangelical* humiliation, not living in a deep sense of his own emptiness, wretchedness, poverty, and absolute dependance on the mere grace of God through Christ. For his convictions of sin, preceding his first consolations in Christ, were exceeding deep and thorough; his trouble and exercise of mind, by a sense of sin and misery, very great, and long continued; and the light let into his mind at his conversion, and in progressive sanctification, appears to have had its genuine humbling influence upon him, to have kept him low in his own eyes, not confiding in himself, but in Christ, "living by the faith "of the Son of God, and looking for the mercy of the Lord "Jesus to eternal life."

Nor can it be pretended, that the reason why he condemned these, and other things, which this sort of people call the very height of vital religion and the power of godliness, was, that he was a *dead Christian*, and lived *in the dark*, (as they express themselves); that his experiences, though they might be true, were not great; that he did not live near to God, had but a small acquaintance with him, and had but a dim sight of spiritual things. If any, after they have read the preceding account of Mr Brainerd's life, will venture to pretend thus, they will only shew that *they themselves* are in the *dark*, and do indeed "put darkness for light, and light for "darkness."

It is common with this sort of people, if there is any one, whom they cannot deny to exhibit good evidences of true godliness, who yet appears to dislike their notions, and condemn those things wherein they place the height of religion, to insinuate, that *they are afraid of the cross*, and have a mind to *curry favour with the world*, and the like. But I presume, this will not be pretended concerning Mr Brainerd, by any one person that has read the preceding account of his life. It must needs appear a thing notorious to such, that he was an extraordinary, and almost unparallelled instance (in these times, and these parts of the world) of the contrary disposition; and *that*, whether we consider what he has recorded of his inward *experience*, from time to time; or his *practice*, how he in fact took up and embraced the *cross*, and bore it constantly, in his great self-denials, labours, and sufferings for the name of Jesus, and went on without fainting, without repenting, or repining, to his dying illness: how he did not only, from time to time, relinquish and renounce the *world* secretly, in his heart, with the full and fervent consent of all the powers of his soul; but openly and actually forsook the *world*, with its possessions, delights, and common comforts, to dwell as it were with wild beasts, in a howling wilderness; with constant cheerfulness, complying with the numerous hardships of a life of toil and travel there, to promote the kingdom of his dear Redeemer. And besides, it appears by the preceding history, that he never did more condemn the things forementioned, never had a greater sense of their delusion, pernicious nature, and ill tendency, and never was more full of pity to those that are led away with them, than in his last illness, and at times when he had the nearest prospect of death, supposed himself to be on the very brink of eternity, and looked on all this lower world as what he never should have any thing more to do with. Surely he did not condemn those things at these seasons, only to *curry favour with the world*.

Besides what has been already related of Mr Brainerd's sentiments in his dying state concerning true and false religion, we have his deliberate and solemn thoughts on this subject, further appearing by his *Preface* to Mr Shepard's diary, before mentioned; which, when he wrote it, he supposed to be (as it proved) one of the *last* things he should ever write. I shall here insert a part of that *Preface*, as follows.

" How much stress is laid by many upon some things as be-
" ing effects and evidences of exalted degrees of religion,
" when they are so far from being of any importance in it,
" that they are really irreligious, a mixture of *self-love*, *ima-*
" *gination*, and spiritual *pride*, or perhaps the influence of
" Satan transformed into an angel of light; I say, how much
" stress is laid on these things by many, I shall not determine;
" but it is much to be feared, that while God was carrying
" on a glorious work of grace, and undoubtedly gathering a

" harvest

"harvest of souls to himself, (which we should always re-
"member with thankfulness), numbers of others have at the
"same time been fatally deluded by the devices of the devil,
"and their own corrupt hearts. It is to be feared, that the
"*conversions* of some have no better foundation than this;
"*viz.* that after they have been under some concern for
"their souls for a while, and it may be manifested some very
"great and uncommon distress and agonies, they have on a
"sudden *imagined they saw Christ*, in some posture or other,
"perhaps on the cross, bleeding and dying for their sins; or
"it may be, smiling on them, and thereby signifying his love
"to them: and that these and the like things, though mere
"imaginations, which have nothing spiritual in them, have in-
"stantly removed all their fears and distresses, filled them
"with raptures of joy, and made them imagine, that they
"loved Christ with all their hearts; when the bottom of all
"was nothing but *self-love*. For when they imagined that
"Christ had been so good to them as to save them, and as it
"were to single them out of all the world, they could not
"but feel some kind of natural gratitude to him; although
"they never had any spiritual view of his divine glory, ex-
"cellency, and beauty, and consequently never had any love
"to him for himself. Or that instead of having some such
"imaginary view of Christ as has been mentioned, in order
"to remove their distress, and give them joy, some having had
"a passage, or perhaps many passages of *scripture* brought
"to their minds *with power*, (as they express it), such as that,
"'Son, be of good cheer, thy sins are forgiven thee,' and the
"like; they have immediately applied these passages to *them-
"selves*, supposing that God hereby manifested his peculiar
"favour to *them*, as if mentioned by name: never consider-
"ing, that they are now giving heed to new revelations,
"there being no such thing revealed in the word of God, as
"that *this* or *that* particular person has, or ever shall have his
"sins forgiven; nor yet remembering, that Satan can, with a
"great deal of seeming pertinency, (and perhaps also with con-
"siderable power), bring scripture to the minds of men, as he
"did to Christ himself. And thus these rejoice upon having
"some scripture suddenly suggested to them, or impressed
"upon their minds, supposing they are now the children of
"God, just as did the other upon their imaginary views of
"Christ. And it is said, that some speak of seeing a great
"*light* which filled all the place where they were, and dis-
"pelled all their darkness, fears, and distresses, and almost ra-
"vished their souls. While others have had it warmly sug-

"gested

"gested to their minds, not by any passage of scripture, but "as it were by a *whisper* or voice from heaven, "That God "loves them, that Christ is theirs," &c. which groundless "imaginations and suggestions of Satan have had the same ef-"fect upon them, that the delusions before mentioned had on "the others.——And as is the conversion of this sort of per-"sons, so are their *after-experiences;* the whole being built "upon imagination, strong impressions, and sudden sugge-"stions made to their minds; whence they are usually extreme "confident (as if immediately informed from God) not only of "the goodness of their own state, but of their infallible know-"ledge, and absolute certainty, of the truth of every thing "they pretend to, under the notion of religion; and thus all "reasoning with some of them is utterly excluded.

"But it is remarkable of these, that they are *extremely de-"ficient* in regard of true poverty of spirit, sense of exceed-"ing vileness in themselves, such as frequently makes truly "gracious souls to *grone, being burdened;* as also in regard "of meekness, love, and gentleness towards mankind, tender-"ness of conscience in their ordinary affairs and dealings in "the world. And it is rare to see them deeply concerned "about the principles and ends of their actions, and under "fears lest they should not eye the glory of God chiefly, but "live to themselves; or this at least is the case in their ordi-"nary conduct, whether civil or religious. But if any one "of their particular *notions*, which their zeal has espoused, "be attacked, they are then so conscientious, they must "*burn*, if called to it, for the defence of it. Yet, at the "same time, when they are so *extremely deficient* in regard "of these precious *divine tempers* which have been men-"tioned, they are usually full of *zeal*, concern, and fervency "in the things of religion, and often *discourse* of them with "much warmth and engagement: and to those who do not "know, or do not consider, wherein the *essence* of true reli-"gion consists, *viz.* in being *conformed to the image of Christ*, "not in point of zeal and fervency only, but in all divine "tempers and practices; I say, to those who do not duly "observe and distinguish, they often appear like the best of "men."

It is common with this sort of people to say, that "God "is amongst them, his Spirit accompanies their exhortations, "and other administrations, and they are sealed by the Holy "Ghost," in the remarkable success they have, in the great affections that are stirred up in God's people, &c.; but to insinuate on the contrary, that "he is not with their oppo-"nents;"

"nents;" and particularly, "that God has forsaken the "standing ministry; and that the time is come, when it is the "will of God that they should be put down, and that God's "people should forsake them; and that no more success is "to be expected to attend their administrations."—But where can they find an instance, among all their most flaming *exhorters*, who has been sealed with so incontestable and wonderful success of his labours, as Mr Brainerd, not only in quickening and comforting God's children, but also in a work of conviction and conversion, (which they own has in a great measure ceased for a long time among themselves), with a most visible and astonishing manifestation of God's power, on subjects so unprepared, and that had been brought up and lived, some of them to old age, in the deepest prejudices against the very first principles of Christianity; the divine power accompanying his labours, producing the most remarkable and abiding change, turning the wilderness into a fruitful field, and causing that which was a desart indeed to bud and blossom as the rose? And this although he was not only one of their greatest *opponents* in their errors; but also one of those they call the *standing ministry;* first examined and licensed to preach by *such ministers,* and sent forth among the Heathen by *such ministers;* and afterwards ordained by *such ministers;* always directed by them, and united with them in their consistories, and administrations: and even abhorring the practice of those who give out, that they ought to be renounced and separated from, and that teachers may be ordained by laymen.

It cannot be pretended by these men, that Mr Brainerd condemned their religion, only because he was *not acquainted with them,* and had not opportunity for full observation of the nature, operation, and tendency of their *experiences:* for he had abundant and peculiar opportunities of such observation and acquaintance. He lived *through* the late extraordinary time of religious commotion, and saw the beginning and end, the good and the bad of it. He had opportunity to see the various operations and effects, that were wrought in this season, more *extensively,* than any person I know of. His native place was about the middle of Connecticut; and he was much conversant in all parts of that colony. He was conversant in the eastern parts of it, after the religion which he condemned, began much to prevail there. He was conversant with the zealous people on Long-Island, from one end of the island to the other; and also in New-Jersey and Pensylvania; with people of various nations. He had some special

cial opportunites in some places in this province, (Massachusetts Bay), where has been very much of this sort of religion, and at a time when it greatly prevailed. He had conversed and disputed with abundance of this kind of people in various parts, as he told me; and also informed me, that he had seen something of the same appearances in some of the Indians, whom he had preached to, and had opportunity to see the beginning and end of them. And besides, Mr Brainerd could speak more feelingly and understandingly concerning these things, because there was once a time when he was drawn away into an esteem of them, and for a short season had united himself to this kind of people, and partook, in some respects, of their spirit and behaviour.

But I proceed to another observation on the foregoing memoirs.

II. This history of Mr Brainerd's may help us to make *distinctions* among the high religious *affections*, and remarkable *impressions* made on the minds of persons, in a time of great *awakening*, and *revival of religion*; and may convince us, that there are not only distinctions in *theory*, invented to save the credit of pretended revivals of religion, and what is called *the experience of the operations of the Spirit*; but distinctions that do actually take place in the course of *events*, and have a real and evident foundation in *fact*.

Many *do* and *will* confound things, blend all together, and say, " It is all alike; it is all of the same sort." So there are many that say concerning the religion most generally prevailing among the Separatists, and the affections they manifest, " It is the same that was all over the land seven years ago." And some that have read Mr Brainerd's Journal, giving an account of the extraordinary things that have come to pass among the Indians in New-Jersey, say, " It is evidently the " same thing that appeared in many places amongst the Eng- " lish, which has now proved naught, and come to that " which is worse than nothing." And all the reason they have thus to determine all to be the *same work*, and the *same spirit*, is, that the one manifested high affections, and so do the other; the great affections of the one had some influence on their bodies, and so have the other; the one use the terms *conviction*, *conversion*, *humiliation*, *coming to Christ*, *discoveries*, *experiences*, &c. and so do the other; the impressions on the one are attended with a great deal of zeal, and so it is with the other; the affections of the one dispose them to speak much about things of religion, and so do the other; the

the one delight much in religious meetings, and so do the other.——The agreement that appears in these, and such like things, make them conclude, that surely all is alike, all is the same work. Whereas, on a closer inspection and critical examination, it would appear, that notwithstanding an agreement in such circumstances, yet indeed there is a vast difference, both in *essence* and *fruits*. A considerable part of the religious operations, that were six or seven years ago, especially towards the latter part of that extraordinary season, was doubtless of the same sort with the religion of the Separatists; but not all: there were many, whose experiences were, like Mr Brainerd's, in a judgment of charity, genuine and incontestable.

Not only do the opposers of all religion consisting in powerful operations and affections, thus confound things; but many of the *pretenders* to *such* religion do so. They that have been the subjects of some sort of vehement, but vain operations on their mind, when they hear the relation of the experiences of some real and eminent Christians, they say, their experiences are of the same sort: so they say, they are just like the experiences of eminent Christians in former times, which we have printed accounts of. So, I doubt not, but there are many deluded people, if they should read the preceding account of Mr Brainerd's life, who reading without much understanding, or careful observation, would say, without hesitation, that some things which they have met with, are of the very same kind with what he expresses: when the agreement is only in some general circumstances, or some particular things that are superficial, and belonging as it were to the profession and outside of religion; but the inward temper of mind, and the fruits in practice, are as opposite and distant as east and west.

Many *honest good* people also, and *true Christians*, do not very well know how to make a difference. The glistering appearance and glaring show of false religion dazzles their eyes; and they sometimes are so deluded by it, that they look on some of these impressions, which hypocrites tell of, as the brightest experiences. And though they have experienced no such things themselves, they think, it is because they are vastly lower in attainments, and but babes, in comparison of these flaming Christians. Yea, sometimes from their differing so much from those who make so great a show, they doubt whether they have any grace at all. And it is a hard thing, to bring many well-meaning people to make proper distinctions in this case; and especially to maintain and stand by them; through a certain weakness they unhappily labour of, whereby they are liable to be overcome with the glare of outward appearances. Thus, if in a sedate hour they are by reasoning brought to allow such and such distinctions, yet the next time they come in the way of the great show of false religion, the dazzling appearance swallows them up, and they are carried away. Thus the devil by his cunning artifices, easily dazzles the feeble sight of men, and puts them beyond a capacity of a proper exercise of consideration, or hearkening to the dictates of calm thought, and cool understanding. When they perceive the great affection, earnest talk, strong voice, assured looks, vast confidence, and bold assertions, of these empty assuming pretenders, they are overborne, lose the possession of their judgment, and say, "Surely these men are in "the right, God is with them of a truth:" and so they are carried away, not with light and reason, but (like children) as it were with a strong wind.

This confounding all things together, that have a fair shew, is but acting the part of a child, that going into a shop, where a variety of wares are exposed to sale, (all of a shining appearance; some vessels of gold and silver, and some diamonds and other precious stones; and other things that are toys of little value, which are of some base metal gilt, or glass polished, and painted with curious colours, or cut like diamonds), should esteem all alike, and give as great a price for the vile as for the precious: or it is like the conduct of some unskilful rash person, who finding himself deceived by some of the wares he had bought at that shop, should at once conclude, all he there saw was of no value; and pursuant to such a conclusion, when afterwards he has true gold and diamonds offered him, enough to enrich him and enable him to live like a prince all his days, he should throw it all into the sea.

But we *must* get into another way. The want of distinguishing in things that appertain to experimental religion, is one of the chief miseries of the professing world. It is attended with very many most dismal consequences: multitudes of souls are fatally deluded about themselves, and their own state; and so are eternally undone: hypocrites are confirmed in their delusions, and exceedingly puffed up with pride: many sincere Christians are dreadfully perplexed, darkened, tempted, and drawn aside from the way of duty; and sometimes sadly tainted with false religion, to the great dishonour of Christianity, and hurt of their own souls: some of the most dangerous and pernicious enemies of religion in the

the world (though called bright Christians) are encouraged and honoured; who ought to be discountenanced and shunned by every body: and prejudices are begotten and confirmed in vast multitudes, against every thing wherein the power and essence of godliness consists; and in the end Deism and Atheism are promoted.

III. The foregoing account of Mr Brainerd's life may afford matter of conviction, that there is indeed such a thing as true *experimental religion*, arising from immediate divine influences, supernaturally enlightening and convincing the mind, and powerfully impressing, quickening, sanctifying, and governing the heart; which religion is indeed an amiable thing, of happy tendency, and of no hurtful consequence to human *society*; notwithstanding there having been so many pretences and appearances of what is called experimental vital religion, that have proved to be nothing but vain, pernicious *enthusiasm*.

If any insist, that Mr Brainerd's religion was *enthusiasm*, and nothing but a strange heat and blind fervour of mind, arising from the strong fancies and dreams of a notional whimsical brain; I would ask, if it be so, that such things as these are the fruits of enthusiasm, *viz.* a great degree of honesty and simplicity, sincere and earnest desires and endeavours, to know and do whatever is right, and to avoid every thing that is wrong; an high degree of love to God, delight in the perfections of his nature, placing the happiness of life in him; not only in contemplating him, but in being active in pleasing and serving him; a firm and undoubting belief in the Messiah, as the Saviour of the world, the great Prophet of God, and King of God's church; together with great love to him, delight and complacence in the way of salvation by him, and longing for the enlargement of his kingdom; earnest desires that God may be glorified and the Messiah's kingdom advanced, whatever instruments are made use of; uncommon resignation to the will of God, and that under vast trials; great and universal benevolence to mankind, reaching all sorts of persons without distinction, manifested in sweetness of speech and behaviour, kind treatment, mercy, liberality, and earnest seeking the good of the souls and bodies of men; attended with extraordinary humility, meekness, forgiveness of injuries, and love to enemies; and a great abhorrence of a contrary spirit and practice; not only as appearing in others, but whereinsoever it had appeared in himself; causing the most bitter repentance, and brokenness of heart on account of any past instances of such a conduct: a modest, discreet, and decent deportment, among superiors, inferiors, and equals; a most diligent improvement of time, and earnest care to lose no part of it; great watchfulness against all sorts of sin, of heart, speech, and action: and this example and these endeavours attended with most happy fruits, and blessed effects on others, in humanizing, civilizing, and wonderfully reforming and transforming some of the most brutish savages; idle, immoral, drunkards, murderers, gross idolaters, and wizards; bringing them to permanent sobriety, diligence, devotion, honesty, conscientiousness, and charity: and the foregoing amiable virtues and successful labours all ending at last in a marvellous peace, unmoveable stability, calmness, and resignation, in the sensible approaches of death; with longing for the heavenly state; not only for the honours and circumstantial advantages of it, but above all for the moral perfection, and holy and blessed employments of it: and these things in a person indisputably of good understanding and judgment: I say, if all these things are the fruits of *enthusiasm*, why should not *enthusiasm* be thought a desirable and excellent thing? for what can true religion, what can the best philosophy do more? If vapours and whimsy will bring men to the most thorough virtue, to the most benign and fruitful morality; and will maintain it through a course of life (attended with many trials) without affectation or self-exaltation, and with an earnest constant bearing testimony against the wildness, the extravagances, the bitter zeal, assuming behaviour, and separating spirit of enthusiasts; and will do all this more effectually, than any thing else has ever done in any plain known instance that can be produced; if it be so, I say, what cause then has the world to prize and pray for this blessed whimsicalness, and these benign sort of vapours?

It would perhaps be a prejudice with some against the whole of Mr Brainerd's religion, if it had begun in the time of the *late religious commotion;* being ready to conclude (however unreasonably) that nothing good could take its rise from those times. But it was not so; his conversion was *before* those times, in a time of general deadness, (as has been before observed); and therefore at a season when it was impossible, that he should receive a taint from any corrupt notions, examples, or customs, that had birth in those times.

And whereas there are many who are not professed opposers of what is called *experimental religion,* who yet doubt of the reality of it, from the *bad lives* of some professors; and are ready to determine that there is nothing in all the talk about being *born again*, being *emptied of self*, *brought to a saving close with Christ*, &c. because many that pretend to these things, and are thought by others to have been the subjects of them, manifest no abiding alteration in their moral disposition and behaviour; are as careless, carnal, covetous, &c. as ever; yea, some much worse than ever: it is to be acknowledged and lamented, that this is the case with some; but by the preceding account they may be sensible, that it is not so with all. There are some indisputable instances of such a change, as the scripture speaks of; an abiding great change, a "renovation of the spirit of the mind," and a "walking in newness of life." In the foregoing instance particularly, they may see the abiding influence of such a work of conversion, as they have heard of from the word of God; the fruits of such experiences through a course of years; under a great variety of circumstances, many changes of state, place, and company; and may see the blessed issue and event of it in life and death.

IV. The preceding history serves to confirm those doctrines usually called *the doctrines of grace*. For if it be allowed that there is truth, substance, or value in the main of Mr Brainerd's religion, it will undoubtedly follow, that those doctrines are divine: since it is evident, that the whole of it, from beginning to end, is according to that scheme of things; all built on those apprehensions, notions, and views, that are produced and established in the mind by those doctrines. He was brought by doctrines of this kind to his awakening, and deep concern about things of a spiritual and eternal nature; and by these doctrines his convictions were maintained and carried on; and his conversion was evidently altogether agreeable to this scheme, but by no means agreeing with the contrary, and utterly inconsistent with the Arminian notion of conversion or repentance. His conversion was plainly founded in a clear strong conviction, and undoubting persuasion of the truth of those things appertaining to these doctrines, which Arminians most object against, and which his own mind had contended most about. And his conversion was no confirming and perfecting of moral principles and habits, by use and practice, and his own labour in an industrious disciplining himself, together with the concurring suggestions and conspiring aids of God's Spirit; but entirely a supernatural work, at once turning him from darkness to marvellous light,

light, and from the power of sin to the dominion of divine and holy principles; an effect, in no regard produced by *his* strength or labour, or obtained by *his* virtue; and not accomplished till he was first brought to a full conviction, that all his own virtue, strength, labours, and endeavours, could never avail any thing to the producing or procuring this effect.

A very little while before, his mind was full of the same cavils against the doctrines of God's sovereign grace, which are made by Arminians; and his heart full even of a raging opposition to them. And God was pleased to perform this good work in him just after a full end had been put to this cavilling and opposition; after he was entirely convinced, that he was dead in sin, and was in the hands of God, as the absolutely sovereign, unobliged, sole disposer and author of true holiness. God's shewing him mercy at such a time, is a confirmation, that this was a preparation for mercy; and consequently, that these things which he was convinced of, were true: while he opposed these things, he was the subject of no such mercy; though he so earnestly sought it, and prayed for it with so much painfulness, care, and strictness in religion: but when once his opposition is fully subdued, and he is brought to submit to the truths, which he before had opposed, with full conviction, then the mercy he sought for is granted, with abundant light, great evidence, and exceeding joy, and he reaps the sweet fruit of it all his life after, and in the valley of the shadow of death.

In his conversion, he was brought to see the glory of that way of salvation by Christ, that is taught in what are called the *doctrines of grace*; and thenceforward, with unspeakable joy and complacence, to embrace and acquiesce in that way of salvation. He was in his conversion, in all respects, brought to those views, and that state of mind, which these doctrines shew to be necessary. And if his conversion was any real conversion, or any thing besides a mere whim, and if the religion of his life was any thing else but a series of freaks of a whimsical mind, then this one grand principle, on which depends the whole difference between Calvinists and Arminians, is undeniable, *viz.* that the grace or virtue of truly good men, not only differs from the virtue of others in *degree*, but even in *nature* and *kind*. If ever Mr Brainerd was truly turned from sin to God at all, or ever became truly religious, none can reasonably doubt but that his conversion was at the time when he supposed it to be: the change he then experienced, was evidently the greatest moral change, that ever he

passed

passed under; and he was then apparently first brought to that kind of religion, that remarkable new habit and temper of mind, which he held all his life after. The narration shews it to be different, in *nature* and *kind*, from all that ever he was the subject of before. It was evidently wrought at once without fitting and preparing his mind, by gradually convincing it more and more of the same truths, and bringing it nearer and nearer to such a temper: for it was soon after his mind had been remarkably full of blasphemy, and a vehement exercise of sensible enmity against God, and great opposition to those truths, which he was now brought with his whole soul to embrace, and rest in, as divine and glorious, and to place his happiness in the contemplation and improvement of. And he himself (who was surely best able to judge) declares, that the dispositions and affections, which were then given him, and thenceforward maintained in him, were most sensibly and certainly, perfectly different, in their *nature*, from all that ever he was the subject of before, or that he ever had any conception of. This he ever stood to, and was peremptory in, (as what he certainly knew), even to his death. He must be looked upon as capable of judging; he had opportunity to know: he had practised a great deal of religion before, was exceeding strict and conscientious, and had continued so for a long time; had various religious affections, with which he often flattered himself, and sometimes pleased himself as being now in a good estate: and after he had those new experiences, that began in his conversion, they were continued to the end of his life; long enough for him thoroughly to observe their nature, and compare them with what had been before. Doubtless he was *compos mentis;* and was at least one of so good an understanding and judgment, as to be pretty well capable of discerning and comparing the things that passed in his own mind.

It is further observable, that his religion all along operated in such a manner as tended to confirm his mind in the doctrines of God's absolute sovereignty, man's universal and entire dependence on God's power and grace, *&c.* The more his religion prevailed in his heart, and the fuller he was of divine love, and of clear and delightful views of spiritual things, and the more his heart was engaged in God's service; the more sensible he was of the certainty and the excellency and importance of these truths, and the more he was affected with them, and rejoiced in them. And he declares particularly, that when he lay for a long while on the verge of the eternal world, often expecting to be in that world in a few minutes,

yet

yet at the same time enjoying great serenity of mind, and clearness of thought, and being most apparently in a peculiar manner at a distance from an enthusiastical frame, he "at that time saw clearly the truth of those great doctrines "of the gospel, which are justly stiled *the doctrines of grace*, "and never felt himself so capable of demonstrating the truth "of them."

So that it is very evident, Mr Brainerd's religion was wholly correspondent to what is called the *Calvinistical scheme*, and was the effect of those doctrines applied to his heart: and certainly it cannot be denied, that the effect was good, unless we turn Atheists, or Deists.——I would ask, whether there be any such thing, in reality, as *Christian devotion?* If there be, what is it? what is its nature? and what its just measure? should it not be in a great degree? we read abundantly in scripture, of "loving God with all the heart, with all the soul, with "all the mind, and with all the strength, of delighting in "God, of rejoicing in the Lord, rejoicing with joy unspeak- "able and full of glory, the soul's magnifying the Lord, "thirsting for God, hungering and thirsting after righteous- "ness, the soul's breaking for the longing it hath to God's "judgments, praying to God with groanings that cannot be "uttered, mourning for sin with a broken heart and contrite "spirit," &c. How full is the book of Psalms, and other parts of scripture, of such things as these! Now wherein do these things, as expressed by and appearing in Mr Brainerd, either the things themselves, or their effects and fruits, differ from the scripture-representations?. These things he was brought to by that strange and wonderful transformation of the man, which he called his conversion. And do not this well agree with what is so often said in Old Testament and New, concerning the "giving of a new heart, creating a "right spirit, a being renewed in the spirit of the mind, a "being sanctified throughout, becoming a new creature?" &c. Now where is there to be found an Arminian conversion or repentance, consisting in so great and admirable a change? Can the Arminians produce an instance, within this age, and so, plainly, within our reach and view, of such a reformation, such a transformation of a man, to scriptural devotion, heavenly mindedness, and true Christian morality, in one that before lived without these things, on the foot of *their* principles, and through the influence of their doctrines?

And here, is worthy to be considered, not only the effect of Calvinistical doctrines (as they are called) on Mr Brainerd himself,

himself, but also the effect of the same doctrines, as taught and inculcated by him, on *others*. It is abundantly pretended and asserted of late, that these doctrines tend to undermine the very foundations of all religion and morality, and to enervate and vacate all reasonable motives to the exercise and practice of them, and lay invincible stumbling-blocks before Infidels, to hinder their embraceing Christianity; and that the contrary doctrines are the fruitful principles of virtue and goodness, set religion on its right basis, represent it in an amiable light, give its motives their full force, and recommend it to the reason and common sense of mankind.—But where can they find an instance of so great and signal an effect of their doctrines, in bringing Infidels, who were at such a distance from all that is civil, human, sober, rational, and Christian, and so full of inveterate prejudices against these things, to such a degree of humanity, civility, exercise of reason, self-denial, and Christian virtue? Arminians place religion in *morality*: let them bring an instance of their doctrines producing such a transformation of a people in point of *morality*. It is strange, if the allwise God so orders things in his providence, that reasonable and proper *means*, and *his own* means, which he himself has appointed, should in no known remarkable instance be instrumental to produce so good an effect; an effect so agreeable to his own word and mind, and that very effect for which he appointed these excellent means; that they should not be so successful, as those means which are *not* his own, but very contrary to them, and of a contrary tendency; means that are in themselves very absurd, and tend to root all religion and virtue out of the world, to promote and establish infidelity, and to lay an insuperable stumbling-block before Pagans, to hinder their embracing the gospel: I say, if this be the true state of the case, it is certainly pretty wonderful, and an event worthy of some attention.

I know, that many will be ready to say, "It is too soon "yet, to glory in the work, that has been wrought among Mr "Brainerd's Indians; it is best to wait and see the final event; "it may be, all will come to nothing by and by." To which I answer, (not to insist, that it will not follow, according to Arminian principles, they are not now true Christians, really pious and godly, though they *should* fall away and come to nothing), that I never supposed, every one of those Indians, who in profession renounced their Heathenism and visibly embraced Christianity, and have had some appearance of piety, will finally prove true converts: if two thirds, or indeed one half of them (as great a proportion as there is in the parable of the *ten virgins*) should persevere; it will be sufficient to shew the work, wrought among them, to have been truly admirable and glorious. But so much of permanence of their religion has already appeared, as shews it to be something else besides an Indian humour or good mood, or any transient effect in the conceits, notions, and affections of these ignorant people, excited at a particular turn, by artful management. For it is now more than *three years* ago, that this work began among them, and a remarkable change appeared in many of them; since which time the number of visible converts has greatly increased: and by repeated accounts, from several hands, they still generally persevere in diligent religion and strict virtue. I think worthy to be here inserted, a *letter* from a young gentleman, a candidate for the ministry, one of those before mentioned, appointed by the honourable commissioners in Boston, as missionaries to the Heathen of the Six Nations, so called; who, by their order, dwelt with Mr John Brainerd among these Christian Indians, in order to their being prepared for the business of their mission. The letter was written from thence, to his parents here in Northampton, and is as follows.

Bethel, in New-Jersey, Jan. 14. 1747-8.

Honoured and dear parents,

AFter a long and uncomfortable journey, by reason of bad weather, I arrived at Mr Brainerd's, the 6th of this instant; where I design to stay this winter: and as yet, upon many accounts, am well satisfied with my coming hither. The state and circumstances of the Indians, spiritual and temporal, much exceed what I expected. I have endeavoured to acquaint myself with the state of the Indians in general, with particular persons, and with the school, as much as the short time I have been here would admit of. And notwithstanding my expectations were very much raised, from Mr David Brainerd's Journal, and from particular informations from him; yet I must confess, that in many respects, they are not equal to that which now appears to me to be true, concerning the glorious work of divine grace amongst the Indians.

The evening after I came to town, I had opportunity to see the Indians together, whilst the Reverend Mr Arthur preached to them: at which time there appeared a very general and uncommon seriousness and solemnity in the congregation:

sation: and this appeared to me to be the effect of an inward sense of the importance of divine truths, and not because they were hearing a stranger: which was abundantly confirmed to me the next Sabbath, when there was the same devout attendance on divine service, and a surprising solemnity appearing in the performance of each part of divine worship. And some, who are hopefully true Christians, appear to have been at that time much enlivened and comforted; not from any observable commotions then, but from conversation afterwards: and others seemed to be under pressing concern for their souls. I have endeavoured to acquaint myself with particular persons; many of whom seem to be very humble and growing Christians; although some of them, (as I am informed), were before their conversion most monstrously wicked.

Religious conversation seems to be very pleasing and delightful to many, and especially that which relates to the exercises of the heart. And many here do not seem to be real Christians only, but growing Christians also; as well in doctrinal, as experimental knowledge. Besides my conversation with particular persons, I have had opportunity to attend upon one of Mr Brainerd's catechetical lectures; where I was surprised at their readiness in answering questions which they had not been used to: although Mr Brainerd complained much of their uncommon deficiency. It is surprising, to see this people, who not long since were led captive by Satan at his will, and living in the practice of all manner of abominations, without the least sense even of moral honesty, yet now living soberly and regularly, and not seeking every man his own, but every man, in some sense, his neighbour's good; and to see those, who but a little while past, knew nothing of the true God, now worshipping him in a solemn and devout manner; not only in public, but in their families and in secret; which is manifestly the case, it being a difficult thing to walk out in the woods in the morning, without disturbing persons at their secret devotion. And it seems wonderful, that this should be the case, not only with adult persons, but with children also. It is observable here, that many children, (if not the children in general), retire into secret places to pray. And, as far as at present I can judge, this is not the effect of custom and fashion, but of real seriousness and thoughtfulness about their souls.

I have frequently gone into the school, and have spent considerable time there amongst the children; and have been surprised to see, not only their diligent attendance upon the business of the school, but also the proficiency they have made in it, in reading and writing, and in their catechisms of divers sorts. It seems to be as pleasing and as natural to these children, to have their books in their hands, as it does for many others to be at play. I have gone into an house where there has been a number of children accidentally gathered together; and observed, that every one had his book in his hand, and was diligently studying of it. There is to the number of about thirty of these children, who can answer to all the questions in the Assembly's catechism; and the bigger part of them are able to do it with the proofs, to the fourth commandment. I wish there were many such schools: I confess, that I never was acquainted with such an one, in many respects. Oh that what God has done here, may prove to be the beginning of a far more glorious and extensive work of grace among the Heathen!

I am your obedient and dutiful son,

JOB STRONG.

P. S. Since the date of this, I have had opportunity to attend upon another of Mr Brainerd's catechetical lectures: and truly I was convinced, that Mr Brainerd did not complain before of his people's defects in answering to questions proposed, without reason: for although their answers at that time exceeded my expectations very much; yet their performances at this lecture very much exceeded them."

Since this, we have had accounts from time to time, and some very late, which shew that religion still continues in prosperous and most desirable circumstances among these Indians.

V. Is there not much in the preceding memoirs of Mr Brainerd to teach, and excite to duty, us who are called to the work of the *ministry*, and all that are *candidates* for that great work? What a deep sense did he seem to have of the greatness and importance of that work, and with what weight did it lie on his mind! how sensible was he of his own insufficiency for this work; and how great was his dependence on God's sufficiency! how solicitous, that he might be fitted for it! and to this end, how much time did he spend in prayer and fasting, as well as reading and meditation; *giving himself to these things!* how did he dedicate his whole life, all his powers and talents to God; and forsake and renounce the world,

world, with all its pleasing and ensnaring enjoyments, that he might be wholly at liberty, to serve Christ in this work; and to "please him who had chosen him to be a soldier, under the Captain of our salvation!" With what solicitude, solemnity, and diligence did he devote himself to God our Saviour, and seek his presence and blessing in secret, at the time of his *ordination!* and how did his whole heart appear to be constantly engaged, his whole time employed, and his whole strength spent in the business he then solemnly undertook and was publicly set apart to!——And his history shews us the right way to *success* in the work of the ministry. He sought it, as a resolute soldier seeks victory, in a siege or battle; or as a man that runs a race, for a great prize. Animated with love to Christ and souls, how did he "labour always fervently," not only in word and doctrine, in public and private, but in *prayers* day and night, "wrestling with God" in secret, and "travailing in birth," with unutterable groans and agonies, "until Christ were formed" in the hearts of the people to whom he was sent! how did he thirst for a blessing on his ministry; and "watch for souls, as one that must give account!" how did he "go forth in the strength of the Lord God;" seeking and depending on a special influence of the *Spirit* to assist and succeed him! and what was the happy fruit at last, though after long waiting, and many dark and discouraging appearances! like a true son of Jacob, he persevered in wrestling, through all the darkness of the night, until the breaking of the day.

And his example of labouring, praying, denying himself, and enduring hardness, with unfainting resolution and patience, and his faithful, vigilant, and prudent conduct in many other respects, (which it would be too long now particularly to recite), may afford instruction to *missionaries* in particular.

VI. The foregoing account of Mr Brainerd's life may afford instruction to *Christians in general;* as it shews, in many respects, the right way of *practising* religion, in order to obtaining the *ends* of it, and receiving the *benefits* of it; or how Christians should "run the race set before them," if they would not "run in vain, or run as uncertainly," but would honour God in the world, adorn their profession, be serviceable to mankind, have the comforts of religion while they live, be free from disquieting doubts and dark apprehensions about the state of their souls; enjoy peace in the approaches of death, and "finish their course with joy."——In general, he much recommended, for this purpose, the *re-*

demption

demption of time, great *diligence* in the business of the Christian life, *watchfulness*, &c. And he very remarkably exemplified these things.

But particularly, his example and success with regard to one duty in special, may be of great use to both ministers and private Christians; I mean the duty of *secret fasting*. The reader has seen, how much Mr Brainerd recommends this duty, and how frequently he exercised himself in it; nor can it well have escaped observation, how much he was owned and blessed in it, and of what great benefit it evidently was to his soul. Among all the many days he spent in secret fasting and prayer, that he gives an account of in his *diary*, there is scarce an instance of one, but what was either attended or soon followed with apparent success, and a remarkable blessing, in special incomes and consolations of God's Spirit; and very often, before the day was ended.——But it must be observed, that when he set about this duty, he did it in good earnest; "stirring up himself to take hold of God," and "continuing instant in prayer," with much of the spirit of Jacob, who said to the Angel, "I will not let thee go, except "thou bless me."

VII. There is much in the preceding account to excite and encourage God's people to earnest prayers and endeavours for the *advancement* and *enlargement* of the *kingdom of Christ* in the *world*. Mr Brainerd set us an excellent example in this respect: he sought the prosperity of Zion with all his might: he preferred Jerusalem above his chief joy. How did his soul long for it, and pant after it! and how earnestly and often did he wrestle with God for it! and how far did he, in these desires and prayers, seem to be carried beyond all private and selfish views! being animated by a pure love to Christ, an earnest desire of his glory, and a disinterested affection to the souls of mankind.

The consideration of this, not only ought to be an *incitement* to the people of God, but may also be a just *encouragement* to them, to be much in seeking and praying for a general outpouring of the Spirit of God, and extensive revival of religion. I confess, that God's giving so much of a spirit of prayer for this mercy to so eminent a servant of his, and exciting him, in so extraordinary a manner, and with such vehement thirstings of soul, to agonize in prayer for it, from time to time, through the course of his life, is one thing, among others, which gives me great hope, that God has a design of accomplishing something very glorious for the interest

terest of his church before long. One such instance as this, I conceive, gives more encouragement, than the common, cold, formal prayers of thousands. As Mr Brainerd's desires and prayers for the coming of Christ's kingdom, were very *special* and *extraordinary;* so, I think, we may reasonably hope, that the God, who excited those desires and prayers, will answer them with something *special* and *extraordinary*. And in a particular manner, do I think it worthy to be taken notice of for our encouragement, that he had his heart (as he declared) unusually, and beyond what had been before, drawn out in longings and prayers for the flourishing of Christ's kingdom on earth, when he was in the approaches of *death;* and that with his dying breath he did as it were breathe out his departing soul into the bosom of his Redeemer, in prayers and pantings after this glorious event; expiring in a very great hope that it would soon begin to be fulfilled. And I wish, that the thoughts which he in his dying state expressed of that explicit agreement, and visible union of God's people, in extraordinary prayer for a general revival of religion, lately proposed in a memorial from Scotland, which has been dispersed among us, may be well considered by those that hitherto have not seen fit to fall in with that proposal.——But I forbear to say any more on this head, having already largely published my thoughts upon it, in a discourse written on purpose to promote that affair; which, I confess, I wish that every one of my readers might be supplied with; not that my honour, but that this excellent design might be promoted.

As there is much in Mr Brainerd's life to encourage Christians to seek the advancement of Christ's kingdom, in general; so there is, in particular, to pray for the conversion of the Indians on this continent, and to exert themselves in the use of proper means for its accomplishment. For it appears, that he in his unutterable longings and wrestlings of soul for the flourishing of religion, had his mind peculiarly intent on the conversion and salvation of these people, and his heart more especially engaged in prayer for them. And if we consider the degree and manner in which he from time to time, sought and hoped for an extensive work of grace among them, I think, we have reason to hope, that the wonderful things, which God wrought among them by him, are but a forerunner of something yet much more glorious and extensive of that kind; and this may justly be an encouragement, to well-disposed charitable persons, to "honour the Lord with their "substance," by contributing, as they are able, to promote the spreading of the gospel among them; and this also may incite

incite and encourage gentlemen who are incorporated, and intrusted with the care and disposal of those liberal benefactions, which have already been made by pious persons, to that end; and likewise the missionaries themselves, that are or may be employed; and it may be of direction unto both, as to the proper qualifications of missionaries, and the proper measures to be taken in order to their success.

One thing in particular, I would take occasion from the foregoing history to mention and propose to the consideration of such as have the care of providing and sending *missionaries* among savages; *viz.* Whether it would not ordinarily be best to send *two* together? It is pretty manifest, that Mr Brainerd's going, as he did, alone into the howling wilderness, was one great occasion of such a prevailing of melancholy on his mind; which was his greatest disadvantage. He was much in speaking of it himself, when he was here in his dying state; and expressed himself, to this purpose, that none could conceive of the disadvantage a missionary in such circumstances was under, by being alone; especially as it exposed him to discouragement and melancholy: and spoke of the wisdom of Christ in sending forth his disciples by two and two; and left it as his dying advice to his brother, never to go to Susquahannah, to travel about in that remote wilderness, to preach to the Indians there, as *he* had often done, without the company of a *fellow missionary*.

VIII. One thing more may not be unprofitably observed in the preceding account of Mr Brainerd; and that is the *special* and *remarkable disposal* of divine providence, with regard to the *circumstances* of his last *sickness and death*.

Though he had been long infirm, his constitution being much broken by his fatigues and hardships; and though he was often brought very low by illness, before he left Kaunaumeek, and also while he lived at the Forks of Delaware: yet his life was preserved, till he had seen that which he had so long and greatly desired and sought, a glorious work of grace among the Indians, and had received the wished-for blessing of God on his labours. Though as it were "in deaths oft," yet he lived to behold the happy fruits of the long continued travail of his soul and labour of his body, in the wonderful conversion of many of the Heathen, and the happy effect of it in the great change of their conversation, with many circumstances which afforded a fair prospect of the continuance of God's blessing upon them; as may appear by what I shall presently further

further observe.——Thus he did not "depart, till his eyes "had seen God's salvation."

Though it was the pleasure of God, that he should be taken off from his labours among that people whom God had made him a spiritual father to, who were so dear to him, and whose spiritual welfare he was so greatly concerned for; yet this was not before they were well initiated and instructed in the Christian religion, thoroughly weaned from their old heathenish and brutish notions and practices, and all their prejudices and jealousies, which tended to keep their minds unsettled, were fully removed; and they were confirmed and fixed in the Christian faith and manners, were formed into a church, had ecclesiastical ordinances and discipline introduced and settled; were brought into a good way with respect to the education of children, had a schoolmaster sent to them in providence, excellently qualified for the business, and had a school set up and established, in good order, among them; had been well brought off from their former idle, strolling, sottish way of living; had removed from their former scattered uncertain habitations; and were collected in a town by themselves, on a good piece of land of their own; were introduced into the way of living by husbandry, and begun to experience the benefits of it, *&c.* These things were but just brought to pass by his indefatigable application and care, and then he was taken off from his work by illness. If this had been but a little sooner, they would by no means have been so well prepared for such a dispensation; and it probably would have been unspeakably more to the hurt of their spiritual interest, and of the cause of Christianity among them.

The time and circumstances of his illness were so ordered, that he had just opportunity to finish his Journal, and prepare it for the press; giving an account of the marvellous display of divine power and grace among the Indians in New-Jersey, and at the Forks of Delaware: his doing which was a thing of great consequence, and therefore urged upon him by the *correspondents*, who have honoured his Journal with a preface. The world being particularly and justly informed of that affair by Mr Brainerd, before his death, a foundation was hereby laid for a concern in *others* for that cause, and proper care and measures to be taken for the maintaining it after his death. As it has actually proved to be of great influence and benefit in this respect; it having excited and engaged many in those parts, and also more distant parts of America, to exert themselves for the upholding and promoting so good and glorious a work, remarkably opening their hearts and hands to that end: and not only in America, but in Great Britain, where that Journal (which is the same that I have earnestly recommended to my readers to possess themselves of) has been an occasion of some large benefactions, made for the promoting the interest of Christianity among the Indians.——If Mr Brainerd had been taken ill but a little sooner, he had not been able to complete this his Journal, and prepare a copy for the press.

He was not taken off from the work of the ministry among his people, till his *brother* was in a capacity and circumstances to *succeed* him in his care of them: who succeeds him in the like spirit, and under whose prudent and faithful care his congregation has flourished, and been very happy, since he left them; and probably could not have been so well provided for, otherwise. If Mr Brainerd had been disabled sooner, his *brother* would by no means have been ready to stand up in his place; having taken his first degree at college but about that very time that he was seized with his fatal consumption.

Though in that winter that he lay sick at Mr Dikinson's in Elisabeth-Town, he continued for a long time in an extremely low state, so that his life was almost despaired of, and his state was sometimes such that it was hardly expected he would live a day to an end; yet his life was spared a while longer; he lived to see his *brother* arrived in New-Jersey, being come to succeed him in the care of his Indians; and he himself had opportunity to assist in his examination and introduction into his business; and to commit the conduct of his dear people to one whom he well knew, and could put confidence in, and use freedom with in giving him particular instructions and charges, and under whose care he could leave his congregation with great cheerfulness.

The providence of God was remarkable in so ordering of it, that before his death he should take a journey into New-England, and go to Boston: which was, in many respects, of very great and happy consequence to the interest of religion, and especially among his own people. By this means, as has been observed, he was brought into acquaintance with many persons of note and influence, ministers and others, belonging both to the town and various parts of the country; and had opportunity, under the best advantages, to bear a testimony for God and true religion, and against those false appearances of it that have proved most pernicious to the interests of Christ's kingdom in the land. And the providence of God is particularly observable in this circumstance

ſtance of the teſtimony he there bore for true religion, *viz.* that he there was brought ſo near the *grave*, and continued for ſo long a time on the very brink of eternity; and from time to time, looked on himſelf, and was looked on by others, as juſt leaving the world; and that in theſe circumſtances he ſhould be ſo particularly directed and aſſiſted in his thoughts and views of religion, to diſtinguiſh between the true and the falſe, with ſuch clearneſs and evidence; and that after this he ſhould be unexpectedly and ſurpriſingly reſtored and ſtrengthened, ſo far as to be able to converſe freely; and have ſuch opportunity, and ſpecial occaſions to declare the ſentiments he had in theſe, which were, to human apprehenſion, his dying circumſtances; and to bear his teſtimony concerning the nature of true religion, and concerning the miſchievous tendency of its moſt prevalent counterfeits and falſe appearances; as things he had a ſpecial, clear, diſtinct view of at that time, when he expected in a few minutes to be in eternity; and the certainty and importance of which were then, in a peculiar manner, impreſſed on his mind.

Among the happy conſequences of his going to Boſton, were thoſe liberal benefactions that have been mentioned, which were made by pious diſpoſed perſons, for the maintaining and promoting the intereſt of religion among his people: and alſo the meeting of a number of gentlemen in Boſton, of note and ability, to conſult upon meaſures for that purpoſe; who were excited by their acquaintance and converſation with Mr Brainerd, and by the account of the great things God had wrought by his miniſtry, to unite themſelves; that by their joint endeavours and contributions they might promote the kingdom of Chriſt, and the ſpiritual good of their fellow-creatures, among the Indians in New-Jerſey, and elſewhere.

It was alſo remarkable, that Mr Brainerd ſhould go to Boſton at *that time*, after the honourable commiſſioners there, of the corporation in London for propagating the goſpel in New-England and parts adjacent, had received Dr William's legacy for the maintaining of two miſſionaries among the Heathen; and at a time when they having concluded on a miſſion to the Indians of the Six Nations (ſo called), were looking out for fit perſons to be employed in that important ſervice. This proved an occaſion of their committing to him the affair of finding and recommending ſuitable perſons: which has proved a ſucceſsful means of two perſons being found and actually appointed to that buſineſs; who ſeem to be well qualified for it, and to have their hearts greatly engaged in it; one of which has been ſolemnly ordained to that work in Boston, and is now gone forth to one of those tribes, who have appeared well disposed to his reception; it being judged not convenient for the other to go till the next spring, by reason of his bodily infirmity *.

These happy consequences of Mr Brainerd's journey to Boston would have been prevented, in case he had died, when he was brought so near to death in New-Jersey. Or if after he came first to Northampton, (where he was much at a loss and long deliberating which way to bend his course), he had determined not to go to Boston.

The providence of God was observable in his going to Boston at a time when not only the honourable commissioners were seeking missionaries to the Six Nations, but just after his Journal, which gives an account of his labours and success among the Indians, had been received and spread in Boston; whereby his name was known, and the minds of serious people were well prepared to receive his person, and the testimony he there gave for God; to exert themselves for the upholding and promoting the interest of religion in his congregation, and amongst the Indians elsewhere; and to regard his judgment concerning the qualifications of missionaries, &c. If he had gone there the fall before, (when he had intended to have made his journey into New-England, but was prevented by a sudden great increase of his illness), it would not have been likely to have been in any measure to so good effect: and also if he had not been unexpectedly detained in Boston; for when he went from my house, he intended to make but a very short stay there; but divine providence by his being brought so low there, detained him long; thereby to make way for the fulfilling its own gracious designs.

The providence of God was remarkable in so ordering, that although he was brought so very near the grave in Boston, that it was not in the least expected he would ever come alive out of his chamber; yet he wonderfully revived, and was preserved several months longer: so that he had opportunity to see, and fully to converse with both his younger

* The appointment of these gentlemen to this mission has been *hitherto* much smiled on in providence; as in other respects, so particularly in the wonderful opening of the hearts of many to contribute liberally to so excellent a design; besides the benefactions in Boston, a number of persons at Northampton with much cheerfulness have given about *L.* 160 (old tenor); and a particular person in Springfield has devoted a considerable part of his estate to this interest.

brethren

brethren before he died; which was a thing he greatly desired; and especially to see his brother John, with whom was left the care of his congregation; that he might by him be fully informed of their state, and might leave with him such instructions and directions as were requisite in order to their spiritual welfare, and to send to them his dying charges and counsels. And he had also opportunity, by means of this suspension of his death, to find and recommend a couple of persons fit to be employed as *missionaries* to the Six Nations, as had been desired of him.

Thus, although it was the pleasure of a sovereign God, that he should be taken away from his congregation, the people that he had begotten through the gospel, who were so dear to him; yet it was granted to him, that before he died he should see them well *provided for*, every way: he saw them provided for with one to instruct them, and take care of their souls; his own brother, whom he could confide in; he saw a good foundation laid for the support of the school among them; those things that before were wanting in order to it, being supplied: and he had the prospect of a *charitable society* being established, of able and well-disposed persons, who seem to make the spiritual interest of his congregation their own; whereby he had a comfortable view of their being well provided for, for the future: and he had also opportunity to leave all his dying charges with his successor in the pastoral care of his people, and by him to send his dying counsels to them. Thus God granted him to see all things happily settled, or in a hopeful way of being so, before his death, with respect to his dear people.—And whereas not only his own congregation, but the souls of the Indians in North-America in general, were very dear to him, and he had greatly set his heart on the propagating and extending the kingdom of Christ among them; God was pleased to grant to him, (however it was his will, that he should be taken away, and so should not be the immediate instrument of their instruction and conversion, yet), that before his death, he should see unexpected extraordinary provision made for this also. And it is remarkable, that God not only allowed him to see such provision made for the maintaining the interest of religion among his own people, and the propagation of it elsewhere; but honoured him by making *him* the means or occasion of it. So that it is very probable, however Mr Brainerd, during the last four months of his life, was ordinarily in an extremely weak and low state, very often scarcely able to speak; yet that he was made the instrument or means of much

much more good in that space of time, than he would have been if he had been well, and in full strength of body. Thus *God's power* was manifested in *his weakness*, and the *life of Christ* was manifested in *his mortal flesh*.

Another thing, wherein appears the merciful disposal of providence with respect to his death, was, that he did not die in the wilderness, among the savages, at Kaunaumeek, or the Forks of Delaware, or at Susquahannah; but in a place where his dying behaviour and speeches might be observed and remembered, and some account given of them for the benefit of survivers; and also where care might be taken of him in his sickness, and proper honours done him at his death.

The providence of God is also worthy of remark, in so over-ruling and ordering the matter, that he did not finally leave absolute orders for the entire suppressing of his *private papers*; as he had intended and fully resolved, insomuch that all the importunity of his friends could scarce restrain him from doing it, when sick at Boston. And one thing relating to this is peculiarly remarkable, *viz.* that his brother, a little before his death, should come from the Jerseys unexpected, and bring his *diary* to him, though he had received no such order. So that he had opportunity of access to these his reserved papers, and for reviewing the same; without which, it appears, he would at last have ordered them to be wholly suppressed: but after this, he the more readily yielded to the desires of his friends, and was willing to leave them in their hands to be disposed of as they thought might be most for God's glory: by which means, "he being dead, yet speaketh," in these memoirs of his life, taken from those private writings: whereby it is to be hoped he may still be as it were the instrument of much promoting the interest of religion in this world; the advancement of which he so much desired, and hoped would be accomplished after his death.

If these circumstances of Mr Brainerd's death be duly considered, I doubt not but they will be acknowledged as a notable instance of God's fatherly care, and covenant-faithfulness towards them that are devoted to him, and faithfully serve him while they live; whereby "he never fails nor "forsakes them, but *is with them* living and dying; so that "whether they live, they live to the Lord; or whether they "die, they die to the Lord;" and both in life and death they are owned and taken care of as *his*.——Mr Brainerd himself, as was before observed, was much in taking notice

(when

(when near his end) of the merciful circumſtances of his death; and ſaid, from time to time, that "God had granted "him all his deſire."

And I would not conclude my obſervations on the merciful circumſtances of Mr Brainerd's death, without acknowledging with thankfulneſs, the gracious diſpenſation of providence to me and my family, in ſo ordering, that he (though the ordinary place of his abode was more than two hundred miles diſtant) ſhould be caſt hither, to my houſe, in his laſt ſickneſs, and ſhould die here: ſo that we had opportunity for much acquaintance and converſation with him, and to ſhew him kindneſs in ſuch circumſtances, and to ſee his dying behaviour, to hear his dying ſpeeches, to receive his dying counſels, and to have the benefit of his dying prayers. May God in infinite mercy grant, that we may ever retain a proper remembrance of theſe things, and make a due improvement of the advantages we have had, in theſe reſpects! The Lord grant alſo, that the foregoing account of Mr Brainerd's life and death may be for the great ſpiritual benefit of all that ſhall read it, and prove a happy means of promoting the rivival of true religion in theſe parts of the world! *Amen.*

FINIS.

Mirabilia Dei inter Indicos;

OR,

The RISE and PROGRESS

OF A

Remarkable WORK of GRACE

Amongſt a NUMBER of the INDIANS

In the Provinces of NEW-JERSEY and PENSYLVANIA,

Juſtly REPRESENTED in a

JOURNAL

Kept by order of the Honourable SOCIETY (in Scotland) for propagating CHRISTIAN KNOWLEDGE.

With ſome general REMARKS.

By DAVID BRAINERD,
Miniſter of the Goſpel, and Miſſionary from the ſaid Society.

Publiſhed by the Reverend and Worthy Correſpondents of the ſaid Society. With a Preface by them.

Iſ. lv. 13. Inſtead of the thorn ſhall come up the fir-tree, and inſtead of the brier ſhall come up the myrtle-tree: and it ſhall be to the Lord for a name, for an everlaſting ſign that ſhall not be cut off.
Iſ. lxv. 1. I am ſought of them that aſked not for me: I am found of them that ſought me not: I ſaid, Behold me, behold me, unto a nation that was not called by my name.
Pſal. cxlv. 10. 11. All thy works ſhall praiſe thee, O Lord, and thy ſaints ſhall bleſs thee. They ſhall ſpeak of the glory of thy kingdom, and talk of thy power.

Printed in the Year MDCCLXV.

THE

PREFACE.

THE design of this publication, is to give God the glory of his diſtinguiſhing grace, and gratify the pious curioſity of thoſe who are waiting and praying for that bleſſed time, when the Son of God, in a more extenſive ſenſe than has yet been accompliſhed, ſhall receive "the Heathen for his inheritance, "and the uttermoſt parts of the earth for a poſ-"ſeſſion."

Whenever any of the guilty race of mankind are awakened to a juſt concern for their eternal intereſt, are humbled at the footſtool of a ſovereign God, and are perſuaded and enabled to accept the offers of redeeming love, it muſt always be acknowledged a wonderful work of divine grace, which demands our thankful praiſes.------But doubtleſs it is a more affecting evidence of almighty power,---a more illuſtrious diſplay of ſovereign mercy, when thoſe are enlightened with the knowledge of ſalvation, who have for many ages dwelt in the groſſeſt darkneſs and Heatheniſm, and are brought to a cheerful ſubjection to the government of our divine Redeemer, who from generation to generation had remained the voluntary ſlaves of "the prince of "darkneſs."

This is that delightful ſcene which will preſent itſelf to the reader's view, while he attentively peruſes the following pages. Nothing certainly can be more agreeable to a benevolent and religious mind, then to ſee thoſe that were ſunk in the moſt degenerate ſtate of human nature, at once, not only renounce thoſe barbarous cuſtoms that they had been inured to from their infancy, but ſurpriſingly transformed into the character of real and devout Chriſtians.---

This mighty change was brought about by the plain and faithful preaching of the goſpel, attended with an uncommon effuſion of the divine Spirit, under the miniſtry of the Reverend Mr DAVID BRAINERD, a Miſſionary employed by the *Honourable Society in* Scotland, *for propagating* CHRISTIAN KNOWLEDGE.

And ſurely it will adminiſter abundant matter of *praiſe* and *thankſgiving* to that honourable body, to find that their generous attempt to ſend the goſpel among the Indian nations upon the borders of New-York, New-Jerſey, and Penſylvania, has met with ſuch ſurpriſing ſucceſs.---

It would perhaps have been more agreeable to the taſte of politer readers, if the following Journal had been caſt into a different method, and formed into one connect *narrative*.--- But the worthy author amidſt his continued labours, had no time to ſpare for ſuch an undertaking.---Beſides, the pious reader will take a peculiar pleaſure to ſee this work deſcribed in its native ſimplicity, and the operations of the

Spirit

Spirit upon the minds of these poor benighted Pagans, laid down just in the method and order in which they happened.—This, it must be confessed, will occasion frequent repetitions; but these, as they tend to give a fuller view of this amazing dispensation of divine grace in its rise and progress, we trust, will be easily forgiven.

When we see such numbers of the most ignorant and barbarous of mankind, in the space of a few months, "turned from darkness to "light, and from the power of sin and Satan "unto God," it gives us encouragement to wait and pray for that blessed time, when our victorious Redeemer shall, in a more signal manner than he has yet done, display the "banner of his "cross," march on from "conquering to con-"quer, till the kingdoms of this world are be-"come the kingdoms of our Lord and of his "Christ."—Yea, we cannot but lift up our heads with joy, and hope that it may be the dawn of that bright and illustrious day, when the SUN OF RIGHTEOUSNESS shall "arise and shine from "one end of the earth to the other;"---when, to use the language of the inspired prophets, "the Gentiles shall come to his light, and kings "to the brightness of his rising;" in consequence of which, "the wilderness and solitary "places shall be glad, and the desert rejoice and "blossom as the rose."

It is doubtless the duty of all, in their different stations, and according to their respective capacities, to use their utmost endeavours to bring forward this promised---this desired day.

----There

——There is a great want of *ſchoolmaſters* among theſe Chriſtianized Indians, to inſtruct their youth in the *Engliſh language*, and the principles of the *Chriſtian faith*: for this, as yet, there is no certain proviſion made; if any are inclined to contribute to ſo good a deſign, we are perſuaded they will do an acceptable ſervice to the "kingdom of the Redeemer." And we earneſtly deſire the moſt indigent to join, at leaſt, in their wiſhes and prayers, that *this work* may *proſper* more and more, till the "whole earth "is filled with the glory of the Lord."

The CORRESPONDENTS.

THE

RISE and PROGRESS

OF A

Remarkable WORK of GRACE, &c.

Crosweeksung, in New-Jersey, June 19. 1745.

HAVING spent most of my time for more than a year past amongst the Indians in the Forks of Delaware in Pensylvania; and having in that time made two journeys to Susquahannah river, far back in that province, in order to treat with the Indians there, respecting Christianity; and not having had any considerable appearance of *special* success in either of those places, which damped my spirits, and was not a little discouraging to me; upon hearing that there was a number of Indians in and about a place called (by the Indians) Crosweeksung in New-Jersey, near fourscore miles south-eastward from the Forks of Delaware, I determined to make them a visit, and see what might be done towards the Christianizing of them; and accordingly arrived among them this day.

I found very few persons at the place I visited, and perceived the Indians in these parts were very much scattered, there being not more than two or three families in a place, and these small settlements six, ten, fifteen, twenty, and thirty miles, and some more, from the place I was then at. However, I preached to those few I found, who appeared well disposed, and not inclined to object and cavil, as the Indians had frequently done otherwhere.

When I had concluded my discourse, I informed them (there being none but a few women and children) that I would willingly visit them again the next day. Whereupon they readily set out, and travelled ten or fifteen miles, in order to give notice to some of their friends at that distance. These women,

women, like the woman of Samaria, seemed desirous that others might "see the man that told them what they had "done" in their lives past, and the misery that attended their *idolatrous* ways.

June 20. Visited and preached to the Indians again as I proposed. Numbers more were gathered at the invitations of their friends, who heard me the day before. These also appeared as attentive, orderly, and well disposed as the others. And none made any objection, as Indians in other places have usually done.

June 22. Preached to the Indians again. Their number which at first consisted of about seven or eight persons, was now increased to near thirty.

There was not only a solemn attention among them, but some considerable impressions (it was apparent) were made upon their minds by divine truths. Some began to feel their misery and perishing state, and appeared concerned for a deliverance from it.

Lord's day, June 23. Preached to the Indians, and spent the day with them.——Their number still increased; and all with one consent seemed to rejoice in my coming among them. Not a word of opposition was heard from any of them against Christianity, although in times past they had been as opposite to any thing of that nature, as any Indians whatsoever. And some of them not many months before, were enraged with my interpreter because he attempted to teach them something of Christianity.

June 24. Preached to the Indians at their desire, and upon their own motion. To see poor Pagans desirous of hearing the gospel of Christ, animated me to discourse to them, although I was now very weakly, and my spirits much exhausted. They attended with the greatest seriousness and diligence; and there was some concern for their souls salvation apparent among them.

June 27. Visited and preached to the Indians again. Their number now amounted to about *forty* persons. Their solemnity and attention still continued; and a considerable concern for their souls became very apparent among sundry of them.

June 28. The Indians being now gathered a considerable number of them, from their several and distant *habitations*, requested me to preach twice a-day to them, being desirous to hear as much as they possibly could while I was with them. I cheerfully complied with their motion, and could not but admire

admire at the goodneſs of God, who, I was perſuaded, had inclined them thus to inquire after the way of ſalvation.

June 29. Preached again twice to the Indians. Saw (as I thought) the hand of God very evidently, and in a manner ſomewhat remarkable, making proviſion for their ſubſiſtence together, in order to their being inſtructed in divine things. For this day and the day before, with only walking a little way from the place of our daily meeting, they killed *three deer*, which were a ſeaſonable ſupply for their wants, and without which, it ſeems, they could not have ſubſiſted together in order to attend the means of grace.

Lord's day, June 30. Preached twice this day alſo. Obſerved yet more concern and affection among the poor Heathens than ever; ſo that they even conſtrained me to tarry yet longer with them; although my conſtitution was exceedingly worn out, and my health much impaired by my late fatigues and labours, and eſpecially by my late journey to Suſquahannah in May laſt, in which I lodged on the ground for ſeveral weeks together.

July 1. Preached again twice to a very ſerious and attentive aſſembly of Indians, they having now learned to attend the worſhip of God with *Chriſtian decency* in all reſpects.

There were now between *forty* and *fifty* perſons of them preſent, old and young.

I ſpent ſome conſiderable time in diſcourſing with them in a more private way, inquiring of them what they remembered of the great truths that had been taught them from day to day; and may juſtly ſay, it was amazing to ſee how they had received and retained the inſtructions given them, and what a meaſure of knowledge ſome of them had acquired in a few days.

July 2. Was obliged to leave theſe Indians at Croſweekſung, thinking it my duty, as ſoon as health would admit, again to viſit thoſe at the Forks of Delaware. When I came to take leave of them, and ſpoke ſomething particularly to each of them, they all earneſtly inquired when I would come again, and expreſſed a great deſire of being further inſtructed. And of their own accord agreed, that when I ſhould come again, they would all meet and live together during my continuance with them; and that they would do their utmoſt endeavours to gather all the other Indians in theſe parts that were yet further remote. And when I parted, one told me with many tears, "She wiſhed God would change her heart:" another, that "ſhe wanted to find Chriſt:" and an old man that had been one of their *chiefs*, wept bitterly with concern for his ſoul. I then promiſed them to return as ſpeedily as my health, and business elsewhere would admit, and felt not a little concerned at parting, lest the good impressions then apparent upon numbers of them, might decline and wear off, when the means came to cease; and yet could not but hope that he who, I trusted, had begun a good work among them, and who I knew did not stand in need of means to carry it on, would maintain and promote it in the absence of them, although at the same time I must confess, that I had so often seen such encouraging appearances among the Indians otherwhere prove wholly abortive; and it appeared the favour would be so great, if God should now, after I had passed through so considerable a series of almost fruitless labours and fatigues, and after my rising hopes had been so often frustrated among these poor Pagans, give me any *special* success in my labours with them, that I could not believe, and scarce dared to hope that the event would be so happy, and scarce ever found myself more suspended between hope and fear, in any affair, or at any time than this.

This encouraging disposition and readiness to receive instruction, now apparent among these Indians, seems to have been the happy effect of the conviction that one or two of them met with some time since at the Forks of Delaware, who have since endeavoured to shew their friends the evil of idolatry, *&c.* And although the other Indians seemed but little to regard, but rather to deride them, yet this, perhaps, has put them into a *thinking* posture of mind, or at least, given them some thoughts about Christianity, and excited in some of them a *curiosity to hear*, and so made way for the present encouraging attention. An apprehension that this might be the case here, has given me encouragement that God may in *such* a manner bless the means I have used with Indians in other places, where there is as yet no appearance of it. If so, may his name have the glory of it; for I have learned by experience that he only can open the ear, engage the attention, and incline the heart of poor benighted prejudiced Pagans to receive instruction.

Forks of Delaware, in Pensylvania, 1745.

Lord's day, July 14. Discoursed to the Indians twice, several of whom appeared concerned, and were, I have reason to think, in some measure convinced by the divine Spirit of their sin and misery; so that they wept much the whole time of divine service.

Afterwards

Afterwards discoursed to a number of white people then present.——

July 18. Preached to my people, who attended diligently, beyond what had been common among these Indians: and some of them appeared concerned for their souls.

Lord's day, July 21. Preached to the Indians first, then to a number of white people present, and in the afternoon to the Indians again.—Divine truths seemed to make very considerable impressions upon several of them, and caused the tears to flow freely.

Afterwards I baptized my *interpreter* and his *wife*, who were the first I baptized among the Indians.

They are both persons of some *experimental* knowledge in religion; have both been awakened to a solemn concern for their souls; have to appearance been brought to a sense of their misery and *undoneness* in themselves; have both appeared to be comforted with divine consolations; and it is apparent both have passed a *great*, and I cannot but hope a *saving* change.

It may perhaps be satisfactory and agreeable that I should give some brief relation of the man's exercise and experience since he has been with me, especially seeing he is improved as my interpreter to others.

When I first employed him in this business in the beginning of summer 1744, he was well fitted for his work in regard of his acquaintance with the Indian and English language, as well as with the manners of both nations; and in regard of his desire that the Indians should conform to the customs and manners of the English, and especially to their manner of living. But he seemed to have little or no impression of religion upon his mind, and in that respect was very *unfit* for his work, being uncapable of understanding and communicating to others many things of importance; so that I laboured under great disadvantages in addressing the Indians, for want of his having an experimental, as well as more doctrinal acquaintance with divine truths; and, at times, my spirits sank, and were much discouraged under this difficulty, especially when I observed that divine truths made little or no impressions upon his mind for many *weeks* together.

He indeed behaved soberly after I employed him, (although before he had been a *hard drinker*), and seemed honestly engaged as far as he was capable in the performance of his work; and especially he appeared very desirous that the Indians should renounce their Heathenish notions and practices, and conform to the customs of the Christian world. But still seemed to have no concern about his own soul, till he had been with me a considerable time.

Near the latter end of July 1744. I preached to an assembly of white people, with more freedom and fervency than I could possibly address the Indians with, without their having first attained a greater measure of doctrinal knowledge: at which time he was present, and was somewhat awakened to a concern for his soul; so that the next day he discoursed freely with me about his spiritual concerns, and gave me an opportunity to use further endeavours to fasten the impressions of his perishing state upon his mind: and I could plainly perceive for some time after this, that he addressed the Indians with more concern and fervency than he had formerly done.

But these impressions seemed quickly to decline, and he remained in a great measure careless and secure, until some time late in the *fall* of the year following, at which time he fell into a weak and languishing state of body, and continued much disordered for several weeks together. And at this season divine truth took hold of him, and made deep impressions upon his mind. He was brought under great concern for his soul, and his exercise was not now *transient* and unsteady, but *constant* and abiding, so that his mind was burdened from day to day; and it was now his great inquiry, "What "he should do to be saved?" His spiritual trouble prevailed, till at length his sleep, in a measure, departed from him, and he had little rest day or night; but walked about under a great pressure of mind, (for though he was disordered he was still able to walk), and appeared like *another* man to his neighbours, who could not but observe his behaviour with wonder.

After he had been sometime under this exercise, while he was striving for mercy, he says, there seemed to be an *impassable mountain* before him. He was pressing towards heaven, as he thought, but "his way was hedged up with thorns, that "he could not stir an inch further." He looked this way and that way, but could find no way at all. He thought if he could but make his way through these thorns and briers, and climb up the first *steep pitch* of the mountain, that then there might be hope for him; but no way or means could he find to accomplish this. Here he laboured for a time, but all in vain; he saw it was *impossible*, he says, for him ever to help himself through this insupportable difficulty. He felt it signified nothing, "it signified just nothing at all for him to "strive and struggle any more." And here, he says, he gave over striving, and felt that it was a gone case with him, as to

his

his *own* power, and that all his attempts were, and for ever would be vain and fruitless. And yet was more calm and composed under this view of things, than he had been while striving to help himself.

While he was giving me this account of his exercise, I was not without fears that what he related was but the working of his own *imagination*, and not the effect of any divine *illumination* of mind. But before I had time to discover my fears, he added, that at this time he felt himself in a miserable and perishing condition; that he saw plainly what he had been doing all his days, and that he had never done one good thing, (as he expressed it). He knew, he said, he was not guilty of some wicked actions that he knew some others guilty of. He had not been used to steal, quarrel, and murder; the latter of which vices are common among the Indians. He likewise knew that he had done many things that were right; he had been kind to his neighbours, *&c.* But still his cry was, "that he had never done one good thing." I knew, said he, that I had not been so bad as some others in some things, and that I had done many things which folks call good; but all this did me no good now, I saw that "all was bad, and that I never had done one good thing," (meaning that he had never done any thing from a right *principle*, and with a right *view*, though he had done many things that were *materially* good and right). And now I thought, said he, that I must sink down to hell, that there was no hope for me, "because I never could do any thing that was "good;" and if God let me alone never so long, and I should try never so much, still I should do nothing but what is bad, *&c.*

This further account of his exercise, satisfied me that it was not the mere working of his imagination, since he appeared so evidently to die to himself, and to be divorced from a dependence upon his own righteousness, and good deeds, which mankind in a *fallen* state, are so much attached to, and inclined to hope for salvation upon.

There was one thing more in his view of things at this time that was very remarkable. He not only saw, he says, what a miserable state he himself was in, but he likewise saw the world around him, in general, were in the same perishing circumstances, notwithstanding the profession many of them made of Christianity, and the hope they entertained of obtaining everlasting happiness. And this he saw clearly, "as "if he was now awaked out of sleep, or had a cloud taken "from

" from before his eyes." He saw that the life he had lived was the way to eternal death, that he was now on the brink of endless misery: and when he looked round, he saw multitudes of others who had lived the same life with himself,——had no more goodness than he, and yet dreamed that they were safe enough, as he had formerly done. He was fully persuaded by their conversation and behaviour, that they had never felt their sin and misery, as he now felt his.

After he had been for some time in this condition, sensible of the impossibility of his helping himself by any thing he could do, or of being delivered by any *created* arm, so that he "had given up all for lost," as to his own attempts, and was become more calm and composed; then, he says, it was borne in upon his mind as if it had been audibly spoken to him, "There is hope, there is hope." Whereupon his soul seemed to rest and be in some measure satisfied, though he had no considerable joy.

He cannot here remember distinctly any views he had of Christ, or give any clear account of his soul's acceptance of him, which makes his experience appear the more doubtful, and renders it less satisfactory to himself and others, than (perhaps) it might be, if he could remember distinctly the apprehensions and actings of his mind at this season.

But these exercises of soul were attended and followed with a very great change in the man, so that it might justly be said, he was become *another man*, if not a *new man*. His conversation and deportment were much altered, and even the careless world could not but admire what had befallen him to make so great a change in his temper, discourse, and behaviour.——

And especially there was a surprising alteration in his public performances. He now addressed the Indians with admirable fervency, and scarce knew when to leave off: and sometimes when I had concluded my discourse, and was returning homeward, he would tarry behind to repeat and inculcate what had been spoken.

His change is *abiding*, and his life, so far as I know, *unblemished* to this day, though it is now more than six months since he experienced this change; in which space of time he has been as much exposed to *strong drink*, as possible, in divers places where it has been moving free as water; and yet has never, as I know of, discovered any hankering desire after it.

He seems to have a very considerable experience of spiritual exercise, and discourses feelingly of the conflicts and consolations

solations of a real Christian. His heart echoes to the *soul-humbling* doctrines of grace, and he never appears better pleased than when he hears of the *absolute sovereignty of God*, and the salvation of sinners in a way of *mere free grace*. He has likewise of late had more satisfaction respecting his own state, has been much enlivened and assisted in his work, so that he has been a great comfort to me.

And upon a view and strict observation of his serious and savoury conversation, his Christian temper, and unblemished behaviour for so considerable a track of time, as well as his experience I have given an account of, I think that I have reason to hope that he is "created anew in Christ Jesus to "good works."

His name is Moses Tinda Tautamy; he is about fifty years of age, and is pretty well acquainted with the Pagan notions and customs of his countrymen, and so is the better able now to expose them. He has, I am persuaded, already been, and I trust will yet be a blessing to the other Indians.

July 23. Preached to the Indians, but had few hearers: those who are constantly at home seem of late to be under some serious impressions of a religious nature.

July 26. Preached to my people, and afterwards baptized my *interpreter's children*.

Lord's day, July 28. Preached again, and perceived my people, at least some of them, more thoughtful than ever about their souls concerns. I was told by some, that seeing my interpreter and others baptized made them more concerned than any thing they had ever seen or heard before. There was indeed a considerable appearance of divine power amongst them at the time that ordinance was administered. May that divine influence spread and increase more abundantly!

July 30. Discoursed to a number of my people, and gave them some particular advice and direction, being now about to leave them for the present, in order to renew my visit to the Indians in New-Jersey. They were very attentive to my discourse, and earnestly desirous to know when I designed to return to them again.

Crosweeksung in New-Jersey, 1745.

August 3. Having visited the Indians in these parts in June last, and tarried with them some considerable time, preaching almost daily; at which season God was pleased to pour upon them a spirit of awakening and concern for their souls, and surprisingly

ſurpriſingly to engage their attention to divine truths. I now found them ſerious, and a number of them under deep concern for an intereſt in Chriſt: their convictions of their ſinful and periſhing ſtate having, in my abſence from them, been much promoted by the labours and endeavours of the Reverend Mr William Tennent, to whom I had adviſed them to apply for direction, and whoſe houſe they frequented much while I was gone.——I preached to them this day with ſome view to Rev. xxii. 17. "And whoſoever will, let him take the water "of life freely:" though I could not pretend to handle the ſubject methodically among them.

The Lord, I am perſuaded, enabled me, in a manner ſomewhat *uncommon,* to ſet before them the Lord Jeſus Chriſt as a kind and compaſſionate Saviour, inviting diſtreſſed and periſhing ſinners to accept everlaſting mercy. And a ſurpriſing concern ſoon became apparent among them. There were about twenty adult perſons together, (many of the Indians at remote places not having as yet had time to come ſince my return hither), and not above two that I could ſee with dry eyes. Some were much concerned, and diſcovered vehement longings of ſoul after Chriſt, to ſave them from the miſery they felt and feared.

Lord's day, Auguſt 4. Being invited by a neighbouring miniſter to aſſiſt in the adminiſtration of the Lord's ſupper, I complied with his requeſt, and took the Indians along with me; not only thoſe that were together the day before, but many more that were coming to hear me; ſo that there were near fifty in all, old and young.

They attended the ſeveral diſcourſes of the day, and ſome of them that could underſtand Engliſh, were much affected, and all ſeemed to have their concern in ſome meaſure raiſed.

Now a change in their manners began to appear very viſible. In the evening when they came to ſup together, they would not taſte a morſel till they had ſent to me to come and aſk a bleſſing on their food; at which time ſundry of them wept, eſpecially when I minded them how they had in times paſt eat their feaſts in *honour* to *devils,* and neglected to thank God for them.

Auguſt 5. After a ſermon had been preached by another miniſter, I preached, and concluded the public work of the ſolemnity from John vii. 37.; and in my diſcourſe addreſſed the Indians in particular, who ſat by themſelves in a part of the houſe; at which time one or two of them were ſtruck with deep concern, as they afterwards told me, who had been little affected before: others had their concern increaſed to a conſiderable

considerable degree. In the evening (the greater part of them being at the house where I lodged) I discoursed to them, and found them universally engaged about their soul's concern, inquiring, "What they should do to be saved?" And all their conversation among themselves turned upon *religious* matters, in which they were much assisted by my interpreter, who was with them day and night.

This day there was one woman, that had been much concerned for her soul, ever since she first heard me preach in June last, who obtained comfort, I trust, solid and well grounded: she seemed to be filled with love to Christ, at the same time behaved humbly and tenderly, and appeared afraid of nothing so much as of grieving and offending him whom her soul loved.

August 6. In the morning I discoursed to the Indians at the house where we lodged: many of them were then much affected, and appeared surprisingly tender, so that a few words about their souls concerns would cause the tears to flow freely, and produce many sobs and groans.——

In the afternoon, they being returned to the place where I have usually preached amongst them, I again discoursed to them there. There were about fifty-five persons in all, about forty that were capable of attending divine service with understanding: I insisted upon 1 John iv. 10. "Herein is "love," &c. They seemed eager of hearing; but there appeared nothing very remarkable, except their attention, till near the close of my discourse; and then divine truths were attended with a surprising influence, and produced a great concern among them. There was scarce *three* in *forty* that could refrain from tears and bitter cries. They all, as one, seemed in an agony of soul to obtain an interest in Christ; and the more I discoursed of the love and compassion of God in sending his Son to suffer for the sins of men; and the more I invited them to come and partake of his love, the more their distress was aggravated, because they felt themselves unable to come.

It was surprising to see how their hearts seemed to be pierced with the tender and melting invitations of the gospel, when there was not a word of terror spoken to them.

There were this day two persons that obtained relief and comfort, which (when I came to discourse with them particularly) appeared solid, rational, and scriptural. After I had inquired into the grounds of their comfort, and said many things I thought proper to them, I asked them what they

 wanted

wanted God to do further for them? They replied, "They "wanted Christ should wipe their hearts quite clean," &c.

Surprising were now the *doings of the Lord*, that I can say no less of this day (and I need say no more of it) than that the *arm of the Lord* was powerfully and marvellously *revealed* in it.

August 7. Preached to the Indians from If. liii. 3.——10. There was a remarkable influence attending the word, and great concern in the assembly; but scarce equal to what appeared the day before, that is, not quite so universal. However, most were much affected, and many in great distress for their souls; and some few could neither go nor stand, but lay flat on the ground, as if pierced at heart, crying incessantly for mercy: several were newly awakened, and it was remarkable, that as fast as they came from remote places round about, the Spirit of God seemed to seize them with concern for their souls.

After public service was concluded, I found two persons more that had newly met with comfort, of whom I had good hopes; and a third that I could not but entertain some hopes of, whose case did not appear so clear as the other; so that here were now six in all that had got some relief from their spiritual distresses, and five whose experience appeared very clear and satisfactory. And it is worthy of remark, that those who obtained comfort first, were in general deeply affected with concern for their souls, when I preached to them in June last.

August 8. In the afternoon I preached to the Indians, their number was now about sixty-five persons, men, women, and children: I discoursed from Luke xiv. 16.—23. and was favoured with *uncommon* freedom in my discourse.

There was much visible concern among them while I was discoursing publicly; but afterwards when I spoke to one and another more particularly, whom I perceived under much concern, the power of God seemed to descend upon the assembly "like a rushing mighty wind," and with an astonishing energy bore down all before it.

I stood amazed at the influence that seized the audience almost universally, and could compare it to nothing more aptly, than the irresistible force of a mighty torrent, or swelling deluge, that with its insupportable weight and pressure, bears down and sweeps before it whatever is in its way. Almost all persons of all ages were bowed down with concern together, and scarce one was able to withstand the *shock* of this surprising operation. Old men and women, who had been drunken

drunken wretches for many years, and some little children, not more than six or seven years of age, appeared in distress for their souls, as well as persons of middle age. And it was apparent these children (some of them at least) were not *merely* frighted with seeing the general concern; but were made sensible of their danger, the badness of their hearts, and their misery without Christ, as some of them expressed it. The most stubborn hearts were now obliged to bow. A principal man among the Indians, who before was most secure and self-righteous, and thought his state good because he knew more than the generality of the Indians had formerly done, and who with a great degree of confidence the day before, told me, "he had been a Christian more than ten years," was now brought under solemn concern for his soul, and wept bitterly. Another man considerable in years, who had been a *murderer*, a *powwow*, (or conjurer), and a notorious drunkard, was likewise brought now to cry for mercy with many tears, and to complain much that he could be no more concerned when he saw his danger so very great.

They were almost universally praying and crying for mercy in every part of the house, and many out of doors, and numbers could neither go nor stand: their concern was so great, each one for himself, that none seemed to take any notice of those about them, but each prayed as freely for themselves; and (I am apt to think) were, to their own apprehension, as much retired as if they had been every one by themselves in the thickest desart; or, I believe rather, that they thought nothing about *any* but themselves, and their own states, and so were every one praying *apart*, although all *together*.

It seemed to me there was now an exact fulfilment of that prophecy, Zech. xii. 10. 11. 12.; for there was now "a great "mourning, like the mourning of Hadadrimmon;"——and each seemed to "mourn apart." Methought this had a near resemblance to the day of God's power, mentioned Josh. x. 14.; for I must say, I never see *any day like it* in all respects: it was a day wherein I am persuaded the Lord did much to destroy the kingdom of darkness among this people.

This concern in general was most rational and just, those who had been awakened any considerable time, complained more especially of the badness of their *hearts*; and those newly awakened, of the badness of their *lives* and *actions* past; and all were afraid of the anger of God, and of everlasting misery as the desert of their sins.

Some of the *white* people, who came out of curiosity to

"hear what this babbler would say" to the poor ignorant Indians, were much awakened, and some appeared to be wounded with a view of their perishing state.

Those who had lately obtained relief, were filled with comfort at this season; they appeared calm and composed, and seemed to rejoice in Christ Jesus; and some of them took their distressed friends by the hand, telling them of the goodness of Christ, and the comfort that is to be enjoyed in him, and thence invited them to come and give up their hearts to him. And I could observe some of them, in the most honest and unaffected manner, (without any design of being taken notice of), lifting up their eyes to heaven, as if crying for mercy, while they saw the distress of the poor souls around them.

There was one remarkable instance of awakening this day, that I cannot but take particular notice of here. A young Indian woman, who, I believe, never knew before she had a soul, nor ever thought of any such thing, hearing that there was something strange among the Indians, came (it seems) to see what was the matter: she in her way to the Indians, called at my lodgings, and when I told her I designed presently to preach to the Indians, laughed, and seemed to mock; but went however to them. I had not proceeded far in my public discourse, before she felt *effectually* that she had a soul; and before I had concluded my discourse, was so convinced of her sin and misery, and so distressed with concern for her soul's salvation, that she seemed like one pierced through with a dart, and cried out incessantly. She could neither go nor stand, nor sit on her seat without being held up. After public service was over, she lay flat on the ground praying earnestly, and would take no notice of, nor give any answer to any that spoke to her. I hearkened to hear what she said, and perceived the burden of her prayer to be, *Guttummaukalummeh wechaumeh kmeleh Ndah*, i. e. "Have mercy on me, "and help me to give you my heart." And thus she continued praying incessantly for many hours together.

This was indeed a surprising day of God's power, and seemed enough to convince an Atheist of the truth, importance, and power of God's word.

August 9. Spent almost the whole day with the Indians, the former part of it in discoursing to many of them privately, and especially to some who had lately received comfort, and endeavouring to inquire into the grounds of it, as well as to give them some proper instructions, cautions, and directions.

In

In the afternoon discoursed to them publicly. There were now present about seventy persons, old and young. I opened and applied the parable of the sower, Matth. xiii. Was enabled to discourse with much plainness, and found afterwards that this discourse was very instructive to them. There were many tears among them while I was discoursing publicly, but no considerable cry: yet some were much affected with a few words spoken from Matth. xi. 28. with which I concluded my discourse. But while I was discoursing near night to two or three of the awakened persons, a divine influence seemed to attend what was spoken to them in a powerful manner, which caused the persons to cry out in anguish of soul, although I spoke not a word of terror; but, on the contrary, set before them the fulness and all-sufficiency of Christ's merits, and his willingness to save all that came to him; and thereupon pressed them to come without delay.

The cry of these was soon heard by others, who, though scattered before, immediately gathered round. I then proceeded in the same strain of gospel-invitation, till they were all melted into tears and cries, except two or three; and seemed in the greatest distress to find and secure an interest in the great Redeemer.——Some who had but little more than a *ruffle* made in their *passions* the day before, seemed now to be deeply affected and wounded at heart: and the concern in general appeared near as prevalent as it was the day before. There was indeed a very *great mourning* among them, and yet every one seemed to *mourn apart*. For so great was their concern, that almost every one was praying and crying for himself, as if none had been near. *Guttummaukalummeh, guttummaukalummeh*, i. e. "Have mercy upon me, have "mercy upon me;" was the common cry.

It was very affecting to see the poor Indians, who the other day were hallooing and yelling in their *idolatrous* feasts and *drunken* frolics, now crying to God with such importunity for an interest in his dear Son!

Found two or three persons, who I had reason to hope had taken comfort upon good grounds since the *evening* before: and these, with others that had obtained comfort, were together, and seemed to rejoice much that God was carrying on his work with such power upon others.

August 10. Rode to the Indians, and began to discourse more privately to those who had obtained comfort and satisfaction; endeavouring to instruct, direct, caution, and comfort them. But others being eager of hearing every word that related to spiritual concerns, soon came together one after

ter another: and when I had discoursed to the *young converts* more than half an hour, they seemed much melted with divine things, and earnestly desirous to be with Christ. I told them of the godly soul's perfect purity, and full enjoyment of Christ, immediately upon its separation from the body; and that it would be for ever inconceivably more happy, than *they* had ever been for any short space of time, when Christ seemed near to them, in prayer or other duties. And that I might make way for speaking of the resurrection of the body, and thence of the complete blessedness of the man, I said, But perhaps some of you will say, I love my body as well as my soul, and I cannot bear to think that my body should lie dead, if my soul is happy. To which they all cheerfully replied, *Muttoh, muttoh,* (before I had opportunity to prosecute what I designed respecting the resurrection), No, no. They did not regard their bodies, if their souls might be but with Christ. Then they appeared "willing to be absent from the "body, that they might be present with the Lord."

When I had spent some time with these, I turned to the other Indians, and spoke to them from Luke xix. 10. I had not discoursed long before their concern rose to a great degree, and the house was filled with cries and groans. And when I insisted on the compassion and care of the Lord Jesus Christ for *those that were lost*, who thought themselves *undone*, and could find no way of escape, this melted them down the more, and aggravated their distress, that they could not find, and come to so kind a Saviour.

Sundry persons who before had been but slightly awakened, were now deeply wounded with a sense of their sin and misery. And one man in particular, who was never before awakened, was now made to feel, that "the word of the Lord was quick "and powerful, sharper than any two-edged sword." He seemed to be pierced at heart with distress, and his concern appeared most rational and scriptural: for he said, "all the "wickedness of his past life was brought fresh to his remem"brance, and he saw all the vile actions he had done former"ly, as if done but yesterday."

Found one that had newly received comfort, after pressing distress from day to day. Could not but rejoice and admire at divine goodness in what appeared this day. There seems to be some good done by every discourse; some newly awakened every day, and some comforted.

It was refreshing to observe the conduct of those that had obtained comfort, while others were distressed with fear and concern; *those* were lifting up their hearts to God for them.

Lord's

Lord's day, August 11. Discoursed in the forenoon from the parable of the *prodigal son*, Luke xv. Observed no such remarkable effect of the word upon the assembly as in days past.——There were numbers of careless spectators of the white people; some Quakers, and others.

In the afternoon I discoursed upon a part of St Peter's sermon, Acts ii.; and at the close of my discourse to the Indians, made an address to the *white* people, and divine truths seemed then to be attended with power both to English and Indians. Several of the *white Heathen* were awakened, and could not longer be idle spectators, but found they had souls to save or lose as well as the Indians, and a great concern spread through the whole assembly, so that this also appeared to be a day of God's power, especially towards the conclusion of it, as well as several of the former, although the influence attending the word seemed scarce so powerful now as in some days past.

The number of the Indians, old and young, was now upwards of seventy, and one or two were newly awakened this day, who never had appeared to be moved with concern for their souls before.

Those that had obtained relief and comfort, and had given hopeful evidences of having passed a saving change, appeared humble and devout, and behaved in an agreeable and Christian manner. I was refreshed to see the tenderness of conscience manifest in some of them, one instance of which I cannot but take notice of. Perceiving one of them very sorrowful in the morning, I inquired into the cause of her sorrow, and found the difficulty was, she had been angry with her child the evening before, and was now exercised with fears, lest her anger had been inordinate and sinful, which so grieved her that she waked and began to sob before daylight, and continued weeping for several hours together.

August 14. Spent the day with the Indians. There was one of them who had some time since put away his wife, (as is common among them), and taken another woman, and being now brought under some serious impressions, was much concerned about that affair in particular, and seemed fully convinced of the wickedness of that practice, and earnestly desirous to know what God would have him do in his present circumstances. When the law of God respecting *marriage* had been opened to them, and the cause of his leaving his wife inquired into; and when it appeared she had given him no just occasion by *unchastity* to desert her, and that she was willing to forgive his past misconduct, and to live peaceably with

with him for the future, and that ſhe moreover inſiſted on it as *her right* to enjoy him; he was then told, that it was his indiſpenſible duty to renounce the woman he had laſt taken, and receive the other who was his proper wife, and live peaceably with her during life; with which he readily and cheerfully complied, and thereupon publicly renounced the woman he had laſt taken, and publicly promiſed to live with and be kind to his wife during life, ſhe alſo promiſing the ſame to him.——And here appeared a clear demonſtration of the power of God's word upon their hearts. I ſuppoſe a few weeks before the whole world could not have perſuaded this man to a compliance with Chriſtian rules in this affair..

I was not without fears, leſt this proceeding might be like putting "new wine into old bottles," and that ſome might be prejudiced againſt Chriſtianity, when they ſaw the overtures made by it. But the man being much concerned about the matter, the determination of it could be deferred no longer, and it ſeemed to have a good, rather than an ill effect among the Indians, who generally owned, that the laws of Chriſt were good and right reſpecting the affairs of marriage.

In the afternoon I preached to them from the apoſtle's diſcourſe to Cornelius, Acts x. 34. *&c.* There appeared ſome affectionate concern among them, though not equal to what appeared in ſeveral of the former days. They ſtill attended and heard as for their lives, and the Lord's work ſeemed ſtill to be promoted, and propagated among them.

Auguſt 15. Preached from Luke iv. 16.——21. The word was attended with power upon the hearts of the hearers. There was much concern, many tears, and affecting cries among them, and ſome in a ſpecial manner were deeply wounded and diſtreſſed for their ſouls. There were ſome newly awakened who came but this week, and convictions ſeemed to be promoted in others.—Thoſe that had received comfort, were likewiſe refreſhed and ſtrengthened, and the work of grace appeared to advance in all reſpects. The *paſſions* of the congregation in general were not ſo much moved, as in ſome days paſt, but their *hearts* ſeemed as ſolemnly and deeply affected with divine truths as ever, at leaſt in many inſtances, although the concern did not ſeem to be ſo univerſal, and to reach every individual in ſuch a manner as it had appeared to do ſome days before.

Auguſt 16. Spent conſiderable time in converſing privately with ſundry of the Indians. Found one that had got relief and comfort, after preſſing concern, and could not but hope,

when

when I came to discourse particularly with her, that her comfort was of the right kind.

In the afternoon preached to them from John vi. 26.—34. Toward the close of my discourse, divine truths were attended with considerable power upon the audience, and more especially after public service was over, when I particularly addressed sundry distressed persons.

There was a great concern for their souls spread pretty generally among them: but especially there were two persons newly awakened to a sense of their sin and misery, one of whom was lately come, and the other had all along been very attentive, and desirous of being awakened, but could never before have any lively view of her perishing state. But now her concern and spiritual distress was such, that, I thought, I had never seen *any* more pressing. Sundry *old* men were also in distress for their souls; so that they could not refrain from weeping and crying out aloud, and their bitter groans were the most convincing, as well as affecting evidence of the reality and depth of their inward anguish.—God is powerfully at work among them! True and genuine convictions of sin are daily promoted in many instances, and some are newly awakened from time to time, although some few, who felt a commotion in their *passions* in days past, seem now to discover that their *hearts* were never duly affected. I never saw the work of God appear so independent of means as at this time. I discoursed to the people, and spoke what (I suppose) had a proper tendency to promote convictions; and God's *manner* of working upon them appeared so entirely *supernatural*, and *above* means, that I could scarce believe he used me as an *instrument*, or what I spake as *means* of carrying on his work; for it seemed, as I thought, to have no connection with, nor dependence upon means in any respect. And although I could not but continue to use the means I thought proper for the promotion of the work, yet God seemed (as I apprehended) to work entirely without them: so that I seemed to do nothing, and indeed to have nothing to do, but to "stand still and see the salvation of God;" and found myself obliged and delighted to say, "Not unto us," not unto instruments and means, "but to thy name be glory." God appeared to work entirely alone, and I saw no room to attribute any part of this work to any created arm.

August 17. Spent much time in private conferences with the Indians. Found one who had newly obtained relief and comfort, after a long season of spiritual trouble and distress, (he having been one of my hearers in the Forks of Delaware for more than a year, and now followed me here under deep concern for his soul), and had abundant reason to hope that his comfort was well grounded, and truly divine.

Afterwards discoursed publicly from Acts viii. 29.—39. and took occasion to treat concerning *baptism*, in order to their being instructed and prepared to partake of that ordinance. They were yet hungry and thirsty for the word of God, and appeared *unwearied* in their attendance upon it.—

Lord's day, August 18. Preached in the forenoon to an assembly of *white* people, made up of Presbyterians, Baptists, Quakers, &c. Afterwards preached to the Indians from John vi. 35.—40. There was considerable concern visible among them, though not equal to what has frequently appeared of late.

August 19. Preached from If. lv. 1. Divine truths were attended with power upon those who had received comfort, and others also. The former were sweetly melted and refreshed with divine invitations, the latter much concerned for their souls, that they might obtain an interest in these glorious gospel-provisions that were set before them. There were numbers of poor *impotent* souls that waited at the *pool* for *healing*, and the *Angel* seemed, as at other times of late, *to trouble the waters:* so that there was yet a most desirable and comfortable prospect of the spiritual recovery of diseased perishing sinners.

August 23. Spent some time with the Indians in private discourse; afterwards preached to them from John vi. 44.—50. There was, as has been usual, a great attention and some affection among them. Several appeared deeply concerned for their souls, and could not but express their inward anguish by tears and cries. But the amazing divine influence that has been so powerfully among them in general, seems, at present, in some degree abated, at least in regard of its *universality*, though many that have got no special comfort, still retain deep impressions of divine things.

August 24. Spent the forenoon in discoursing to some of the Indians, in order to their receiving the ordinance of *baptism*. When I had opened the nature of the ordinance, the obligations attending it, the duty of devoting ourselves to God in it, and the privilege of being *in covenant* with him, sundry of them seemed to be filled with love to God, and delighted with the thoughts of giving up themselves to him in that solemn and public manner, melted and refreshed with the hopes of enjoying the blessed Redeemer.

Afterwards I discoursed publicly from 1 Thess. iv. 13.—17.

There

There was a solemn attention, and some visible concern and affection in the time of public service, which was afterwards increased by some further exhortation given them to come to Christ, and give up their hearts to him, that they might be fitted to "ascend up and meet him in the air," when he shall "descend with a shout, and the voice of the archangel."

There were several Indians newly come, who thought their state good, and themselves happy, because they had sometimes lived with the *white people* under gospel-light, had learned to read, were civil, *&c.* although they appeared utter strangers to their own hearts, and altogether unacquainted with the power of religion, as well as with the *doctrines of grace*. With those I discoursed particularly after public worship, and was surprised to see their self-righteous disposition, their strong attachment to the covenant of works for salvation, and the high value they put upon their supposed attainments. Yet after much discourse, one appeared in a measure convinced, that "by the deeds of the law no flesh "living should be justified," and wept bitterly, inquiring, "what he must do to be saved?"

This was very comfortable to others, who had gained some *experimental* acquaintance with their own hearts; for before they were grieved with the conversation and conduct of these *new-comers*, who boasted of their knowledge, and thought well of themselves, but evidently discovered to those that had any experience of divine truths, that they knew nothing of their own hearts.

Lord's day, August 25. Preached in the forenoon from Luke xv. 3.—7. There being a multitude of *white* people present, I made an address to them at the close of my discourse to the Indians: but could not so much as keep them orderly; for scores of them kept walking and gazing about, and behaved more indecently than *any Indians* I ever addressed; and a view of their abusive conduct so sunk my spirits, that I could scarce go on with my work.

In the afternoon discoursed from Rev. iii. 20. at which time the Indians behaved seriously, though many others were vain.

Afterwards baptized *twenty-five* persons of the Indians, fifteen adults, and ten children. Most of the adults I have comfortable reason to hope are renewed persons; and there was not one of them but what I entertained some hopes of in that respect, though the case of two or three of them appeared more doubtful.

After the croud of spectators was gone, I called the baptized persons together, and discoursed to them in particular, at the same time inviting others to attend, minded them of the solemn obligations they were now under to live to God, warned them of the evil and dreadful consequences of careless living, especially after this public profession of Christianity; gave them directions for their future conduct, and encouraged them to watchfulness and devotion, by setting before them the *comfort* and happy *conclusion* of a religious life.——This was a desirable and sweet season indeed! Their hearts were engaged and cheerful in duty, and they rejoiced that they had in a public and solemn manner dedicated themselves to God.—Love seemed to reign among them! They took each other by the hand with tenderness and affection, as if their hearts were knit together, while I was discoursing to them: and all their deportment toward each other was such, that a *serious spectator* might justly be excited to cry out with admiration, "Behold how they love one another!" Sundry of the other Indians at seeing and hearing these things, were much affected and wept bitterly, longing to be partakers of the same joy and comfort that these discovered by their very countenances as well as conduct.

August 26. Preached to my people from John vi. 51.—55. After I had discoursed some time, I addressed those in particular who entertained hopes that they were "passed from "death to life." Opened to them the persevering nature of those consolations Christ gives his people, and which I trusted he had bestowed upon some in that assembly, shewed them that such have already the "beginnings of eternal life," (vers. 54.) and that their *heaven* shall speedily be completed, &c.

I no sooner began to discourse in this strain, but the *dear Christians* in the congregation began to be melted with affection to, and desire of the enjoyment of Christ, and of a state of perfect purity. They wept affectionately and yet joyfully, and their tears and sobs discovered *brokenness* of heart, and yet were attended with *real comfort* and *sweetness;* so that this was a tender, affectionate, humble, delightful melting, and appeared to be the genuine effect of a Spirit of *adoption*, and very far from that Spirit of *bondage* that they not long since laboured under. The influence seemed to spread from these through the whole assembly, and there quickly appeared a wonderful concern among them. Many who had not yet found Christ as an all-sufficient Saviour, were surprisingly engaged in seeking after him. It was indeed a lovely and very desirable assembly. Their number was now about *ninety-*

five

five persons, old and young, and almost all affected either with *joy* in Christ Jesus, or with *utmost concern* to obtain an interest in him.

Being fully convinced it was now my duty to take a journey far back to the Indians on Susquahannah river, (it being now a proper season of the year to find them generally at home), after having spent some hours in public and private discourses with my people, I told them that I must now leave them for the present, and go to their *brethren* far remote, and preach to them; that I wanted the Spirit of God should go with me, without whom nothing could be done to any good purpose among the Indians, as they themselves had had opportunity to see and observe by the barrenness of our meetings at some times, when there was much pains taken to affect and awaken sinners, and yet to little or no purpose: and asked them, if they could not be willing to spend the remainder of the day in prayer for me, that God would go with me, and succeed my endeavours for the conversion of those poor souls. They cheerfully complied with the motion, and soon after I left them (the sun being then about an hour and half high at night) they began, and continued praying all night till *break of day*, or very near, never mistrusting (they tell me) till they went out and viewed the stars, and saw the *morning-star* a considerable height, that it was later than common bed-time. Thus eager and unwearied were they in their devotions! A remarkable night it was, attended (as my interpreter tells me) with a powerful influence upon those who were yet under concern, as well as those that had received comfort.

There were, I trust, this day two distressed souls brought to the enjoyment of solid comfort in him, in whom the *weary* find rest.

It was likewise remarkable, that this day an *old* Indian, who has all his days been an obstinate *idolater*, was brought to give up his *rattles* (which they use for music in their *idolatrous* feasts and dances) to the other Indians, who quickly destroyed them; and this without any attempt of mine in the affair, I having said nothing to him about it; so that it seemed it was nothing but just the power of God's word, without any particular application to this sin, that produced this effect. Thus God has begun, thus he has hitherto surprisingly carried on a work of grace amongst these Indians. May the glory be ascribed to him, who is the sole author of it!

Forks

Forks of Delaware in Pennſylvania, 1745.

Lord's day, September 1. Preached to the Indians here from Luke xiv. 16.——23. The word appeared to be attended with ſome power, and cauſed ſome tears in the aſſembly.

Afterwards preached to a number of *white* people preſent, and obſerved many of them in tears, and ſome who had formerly been as careleſs and unconcerned about religion perhaps as the Indians.

Towards night diſcourſed to the Indians again, and perceived a greater attention, and more viſible concern among them than has been uſual in *theſe parts*.

September 3. Preached to the Indians from Iſ. liii. 3.—6. The divine preſence ſeemed to be in the midſt of the aſſembly, and a conſiderable concern ſpread amongſt them. Sundry perſons ſeemed to be awakened, amongſt whom were two ſtupid creatures that I could ſcarce ever before keep awake while I was diſcourſing to them. Could not but rejoice at this appearance of things, although at the ſame time I could not but fear leſt the concern they at preſent manifeſted, might prove *like a morning-cloud*, as ſomething of that nature had formerly done in theſe parts.

September 5. Diſcourſed to the Indians from the parable of the ſower, afterwards converſed particularly with ſundry perſons, which occaſioned them to weep, and even to cry out in an affecting manner, and ſeized others with ſurpriſe and concern; and I doubt not but that a divine power accompanied what was then ſpoken. Sundry of theſe perſons had been with me to Croſweekſung, and had there ſeen, and ſome of them, I truſt, felt the power of God's word in an *effectual* and ſaving manner. I aſked one of them, who had obtained comfort, and given hopeful evidences of being truly religious, why he now cried? He replied, "When he "thought how Chriſt was ſlain like a lamb, and ſpilt his "blood for ſinners, he could not help crying, when he was "all alone:" and thereupon burſt out into tears and cries again. I then aſked his wife, who had likewiſe been abundantly comforted, wherefore ſhe cried? She anſwered, "She was grieved that the Indians here would not come to "Chriſt, as well as thoſe at Croſweekſung." I aſked her if ſhe found a heart to pray for them, and whether Chriſt had ſeemed to be near to her of late in prayer, as in time paſt? (which is my uſual method of expreſſing a ſenſe of the divine preſence.)

presence.) She replied, "Yes, he had been near to her; "and that at some times when she had been praying alone, "her heart loved to pray so, that she could not bear to leave "the place, but wanted to stay and pray longer."

September 7. Preached to the Indians from John vi. 35.—39. There was not so much appearance of concern among them as at several other times of late; yet they appeared serious and attentive.

Lord's day, September 8. Discoursed to the Indians in the forenoon from John xii. 44. 50. in the afternoon from Acts ii. 36.—39. The word of God at this time seemed to fall with *weight* and influence upon them. There were but few present, but most that were, were in tears, and sundry cried out under distressing concern for their souls.

There was one man considerably awakened, who never before discovered any concern for his soul. There appeared a remarkable work of the divine Spirit among them, almost generally, not unlike what has been of late at Crosweeksung. It seemed as if the divine influence had spread from thence to this place; although something of it appeared here in the awakening of my interpreter, his wife, and some few others.

Sundry of the careless white people now present were awakened, (or at least startled), seeing the power of God so prevalent among the Indians. I then made a particular address to them, which seemed to make some impression upon them, and excite some affection in them.

There are sundry Indians in these parts who have always refused to hear me preach, and have been enraged against those that have attended my preaching. But of late they are more bitter than ever, scoffing at Christianity, and sometimes asking my hearers, "How often they have cried?" and "whe- "ther they have not now cried enough to do the turn?" &c. So that they have already "trial of cruel mockings."

September 9. Left the Indians in the Forks of Delaware, and set out on a journey towards Susquahannah-river, directing my course towards the Indian-town more than an hundred and twenty miles west-ward from the Forks. Travelled about fifteen miles, and there lodged.

September 13. After having lodged out three nights, arrived at the Indian-town I aimed at on Susquahannah, called Shaumoking, (one of the places, and the largest of them, that I visited in May last), and was kindly received and entertained by the Indians: but had little satisfaction by reason of the Heathenish dance and revel they then held in the house where I was obliged to lodge, which I could not suppress, though

though I often intreated them to desist, for the sake of one of their own friends who was then sick in the house, and whose disorders was much aggravated by the noise.——Alas! how destitute of *natural affection* are these poor uncultivated Pagans! although they seem somewhat kind in their own way. Of a truth, "the dark corners of the earth are full of "the habitations of cruelty."

This town (as I observed in my Journal of May last) lies partly on the east side of the river, partly on the west, and partly on a large island in it, and contains upwards of fifty houses, and (they tell me) near three hundred persons, though I never saw much more than half that number in it; but of three different tribes of Indians, speaking three languages wholly *unintelligible* to each other. About one half of its inhabitants are Delawares, the others called Senakas, and Tutelas. The Indians of this place are counted the most drunken, mischievous, and ruffainly *fellows* of any in these parts; and *Satan* seems to have his *seat* in this *town* in an eminent manner.

September 14. Visited the Delaware king, (who was supposed to be at the point of death when I was here in May last, but was now recovered), and discoursed with him and others respecting Christianity, and spent the afternoon with them, and had more encouragement than I expected. The *king* appeared kindly disposed, and willing to be instructed: this gave me some encouragement that God would open an *effectual door* for my preaching the gospel here, and set up his kingdom in this place. Which was a support and refreshment to me in the wilderness, and rendered my *solitary* circumstances comfortable and pleasant.

Lord's day, September 15. Visited the *chief* of the Delawares again; was kindly received by him, and discoursed to the Indians in the afternoon. Still entertained hopes that God would open their hearts to receive the gospel, though many of them in the place were so drunk from day to day, that I could get no opportunity to speak to them. Towards night discoursed with one that understood the languages of the Six Nations, (as they are usually called), who discovered an inclination to hearken to Christianity; which gave me some hopes that the gospel might hereafter be sent to those nations far remote.

September 16. Spent the forenoon with the Indians, endeavouring to instruct them from house to house, and to engage them, as far as I could, to be friendly to Christianity.

Towards night went to one part of the town where they were

were *sober*, and got together near fifty persons of them, and discoursed to them, having first obtained the king's *cheerful* consent.——There was a surprising attention among them, and they manifested a considerable desire of being further instructed. There was also one or two that seemed to be touched with some concern for their souls, who appeared well pleased with some conversation in private, after I had concluded my public discourse to them.

My spirits were much refreshed with this appearance of things, and I could not but return with my interpreter (having no *other companion* in this journey) to my poor hard lodgings, rejoicing in hopes that God designed to set up his kingdom here, where Satan now reigns in the most eminent manner; and found uncommon freedom in addressing the throne of grace for the accomplishment of so great and glorious a work.

September 17. Spent the forenoon in visiting and discoursing to the Indians. About noon left Shaumoking, (most of the Indians going out this day on their hunting design), and travelled down the river south-westward.

September 19. Visited an Indian town called *Juneauta*, situate on an island in Susquahannah. Was much discouraged with the temper and behaviour of the Indians here, although they appeared friendly when I was with them the last spring, and then gave me encouragement to come and see them again. But they now seemed resolved to retain their Pagan notions, and persist in their *idolatrous* practices.

September 20. Visited the Indians again at Juneauta island, and found them almost universally very busy in making preparations for a great *sacrifice* and *dance*. Had no opportunity to get them together in order to discourse with them about Christianity, by reason of their being so much engaged about their *sacrifice*. My spirits were much sunk with a prospect so very discouraging, and especially seeing I had now no interpreter but a Pagan, who was as much attached to *idolatry* as any of them, (my own interpreter having left me the day before, being obliged to attend upon some important business otherwhere, and knowing that he could neither speak nor understand the language of *these* Indians); so that I was under the greatest disadvantages imaginable. However, I attempted to discourse privately with some of them, but without any appearance of success: notwithstanding I still tarried with them.

In the evening they met together, near a hundred of them, and danced round a large fire, having prepared ten fat deer for the *sacrifice*. The fat of whose inwards they burnt in the fire while they were dancing, and sometimes raised the flame to a prodigious height, at the same time yelling and shouting in such a manner, that they might easily have been heard two miles or more.

They continued their *sacred dance* all night, or near the matter; after which they ate the *flesh* of the *sacrifice*, and so retired each one to his lodging.

I enjoyed little satisfaction this night, being entirely alone on the island, (as to any Christian company), and in the midst of this *idolatrous* revel; and having walked to and fro till body and mind were pained and much oppressed, I at length crept into a little crib made for corn, and there slept on the poles.

Lord's day, September 21. Spent the day with the Indians on the island. As soon as they were well up in the morning, I attempted to instruct them, and laboured for that purpose to get them together, but quickly found they had something else to do; for near noon they gathered together all their *powwows*, (or conjurers), and set about half a dozen of them to playing their juggling tricks, and acting their frantic distracted postures, in order to find out why they were then so sickly upon the island, numbers of them being at that time disordered with a *fever*, and bloody *flux*. In this exercise they were engaged for several hours, making all the wild, ridiculous, and distracted motions imaginable; sometimes singing; sometimes howling; sometimes extending their hands to the utmost stretch, spreading all their fingers, and seemed to push with them, as if they designed to fright something away, or at least keep it off at arms-end; sometimes stroking their faces with their hands, then spurting water as fine as mist; sometimes setting flat on the earth, then bowing down their faces to the ground; wringing their sides, as if in pain and anguish; twisting their faces, turning up their eyes, grunting, puffing, &c.

Their monstrous actions tended to excite ideas of horror, and seemed to have something in them (as I thought) peculiarly suited to raise the devil, if he could be raised by any thing odd, ridiculous, and frightful. Some of them, I could observe, were much more fervent and devout in the business than others, and seemed to *chant*, *peep*, and *mutter* with a great degree of warmth and vigour, as if determined to awaken and engage the powers below. I sat at a small distance, not more than thirty feet from them, (though undiscovered), with my Bible in my hand, resolving, if possible, to spoil their sport, and

and prevent their receiving any anſwers from the *infernal* world, and there viewed the whole ſcene. They continued their hideous charms and incantations for more than three hours, until they had all wearied themſelves out, although they had in that ſpace of time taken ſundry intervals of reſt; and at length broke up, I apprehended, without receiving any anſwer at all.

After they had done powwowing, I attempted to diſcourſe with them about Chriſtianity; but they ſoon ſcattered, and gave me no opportunity for any thing of that nature. A view of theſe things, while I was entirely alone in the wilderneſs, deſtitute of the ſociety of any one that ſo much as "named "the name of Chriſt," greatly ſunk my ſpirits, gave me the moſt gloomy turn of mind imaginable, almoſt ſtripped me of all reſolution and hope reſpecting further attempts for propagating the goſpel, and converting the Pagans, and rendered this the moſt burdenſome and diſagreeable Sabbath that ever I ſaw. But nothing, I can truly ſay, ſunk and diſtreſſed me like the loſs of my hope reſpecting *their converſion*. This concern appeared ſo great, and ſeemed to be ſo much *my own*, that I ſeemed to have nothing to do on *earth*, if this failed: and a proſpect of the greateſt ſucceſs in the ſaving converſion of ſouls under *goſpel-light*, would have done little or nothing towards compenſating for the loſs of my hope in this reſpect; and my ſpirits now were ſo damped and depreſſed, that I had no heart nor power to make any further attempts among them for that purpoſe, and could not poſſibly recover my hope, reſolution, and courage, by the utmoſt of my endeavours.

The Indians of this iſland can many of them underſtand the Engliſh language conſiderably well, having formerly lived in ſome part of Maryland among or near the white people, but are very vicious, drunken, and profane, although not ſo *ſavage* as thoſe who have leſs acquaintance with the Engliſh. Their cuſtoms in divers reſpects, differ from thoſe of other Indians upon this river. They do not bury their dead in a common form, but let their fleſh conſume above ground in cloſe cribs made for that purpoſe; and at the end of a year, or perhaps ſometimes a longer ſpace of time, they take the bones, when the fleſh is all conſumed, and waſh and ſcrape them, and afterwards bury them with ſome ceremony.—— Their method of *charming* or conjuring over the ſick, ſeems ſomewhat different from that of other Indians, though for ſubſtance the ſame: and the whole of it, among theſe and others, perhaps is an imitation of what ſeems, by Naaman's expreſſion, 2 Kings v. 11. to have been the cuſtom of the ancient Heathens. For it seems chiefly to consist in their "striking their hands over the diseased," repeatedly stroking of them, "and calling upon their gods," excepting the spurting of water like a mist, and some other frantic ceremonies common to the other *conjurations*, I have already mentioned.

When I was in these parts in May last, I had an opportunity of learning many of the notions and customs of the Indians, as well as of observing many of their practices: I then travelling more than an hundred and thirty miles upon the river above the English settlements; and having in that journey a view of some persons of *seven* or *eight* distinct tribes, speaking so many different languages. But of all the sights I ever saw among them, or indeed any where else, none appeared so frightful, or so near a-kin to what is usually imagined of *infernal powers*; none ever excited such images of terror in my mind, as the appearance of one who was a devout and zealous reformer, or rather restorer of what he supposed was the ancient religion of the Indians. He made his appearance in his *pontifical garb*, which was a coat of *bears skins*, dressed with the hair on, and hanging down to his toes, a pair of bear-skin stockings, and a great *wooden* face, painted the one half black, and the other tawny, about the colour of an Indian's skin, with an extravagant mouth, cut very much awry; the face fastened to a bear-skin cap, which was drawn over his head. He advanced toward me with the instrument in his hand that he used for music in his *idolatrous worship*, which was a dry *tortoise-shell*, with some corn in it, and the neck of it drawn on to a piece of wood, which made a very convenient handle. As he came forward, he beat his tune with the *rattle*, and danced with all his might, but did not suffer any part of his body, not so much as his fingers, to be seen: and no man would have guessed by his appearance and actions, that he could have been a human creature, if they had not had some intimation of it otherwise. When he came near me, I could not but shrink away from him, although it was then noon-day, and I knew who it was, his appearance and gestures were so prodigiously frightful. He had a house consecrated to religious uses, with divers images cut out upon the several parts of it; I went in and found the ground beat almost as hard as a rock with their frequent dancing in it.—I discoursed with him about Christianity, and some of my discourse he seemed to like, but some of it he disliked entirely. He told me that God had taught him his religion, and that he never would turn from it, but wanted to find some that would join heartily with him in it; for the Indians, he said, were

grown

grown very degenerate and corrupt. He had thoughts, he ſaid, of leaving all his friends, and travelling abroad, in order to find ſome that would join with him; for he believed God had ſome good people ſome where that felt as he did. He had not always, he ſaid, felt as he now did, but had *formerly* been like the reſt of the Indians, until about four or five years before that time: then, he ſaid, his heart was very much diſtreſſed, ſo that he could not live among the Indians, but got away into the woods, and lived alone for ſome months. At length, he ſays, God comforted his heart, and ſhowed him what he ſhould do; and ſince that time he had known God, and tried to ſerve him; and loved all men, be they who they would, ſo as he never did before.——He treated me with uncommon courteſy, and ſeemed to be hearty in it. ——And I was told by the Indians, that he oppoſed their drinking ſtrong liquor with all his power; and if at any time he could not diſſuade them from it, by all he could ſay, he would leave them, and go crying into the woods. It was manifeſt he had a ſet of religious notions that he had looked into *for himſelf*, and not taken for *granted* upon bare tradition; and he reliſhed or diſreliſhed whatever was ſpoken of a religious nature, according as it either agreed or diſagreed with *his ſtandard.* And while I was diſcourſing he would ſometimes ſay, "Now that I like: ſo God has taught me," *&c.* And ſome of his ſentiments ſeemed very juſt. Yet he utterly denied the being of a *devil*, and declared there was no ſuch a creature known among the Indians of old times, whoſe religion he ſuppoſed he was attempting to revive. He likewiſe told me, that departed ſouls all went ſouthward, and that the difference between the good and bad was this, that the *former* were admitted into a beautiful town with *ſpiritual* walls, or walls agreeable to the nature of ſouls; and that the *latter* would for ever hover round thoſe walls, and in vain attempt to get in. He ſeemed to be ſincere, honeſt, and conſcientious in his *own way*, and according to his own religious notions, which was more than I ever ſaw in any other Pagan: and I perceived he was looked upon, and derided amongſt moſt of the Indians as a *preciſe zealot*, that made a needleſs noiſe about religious matters. But I muſt ſay, there was ſomething in his temper and diſpoſition that looked more like true religion than any thing I ever obſerved amongſt other Heathens.

But; alas! how deplorable is the ſtate of the Indians upon this river! The brief repreſentation I have here given of their notions and manners, is ſufficient to ſhew that they are "led

"captive

"captive by Satan at his will," in the most eminent manner; and, methinks, might likewise be sufficient to excite the compassion, and engage the prayers of pious souls for these their fellow-men, who sit in "the regions of the shadow of death."

September 22. Made some further attempts to instruct and christianize the Indians on this island, but all to no purpose. They live so near the white people, that they are always in the way of strong liquor, as well as the ill examples of *nominal* Christians; which renders it so unspeakably difficult to treat with them about Christianity.

Forks of Delaware, 1745.

October 1. Discoursed to the Indians here, and spent some time in private conferences with them about their souls concerns, and afterwards invited them to accompany, or if not, to follow me down to Crosweeksung as soon as their conveniency would admit; which invitation sundry of them cheerfully accepted.

Crosweeksung in New-Jersey, 1745.

Preached to my people from John xiv. 1.—6. The divine presence seemed to be in the assembly. Numbers were affected with divine truths, and it was a season of comfort to some in particular.

O what a difference is there between these and the Indians I had lately treated with upon Susquahannah! To be with *those* seemed like being banished from God, and all his people; to be with *these* like being admitted into his family, and to the enjoyment of his divine presence! How great is the change lately made upon numbers of these Indians, who not many months ago were many of them as thoughtless, and averse to Christianity, as those upon Susquahannah! and how astonishing is that grace that has made this change!

Lord's day, October 6. Preached in the forenoon from John x. 7.—11. There was a considerable melting among my people; the dear young Christians were refreshed, comforted, and strengthened, and one or two persons newly awakened.

In the afternoon I discoursed on the story of the jailor, Acts xvi. and in the evening expounded Acts xx. 1.—12. There was at this time a very agreeable melting spread through the whole assembly. I think I scarce ever saw a more

more desirable affection in any number of people in my life. There was scarce a dry eye to be seen among them, and yet nothing *boisterous* or *unseemly*, nothing that tended to disturb the public worship; but rather to encourage and excite a Christian ardour and spirit of devotion.

Those who, I have reason to hope, were savingly renewed, were first affected, and seemed to rejoice much, but with brokenness of spirit and godly fear; their exercises were much the same with those mentioned in my Journal of August 26, evidently appearing to be the genuine effect of a Spirit of adoption.

After public service was over I withdrew, (being much tired with the labours of the day), and the Indians continued praying among themselves for near two hours together; which continued exercises appeared to be attended with a blessed quickening influence from on high.

I could not but earnestly *wish* that numbers of God's people had been present at this season, to see and hear these things which I am sure must refresh the heart of every true lover of Zion's interest. To see those, who very lately were savage Pagans and idolaters, "having no hope, and without God in "the world," now filled with a sense of divine love and grace, and worshipping the "Father in spirit and in truth," as numbers here appeared to do, was not a little affecting; and especially to see them appear so tender and humble, as well as lively, fervent, and devout in the divine service.

October 24. Discoursed from John iv. 13.—14. There was a great attention, a desirable affection, and an unaffected melting in the assembly.—It is surprising to see how eager they are of hearing the word of God. I have oftentimes thought they would cheerfully and diligently attend divine worship twenty-four hours together, had they an opportunity so to do.

October 25. Discoursed to my people respecting the *resurrection*, from Luke xx. 27.—36. And when I came to mention the blessedness the godly shall enjoy at that season; their final freedom from death, sin, and sorrow; their equality to the *angels* in regard of their nearness to, and enjoyment of Christ, (some imperfect degree of which they are favoured with in the present life, from whence springs their sweetest comfort); and their being the *children of God*, openly acknowledged by him *as such*: I say, when I mentioned these things, numbers of them were much affected, and melted with a view of this blessed state.

October 26. Being called to assist in the administration of the

the Lord's supper, in a neighbouring congregation, I invited my people to go with me, who in general embraced the opportunity cheerfully, and attended the several discourses of that solemnity with diligence and affection, most of them now understanding something of the English language.

Lord's day, October 27. While I was preaching to a vast assembly of people abroad, who appeared generally easy and secure enough, there was one Indian woman, a stranger, who never heard me preach before, nor ever regarded any thing about religion, (being now persuaded by some of her friends to come to meeting, though much against her will), was seized with pressing concern for her soul, and soon after expressed a great desire of going home, (more than forty miles distant), to call her husband, that he also might be awakened to a concern for his soul. Some other of the Indians also appeared to be affected with divine truths this day.

The pious people of the English (numbers of whom I had opportunity to converse with) seemed refreshed with seeing the Indians worship God in that devout and solemn manner with the assembly of his people: and with those mentioned Acts xi. 18. they could not but "glorify God, saying, Then "hath God also to the Gentiles granted repentance unto "life."

October 28. Preached again to a great assembly, at which time some of my people appeared affected; and when public worship was over, were inquisitive whether there would not be another sermon in the evening, or before the *sacramental* solemnity was concluded; being still desirous to hear God's word.

Crosweeksung,

October 28. Discoursed from Matth. xxii. 1.—13. I was enabled to open the scripture, and adapt my discourse and expressions to the capacities of my people, "I know not "how," in a plain, easy, and familiar manner, beyond all that I could have done by the utmost study: and this, without any *special* difficulty, with as much freedom as if I had been addressing a common audience, who had been instructed in the doctrine of Christianity all their days.

The word of God at this time seemed to fall upon the assembly with a divine power and influence, especially toward the close of my discourse: there was both a sweet melting and bitter mourning in the audience.—The dear Christians were refreshed and comforted,—convictions revived in others, and sundry persons newly awakened who had never been with us before; and so much of the divine presence appeared in the assembly,

assembly, that it seemed, "this was no other than the house "of God, and the gate of heaven." And all that had any favour and relish of divine things were even constrained by the sweetness of that season to say, "Lord, it is good for us "to be here!" If ever there was amongst my people an appearance of the New Jerusalem——"as a bride adorned for "her husband," there was much of it at this time; and so agreeable was the entertainment where such tokens of the divine presence were, that I could scarce be willing in the evening to leave the place, and repair to my lodgings. I was refreshed with a view of the continuance of this blessed work of grace among them, and its influence upon strangers of the Indians that had of late, from time to time, providentially fallen into these parts.

November 1. Discoursed from Luke xxiv. briefly explaining the whole chapter, and insisting especially upon some particular passages.

The discourse was attended with some affectionate concern upon some of the hearers, though not equal to what has often appeared among them.

Lord's day, November 3. Preached to my people from Luke xvi. 17. more especially for the sake of several lately brought under deep concern for their souls. There was some apparent concern and affection in the assembly, though far less than has been usual of late.

Afterwards I baptized *fourteen* persons of the Indians, six adults and eight children: one of these was near *fourscore* years of age, and I have reason to hope God has brought her savingly home to himself: two of the others were men of *fifty* years old, who had been singular and remarkable, even among the Indians, for their wickedness; one of them had been a *murderer*, and both notorious drunkards, as well as excessive quarrelsome; but now I cannot but hope both are become subjects of God's special grace, especially the worst of them *. I deferred their *baptism* for many weeks after they had given evidences of having passed a great change, that I might have more opportunities to observe the fruits of those impressions they had been under, and apprehended the way was now clear: and there was not one of the adults I baptized, but what had given me some comfortable grounds to hope, that God had wrought a work of special grace in their hearts;

* The man particularly mentioned in my Journal of August 10th, as being then awakened.

hearts; although I could not have the same degree of satisfaction respecting one or two of them, as the rest.

November 4. Discoursed from John xi. briefly explaining most of the chapter.——Divine truths made deep impressions upon many in the assembly; numbers were affected with a view of the power of Christ, manifested in his raising the dead; and especially when this instance of his power was improved to shew his power and ability to raise dead souls (such as many of them then felt themselves to be) to a spiritual life; as also to raise the dead at the last day, and dispense to them due rewards and punishments.

There were sundry of the persons lately come here from remote places, that were now brought under deep and pressing concern for their souls, particularly one, who not long since came half drunk, and railed on us, and attempted by all means to disturb us while engaged in the divine worship, was now so concerned and distressed for her soul, that she seemed unable to get any ease without an interest in Christ. There were many tears and affectionate sobs and groans in the assembly in general, some weeping for themselves, others for their friends. And although persons are doubtless much easier affected now, than they were in the beginning of this religious concern, when tears and cries for their souls were things unheard of among them; yet I must say, their affection in general appeared *genuine* and *unfeigned*; and especially this appeared very conspicuous in those newly awakened. So that true and genuine convictions of sin, seem still to be begun and promoted in many instances.

Baptized a child this day, and perceived sundry of the baptized persons affected with the administration of this ordinance, as being thereby minded of their own solemn engagements.

I have now baptized in all *forty-seven* persons of the Indians, twenty-three adults, and twenty-four children; thirty-five of them belonging to these parts, and the rest to the Forks of Delaware: and (through rich grace) they have none of them as yet been left to disgrace their profession of Christianity by any scandalous or unbecoming behaviour.

I might now justly make many remarks on a work of grace so very remarkable as this has been in divers respects; but shall confine myself to a few general hints only.

1st, It is remarkable that God began this work among the Indians at a time when I had the least hope, and (to my apprehension) the least rational prospect of seeing a work of grace

grace propagated amongst them. My bodily strength being then much wasted by a late tedious journey to Susquahannah, where I was necessarily exposed to hardships and fatigues among the Indians: my mind being also exceedingly depressed with a view of the unsuccessfulness of my labours, (since I had little reason so much as to hope that God had made me instrumental of the saving conversion of any of the Indians, except my interpreter and his wife); whence I was ready to look upon myself as a burden to the Honourable Society, that employed and supported me in this business, and began to entertain serious thoughts of giving up my *mission*; and almost resolved I would do so, at the conclusion of the present year, if I had then no better prospect of special success in my work than I had hitherto had: although I cannot say I entertained these thoughts because I was weary of the labours and fatigues that necessarily attended my present business, or because I had light and freedom in my own mind to turn any other way; but purely through dejection of spirit, pressing discouragement, and an apprehension of its being unjust to spend money consecrated to religious uses, only to civilize the Indians, and bring them to an *external* profession of Christianity, which was all that I could then see any prospect of having effected, while God seemed (as I thought) evidently to frown upon the design of their saving conversion, by with-holding the convincing and renewing influences of his blessed Spirit from attending the means I had hitherto used with them for that end.

And in this frame of mind I first visited these Indians at Crosweeksung, apprehending it was my indispensible duty (seeing I had heard there was a number in these parts) to make some attempts for their conversion to God, though I cannot say, I had any hope of success, my spirits were now so extremely sunk. And I do not know that my hopes respecting the conversion of the Indians were ever reduced to so low an ebb, since I had any *special* concern for them, as at this time.

And yet *this* was the very season that God saw fittest to begin this glorious work in! And thus he "ordained strength "out of weakness," by making bare his almighty arm at a time when *all hopes* and *human probabilities* most evidently appeared to fail.——"Whence I learn, that it is good to "follow the path of duty, though in the midst of darkness "and discouragement."

2*dly*, It is remarkable how God providentially, and in a manner almost *unaccountable*, called these Indians together to be instructed in the great things that concerned their souls; and how he seized their minds with the most solemn and weighty concern for their eternal salvation as fast as they came to the place where his word was preached. When I first came into these parts in June, I found not one man at the place I visited, but only *four* women and a few children: but before I had been here many days, they gathered from all quarters, some from more than twenty miles distant; and when I made them a second visit in the beginning of August, some came more than forty miles to hear me.

And many came without any intelligence of what was going on here, and consequently without any design of *theirs*, so much as to gratify their curiosity; so that it seemed as if God had summoned them together from all quarters for nothing else but to deliver his message to them; and that he did this, (with regard to some of them), without making use of any *human* means; although there was pains taken by some of them to give notice to others at remote places.

Nor is it less surprising that they were one after another affected with a solemn concern for their souls, almost as soon as they came upon the spot where divine truths were taught them. I could not but think often that their coming to the place of our public worship, was like Saul and his messengers coming among the prophets; they no sooner came but they prophesied; and these were almost as soon affected with a sense of their sin and misery, and with an earnest concern for deliverance, as they made their appearance in our assembly. —After this work of *grace* began with power among them, it was common for *strangers* of the Indians, before they had been with us one day, to be much awakened, deeply convinced of their sin and misery, and to inquire with great solicitude, "What they should do to be saved?"

3dly, It is likewise remarkable how God preserved these poor ignorant Indians from being prejudised against me, and the truths I taught them, by those means that were used with them for that purpose by ungodly people. There were many attempts made by some ill-minded persons of the *white* people to prejudise them against, or fright them from Christianity. They sometimes told them, the Indians were well enough on it already:—that there was no need of all this *noise* about Christianity:—that if they were Christians, they would be in no better, no safer, or happier state, than they were already in, &c.

Sometimes they told them, that I was a *knave*, a *deceiver*, and the like: that I daily taught them a company of lies, and had no other design but to impose upon them, &c.

And

And when none of these, and such like suggestions, would avail to their purpose, they then tried another expedient, and told the Indians, "My design was to gather together as large "a body of them as I possibly could, and then sell them to "England for slaves." Than which nothing could be more likely to terrify the Indians, they being naturally of a jealous disposition, and the most averse to a state of servitude perhaps of any people living.

But all these wicked insinuations (through divine goodness over-ruling) constantly turned against the *authors* of them, and only served to engage the affections of the Indians more firmly to me: for they being awakened to a solemn concern for their souls, could not but observe, that the persons who endeavoured to imbitter their minds against me, were altogether unconcerned about their own souls, and not only so, but vicious and profane; and thence could not but argue, that if they had no concern for their *own*, it was not likely they should have for the souls of *others*.

It seems yet the more wonderful that the Indians were preserved from once hearkening to these suggestions, in as much as I was an utter stranger among them, and could give them no assurance of my sincere affection to, and concern for them, by any thing that was past,—while the persons that insinuated these things were their old acquaintance, who had had frequent opportunites of gratifying their *thirsty appetites* with strong drink, and consequently, doubtless, had the greatest interest in their affections.——But from this instance of their preservation from fatal prejudices, I have had occasion with admiration to say, "If God will work, who can hinder or "resist?"

4thly, Nor is it less wonderful how God was pleased to provide a *remedy* for my want of skill and freedom in the Indian language, by remarkably fitting my interpreter for, and assisting him in the performance of his work. It might reasonably be supposed I must needs labour under a vast disadvantage in addressing the Indians by an interpreter; and that divine truths would unavoidably loose much of the *energy* and *pathos* with which they might at first be delivered, by reason of their coming to the audience from a *second hand*. But although this has often (to my sorrow and discouragement) been the case in times past, when my interpreter had little or no sense of divine things, yet now it was quite otherwise. I cannot think my addresses to the Indians ordinarily since the beginning of this season of grace, have lost any thing of the power or pungency with which they were made, unless it it were sometimes for want of pertinent and pathetic terms and expressions in the Indian language; which difficulty could not have been much redressed by my personal acquaintance with their language. My interpreter had before gained some good degree of *doctrinal* knowledge, whereby he was rendered capable of understanding and communicating, without mistakes, the *intent* and *meaning* of my discourses, and that without being confined *strictly*, and obliged to interpret *verbatim*. He had likewise, to appearance, an *experimental* acquaintance with divine things; and it pleased God at this season to inspire his mind with longing desires for the conversion of the Indians, and to give him admirable zeal and fervency in addressing them in order thereto. And it is remarkable, that when I was favoured with any *special assistance* in any work, and enabled to speak with more than common *freedom, fervency*, and *power*, under a *lively* and *affecting sense* of divine things, he was usually affected in the *same manner* almost instantly, and seemed at once quickened and enabled to speak in the same *pathetic* language, and under the same influence that I did. And a *surprising energy* often accompanied the word at such seasons; so that the face of the whole assembly would be apparently changed almost in an instant, and tears and sobs became common among them.

He also appeared to have such a clear doctrinal view of God's usual methods of dealing with souls under a preparatory work of *conviction* and *humiliation* as he never had before; so that I could, with his help, discourse freely with the distressed persons about their *internal* exercises, their fears, discouragements, temptations, *&c.*

He likewise took pains day and night to repeat and inculcate upon the minds of the Indians the truths I taught them daily; and this he appeared to do, not from spiritual pride, and an affectation of setting himself up as a *public teacher*, but from a spirit of faithfulness, and an honest concern for their souls.

His conversation among the Indians has likewise (so far as I know) been savoury, as becomes a Christian, and a person employed in his work; and I may justly say, he has been a great comfort to me, and a great instrument of promoting this good work among the Indians: so that whatever be the state of his own soul, it is apparent God has remarkably fitted him for this work.

And thus God has manifested that, without bestowing on me the *gift of tongues*, he could find a way wherein I might

be-

be as effectually enabled to convey the truths of his glorious gospel to the minds of these poor benighted Pagans.

5thly, It is further remarkable, that God has carried on his work here by *such means*, and in *such a manner* as tended to obviate, and leave no room for those prejudices and objections that have often been raised against such a work. When persons have been awakened to a solemn concern for their souls, by hearing the more *awful* truths of God's word, and the *terrors* of the divine law insisted upon, it has usually in such cases been objected by some, that such persons were only *frighted* with a *fearful noise* of *hell* and *damnation*; and that there was no evidence that their concern was the effect of a divine influence. But God has left no room for this objection in the present case, this work of grace having been begun and carried on, by almost one continued strain of gospel-invitation to perishing sinners, as may reasonably be guessed, from a view of the *passages* of *scripture* I chiefly insisted upon in my discourses from time to time; which I have for that purpose inserted in my Journal.

Nor have I ever seen so general an awakening in any assembly in my life as appeared here, while I was opening and insisting upon the parable of the *great supper*, Luke xiv. In which discourse I was enabled to set before my hearers the *unsearchable riches* of gospel-grace.

Not that I would be understood here, that I never instructed the Indians respecting their fallen state, and the sinfulness and misery of it: for *this* was what I at first chiefly insisted upon with them, and endeavoured to repeat and inculcate in almost every discourse, knowing that without this *foundation* I should but build upon the *sand*; and that it would be in vain to invite them to Christ, unless I could convince them of their *need* of him, Mark ii. 17.

But still this great awakening, this surprising concern was never excited by any *harangues* of *terror*, but always appeared most remarkable when I insisted upon "the compositions "of a dying Saviour," the "plentiful provisions of the gospel," and the "free offers of divine grace to needy distressed sinners."

Nor would I be understood to insinuate, that such a religious concern might *justly* be suspected as not being genuine, and from a divine influence, because produced by the preaching of *terror*: for this is perhaps God's more usual way of awakening sinners, and appears entirely agreeable to scripture, and sound reason.—But what I meant here to observe is, that God saw fit to *improve* and bless *milder* means for the effectual

tual awakening of these Indians, and thereby obviated the forementioned objection, which the world might otherwise have had a more *plausible* colour of making.

And as there has been no room for any plausible objection against this work, in regard of the *means;* so neither in regard of the *manner* in which it has been carried on.——It is true, persons concern for their souls has been exceeding great, the convictions of their sin and misery have risen to a *high* degree, and produced many tears, cries, and groans: but then they have not been attended with those disorders, either bodily or mental, that have sometimes prevailed among persons under religious impressions.——There has here been no appearance of those "convulsions, bodily agonies, frightful "screamings, swoonings," and the like, that have been so much complained of in some places; although there have been some who (with the jailor) have been made to *tremble* under a sense of their sin and misery,——numbers who have been made to cry out from a distressing view of their perishing state,——and some that have been, for a time, in a great measure, deprived of their bodily strength, yet without any such *convulsive* appearances.

Nor has there been any appearance of *mental* disorders here, such as "visions, trances, imaginations of being under prophetic inspiration," and the like; or scarce any unbecoming disposition to appear remarkably affected either with concern or joy; though I must confess, I observed one or two persons, whose concern, I thought, was in a considerable measure affected; and one whose joy appeared to be of the same kind. But these workings of *spiritual pride*, I endeavoured to crush in their first appearances, and have not since observed any affection, either of joy or sorrow, but what appeared *genuine* and *unaffected*. But,

6thly, and *lastly*, The *effects* of this work have likewise been very remarkable. I doubt not but that many of these people have gained more *doctrinal* knowledge of divine truths, since I first visited them in June last, than could have been instilled into their minds by the most diligent use of proper and instructive means for whole *years* together, without such a divine influence. Their Pagan notions and *idolatrous* practices seem to be entirely abandoned in these parts. They are regulated, and appear regularly disposed in the affairs of *marriage;* an instance whereof I have given in my Journal of August 14. They seem generally divorced from *drunkenness*, their darling vice, and the "sin that easily besets them:" so that I do not know of more than two or three who have been

my

my steady hearers, that have drank to excess since I first visited them, although before it was common for some or other of them to be drunk almost every day: and some of them seem now to fear this sin in particular more than death itself. A principle of honesty and justice appears in many of them, and they seem concerned to discharge their old debts, which they have neglected, and, perhaps, scarce thought of for years past. Their manner of living is much more decent and comfortable than formerly, having now the benefit of that money which they used to consume upon strong drink. *Love* seems to reign among them, especially those who have given evidences of having passed a saving change: and I never saw any appearance of *bitterness* or *censoriousness* in these, nor any disposition to "esteem themselves better than others," who had not received the like mercy.

As their sorrows under *convictions* have been great and pressing, so many of them have since appeared to "rejoice "with joy unspeakable, and full of glory:" and yet I never saw any thing *ecstatic* or *flighty* in their joy. Their consolations do not incline them to *air* and *lightness*; but, on the contrary, are attended with *solemnity*, and oftentimes with *tears*, and an apparent *brokenness of heart*, as may be seen in several passages of my Journal: and in this respect some of them have been surprised at themselves, and have with concern observed to me, that "when their hearts have been glad," (which is a phrase they commonly make use of to express spiritual joy), "they could not help crying for all."

And now, upon the whole, I think, I may justly say, here are all the symptoms and evidences of a remarkable work of grace among these Indians, that can reasonably be desired or looked for. May the *great Author* of this work maintain and promote the same *here*, and propagate it *every where*, till "the whole earth be filled with his glory!" Amen.

I have now rode more than three thousand miles, that I have kept an exact account of, since the beginning of March last; and almost the whole of it has been in my own proper business as a *missionary*, upon the design (either immediately or more remotely) of propagating *Christian knowledge* among the Indians. I have taken pains to look out for a *colleague*, or *companion*, to travel with me; and have likewise used endeavours to procure something for his support, among religious persons in New-England, which cost me a journey of several hundred miles in length; but have not as yet found any person qualified and disposed for this good work, although I had ſome encouragement from *miniſters* and others, that it was hopeful a maintenance might be procured for one, when *the man* ſhould be found.

I have likewiſe of late repreſented to the gentlemen concerned with this *miſſion*, the neceſſity of having an Engliſh ſchool ſpeedily ſet up among theſe Indians, who are now willing to be at the pains of gathering together in a body for this purpoſe. And in order hereto, have humbly propoſed to them the collecting of money for the maintenance of a ſchoolmaſter, and defraying of other neceſſary charges in the promotion of this good work; which they are now attempting in the ſeveral congregations of Chriſtians to which they reſpectively belong.

The ſeveral companies of Indians I have preached to in the ſummer paſt, live at *great diſtances* from each other. It is more than ſeventy miles from Croſweekſung in New-Jerſey, to the Forks of Delaware in Penſylvania. And from thence to ſundry of the Indian ſettlements I viſited on Suſquahannah, is more than an hundred and twenty miles. And ſo much of my time is neceſſarily conſumed in journeying, that I can have but little for *any* of my neceſſary ſtudies, and conſequently for the ſtudy of the Indian languages in particular; and eſpecially ſeeing I am obliged to diſcourſe ſo frequently to the Indians at each of theſe places while I am with them, in order to redeem time to viſit the reſt. I am, at times, almoſt diſcouraged from attempting to gain any acquaintance with the Indian languages, they are ſo very numerous, (ſome account of which I gave in my Journal of May laſt), and eſpecially ſeeing my other labours and fatigues ingroſs almoſt the whole of my time, and bear exceeding hard upon my *conſtitution*, ſo that my health is much impaired.—— However, I have taken conſiderable pains to learn the Delaware language, and propoſe ſtill to do ſo, as far as my other buſineſs and bodily health will admit. I have already made ſome proficiency in it, though I have laboured under many and great diſadvantages in my attempts of that nature. And it is but juſt to obſerve here, that all the pains I took to acquaint myſelf with the language of the Indians I ſpent my firſt year with, were of little or no ſervice to me here among the Delawares; ſo that my work, when I came among theſe Indians, was all to begin anew.

As theſe poor ignorant Pagans ſtood in need of having "line "upon line, and precept upon precept," in order to their being inſtructed and grounded in the principles of Chriſtianity; ſo I preached "publicly, and taught from houſe to houſe," almoſt

almost every day for *whole weeks* together, when I was with them. And my *public* discourses did not then make up the one half of my work, while there was so many constantly coming to me with that important inquiry, "What must "we do to be saved?" and opening to me the various exercises of their minds. And yet I can say, (to the praise of rich grace), that the apparent success with which my labours were crowned, unspeakably more than compensated for the labour itself, and was likewise a great means of supporting and carrying me through the business and fatigues, which (it seems) my nature would have sunk under, without such an encouraging prospect. But although this success has afforded matter of support, comfort, and thankfulness; yet in this season I have found great need of assistance in my work, and have been much oppressed for want of *one* to bear a *part* of my *labours* and *hardships*.——

"May the Lord of the harvest send forth other labourers "into this part of his harvest, that those who sit in darkness "may see great light, and that the whole earth may be filled "with the knowledge of himself! Amen."

November 20. 1745. DAVID BRAINERD.

Divine Grace displayed;

OR,

The Continuance and Progress

OF A

Remarkable Work of Grace

Among some of the INDIANS

Belonging to the Provinces of New-Jersey and Pensylvania,

Justly Represented in a

JOURNAL

Kept by order of the Honourable Society (in Scotland) for propagating Christian Knowledge.

With some general REMARKS.

To which is subjoined an APPENDIX, containing some account of sundry things, especially of the difficulties attending the work of a Missionary among the INDIANS.

By DAVID BRAINERD,

Minister of the Gospel, and Missionary from the said Society.

Published by the Reverend and Worthy Correspondents of the said Society.

Rom. ix. 25. 26. I will call them my people, that were not my people; and her, beloved, that was not beloved. And it shall come to pass, that in the place where it was said unto them, Ye are not my people; there shall they be called, The children of the living God.

Eph. v. 8. Ye were sometimes darkness, but now are ye light in the Lord.

Psal. cxviii. 23. This is the Lord's doing, it is marvellous in our eyes.

Printed in the Year MDCCLXV.

Crosweeksung in New-Jersey, 1745.

LOrd's day, November 24. Preached both parts of the day from the story of Zaccheus, Luke xix. 1.—9. In the latter exercise, when I opened and insisted upon the *salvation* that *comes to the sinner*, upon his becoming a *son of Abraham*, or a true believer, the word seemed to be attended with divine power to the hearts of the hearers.——Numbers were much affected with divine truths;—former convictions were revived;—one or two persons newly awakened;—and a most affectionate engagement in divine service appeared among them universally.

The impressions they were under appeared to be the genuine effect of God's word brought home to their hearts, by the power and influence of the divine Spirit.

November 26. After having spent some time in private conferences with my people, I discoursed publicly among them from John v. 1. 9. I was favoured with some *special* freedom and fervency in my discourse, and a powerful energy accompanied divine truths. Many wept and sobed affectionately, and scarce any appeared unconcerned in the whole assembly. The influence that seized the audience appeared gentle, and yet pungent and efficacious. It produced no boisterous commotion of the passions, but seemed deeply to affect the heart; and excited in the persons under convictions of their lost state, heavy groans and tears:——and in others who had obtained comfort, a sweet and humble melting. It seemed like the gentle but steady showers that effectually water the earth, without violently beating upon the surface.

The persons lately awakened, were, some of them, deeply distressed for their souls, and appeared earnestly solicitous to obtain an interest in Christ: and some of them, after public worship was over, in anguish of spirit, said, "They knew "not what to do, nor how to get their wicked hearts chan-"ged," *&c.*

November 28. Discoursed to the Indians publicly, after having used some private endeavours to instruct and excite some in the duties of Christianity. Opened and made remarks

marks upon the sacred story of our Lord's *transfiguration*, Luke ix. 28.—36 Had a principal view in my insisting upon this passage of scripture to the edification and consolation of God's people. And observed some, that I have reason to think are truly such, exceedingly affected with an account of the glory of Christ in his transfiguration; and filled with longing desires of being with him, that they might with *open face* behold his glory.

After public service was over, I asked one of them, who wept and sobed most affectionately, "What she now wanted?" She replied, "Oh to be with Christ! she did not "know how to stay," &c. This was a blessed refreshing season to the religious people in general. The Lord Jesus Christ seemed to manifest his divine glory to them, as when *transfigured* before his disciples. And they, with the disciples, were ready universally to say, "Lord, it is good for "us to be here."

The influence of God's word was not *confined* to those who had given evidences of being truly gracious, though at this time, I calculated my discourse for, and directed it *chiefly* to such: but it appeared to be a season of divine power in the whole assembly; so that most were, in some measure, affected. And one aged man in particular, lately awakened, was now brought under deep and pressing concern for his soul, and was earnestly inquisitive "how he might find Jesus Christ."

God seems still to vouchsafe his divine presence and the influence of his blessed Spirit to accompany his word, at least in some measure, in all our meetings for divine worship.

November 30. Preached near night, after having spent some hours in private conference with some of my people about their souls concerns. Explained and insisted upon the story of the rich man and Lazarus, Luke xvi. 19. 26. The word made powerful impressions upon many in the assembly, especially while I discoursed of the blessedness of "Lazarus "in Abraham's bosom." *This* I could perceive, affected them much more than what I spoke of the *rich man's* misery and torments. And thus it has been usually with them. They have almost always appeared much more affected with the *comfortable* than the *dreadful* truths of God's word. And that which has distressed many of them under convictions, is, that they found they wanted, and could not obtain the happiness of the godly; at least they have often appeared to be more affected with *this*, than with the *terrors* of hell. But whatever be the *means* of their awakening, it is plain, numbers are made *deeply sensible* of their sin and misery. the

wickedness

wickedneſs and ſtubbornneſs of their own hearts, their *utter inability* to help themſelves, or to come to Chriſt for help, without divine aſſiſtance; and ſo are brought to ſee their *periſhing* need of Chriſt to do all for them, and to lie at the foot of *ſovereign mercy*.

Lord's day, December 1. Diſcourſed to my people in the forenoon from Luke xvi. 27. 31. There appeared an unfeigned affection in divers perſons, and ſome ſeemed deeply impreſſed with divine truths.

In the afternoon preached to a number of white people; at which time the Indians attended with diligence, and many of them were able to underſtand a conſiderable part of the diſcourſe.

At night diſcourſed to my people again, and gave them ſome particular cautions and directions relating to their conduct in divers reſpects. And preſſed them to *watchfulneſs* in all their deportment, ſeeing they were encompaſſed with thoſe that "waited for their halting," and who *ſtood ready* to draw them into *temptations* of every kind, and then to expoſe religion for their miſſteps.

Lord's day, December 8. Diſcourſed on the ſtory of the blind man, John ix. There appeared no remarkable effect of the word upon the aſſembly at this time. The perſons who have lately been much concerned for their ſouls, ſeemed now not ſo affected nor ſolicitous to obtain an intereſt in Chriſt as has been uſual; although they attended divine ſervice with ſeriouſneſs and diligence.

Such have been the *doings of the Lord* here, in awakening ſinners, and affecting the hearts of thoſe who are brought to ſolid comfort, with a freſh ſenſe of divine things from time to time, that it is now ſtrange to ſee the aſſembly ſit with *dry* eyes, and without ſobs and groans.

December 12. Preached from the parable of the ten virgins, Matth. xxv. The divine power ſeemed in ſome meaſure to attend this diſcourſe, in which I was favoured with *uncommon* freedom and plainneſs of addreſs, and enabled to open divine truths, and explain them to the capacities of my people, in a manner *beyond myſelf*.——There appeared in many perſons an affectionate concern for their ſouls; although the concern in general ſeemed not ſo deep and preſſing as it had formerly done. Yet it was refreſhing to ſee many melted into tears and unaffected ſobs; ſome with a *ſenſe* of divine love, and ſome for *want* of it.

Lord's day, December 15. Preached to the Indians from Luke xiii. 24. 28. Divine truths fell with weight and power upon the audience, and seemed to reach the hearts of many. Near night discoursed to them again from Matth. xxv. 31. to 46. At which season also, the word appeared to be accompanied with a divine influence, and made powerful impressions upon the assembly in general, as well as upon divers persons in a very special and particular manner. This was an amazing season of grace! "The word of the Lord," this day, "was quick and powerful, sharper than a two-edged sword," and pierced to the hearts of many. The assembly was greatly affected, and *deeply* wrought upon; yet without so much *apparent* commotion of the passions, as was usual in the beginning of this work of grace. The impressions made by the word of God upon the audience appeared solid, rational, and deep, worthy of the solemn truths by means of which they were produced, and far from being the effects of any *sudden fright*, or *groundless* perturbation of mind.

O how did the hearts of the hearers seem to bow under the weight of divine truths! And how evident did it now appear that they *received* and *felt* them, "not as the word of man, "but as the word of God!" None can frame a just idea of the appearance of our assembly at this time, but those who have seen a congregation solemnly *awed*, and deeply *impressed* by the *special* power and influence of divine truths delivered to them in the name of God.

December 16. Discoursed to my people in the evening from Luke xi. 1.—13. After having insisted some time upon the 9th verse, wherein there is a command and encouragement to ask for divine favours, I called upon them to ask for a *new heart* with utmost importunity, as the man mentioned in the parable, I was discoursing upon, pleaded for *loaves of bread* at midnight.

There was much affection and concern in the assembly; and especially one woman appeared in great distress for her soul. She was brought to such an *agony* in seeking after Christ, that the sweet ran off her face for a considerable time together, although the evening was very cold; and her bitter cries were the most affecting indication of the *inward* anguish of her heart.

December 21. My people having now attained to a considerable degree of knowledge in the principles of Christianity, I thought it proper to set up a *catechetical lecture* among them; and this evening attempted something in *that form;* proposing questions to them agreeable to the Reverend Assembly's *Shorter Catechism*, receiving their answers, and then explaining and insisting as appeared necessary and proper upon

each

each question. After which I endeavoured to make some practical improvement of the whole. This was the method I entered upon.——They were able readily and *rationally* to answer many important questions I proposed to them: so that, upon trial, I found their *doctrinal* knowledge to exceed my own expectations.——In the improvement of my discourse, when I came to infer and open the blessedness of those who have so great and glorious a God, as had before been spoken of, "for their everlasting friend and portion," sundry were much affected; and especially when I exhorted, and endeavoured to persuade them "to be reconciled to God," through his dear Son, and *thus* to secure an interest in his everlasting favour. So that they appeared to be not only *enlightened* and *instructed*, but *affected* and engaged in their souls concern by this method of discoursing.

Lord's day, December 22. Discoursed upon the story of the young man in the gospel, Matth. ix. 16.—22. God made it a seasonable word, I am persuaded, to some souls.

There were sundry persons of the Indians newly come here, who had frequently lived among Quakers; and being more civilized and conformed to English manners than the generality of the Indians, they had imbibed some of the Quakers errors, especially this fundamental one, *viz.* That if men will but live soberly and honestly, according to the dictates of their own consciences, (or the *light within*), there is then no danger or doubt of their salvation, *&c.*——These persons I found much worse to deal with than those who are wholly under Pagan darkness, who make no *pretences* to knowledge in Christianity at all, nor have any *self-righteous* foundation to stand upon. However, they all, except one, appeared now convinced, that this *sober, honest life*, of itself, was not sufficient to salvation; since Christ himself had declared it so in the case of the young man. And seemed in some measure concerned to obtain that change of heart which I had been labouring to shew them the necessity of.

This was likewise a season of *comfort* to some souls, and in particular to one, (the same mentioned in my Journal of the 16th instant), who never before obtained any settled comfort, though I have abundant reason to think she had passed a saving change some days before.

She now appeared in a heavenly frame of mind, composed and delighted with the divine will. When I came to discourse particularly with her, and to enquire of her, how she got relief and deliverance from the spiritual distresses she had lately been under, ſhe anſwered in broken Engliſh, * "Me try, me "try, ſave myſelf, laſt my ſtrength be all gone, (meaning "her ability to ſave herſelf), could not me ſtir bit further. "Den laſt, me forced let Jeſus Chriſt alone, ſend me hell if "he pleaſe." I ſaid, But you was not willing to go to hell, was you? She replied, † "Could not me help it. My "heart he would wicked for all. Could not me make him "good;" (meaning ſhe ſaw it was right ſhe ſhould go to hell, becauſe her heart was wicked, and would be ſo after all ſhe could do to mend it). I aſked her, How ſhe got out of this caſe? She anſwered ſtill in the ſame broken language, ‡ "By, "by my heart be grad deſperately." I aſked her why her heart was glad? She replied, "Grad my heart Jeſus Chriſt "do what he pleaſe with me. Den me tink, grad my heart "Jeſus Chriſt ſend me hell. Did not me care where he put "me, me lobe him for all," &c.

And ſhe could not readily be convinced, but that ſhe was willing to go to hell, if Chriſt was pleaſed to ſend her there. Though the truth evidently was, her will was ſo ſwallowed up in the divine will, that ſhe could not frame any hell in her imagination that would be dreadful or undeſirable, provided it was but the will of God to ſend her to it.

Toward night diſcourſed to them again in the *catechetical* method I entered upon the evening before. And when I came to improve the truths I had explained to them, and to anſwer that queſtion, "But how ſhall I know whether God "has choſen me to everlaſting life," by preſſing them to come and give up their hearts to Chriſt, and thereby "to "make their election ſure;" they then appeared much affected: and the perſons under concern were afreſh engaged in ſeeking after an intereſt in him; while ſome others, who had obtained comfort before, were refreſhed to find that love to

* In proper Engliſh thus, "I tried and tried to ſave myſelf, till "at laſt my ſtrength was all gone, and I could not ſtir any further. "Then at laſt I was forced to let Jeſus Chriſt alone to ſend me to "hell if he pleaſed."

† In plain Engliſh thus, "I could not help it. My heart would "be wicked for all what I could do. I could not make it good."

‡ "By and by my heart was exceeding glad.——My heart was "glad that Jeſus Chriſt would do with me what he pleaſed. Then "I thought my heart would be glad although Chriſt ſhould ſend "me to hell. I did not care where he put me, I ſhould love him "for all; *i. e.* do what he would with me."

God

God in themselves, which was an evidence of his *electing* love to them.

December 25. The Indians having been used upon Christmas-days to drink and revel among some of the *white* people in these parts, I thought it proper this day to call them together, and discourse to them upon divine things: which I accordingly did from the parable of the barren fig-tree, Luke xiii. 6.—9. A divine influence, I am persuaded, accompanied the word at this season. The power of God appeared in the assembly, not by producing any remarkable *cries*, but by shocking and rousing at heart (as it seemed) several stupid creatures, that were scarce ever moved with any concern before. The power attending divine truths seemed to have the influence of the *earthquake* rather than the *whirlwind* upon them. Their *passions* were not so much alarmed as has been common here in times past, but their *judgments* appeared to be powerfully convinced by the *masterly* and *conquering* influence of divine truths. The impressions made upon the assembly in general, seemed not *superficial*, but *deep* and heart-affecting. O how ready did they now appear universally to embrace and comply with every thing they heard and were convinced was duty! God was in the midst of us of a truth, bowing and melting stubborn hearts! How many tears and sobs were then to be seen and heard among us! What liveliness and strict attention! what eagerness and intenseness of mind appeared in the whole assembly in the time of divine service! They seemed to watch and wait for the dropping of God's word, as the thirsty earth for the "former and latter "rain."

Afterwards I discoursed to them on the duty of husbands and wives, from Eph. v. 22.—33.; and have reason to think this was a word in season.——Spent some time further in the evening, in inculcating the truths I had insisted upon in my former discourse respecting the barren fig-tree, and observed a powerful influence still accompany what was spoken.

December 26. This evening I was visited by a person under great spiritual exercise. The most remarkable instance of this kind I ever saw. She was a woman of (I believe) more than *fourscore* years old, and appeared to be much broken and very *childish* through age, so that it seemed impossible for man to instil into her mind any *notions* of divine things, not so much as to give her any *doctrinal* instruction, because she seemed uncapable of being taught.——She was led by the hand into my house, and appeared in extreme anguish. I asked her, what ailed her? She answered, "That her heart was "distressed,

"distressed, and she feared she should never find Christ." I asked her, when she began to be concerned? with divers other questions relating to her distress. To all which she answered, for substance, to this effect, *viz.* That she had heard me preach many times, but never knew any thing about it, never "felt it in her heart" till the last Sabbath; and then it came (she said) "all one as if a needle had been thrust into "her heart;" since which time, she had no rest day nor night. She added, that on the evening before Christmas, a number of Indians being together at the house where she was, and discoursing about *Christ*, their talk *pricked her heart*, so that she could not sit up, but fell down on her bed; at which time *she went away*, (as she expressed it), and felt as if she dreamed, and yet is confident she did not dream. When she was thus gone, she saw, she says, two paths, one appeared very broad and crooked; and that, she says, turned to the left hand. The other appeared strait and very narrow; and that went up the hill to the right hand. She travelled, she said, for some time up the narrow right-hand path, till at length something seemed to obstruct her journey. She sometimes called it darkness, and then described it otherwise, and seemed to compare it to a block or bar. She then remembered, she says, what she had heard me say about "striving to enter in at the strait "gate," (although she took little notice of it, at the time when she heard me discourse upon that subject), and thought she would climb over this bar. But just as she was thinking of this, she came back again, as she termed it, meaning that she came to herself; whereupon her soul was extremely distressed, apprehending she had now turned back and forsaken Christ, and that there was therefore no hope of mercy for her.

As I was sensible that *trances*, and *imaginary* views of things, are of *dangerous* tendency in religion, when sought after, and depended upon; so I could not but be much concerned about this exercise, especially at first; apprehending this might be a design of Satan to bring a blemish upon the work of God here, by introducing *visionary* scenes, imaginary terrors, and all manner of mental disorders and *delusions*, in the room of genuine convictions of sin, and the enlightening influences of the blessed Spirit; and I was almost resolved to declare, that I looked upon this to be one of *Satan's devices*, and to caution my people against it, and the like exercises, *as such*. —However, I determined first to enquire into her knowledge, to see whether she had any just views of things, that might be the occasion of her present distressing concern, or whether it it was a *mere fright* arising only from *imaginary* terrors. I asked her divers questions respecting man's primitive, and more especially his present state, and respecting her own heart; which she answered rationally, and to my surprise. And I thought it was next to impossible, if not altogether so, that a Pagan who was become a *child* through age, should in that state gain so much knowledge by any mere human instruction, without being remarkably enlightened by a divine influence.

I then proposed to her the provision made in the gospel for the salvation of sinners, and the ability and willingness of Christ "to save to the uttermost all (old as well as young) "that come to him." To which she seemed to give a hearty assent. But instantly replied, "Ay, but I cannot come; "my wicked heart will not come to Christ; I do not know "how to come," *&c.* And this she spoke in anguish of spirit, striking on her breast, with tears in her eyes, and with such *earnestness* in her looks as was indeed piteous and affecting.

She seems to be really convinced of her sin and misery, and her need of a change of heart: and her concern is abiding and constant. So that nothing appears but that this exercise may have a saving issue. And indeed it seems hopeful, seeing she is so solicitous to obtain an interest in Christ, that her heart (as she expresses it) prays day and night.

How far God may make use of the *imagination* in awakening some persons under *these*, and such like circumstances, I cannot pretend to determine. Or whether this exercise I have given an account of, be from a divine influence, I shall leave others to judge. But this I must say, that its effects hitherto bespeak it to be *such*: nor can it (as I see) be accounted for, in a rational way, but from the influence of some spirit, either good or evil. For the woman I am sure, never heard divine things treated of in the *manner* she now viewed them in; and it would seem strange she should get such a *rational* notion of them from the *mere* working of her own fancy, without some superior, or at least foreign aid.—And yet I must say, I have looked upon it as one of the glories of this work of grace among the Indians, and a *special* evidence of its being from a divine influence, that there has, till now, been no appearance of such things, no visionary notions, trances, and imaginations intermixed with those rational convictions of sin, and solid consolations, that numbers have been made the subjects of. And might I have had my desire, there

there had been no appearance of any thing of this nature at all.

December 28. Discoursed to my people in the catechetical method I lately entered upon. And in the improvement of my discourse, wherein I was comparing man's *present* with his *primitive* state; and shewing what he had fallen from, and the miseries he is now involved in, and exposed to in his natural estate; and pressing sinners to take a view of their deplorable circumstances without Christ; as also to strive that they might obtain an interest in him; the Lord, I trust, granted a remarkable influence of his blessed Spirit to accompany what was spoken, and there was a great concern appeared in the assembly: many were melted into tears and sobs, and the impressions made upon them seemed *deep* and heart-affecting. And in particular, there were two or three persons who appeared to be brought to the last exercises of a *preparatory* work, and reduced almost to extremity; being in a great measure convinced of the impossibility of their helping themselves, or of mending their own hearts; and seemed to be upon the *point* of giving up all hope *in themselves*, and of venturing upon Christ as naked, helpless, and *undone*. And yet were in distress and anguish because they saw no safety in so doing, unless they could do *something* towards saving themselves.

One of these persons was the very aged woman above mentioned, who now appeared "weary and heavy laden" with a sense of her sin and misery, and her perishing need of an interest in Christ.

Lord's day, December 29. Preached from John iii. 1.—5. A number of white people were present, as is usual upon the Sabbath. The discourse was accompanied with power, and seemed to have a *silent*, but *deep* and *piercing* influence upon the audience. Many wept and sobed affectionately. And there were some tears among the white people, as well as the Indians. Some could not refrain from crying *out*, though there were not many so exercised. But the impressions made upon their hearts, appeared chiefly by the extraordinary earnestness of their attention, and their heavy sighs and tears.

After public worship was over, I went to my house, proposing to preach again after a short season of intermission. But they soon came in one after another, with tears in their eyes, to know "what they should do to be saved." And the divine Spirit in such a manner set home upon their hearts what I spoke to them, that the house was soon filled with cries,

cries, and groans.——They all flocked together upon this occasion, and those whom I had reason to think in a Christless state, were almost universally seized with concern for their souls.

It was an amazing season of *power* among them, and seemed as if God had "bowed the heavens, and come down." So astonishingly prevalent was the operation upon *old* as well as young, that it seemed as if none would be left in a secure and natural state, but that God was now about to convert *all the world*. And I was ready to think *then*, that I should never again despair of the conversion of any man or woman living, be they *who* or *what* they would.

It is impossible to give a just and lively description of the appearance of things at this season, at least *such* as to convey a bright and adequate idea of the effects of this influence. A number might now be seen rejoicing that God had not taken away the powerful influence of his blessed Spirit from this place.——Refreshed to see so many "striving to enter in "at the strait gate;"—and animated with such concern for them, that they wanted "to push them forward," as some of them expressed it.——At the same time numbers both of men and women, old and young, might be seen in tears, and some in anguish of spirit, appearing in their very countenances, like condemned malefactors bound towards the place of execution, with a heavy solicitude sitting in their faces: so that there seemed here (as I thought) a lively emblem of the solemn day of accounts: a mixture of heaven and hell; of joy unspeakable, and anguish inexpressible.

The concern and religious affection was *such*, that I could not pretend to have any *formal* religious exercise among them; but spent the time in discoursing to one and another, as I thought most proper, and seasonable for each, and sometimes addressed them all together, and finally concluded with prayer. ——*Such* were their circumstances at this season, that I could scarce have *half an hour's* rest from speaking from about half an hour before twelve o'clock, (at which time I began public worship), till past *seven* at night.

There appeared to be four or five persons newly awakened this day and the evening before, some of whom but very lately came among us.

December 30. Was visited by four or five young persons under concern for their souls, most of whom were very lately awakened. They wept much while I discoursed to them, and endeavoured to press upon them the necessity of *flying* to Christ, without delay, for salvation.

December 31. Spent ſome hours this day in viſiting my people from houſe to houſe, and converſing with them about their ſpiritual concerns; endeavouring to preſs upon Chriſtleſs ſouls the neceſſity of a renovation of heart: and ſcarce left a houſe, without leaving ſome or other of its inhabitants in tears, appearing ſolicitouſly engaged to obtain an intereſt in Chriſt.

The Indians are now gathered together from all quarters to this place, and have built them little cottages, ſo that more than *twenty* families live within a quarter of a mile of me. A very convenient ſituation in regard both of public and private inſtruction.

January 1. 1745-6. Spent ſome conſiderable time in viſiting my people again. Found ſcarce one but what was under ſome ſerious impreſſions reſpecting their ſpiritual concerns.

January 2. Viſited ſome perſons newly come among us, who had ſcarce ever heard any thing of Chriſtianity (except the empty name) before. Endeavoured to inſtruct them *particularly* in the firſt principles of religion, in the moſt eaſy and familiar manner I could.

There are ſtrangers from remote parts almoſt continually dropping in among us, ſo that I have occaſion repeatedly to open and inculcate the *firſt principles* of Chriſtianity.

January 4. Proſecuted my catechetical method of inſtructing.——Found my people able to anſwer queſtions with propriety, beyond what could have been expected from perſons ſo lately brought out of Heatheniſh darkneſs.

In the improvement of my diſcourſe, there appeared ſome concern and affection in the aſſembly: and eſpecially thoſe of whom I entertained hopes as being truly gracious, at leaſt divers of them were much affected and refreſhed.

Lord's day, January 5. Diſcourſed from Matth. xii. 10. to 13. There appeared not ſo much livelineſs and affection in divine ſervice as uſual. The ſame truths that have often produced many tears and ſobs in the aſſembly, ſeemed now to have no *ſpecial* influence upon any in it.

Near night I propoſed to have proceeded in my uſual method of catechiſing. But while we were engaged in the firſt prayer, the power of God ſeemed to deſcend upon the aſſembly in ſuch a remarkable manner, and ſo many appeared under preſſing concern for their ſouls, that I thought it much more expedient to inſiſt upon the plentiful proviſion made by divine grace for the redemption of periſhing ſinners, and to preſs them to a *ſpeedy* acceptance of the *great ſalvation*, than to aſk them queſtions about *doctrinal* points. What was moſt

practical,

practical, seemed most *seasonable* to be insisted upon, while numbers appeared so extraordinarily solicitous to obtain an interest in the great Redeemer.

Baptized two persons this day; one adult (the woman particularly mentioned in my Journal of December 22.) and one child.

This woman has discovered a very sweet and heavenly frame of mind, from time to time, since her first reception of comfort. One morning in particular she came to see me, discovering an unusual joy and satisfaction in her countenance; and when I inquired into the reason of it, she replied, "That "God had made her feel that it was *right* for him to do what "he pleased with all things; and that it would be right if he "should cast her husband and son both into hell; and she saw "it was so right for God to do what he pleased with them, "that she could not but rejoice if God should send them into "hell;" though it was apparent she loved them dearly. She moreover inquired, whether I was not sent to preach to the Indians, by some good people a great way off. I replied, Yes, by the good people in Scotland. She answered, that her heart loved those good people so, the evening before, "that she could scarce help praying for them all night, her "heart would go to God for them," *&c.*; so that "the bless-"ing of those ready to perish is like to come upon those "pious persons who have communicated of their substance "to the propagation of the gospel."

January 11. Discoursed in a catechetical method, as usual of late. And having opened our *first parents* primitive apostacy from God, and our fall *in him*; I proceeded to improve my discourse, by shewing the necessity we stood in of an almighty Redeemer, and the *absolute* need every sinner has of an interest in his merits and mediation. There was some tenderness and affectionate concern appeared in the assembly.

Lord's day, January 12. Preached from Is. lv. 6. The word of God seemed to fall upon the audience with a divine weight and influence, and evidently appeared to be "not the "word of man." The blessed Spirit, I am persuaded, accompanied what was spoken to the hearts of many. So that there was a powerful revival of conviction in numbers who were under spiritual exercise before.

Toward night, catechised in my usual method. Near the close of my discourse, there appeared a great concern, and much affection in the audience. Which increased while I continued

tinued to invite them to come to an all-sufficient Redeemer for eternal salvation.

The Spirit of God seems, from time to time, to be striving with numbers of souls here. They are so frequently and repeatedly rouzed, that they seem unable at present to lull themselves asleep.

January 13. Was visited by divers persons under deep concern for their souls; one of whom was newly awakened.—It is a most agreeable work to treat with souls who are solicitously inquiring "what they shall do to be saved." And as we are never to "be weary in well-doing," so the obligation seems to be peculiarly strong when the work is so very desirable. And yet I must say, my health is so much impaired, and my spirits so wasted with my labours, and solitary manner of living, (there being no human creature in the house with me), that their repeated and almost incessant application to me for help and direction, are sometimes exceeding burdensome, and so exhaust my spirits, that I become fit for nothing at all, entirely unable to prosecute any business sometimes for days together. And what contributes much toward this difficulty is, that I am obliged to spend *much* time in communicating a *little* matter to them; there being oftentimes many things necessary to be premised, before I can speak directly to what I principally aim at; which things would readily be taken for granted, where there was a competency of doctrinal knowledge.

January 14. Spent some time in private conferences with my people, and found some disposed to take comfort, as I thought, upon slighty grounds.——They are now generally awakened, and it is become so disgraceful, as well as terrifying to the conscience, to be destitute of religion, that they are in eminent danger of taking up with any *appearances* of grace, rather than to live under the fear and disgrace of an unregenerate state.

January 18. Prosecuted my catechetical method of discoursing. There appeared a great solemnity, and some considerable affection in the assembly.

This method of instructing I find very profitable. When I first entered upon it, I was exercised with fears, lest my discourses would unavoidably be so *doctrinal*, that they would tend only to enlighten the *head*, but not to *affect* the *heart*. But the *event* proves quite otherwise; for these exercises have hitherto been remarkably blessed in the *latter*, as well as the *former* respects.

Lord's day, January 19. Discoursed to my people from Is.

lv.

Nov. 7.—Toward night catechised in my ordinary method. And this appeared to be a powerful season of grace among us. Numbers were much affected.—Convictions powerfully revived.—Divers of the Christians refreshed and strengthened. —And one weary *heavy laden* soul, I have abundant reason to hope, brought to true rest and solid comfort in Christ, who afterwards gave me such an account of God's dealing with his soul, as was abundantly *satisfying*, as well as *refreshing* to me.

He told me, he had often heard me say, that persons must *see* and *feel* themselves utterly helpless and *undone;* that they must be emptied of a dependance upon themselves, and of all hope of saving themselves by their *own doings*, in order to their coming to Christ for salvation. And he had long been striving after this view of things; supposing this would be an excellent frame of mind to be thus emptied of a dependance upon his own goodness: that God would have respect to *this* frame, would *then* be well pleased with him, and bestow eternal life upon him.——But when he came to feel himself in this helpless *undone* condition, he found it quite contrary to all his thoughts and expectations; so that it was not the *same*, nor indeed any thing *like* the frame he had been seeking after. Instead of its being a *good* frame of mind, he now found nothing but *badness* in himself, and saw it was for ever impossible for him to make himself any better. He wondered, he said, that he had ever hoped to mend his own heart. He was amazed he had never *before* seen that it was utterly impossible for him, by all his contrivances and endeavours, to do any thing *that way*, since the matter *now* appeared to him in so clear a light.——Instead of imagining now, that God would be pleased with him for the sake of this frame of mind, and this view of his *undone* estate, he saw clearly, and felt it would be just with God to send him to eternal misery; and that there was *no goodness* in what he then felt; for he could not help seeing, that he was naked, sinful, and miserable, and there was nothing in such a sight to deserve God's love or pity.

He saw these things in a manner so clear and convincing, that it seemed to him, he said, he could convince every body of their utter *inability* ever to help themselves, and their *unworthiness* of any help from God.

In *this* frame of mind he came to public worship this evening, and while I was inviting sinners to come to Christ naked and empty, without *any* goodness of *their own* to recommend them to his acceptance; then he thought with himself, that he had often tried to come and give up his heart to Christ, and he he used to hope, that some time or other he should be *able to* do so. But now he was convinced *he could not*, and it seemed utterly vain for him ever to try *any more:* and he could not, he said, find a heart to make any further attempt, because he saw it would signify *nothing at all:* nor did he now hope for a better opportunity, or more *ability* hereafter, as he had formerly done, because he saw, and was fully convinced, his own strength would for ever fail.

While he was musing in this manner, he saw, he said, with his heart (which is a common phrase among them) something that was unspeakably good and lovely, and what he had never seen before; and "this stole away his heart whether he "would or no." He did not, he said, know what it was he saw. He did not say, "this is Jesus Christ;" but it was such glory and beauty as he never saw before. He did not now give away his heart *so* as he had formerly intended and attempted to do, but it *went away of itself* after that glory he then discovered. He used to try to make a bargain with Christ, to give up his heart to him, that he might have eternal life *for it*. But now he thought nothing about himself, or what would become of him hereafter; but was pleased, and his mind wholly taken up with the unspeakable excellency of what he then beheld.

After some time he was wonderfully pleased with the way of salvation by Christ: so that it seemed unspeakably better to be saved altogether by the *mere free grace* of God in Christ, than to have *any hand* in saving himself.——And the consequence of this exercise is, that he appears to retain a sense and relish of divine things, and to maintain a life of seriousness and true religion.

January 28. The Indians in these parts having in times past run themselves in debt by their excessive drinking; and some having taken the advantage of them, and put them to trouble and charge by arresting sundry of them; whereby it was supposed a great body of their hunting lands were much endangered, and might speedily be taken from them. And I being sensible that they could not subsist together in these parts, in order to their being a Christian congregation, if these lands should drop out of their hands, which was thought very likely, thought it my duty to use my utmost endeavours to prevent so unhappy an event. And having acquainted the gentlemen concerned with this *mission* of this affair, according to the best information I could get of it, they thought it proper to expend the money they had been, and still were collecting for the *religious* interests of the Indians, (at least a part of it), for

for the discharging of their debts, and securing of these lands, that there might be no entanglement lying upon them to hinder the settlement and hopeful enlargement of a *Christian congregation* of Indians in these parts.——And having received orders from them, I answered, in behalf of the Indians, *Eighty-two pounds five shillings*, New-Jersey currency, at *eight shillings per* ounce; and so prevented the danger of difficulty in this respect.

As God has wrought a wonderful *work of grace* among these Indians, and now inclines others from remote places to fall in among them almost continually; and as he has opened a door for the prevention of the difficulty now mentioned, which seemed greatly to threaten their religious interests, as well as worldly comfort; it is hopeful he designs to establish a *church* for himself among them, and to hand down true religion to their *posterity*.

January 30. Preached to the Indians from John iii. 16. 17. There was a solemn attention and some affection visible in the audience; especially divers persons who had long been concerned for their souls, seemed afresh excited and engaged in seeking after an interest in Christ. And one, with much concern, afterwards told me, "his heart was so pricked with "my preaching, he knew not where to turn, nor what to "do."

January 31. This day the person I had made choice of and engaged for a *schoolmaster* among the Indians, arrived among us, and was heartily welcomed by my people universally.——Whereupon I distributed several dozen of *primers* among the children and young people.

February 1. 1745-6. My schoolmaster entered upon his business among the Indians.——He has generally about thirty children and young persons in his school in the day-time, and about *fifteen* married people in his evening-school. The number of the latter sort of persons being less than it would be, if they could be more constant at home, and spare time from their necessary employments for an attendance upon these instructions.

In the evening catechised in my usual method. Towards the close of my discourse, a surprising power seemed to attend the word, especially to some persons.—One man considerably in years, who had been a remarkable drunkard, a conjurer and murderer, that was awakened some months before, was now brought to great extremity under his spiritual distress, so that he trembled for hours together, and apprehended himself just dropping into hell, without any power to rescue or relieve himself.—Divers others appeared under great concern as well as he, and solicitous to obtain a saving change.

Lord's day, February 2. Preached from John v. 24. 25. There appeared (as usual) some concern and affection in the assembly.

Toward night proceeded in my usual method of catechising. Observed my people more ready in answering the questions proposed to them than ever before. It is apparent they advance daily in *doctrinal* knowledge. But what is still more desirable, the Spirit of God is yet operating among them, whereby *experimental*, as well as *speculative* knowledge is propagated in their minds.

February 5. Discoursed to a considerable number of the Indians in the evening; at which time divers of them appeared much affected and melted with divine things.

February 8. Spent a considerable part of the day in visiting my people from house to house, and conversing with them about their souls concerns. Divers persons wept while I discoursed to them, and appeared concerned for nothing so much as for an interest in the great Redeemer.

In the evening catechised as usual. Divine truths made some impression upon the audience, and were attended with an affectionate engagement of soul in some.

Lord's day, February 9. Discoursed to my people from the story of the blind man, Matth. x. 46.—52. The word of God seemed weighty and powerful upon the assembly at this time, and made considerable impressions upon many; divers in particular who have generally been remarkably stupid and careless under the means of grace, were now awakened, and wept affectionately. And the most earnest attention, as well as tenderness and affection, appeared in the audience universally.

Baptized three persons, two adults and one child. The adults, I have reason to hope, were both truly pious. There was a considerable melting in the assembly, while I was discoursing particularly to the persons, and administering the ordinance.

God has been pleased to own and bless the administration of *this*, as well as of his other *ordinances*, among the Indians. There are some here that have been powerfully awakened at seeing others baptized. And some that have obtained relief and comfort, just in the season when this ordinance has been administered.

Toward night catechised. God made this a powerful season to some. There were many affected.——Former convictions

victions appeared to be powerfully revived. There was likewise one, who had been a vile drunkard, remarkably awakened. He appeared to be in great anguish of soul, wept and trembled, and continued so to do till near midnight.——There was also a poor *heavy laden* soul, who had been long under spiritual distress, as constant and pressing as ever I saw, that was now brought to a comfortable *calm*, and seemed to be bowed and reconciled to divine *sovereignty;* and told me, "She now saw and felt it was right God should do with her "as he pleased. And her heart felt pleased and satisfied it "should be so." Although of late she had often found her heart rise and quarrel with God because he would, *if he pleased*, send her to hell after all she had done, or could do to save herself, *&c.* And added, that the *heavy burden* she had lain under, was now removed: that she had tried to recover her concern and distress again, (fearing that the Spirit of God was departing from her, and would leave her wholly careless), but that she could not recover it: that she felt she never could do any thing to save herself, but must perish for ever if Christ did not *do all* for her: that she did not deserve he should help her; and that it would be *right* if he should leave her to perish. But Christ could save her, though she could *do nothing* to save herself, *&c.* And here she seemed to rest.

Forks of Delaware in Pennsylvania, 1745-6.

Lord's day, February 16. I knowing that divers of the Indians in those parts were obstinately set against Christianity, and that some of them had refused to hear me preach in times past, thought it might be proper and beneficial to the Christian interest here, to have a number of my religious people from Crosweeksung with me, in order to converse with them about religious matters; hoping it might be a means to convince them of the truth and importance of Christianity, to see and hear some of their own nation discoursing of divine things, and manifesting earnest desires that others might be brought out of Heathenish darkness, as themselves were.

And having taken *half a dozen* of the most serious and knowing persons for this purpose, I this day met with them and the Indians of this place, (sundry of whom probably could not have been prevailed upon to attend the meeting, had it not been for these religious Indians that accompanied me here), and preached to them.——Some of them who had, in times past, been extremely averse to Christianity, now behaved

haved soberly, and some others laughed and mocked. However the word of God fell with such weight and power, that sundry seemed to be stunned, and expressed a willingness to "hear me again of these matters."

Afterwards prayed with, and made an address to the white people present, and could not but observe some visible effects of the word, such as tears and sobs, among them.

After public worship, spent some time and took pains to convince those that mocked, of the truth and importance of what I had been insisting upon; and so endeavoured to awaken their attention to divine truths. And had reason to think, from what I observed then and afterwards, that my endeavours took considerable effect upon one of the worst of them.

Those few Indians then present, who used to be my hearers in these parts, (some having removed from hence to Crosweeksung), seemed somewhat kindly disposed toward, and glad to see me again, although they had been so much attacked by some of the opposing Pagans, that they were almost ashamed or afraid to manifest their friendship.

February 17. After having spent much time in discoursing to the Indians in their respective houses, I got them together, and repeated and inculcated what I had before taught them.——

Afterwards discoursed to them from Acts viii. 5.—8. A divine influence seemed to attend the word. Sundry of the Indians here appeared to be somewhat awakened, and manifested a concern of mind, by their earnest attention, tears and sobs. My people from Crosweeksung continued with them day and night, repeating and inculcating the truths I had taught them: and sometimes prayed and sung psalms among them; discoursing with each other, in their hearing, of the great things God had done for *them*, and for the Indians from whence they came: which seemed (as my people told me) to take more effect upon them, than when they directed their discourses immediately to them.

February 18. Preached to an assembly of Irish people near fifteen miles distant from the Indians.

February 19. Preached to the Indians again, after having spent considerable time in conversing with them more privately. There appeared a great solemnity, and some concern and affection among the Indians belonging to these parts, as well as a sweet melting among those who came with me.—— Divers of the Indians here seemed to have their prejudices and

and aversion to Christianity removed, and appeared well disposed and inclined to hear the word of God.

February 20. Preached to a small assembly of High-Dutch people, who had seldom heard the gospel preached, and were (some of them at least) very ignorant; but have divers of them lately been put upon an inquiry after the way of salvation, with some thoughtfulness. They gave wonderful attention, and some of them were much affected under the word, and afterwards said, (as I was informed), that they never had been so much enlightened about the way of salvation in their whole lives before. They requested me to tarry with them, or come again and preach to them. And it grieved me that I could not comply with their request, for I could not but be affected with their circumstances; they being as "sheep not "having a shepherd," and some of them appearing under some degree of soul-trouble, standing in peculiar need of the assistance of an *experienced* spiritual guide.

February 21. Preached to a number of people, many of them Low-Dutch. Sundry of the fore-mentioned High-Dutch attended the sermon, though *eight* or *ten* miles distant from their houses.——Divers of the Indians also belonging to these parts, came of their own accord with my people (from Crosweeksung) to the meeting. And there were two in particular, who, the last Sabbath, opposed and ridiculed Christianity, that were now present and behaved soberly. May the present encouraging appearance continue.

February 22. Preached to the Indians. They appeared more free from prejudice, and more cordial to Christianity than before. And some of them appeared affected with divine truths.

Lord's day, February 23. Preached to the Indians from John vi. 35.—37.—After public service, discoursed particularly with sundry of them, and invited them to go down to Crosweeksung, and tarry there at least for some time; knowing they would then be free from the scoffs and temptations of the opposing Pagans, as well as *in the way* of hearing divine truths discoursed of, both in public and private. And got a promise of some of them, that they would speedily pay us a visit, and attend some further instructions. They seemed to be considerably enlightened, and much freed from their prejudices against Christianity. But it is much to be feared their prejudices will revive again, unless they could enjoy the means of instruction here, or be removed where they might be under such advantages, and out of the way of their Pagan acquaintance.

Crosweeksung in New-Jersey, 1745-6.

March 1. Catechised in my ordinary method. Was pleased and refreshed to see them answer the questions proposed to them with such remarkable readiness, discretion, and knowledge.

Toward the close of my discourse, divine truths made considerable impressions upon the audience, and produced tears and sobs in some under concern; and more especially a sweet and humble melting in sundry that, I have reason to hope, were truly gracious.

Lord's day, March 2. Preached from John xv. 1.—6.—— The assembly appeared not so lively in their attention as usual, nor so much affected with divine truths in general as has been common.

Some of my people who went up to the Forks of Delaware with me, being now returned, were accompanied by two of the Indians belonging to the Forks, who had promised me a speedy visit. May the Lord meet with them here. They can scarce go into a house now, but they will meet with Christian conversation, whereby, it is hopeful, they may be both instructed and awakened.

Discoursed to the Indians again in the afternoon, and observed among them some liveliness and engagement in divine service, though not equal to what has often appeared here.

I know of no assembly of Christians, where there seems to be so much of the presence of God, where brotherly love so much prevails, and where I should take so much delight in the public worship of God, in the general, as in my *own congregation*: although not more than nine months ago, they were worshipping *devils* and *dumb idols* under the power of Pagan darkness and superstition. Amazing change this! effected by nothing less than divine power and grace! "This is the " doing of the Lord, and it is justly marvellous in our eyes!

March 5. Spent some time just at evening in prayer, singing, and discoursing to my people upon divine things; and observed some agreeable tenderness and affection among them.

Their present situation is so compact and commodious, that they are easily and quickly called together with only the sound of a Conk-shell, (a shell like that of a Perwinkle), so that they have frequent opportunities of attending religious exercises publicly; which seems to be a great means, under God,

God, of keeping alive the impressions of divine things in their minds.

March 8. Catechised in the evening. My people answered the questions proposed to them well. I can perceive their knowledge in religion increases daily.——And what is still more desirable, the divine influence that has been so remarkable among them, appears still to continue in some good measure. The divine presence seemed to be in the assembly this evening. Some, who I have good reason to think are Christians *indeed*, were melted with a sense of the divine goodness, and their own barrenness and ingratitude, and seemed to *hate themselves*, as one of them afterwards expressed it.——Convictions also appeared to be revived in several instances; and divine truths were attended with such influence upon the assembly in general, that it might justly be called, "an evening "of divine power."

Lord's day, March 9. Preached from Luke x. 38.—42.—The word of God was attended with power and energy upon the audience. Numbers were affected and concerned to obtain the *one thing needful*. And sundry that have given good evidences of being truly gracious, were much affected with a sense of their want of spirituality; and saw the need they stood in of *growing in grace*. And most that had been under any impressions of divine things in times past, seemed now to have those impressions revived.

In the afternoon proposed to have catechised in my usual method. But while we were engaged in the first prayer in the Indian language, (as usual), a great part of the assembly was so much moved, and affected with divine things, that I thought it seasonable and proper to omit the proposing of questions for that time, and insist upon the most practical truths. And accordingly did so; making a further improvement of the passage of scripture I discoursed upon in the former part of the day.

There appeared to be a powerful divine influence in the congregation. Sundry that I have reason to think are truly pious, were so deeply affected with a sense of their own *barrenness*, and their unworthy treatment of the blessed Redeemer, that they *looked on him as pierced* by themselves, *and mourned*, yea, some of them were *in bitterness as for a firstborn*.—Some poor awakened sinners also appeared to be in anguish of soul to obtain an interest in Christ. So that there was *a great mourning* in the assembly: many heavy groans, sobs, and tears! and one or two persons newly come among us, were considerably awakened.

Methinks

Methinks it would have refreshed the heart of any who truly love Zion's interest, to have been in the midst of this divine influence, and seen the effects of it upon saints and sinners. The place of divine worship appeared both *solemn* and *sweet!* and was so endeared by a display of the divine presence and grace, that those who had any relish of divine things, could not but cry, "How amiable are thy tabernacles, O Lord "of hosts!"

After public worship was over, numbers came to my house, where we sang and discoursed of divine things; and the presence of God seemed here also to be in the midst of us.

While we were singing, there was one (the woman mentioned in my Journal of February 9.) who, I may venture to say, if I may be allowed to say so much of any person I ever saw, was "filled with joy unspeakable and full of glory," and could not but burst forth in prayer and praises to God before us all, with many tears, crying sometimes in English and sometimes in Indian, "O blessed Lord, do come, do "come! O do take me away, do let me die and go to Jesus "Christ! I am afraid if I live I shall sin again! O do let me "die now! O dear Jesus, do come! I cannot stay, I cannot "stay! O how can I live in this world! do take my soul a-"way from this sinful place! O let me never sin any more! "O what shall I do, what shall I do! dear Jesus, O dear "Jesus," *&c.*——In this ecstasy she continued some time, uttering these and such like expressions incessantly.—And the grand argument she used with God to take her away immediately, was, that "if she lived, she should sin against "him."

When she had a little recovered herself, I asked her, if Christ was not now sweet to her soul? Whereupon, turning to me with tears in her eyes, and with all the tokens of deep humility I ever saw in any person, she said, "I have many "times heard you speak of the goodness and the sweetness "of Christ, that he was better than all the world. But O! "I knew nothing what you meant, I never believed you! I "never believed you! But now I know it is true!" Or words to that effect.—I answered, And do you see enough in Christ for the greatest of sinners? She replied, "O! enough, e-"nough! for all the sinners in the world if they would but "come." And when I asked her, if she could not tell them of the goodness of Christ; turning herself about to some poor Christless souls who stood by, and were much affected, she said, "O! there is enough in Christ for you, if you would "but come! O strive, strive to give up your hearts to him!" *&c.*—

&c.—And upon hearing something of the glory of heaven mentioned, that there was no sin in that world, &c. she again fell into the same ecstasy of joy, and desire of Christ's coming; repeating her former expressions, "O dear Lord, "do let me go! O what shall I do, what shall I do! I want "to go to Christ! I cannot live! O do let me die!" &c.

She continued in this sweet frame for more than two hours, before she was well able to get home.

I am very sensible there may be great joys arising even to an ecstasy, where there is still no substantial evidence of their being well-grounded. But in the present case there seemed to be no evidence wanting, in order to prove this joy to be divine, either in regard of its preparatives, attendants, or consequents.

Of all the persons I have seen under spiritual exercise, I scarce ever saw one appear more bowed and broken under convictions of sin and misery (or what is usually called a *preparatory work*) than this woman. Nor scarce any who seemen to have a greater acquaintance with her own heart than she had. She would frequently complain to me of the hardness and rebellion of her heart. Would tell me, her heart rose and quarrelled with God, when she thought he would do with her as he pleased, and send her to hell notwithstanding her prayers, good frames, &c. That her heart was not willing to come to Christ for salvation, but tried every where else for help.

And as she seemed to be remarkably sensible of her stubbornness and contrariety to God, under conviction, so she appeared to be no less remarkably bowed and reconciled to divine *sovereignty* before she obtained any relief or comfort. Something of which I have before noticed in my Journal of February 9. Since which time she has seemed constantly to breathe the spirit and temper of the new creature: crying after Christ, not through fear of *hell* as before, but with strong desires after him as her only satisfying *portion;* and has many times wept and sobbed bitterly, because (as she apprehended) she did not and could not love him.—When I have sometimes asked her, Why she appeared so sorrowful, and whether it was because she was afraid of hell? She would answer, "No, I be not distressed about *that*; but my heart is "so wicked I *cannot love* Christ;" and thereupon burst out into tears.—But although this has been the habitual frame of her mind for several weeks together, so that the exercise of grace appeared evident to *others*, yet *she* seemed wholly insensible

sensible of it herself, and never had any remarkable comfort, and sensible satisfaction till this evening.

This sweet and surprising ecstasy, appeared to *spring* from a true *spiritual* discovery of the glory, ravishing beauty and excellency of Christ: and not from any *gross* imaginary notions of his human nature; such as that of seeing him in *such* a place or posture, as hanging on the cross, as bleeding, dying, as gently smiling, and the like; which delusions some have been carried away with. Nor did it rise from a *sordid, selfish* apprehension of *her* having any benefit whatsoever conferred on her, but from a view of his *personal* excellency, and *transcendent* loveliness, which drew forth those vehement desires of enjoying him she now manifested, and made her long "to be absent from the body, that she might be present with "the Lord."

The *attendants* of this ravishing comfort, were such as abundantly discovered its spring to be divine, and that it was truly a "joy in the Holy Ghost."——*Now* she viewed divine truths as *living realities*; and could say, "I know these things "are so, I feel they are true!"——*Now* her soul was resigned to the divine will in the most tender points; so that when I said to her, What if God should take away your * husband from you, (who was then very sick), how do you think you could bear that? She replied, "He belongs to God, and not to "me; he may do with him just what he pleases."——*Now* she had the most tender sense of the evil of sin, and discovered the utmost aversion to it; longing to die that she might be delivered from it.——*Now* she could freely trust her *all* with God for time and eternity. And when I queried with her, how she could be willing to die, and leave her little infant; and what she thought would become of it in case she should? She answered, "God will take care of it. It belongs to him, "he will take care of it."——*Now* she appeared to have the most humbling sense of her own meanness and unworthiness, her weakness and inability to preserve herself from sin, and to persevere in the way of holiness, crying, "If I live, I "shall sin." And I then thought I had never seen such an appearance of *ecstasy* and *humility* meeting in any one person in all my life before.

The consequents of this joy are no less desirable and satisfactory than its attendants. She since appears to be a most tender, broken-hearted, affectionate, devout, and humble Christian, as exemplary in life and conversation as any person

* The man particularly mentioned in my Journal of January 19.

in

in my congregation. May ſhe ſtill "grow in grace, and in "the knowledge of Chriſt."

March 10. Toward night the Indians met together of their own accord, and ſang, prayed, and diſcourſed of divine things among themſelves. At which time there was much affection among them. Some who are hopefully gracious, appeared to be melted with divine things. And ſome others ſeemed much concerned for their ſouls.——Perceiving their engagement and affection in religious exerciſes, I went among them, and prayed, and gave a word of exhortation; and obſerved two or three ſomewhat affected and concerned, who ſcarce ever appeared to be under any religious impreſſions before. It ſeemed to be a day and evening of divine power. Numbers retained the warm impreſſions of divine things that had been made upon their minds the day before.

March 14. Was viſited by a conſiderable number of my people, and ſpent ſome time in religious exerciſes with them.

March 15. In the evening catechiſed. My people anſwered the queſtions put to them with ſurpriſing readineſs and judgment. There appeared ſome warmth and feeling ſenſe of divine things among thoſe, I have reaſon to hope, are *real* Chriſtians, while I was diſcourſing upon "peace of conſcience, and joy in the Holy Ghoſt." *Theſe* ſeemed quickened and enlivened in divine ſervice, though there was not ſo much appearance of concern among thoſe I have reaſon to think in a Chriſtleſs ſtate.

Lord's day, March 16. Preached to my congregation from Heb. ii. 1.—3. Divine truths ſeemed to have ſome conſiderable influence upon many of the hearers; and produced many tears, as well as heavy ſighs and ſobs among both thoſe who have given evidences of being real Chriſtians, and others alſo. And the impreſſions made upon the audience, appeared in general *deep* and heart-affecting, not ſuperficial, *noiſy*, and affected.

Toward night diſcourſed again on the *great ſalvation.* The word was again attended with ſome power upon the audience. Numbers wept affectionately, and, to appearance, *unfeignedly;* ſo that the Spirit of God ſeemed to be *moving upon the face* of the aſſembly.

Baptized the *woman* particularly mentioned in my Journal of laſt Lord's day; who now, as well as then, appeared to be in a devout, humble, and excellent frame of mind.

My houſe being thronged with my people in the evening, I ſpent the time in religious exerciſes with them, till my nature was almoſt ſpent.——They are ſo unwearied in religious exercises, and unsatiable in their thirsting after *Christian knowledge*, that I can sometimes scarce avoid labouring so, as greatly to exhaust my strength and spirits.

March 19. Sundry of the persons that went with me to the Forks of Delaware in February last, having been detained there by the *dangerous* illness of one of their company, returned home but this day. Whereupon my people generally met together of their own accord, in order to spend some time in religious exercises; and in special to give thanks to God for his preserving goodness to those who had been absent from them for several weeks, and recovering mercy to him that had been sick; and that he had now returned them all in safety. I being then absent, they desired my schoolmaster to assist them in carrying on their religious solemnity; who tells me they appeared engaged and affectionate in repeated prayer, singing, &c.

March 22. Catechised in my usual method in the evening.— My people answered questions to my great satisfaction. There appeared nothing very remarkable in the assembly, considering what has been common among us. Although I may justly say, the strict attention, the tenderness and affection, the many tears, and heart-affecting sobs appearing in numbers in the assembly would have been *very remarkable*, were it not that God has made these things *common* with us, and even with *strangers* soon after their coming among us, from time to time. Although I am far from thinking that every *appearance*, and particular instance of affection, that has been among us, has been truly genuine, and *purely* from a divine influence. I am sensible of the contrary; and doubt not, but that there has been some *corrupt mixtures*, some chaff as well as wheat, especially since religious concern became so common and prevalent here.

Lord's day, March 23. There being about fifteen *strangers*, adult persons, come among us in the *week* past; divers of whom had never been in any religious meeting till now, I thought it proper to discourse this day in a manner peculiarly suited to their circumstances and capacities: and accordingly attempted it from Hos. xiii. 9.; in the forenoon opening in the plainest manner I could, man's apostacy and ruined state, after having spoken some things respecting the being and perfections of God, and his creation of man in a state of uprightness and happiness. In the afternoon, endeavoured to open the glorious provision God has made for the redemption of apostate creatures, by giving his own dear Son to suffer for them, and satisfy divine justice on their behalf.

There

There was not that affection and concern in the assembly that has been common among us, although there was a desirable attention appearing in general, and even in most of the *strangers*.

Near sun-set I felt an uncommon concern upon my mind, especially for the poor *strangers*, that God had so much withheld his presence, and the powerful influence of his Spirit, from the assembly in the exercises of the day; and thereby denied them of that matter of conviction which I hoped they might have had. And in this frame I visited sundry houses, and discoursed with some concern and affection to divers persons particularly; but without much appearance of success, till I came to a house where divers of the strangers were; and there the solemn truths I discoursed of appeared to take *effect*, first upon some *children*, then upon divers *adult* persons that had been somewhat awakened before, and afterwards upon several of the Pagan *strangers*.

I continued my discourse, with some fervency, till almost every one in the house was melted into tears; and divers wept aloud, and appeared earnestly concerned to obtain an interest in Christ. Upon this, numbers soon gathered from all the houses round about, and so thronged the place, that we were obliged to remove to the house where we usually meet for public worship. And the congregation gathering immediately, and many appearing remarkably affected, I discoursed some time from Luke xix. 10. Endeavouring to open the mercy, compassion, and concern of Christ for *lost*, *helpless*, and *undone* sinners.

There was much visible concern and affection in the assembly; and I doubt not but that a divine influence accompanied what was spoken to the hearts of many. There were five or six of the *strangers* (men and women) who appeared to be considerable awakened. And in particular one very rugged young man, who seemed as if nothing would move him, was now brought to tremble like the jailor, and weep for a long time.

The Pagans that were awakened seemed at once to put off their *savage* roughness and Pagan manners, and became sociable, orderly, and *humane* in their carriage. When they first came, I exhorted my religious people to take pains with them (as they had done with other strangers from time to time) to instruct them in Christianity. But when some of them attempted something of that nature, the strangers would soon rise up and walk to other houses, in order to avoid the hearing of such discourses. Whereupon some of the serious persons agreed to disperse themselves into the several parts of the settlement. So that where-ever the *strangers* went, they met with some instructive discourse, and warm addresses respecting their soul's concern.——But *now* there was no need of using policy in order to get an opportunity of conversing with some of them about their spiritual concerns: for they were so far touched with a sense of their perishing state, as made them *tamely* yield to the *closest* addresses that were made them, respecting their sin and misery, their need of an acquaintance with, and interest in the great Redeemer.

March 24. Numbered the Indians, to see how many souls God had gathered together here, since my coming into these parts; and found there was now about an *hundred and thirty* persons together, old and young. Sundry of those that are my stated hearers, perhaps to the number of *fifteen* or *twenty*, were absent at this season. So that if all had been together, the number would now have been very considerable; especially considering how *few* were together at my first coming into these parts, the whole number not amounting to *ten* persons at that time.

My people going out this day upon the design of clearing some of their lands above fifteen miles distant from this settlement, in order to their settling there in a compact form, where they might be under advantages of attending the public worship of God, of having their children schooled, and at the same time have a conveniency for planting, &c.; their land in the place of our *present* residence being of little or no value for that purpose. And the design of their settling thus in a body, and cultivating their lands (which they have done very little at in their Pagan state) being of such necessity and importance to their religious interest, as well as worldly comfort, I thought it proper to call them together, and shew them the duty of labouring with faithfulness and industry; and that they must not now "be slothful in business," as they had ever been in their Pagan state. And endeavoured to press the importance of their being laborious, diligent, and vigorous in the prosecution of their business, especially at the present juncture, (the season of planting being now near), in order to their being in a capacity of living together, and enjoying the means of grace and instruction. And having given them directions for their work, (which they very much wanted, as well as for their behaviour in divers respects, I explained, sang, and endeavoured to inculcate upon them Psal. cxxvii. common metre, Dr Watts's version. And having recommended them,

and

and the design of their going forth, to God, by prayer with them, I dismissed them to their business.

In the evening read and expounded to my people (those of them who were yet at home, and the *strangers* newly come) the substance of the third chapter of the Acts. Numbers seemed to melt under the word, especially while I was discoursing upon vers. 19. Sundry of the *strangers* also were affected. ——When I asked them afterwards, whether they did not now feel that their *hearts* were *wicked*, as I had taught them? One replied, "Yes, she felt it now." Although before she came here, (upon hearing that I taught the Indians their hearts were all bad by nature, and needed to be changed and made good by the power of God), she had said, "Her heart "was not wicked, and she never had done any thing that "was bad in her life." And *this* indeed seems to be the case with them, I think, universally in their Pagan state.

They seem to have no *consciousness* of sin and guilt, unless they can charge themselves with some *gross acts* of sin contrary to the commands of the *second table*.

March 27. Discoursed to a number of my people in one of their houses in a more private manner. Enquired particularly into their spiritual states, in order to see what impressions of a religions nature they were under. Laid before them the marks and tokens of a *regenerate*, as well as *unregenerate* state: and endeavoured to suit and direct my discourse to them severally according as I apprehended their states to be.

There was a considerable number gathered together, before I finished my discourse; and divers seemed much affected, while I was urging the necessity and infinite importance of getting into a renewed state.——I find particular and close dealing with souls in private, is often very successful.

March 29. In the evening catechised as usual upon Saturday.—Treated upon the "benefits which believers receive from "Christ at death."——The questions were answered with great readiness and propriety. And those who, I have reason to think, are the dear people of God, were sweetly melted almost in general. There appeared such a liveliness and vigour in their attendance upon the word of God, and such eagerness to be made partakers of the *benefits* then mentioned, that they seemed to be not only "looking for, but ha-"sting to the coming of the day of God." Divine truths seemed to distil upon the audience with a gentle, but melting efficacy, as the refreshing "showers upon the new mown grass." The assembly in general, as well as those who appear truly religious,

religious, were affected with some brief account of the blessedness of the godly at death: and most then discovered an affectionate inclination to cry, "Let me die the death of the "righteous," &c. Although many were not duly engaged to obtain the change of heart that is necessary in order to that blessed end.

Lord's day, March 30. Discoursed from Matth. xxv. 31. to 40. There was a very considerable moving and affectionate melting in the assembly. I hope there were some real, deep, and abiding impressions of divine things made upon the minds of many.——There was one aged man newly come among us, who appeared to be considerably awakened, that never was touched with any concern for his soul before.

In the evening catechised. There was not that tenderness and melting engagement among God's people that appeared the evening before, and at many other times. Although they answered the *questions* distinctly and well, and were devout and attentive in divine service.

March 31. Called my people together, as I had done the Monday morning before, and discoursed to them again on the necessity and importance of their labouring industriously, in order to their living together, and enjoying the means of grace, &c. And having engaged in solemn prayer to God among them, for a blessing upon their attempts, I dismissed them to their work.

Numbers of them (both men and women) seemed to offer themselves willingly to this service; and some appeared affectionately concerned that God might go with them, and begin their *little town* for them; that by his blessing it might be a place comfortable for them and theirs, in regard both of procuring the necessaries of life, and of attending the worship of God.

April 5. 1746. Catechised towards evening. There appeared to be some affection and fervent engagement in divine service through the assembly in general; especially towards the conclusion of my discourse.

After public worship, a number of those I have reason to think are truly religious, came to my house, and seemed eager of some further entertainment upon divine things. And while I was conversing with them about their spiritual exercises, observing to them, that God's work in the hearts of all his children, was, for substance, the same; and that their trials and temptations were also alike; and shewing the obligations *such* were under to *love* one another in a peculiar manner, they seemed to be melted into tenderness and affection toward each other: and I thought that particular token of their being the *disciples* of Christ, *viz.* of their "having "love one toward another," had scarce ever appeared more evident than at this time.

Lord's day, April 6. Preached from Matth. vii. 21.—23. ——There were considerable effects of the word visible in the audience, and *such* as were very desirable: an earnest attention, a great solemnity, many tears and heavy sighs, which were modestly suppressed in a considerable measure, and appeared unaffected, and without any indecent commotion of the passions. Divers of the religious people were put upon serious and close examination of their spiritual states, by hearing that "not every one that saith to Christ, Lord, Lord, "shall enter into his kingdom." And some of them expressed fears least they had deceived themselves, and taken up a false hope, because they found they had done so little of the "will "of his Father who is in heaven."

There was also one man brought under very great and pressing concern for his soul; which appeared more especially after his *retirement* from public worship. And that which, he says, gave him his great uneasiness, was, not so much any particular sin, as that he had never done the will of God at *all*, but had sinned continually, and so had no claim to the kingdom of heaven.

In the afternoon I opened to them the *discipline* of Christ in his church, and the method in which *offenders* are to be dealt with. At which time the religious people were much affected, especially when they heard, that the offender continuing obstinate, must finally be esteemed and treated "as "an Heathen man," as a Pagan, that has no part nor lot among God's visible people. *This* they seemed to have the most awful apprehensions of; a state of Heathenism, out of which they were so lately brought, appearing very dreadful to them.

After public worship I visited sundry houses to see how they spent the remainder of the Sabbath, and to treat with them solemnly on the great concerns of their souls: and the Lord seemed to smile upon my private endeavours, and to make these particular and *personal* addresses more effectual upon some, than my public discourses.

April 7. Discoursed to my people at evening from 1 Cor. xi. 23. 26. And endeavoured to open to them the institution, nature, and ends of the Lord's supper, as well as the qualifications and preparations necessary to the right participation of that ordinance.——Sundry persons appeared much affected ed with the love of Christ manifested in his making this provision for the comfort of his people, at a season when himself was just entering upon his sharpest sufferings.

Lord's day, April 20. Discoursed both forenoon and afternoon from Luke xxiv. explaining most of the chapter, and making remarks upon it. There was a desirable attention in the audience, though there was not so much appearance of affection and tenderness among them as has been usual.—Our meeting was very full, there being sundry *strangers* present, who had never been with us before.

In the evening catechised. My people answered the questions proposed to them, readily and distinctly; and I could perceive they advanced in their knowledge of the *principles* of Christianity.

There appeared an affectionate melting in the assembly at this time. Sundry who, I trust, are truly religious, were refreshed and quickened, and seemed, by their discourse and behaviour, after public worship, to have their "hearts knit "together in love."——This was a sweet and blessed season, like many others, that my poor people have been favoured with in months past. God has caused *this little fleece* to be repeatedly wet with the blessed *dews* of his divine grace, while all the earth around has been comparatively dry.

April 25. Having of late apprehended that a number of persons in my congregation, were proper subjects of the ordinance of the *Lord's supper*, and that it might be *seasonable* speedily to administer it to them: and having taken advice of some of the reverend *correspondents* in this solemn affair; and accordingly having proposed and appointed the next Lord's day (with leave of divine providence) for the administration of this ordinance, this day, as preparatory thereto was set apart for solemn *fasting* and *prayer*, to implore the blessing of God upon our design of renewing covenant with him, and with one another, to walk together in the fear of God, in love and Christian fellowship; and to intreat that his divine presence might be with us in our designed approach to his table; as well as to humble ourselves before God on account of the apparent withdrawment (at least in a measure) of that blessed influence that has been so prevalent upon persons of all ages among us; as also on account of the rising appearance of carelessness, vanity, and vice among some, who, some time since, appeared to be touched and affected with divine truths, and brought to some sensibility of their miserable and perishing state by nature. And that we might also importunately pray for the peaceable *settlement* of the Indians

dians together in a body, that they might be a commodious congregation for the worship of God; and that God would blast and defeat all the attempts that were or might be made against that pious design *.

The solemnity was observed and seriously attended, not only by those who proposed to communicate at the Lord's table, but by the whole congregation universally.—In the former part of the day, I endeavoured to open to my people the nature and design of a *fast*, as I had attempted more briefly to do before, and to instruct them in the duties of such a solemnity.——In the afternoon, I insisted upon the special reasons there were for our engaging in these solemn exercises at this time; both in regard of the need we stood in of divine assistance, in order to a due preparation for that sacred ordinance we were some of us proposing (with leave of divine providence) speedily to attend upon; and also in respect of the manifest *decline* of God's work here, as to the effectual conviction and conversion of sinners, there having been few of late deeply awakened out of a state of security.

The worship of God was attended with great solemnity and reverence, with much tenderness and many tears, by those who appear to be truly religious: and there was some appearance of divine power upon those who had been awakened some time before, and who were still under concern.

After repeated prayer and attendance upon the word of God, I proposed to the religious people with as much brevity and plainness as I could, the substance of the *doctrine* of the *Christian faith*, as I had formerly done, previous to their *baptism*, and had their renewed cheerful assent to it.——I then led them to a solemn renewal of their *baptismal covenant*, wherein they had explicitly and publicly given up themselves to God, the Father, Son, and Holy Ghost, avouching him to be their God; and at the same time renouncing their Heathenish vanities, their *idolatrous* and *superstitious* practices, and solemnly engaging to take the word of God, so far as it was, or might be made known to them, for the *rule*

* There being at this time a terrible clamour raised against the Indians in various places in the country, and insinuations as though I was training them up to cut people's throats. Numbers wishing to have them banished out of these parts, and some giving out great words, in order to fright and deter them from settling upon the best and most convenient track of their own lands, threatening to molest and trouble them in the law, pretending a claim to these lands themselves, although never purchased of the Indians.

of their lives, promising to walk together in love, to watch over themselves, and one another; to lead lives of seriousness and devotion, and to discharge the *relative* duties incumbent upon them respectively, *&c*.

This solemn transaction was attended with much gravity and seriousness; and at the same time with utmost readiness, freedom, and cheerfulness; and a religious union and harmony of soul, seemed to crown the whole solemnity. I could not but think in the evening, that there had been manifest tokens of the divine presence with us in all the several services of the day; though it was also manifest there was not that concern among Christless souls that has often appeared here.

April 26. Toward noon prayed with a *dying* child, and gave a word of exhortation to the by-standers to prepare for death, which seemed to take effect upon some.

In the afternoon discoursed to my people from Matth. xxvi. 26.—30. of the author, the nature and design of the Lord's supper; and endeavoured to point out the *worthy* receivers of that ordinance.

The religious people were affected, and even melted with divine truths,—with a view of the dying love of Christ. Sundry others who had been for some months under convictions of their perishing state, appeared now to be much moved with concern, and afresh engaged in seeking after an interest in Christ; although I cannot say, "the word of God" appeared "so quick and powerful," so sharp and piercing to the assembly, as it had sometimes formerly done.

Baptized *two* adult persons, both serious and exemplary in their lives, and, I hope, truly religious. One of them was the man particularly mentioned in my Journal of the 6th instant; who although he was then greatly distressed, because "he had "never done the will of God," has since (it is hopeful) obtained spiritual comfort upon good grounds.

In the evening I catechised those that were designed to partake of the Lord's supper the next day, upon the institution, nature, and end of that ordinance; and had abundant satisfaction respecting their doctrinal knowledge and fitness in *that* respect for an attendance upon it. They likewise appeared, in general, to have an affecting sense of the solemnity of this sacred ordinance, and to be humbled under a sense of their own unworthiness to approach to God in it; and to be earnestly concerned that they might be duly prepared for an attendance upon it. Their hearts were full of love one toward another, and *that* was the frame of mind they seemed much

much concerned to maintain, and bring to the Lord's table with them.

In singing and prayer, after catechising, there appeared an agreeable tenderness and melting among them, and such tokens of brotherly love and affection, that would even constrain one to say, "Lord, it is good to be here;" it is good to dwell where such an heavenly influence distills.

Lord's day, April 27. Preached from Tit. ii. 14. "Who "gave himself for us," *&c.*——The word of God at this time was attended with some appearance of divine power upon the assembly; so that the attention and gravity of the audience was *remarkable*; and especially towards the conclusion of the exercise divers persons were much affected.

Administered the *sacrament* of the Lord's supper to *twenty-three* persons of the Indians, (the number of *men* and *women* being near equal), divers others, to the number of *five* or *six*, being now absent at the Forks of Delaware, who would otherwise have communicated with us.

The ordinance was attended with great solemnity, and with a most desirable tenderness and affection. And it was remarkable, that in the season of the performance of the *sacramental* actions, especially in the distribution of the *bread*, they seemed to be affected in a most lively manner, as if "Christ had been" really "crucified before them." And the words of the institution, when repeated and enlarged upon in the season of the administration, seemed to meet with the same reception, to be entertained with the *same full* and *firm* belief and affectionate engagement of soul, as if the Lord Jesus Christ himself had been present, and had *personally* spoken to them.

The affections of the communicants, although considerably raised, were notwithstanding agreeably *regulated*, and kept within proper bounds. So that there was a sweet, gentle, and affectionate melting, without any *indecent* or boisterous commotion of the passions.

Having rested some time after the administration of the *sacrament*, (being extremely tired with the necessary prolixity of the work), I walked from house to house, and conversed particularly with most of the *communicants*, and found they had been almost universally refreshed at the Lord's table "as "with new wine." And never did I see such an appearance of *Christian love* among any people in all my life. It was so remarkable, that one might well have cried with an agreeable surprise, "Behold how they love one another!" I think there could be no greater tokens of mutual affection among the people of God in the early days of Christianity, than what now appeared here. The sight was so desirable, and so well *becoming* the gospel, that nothing less could be said of it, than that it was "the doing of the Lord," the genuine operations of him "who is love!"

Toward night discoursed again on the forementioned Tit. ii. 14. and insisted on the immediate end and design of Christ's death, *viz.* "That he might redeem his people from "all iniquity," *&c.*

This appeared to be a season of divine power among us. The religious people were much refreshed, and seemed remarkably tender and affectionate, full of love, joy, peace, and desires of being completely "redeemed from all iniquity;" so that some of them afterwards told me, "they had never "felt the like before."—Convictions also appeared to be revived in many instances; and divers persons were awakened whom I had never observed under any religious impressions before.

Such was the influence that attended our assembly, and so unspeakably desirable the frame of mind that many enjoyed in the divine service, that it seemed almost grievous to conclude the public worship. And the congregation when dismissed, although it was then almost dark, appeared loth to leave the place and employments that had been rendered *so dear* to them by the benefits enjoyed, while a blessed quickening influence distilled upon them.

And upon the whole, I must say, I had great satisfaction with relation to the administration of this ordinance in divers respects. I have abundant reason to think, that those who came to the Lord's table, had a good degree of *doctrinal* knowledge of the *nature* and *design* of the ordinance; and that they acted *understandingly* in what they did.

In the preparatory services I found (I may justly say) uncommon freedom in opening to their understandings and capacities, the *covenant of grace*, and in shewing them the *nature* of this ordinance as a *seal* of that covenant. Although many of them knew of no such thing as a seal before my coming among them, or at least of the use and design of it in the common affairs of life.—— They were likewise thoroughly sensible that it was no more than a *seal* or *sign*, and not the *real* body and blood of Christ.—That it was designed for the refreshment and edification of the *soul*, and not for the *feasting* of the *body*.—— They were also acquainted with the end of the ordinance, that they were therein called to *commemorate* the dying love of Christ, *&c.*

And

And this competency of doctrinal knowledge, together with their grave and decent attendance upon the ordinance; their affectionate melting under it; and the sweet and Christian frame of mind they discovered consequent upon it, gave me great satisfaction respecting my administration of it to them.

And O what a sweet and blessed season was this! God himself, I am persuaded, was in the midst of his people, attending his own ordinances. And I doubt not but many in the conclusion of the day, could say, with their whole hearts, "Verily, a day thus spent in God's house, is better than a "thousand elsewhere." There seemed to be but *one heart* among the pious people. The sweet union, harmony, and endearing love and tenderness subsisting among them, was (I thought) the most lively emblem of the heavenly world I had ever seen.

April 28. Concluded the sacramental solemnity with a discourse upon John xiv. 15. "If ye love me, keep my com-"mandments." At which time there appeared a very agreeable tenderness in the audience in general, but especially in the *communicants*.——O how free, how engaged and affectionate did *these* appear in the service of God! they seemed willing to have their "ears bored to the door-posts of God's "house," and to be his servants for ever.

Observing numbers in this excellent frame, and the assembly in general affected, and that by a divine influence, I thought it proper to improve this advantageous season, as Hezekiah did the desirable season of his great *passover*, (2 Chron. xxxi.) in order to promote the blessed reformation begun among them; and to engage those that appear serious and religious, to persevere therein; and accordingly proposed to them, that they should *renewedly* enter into covenant before God, that they would watch over themselves and one another, lest they should dishonour the name of Christ by falling into sinful and unbecoming practices. And especially that they would watch against the sin of *drunkenness*, (the sin that easily besets them), and the temptations leading thereto; as well as "the appearance of evil" in that respect.——They cheerfully complied with the *proposal*, and *explicitly* joined in that covenant; whereupon I proceeded in the most solemn manner I was capable of, to call God to *witness* respecting their sacred engagement; and minded them of the greatness of the guilt they would contract to themselves in the violation of it; as well as observed to them, that God would be a terrible *witness*

ness against those who should presume to do so, in the "great "and notable day of the Lord."

It was a season of amazing solemnity! and a *divine awe* appeared upon the face of the whole assembly in this transaction! Affectionate sobs, sighs, and tears, were now frequent in the audience: and I doubt not but that many silent cries were then sent up to the *fountain* of grace, for supplies of grace sufficient for the fulfilment of these solemn engagements.

Baptized *six* children this day.

Lord's day, May 4. My people being now removed to their *lands*, mentioned in my Journal of March 24. where they were then, and have since been making provision for a *compact settlement*, in order to their more convenient enjoyment of the gospel, and other means of instruction, as well as the comforts of life; I this day visited them, (being now obliged to board with an English family at some distance from them), and preached to them in the forenoon from Mark iv. 5. Endeavoured to shew them the reason there was to fear lest many promising appearances and hopeful beginnings in religion, might prove abortive, like the "seed dropped upon "stony places."

In the afternoon discoursed upon Rom. viii. 9. "Now if "any man have not the Spirit of Christ, he is none of his." ——I have reason to think this discourse was peculiarly seasonable, and that it had a good effect upon some of the hearers.

Spent some hours afterwards in private conferences with my people, and laboured to regulate some things I apprehended amiss among some of them.

May 5. Visited my people again, and took care of their *worldly* concerns, giving them directions relating to their business.

I daily discover more and more of what importance it is like to be to their *religious* interests, that they become laborious and industrious, acquainted with the affairs of *husbandry*, and able, in a good measure, to raise the necessaries and comforts of life *within themselves;* for their present method of living greatly exposes them to temptations of various kinds.

May 9. Preached from John v. 40. in the open wilderness; the Indians having as yet no house for public worship in this place, nor scarce any *shelters* for themselves.——Divine truths made considerable impressions upon the audience, and

and it was a season of solemnity, tenderness, and affection.

Baptized one man this day, (the conjurer, murderer, &c. mentioned in my Journal of August 8. 1745. and Feburary 1. 1745-6.), who appears to be such a remarkable instance of divine grace, that I cannot omit somo brief account of him here.

He lived near, and sometimes attended my meeting in the Forks of Delaware for more than a year together; but was (like many others of them) extremely attached to strong drink, and seemed to be no ways reformed by the means I used with them for their instruction and conversion. In this time he likewise *murdered* a likely young Indian, which threw him into some kind of *horror* and *desperation*, so that he kept at a distance from me, and refused to hear me preach for several months together, (as I noted in a formal Journal of March 4. 1744-5), till I had an opportunity of conversing freely with him, and giving him encouragement, that his sin might be forgiven for Christ's sake. After which he again attended my meeting at some times.

But that which was the worst of all his conduct, was his *conjuration*. He was one of them who are sometimes called *powwows* among the Indians: and notwithstanding his frequent attendance upon my preaching, he still followed his old *charms* and juggling tricks, "giving out that himself was "some great one, and to him they gave heed," supposing him to be possessed of a *great power*. So that when I have instructed them respecting the *miracles* wrought by Christ in healing the sick, &c. and mentioned them as evidences of his *divine* mission, and the truth of his doctrines, they have quickly observed the wonders of that kind which this man had performed by his *magic charms*: whence they had a high opinion of him, and his superstitious notions, which seemed to be a fatal obstruction to some of them in regard of their receiving the gospel. And I have often thought, it would be a great favour to the design of gospellizing the Indians, if God would take that wretch out of the world; for I had scarce any hope of his ever coming to good: but God, "whose "thoughts are not as man's thoughts," has been pleased to take a much more desirable method with him; a method agreeable to his own merciful nature, and, I trust, advantageous to his own interest among the Indians, as well as effectual to the salvation of the poor soul himself. "And to him "be the glory of it."

The first genuine concern for his soul that ever appeared in in him, was excited by seeing my interpreter and his wife baptized at the Forks of Delaware, July 21. 1745. Which so prevailed upon him, that, with the invitation of an Indian, who was a friend to Christianity, he followed me down to Crosweeksung in the beginning of August following, in order to hear me preach, and there continued for several weeks, in the season of the most remarkable and powerful awakening among the Indians; at which time he was more effectually awakened, and brought under great concern for his soul: and then, he says, upon his "feeling the word of God in his "heart," (as he expresses it), his spirit of conjuration left him entirely; that he has had no more power of that nature since, than any other man living. And declares that he does not now so much as know how he used to *charm* and conjure; and that he could not do any thing of that nature if he was never so desirous of it.

He continued under convictions of his sinful and perishing state, and a considerable degree of concern for his soul, all the fall and former part of the winter past, but was not so deeply exercised till sometime in January; and then the word of God took such hold upon him, that he was brought into great distress, and knew not what to do, nor where to turn himself.——He then told me, that when he used to hear me preach from time to time in the fall of the year, my preaching pricked his heart and made him very *uneasy*, but did not bring him to so *great* distress, because he still hoped he could do *something* for his own relief: but now, he said, I drave him up into "such a sharp corner," that he had no way to turn, and could not avoid being in distress.

He continued constantly under the heavy burden and pressure of a *wounded spirit*, till at length he was brought into the acute anguish and utmost *agony of soul*, mentioned in my Journal of February 1. which continued that night, and part of the next day.

After this, he was brought to the utmost calmness and composure of mind, his trembling and heavy burden were removed, and he appeared perfectly sedate; although he had, to his apprehensions, scarce any hope of salvation.

I observed him to appear remarkably composed, and thereupon asked him how he did? He replied, "It is done, it is "done, it is all done now." I asked him what he meant? He answered, "I can never do any more to save myself; it "is all done for ever, I can do no more." I queried with him, whether he could not do a *little* more rather than to go to hell. He replied, "My heart is dead, I can never help my-"self."

"self." I asked him, what he thought would become of him then? He answered, "I must go to hell." I asked him, if he thought it was right that God should send him to hell? He replied, "O it is right. The devil has been in me ever "since I was born." I asked him, if he felt this when he was in such great distress the evening before? He answered, "No, I did not then think it was right. I thought God "would send me to hell, and that I was then dropping into it; "but my heart quarrelled with God, and would not say it was "*right* he should send me there. But now I know it is right, "for I have always served the devil, and my heart has no "goodness in it now, but is as bad as ever it was," &c.—— I thought I had scarce ever seen any person more effectually brought off from a dependence upon his own contrivances and endeavours for salvation, or more apparently to lie at the foot of *sovereign* mercy, than this man now did under these views of things.

In this frame of mind he continued for several days, passing sentence of condemnation upon himself, and constantly owning, that it would be right he should be damned, and that he expected this would be his portion for the greatness of his sins. And yet it was plain he had a secret hope of mercy, though imperceptible to himself, which kept him not only from despair, but from any pressing distress: so that instead of being sad and dejected, his very countenance appeared pleasant and agreeable.

While he was in this frame, he sundry times asked me, "When I would preach again?" and seemed desirous to hear the word of God every day. I asked him why he wanted to hear me preach, seeing "his heart was dead, and all was done?" That "he could never help himself, and expected that he must "go to hell?" He replied, "I love to hear you speak about "Christ for all." I added, But what good will that do you, if you must go to hell at last? (using now his own language with him; having before, from time to time, laboured in the best manner I could, to represent to him the excellency of Christ, his all-sufficiency and willingness to save lost sinners, and persons just in his case; although to no purpose, as to yielding him any special comfort). He answered, "I would "have others come to Christ, if I must go to hell myself."— It was remarkable in this season that he seemed to have a great love to the people of God, and nothing affected him so much as the thoughts of being separated from them. This seemed to be a very dreadful part of the hell he thought himself doomed to.——It was likewise remarkable, that in this season he was most diligent in the use of all means for his soul's salvation; although he had the clearest view of the *insufficiency* of means to afford him help. And would frequently say, "That "all he did, signified nothing at all;" and yet was never more constant in doing, attending secret and family prayer daily, and surprisingly diligent and attentive in hearing the word of God: so that he neither despaired of mercy, nor yet presumed to hope upon his own doings, but used means, because appointed of God in order to salvation; and because he would wait upon God in his own way.

After he had continued in this frame of mind more than a *week*, while I was discoursing publicly, he seemed to have a lively, soul-refreshing view of the excellency of Christ, and the way of salvation by him, which melted him into tears, and filled him with admiration, comfort, satisfaction, and praise to God; since which he has appeared to be a humble, devout, and affectionate Christian; serious and exemplary in his conversation and behaviour, frequently complaining of his barrenness, his want of spiritual warmth, life, and activity, and yet frequently favoured with quickening and refreshing influences. And in all respects, so far as I am capable to judge, he bears the marks and characters of one "created anew in "Christ Jesus to good works."

His zeal for the cause of God was pleasing to me, when he was with me at the Forks of Delaware in February last. There being an old Indian at the place where I preached, who threatened to *bewitch* me and my religious people who accompanied me there; *this* man presently challenged him to do his worst, telling him, that himself had been as great a *conjurer* as he, and that notwithstanding as soon as he felt that word in his heart which these people loved, (meaning the word of God), his power of conjuring immediately left him.—And so it would you, said he, if you did but once feel it in your heart; and you have no power to hurt them, nor so much as to touch one of them, &c.

So that I may conclude my account of him, by observing, (in allusion to what was said of St Paul), that he now zealously defends, and practically "preaches the faith which he once "destroyed," or at least was instrumental of obstructing.——May God have the glory of the amazing change he has wrought in him!

Lord's day, May 18. Discoursed both parts of the day from Rev. iii. 20. There appeared some affectionate melting towards the conclusion of the forenoon exercise, and one or two instances of fresh awakening.——In the intermission of public

lic worship, I took occasion to discourse to numbers in a more private way, on the *kindness* and *patience* of the blessed Redeemer in *standing* and *knocking*, in continuing his gracious calls to sinners, who had long neglected and abused his grace; which seemed to take some effect upon sundry.

In the afternoon, divine truths were attended with solemnity, and with some tears, although there was not that powerful, awakening, and quickening influence, which in times past has been common in our assemblies. The appearance of the audience under divine truths, was comparatively discouraging; and I was ready to fear, that God was about to withdraw the blessed influence of his Spirit from us.

May 19. Visited and preached to my people from Acts xx. 18. 19. and endeavoured to rectify their notions about *religious affections*: shewing them, on the one hand, the *desirableness* of religious affection, tenderness, and fervent engagement in the worship and service of God, when such affection flows from a *true spiritual* discovery of divine glories, from a justly-affecting sense of the transcendent excellency and perfections of the blessed God,—a view of the glory and loveliness of the great Redeemer: and that such views of divine things, will *naturally* excite us to "serve the "Lord with many tears," with much affection and fervency, and yet "with all humility of mind."—And, on the other hand, observing the *sinfulness* of seeking after high affections *immediately*, and for their own sakes, that is, of making them the object our eye and heart is *nextly* and *principally* set upon, when the glory of God ought to be so. Shewed them, that if the heart be *directly* and *chiefly* fixed on God, and the soul engaged to glorify him, some degree of religious affection will be the effect and attendant of it. But to seek after affection, *directly* and *chiefly*, to have the heart *principally* set upon *that*, is to place it in the room of God and his glory. If it be sought, that others may take notice of, and admire us for our spirituality and forwardness in religion, it is then abominable *pride*: if for the sake of feeling the pleasure of being affected, it is then *idolatry* and self-gratification. —Laboured also to expose the *disagreeableness* of those affections that are sometimes wrought up in persons by the power of fancy, and their own attempts for that purpose, while I still endeavoured to recommend to them *that* religious affection, fervency, and devotion which ought to attend all our religious exercises, and without which religion will be but an *empty* name and *lifeless* carcase.

This appeared to be a seasonable discourse, and proved very

 satisfactory

satisfactory to some of the religious people, who before were exercised with some difficulties relating to this point.

Afterwards took care of, and gave my people directions about their worldly affairs.

May 24. Visited the Indians, and took care of their secular business, which they are not able to manage themselves, without the constant care and advice of others.

Afterwards discoursed to some particularly about their spiritual concerns.

Lord's day, May 25. Discoursed both parts of the day from John xii. 44.—48. There was some degree of divine power attending the word of God. Sundry wept and appeared considerably affected: and one who had long been under spiritual trouble, now obtained clearness and comfort, and appeared to "rejoice in God her Saviour." It was a day of grace and divine goodness; a day wherein something, I trust, was done for the cause of God among my people: a season of sweetness and comfort to divers of the religious people, although there was not that powerful influence upon the congregation which was common some months ago.

Lord's day, June 1. 1746. Preached both forenoon and afternoon from Matth. xi. 27. 28. The presence of God seemed to be in the assembly, and numbers were considerably melted and affected under divine truths. There was a desirable appearance in the congregation in general, an earnest attention and agreeable tenderness, and it seemed as if God designed to visit us with further showers of divine grace.——I then baptized *ten* persons, five adults and five children, and was not a little refreshed with this "addition made to the "church of such as (I hope) shall be saved."

I have reason to hope, that God has lately (at and since our celebration of the Lord's supper) brought home to himself sundry souls who had long been under spiritual trouble and concern: although there have been few instances of persons lately awakened out of a state of security. And those comforted of late, seem to be brought in, in a more *silent* way, neither their concern nor consolation being so powerful and *remarkable*, as appeared among those more suddenly wrought upon in the beginning of this work of grace.

June 6. Discoursed to my people from part of If. liii.— The divine presence appeared to be amongst us in some measure. Divers persons were much melted and refreshed; and one man in particular, who had long been under concern for his soul, was now brought to see and feel, in a very lively

manner,

manner, the impoſſibility of his doing any thing to help himſelf, or to bring him into the favour of God, by his tears, prayers, and other religious performances; and found himſelf *undone* as to any power or goodneſs of his own, and that there was no way left him, but to leave himſelf with God to be diſpoſed of as he pleaſed.

June 7. Being deſired by the Reverend Mr William Tennent to be his *aſſiſtant* in the adminiſtration of the Lord's ſupper; my people alſo being invited to attend the *ſacramental* ſolemnity, they cheerfully embraced the opportunity, and this day attended the preparatory ſervices with me.

Lord's day, June 8. Moſt of my people, who had been *communicants* at the Lord's table before, being preſent at this ſacramental occaſion, communicated, with others, in this holy ordinance, at the deſire, and, I truſt, to the ſatiſfaction and comfort of numbers of God's people, who had longed to ſee *this* day, and whoſe hearts had rejoiced in *this* work of grace among the Indians, which prepared the way for what appeared ſo agreeable at this time.

Thoſe of my people who communicated, ſeemed in general agreeably affected at the Lord's table, and ſome of them conſiderably melted with the love of Chriſt; although they were not ſo remarkably refreſhed and feaſted at this time, as when I adminiſtered this ordinance to them in our own congregation only.

Some of the *by-ſtanders* were affected with ſeeing theſe, who had been "aliens from the commonwealth of Iſrael, "and ſtrangers to the covenant of promiſe," who of all men had lived "without God, and without hope in the world," now brought *near to God* as his profeſſing people, and ſealing covenant with him, by a ſolemn and devout attendance upon this ſacred ordinance. And as numbers of God's people were refreſhed with this ſight, and thereby excited to bleſs God for the enlargement of his kingdom in the world, ſo ſome others (I was told) were awakened by it, apprehending the danger they were in of being themſelves finally *caſt out*, while they ſaw others, "from the eaſt and weſt," preparing, and hopefully prepared in ſome good meaſure, to "ſit down "in the kingdom of God."

At this ſeaſon others of my people alſo, who were not *communicants*, were conſiderably affected; convictions were revived in divers inſtances; and one (the man particularly mentioned in my Journal of the 6th inſtant) obtained comfort and ſatisfaction; and has ſince given me ſuch an account of his ſpiritual exerciſes, and the *manner* in which he obtained relief,

relief, as appears very hopeful. It seems as if he "who commanded the light to shine out of darkness," had now "shined in his heart, and given him the light of" an experimental "knowledge of the glory of God in the face of Jesus Christ."

June 9. A considerable number of my people met together early in the day in a *retired* place in the *woods*, and prayed, sang, and conversed of divine things, and were seen by some religious persons of the white people, to be affected and engaged, and divers of them in tears in these religious exercises.

Afterwards they attended the concluding exercises of the sacramental solemnity, and then returned home, divers of them "rejoicing for all the goodness of God" they had seen and felt: so that this appeared to be a profitable, as well as a comfortable season to numbers of my congregation. And their being present at this occasion, and a number of them communicating at the Lord's table with others of God's people, was, I trust, for the honour of God, and the interest of religion in these parts, as numbers, I have reason to think, were quickened by means of it.

June 13. Preached to my people upon the new creature, from 2 Cor. v. 17. The presence of God appeared to be in the assembly.—It was a sweet and agreeable meeting, wherein the people of God were refreshed and strengthened, beholding their faces in the glass of God's word, and finding in themselves the *marks* and *lineaments* of the *new creature*.—— Some sinners under concern, were also renewedly affected; and afresh engaged for the securing of their eternal interests.

Baptized *five* persons at this time, three adults and two children. One of these was the very *aged woman* of whose exercise I gave an account in my Journal of December 26. She now gave me a very punctual, rational, and satisfactory account of the remarkable change she experienced some months after the beginning of her concern, which, I must say, appeared to be the genuine operations of the divine Spirit, so far as I am capable of judging. And although she was become so childish through old age, that I could do nothing in a way of *questioning* with her, nor scarce make her understand any that I asked her; yet when I let her alone to go on with her own story, she could give a very distinct and particular relation of the many and various exercises of soul she had experienced; so deep were the impressions left upon her mind by that influence and exercise she had been under! And I have

have great reason to hope, she is *born anew* in her old age, she being, I presume, upwards of *fourscore.*——I had good hopes of the other adults, and trust they are such as God will own "in the day when he makes up his jewels."

June 19. Visited my people with two of the Reverend correspondents. Spent some time in conversation with some of them upon spiritual things; and took some care of their worldly concerns.

This day makes up a complete year from the first time of my preaching to these Indians in New-Jersey.——What amazing things has God wrought in this space of time for these poor people! What a surprising change appears in their tempers and behaviour! How are morose and savage Pagans in this short space of time transformed into agreeable, affectionate, and humble Christians! and their drunken and Pagan howlings, turned into devout and fervent prayers and praises to God! They "who were sometimes darkness, are now become light in the Lord. May they walk as children of the light, and of the day. And now to him that is of power to stablish them according to the gospel, and the preaching of Christ——To God only wise, be glory, through Jesus Christ, for ever and ever! Amen."

Before I conclude the present *Journal,* I would make a few *general remarks* upon what to me appears worthy of notice, relating to the continued work of grace among my people.

And, *first,* I cannot but take notice that I have in the general, ever since my first coming among these Indians in New-Jersey, been favoured with that assistance, which (to me) is *uncommon,* in preaching *Christ crucified,* and making him the *centre* and *mark* to which all my discourses among them were directed.

It was the principal scope and drift of all my discourses to this people for several months together, (after having taught them something of the being and perfections of God, his creation of man in a state of rectitude and happiness, and the obligations mankind were thence under to love and honour him), to lead them into an acquaintance with their deplorable state by nature, *as fallen creatures:* their *inability* to extricate and deliver themselves from it: the *utter insufficiency* of any *external* reformations and amendments of life, or of any religious performances, *they* were capable of, while in this state, to bring them into the favour of God, and interest them in his eternal mercy. And thence to shew them their *absolute* need of Christ to redeem and save them from the misery

ſery of their fallen ſtate.——To open his all-ſufficiency and willingneſs to ſave the chief of ſinners.——The *freeneſs* and *riches* of his divine grace, propoſed "without money, and "without price," to all that will accept the offer.—And thereupon to preſs them *without delay* to betake themſelves to him, under a ſenſe of their miſery and *undone* eſtate, for relief and everlaſting ſalvation.——And to ſhew them the abundant encouragement the goſpel propoſes to needy, periſhing, and helpleſs ſinners, in order to engage them ſo to do. Theſe things I repeatedly and largely inſiſted upon from time to time.

And I have oftentimes remarked with admiration, that whatever ſubject I have been treating upon, after having ſpent time ſufficient to explain and illuſtrate the truths contained therein, I have been *naturally* and *eaſily* led to *Chriſt* as the *ſubſtance* of every ſubject. If I treated on the being and glorious perfections of God, I was thence *naturally* led to diſcourſe of Chriſt as the only "way to the Father."—If I attempted to open the deplorable miſery of our fallen ſtate, it was natural from thence to ſhew the neceſſity of Chriſt to undertake for us, to atone for our ſins, and to redeem us from the power of them.—If I taught the commands of God, and ſhewed our violation of them, this brought me in the moſt *eaſy* and natural way, to ſpeak of, and recommend the Lord Jeſus Chriſt, as one who had "magnified the law" we had broken, and who was "become the end of it for righ-"teouſneſs, to every one that believes." And never did I find ſo much freedom and aſſiſtance in making all the various lines of my diſcourſes meet together, and centre in Chriſt, as I have frequently done among theſe Indians.

Sometimes when I have had thoughts of offering but a few words upon ſome particular ſubject, and ſaw no occaſion, nor indeed much room for any conſiderable enlargement, there has at unawares appeared ſuch a fountain of goſpel-grace ſhining forth in, or *naturally* reſulting from a juſt explication of it, and Chriſt has ſeemed in ſuch a manner to be pointed out as the *ſubſtance* of what I was conſidering and explaining, that I have been drawn in a way not only *eaſy* and *natural*, *proper* and *pertinent*, but almoſt *unavoidable* to diſcourſe of him, either in regard of his undertaking, incarnation, ſatisfaction, admirable fitneſs for the work of man's redemption, or the infinite need that ſinners ſtand in of an intereſt in him; which has opened the way for a continued ſtrain of goſpel-invitation to periſhing ſouls, to come *empty*

and

and *naked*, *weary* and *heavy laden*, and cast themselves upon him.

And as I have been remarkably influenced and assisted to dwell upon the Lord Jesus Christ, and the way of salvation by him, in the general current of my discourses here, and have been, at times, surprisingly furnished with pertinent *matter* relating to him, and the design of his incarnation: so I have been no less assisted oftentimes in regard of an advantageous *manner* of opening the mysteries of divine grace, and representing the infinite excellencies, and "unsearchable riches "of Christ," as well as of recommending him to the acceptance of perishing sinners. I have frequently been enabled to represent the divine glory, the infinite preciousness and transcendent loveliness of the great Redeemer; the suitableness of his person and purchase to supply the wants, and answer the utmost desires of immortal souls.—To open the infinite riches of his grace, and the wonderful encouragement proposed in the gospel to unworthy, helpless sinners.—To call, invite, and beseech them to come and give up themselves to him, and be reconciled to God through him.—To expostulate with them respecting their neglect of one so infinitely lovely, and freely offered.—And *this* in *such a manner*, with *such* freedom, pertinency, pathos, and application to the conscience, as (I am sure) I never could have made myself master of by the most assiduous application of mind I am capable of. And have frequently at such seasons been surprisingly helped in adapting my discourses to the *capacities* of my people, and bringing them down into such easy, vulgar, and familiar methods of expression, as has rendered them intelligible even to Pagans.

I do not mention these things as a recommendation of my own performances; for, I am sure, I found, from time to time, that I had no skill or wisdom for my great work; and knew not how "to chuse out acceptable words" proper to address poor benighted Pagans with. But thus God was pleased to help me, "not to know any thing among them, save Jesus "Christ, and him crucified." Thus I was *enabled* to shew them their misery and undoneness without him, and to represent his complete *fitness* to redeem and save them.

And *this* was the preaching God made use of for the awakening of sinners, and the propagation of this "work of grace "among the Indians."——And it was remarkable, from time to time, that when I was favoured with any *special* freedom, in discoursing of the "ability and willingness of Christ to save "sinners," and the "need they stood in of such a Saviour," there was then the greatest appearance of divine power in awakening numbers of secure souls, promoting convictions begun, and comforting the distressed.

I have sometimes formerly, in reading the apostle's discourse to Cornelius, (Acts x.), admired to see him so quickly introduce the Lord Jesus Christ into his sermon, and so entirely dwell upon him through the whole of it, observing him in this point very widely to differ from many of our *modern* preachers: but latterly this has not seemed strange, since Christ has appeared to be the *substance* of the gospel, and the *centre* in which the several lines of divine revelation meet. Although I am still sensible there are many things necessary to be spoken to persons under Pagan darkness, in order to make way for a proper introduction of the name of Christ, and his undertaking in behalf of fallen man.

Secondly, It is worthy of remark, that numbers of these people are brought to a strict compliance with the rules of *morality* and *sobriety*, and to a conscientious performance of the *external duties* of Christianity, by the *internal* power and influence of divine truths (the peculiar doctrines of grace) upon their minds; without their having these *moral duties* frequently repeated and inculcated upon them, and the contrary vices particularly exposed and spoken against. What has been the general *strain* and *drift* of my preaching among these Indians; what were the truths I principally insisted upon, and how I was influenced and enabled to dwell from time to time upon the peculiar doctrines of grace, I have already observed in the preceding remark. Those doctrines, which had the most direct tendency to humble the *fallen* creature; to shew him the misery of his *natural* state; to bring him down to the foot of *sovereign mercy*; and to exalt the great Redeemer, discover his transcendent excellency and infinite preciousness, and so to recommend him to the sinner's acceptance, were the subject-matter of what was delivered in public and private to them, and from time to time repeated and inculcated upon them.

And God was pleased to give these divine truths such a powerful influence upon the minds of these people, and so to bless them for the effectual awakening of numbers of them, that their lives were quickly reformed, without my insisting upon the *precepts* of *morality*, and spending time in repeated harangues upon *external* duties. There was indeed no room for any kind of discourses but those that respected the *essentials* of religion, and the *experimental* knowledge of divine things, whilst there were so many inquiring daily, not how

they

they should regulate their *external* conduct, (for that, persons who are honestly disposed to comply with duty, when known, may, in ordinary cases, be easily satisfied about); but how they should escape from the wrath they feared and felt a desert of,—obtain an *effectual change of heart*,—get an interest in Christ,—and come to the enjoyment of eternal blessedness. ——So that my *great work* still was to lead them into a further view of their *utter undoneness* in themselves, the total depravity and corruption of their hearts; that there was no manner of goodness in them; no good dispositions nor desires; no love to God, nor delight in his commands: but, on the contrary, hatred, enmity, and all manner of wickedness reigning in them.—And at the same time to open to them the glorious and complete remedy provided in Christ for helpless perishing sinners, and offered freely to those who have no goodness of their own, no "works of righteousness which "they have done," to recommend them to God.

This was the continued strain of my preaching; this my great concern and constant endeavour, so to enlighten the mind, as thereby duly to affect the *heart*, and, as far as possible, give persons a *sense* and *feeling* of these precious and important doctrines of grace, at least, so far as means might conduce to it. And these were the doctrines,—this the method of preaching which were blessed of God for the awakening, and, I trust, the saving conversion of numbers of souls,—and which were made the means of producing a remarkable reformation among the hearers in general.

When these truths were felt *at heart*, there was now no vice unreformed,—no external duty neglected.——Drunkenness, the darling vice, was broken off from, and scarce an instance of it known among my hearers for months together. The abusive practice of *husbands* and *wives* in putting away each other, and taking others in their stead, was quickly reformed; so that there are three or four couple who have voluntarily dismissed those they had wrongfully taken, and now live together again in love and peace. The same might be said of all other vicious practices.——The reformation was general; and all springing from the *internal* influence of divine truths upon their hearts; and not from any *external* restraints, or because they had heard these vices particularly exposed, and repeatedly spoken against: for some of them I never so much as mentioned; particularly that of the parting of men and their wives, till some, having their conscience awakened by God's word, came, and, of their own accord, confessed themselves guilty in that respect. And when I did

 at

at any time mention their wicked practices, and the sins they were guilty of contrary to the light of nature, it was not with design, nor indeed with any hope, of working an effectual reformation in their external manners by this means, for I knew that while the *tree* remained corrupt, the *fruit* would naturally be so; but with design to lead them, by observing the wickedness of their *lives*, to a view of the corruption of their *hearts*, and so to convince them of the necessity of a renovation of nature, and to excite them diligently to seek after that great change, which if once obtained, would of course produce a reformation of external manners in every respect.

And as all vice was reformed upon their feeling the power of divine truth upon their hearts, so the external duties of Christianity were complied with, and conscientiously performed from the same internal influence. Family-prayer was set up, and constantly maintained, unless among some few more lately come, who had felt little of this divine influence. This duty constantly was performed even in some families where there were none but females, and scarce a prayerless person to be found among near a hundred of them. The Lord's day was seriously and religiously observed, and care taken by parents to keep their children orderly upon that sacred day. And this, not because I had driven them to the performance of these duties by a frequent inculcation of them, but because they had felt the power of God's word upon their hearts; were made sensible of their sin and misery, and thence could not but pray, and comply with every thing they knew was duty, from what they felt within themselves. When their hearts were touched with a sense of their eternal concerns, they could pray with great freedom, as well as fervency, without being at the trouble first to learn set forms for that purpose. And some of them who were suddenly awakened at their first coming among us, were brought to pray and cry for mercy with the utmost importunity, without ever being instructed in the duty of prayer, or so much as once directed to a performance of it.

The happy effects of these peculiar doctrines of grace, which I have so much insisted upon with this people, plainly discover, even to demonstration, that instead of their opening a door to licentiousness, as many vainly imagine, and slanderously insinuate, they have a direct contrary tendency; so that a close application, a sense and feeling of them, will have the most powerful influence toward the renovation, and effectual reformation both of heart and life.

Happy experience, as well as the word of God and the example of Christ and his apostles, has taught me, that that method of preaching which is best suited to awaken in mankind a sense and lively apprehension of their depravity and misery in a fallen state,—to excite them earnestly to seek after a change of heart, and to fly for refuge to free and sovereign grace in Christ, as the only hope set before them, is likely to be most successful toward the reformation of their external conduct. I have found that close addresses, and solemn applications of divine truth to the conscience, tend directly to strike death to the root of all vice; while smooth and plausible harangues upon *moral virtues* and external duties, at best are likely to do no more than lop off the branches of corruption, while the *root* of all vice remains still untouched.

A view of the blessed effect of honest endeavours to bring home truth to the conscience, and duly to affect the heart, has often reminded me of those words of our Lord, which I have thought might be a proper exhortation for ministers in treating with others, as well as for persons in general with regard to themselves;—"Cleanse first the inside of the cup and platter, that the outside may be clean also." Cleanse, says he, the inside, *that* the outside may be clean. *q. d.* The only effectual way to have the outside clean, is to begin with what is *within;* and if the fountain be purified, the streams will naturally be pure. Most certain it is, if we can awaken in sinners a lively sense of their inward pollution and depravity, their need of a change of heart, and so engage them to seek after inward cleansing; their external defilement will naturally be cleansed, their vicious ways of course be reformed, and their conversation and behaviour become regular. And though I cannot pretend that the reformation among my people does, in every instance, spring from a saving change of heart; yet I may truly say, it flows from some *heart affecting* view and sense of divine truth, which all have had in a greater or lesser degree.

I do not intend, by what I have observed here, to represent the preaching of *morality*, and pressing persons to the external performance of duty, to be altogether unnecessary and useless at any time, and especially at times when there is less of divine power attending the means of grace;—when for want of *internal* influences, there is need of *external* restraints. It is doubtless among the things that "ought to be done," while "others are not to be left undone." But what I principally designed by this remark was to discover plain matter of fact, *viz*. That the reformation, the sobriety, and external compliance with the rules and duties of Christianity, appearing among my people, are not the effect of any *mere* doctrinal instruction, or *merely* rational view of the beauty of *morality*, but from the *internal* power and influence that divine truths (the soul-humbling doctrines of grace) have had upon their hearts.

Thirdly, It is remarkable, that God has so *continued* and *renewed* the showers of his grace here:—so *quickly* set up his visible kingdom among these people; and so *smiled* upon them in relation to their acquirement of knowledge, both divine and human. It is now near a year since the beginning of this gracious outpouring of the divine Spirit among them: and although it has often seemed to decline and abate for some short space of time, (as may be observed by several passages of my Journal, where I have endeavoured to note things just as they appeared to me from time to time); yet the shower has seemed to be *renewed*, and the work of grace *revived* again: so that a divine influence seems still apparently to attend the means of grace, in a greater or less degree, in most of our meetings for religious exercises: whereby religious persons are refreshed, strengthened, and established,—convictions revived and promoted in many instances,—and some few persons newly awakened from time to time. Although it must be acknowledged, that for some time past, there has, in the general, appeared a more manifest decline of this work, and the divine Spirit has seemed, in a considerable measure, withdrawn, especially in regard of his awakening influences; so that the *strangers* who come latterly, are not seized with concern as formerly; and some few who have been much affected with divine truths in time past, now appear less concerned. Yet (blessed be God) there is still an appearance of divine power and grace, a desirable degree of tenderness, religious affection, and devotion in our assemblies.

And as God has continued and renewed the showers of his grace among this people for some time; so he has with uncommon *quickness* set up his visible kingdom, and gathered himself a church in the midst of them. I have now *baptized*, since the conclusion of my last Journal, *thirty* persons, *fifteen* adults and *fifteen* children. Which added to the number there mentioned, makes *seventy-seven* persons; whereof *thirty-eight* are adults, and *thirty-nine* children; and all within the space of *eleven* months past.—And it must be noted, that I have baptized no adults, but such as appeared to have a work of special grace wrought in their hearts; I mean such who

who have had the experience not only of the awakening and humbling, but (in a judgment of charity) of the renewing and comforting influences of the divine Spirit. Although there are many others under solemn concern for their souls, who (I apprehend) are persons of sufficient knowledge, and visible seriousness, *at present*, to render them proper subjects of the ordinance of baptism. Yet since they give no comfortable evidences of having as yet passed a saving change, but only appear under convictions of their sin and misery, and having no principle of spiritual life wrought in them, are liable to lose the impressions of religion they are now under: and considering the great propensity there is in this people *naturally* to abuse themselves with strong drink, and fearing lest some, who at present appear serious and concerned for their souls, might lose their concern, and return to *this* sin, and so (if baptized) prove a scandal to their profession, I have thought proper hitherto to omit the baptism of any but such who give some *hopeful* evidences of a saving change, although I do not pretend to determine positively respecting the states of any.

I likewise administered the Lord's supper to a number of persons, who I have abundant reason to think (as I elsewhere observed) were proper subjects of that ordinance, within the space of *ten months* and *ten days*, after my first coming among these Indians in New-Jersey. And from the time that I am informed, some of them were attending an *idolatrous feast* and *sacrifice* in honour to *devils*, to the time they sat down at the Lord's table (I trust) to the honour of God, was not more than a *full year*. Surely Christ's little flock here, so suddenly gathered from among Pagans, may justly say, in the language of the church of old, "The Lord hath done "great things for us, whereof we are glad."

Much of the goodness of God has also appeared in relation to their acquirement of knowledge, both in religion and in the affairs of common life. There has been a wonderful thirst after *Christian knowledge* prevailing among them in general, and an eager desire of being instructed in Christian doctrines and manners. This has prompted them to ask many pertinent as well as important questions; the answers to which have tended much to enlighten their minds, and promote their knowledge in divine things. Many of the doctrines I have delivered, they have queried with me about, in order to gain further light and insight into them; particularly the doctrine of *predestination*: and have from time to time manifested a good understanding of them, by their answers

ſwers to the queſtions propoſed to them in my *catechetical lectures.*

They have likewiſe queried with me, reſpecting a proper *method* as well as proper *matter* of prayer, and expreſſions ſuitable to be made uſe of in that religious exerciſe; and have taken pains in order to the performance of this duty with underſtanding.

They have likewiſe taken pains, and appeared remarkably apt in learning to ſing *Pſalm-tunes*, and are now able to ſing with a good degree of decency in the worſhip of God.

They have alſo acquired a conſiderable degree of uſeful knowledge in the affairs of common life: ſo that they now appear like *rational* creatures, fit for human ſociety, free of that ſavage roughneſs and brutiſh ſtupidity, which rendered them very diſagreeable in their Pagan ſtate.

They ſeem ambitious of a thorough acquaintance with the Engliſh language, and for that end frequently ſpeak it among themſelves; and many of them have made good proficiency in their acquirement of it, ſince my coming among them; ſo that moſt of them can underſtand a conſiderable part, and ſome the ſubſtance of my diſcourſes, without an *interpreter*, (being uſed to my low and vulgar methods of expreſſion), though they could not well underſtand other miniſters.

And as they are deſirous of inſtruction, and ſurpriſingly apt in the reception of it, ſo divine providence has ſmiled upon them in regard of *proper means* in order to it.——The attempts made for the procurement of a *ſchool* among them have been ſucceeded, and a kind providence has ſent them a *ſchoolmaſter*, of whom I may juſtly ſay, I know of "no "man like minded, who will naturally care for their ſtate."

He has generally *thirty* or *thirty-five* children in his ſchool: and when he kept an evening ſchool (as he did while the length of the evenings would admit of it) he had *fifteen* or *twenty* people, married and ſingle.

The children learn with ſurpriſing readineſs; ſo that their *maſter* tells me, he never had an Engliſh ſchool that learned, in general, comparably ſo faſt. There were not above *two* in *thirty*, although ſome of them were very ſmall, but what learned to know all the *letters* in the *alphabet* diſtinctly, within three days after his entrance upon his buſineſs; and divers in that ſpace of time learned to *ſpell* conſiderably: and ſome of them, ſince the beginning of February laſt (at which time the ſchool was ſet up) have learned ſo much, that they are able to read in a *Pſalter* or *Teſtament* without ſpelling.

They are inſtructed twice a week in the Reverend Aſſembly's

bly's *Shorter Catechism, viz.* on Wednesday and Saturday. And some of them, since the latter end of February, (at which time they began), have learned to say it pretty distinctly *by heart* considerably more than half through; and most of them have made some proficiency in it.

They are likewise instructed in the duty of secret prayer, and most of them constantly attend it night and morning, and are very careful to inform their master if they apprehend any of their little school-mates neglect that religious exercise.

Fourthly, It is worthy to be noted, (to the praise of sovereign grace), that amidst *so great* a work of conviction,—so much concern and religious affection, there has been no *prevalency,* nor indeed any considerable *appearance* of *false religion,* (if I may so term it), or heats of imagination, intemperate zeal, and spiritual pride; which corrupt mixtures too often attend the revival and powerful propagation of religion; and that there have been so very few instances of irregular and scandalous behaviour among those who have appeared serious.—I may justly repeat what I observed in a *remark* at the conclusion of my last Journal, *viz.* That there has here been no appearance of "bodily agonies, convulsions, frightful screamings, swoonings," and the like: and may now further add, that there has been no *prevalency* of visions, trances, and imaginations of any kind; although there has been *some* appearance of something of that nature since the conclusion of that Journal. An instance of which I have given an account of in my Journal of December 26.

But this *work of grace* has, in the *main,* been carried on with a surprising degree of *purity,* and freedom from *trash* and corrupt mixture. The religious concern that persons have been under, has generally been *rational* and *just;* arising from a *sense* of their sins, and exposedness to the divine displeasure on the account of them; as well as their utter inability to deliver themselves from the misery they felt and feared. And if there has been in any instances an *appearance* of irrational concern and perturbation of mind, when the subjects of it knew not why, yet there has been no *prevalency* of any such thing; and indeed I scarce know of any instance of that nature at all.—And it is very remarkable, that although the concern of many persons under convictions of their perishing state has been very great and pressing, yet I have never seen any thing like *desperation* attending it in any one instance. They have had the most *lively sense* of their *undoneness* in themselves; have been brought to give up *all hopes* of deliverance from themselves; and their spiritual exercises leading hereto, have been attended with great diſtreſs and anguiſh of ſoul: and yet in the ſeaſons of the greateſt extremity, there has been no appearance of *deſpair* in any of them,—nothing that has diſcouraged, or in any wiſe hindered them from the moſt diligent uſe of all proper means for their converſion and ſalvation; whence it is apparent, there is not that danger of perſons being driven into deſpair under *ſpiritual trouble*, (unleſs in caſes of deep and habitual melancholy), that the world in general is ready to imagine.

The *comfort* that perſons have obtained after their diſtreſſes, has likewiſe in general appeared ſolid, well grounded, and ſcriptural; ariſing from a ſpiritual and *ſupernatural illumination* of mind,—a view of divine things (in a meaſure) *as they are*,—a complacency of ſoul in the divine perfections,—and a peculiar ſatisfaction in the *way of ſalvation* by free *ſovereign grace* in the great Redeemer.

Their joys have ſeemed to riſe from a variety of views and conſiderations of divine things, although for ſubſtance the ſame. Some, who under *conviction* ſeemed to have the hardeſt ſtruggles and heart-riſings againſt divine ſovereignty, have ſeemed, at the firſt dawn of their comfort, to rejoice in a peculiar manner in *that* divine perfection,—have been delighted to think that themſelves, and all things elſe, were in the hand of God, and that he would diſpoſe of them "juſt as "he pleaſed."

Others, who juſt before their reception of comfort, have been remarkably oppreſſed with a ſenſe of their *undoneneſs* and poverty, who have ſeen themſelves, as it were, falling down into remedileſs perdition, have been at firſt more peculiarly delighted with a view of the *freeneſs* and *riches* of divine grace, and the offer of ſalvation made to periſhing ſinners "without money, and without price."

Some have at firſt appeared to rejoice eſpecially in the *wiſdom* of God, diſcovered in the way of ſalvation by Chriſt; it then appearing to them "a new and living way," a way they had never thought, nor had any juſt conception of, until opened to them by the *ſpecial* influence of the divine Spirit. And ſome of them, upon a lively *ſpiritual* view of this way of ſalvation, have wondered at their paſt folly in ſeeking ſalvation other ways, and have admired that they never ſaw *this* way of ſalvation before, which now appeared ſo *plain* and *eaſy*, as well as *excellent* to them.

Others again have had a more *general* view of the beauty and excellency of Chriſt, and have had their ſouls delighted with an apprehenſion of his divine glory, as unſpeakably exceeding

ceeding *all* they had ever conceived of before; yet without singling out (as it were) any one of the divine perfections in particular; so that although their comforts have seemed to arise from a *variety* of views and considerations of divine glories, still they were *spiritual* and *supernatural* views of them, and not groundless fancies, that were the spring of their joys and comforts.

Yet it must be acknowledged, that when this work became so *universal* and *prevalent*, and gained such *general* credit and esteem among the Indians, that Satan seemed to have little advantage of working against it in his own proper garb; he then *transformed* himself "into an angel of light," and made some vigorous attempts to introduce turbulent commotions of the passions in the *room* of genuine convictions of sin, imaginary and fanciful notions of Christ, as appearing to the mental eye in a human shape, and being in some particular postures, &c. in the room of *spiritual* and *supernatural* discoveries of his divine glory and excellency, as well as divers other delusions. And I have reason to think, that if these things had met with countenance and encouragement, there would have been a very considerable *harvest* of this kind of converts here. *Spiritual pride* also discovered itself in various instances. Some persons who had been under great affections, seemed very desirous from thence of being thought truly gracious; who, when I could not but express to them my fears respecting their spiritual states, discovered their resentments to a considerable degree upon that occasion. There also appeared in *one* or *two* of them an unbecoming ambition of being *teachers* of others. So that *Satan* has been *a busy adversary* here, as well as elsewhere. But (blessed be God) though something of this nature has appeared, yet nothing of it has *prevailed*, nor indeed made any considerable progress at all. My people are now apprised of these things, are acquainted that *Satan* in such a manner "transformed himself "into an angel of light," in the first season of the great *outpouring* of the divine Spirit in the days of the apostles; and that something of this nature, in a greater or lesser degree, has attended almost every revival and remarkable propagation of true religion ever since. And they have learned *so* to distinguish between the *gold* and *dross*, that the credit of the latter "is trode down like the mire of the streets:" and it being natural for this kind of *stuff* to die with its *credit*, there is now scarce any *appearance* of it among them.

And as there has been no *prevalency* of irregular heats, imaginary notions, spiritual pride, and Satanical delusions among my people; so there has been a very few instances of *scandalous* and *irregular* behaviour among those who have made a *profession*, or even an *appearance* of seriousness. I do not know of more than three or four *such* persons that have been guilty of any open misconduct, since their first acquaintance with Christianity, and not one that persists in any thing of that nature. And perhaps the remarkable purity of this work in the *latter* respect, its freedom from frequent instances of scandal, is very much owing to its purity in the *former* respect, its freedom from corrupt mixtures of spiritual pride, wild-fire, and delusion, which naturally lay a foundation for scandalous practices.

" May this blessed work in the power and purity of it prevail among the poor Indians here, as well as spread elsewhere, till their remotest tribes shall see the salvation of God! Amen."

Money collected and expended for the Indians.

As mention has been made in the preceding Journal, of an English *school* erected and continued among these Indians, dependent entirely upon charity; and as *collections* have already been made in divers places for the support of it, as well as for defraying other charges that have necessarily arisen in the promotion of the religious interests of the Indians, it may be satisfactory, and perhaps will be thought by some but a piece of justice to the world, that an exact account be here given of the money already received by way of collection for the benefit of the Indians, and the *manner* in which it has been expended.

The following is therefore a just account of this matter.

Money

Money received since October last, by way of public collection, for promoting the religious interests of the Indians in New-Jersey, *viz.*

	l.	*s.*	*d.*
From New-York, - - - - -	23	10	2
Jamaica on Long-Island, - -	3	0	0
Elisabeth-Town, - - -	7	5	0
Elisabeth-Town farms, - - -	1	18	9
Newark, - - - -	4	5	7
Woodbridge, - - - -	2	18	2
Morris-Town, - -	1	5	3
Freehold, - - - - -	12	11	0
Freehold Dutch congregation, - -	4	14	3
Shrewsbury and Shark-river, - -	3	5	0
Middle-Town Dutch congregation, -	2	0	6
The Dutch congregation in and about New-Brunswick, - - - -	3	5	0
Kings-Town, - - - -	5	11	0
Neshaminy, and places adjacent in Pennsylvania,	14	5	10
Abington and New-Providence, by the hand of the Reverend Mr Treat, - - -	10	5	0
The whole amounting to *L.*	100	0	0

Money paid out since October last for promoting the religious interests of the Indians in New-Jersey, *viz.*

	l.	*s.*	*d.*
Upon the occasion mentioned in my Journal of January 28. - - -	82	5	0
For the building a schoolhouse, -	3	5	0
To the schoolmaster as a part of his reward for his present year's service, - -	17	10	0
For books for the children to learn in, -	3	0	0
The whole amounting to *L.*	106	0	0

DAVID BRAINERD.

APPENDIX to the Journal.

I Should have concluded what I had, at present, to offer upon the affairs respecting my *mission*, with the preceding account of the money collected and expended for the *religious interests* of the Indians, but that I have not long since received from the Reverend President of the correspondents, the copy of a letter directed to him from the Honourable Society for propagating Christian knowledge, dated at Edinburgh, March 21. 1745. Wherein I find it is expresly enjoined upon their missionaries, "That they give an exact account of " the methods they make use of for instructing themselves in " the Indians language, and what progress they have already " made in it. What methods they are now taking to instruct " the Indians in the principles of our holy religion. And " *particularly*, that they set forth in their Journals what dif- " ficulties they have already met with, and the methods they " make use of for surmounting the same."

As to the *two former* of these particulars, I trust that what I have already noted in my Journals from time to time, might have been in a good measure satisfactory to the Honourable Society, had these Journals arrived *safely* and *seasonably*, which I am sensible they have not in general done, by reason of their falling into the hands of the enemy, although I have been at the pains of sending two copies of every Journal, for more than two years past, lest one might miscarry in the passage. But with relation to the *latter* of these particulars, I have purposely omitted saying any thing considerable, and that for these two reasons. *First*, Because I could not oftentimes give any tolerable account of the *difficulties* I met with in my work, without speaking somewhat particularly of the *causes* of them, and the *circumstances* conducing to them, which would necessarily have rendered my Journals very lengthy and tedious. Besides, some of the causes of my difficulties I thought more fit to be concealed than divulged.— And, *secondly*, Because I thought a frequent mentioning of the difficulties attending my work, might appear as an *unbecoming* complaint under my burdens; or as if I would rather be thought to be endowed with a singular measure of self-denial, constancy,

constancy, and holy resolution, to meet and confront so many difficulties, and yet to hold on and go forward amidst them all. But since the Honourable Society are pleased to require a more *exact* and *particular* account of these things, I shall cheerfully endeavour something for their satisfaction in relation to each of these particulars: although in regard of the latter, I am ready to say, *Infandum ——jubes renovare dolorem.*

The most successful *method* I have taken for instructing myself in any of the Indian languages, is, to translate English discourses by the help of an interpreter or two, into their language, as near verbatim as the sense will admit of, and to observe strictly how they use words, and what construction they will bear in various cases; and thus to gain some acquaintance with the root from whence particular words proceed, and to see how they are thence varied and diversified. But here occurs a very great difficulty; for the interpreters being unlearned, and unacquainted with the rules of language, it is impossible sometimes to know by them what part of speech some particular words is of, whether *noun*, *verb*, or *participle*; for they seem to use *participles* sometimes where we should use *nouns*, and sometimes where we should use *verbs* in the English language. But I have, notwithstanding many difficulties, gained some acquaintance with the grounds of the Delaware language, and have learned most of the *defects* in it; so that I know what English words can, and what cannot be translated into it. I have also gained some acquaintance with the particular phraseologies, as well as *peculiarities* of their language, one of which I cannot but mention. Their language does not admit of their speaking any word denoting relation, such as, father, son, *&c. absolutely*; that is, without prefixing a pronoun-passive to it, such as *my*, *thy*, *his*, &c. Hence they cannot be baptized in their own language in the name of *the* Father, and *the* Son, *&c.*; but they may be baptized in the name of Jesus Christ and *his* Father, *&c.* I have gained so much knowledge of their language, that I can understand a considerable part of what they say, when they discourse upon divine things, and am frequently able to correct my interpreter, if he mistakes my sense. But I can do nothing to any purpose at speaking the language myself.

And as an apology for this defect, I must renew, or rather enlarge my former complaint, *viz.* That "while so much of "my time is necessarily consumed in journeying," while I am obliged to ride four thousand miles a-year, (as I have done in the year past), "I can have little left for any of my necessary "studies,

"studies, and consequently for the study of the Indian languages." And this I may venture to say, is the great, if not the only reason why the Delaware language is not familiar to me before this time. And it is impossible I should ever be able to speak it without close application, which (at present) I see no prospect of having time for. To preach and catechise frequently; to converse privately with persons that need so much instruction and direction as these poor Indians do; to take care of all their *secular* affairs, as if they were a company of children; to ride abroad frequently in order to procure collections for the support of the *school*, and for their help and benefit in other respects; to hear and decide all the petty differences that arise among any of them; and to have the constant oversight and management of all their affairs of every kind, must needs ingross most of my time, and leave me little for application to the study of the Indian languages. And when I add to this, the time that is necessarily consumed upon my Journals, I must say I have little to spare for other business. I have not (as was observed before) sent to the Honourable Society less than two copies of every Journal, for more than two years past; most of which, I suppose, have been taken by the French in their passage. And a third copy I have constantly kept by me, lest the others should miscarry; which has caused me not a little labour, and so straitened me for time, when I have been at liberty from other business, and had opportunity to sit down to writing, (which is but rare), I have been obliged to write twelve and thirteen hours in a day, till my spirits have been extremely wasted, and my life almost spent, to get these writings accomplished. And after all; after diligent application to the various parts of my work, and after the most industrious improvement of time I am capable of, both early and late, I cannot oftentimes possibly gain two hours in a week for reading, or any other studies, unless just for what urges and appears of absolute necessity *for the present*. And frequently when I attempt to redeem time, by sparing it out of my sleeping hours, I am by that means thrown under bodily indisposition, and rendered fit for nothing.

This is truly my present state, and is like to be so, for aught I can see, unless I could procure an *assistant* in my work, or quit my present business.

But although I have not made that proficiency I could wish to have done, in learning the Indian languages; yet I have used all endeavours to instruct them in the English tongue, which perhaps will be more advantageous to the Christian interest

terest among them, than if I should preach in their own language; for that is very defective, (as I shall hereafter observe), so that many things cannot be communicated to them without introducing English terms. Besides, they can have no *books* translated into their language, without great difficulty and expence; and if still accustomed to their own language only, they would have no advantage of hearing other ministers occasionally, or in my absence. So that my having a perfect acquaintance with the Indian language, would be of no great importance with regard to this congregation of Indians in New-Jersey, although it might be of great service to me in treating with the Indians elsewhere.

The methods I am taking to instruct the Indians in the principles of our holy religion, are, to preach, or open and improve some particular points of doctrine; to expound particular paragraphs, or sometimes whole chapters of God's word to them; to give historical relations from scripture of the most material and remarkable occurrences relating to the church of God from the beginning; and frequently to catechise them upon the principles of Christianity. The latter of these methods of instructing, I manage in a twofold manner. I sometimes catechise *systematically*, proposing questions agreeable to the Reverend Assembly's *Shorter Catechism*. This I have carried on to a considerable length. At other times I catechise upon any important subject that I think difficult to them. Sometimes when I have discoursed upon some particular point, and made it as plain and familiar to them as I can, I then catechise them upon the most material branches of my discourse, to see whether they had a thorough understanding of it. But I as have catechised chiefly in a *systematical* form, I shall here give some specimen of the method I make use of in it, as well as of the propriety and justness of my people's answers to the questions proposed to them.

Questions upon the benefits believers receive from Christ at death.

Q. I have shewn you, that the children of God receive a great many good things from Christ while they live, now have they any more to receive when they come to die? A. *Yes.*

Q. Are the children of God then made perfectly free from sin? A. *Yes.*

Q. Do you think they will never more be troubled with

 vain,

vain, foolish, and wicked thoughts? A. *No, never at all.*

Q. Will not they then be like the good angels I have so often told you of? A. *Yes.*

Q. And do you call *this* a great mercy to be freed from all sin? A. *Yes.*

Q. Do all God's children count it so?

A. *Yes, all of them.*

Q. Do you think this is what they would ask for above *all things*, if God should say to them, Ask what you will, and it shall be done for you?

A. *O yes, be sure, this is what they want.*

Q. You say the souls of God's people at death are made perfectly free from sin, where do they go then?

A. *They go and live with Jesus Christ.*

Q. Does Christ shew them more respect and honour, and make them more happy * than we can possibly think of in this world? A. *Yes.*

Q. Do they go *immediately* to live with Christ in heaven, as soon as their bodies are dead? or do they tarry somewhere else a while? A. *They go immediately to Christ.*

Q. Does Christ take any care of the bodies of his people when they are dead, and their souls gone to heaven, or does he forget them?

A. *He takes care of them.*

These questions were all answered with surprising readiness, and without once missing, as I remember. And in answering several of them which respected deliverance from sin, they were much affected, and melted with the hopes of that happy state.

Questions upon the benefits believers receive from Christ at the resurrection.

Q. You see I have already shewn you what good things Christ gives his good people while they live, and when they come to die: now, will he raise their bodies, and the bodies of others, to life again at the last day?

A. *Yes, they shall all be raised.*

Q. Shall they then have the same bodies they now have?

A. *Yes.*

* The only way I have to express their "entering into glory," or being glorified; there being no word in the Indian language answering to that general term.

Q. Will

Q. Will their bodies then be weak, will they feel cold, hunger, thirst, and weariness, as they now do?

A. *No, none of these things.*

Q. Will their bodies ever die any more after they are raised to life? A. *No.*

Q. Will their souls and bodies be joined together again?

A. *Yes.*

Q. Will God's people be more happy then, than they were while their bodies were asleep? A. *Yes.*

Q. Will Christ then own these to be his people before all the world? A. *Yes.*

Q. But God's people find so much sin in themselves, that they are often ashamed of themselves, and will not Christ be ashamed to own such for his friends at that day?

A. *No, he will never be ashamed of them.*

Q. Will Christ then show all the world, that he has put away these peoples sins *, and that he looks upon them as if they had never sinned at all? A. *Yes.*

Q. Will he look upon them as if they had never sinned, for the sake of any good things they have done themselves, or for the sake of his righteousness accounted to them as if it was theirs?

A. *For the sake of his righteousness counted to them, not for their own goodness.*

Q. Will God's children then be as happy as they can desire to be? A. *Yes.*

Q. The children of God while in this world, can but now and then draw near to him, and they are ready to think they can never have enough of God and Christ, but will they have enough there, as much as they can desire?

A. *O yes, enough, enough.*

Q. Will the children of God love him then as much as they desire, will they find nothing to hinder their love from going to him?

A. *Nothing at all, they shall love him as much as they desire.*

Q. Will they never be weary of God and Christ, and the pleasures of heaven, so as we are weary of our friends and enjoyments here, after we have been pleased with them a while?

A. *No, never.*

Q. Could God's people be happy if they knew God loved

* The only way I have to express their being *openly—acquitted.* As when I speak of justification, I have no other way but to call it God's looking upon us as good creatures.

them, and yet felt at the same time that they could not love and honour him? A. *No, no.*

Q. Will this then make God's people perfectly happy, to love God above all, to honour him continually, and to feel his love to them? A. *Yes.*

Q. And will this happiness last for ever?

A. *Yes, for ever, for ever!*

These questions, like the former, were answered without hesitation or missing, as I remember, in any one instance.

Questions upon the duty which God requires of man.

Q. Has God let us know any thing of his will, or what he would have us to do to please him? A. *Yes.*

Q. And does he require us to do his will, and to please him? A. *Yes.*

Q. Is it right that God should require this of us, has he any business to command us as a father does his children?

A. *Yes.*

Q. Why is it right that God should command us to do what he pleases?

A. *Because he made us, and gives us all our good things.*

Q. Does God require us to do any thing that will hurt us, and take away our comfort and happiness? A. *No.*

Q. But God requires sinners to repent and be sorry for their sins, and to have their hearts broken; now, does not this hurt them, and take away their comfort, to be made sorry, and to have their hearts broken?

A. *No, it does them good.*

Q. Did God teach man his will at first by writing it down in a book, or did he put it into his heart, and teach him without a book what was right?

A. *He put it into his heart, and made him know what he should do.*

Q. Has God since that time writ down his will in a book?

A. *Yes.*

Q. Has God written his whole will in his book; has he there told us all that he would have us believe and do?

A. *Yes.*

Q. What need was there of this book, if God at first put his will into the heart of man, and made him feel what he should do?

A. *There was need of it, because we have sinned, and made our hearts blind.*

Q. And

Q. And has God writ down the same things in his book, that he at first put into the heart of man? A. *Yes.*

In this manner I endeavour to adapt my instructions to the capacities of my people; although they may perhaps seem strange to others who have never experienced the difficulty of the work. And these I have given an account of, are the methods I am from time to time pursuing, in order to instruct them in the principles of Christianity. And I think I may say, it is my great concern that these instructions be given them in such a *manner*, that they may not only be *doctrinally taught*, but *duly affected* thereby, that divine truths may come to them, "not in word only, but in power, and in the "Holy Ghost," and be received "not as the word of man."

Difficulties attending the Christianizing of the Indians.

I shall now attempt something with relation to the last particular required by the Honourable Society in their letter, *viz.* To give some account of the "difficulties I have already "met with in my work, and the methods I make use of for "surmounting the same." And what I have to say upon this subject, I shall reduce to the following heads.

First, I have met with great difficulty in my work among these Indians, "from the rooted aversion to Christianity that "generally prevails among them." They are not only brutishly stupid and ignorant of divine things, but many of them are obstinately set against Christianity, and seem to abhor even the Christian *name*.

This aversion to Christianity arises partly from a view of the "immorality and vicious behaviour of many who are call-"ed Christians." They observe that horrid wickedness in nominal Christians, which the light of nature condemns in themselves: and not having distinguishing views of things, are ready to look upon all the white people *alike*, and to condemn them *alike*, for the abominable practices of *some*.—Hence when I have attempted to treat with them about Christianity, they have frequently objected the scandalous practices of Christians, and cast in my teeth all they could think of that was odious in the conduct of any of them. Have observed to me, that the white people lie, defraud, steal, and drink worse than the Indians; that they have taught the Indians these things, especially the latter of them; who before the coming of the English, knew of no such thing as strong drink: that the English have, by these means, made them quarrel and kill one another; and, in a word, brought them to the practice of all those vices that now prevail among them. So that they are now vastly more vicious, as well as much more miserable, than they were before the coming of the white people into the country.

These, and such like objections, they frequently make against Christianity, which are not easily answered to their satisfaction; many of them being *facts* too notoriously true.

The only way I have to take in order to *surmount this difficulty*, is to distinguish between *nominal* and *real* Christians; and to shew them, that the ill conduct of many of the *former* proceed not from their being Christians, but from their being Christians only in *name*, not in *heart*, &c. To which it has sometimes been objected, that if all those who will cheat the Indians are Christians only in *name*, there are but few left in the country to be Christians in *heart*. This, and many other of the remarks they pass upon the white people, and their miscarriages, I am forced to own, and cannot but grant, that many *nominal* Christians are more abominably wicked than the Indians. But then I attempt to show them, that there are some who feel the power of Christianity, that are not so. And I ask them, when they ever saw me guilty of the vices they complain of, and charge Christians in general with? But still the great difficulty is, that the people who live back in the country nearest to them, and the *traders* that go among them, are generally of the most irreligious and vicious sort; and the conduct of one or two persons, be it never so exemplary, is not sufficient to counterbalance the vicious behaviour of so many of the same denomination, and so to recommend Christianity to Pagans.

Another thing that serves to make them more averse to Christianity, is a "fear of being enslaved." They are, perhaps, some of the most jealous people living, and extremely averse to a state of servitude, and hence are always afraid of some design forming against them. Besides, they seem to have no sentiments of generosity, benevolence, and goodness; that if any thing be proposed to them, as being for their good, they are ready rather to suspect, that there is at bottom some design forming against them, than that such proposals flow from goodwill to them, and a desire of their welfare. And hence, when I have attempted to recommend Christianity to their acceptance, they have sometimes objected, that the white people have come among them, have cheated them out of their lands, driven them back to the mountains, from the pleasant places they used to enjoy by the sea-side, &c.: that

that therefore they have no reason to think the white people are now seeking their welfare; but rather that they have sent me out to draw them together, under a pretence of kindness to them, that they may have an opportunity to make slaves of them, as they do of the poor negroes, or else to ship them on board their vessels, and make them fight with their enemies, *&c.* Thus they have oftentimes construed all the kindness I could shew them, and the hardships I have endured in order to treat with them about Christianity. "He "never would (say they) take all this pains to do us good, "he must have some wicked design to hurt us some way or "other." And to give them assurance of the contrary, is not an easy matter, while there are so many, who (agreeable to their apprehension) are only "seeking their own," not the good of others.

To remove this difficulty I inform them, that I am not sent out among them by those persons in *these provinces*, who, they suppose, have cheated them out of their lands; but by pious people at a great distance, who never had an inch of their lands, nor ever thought of doing them any hurt, *&c.*

But here will arise so many frivolous and impertinent questions, that it would tire one's patience, and wear out one's spirits to hear them; such as that, "But why did not "*these good people* send you to teach us before, while we had "our lands down by the sea-side, *&c.* If they had sent you "then, we should likely have heard you, and turned Chri-"stians." The poor creatures still imagining, that I should be much beholding to them, in case they would hearken to Christianity; and insinuating, that this was a favour they could not now be so good as to shew me, seeing they had received so many injuries from the *white* people.

Another spring of aversion to Christianity in the Indians, is, "their strong attachment to their own religious notions, "(if they may be called religious), and the early prejudices "they have imbibed in favour of their own frantic and ridi-"culous kind of worship." What their notions of God are, in their Pagan state, is hard precisely to determine. I have taken much pains to inquire of my Christian people, whether they, before their acquaintance with Christianity, imagined there was a *plurality* of great invisible powers, or whether they supposed but *one* such being, and worshipped him in a variety of forms and shapes: but cannot learn any thing of them so distinct as to be fully satisfying upon the point. Their notions in that state were so prodigiously dark and confused,

fused, that they seemed not to know what they thought themselves. But so far as I can learn, they had a notion of a plurality of invisible *deities*, and paid some kind of homage to them promiscuously, under a great variety of forms and shapes. And it is certain, those who yet remain Pagans pay some kind of superstitious reverence to beasts, birds, fishes, and even reptiles; that is, some to one kind of animal, and some to another. They do not indeed suppose a divine power *essential* to, or *inhering* in these creatures, but that some invisible beings (I cannot learn that it is always one such being only, but divers; not distinguished from each other by certain names, but only notionally) communicate to these animals a *great power*, either one or other of them, (just as it happens), or perhaps sometimes all of them, and so make these creatures the immediate authors of good to certain persons. Whence such a creature becomes *sacred* to the persons to whom he is supposed to be the immediate author of good, and through him they must worship the invisible powers, though to others he is no more than another creature. And perhaps another animal is looked upon to be the immediate author of good to *another*, and consequently *he* must worship the invisible powers in that animal. And I have known a Pagan burn fine tobacco for incense, in order to appease the anger of that invisible power which he supposed presided over *rattle-snakes*, because one of these animals was killed by another Indian near his house.

But after the strictest inquiry respecting their notions of the Deity, I find, that in ancient times, before the coming of the white people, some supposed there were *four* invisible powers, who presided over the four corners of the earth. Others imagined the *sun* to be the *only* deity, and that all things were made by him: others at the same time having a confused notion of a certain *body* or fountain of *deity*, somewhat like the *anima mundi*, so frequently mentioned by the more learned ancient Heathens, diffusing itself to various animals, and even to inanimate things, making them the immediate authors of good to certain persons, as was before observed, with respect to *various* supposed deities. But after the coming of the white people, they seemed to suppose there were three deities, and three only, because they saw people of three different kinds of complexion, *viz.* English, Negroes, and themselves.

It is a notion pretty generally prevailing among them, that it was not the *same God* made them, who made us; but that they were made after the white people; which further shews, that

that they imagine a plurality of divine powers. And I fancy they suppose their God gained some special skill by seeing the white people made, and so made *them* better: for it is certain they look upon themselves, and their methods of living, (which, they say, their God expressly prescribed for them), vastly preferable to the white people, and their methods. And hence will frequently sit and laugh at them, as being good for nothing else but to plow and fatigue themselves with hard labour; while *they* enjoy the satisfaction of stretching themselves on the ground, and sleeping as much as they please; and have no other trouble but now and then to chase the deer, which is often attended with pleasure rather than pain. Hence, by the way, many of them look upon it as disgraceful for them to become Christians, as it would be esteemed among Christians for any to become Pagans. And now although they suppose our religion will do well enough for us, because prescribed by *our* God, yet it is no ways proper for them, because not of the same make and original. This they have sometimes offered as a reason why they did not incline to hearken to Christianity.

They seem to have some confused notion about a future state of existence, and many of them imagine that the *chichung*, (*i. e.* the shadow), or what survives the body, will at death go *southward*, and in an unknown but curious place, will enjoy some kind of happiness, such as, hunting, feasting, dancing, and the like. And what they suppose will contribute much to their happiness in that state is, that they shall never be weary of those entertainments. It seems by this notion of their going *southward* to obtain happiness, as if they had their course into these parts of the world from some very cold climate, and found the further they went *southward* the more comfortable they were; and thence concluded, that perfect felicity was to be found further towards the same point.

They seem to have some faint and glimmering notion about *rewards* and *punishments*, or at least *happiness* and *misery* in a future state, that is, some that I have conversed with, though others seem to know of no such thing. Those that suppose this, seem to imagine that most will be happy, and that those who are not so, will be punished only with *privation*, being only excluded the walls of that good world where happy souls shall dwell.

These rewards and punishments they suppose to depend entirely upon their conduct with relation to the duties of the *second* table, *i. e.* their behaviour towards mankind, and seem, so far as I can see, not to imagine that they have any reference to their *religious* notions or practices, or any thing that relates to the worship of God. I remember I once consulted a very ancient, but intelligent Indian upon this point, for my own satisfaction; asked him whether the Indians of old times had supposed there was any thing of the man that would survive the body? He replied, Yes. I asked him, where they supposed its abode would be? He replied, "It would go "southward." I asked him further, whether it would be happy there? He answered, after a considerable pause, "that "the souls of *good* folks would be happy, and the souls of "*bad* folks miserable." I then asked him, who he called *bad folks?* His answer (as I remember) was, "Those who lie, "steal, quarrel with their neighbours, are unkind to their "friends, and especially to aged parents, and, in a word, "such as are a plague to mankind." These were his *bad folks;* but not a word was said about their neglect of divine worship, and their badness in that respect.

They have indeed some kind of religious worship, are frequently offering *sacrifices* to some supposed invisible powers, and are very ready to impute their calamities in the *present* world, to the neglect of these sacrifices; but there is no appearance of reverence and devotion in the homage they pay them; and what they do of this nature, seems to be done only to appease the supposed anger of their deities, to engage them to be placable to themselves, and do them no hurt, or at most, only to invite these *powers* to succeed them in those enterprises they are engaged in respecting the *present* life. So that in offering these sacrifices, they seem to have no reference to a future state, but only to present comfort. And this is the account my interpreter always gives me of this matter. "They sacrifice (says he) that they may have suc"cess in hunting and other affairs, and that sickness and "other calamities, may not befal them, which they fear in "the present world, in case of neglect; but they do not sup"pose God will ever punish them in the *coming* world for "neglecting to sacrifice," &c. And indeed they seem to imagine, that those whom they call *bad folks*, are excluded from the company of good people in that state, not so much because God remembers, and is determined to punish them for their sins of any kind, either immediately against himself or their neighbour, as because they would be a *plague* to society, and would render others unhappy if admitted to dwell with them. So that they are excluded rather of *necessity*, than by God acting as a *righteous judge*.

They

They give much heed to *dreams*, because they suppose these invisible powers give them directions at such times about certain affairs, and sometime informs them what *animal* they would chuse to be worshipped in. They are likewise much attached to the traditions and fabulous notions of their fathers, who have informed them of divers miracles that were anciently wrought among the Indians, which they firmly believe, and thence look upon their ancestors to have been the best of men. They also mention some wonderful things which, they say, have happened since the memory of some who are now living. One I remember affirmed to me, that himself had once been dead four days, that most of his friends in that time were gathered together to his funeral, and that he should have been buried, but that some of his relations at a great distance, who were sent for upon that occasion, were not arrived, before whose coming he came to life again. In this time, he says, he went to the place where the sun *rises*, (imagining the earth to be plain), and directly over that place, at a great height in the air, he was admitted, he says, into a great house, which he supposes was several miles in length, and saw many wonderful things, too tedious as well as ridiculous to mention. Another person, a woman, whom I have not seen, but been credibly informed of by the Indians, declares, that she was dead several days, that her soul went *southward*, and feasted and danced with the happy spirits, and that she found all things exactly agreeable to the Indian notions of a future state.

These superstitious notions and traditions, and this kind of ridiculous worship I have mentioned, they are extremely attached to, and the prejudice they have imbibed in favour of these things, renders them not a little averse to the doctrines of Christianity. Whence some of them have told me, when I have endeavoured to instruct them, "that their fathers had "taught them already, and that they did not want to learn "now."

It will be too tedious to give any considerable account of the methods I make use of for surmounting this difficulty. I will just say, I endeavour, as much as possible, to shew them the *inconsistency* of their own notions, and so to confound them out of their own mouths. But I must also say, I have sometimes been almost nonplussed with them, and scarce knew what to answer them: but never have been more perplexed with them, than when they have pretended to yield to me as knowing more than they, and consequently have asked me numbers of impertinent, and yet difficult questions, as,

"How the Indians came first into this part of the world, a-"
"way from all the white people, if what I said was true," *viz.* that the same God made them who made us? "How the In-"
"dians became *black*, if they had the same original parents"
"with the *white* people?" And numbers more of the like nature.

These things, I must say, have been not a little difficult and discouraging, especially when withal, some of the Indians have appeared angry and malicious against Christianity.

What further contributes to their aversion to Christianity is, the influence that their powwows (conjurers or diviners) have upon them. These are a sort of persons who are supposed to have a power of *foretelling future events*, of *recovering the sick*, at least oftentimes, and of *charming*, *inchanting*, or *poisoning persons to death* by their *magic* divinations. And their spirit, in its various operations, seems to be a Satanical imitation of the spirit of prophecy that the church in early ages was favoured with. Some of these diviners are endowed with this spirit in infancy;—others in adult age.—It seems not to depend upon their own will, nor to be acquired by any endeavours of the person who is the subject of it, although it is supposed to be given to children sometimes in consequence of some means the parents use with them for that purpose; one of which is to make the child swallow a small living frog, after having performed some superstitious rites and ceremonies upon it. They are not under the influence of this spirit always alike,—but it comes upon them at times. And those who are endowed with it, are accounted singularly favoured.

I have laboured to gain some acquaintance with this affair of their conjuration, and have for that end consulted and queried with the man mentioned in my Journal of May 9. who, since his conversion to Christianity, has endeavoured to give me the best intelligence he could of this matter. But it seems to be such a *mystery of iniquity*, that I cannot well understand it, and does not know oftentimes what ideas to affix to the terms he makes use of; and, so far as I can learn, he himself has not any clear notions of the thing, now his spirit of divination is gone from him. However, the manner in which he says he obtained this spirit of divination was this, he was admitted into the presence of a *great man*, who informed him, that he loved, pitied, and desired to do him good. It was not in this world that he saw the great man, but in a world *above* at a vast distance from this. The great man, he says, was clothed with the day; yea, with the brightest

brightest day he ever saw; a day of many years, yea, of everlasting continuance! this whole world, he says, was drawn upon him, so that *in* him, the earth, and all things in it, might be seen. I asked him, if rocks, mountains, and seas was drawn upon, or appeared in him? He replied, that every thing that was beautiful and lovely in the earth was upon him, and might be seen by looking on him, as well as if one was on the earth to take a view of them there. By the side of the great man, he says, stood his *shadow* or spirit; for he used (*chichung*), the word they commonly make use of to express that of the man which survives the body, which word properly signifies a *shadow*. This shadow, he says, was as lovely as the man himself, and filled *all places*, and was most agreeable as well as wonderful to him.—Here he says, he tarried some time, and was unspeakably entertained and delighted with a view of the great man, of his shadow or spirit, and of all things *in him*. And what is most of all astonishing, he imagines all this to have passed before he was born. He never had been, he says, in this world at that time. And what confirms him in the belief of this, is, that the great man told him, that he must come down to earth, be born of *such* a woman, meet with *such* and *such* things, and in particular, that he should once in his life be guilty of *murder*. At this he was displeased, and told the great man, he would never murder. But the great man replied, "I have said it, "and it shall be so." Which has accordingly happened. At this time, he says, the great man asked him what he would chuse in life. He replied, first to be a *hunter*, and afterwards to be a *powwow* or *diviner*. Whereupon the great man told him, he should have what he desired, and that his *shadow* should go along with him down to earth, and be with him for ever. There was, he says, all this time no words spoken between them. The conference was not carried on by any *human* language, but they had a kind of mental intelligence of each others thoughts, dispositions, and proposals. After this, he says, he saw the great man no more; but supposes he now came down to earth to be born, but the spirit or shadow of the great man still attended him, and ever after continued to appear to him in dreams and other ways, until he felt the power of God's word upon his heart; since which it has entirely left him.

This spirit, he says, used sometimes to direct him in dreams to go to such a place and hunt, assuring him he should there meet with success, which accordingly proved so. And when he had been there some time, the spirit would order him to

another

another place. So that he had succefs in hunting, according to the great man's promife made to him at the time of his chufing this employment.

There were fome times when this fpirit came upon him in a *fpecial* manner, and he was full of what he faw in the great man; and then, he fays, he was *all light*, and not only *light* himfelf, but it was light all *around him*, fo that he could fee through men, and knew the thoughts of their hearts, &c. Thefe *depths of Satan* I leave to others to fathom or to dive into as they pleafe, and do not pretend, for my own part, to know what ideas to affix to fuch terms, and cannot well guefs what conceptions of things thefe creatures have at thefe times when they call themfelves *all light*. But my interpreter tells me, that he heard one of them tell a certain Indian the fecret thoughts of his heart, which he had never divulged. The cafe was this, the Indian was bitten with a fnake, and was in extreme pain with the bite. Whereupon the *diviner* (who was applied to for his recovery) told him, that at *fuch a time* he had promifed, that the next deer he killed, he would facrifice it to fome *great power*, but had broken his promife. And now, faid he, that great power has ordered this fnake to bite you for your neglect. The Indian confeffed it was fo, but faid he had never told any body of it. But as *Satan*, no doubt, excited the Indian to make that promife, it was no wonder he fhould be able to communicate the matter to the conjurer.

Thefe things ferve to fix them down in their *idolatry*, and to make them believe there is no fafety to be expected, but by their continuing to *offer fuch facrifices*. And the influence that thefe powwows have upon them, either through the efteem or fear they have of them, is no fmall hindrance to their embracing Chriftianity.

To remove this difficulty, I have laboured to fhew the Indians, that thefe diviners have no power to recover the fick, when the God whom Chriftians ferve, has determined them for death, and that the fuppofed *great power* who influences thefe *diviners* has himfelf no power in this cafe: and that if they feem to recover any by their *magic charms*, they are only fuch as the God I preached to them, had determined fhould recover, and who would have recovered without their conjurations, &c. And when I have apprehended them afraid of embracing Chriftianity, left they fhould be inchanted and poifoned, I have endeavoured to relieve their minds of this fear, by afking them, why their powwows did not inchant and poifon me, feeing they had as much reafon to hate me me for preaching to, and desiring them to become Christians, as they could have to hate them in case they should actually become such. And that they might have an evidence of the power and goodness of God engaged for the protection of Christians, I ventured to bid a challenge to all their powwows and *great powers* to do their worst on me first of all, and thus laboured to tread down their influence.

Many things further might be offered upon this head, but thus much may suffice for a representation of their aversion to, and prejudice against Christianity, the springs of it, and the difficulties thence arising.

Secondly, Another great difficulty I have met with in my attempts to Christianize the Indians, has been to "convey divine truths to their understandings, and to gain their assent to them as such."

In the first place, I laboured under a very great disadvantage for want of an interpreter, who had a good degree of *doctrinal* as well as *experimental* knowledge of divine things: in both which respects my present interpreter was very defective when I first employed him, as I noted in the account I before gave of him. And it was sometimes extremely discouraging to me, when I could not make him understand what I designed to communicate; when truths of the last importance appeared *foolishness to him* for want of a spiritual understanding and relish of them; and when he addressed the Indians in a lifeless indifferent manner, without any heart-engagement or fervency; and especially when he appeared heartless and irresolute about making attempts for the conversion of the Indians to Christianity, as he frequently did. For although he had a desire that they should conform to Christian manners, (as I elsewhere observed), yet being abundantly acquainted with their strong attachment to their own superstitious notions, and the difficulty of bringing them off, and having no sense of divine power and grace, nor dependence upon an almighty Arm for the accomplishment of this work, he used to be discouraged, and tell me, "It signifies nothing "for us to try, they will never turn," *&c*. So that he was a distressing weight and burden to me. And here I should have sunk scores of times, but that God in a remarkable manner supported me; sometimes by giving me full satisfaction that he himself had called me to this work, and thence a secret hope that sometime or other I might meet with success in it; or if not, that "my judgment should notwithstanding be "with the Lord, and my work with my God." Sometimes by giving me a sense of his almighty power, and that "his "hand

"hand was not shortened." Sometimes by affording me a fresh and lively view of some remarkable freedom and assistance I had been repeatedly favoured with in prayer for the ingathering of these Heathens some years before, even before I was a missionary, and a refreshing sense of the stability and faithfulness of the divine promises, and that the *prayer of faith* should not fail.

Thus I was supported under these trials, and the method God was pleased to take for the removal of this difficulty, (respecting my interpreter), I have sufficiently represented elsewhere.

Another thing that rendered it very difficult to convey divine truths to the understandings of the Indians, was the *defectiveness* of their language, the want of terms to express and convey ideas of spiritual things. There are no words in the Indian language to answer our English words, "Lord, "Saviour, salvation, sinner, justice, condemnation, faith, "repentance, justification, adoption, sanctification, grace, "glory, heaven," with scores of the like importance.

The only methods I can make use of for surmounting this difficulty, are, either to describe the things at large designed by these terms, as if I was speaking of regeneration, to call it, the "heart's being changed" by God's Spirit, or the "heart's being made good." Or else I must introduce the English terms into their language, and fix the precise meaning of them, that they may know what I intend whenever I use them.

But what renders it much more difficult to convey divine truths to the understandings of these Indians, is, that "there "seems to be no foundation in their minds to begin upon," I mean no truths that may be taken for granted as being already known, while I am attempting to instill others. And divine truths having such a necessary connection with, and dependence upon each other, I find it extremely difficult in my first addresses to Pagans to begin and discourse of them in their proper order and connection, without having reference to truths not yet known,—without taking for granted such things as need first to be taught and proved. There is no point of Christian doctrine but what they are either wholly ignorant of, or extremely confused in their notions about. And therefore it is necessary they should be instructed in every truth, even in those that are the most easy and obvious to the understanding, and which a person educated under gospel-light would be ready to pass over in silence, as not imagining that any rational creature could be ignorant of.

The

The method I have usually taken in my first addresses to Pagans, has been to introduce myself by saying, that I was come among them with a desire and design of teaching them some things which I presumed they did not know, and which, I trusted, would be for their comfort and happiness, if known, desiring they would give their attention, and hoping they might meet with satisfaction in my discourse. And thence have proceeded to observe, that there are two things belonging to every man, which I call the *soul* and *body*. These I endeavour to distingush from each other, by observing to them, that there is something in them that is capable of joy and pleasure, when their *bodies* are sick and much pained: and, on the contrary, that they find something within them, that is fearful, sorrowful, ashamed, &c. and consequently very uneasy, when their bodies are in perfect health. I then observe to them, that this which rejoices in them (perhaps at the sight of some friend who has been long absent) when their bodies are sick and in pain,—this which is sorrowful, frighted, ashamed, &c. and consequently uneasy, when their bodies are perfectly at ease,—*this* I call the *soul*. And although it cannot be seen like the other part of the man, *viz*. the body, yet it is as real as their thoughts, desires, &c. which are likewise things that cannot be seen.

I then further observe, that this part of the man which thinks, rejoices, grieves, &c. will live after the body is dead. For the proof of this, I produce the opinion of their fathers, who (as I am told by very aged Indians now living) always supposed there was something of the man that would survive the body. And if I can, for the proof of any thing I assert, say, as St Paul to the Athenians, "As certain also of your "own sages have said," it is sufficient. And having established this point, I next observe, that what I have to say to them, respects the *conscious* part of this man; and that with relation to its state after the death of the body; and that I am not come to treat with them about the things that concern the *present* world.

This method I am obliged to take, because they will otherwise entirely mistake the design of my preaching, and suppose the business I am upon, is something that relates to the present world, having never been called together by the white people upon any other occasion, but only to be treated with about the sale of lands, or some other secular business. And I find it almost impossible to prevent their imagining that I am engaged in the same, or such like affairs, and to beat it into them, that my concern is to treat with them about their *invisible* part, and that with relation to its future ſtate.

But having thus opened the way, by diſtinguiſhing between ſoul and body, and ſhewing the immortality of the former, and that my buſineſs is to treat with them in order to their happineſs in a future ſtate; I proceed to diſcourſe of the being and perfections of God, particularly of his "eternity, "unity, ſelf-ſufficiency, infinite wiſdom, and almighty power." It is neceſſary, in the firſt place, to teach them, that God is from *everlaſting*, and ſo diſtinguiſhed from all creatures; though it is very difficult to communicate any thing of that nature to them, they having no terms in their language to ſignify an eternity *a parte ante*. It is likewiſe neceſſary to diſcourſe of the divine *unity*, in order to confute the notions they ſeem to have of a *plurality* of gods. The divine *all-ſufficiency* muſt alſo neceſſarily be mentioned, in order to prevent their imagining that God was unhappy while alone, before the formation of his creatures. And ſomething reſpecting the divine *wiſdom* and *power* ſeems neceſſary to be inſiſted upon, in order to make way for diſcourſing of God's works.

Having offered ſome things upon the divine perfections mentioned, I proceed to open the work of *creation* in general, and in particular God's creation of man in a ſtate of uprightneſs and happineſs, placing them in a garden of pleaſure; the means and manner of their apoſtaſy from that ſtate, and loſs of that happineſs. But before I can give a relation of their fall from God, I am obliged to make a large digreſſion, in order to give an account of the original and circumſtances of their tempter, his capacity of aſſuming the ſhape of a ſerpent, from his being a ſpirit without a body, &c. Whence I go on to ſhow, the *ruins* of our *fallen* ſtate, the mental blindneſs and vicious diſpoſitions our firſt parents then contracted to themſelves, and propagated to all their poſterity; the numerous calamities brought upon them and theirs by this apoſtaſy from God, and the expoſedneſs of the whole human race to eternal perdition. And thence labour to ſhew them, the neceſſity of an almighty Saviour to deliver us from this deplorable ſtate, as well as of a divine *revelation* to inſtruct us in, and direct us agreeable to the will of God.

And thus the way, by ſuch an introductory diſcourſe, is prepared for opening the goſpel-ſcheme of ſalvation through the great Redeemer, and for treating of thoſe doctrines that immediately relate to the ſoul's renovation by the divine Spirit, and preparation for a ſtate of everlaſting bleſſedneſs.

In

In giving ſuch a relation of things to Pagans, it is not a little difficult (as was obſerved before) to deliver truths in their proper order, without interfering, and without taking for granted things not as yet known: to diſcourſe of them in a familiar manner, ſuited to the capacities of Heathen: to illuſtrate them by eaſy and natural ſimilitudes: to obviate or anſwer the objections they are diſpoſed to make againſt the ſeveral particulars of it, as well as to take notice of, and confute their contrary notions.

What has ſometimes been very diſcouraging in my firſt diſcourſes to them, is, that when I have diſtinguiſhed between the *preſent* and *future* ſtate, and ſhown them, that it was my buſineſs to treat of theſe things that concern the life to come, they have ſome of them mocked, looked upon theſe things of no importance; have ſcarce had a curioſity to hear, and perhaps walked off before I had half done my diſcourſe. And in ſuch a caſe no impreſſions can be made upon their minds to gain their attention. They are not awed by hearing of the anger of God engaged againſt ſinners, of everlaſting puniſhment as the portion of goſpel-neglecters. They are not allured by hearing of the bleſſedneſs of thoſe who embrace and obey the goſpel. So that to gain their attention to my diſcourſes, has often been as difficult as to give them a juſt notion of the deſign of them, or to open truths in their proper order.

Another difficulty naturally falling under this head I am now upon, is, that "it is next to impoſſible to bring them to "a rational conviction that they are ſinners by nature, and "that their hearts are corrupt and ſinful," unleſs one could charge them with ſome groſs acts of immorality, ſuch as the *light of nature* condemns. If they can be charged with behaviour contrary to the commands of the *ſecond table*,—with manifeſt abuſes of their neighbour, they will generally own ſuch actions to be wrong; but then they ſeem as if they thought it was only the *actions* that were ſinful, and not their *hearts*. But if they cannot be charged with ſuch ſcandalous actions, they ſeem to have no conſciouſneſs of ſin and guilt at all, as I had occaſion to obſerve in my Journal of March 24. So that it is very difficult to convince them rationally of that which is readily acknowledged (though, alas! rarely felt) in the Chriſtian world, *viz.* "That we are all ſinners."

The method I take to convince them "we are ſinners by "nature," is, to lead them to an obſervation of their *little children*, how they will appear in a rage, fight and ſtrike their mothers, before they are able to ſpeak or walk, while they are so young that it is plain they are incapable of learning such practices. And the light of nature in the Indians condemning such behaviour in children towards their parents, they must own these tempers and actions to be wrong and sinful. And the children having never learned these things, they must have been in their natures, and consequently they must be allowed, to be "by nature the children of wrath." The same I observe to them with respect to the sin of *lying*, (which their children seem much inclined to). They tell lies without being taught so to do, from their own *natural* inclination, as well as against restraints, and after corrections for that vice, which proves them sinners *by nature*, &c.

And further, in order to shew them their *hearts* are all *corrupted* and *sinful*, I observe to them, that this may be the case, and they not be sensible of it through the blindness of their minds. That it is no evidence they are not *sinful*, because they do not know and feel it. I then mention all the vices I know the Indians to be guilty of, and so make use of these sinful *streams* to convince them the *fountain* is corrupt. And this is the end for which I mention their wicked practices to them, not because I expect to bring them to an *effectual* reformation merely by inveighing against their immoralities; but hoping they may hereby be convinced of the corruption of their hearts, and awakened to a sense of the depravity and misery of their *fallen* state.

And for the same purpose, *viz.* "to convince them they "are sinners," I sometimes open to them, the great command of "loving God with all the heart, strength, and mind." Shew them the reasonableness of *loving him* who has made, preserved, and dealt bountifully with us: and then labour to shew them their utter neglect in this regard, and that they have been so far from *loving* God in this manner, that, on the contrary, he has not been "in all their thoughts."

These, and such like, are the means I have made use of in order to remove this difficulty; but if it be asked after all, "how it was surmounted?" I must answer, God himself was pleased to do it with regard to a number of *these* Indians, by taking his work into his own hand, and making them *feel at heart*, that they were both sinful and miserable. And in the *day of God's power*, whatever was spoken to them from God's word, served to convince them they were *sinners*, (even the most melting invitations of the gospel), and to fill them with solicitude to obtain a deliverance from that deplorable state.

Further, it is extremely difficult to give them any just notion

tion of the undertaking of Chriſt in behalf of ſinners; of his obeying and ſuffering in their *room* and *ſtead*, in order to atone for their ſins, and procure their ſalvation; and of their being juſtified by his righteouſneſs *imputed* to them.—They are in general wholly unacquainted with *civil laws* and proceedings, and know of no ſuch thing as one perſon's being ſubſtituted as a *ſurety* in the *room* of another, nor have any kind of notion of *civil* judicatures, of perſons being arraigned, tried, judged, condemned, or acquitted. And hence it is very difficult to treat with them upon any thing of this nature, or that bears any relation to *legal* procedures. And although they cannot but have ſome dealings with the white people, in order to procure cloathing and other neceſſaries of life, yet it is ſcarce ever known that any one pays a *penny* for another, but each one ſtands for himſelf. Yet this is a thing that may be ſuppoſed, though ſeldom practiſed among them, and they may be made to underſtand, that if a friend of theirs pays a debt for them, it is right that upon that conſideration they themſelves ſhould be diſcharged.

And this is the only way I can take in order to give them a proper notion of the *undertaking* and *ſatisfaction* of *Chriſt* in behalf of ſinners. But here naturally ariſe two queſtions. *Firſt*, "What need there was of Chriſt's obeying and ſuffering "for us; why God would not look upon us to be good crea-"tures (to uſe my common phraſe for juſtification) on ac-"count of our own good deeds?" In anſwer to which I ſometimes obſerve, that a child's being never ſo orderly and obedient to its parents to-day, does by no means ſatisfy for its contrary behaviour yeſterday; and that if it be loving and obedient at *ſome* times only, and at *other* times croſs and diſobedient, it never can be looked upon a good child for its own doings, ſince it ought to have behaved in an obedient manner *always*. This ſimile ſtrikes their minds in an eaſy and forcible manner, and ſerves, in a meaſure, to illuſtrate the point. For the *light of nature* (as before hinted) teaches them, that their children ought to be obedient to them, and that at *all times*; and ſome of them are very ſevere with them for the contrary behaviour. This I apply in the plaineſt manner to our behaviour towards God; and ſo ſhew them, that it is impoſſible for us, ſince we have ſinned againſt God, to be juſtified before him by our own doings, ſince preſent and future goodneſs, *although perfect* and *conſtant*, could never ſatisfy for paſt miſconduct.

A *ſecond* queſtion, is, "If our debt was ſo great, and if "we all deſerved to ſuffer, how one perſon's ſuffering was "ſufficient

" sufficient to answer for the whole?" Here I have no better way to illustrate the infinite value of Christ's obedience and sufferings, arising from the dignity and excellency of his *person*, than to shew them the superior value of *gold* to that of baser metals, and that a small quantity of *this* will discharge a greater debt, than a vast quantity of the common *copper pence*.

But after all, it is extremely difficult to treat with them upon this great doctrine of "justification by imputed righ-" teousness."

I scarce know how to conclude this head, so many things occurring that might properly be added here: but what has been mentioned, may serve for a specimen of the difficulty of conveying divine truths to the understandings of these Indians, and of gaining their assent to them *as such*.

Thirdly, Their "inconvenient situations, savage manners, " and unhappy method of living," have been an unspeakable difficulty and discouragement to me in my work.

They generally live in the wilderness, and some that I have visited, at great distances from the English settlements, which has obliged me to travel much, and oftentimes over hideous rocks, mountains, and swamps,—frequently to lie out in the open woods,—deprived me of the common comforts of life, and greatly impaired my health.

When I have got among them in the wilderness, I have often met with great difficulty in my attempts to discourse to them.——Have sometimes spent hours with them in attempting to answer their objections, and remove their jealousies, before I could prevail upon them to give me a hearing upon Christianity.——Have been often obliged to preach in their houses in cold and windy weather, when they have been full of smoak and cinders, as well as unspeakably filthy; which has many times thrown me into violent sick head-achs.

While I have been preaching, their children have frequently cried to that degree, I could scarcely be heard, and their Pagan mothers would take no manner of care to quiet them. At the same time, perhaps, some have been laughing and mocking at divine truths.——Others playing with their dogs, —whittleing sticks, and the like. And this, in many of them, not from spite and prejudice, but for want of better manners.

A view of these things has been not a little sinking and discouraging to me;—has sometimes so far prevailed upon me as to render me entirely dispirited, and wholly unable to go on with my work; and given me such a melancholy turn of mind,

mind, that I have many times thought I could never more address an Indian upon religious matters.

The solitary manner in which I have generally been obliged to live, on account of their inconvenient situations, has been not a little pressing. I have spent the greater part of my time, for more than three years past, entirely alone, as to any agreeable society; and a very considerable part of it have lived in houses by myself, without having the company of any human creature. And sometimes have scarcely seen an Englishman for a month or six weeks together.——Have had my spirits so depressed with melancholy views of the tempers and conduct of Pagans, when I have been for some time confined with them, that I have felt as if banished from all the people of God.

I have likewise been wholly alone in my work, there being no other *missionary* among the Indians in either of these provinces. And other *ministers* neither knowing the *peculiar* difficulties, nor most *advantageous* methods of performing my work, have been capable to afford me little assistance or support in any respect.

A feeling of the great disadvantages of being alone in this work, has discovered to me the wisdom and goodness of the great Head of the church, in sending forth his disciples two and two, in order to proclaim the sacred mysteries of his kingdom; and has made me long for a *colleague* to be a *partner* of my cares, hopes, and fears, as well as labours amongst the Indians; and excited me to use some means in order to procure such an assistant, although I have not as yet been so happy as to meet with success in that respect.

I have not only met with great difficulty in travelling to, and for some time residing among the Indians far remote in the wilderness, but also in living with them in one place and another more statedly.——Have been obliged to remove my residence from place to place.——Have procured, and after some poor fashion, furnished three houses for living among them, in the space of about three years past.——One at Kaunaumeek, about twenty miles distant from the city of Albany; one at the Forks of Delaware in Pennsylvania; and one at Crosweeksung in New-Jersey. And the Indians in the latter of these provinces (with whom I have latterly spent most of my time) being not long since removed from the place where they lived the last winter, (the reason of which I mentioned in my Journal of March 24. and May 4.), I have now no house at all of my own, but am obliged to lodge with an English family at a considerable distance from them, to the great

disadvantage

disadvantage of my work among them, they being like *children* that continually need advice and direction, as well as incitement to their worldly business.

The houses I have formerly lived in are at great distances from each other; the two nearest of them being more than *seventy* miles apart, and neither of them within *fifteen* miles of the place where the Indians now live.

The Indians are a people very poor and indigent, and so destitute of the comforts of life, at some seasons of the year especially, that it is impossible for a person who has any pity to them, and concern for the Christian interest, to live among them without considerable expence, especially in time of sickness. If any thing be bestowed on one, (as in some cases it is peculiarly necessary, in order to remove their Pagan jealousies, and engage their friendship to Christianity), others, be there never so many of them, expect the same treatment. And while they retain their Pagan tempers, they discover little gratitude, or even manhood, amidst all the kindnesses they receive.——If they make any presents, they expect double satisfaction. And Christianity itself does not at *once* cure them of these ungrateful and unmanly tempers.

They are in general unspeakably indolent and slothful,—have been bred up in idleness,—know little about cultivating land, or indeed of engaging vigorously in any other business.—So that I am obliged to instruct them in, as well as press them to the performance of their work, and take the oversight of all their secular business. They have little or no ambition or resolution.——Not one in a thousand of them that has the spirit of a man. And it is next to impossible to make them sensible of the duty and importance of being active, diligent, and industrious in the management of their worldly business; and to excite any spirit and promptitude of that nature in them. When I have laboured to the utmost of my ability to shew them of what importance it would be to the Christian interest among them, as well as to their worldly comfort, for them to be laborious and prudent in their business, and to furnish themselves with the comforts of life; how this would incline the Pagans to come among them, and so put them under the means of salvation, how it would encourage religious persons of the white people to help them, as well as stop the mouths of others that were disposed to cavil against them; how they might by this means pay those they owe their just dues, and so prevent trouble from coming upon themselves, and reproach upon their Christian *profession*: I say, when I have endeavoured to represent this matter in the most advantageous

tageous light I possibly could, they have indeed assented to all I said, but been little moved, and consequently have acted *like themselves*, or at least too much so. Though it must be acknowledged, that those who appear to have a sense of divine things, are considerably amended in this respect, and it is hopeful, that time will make a yet greater alteration upon them for the better.

The concern I have had for the settling of these Indians in New-Jersey in a compact form, in order to their being a Christian congregation, in a capacity of enjoying the means of grace; the care of managing their worldly business in order to this end, and to their having a comfortable livelihood, have been more pressing to my mind, and cost me more labour and fatigue, for several months past, than all my other work among them.

Their "wandering to and fro in order to procure the ne- "cessaries of life," is another difficulty that attends my work. This has often deprived me of opportunities to discourse to them:---has thrown them in the way of temptation, either among Pagans further remote where they have gone to hunt, who have laughed at them for hearkening to Christianity: or among white people more horribly wicked, who have often made them drunk; and then got their commodities, such as skins, baskets, brooms, shovels, and the like, (with which they designed to have bought corn, and other necessaries of life, for themselves and families), for, it may be, nothing but a little strong liquor, and then sent them home empty. So that for the labour, perhaps, of several weeks, they have got nothing but the satisfaction of being drunk once; and have not only lost their labour, but (which is infinitely worse) the impressions of divine things that were made upon their minds before.

But I forbear enlarging upon this head. The few hints I have given may be sufficient to give *thinking* persons some apprehensions of the difficulties attending my work, on account of the *inconvenient situations* and *savage manners* of the Indians, as well as of their *unhappy method of living*.

Fourthly, The last difficulty I shall mention, as having attended my work, is, "what has proceeded from the attempts "that some ill-minded persons have designedly made, to "hinder the propagation of the gospel, and a work of divine "grace among the Indians."

The Indians are not only of themselves prejudised against Christianity, on the various accounts I have already mentioned, but, as if this was not enough, there are some in all parts of the country where I have preached to them, who have taken pains induſtriouſly to bind them down in Pagan darkneſs: "neglecting to enter into the kingdom of God them-"ſelves, and labouring to hinder others."

After the beginning of the religious concern among the Indians in New-Jerſey, ſome endeavoured to prejudiſe them againſt me and the truths I taught them, by the moſt ſneaking, unmanly, and falſe ſuggeſtions of things that had no manner of foundation but in their own brains. Some particulars of this kind I formerly took notice of in one of the remarks made upon my Journal concluded the 20th of November laſt. And might have added yet more, and of another nature, than thoſe there mentioned, had not modeſty forbidden me to mention what was too obſcene to be thought of. But, through the mercy of God, they were never able, by all their abominable inſinuations, flouting jeers, and downright lies, to create in the Indians thoſe jealouſies they deſired to poſſeſs them with, and ſo were never ſuffered to hinder the work of grace among them.

But when they ſaw they could not prejudiſe the Indians againſt me, nor hinder them from receiving the goſpel, they then noiſed it through the country, that I was undoubtedly a *Roman catholic*, and that I was gathering together, and training up the Indians in order to ſerve a Popiſh intereſt; that I ſhould quickly head them, and cut people's throats.

What they pretended gave them reaſon for this opinion, was, that they underſtood I had a commiſſion from Scotland. Whereupon they could with great aſſurance ſay, "All Scot-"land is turned to the *Pretender*, and this is but a Popiſh "plot to make a party for him here," *&c.* And ſome (I am informed) actually went to the *civil* authority with complaints againſt me, but only laboured under this unhappineſs, that when they came, they had nothing to complain of, and could give no colour of reaſon why they attempted any ſuch thing, or deſired the civil authority to take cognizance of me, having not a word to alledge againſt my *preaching* or *practice*, only they ſurmiſed that becauſe the Indians appeared ſo very *loving* and *orderly*, they had a deſign of impoſing upon people, by that means, and ſo of getting a better advantage to cut their throats. And what temper they would have had the Indians appear with in order to have given no occaſion, nor have left any room for ſuch a ſuſpicion, "I cannot tell." I preſume if they had appeared with the *contrary* temper, it would quickly have been obſerved of them, that "they were now "grown

"grown surly," and in all probability were preparing to "cut people's throats."

From a view of these things, I have had occasion to admire the wisdom and goodness of God in providing so *full* and *authentic* a commission for the undertaking and carrying on of this work, without which (notwithstanding the charitableness of the design) it had probably met with molestation.

The Indians who have been my hearers in New-Jersey, have likewise been sued for debt, and threatened with imprisonment more since I came among them (as they inform me) than in *seven* years before. The reason of this, I suppose, was, they left frequenting those *tippling* houses where they used to consume most of what they gained by hunting and other means. And these persons seeing that "the hope "of future gain was lost," were resolved to make sure of what they could. And perhaps some of them put the Indians to trouble, purely out of spite at their embracing Christianity.

This conduct of theirs has been very distressing to me; for I was sensible, that if they did imprison any *one* that embraced, or hearkened to Christianity, the news of it would quickly spread among the Pagans hundreds of miles distant, who would immediately conclude I had involved them in this difficulty, and thence be filled with prejudice against Christianity, and strengthened in their jealousy that the whole of my design among them, was to ensnare and enslave them. And I knew that some of the Indians upon Susquahannah had made this objection against hearing me preach, *viz.* That they understood a number of Indians in Maryland, some hundred of miles distant, who had been uncommonly free with the English, were after a while put in jail, sold, *&c.* Whence they concluded, it was best for them to keep at a distance, and have nothing to do with Christians.

The method I took in order to remove this difficulty, was, to press the Indians with all possible speed to pay their debts, and to exhort those of them that had *skins* or *money*, and were themselves in a good measure free of debt, to help others that were oppressed. And frequently upon such occasions I have paid money out of my own pocket, which I have not as yet received again.

These are some of the difficulties I have met with from the conduct of those who, notwithstanding their actions so much tend to hinder the propagation of Christianity, would (I suppose) be loth to be reputed Pagans.

Thus I have endeavoured to anſwer the demands of the Honourable Society in relation to *each* of the particulars mentioned in their *letter*.

If what I have written may be in any meaſure agreeable and ſatisfactory to them, and ſerve to excite in them, or any of God's people, a ſpirit of *prayer* and *ſupplication* for the furtherance of a work of grace among the Indians *here*, and the propagation of it to their *diſtant tribes*, I ſhall have abundant reaſon to rejoice and bleſs God in this, as well as other reſpects.

June 20. 1746. DAVID BRAINERD.

P. S. Since the concluſion of the preceding Journal, (which was deſigned to repreſent the operations of one year only, from the firſt time of my preaching to the Indians in New-Jerſey), I adminiſtered the *ſacrament* of the *Lord's ſupper* a ſecond time in my congregation, *viz.* on the 13th of July. At which ſeaſon, there were more than *thirty* communicants of the Indians, although divers were abſent who ſhould have communicated: ſo conſiderably has God enlarged our number ſince the former ſolemnity of this kind, deſcribed ſomewhat particularly in my Journal. This appeared to be a ſeaſon of divine power and grace, not unlike the former; a ſeaſon of refreſhing to God's people in general, and of awakening to ſome others, although the divine influence manifeſtly attending the ſeveral ſervices of the ſolemnity, ſeemed not ſo great and powerful as at the former ſeaſon.

D. BRAINERD.

The

The Attestation of the Reverend Mr WILLIAM TENNENT of Freehold.

SINCE my dear and Reverend brother Brainerd has at length consented to the publication of his Journal, I gladly embrace this opportunity of testifying, that our altogether glorious Lord and Saviour Jesus Christ has given such a *display* of his almighty power and sovereign grace, not only in the external *reformation*, but (in a judgment of charity) the saving conversion of a considerable number of Indians, that it is really wonderful to all beholders! though some, alas! notwithstanding sufficient grounds of conviction to the contrary, do join with the devil, that avowed enemy of God and man, in endeavouring to prevent this glorious work, by such ways and means as are mentioned in the aforesaid Journal, to which I must refer the reader for a faithful, though very brief, account of the time when, the place where, the means by which, and manner how, this wished-for work has been begun and carried on, by the great Head of the church.—And this I can more confidently do, not only because I am intimately acquainted with the author of the Journal, but on account of my own personal knowledge of the matters of fact recorded in it respecting the work itself.——As I live not far from the Indians, I have been much conversant with them, both at their own place, and in my own parish, (where they generally convene for public worship in Mr Brainerd's absence); and I think it my duty to acknowledge, that their conversation hath often, under God, refreshed my soul.

To conclude; it is my opinion, that the change wrought in those *savages*, namely, from the darkness of Paganism, to the knowledge of the pure gospel of Christ; from sacrificing to devils, to "present themselves, body and soul, a living sacrifice to God," and that not only from the persuasion of their minister, but from a clear heart-affecting sense of its being their *reasonable service*: this change, I say, is so great, that none could effect it but he "who worketh all things after the good pleasure of his own will." And I would humbly hope, that this is only the first-fruits of a much greater harvest to be brought in from among the Indians, by HIM who has promised to give his Son "the Heathen for his inheritance, and the uttermost ends of the earth for his possession:"—and hath also declared, "That the whole earth shall be filled with the knowledge of the Lord, as the waters cover the sea.

" sea.—Even so, Lord Jesus come quickly. Amen and A-
" men."

I am, courteous reader,
thy soul's well-wisher,

Freehold, August 16. 1746.

WILLIAM TENNENT.

The Attestation of the Reverend Mr MACNIGHT of Croswicks.

AS it must needs afford a sacred pleasure to such as cordially desire the prosperity and advancement of the Redeemer's kingdom and interest in the world, to hear that our merciful and gracious God is in very deed fulfilling such precious promises as relate to the poor Heathen, by sending his everlasting gospel among them, which, with the concurrence of his holy Spirit, is removing that worse than Egyptian darkness, whereby the god of this world has long held them in willing subjection; so this narrative will perhaps be more acceptable to the world, when it is confirmed by the testimony of such as were either eye-witnesses of this glorious dawn of gospel-light among the benighted Pagans, or personally acquainted with those of them, in whom (in a judgment of charity) a gracious change has been wrought. Therefore I the more willingly join with my brethren Mr William Tennent and Mr Brainerd, in affixing my attestation to the foregoing narrative, and look upon myself as concerned in point of duty both to God and his people to do so, by reason that I live contiguous to their settlement, and have had frequent opportunities of being present at their religious meetings, where I have, with pleasing wonder, beheld, what I am strongly inclined to believe were the effects of God's almighty power accompanying his own truths; more especially on the 8th day of August 1745. in which, while the word of God was preached by Mr Brainerd, there appeared an uncommon solemnity among the Indians in general: but I am wholly unable to give a full representation of the surprising effects of God's almighty power that appeared among them when public service was over; while Mr Brainerd urged upon some of them the absolute necessity of a speedy closure with Christ, the holy Spirit seemed to be poured out upon them in a plenteous measure, insomuch as the Indians present in the *wigwam* seemed to be brought to the jailor's case, Acts xvi. 30. utterly unable to conceal

conceal the diſtreſs and perplexity of their ſouls; this prompted the pious among them to bring the diſperſed congregation together, who ſoon ſeemed to be in the greateſt extremity, ſome earneſtly begging for mercy, under a ſolemn ſenſe of their periſhing condition, (in their language), while others were unable to ariſe from the earth, to the great wonder of thoſe white people that were preſent, (one of whom is by this means, I truſt, ſavingly brought to Chriſt ſince); nay, ſo very ſtrange was the concern that appeared among theſe poor Indians in general, that I am ready to conclude, it might have been ſufficient to have convinced an Atheiſt, that the Lord was indeed in the place. I am, for my part, fully perſuaded, that this glorious work is true and genuine, whilſt with ſatisfaction I behold ſeveral of theſe Indians diſcovering all the ſymptoms of *inward holineſs* in their lives and converſation.——I have had the ſatisfaction of joining with them in their ſervice on the 11th of Auguſt 1746, which was a day ſet apart for imploring the divine bleſſing on the labours of their miniſter among other tribes of Indians at Suſquahannah, in all which they conducted themſelves with a very decent and becoming gravity; and, as far as I am capable of judging, they may be propoſed as examples of piety and godlineſs to all the white people around them, which indeed is juſtly "marvellous in our eyes," eſpecially conſidering what they lately have been.

O may the glorious God ſhortly bring about that deſirable time, when our exalted Immanuel ſhall have "the Heathen given for his inheritance, and the uttermoſt parts of the earth for his poſſeſſion!"

CHARLES MACNIGHT.

Auguſt 29. 1746.

Atteſtation of the elders and deacons of the Presbyterian church in Freehold.

WE whoſe names are underwritten, being elders and deacons of the Preſbyterian church in Freehold, do hereby teſtify, that, in our humble opinion, God, even our Saviour, has brought a conſiderable number of the Indians in theſe parts, to a ſaving union with himſelf.

This we are perſuaded of from a perſonal acquaintance with them, whom we not only hear ſpeak of the great doctrines

trines of the gospel with humility, affection, and understanding, but we see them walk (as far as man can judge) soberly, righteously, and godly. We have joined with them at the Lord's supper, and do from our hearts esteem them our brethren in Jesus. For "these who were not God's people, may "now be called the children of the living God: it is the "Lord's doing, and it is marvellous in our eyes." O that he may go on "conquering and to conquer," until he has subdued all things to himself! This is, and shall be the unfeigned desires and prayers of,

Walter Ker,
Robert Cummins,
David Rhe,
John Henderson,
John Anderson,
Joseph Ker, } Elders.

William Ker,
Samuel Ker,
Samuel Craig, } Deacons.

Freehold, August 16.
1746.

FINIS.

A SERMON

PREACHED

In New-Ark, June 12. 1744.

AT THE

ORDINATION

OF

Mr *David Brainerd*,

A Miſſionary among the Indians

Upon the Borders of the Provinces of New-York, New-Jerſey, and Pennſylvania.

By E. PEMBERTON, A. M.

Paſtor of the Preſbyterian Church in the City of New-York.

WITH

An APPENDIX, touching the Indian Affairs.

EDINBURGH:

Printed in the Year MDCCLXV.

****

AN

Ordination SERMON.

LUKE xiv. 23.

And the Lord said unto the servant, Go out into the high-ways and hedges, and compel them to come in, that my house may be filled.

GOD erected this visible world as a monument of his glory,—a theatre for the display of his adorable perfections.—The heavens proclaim his wisdom and power in shining characters, and the whole earth is full of his goodness. Man was in his original creation excellently fitted for the service of God, and for perfect happiness in the enjoyment of the divine favour.

But sin has disturbed the order of nature, defaced the beauty of the creation, and involved man, the lord of this lower world, in the most disconsolate circumstances of guilt and misery.

The all-seeing eye of God beheld our deplorable state; infinite pity touched the heart of the Father of mercies; and infinite wisdom laid the plan of our recovery. The Majesty of heaven did not see meet to suffer the enemy of mankind, eternally to triumph in his success; nor leave his favourite workmanship, irrecoverably to perish in the ruins of the apostasy. By a method, which at once astonishes and delights the sublimest spirits above, he opened a way for the display of his mercy, without any violation of the sacred claims of his justice; in which, the honour of the law is vindicated, and the guilty offender acquitted; sin is condemned, and the sinner eternally saved. To accomplish this blessed design, the beloved Son of God assumed the nature of man,—in our nature died a spotless sacrifice for sin,—by the atoning virtue of his blood he "made reconciliation for iniquity,"—and by his perfect obedience to the law of God, "brought in everlasting righteousness."

3 O 2 Having

Having finiſhed his work upon earth, before he aſcended to his heavenly Father, he commiſſioned the miniſters of his kingdom, to "preach the goſpel to every creature." He ſent them forth to make the moſt extenſive offers of ſalvation to rebellious ſinners, and by all the methods of holy violence to "compel them to come in," and accept the invitations of his grace.—We have a lively repreſentation of this in the *parable*, in which our text is contained.

The evident deſign of which is, under the figure of a *marriage-ſupper*, to ſet forth the plentiful proviſion, which is made in our Lord Jeſus Chriſt for the reception of his people, and the freedom and riches of divine grace, which invites the moſt unworthy and miſerable ſinners, to partake of this ſacred entertainment. The firſt invited gueſts were the Jews, the favourite people of God, who were heirs of divine love, while the reſt of the world were "aliens from the common-"wealth of Iſrael, and ſtrangers from the covenants of "promiſe:" but theſe, through the power of prevailing prejudice, and the influence of carnal affections, obſtinately rejected the invitation, and were therefore finally excluded from theſe invaluable bleſſings.

But it was not the deſign of infinite wiſdom, that theſe coſtly preparations ſhould be loſt, and the table he had ſpread, remain unfurniſhed with gueſts. Therefore he ſent forth his ſervant "into the ſtreets and lanes of the city," and commanded him to bring in "the poor, the maimed, the halt, "and the blind,"—*i. e.* the moſt neceſſitous and miſerable of mankind;—yea, to "go out into the high-ways and hedges," to the wretched and periſhing Gentiles, and not only invite, but even "compel them to come in, that his houſe might be "filled."

The words of the text repreſent to us,

I. The *melancholy ſtate* of the Gentile world. They are deſcribed as "in the high-ways and hedges," in the moſt periſhing and helpleſs condition.

II. The *compaſſionate care*, which the bleſſed Redeemer takes of them in theſe their deplorable circumſtances. He "ſends out his ſervants" to them, to invite them to partake of the entertainments of *his houſe*.

III. The duty of the *miniſters* of the goſpel, to "compel "them to come in," and accept of his gracious invitation.

Theſe I ſhall conſider in their order, and then apply them to the preſent occaſion.

I. I am to consider the *melancholy state* of the Heathen world, while in the darkness of nature, and destitute of divine revelation.—It is easy to harangue upon the excellency and advantage of the *light of nature*. It is agreeable to the pride of mankind, to exalt the powers of human reason, and pronounce it a sufficient guide to eternal happiness. But let us inquire into the records of *antiquity*, let us consult the experience of all ages; and we shall find that those who had no guide but the light of nature, no instructor but unassisted reason, have wandered in perpetual uncertainty, darkness, and error. Or let us take a view of the *present* state of those countries that have not been illuminated by the gospel; and we shall see, that notwithstanding the improvements of near six thousand years, they remain to this day covered with the grossest darkness, and abandoned to the most immoral and vicious practices.

The beauty and good order, every where discovered in the visible frame of nature, evidences beyond all reasonable dispute, the existence of an infinite and almighty cause, who first gave being to the universe, and still preserves it by his powerful providence. Says the apostle to the Gentiles, (Rom. i. 20.) " The invisible things of God, from the creation of " the world, are clearly seen, being understood by the things " that are made, even his eternal power and Godhead." And yet many, even among the philosophers of the Gentile nations, impiously denied the eternal Deity, from whose hands they received their existence; and blasphemed his infinite perfections, when surrounded with the clearest demonstrations of his power and goodness.—Those who acknowledged a Deity, entertained the most unworthy conceptions of his nature and attributes, and worshipped *the creature*, in the place of *the Creator*, " who is God blessed for ever."—Not only the illustrious heroes of antiquity, and the public benefactors of mankind, but even the most despicable beings in the order of nature, were enrolled in the catalogue of their gods, and became the object of their impious adoration. " They " changed the glory of the incorruptible God, into an image " made like to corruptible man, to birds and four-footed beasts, " and creeping things," Rom. i. 23.

A few of the sublimest genius's of Rome and Athens, had some faint discoveries of the spiritual nature of the human *soul*, and formed some probable conjectures, that man was designed for a future state of existence. When they considered the extensive capacities of the human mind, and the deep impressions of futurity, engraven in every breast, they could not

not but infer, that the soul was immortal, and at death would be translated to some new and unknown state. When they saw the virtuous oppressed with various and successive calamities, and the vilest of men triumphing in prosperity and pleasure, they entertained distant hopes, that in a future revolution, these seeming inequalities would be rectified, these inconsistencies removed,—the righteous distinguishingly rewarded, and the wicked remarkably punished.—But after all their inquiries upon this important subject, they attained no higher than some probable conjectures, some uncertain expectations.—And when they came to describe the nature and situation of these invisible regions of happiness or misery, they made the wildest guesses, and run into the most absurd and vain imaginations. The *heaven* they contrived for the entertainment of the virtuous, was made up of sensual pleasures, beneath the dignity of human nature, and inconsistent with perfect felicity: the *hell* they described for the punishment of the vicious, consisted in ridiculous terrors, unworthy the belief of a rational and religious creature.

Their *practices* were equally corrupt with their principles. As the most extravagant errors were received among the established articles of their faith, so the most infamous vices obtained in their practice, and were indulged not only with impunity, but authorised by the sanction of their laws. They stupidly erected altars to idols of wood and stone; paid divine honours to those, who in their lives had been the greatest monsters of lust and cruelty; yea, offered up their sons and daughters as sacrifices to devils. The principles of honour, the restraints of shame, the precepts of their philosophers, were all too weak, to keep their corruptions within any tolerable bounds. The wickedness of their hearts broke through every inclosure, and deluged the earth with rapine and violence, blood and slaughter, and all manner of brutish and detestable impurities.—It is hardly possible to read the melancholy description of the principles and manners of the Heathen world, given us by St Paul, without horror and surprise. To think, that man once the "friend of God," and "the lord of this "lower world," should thus "deny the God that made him," and bow down to *dumb idols;* should thus by lust and intemperance, degrade himself into the character of the *beast*, "which hath no understanding;" and by pride, malice, and revenge, transform himself into the very image of the *devil*, "who was a murderer from the beginning."

This was the state of the Gentile nations, when the light of the gospel appeared, to scatter the darkness that overspread the

the face of the earth. And this has been the case, so far as has yet appeared, of all the nations ever since, upon whom the Sun of righteousness has not arose with healing in his wings. Every new discovered country opens a new scene of astonishing ignorance and barbarity; and gives us fresh evidence of the universal corruption of human nature.

II. I proceed now to consider the *compassionate care* and *kindness* of our blessed Redeemer towards mankind, in these their deplorable circumstances. He "sends out his servants," to invite them "to come in," and accept the entertainments of *his house*.

God might have left his guilty creatures, to have eternally suffered the dismal effects of their apostasy, without the least imputation of injustice, or violence of his infinite perfections. The fall was the consequence of man's criminal choice, and attended with the highest aggravations.—The *angels that sinned* were made examples of God's righteous severity, and are reserved "in chains" of guilt, "to the judgment of the great "day." Mercy, that tender attribute of the divine nature, did not interpose in their behalf, to suspend the execution of their sentence, or avert God's threatened displeasure: their punishment is unalterably decreed, their judgment is irreversible; they are the awful monuments of revenging wrath, and are condemned "to blackness of darkness for ever."—Now justice might have shewn the same inflexible severity to rebellious man, and have left the universal progeny of Adam, to perish in their guilt and misery. It was unmerited mercy, that distinguished the human race, in providing a Saviour for us; and the most signal compassion, that revealed the counsels of Heaven for our recovery.

But though justice did not oblige the divine Being to provide for our relief, yet the goodness of the indulgent Father of the universe inclined him to shew pity to his guilty creatures, who fell from their innocence, through the subtlety and malice of seducing and apostate spirits. It was agreeable to the divine wisdom, to disappoint the devices of Satan, the enemy of God and goodness, and recover the creatures he had made, from their subjection to the powers of darkness.

He therefore gave early discoveries of his designs of mercy to our first parents, and immediately upon the apostasy opened a door of hope for their recovery. He revealed a Saviour to the ancient Patriarchs, under dark types, and by distant promises; made clearer declarations of his will, as the appointed time drew near, for the accomplishment of the promises, and the

the manifestation of the Son of God in human flesh.—" And " when the fulness of time was come, God sent forth his " Son, made of a woman, made under the law, to redeem " them that were under the law, that we might receive the " adoption of sons."

This divine and illustrious person left the bosom of his Father, that he might put on the character of a servant;—descended from the glories of heaven, that he might dwell on this inferior earth;—was made under the law, that he might fulfil all righteousness;—submitted to the infirmities of human nature, to the sorrows and sufferings of an afflicted life, and to the agonies of a painful ignominious death on a cross, that he might destroy the power of sin, abolish the empire of death, and purchase immortality and glory for perishing man.

While our Lord Jesus resided in this lower world, he preached the glad tidings of salvation, and published the kingdom of God; confirming his doctrine by numerous and undoubted miracles, and recommending his instructions by the charms of a spotless life and conversation. He sent forth his apostles to pursue the same gracious design of gospellizing the people, and furnished them with sufficient powers to proselyte the nations to the faith. He also appointed a standing ministry, to carry on a treaty of peace with rebellious sinners, in the successive ages of the church; to continue, till the number of the redeemed is completed, and the whole election of grace placed in circumstances of spotless purity and perfect happiness.

These ministers are stiled "the servants of Christ," by way of eminence: they are in a peculiar manner devoted to the service of their divine Master; from him they receive their commission; by him they are appointed to represent his person, preside in his worship, and teach the laws of his kingdom.—To assume this character without being divinely called, and regularly introduced into this sacred office, is a bold invasion of Christ's royal authority, and an open violation of that order, which he has established in his church.——These not only derive their mission from Christ, but it is *his doctrine* they are to preach, and not the inventions of their own brain:—it is *his glory* they are to promote, and not their own interest or honour:—their business is not to propagate the designs of a party, but *the common salvation*, and to "beseech all, in Christ's name, to be reconciled unto " God."

The

The apoſtles, the primitive heralds of the everlaſting goſpel, were ſent to make the firſt tender of ſalvation to "the "loſt ſheep of the houſe of Iſrael;" they were commanded to begin at Jeruſalem, the centre of the Jewiſh commonwealth: but when the Jews obſtinately perſiſted in their impenitence and unbelief, they were commiſſioned "to preach the goſpel "to every creature under heaven:"—the ſinners of the Gentiles were invited to *come in*, and accept of the offers of ſalvation.

The prophets pointed out a Meſſiah that was to come, and proclaimed the joyful approach of a Redeemer, at the time appointed in the ſovereign counſels of Heaven. The miniſters of the goſpel now are ſent to declare, that the prophecies are accompliſhed, the promiſe fulfilled, juſtice ſatisfied, ſalvation purchaſed; and all that will *come in*, ſhall receive the bleſſings of the goſpel. They are not only freely to invite ſinners, of all orders and degrees, of all ages and nations; but to aſſure them, that "all things are now ready," and to uſe the moſt powerful and perſuaſive methods, that they may engage them to comply with the heavenly call.——Which brings me to the third thing propoſed.

III. I am next to ſhew, that it is the great duty of the miniſters of the goſpel "to compel ſinners to come in," and accept of the bleſſings of the goſpel.——This is ſo plainly contained in my text, that I ſhall not multiply arguments to confirm it. My only buſineſs ſhall be to explain the nature of this compulſion, or ſhew in what manner ſinners are to be "compelled to come in" to the Chriſtian church.——And ſure I am, I muſt anſwer, negatively, not by the deceitful methods of fraud and diſguiſe,—nor the inhuman practices of perſecution and violence. This text indeed has often been alledged by the *perſecuting bigots* of all ages, and applied to ſupport the cauſe of *religious tyranny;* to the infinite ſcandal of the Chriſtian name, and the unſpeakable detriment of the Chriſtian intereſt.—By this means the enemies of our moſt holy faith have been ſtrengthened in their infidelity, the weak have been turned aſide from "the truth, as it is in Jeſus," and the peaceable kingdom of the Meſſiah transformed into a field of blood,—a ſcene of helliſh and horrid cruelties. If this were the *compulſion* recommended in the goſpel, then abſolute unrelenting tyrants would be the proper and moſt infallible teachers; then racks and tortures would be the genuine and moſt ſucceſsful method of propagating the faith. But ſurely every thing of this kind, every violent and driving meaſure, is in direct oppoſition to the precepts and example of our blessed Saviour, and contrary to the very genius of his gospel,--which proclaims, "Glory to God in the highest, "on earth peace, good-will towards men *."

The princes of this world exercise a temporal dominion over mankind, and by fines levied on their estates, and punishments inflicted upon their bodies, force men to an outward subjection to their authority and government.—But the kingdom of our Lord is of a spiritual nature: he erects his empire in the hearts of men, and reigns over "a willing people in the "day of his power." External violence may necessitate men to an external profession of the truth, and procure a dissembled compliance with the institutions of Christ; but can never enlighten the darkness of the mind, conquer the rebellion of the will, nor sanctify and save the soul. It may transfigure men into accomplished hypocrites; but will never convert them into real saints.

The gospel was originally propagated by the powerful preaching of Christ and his apostles, by the astonishing miracles which they wrought in confirmation of their doctrine, and the exemplary lives by which they adorned their profession and character. Instead of propagating their religion by the destructive methods of fire and sword, they submitted to the rage and cruelty of a malignant world with surprising patience, and sacrificed their very lives in the cause of God, without any intemperate discoveries of anger and resentment:--instead of calling for "fire from heaven" to destroy their opposers, they compassionated their ignorance, instructed them with *meekness*, counselled and exhorted them with "all long-"suffering and doctrine," and even spent their dying breath in praying for their conviction and conversion, that they might be saved in the day of the Lord Jesus.

Now, in imitation of these primitive doctors of the Christian church, these wise and successful preachers of the gospel, it is the duty of the ministers of the present day, to use the same methods of compassion and friendly violence. A disinterested zeal for the glory of God, a stedfast adherence to the truth, and unshaken fidelity in our Master's cause, with universal benevolence to mankind, must constantly animate our public discourses, and be conspicuous in our private conversation and behaviour.——We must diligently endeavour to convince the understandings, engage the affections, and direct the practice of our hearers.--Upon this head, it may not be amiss to descend to a few particulars.

* Luke ii. 14.

1. Ministers are to "compel sinners to come in," by setting before them their "guilty and perishing condition by nature." ——Sinners are naturally fond of carnal ease and security; they are delighted with their pleasant and profitable sins; they even "drink in iniquity like water," with great greediness, with insatiable thirst, and incessant gratification, but without fear or remorse. Upon this account, there is the highest necessity to sound an alarm in their ears, that they may be awakened, to see and consider their dangerous state; or else they will never be excited to "flee from the wrath to come." The secure sinner is insensible of his want of a Saviour: "The "whole need not a physician, but they that are sick."

To this end, the ministers of the gospel are to set "the "terrors of the Lord" in array against the sinner, and let him hear the "thunder of divine curses," that utter their voice against the unbelieving. They are to represent in the clearest light, and with the most convincing evidence, the evil of sin, and the danger it exposes to; that "wrath from heaven is re- "vealed against all ungodliness and unrighteousness of men *;" that the flaming sword of incensed justice is unsheathed, and the arm of the Almighty ready to destroy such as are "going "on still in their trespasses," impenitent and secure.——They are not only thus to shew them their danger, but to set before them at the same time their wretched and helpless circumstances;—that there is no human eye can successfully pity them, nor any created arm can bring them effectual deliverance;—that, while in a state of unregenerate nature, they are destitute of strength to perform any acceptable service to the blessed God, and unable to make any adequate satisfaction to his offended justice;—that indeed they can neither avoid the divine displeasure, nor endure the punishment that is due to their crimes.——Thus by a faithful application of the law and its threatenings, we should endeavour, by God's blessing, to make way for the reception of the gospel and its promises.— This was the wise method observed by our blessed Saviour, the first preacher of the gospel; and by the apostles, his inspired successors. So John the Baptist, who served as "the "morning-star," to usher in the appearance of the "Sun of "righteousness," did thus "prepare the way of the Lord," by enlightening the minds of men, in the knowledge of their guilt and misery, and inciting them to flee from the "damna- "tion of hell."—The three thousand that were converted to the faith at one sermon, in the infancy of the Christian church,

* Rom. i. 18.

were first awakened with a sense of their aggravated guilt, in "crucifying the Lord of glory;" and brought in agony and distress to cry out, * "Men and brethren, what shall we "do?"

This method, I confess, is disagreeable to the sentiments and inclinations of a secure world; and may expose us to the reproach of those "that are at ease in Zion:" but is agreeable to the dictates of an enlightened mind, conformable to the plan laid down in the sacred scriptures, and has in all ages approved itself the most successful method of promoting the interests of real and vital religion.

2. They are to "compel sinners to come in," by a lively representation of the *power* and *grace* of our Almighty *Redeemer*.—Not all the thunder and terror of curses from mount Ebal, not all the tremendous "wrath revealed from heaven a"gainst the ungodly," not all the anguish and horror of a *wounded spirit* in an awakened sinner, are able to produce an unfeigned and effectual compliance with the gospel-terms of mercy. The ministry of the *law* can only give the *knowledge of sin*, rouse the sinner's conscience, and alarm his fears: it is the dispensation of *grace*, that sanctifies and saves the soul. Nor is the former needful but in order to the latter. So much conviction as gives us a sight of our sin and misery, as inclines us to "flee from the wrath to come," and disposes us to submit to the gospel-method of salvation "by grace "through faith," by sovereign mercy through the Mediator, so much is necessary; and more is neither requisite, nor useful, or desirable.

It is not the office of preachers to be perpetually employed in the language of terror, or exhaust their strength and zeal in awakening and distressing subjects. No; but as it is their distinguishing character, that they are *ministers of the gospel*, so it is their peculiar business to "preach the unsearchable "riches of Christ." The person, and offices, and love of the great Redeemer, the merits of his obedience, and purchases of his cross, the victories of his resurrection, the triumphs of his ascension, and prevalence of his intercession, the power of his Spirit, greatness of his salvation, freeness of his grace, *&c.*; these are to be the chosen and delightful subjects of their discourses.—They are to represent him as one—who has completely answered the demands of the law, rendered the Deity propitious to the sinner, and upon this account is able eternally to save us from the vengeance of an offended

* Acts ii. 36. 37.

God;—who is clothed with almighty power, to ſubdue the inveterate habits of ſin, ſanctify our polluted nature, and reſtore us to ſpiritual health and purity;—who is *Lord of the viſible and inviſible worlds*, who knows how to defeat the moſt artful devices of Satan, and will finally render his people victorious over their moſt malicious and implacable adverſaries;—who having "made reconciliation for iniquity" upon the croſs, is pleading the merits of his blood in heaven, and powerfully interceding for all ſuitable bleſſings in behalf of his people;—"who is there exalted as a Prince and a Saviour to "give repentance and remiſſion of ſins *; and is able to ſave "unto the uttermoſt all thoſe that come to God in and "through him †;"—in fine, who from his illuſtrious throne in glory ſtoops to look down with pity upon guilty and periſhing ſinners, ſtretches forth the ſceptre of grace, and opens the everlaſting arms of his mercy to receive them.—Theſe peculiar doctrines of the goſpel they are frequently to teach, upon theſe they are to dwell with conſtant pleaſure, that ſinners may be perſuaded to hearken to the inviting voice of divine love, and put their truſt in this almighty and compaſſionate Saviour. In order to which,

3. They are to ſhew ſinners the mighty *encouragement*, that the goſpel gives them to *accept* of *Chriſt*, and *ſalvation* through his merits and righteouſneſs.—As for ignorant *preſumers*, theſe hear the glad tidings of the goſpel with a fatal indifference; and ſay in their hearts, "they ſhall have peace," though they go on in their evil way, ſtupidly "neglecting ſo "great ſalvation," and regardleſs of eternal things. But *awakened* minds are rather apt to draw the darkeſt concluſions with reſpect to their caſe, and to judge themſelves excluded from the invitations of the goſpel.——Sometimes they imagine, that the *number* and *aggravations* of their *ſins* exceed the deſigns of pardoning mercy:—at other times, that they have ſo long reſiſted the heavenly call, that now the gate of heaven is irrecoverably barred againſt them:—and Satan further ſuggeſts, that it would be the height of *preſumption* in them to lay claim to the bleſſings of the goſpel, till *better prepared* for the divine reception.——Upon ſuch imaginary and falſe grounds as theſe, multitudes of the invited gueſts make *excuſes*, and exclude themſelves from the "marriage-"ſupper of the Lamb." It is therefore the buſineſs of the ſervants of Chriſt to ſhew, that "there is yet room," even for the greateſt and vileſt ſinners to *come in*, and partake of the goſpel-feſtival; that "all things are now ready," for their wel-

* Acts v. 31. † Heb. vii. 25.

come

come entertainment;—that the *door* is still *open*, and there is free access, not only for those who have escaped the grosser pollutions of the world, but even "for the chief of sinners," whose guilt is of a *crimson* colour and a *scarlet* dye; that neither the number nor aggravations of their iniquities will exclude them a share in the divine mercy, if now they submit to the sceptre of grace;—that whatever their condition and circumstances may be, it is of present obligation upon them to accept the gospel-call, and their instant duty to *come in;* the Master invites them "to come to him, that they may "have life:" and "whosoever do so," the Master of the house has assured them, that "he will in no wise cast them out *."

4. They are to exhibit the unspeakable *advantages*, that will attend a compliance with the gospel-call.——I know indeed, the religion of Jesus is by its enemies often represented in the most frightful and hideous colours,—particularly as laying an unreasonable restraint on the liberties of mankind, and sinking them into melancholy enthusiasts. It becomes us therefore, who are "set for the defence of the gospel," to endeavour the removing this groundless prejudice, and to convince mankind by the light of reason and scripture, that "the ways of wisdom are ways of pleasantness, and all her "paths are peace:" that verily a life of *faith* in the blessed Redeemer is the way to be happy, both here and hereafter.

O what more honourable, than to be "a child of God, "an heir of the kingdom of heaven?" What more pleasing, than to look back, and behold our past iniquities all buried in the depths of eternal oblivion;—than to look forward, and view our dear Saviour acknowledging us his friends and favourites, and adjudging us to a state of unperishing glory? What more advantageous, than to have the divine favour engaged for our protection, the promises of divine grace for our consolation, and an assured title to "an inheritance un-"defiled, incorruptible, and eternal?" This is the portion of the true believer. These the privileges, that attend a compliance with the gospel-call.

These things are to be represented in such a manner as may tend to captivate the hearts of men, and engage them in a solicious care and resolution to renounce the degrading servitude of sin, and resign themselves to the power of redeeming grace. Thus by the most effectual and persuasive methods, the ministers of Jesus are to *compel* sinners "to come in, that "his house may be filled."

* John vi. 37.

It

It was not in my design, to consider the duty of the ministry in its just extent; but only to insist upon those things that more properly belong to my subject, and lie directly in the view of my text.

It will now doubtless be expected, that I APPLY my discourse, more immediately to the *present occasion.*

And suffer me, dear Sir, in the first place, to address myself to you, who are this day coming under a public consecration to the service of Christ, "to bear his name among "the Gentiles; to whom the Master is now sending you "forth, to compel them to come in, that his house may be "filled." We trust, you are *a chosen vessel,* designed for extensive service in this honourable, though difficult employment. We adore the God of nature, who has furnished you with such endowments as suit you to this important charge. We adore the great Head of the church for the nobler gifts and graces of his Spirit; by which, we trust, you are enabled to engage in this mission with an ardent love to God, the universal Father of mankind, with a disinterested zeal for the honour of Christ, the compassionate friend of sinners, and with tender concern for the perishing souls of a "people that sit in darkness, and in the shadow of death;" who have for so many ages been wandering out of the way of salvation, "without Christ, and without God in the "world."

The work of the ministry, in every place, has its difficulties and dangers, and requires much wisdom, fortitude, patience, and self-denial, to discharge it in a right manner, with an encouraging prospect of success: but greater degrees of prudence, humility, and meekness, mortification to the present world, holy courage, and zeal for the honour of God our Saviour, are necessary where any are called to minister the gospel unto those, who through a long succession of ages have dwelt in the darkness of Heathenism, have from their infancy imbibed inveterate prejudices against the Christian faith, and from time immemorial been inured to many superstitious and idolatrous practices, directly opposite to the nature and design of the gospel.

What heavenly *skill* is required, to convey the supernatural mysteries of the gospel into the minds of uninstructed Pagans, who are "a people of a strange speech and hard language?" —What deep *self-denial* is necessary, to enable you cheerfully to forsake the pleasures of your native country, with the agreeable society of your friends and acquaintance, to dwell among

among those who inhabit not indeed "the high-ways and "hedges," but uncultivated desarts, and the remotest recesses of the wilderness?—What unwearied *zeal* and *diligence*, to proselyte those to the faith of the gospel, who have quenched the light of reason, and by their inhumane and barbarous practices have placed themselves upon a level with the brute-creation?

Methinks, I hear you crying out, "Who is sufficient for "these things?"—And indeed, if you had no strength to depend upon, but only your own,—no encouragement, but from human assistance, you might justly sink down in a disconsolate despair, and utter the passionate language of Moses, "O my Lord, send, I pray thee, by the hand of him whom "thou wilt send:" thy servant is insufficient for so great a work.—But it is at the command of Christ, the great Head of the church, that you go forth; who by a train of surprising providences, has been preparing your way for this important embassy; and therefore you may be assured, that he will support you in the faithful discharge of your duty, accept your unfeigned desires to promote the interests of his kingdom, and finally reward your imperfect services with his gracious approbation. You have his divine promise for your security and consolation; "Lo! I am with you alway, even to the "end of the world." This will afford you light in every darkness,—defence in every danger,—strength in every weakness,—a final victory over every temptation. If Christ be with you, "in vain do the Heathen rage," in vain will their confederated tribes unite their forces to obstruct and discourage you. Infinite wisdom will be your guide,—almighty power your shield,—and God himself "your exceeding great "reward." The presence of your divine Master will make amends for the absence of your dearest friends and relatives. This will transform a wild and uncultivated desart into a paradise of joy and pleasure; and the lonely hutts of savages into more delightful habitations than the palaces of princes.

Let not then any difficulties discourage, any dangers affright you. Go forth *in the name* and *strength* of the Lord Jesus, to whom you are now to be devoted in the sacred office of the ministry. "Be not ashamed of the gospel of "Christ; for it is the power of God unto salvation to every "one that believeth, to the Jew first, and also to the Gentile." Let zeal for the honour of God, and compassion for the souls of men, animate your public discourses and private addresses to the people committed to your charge. Always remember, that your character is *a minister of Jesus;* and therefore with the

the inſpired doctor of the Gentiles, you "are to know no-"thing among them, ſave Chriſt and him crucified." Frequently conſider, that the goſpel is a divine diſcipline to purify the heart, and ſet up the kingdom of the Redeemer in the ſouls of men: and therefore it is not ſufficient to bring ſinners to a profeſſion of the name of Chriſt, and an outward ſubjection to the inſtitutions of divine worſhip: "You are ſent to "turn them from darkneſs to light, and from the power of Satan "unto God,—that they may receive forgiveneſs of ſins, and "an inheritance among them that are ſanctified by faith that "is in Chriſt." Unleſs this be effected, (whatever other improvements they gain), they are left under the dominion of ſin, and expoſed to the wrath of God; and their ſuperior degrees of knowledge will only ſerve to light them down to the regions of death and miſery.——*This* then is to be the principal deſign of your miniſtry: for *this* you are to labour with unwearied application,—and with inceſſant importunity to encompaſs the throne of that God, whoſe peculiar prerogative it is "to teach us to profit;" whoſe grace alone can make them "a willing people in the day of his power."

And for your encouragement, I will only add,—when I conſider the many prophecies, in ſacred ſcripture, of the triumphant progreſs of the goſpel in the laſt ages of the world, I cannot but *lift up* my *head with joy*, in an humble expectation, that the *day draws near*, yea, is *even at hand*, when the promiſes made to the Son of God ſhall be more illuſtriouſly fulfilled:—"when he ſhall have the Heathen for his inheritance, "and the utmoſt ends of the earth for his poſſeſſion;—when "his name ſhall be great among the Gentiles, and be *honour-"ed and adored* from the riſing of the ſun to the going "down of the ſame."——But if the appointed time is not yet come, and the attempts made to introduce this glorious day, fail of deſired ſucceſs,— "your judgment will be with "the Lord, and your reward with your God." If the Gentiles "be not gathered" in; you will "be glorious in the eyes "of the Lord," who accepts and rewards his ſervants according to the ſincerity of their deſires, and not according to the ſucceſs of their endeavours.

I ſhall conclude, with a few words to the *body of the people*.

God our Saviour, in infinite condeſcenſion, hath *ſent his ſervants* to invite you to *come in*, and receive the bleſſings, which infinite wiſdom has contrived, and aſtoniſhing grace prepared, for your entertainment. And surely, my brethren, it is your important duty, and incomparable interest, not to despise "the salvation of God sent unto the Gentiles," nor *make light* of the gospel-message to you.

God has been pleased to employ us the messengers of his grace, men of *like passions* with yourselves, subject to the common infirmities of human nature: but the message comes from him, who is King of kings, and Lord of lords; whom you are under the strongest obligations to hear and obey, in point of interest, gratitude, and duty.

What gracious and condescending methods has he taken, to allure and invite you! has he not descended from heaven to earth; from the boundless glories of eternity, to all the sufferings and afflictions of this mortal life, that he might purchase and reveal salvation; that he might engage your love, and persuade you to comply with his saving designs? does he not send his "embassadors to beseech you in his stead, to "be reconciled to God?"

What excuses have you to make, that will stand the trial of an enlightened conscience, or justify you at the awful tribunal of God? will the vanishing enjoyments of sin and sense, or the perishing riches of this transitory world, make amends for the loss of the divine favour, or support you under the terrors of eternal damnation?

Are there any honours comparable to the dignity and character of a child of God,—a title to the privileges of his house and family? Are there any pleasures equal to the smiles of God's reconciled face,—the refreshing visits of his love,—the immortal *joys of his salvation?*

But how deplorable, how desperate will be your case, if you finally refuse the gospel-invitation, and perish in your natural state of guilt and misery? the compassionate Jesus, who now addresses you in the inviting language of love, will then speak to you with the voice of terror, and "swear in his "wrath, that you shall never enter into his rest, that you "shall never taste of his supper," the rich provision which he has made for the eternal entertainment of his guests. "When "once the Master of the house is risen up, and hath shut to "the door," you will in vain *stand without*, and *knock* for admission.

In a word, *Now*, he declares by his servants, that "all "things are ready,"—and all that are *bidden*, shall be welcome, upon their *coming in*, to be *partakers of the benefit*. The blood of Christ is now ready, to cleanse you from all your guilt and pollution;—his righteousness is now ready, to adorn

adorn your naked souls with the garment of salvation,—his Spirit is now ready, to take possession of you, and make you eternal monuments of victorious and redeeming grace. "The Spirit and the bride say, Come; and whosoever (of "the lost and perishing sons of Adam) will, let him come," and participate of the blessings of the gospel "freely, without "money, and without price." The arms of everlasting mercy are open, to receive you: the treasures of divine grace are open, to supply your wants: and every one of you that now sincerely accepts this gracious invitation, shall hereafter be admitted "to sit down with Abraham, Isaac, and Jacob, in "the kingdom of heaven."

For which, God of his infinite mercy prepare us all, through Jesus Christ: to whom be glory and dominion world without end. Amen.

An APPENDIX,

Containing a short Account of the Endeavours that have been used by the Missionaries of the Society in Scotland for propagating Christian Knowledge, to introduce the Gospel among the Indians upon the Borders of New-York, &c.

THE deplorable, perishing state of the Indians in these parts of America, being by several ministers here represented to the Society in Scotland for propagating Christian knowledge; the said Society charitably and cheerfully came into the proposal of maintaining *two missionaries* among these miserable Pagans, to endeavour their conversion "from darkness to light, and from the power of Satan unto God:" and sent their commission to some ministers and other gentlemen here, to act as their *correspondents*, in providing, directing, and inspecting the said mission.

As soon as the Correspondents were authorised by the Society's commission, they immediately looked out for two candidates of the evangelical ministry, whose zeal for the interests of the Redeemer's kingdom, and whose compassion for poor perishing souls, would prompt them to such an exceeding difficult and self-denying undertaking.——They first prevailed with Mr Azariah Horton to relinquish a call to an encouraging parish, and to devote himself to the Indian service.——He was directed to Long-Island, in August 1741, at the east end whereof there are two small towns of the Indians, and from the east to the west end of the island, lesser companies settled at a few miles distance from one another, for the length of above an hundred miles.—At his first coming among these, he was well received by the most, and heartily welcomed by some of them.—They at the east end of the island especially, gave diligent and serious attention to his instructions, and were many of them put upon solemn inquiries about "what they should do to be saved."—A general reformation

ation of manners was soon observable among the most of these Indians.—They were careful to attend, and serious and solemn in attendance, upon both public and private instructions. —A number of them were under very deep convictions of their miserable perishing state; and about *twenty* of them give lasting evidences of their saving conversion to God.—Mr Horton has baptized *thirty-five* adults, and *forty-four* children.—He took pains with them to learn them to read; and some of them have made considerable proficiency. But the extensiveness of his charge, and the necessity of his travelling from place to place, makes him incapable of giving so constant attendance to their instruction in reading, as is needful. In his last letter to the Correspondents, he heavily complains of a great *defection* of some of them, from their first reformation and care of their souls, occasioned by strong drink being brought among them, and their being thereby allured to a relapse into their darling vice of drunkenness: a vice to which the Indians are every where so greatly addicted, and so vehemently disposed, that nothing but the power of divine grace can restrain that impetuous lust, when they have opportunity to gratify it. He likewise complains, that some of them are grown more careless and remiss in the duties of religious worship, than they were when first acquainted with the great things of their eternal peace.—But as a number retain their first impressions, and as they generally attend with reverence upon his ministry, he goes on in his work, with encouraging hopes of the presence and blessing of God with him in his difficult undertaking.

This is a general view of the state of the mission upon Long-Island, collected from several of Mr Horton's letters; which is all that could now be offered, not having as yet a particular account from Mr Horton himself.

It was some time after Mr Horton was employed in the Indian service, before the Correspondents could obtain another qualified candidate for this self-denying mission. At length they prevailed with Mr David Brainerd, to refuse several invitations unto places where he had a promising prospect of a comfortable settlement among the English, to encounter the fatigues and perils that must attend his carrying the gospel of Christ to these poor miserable savages.—A general representation of whose conduct and success in that undertaking, is contained in a letter we lately received from himself, which is as follows.

To

To the Reverend Mr EBENEZER PEMBERTON.

Rev. Sir,

SInce you are pleaſed to require of me ſome brief and general account of my conduct in the affair of my miſſion amongſt the Indians; the pains and endeavours I have uſed to propagate Chriſtian knowledge among them; the difficulties I have met with in purſuance of that great work; and the hopeful and encouraging appearances I have obſerved in any of them: I ſhall now endeavour to anſwer your demands, by giving a brief but faithful account of the moſt material things relating to that important affair, with which I have been, and am ſtill concerned. And this I ſhall do with more freedom, and cheerfulneſs, both becauſe I apprehend it will be a likely means to give pious perſons, who are concerned for the kingdom of Chriſt, ſome juſt apprehenſion of the many and great difficulties that attend the propagation of it amongſt the poor Pagans, and conſequently it is hopeful, will engage their more frequent and fervent prayers to God, that thoſe may be ſucceeded, who are employed in this arduous work: and alſo becauſe I perſuade myſelf, that the tidings of the goſpel's ſpreading among the poor Heathen, will be, to thoſe who are waiting for the accompliſhment of the "glorious things ſpoken of the city of our "God," as "good news from a far country;" and that *theſe* will be ſo far from "deſpiſing the day of ſmall things," that, on the contrary, the leaſt dawn of encouragement and hope, in this important affair, will rather inſpire their pious breaſts with more generous and warm deſires, that "the kingdoms of "this world, may ſpeedily become the kingdoms of our "Lord, and of his Chriſt."

I ſhall therefore immediately proceed to the buſineſs before me, and briefly touch upon the moſt important matters, that have concerned my miſſion, from the beginning to this preſent time.

On March 15. 1743. I waited on the Correſpondents for the Indian miſſion at New-York; and the week following, attended their meeting at Woodbridge in New-Jerſey, and was ſpeedily diſmiſſed by them with orders to attempt the inſtruction of a number of Indians in a place ſome miles diſtant from the city of Albany. And on the firſt day of April following, I arrived among the Indians, at a place called by them Kaunaumeek,

Kaunaumeek, in the county of Albany, near about twenty miles distant from the city eastward.

The place, as to its situation, was sufficiently lonesome, and unpleasant, being encompassed with mountains and woods; twenty miles distant from any English inhabitants; six or seven from any Dutch; and more than two from a family that came, some time since, from the Highlands of Scotland, and had then lived (as I remember) about two years in this wilderness. In this family I lodged about the space of three months, the master of it being the only person with whom I could readily converse in those parts, except my interpreter; others understanding very little English.

After I had spent about three months in this situation, I found my distance from the Indians a very great disadvantage to my work amongst them, and very burdensome to myself; as I was obliged to travel forward and backward almost daily on foot, having no pasture in which I could keep my horse for that purpose. And after all my pains, could not be with the Indians in the evening and morning, which were usually the best hours to find them at home, and when they could best attend my instructions.

I therefore resolved to remove, and live with or near the Indians, that I might watch all opportunities, when they were generally at home, and take the advantage of such seasons for their instruction.

Accordingly I removed soon after; and, for a time, lived with them in one of their *wigwams:* and not long after, built me a small house, where I spent the remainder of that year entirely alone; my interpreter (who was an Indian) choosing rather to live in a wigwam among his own countrymen.

This way of living I found attended with many difficulties, and uncomfortable circumstances, in a place where I could get none of the necessaries and common comforts of life, (no, not so much as a morsel of bread), but what I brought from places fifteen and twenty miles distant, and oftentimes was obliged, for some time together to content myself without, for want of an opportunity to procure the things I needed.

But although the difficulties of this solitary way of living are not the least, or most inconsiderable, (and doubtless are in fact many more and greater to those who *experience*, than they can readily *appear* to those, who only view them at a distance); yet I can truly say, that the burden I felt respecting my *great work* among the poor Indians, the fear and concern

cern that continually hung upon my ſpirit, leſt they ſhould be prejudiſed againſt Chriſtianity, and their minds imbittered againſt me, and my labours among them, by means of the inſinuations of ſome who (although they are called *Chriſtians*) ſeem to have no concern for Chriſt's *kingdom*, but had rather (as their conduct plainly diſcovers) that the Indians ſhould remain Heathens, that they may with the more eaſe cheat, and ſo enrich themſelves by them; the burden, I ſay, the fear and concern I felt in theſe reſpects, were much more preſſing to me, than all the difficulties that attended the circumſtances of my living.

As to the *ſtate* or *temper* of *mind*, in which I found theſe Indians, at my firſt coming among them, I may juſtly ſay, it was much more deſirable, and encouraging, than what appears among thoſe who are altogether uncultivated. Their Heatheniſh jealouſies and ſuſpicion, and their prejudices againſt Chriſtianity, were in a great meaſure removed by the long-continued labours of the Reverend Mr Sargeant among a number of the ſame tribe, in a place little more than twenty miles diſtant: by which means theſe were, in ſome good degree, prepared to entertain the truths of Chriſtianity, inſtead of objecting againſt them, and appearing almoſt entirely untractable, as is common with them at firſt, and as perhaps theſe appeared a few years ago. Some of them, at leaſt, appeared very well diſpoſed toward religion, and ſeemed much pleaſed with my coming among them.

In my labours with them, in order "to turn them from "darkneſs to light," I ſtudied what was moſt *plain* and *eaſy*, and beſt ſuited to their capacities; and endeavoured to ſet before them from time to time (as they were able to receive them) the moſt *important* and *neceſſary* truths of Chriſtianity; ſuch as moſt immediately concerned their ſpeedy converſion to God, and ſuch as I judged had the greateſt tendency (as means) to effect that glorious change in them. But eſpecially I made it the *ſcope* and *drift* of all my labours, to lead them into a thorough acquaintance with theſe two things.—*Firſt*, The *ſinfulneſs* and *miſery* of the eſtate they were *naturally* in; the evil of their hearts, the pollution of their natures; the heavy guilt they were under, and their expoſedneſs to everlaſting puniſhment; as alſo their utter inability to ſave themſelves, either from their ſins, or from thoſe miſeries which are the juſt puniſhment of them; and their unworthineſs of any mercy at the hand of God, on account of any thing they themſelves could do to procure his favour, and conſequently their extreme need of Chriſt to ſave them.——

And

And, *secondly*, I frequently endeavoured to open to them the *fulness*, *all-sufficiency*, and *freeness* of that *redemption*, which the Son of God has wrought out by his obedience and sufferings, for perishing sinners: how this provision he had made, was suited to all their wants; and how he called and invited them to accept of everlasting life freely, notwithstanding all their sinfulness, inability, unworthiness, *&c.*

After I had been with the Indians several months, I composed sundry *forms of prayer*, adapted to their circumstances and capacities; which with the help of my interpreter, I translated into the Indian language; and soon learned to pronounce their words, so as to pray with them in their own tongue. I also translated sundry *psalms* into their language, and soon after we were able to sing in the worship of God.

When my people had gained some acquaintance with many of the truths of Christianity, so that they were capable of receiving and understanding many others, which at first could not be taught them, by reason of their ignorance of those that were necessary to be previously known, and upon which others depended; I then gave them an *historical* account of God's dealings with his ancient professing people the Jews; some of the rites and ceremonies they were obliged to observe, as their sacrifices, *&c.*; and what these were designed to represent to them: as also some of the surprising miracles God wrought for their salvation, while they trusted in him, and the sore punishments he sometimes brought upon them, when they forsook and sinned against him. Afterwards I proceeded to give them a relation of the birth, life, miracles, sufferings, death, and resurrection of Christ; as well as his ascension, and the wonderful effusion of the holy Spirit consequent thereupon.

And having thus endeavoured to prepare the way by such a general account of things, I next proceeded to read, and *expound* to them the gospel of St Matthew (at least the substance of it) in course, wherein they had a more distinct and particular view of what they had before some general notion of.

These expositions I attended almost every *evening*, when there was any considerable number of them at home; except when I was obliged to be absent myself, in order to learn the Indian language with the Reverend Mr Sargeant.——Besides these means of instruction, there was likewise an English *school* constantly kept by my interpreter among the Indians; which I used frequently to visit, in order to give the children and young people some proper instructions, and serious exhortations suited to their age.

The degree of *knowledge* to which ſome of them attained, was conſiderable. Many of the truths of Chriſtianity ſeemed fixed in their minds, (eſpecially in ſome inſtances), ſo that they would ſpeak to me of them, and aſk ſuch queſtions about them, as were neceſſary to render them more plain and clear to their underſtandings.

The children alſo, and young people, who attended the *ſchool*, made conſiderable proficiency (at leaſt ſome of them) in their learning; ſo that had they underſtood the Engliſh language well, they would have been able to read ſomewhat readily in a *pſalter*.

But that which was moſt of all deſirable, and gave me the greateſt encouragement amidſt many difficulties and diſconſolate hours, was, that the truths of God's word ſeemed, at times, to be attended with ſome *power* upon the hearts and conſciences of the Indians. And eſpecially this appeared evident in a few inſtances, who were awakened to ſome ſenſe of their miſerable eſtate by nature, and appeared ſolicitous for deliverance from it. Several of them came, of their own accord, to diſcourſe with me about their ſouls concerns; and ſome, with tears, inquired "what they ſhould do to be "ſaved?" and whether the God that Chriſtians ſerved, would be merciful to thoſe that had been frequently drunk? *&c.*

And although I cannot ſay, I have ſatisfactory evidences of their being "renewed in the ſpirit of their mind," and ſavingly converted to God; yet the Spirit of God did (I apprehend) in ſuch a manner attend the means of grace, and ſo operate upon their minds thereby, as might juſtly afford matter of encouragement to hope, that God deſigned good to them, and that he was preparing his way into their ſouls.

There likewiſe appeared a *reformation* in the lives and manners of the Indians.

Their idolatrous *ſacrifices* (of which there was but one or two, that I know of, after my coming among them) were wholly laid aſide. And their Heatheniſh cuſtom of *dancing*, *hallooing*, &c. they ſeemed in a conſiderable meaſure broken off from. And I could not but hope, that they were reformed in ſome meaſure from the ſin of *drunkenneſs*. They likewiſe manifeſted a regard to the *Lord's day*; and not only behaved ſoberly themſelves, but took care alſo to keep their *children* in order.

Yet after all I muſt confeſs, that as there were many hopeful appearances among them, ſo there were ſome things more *diſcouraging*. And while I rejoiced to obſerve any ſeriouſneſs, and concern among them about the affairs of their ſouls, ſtill I was not without continual fear and concern, leſt ſuch

encouraging

encouraging appearances might prove "like a morning-cloud, "that paſſeth away."

When I had ſpent near a year with the Indians, I informed them that I expected to leave them in the ſpring then approaching, and to be ſent to another tribe of Indians, at a great diſtance from them: upon hearing of which they appeared very ſorrowful, and ſome of them endeavoured to perſuade me to continue with them; urging that they had now heard ſo much about their *ſouls concerns*, that they could never more be willing to live as they had done, without a *miniſter*, and further inſtructions in the way to heaven, *&c.* Whereupon I told them, they ought to be willing that others alſo ſhould hear about their ſouls concerns, ſeeing thoſe needed it as much as themſelves. Yet further to diſſuade me from going, they added, that thoſe Indians, to whom I had thoughts of going (as they had heard) were not willing to become *Chriſtians*, as *they* were, and therefore urged me to tarry with them. I then told them, that *they* might receive further inſtruction without me; but the Indians, to whom I expected to be ſent, could not, there being no miniſter near to teach them. And hereupon I adviſed them, in caſe I ſhould leave them, and be ſent otherwhere, to remove to Stockbridge, where they might be ſupplied with land, and conveniencies of living, and be under the miniſtry of the Reverend Mr Sargeant: which advice, and propoſal, they ſeemed diſpoſed to comply with.

On April 6. 1744. I was ordered and directed by the correſpondents for the Indian miſſion, to take leave of the people, with whom I had then ſpent a full year, and to go (as ſoon as conveniently I could) to a tribe of Indians on Delaware river in Pennſylvania.

Theſe orders I ſoon attended, and on April 29th took leave of my people, who were moſtly removed to Stockbridge under the care of the Reverend Mr Sargeant. I then ſet out on my journey toward Delaware; and on May 10th, met with a number of Indians in a place called Minniſſinks, about an hundred and forty miles from Kaunaumeek, (the place where I ſpent the laſt year), and directly in my way to Delaware river. With theſe Indians I ſpent ſome time, and firſt addreſſed their *king* in a friendly manner; and after ſome diſcourſe, and attempts to contract a friendſhip with him, I told him I had a deſire (for his benefit and happineſs) to inſtruct them in *Chriſtianity*. At which he laughed, turned his back upon me, and went away. I then addreſſed another *principal* man in the ſame manner, who ſaid he was willing to hear me. After ſome time, I followed the *king* into his houſe, and renewed my difcourfe to him: but he declined talking, and left the affair to another, who appeared to be a rational man. He began, and talked very warmly near a quarter of an hour together: he inquired why I defired the Indians to become *Chriftians*, feeing the Chriftians were fo much worfe than the Indians are in their prefent ftate. The Chriftians, he faid, would lie, fteal, and drink, worfe than the Indians. It was *they* firft taught the Indians to be drunk: and *they* ftole from one another, to that degree, that their rulers were obliged to hang them for it, and that was not fufficient to deter others from the like practice. But the Indians, he added, were none of them ever hanged for ftealing, and yet they did not fteal half fo much; and he fuppofed that if the Indians fhould become Chriftians, they would then be as bad as thefe. And hereupon he faid, they would live as their *fathers* lived, and go where their *fathers* were when they died. I then freely *owned*, *lamented*, and joined with him in *condemning* the ill conduct of fome who are called *Chriftians*: told him, thefe were not *Chriftians* in *heart;* that I hated fuch wicked practices, and did not defire the Indians to become fuch as thefe. —And when he appeared calmer, I afked him if he was willing that I fhould come and fee them again: he replied, he fhould be willing to fee me again, as a *friend*, if I would not defire them to become *Chriftians*.—I then bid them farewell, and profecuted my journey toward Delaware. And May 13th I arrived at a place called by the Indians, Sakhauwotung, within the Forks of Delaware in Pennfylvania.

Here alfo, when I came to the Indians, I faluted their king, and others, in a manner I thought moft engaging. And foon after informed the king of my defire to inftruct them in the *Chriftian religion*. After he had confulted a few minutes with two or three old men, he told me, he was willing to hear. I then preached to thofe few that were prefent; who appeared very attentive, and well difpofed. And the king in particular feemed both to wonder, and at the fame time to be well pleafed with what I taught them, refpecting the divine Being, *&c.* And fince that time he has ever fhewn himfelf friendly to me, giving me free liberty to preach in his houfe, whenever I think fit.—Here therefore I have fpent the greater part of the fummer paft, preaching ufually in the king's houfe.

The number of Indians in this place is but fmall; moft of thofe that formerly belonged here, are difperfed, and removed to places farther back in the country. There are not more than ten houfes hereabouts, that continue to be inhabited; and fome of thefe are feveral miles diftant from others, which

which makes it difficult for the Indians to meet together ſo frequently as could be deſired.

When I firſt began to preach here, the number of my *hearers* was very ſmall; often not exceeding twenty or twenty-five perſons: but towards the latter part of the ſummer, their number increaſed, ſo that I have frequently had forty perſons, or more, at once: and oftentimes the moſt of thoſe belonging to thoſe parts, came together to hear me preach.

The *effects* which the truths of God's word have had upon ſome of the Indians, in this place, are ſomewhat encouraging. Sundry of them are brought to renounce *idolatry*, and to decline partaking of thoſe *feaſts* which they uſed to offer in ſacrifice to certain ſuppoſed unknown powers. And ſome few inſtances among them have, for a conſiderable time, manifeſted a ſerious concern for their ſouls eternal welfare, and ſtill continue to "inquire the way to Zion," with ſuch diligence, affection, and becoming ſolicitude, as gives me reaſon to hope, that "God who (I truſt) has begun this work "in them," will carry it on, until it ſhall iſſue in their ſaving converſion to himſelf. Theſe not only deteſt their old idolatrous notions, but ſtrive alſo to bring their friends off from them. And as they are ſeeking ſalvation for their own ſouls, ſo they ſeem deſirous, and ſome of them take pains, that others might be excited to do the like.

In July laſt I heard of a number of Indians reſiding at a place called Kaukſeſauchung, more than thirty miles weſtward from the place where I uſually preach. I viſited them, found about thirty perſons, and propoſed my deſire of preaching to them; they readily complied, and I preached to them only twice, they being juſt then removing from this place, where they only lived for the preſent, to Suſquahannah-river where they belonged.

While I was preaching, they appeared ſober, and attentive; and were ſomewhat ſurpriſed, having never before heard of theſe things. There were two or three, who ſuſpected that I had ſome ill deſign upon them; and urged, that the white people had abuſed them, and taken their lands from them, and therefore they had no reaſon to think that they were now concerned for their happineſs; but, on the contrary, that they deſigned to make them ſlaves, or get them on board their veſſels, and make them fight with the people over the water, (as they expreſſed it), meaning the French and Spaniards. However, the moſt of them appeared very friendly, and told me, they were then going directly home to Suſquahannah, and deſired I would make them a viſit there, and manifeſted a conſiderable deſire of farther inſtruction.

This

This invitation gave me ſome encouragement in my great work; and made me hope, that God deſigned to "open an "effectual door to me" for ſpreading the goſpel among the poor Heathen farther weſtward.

In the beginning of October laſt, with the advice and direction of the correſpondents for the Indian miſſion, I undertook a journey to Suſquahannah. And after three days tedious travel, two of them through a wilderneſs almoſt unpaſſable by reaſon of mountains and rocks, and two nights lodging in the open wilderneſs, I came to an Indian ſettlement on the ſide of Suſquahannah-river, called Opeholhaupung; where were twelve Indian houſes, and (as nigh as I could learn) about ſeventy ſouls, old and young, belonging to them.

Here alſo, ſoon after my arrival, I viſited the king, addreſſing him with expreſſions of kindneſs: and after a few words of friendſhip, informed him of my deſire to teach them the knowledge of Chriſtianity. He heſitated not long before he told me, that he was willing to hear. I then preached; and continued there ſeveral days, preaching every day, as long as the Indians were at home. And they in order to hear me, deferred the deſign of their general hunting (which they were juſt then entering upon) for the ſpace of three or four days.

The *men*, I think, univerſally (except one) attended my preaching. Only, the *women*, ſuppoſing the affair we were upon was of a public nature, belonging only to the men, and not what every individual perſon ſhould concern himſelf with, could not readily be perſuaded to come and hear: but, after much pains uſed with them for that purpoſe, ſome few ventured to come, and ſtand at a diſtance.

When I had preached to the Indians ſeveral times, ſome of them very frankly propoſed what they had to object againſt Chriſtianity; and ſo gave me a fair opportunity for uſing my beſt endeavours to remove from their minds thoſe ſcruples and jealouſies they laboured under: and when I had endeavoured to anſwer their objections, ſome appeared much ſatisfied. I then aſked the king, if he was willing I ſhould viſit, and preach to them again, if I ſhould live to the next ſpring: he replied, he ſhould be heartily willing for his own part, and added, he wiſhed the young people would learn, &c I then put the ſame queſtion to the reſt: ſome anſwered, they ſhould be very glad, and none manifeſted any diſlike to it.

There were ſundry other things in their behaviour, which appeared with a comfortable and encouraging aſpect; that, upon the whole, I could not but rejoice I had taken that journey among them, although it was attended with many difficulties

culties and hardſhips. The method I uſed with them, and the inſtructions I gave them, (I am perſuaded), were means in ſome meaſure, to remove their heatheniſh jealouſies, and prejudices againſt Chriſtianity: and I could not but hope, the God of all grace was preparing their minds to receive "the truth as it is in Jeſus." If this may be the happy conſequence, I ſhall not only rejoice in my paſt labours and fatigues; but ſhall, I truſt, alſo "be willing to ſpend and be "ſpent," if I may thereby be inſtrumental "to turn them "from darkneſs to light, and from the power of Satan to God."

Thus, *Sir*, I have given you a faithful account of what has been moſt conſiderable reſpecting my miſſion among the Indians; in which I have ſtudied all convenient brevity. I ſhall only now take leave to add a word or two reſpecting the *difficulties* that attend the Chriſtianizing of theſe poor Pagans.

In the firſt place, their minds are filled with *prejudices* againſt Chriſtianity, on account of the *vicious* lives and *unchriſtian* behaviour of ſome that are called Chriſtians. Theſe not only ſet before them the worſt examples, but ſome of them take pains, expreſsly in words, to diſſuade them from becoming Chriſtians; foreſeeing, that if theſe ſhould be converted to God, "the hope of their unlawful gain" would thereby be loſt.

Again, theſe poor Heathens are extremely attached to the cuſtoms, traditions, and fabulous notions of their fathers. And this one ſeems to be the foundation of all their other notions, *viz.* that "it was not the ſame God made them, "who made the white people," but another, who commanded them to live by hunting, *&c.* and not conform to the cuſtoms of the white people.——Hence when they are deſired to become Chriſtians, they frequently reply, that "they will live "as their fathers lived, and go to their fathers when they "die." And if the miracles of Chriſt and his apoſtles be mentioned, to prove the truth of Chriſtianity; they alſo mention ſundry miracles, which their fathers have told them were anciently wrought among the Indians, and which Satan makes them believe were ſo.——They are much attached to idolatry; frequently making feaſts, which they eat in honour to ſome *unknown* beings, who, they ſuppoſe, ſpeak to them in *dreams;* promiſing them ſucceſs in hunting, and other affairs, in caſe they will ſacrifice to them. They oftentimes alſo offer their ſacrifices to the ſpirits of the dead; who, they ſuppoſe, ſtand in need of favours from the living, and yet are in ſuch a ſtate as that they can well reward all the offices of kindneſs that are ſhewn them. And they impute all their calamities to the neglect of theſe ſacrifices.

Furthermore,

Furthermore, they are much awed by those among themselves, who are called powwows, who are supposed to have a power of inchanting, or poisoning them to death, or at least in a very distressing manner. And they apprehend it would be their sad fate to be thus inchanted, in case they should become Christians.

Lastly, The *manner of their living* is likewise a great disadvantage to the design of their being Christianized. They are almost continually roving from place to place; and it is but rare, that an opportunity can be had with some of them for their instruction. There is scarce any time of the year, wherein the *men* can be found generally at home, except about six weeks before, and in, the season of planting their corn, and about two months in the latter part of summer, from the time they begin to roast their corn, until it is fit to gather in.

As to the *hardships* that necessarily attend a mission among them, the fatigues of frequent journeying in the wilderness, the unpleasantness of a mean and hard way of living, and the great difficulty of addressing "a people of a strange language," these I shall, at present, pass over in silence; designing what I have already said of difficulties attending this work, not for the discouragement of any, but rather for the incitement of *all*, who "love the appearing and kingdom of Christ," to frequent the throne of grace with earnest supplications, that the Heathen, who were anciently promised to Christ "for "his inheritance," may now *actually* and *speedily* be brought into his kingdom of grace, and made heirs of immortal glory.——I am,

From the Forks of Delaware in Pennsylvania, Nov. 5. 1744.

Sir,
Your obedient, humble servant,
DAVID BRAINERD.

P. S. It should have been observed in the *preceding account*, that although the number of Indians in the place I visited on Susquahannah-river, in October last, is but small, yet their numbers in the adjacent places are very considerable; who, it is hopeful, might be brought to embrace Christianity by the example of others. But being at present somewhat more savage, and unacquainted with the English, than these I visited, I thought it not best to make my first attempts among them; hoping I might hereafter be better introduced among them by means of these.——Sundry of the neighbouring settlements are much larger than this: so that there are, probably, several hundreds of the Indians not many miles distant. D. B.

FINIS.

13412664R10292

Made in the
USA
Monee, IL